Rethinking Corporate Governance

The standard approach to the legal foundations of corporate governance is based on the view that corporate law promotes separation of ownership and control by protecting non-controlling shareholders from expropriation. This book takes a broader perspective by showing that investor protection is a necessary, but not sufficient, legal condition for the efficient separation of ownership and control. Supporting the control powers of managers or controlling shareholders is as important as protecting investors from the abuse of these powers.

Rethinking Corporate Governance reappraises the existing framework for the economic analysis of corporate law based on three categories of private benefits of control. Some of these benefits are not necessarily bad for corporate governance. The areas of law mainly affecting private benefits of control – including the distribution of corporate powers, self-dealing, and takeover regulation – are analyzed in five jurisdictions, namely the US, the UK, Italy, Sweden, and the Netherlands. Not only does this approach to corporate law explain separation of ownership and control better than just investor protection, it also suggests that the law can improve the efficiency of corporate governance by allowing non-controlling shareholders to be less powerful.

Alessio M. Pacces is Professor of Law and Finance at the Erasmus School of Law, Erasmus University Rotterdam, and since 2009 he has been a Research Associate of the European Corporate Governance Institute (ECGI). Before joining academia, Professor Pacces was a senior researcher in the Law and Economics Research Department of the Bank of Italy, a financial economist at the Italian Securities Authority (Consob), and he served as junior officer in the Italian Financial Police. His research is mainly concerned with the economic analysis of corporate law and financial regulation.

Routledge Research in Corporate Law

Available titles in this series include:

Corporate Social Responsibility, Human Rights and the Law
Multinational corporations in developing countries
Olufemi Amao

The Political Determinants of Corporate Governance in China
Chenxia Shi

The Enlightened Shareholder Value Principle and Corporate Governance
Andrew Keay

Progressive Corporate Governance for the 21st Century
Lorraine Talbot

Rethinking Corporate Governance
The law and economics of control powers
Alessio Pacces

Forthcoming titles in this series include:

Directors' Decisions and the Law
Promoting success
Alice Belcher

Rethinking Corporate Governance

The law and economics of control powers

Alessio M. Pacces

Routledge
Taylor & Francis Group

LONDON AND NEW YORK

First published 2012
by Routledge

2 Park Square, Milton Park, Abingdon, Oxfordshire OX14 4RN

Simultaneously published in the USA and Canada
by Routledge
711 Third Avenue, New York, NY 10017

Routledge is an imprint of the Taylor and Francis Group, an informa business

First issued in paperback 2015

British Library Cataloguing in Publication Data
A catalogue record for this book is available from the British Library

Library of Congress Cataloging in Publication Data
A catalog record for this book has been requested

ISBN 978-0-415-56519-6 (hbk)

ISBN 978-1-138-19125-9 (pbk)

ISBN 978-0-203-07242-4 (ebk)

Typeset in Garamond
by RefineCatch Limited, Bungay, Suffolk

Endorsements

Alessio Pacces' book represents a substantial contribution to the growing field of law and finance. It sheds new light on the problems of corporate governance from both economic and legal perspectives in countries with concentrated corporate ownership.

Andrei Shleifer, Professor of Economics, Harvard University,
Cambridge, Massachusetts, USA

Alessio Pacces has written an important, thought provoking book on corporate governance that invites researchers in law and finance to rethink the relevance and regulation of control powers, in particular in the context of private benefits of control, conflicts of interest, self-dealing and takeovers.

Klaus J. Hopt, Professor and Director (emeritus),
Max Planck Institute for Comparative and International Private Law,
Hamburg, Germany

Contents

Acknowledgements

This book benefited from the contribution of many more people than can be acknowledged in a few sentences. I would never have been able to write such a study from scratch. Therefore, the first contribution to be acknowledged is that of by the two books that have preceded this one, namely *Proprietà e controllo delle imprese in Italia* (with Marcello Bianchi, Magda Bianco, Silvia Giacomelli and Sandro Trento; Bologna: Il Mulino, 2005) and *Featuring Control Power: Corporate Law and Economics Revisited* (Rotterdam: PhD Dissertation, 2007). For the latter I am particularly indebted to Roberto Pardolesi and to my supervisor, Roger Van den Bergh.

Short of the people that contributed to the development of the previous studies – they are simply too many to mention, I have benefited enormously from the comments and encouragement by colleagues and friends on my related work of the past few years. I thank Theodor Baums, Richard Buxbaum, Bill Carney, Brian Cheffins, Abe de Jong, Luca Enriques, Eilis Ferran, Ron Gilson, Magnus Henrekson, Klaus Hopt, Mats Isaksson, Jon Klick, Harold Koster, Maarten Kroeze, Henry Manne, and Andrei Shleifer for this. I hope that I was able to address some of the issues they have been so generous to discuss with me. This book also benefited from four very insightful anonymous referees. Thanks to them, and to the patience of Katie Carpenter and Stephen Gutierrez at Routledge, my earlier PhD dissertation could become a real monograph. Finally, I would like to thank Meltem Bayramli for valuable research assistance and the Erasmus School of Law for the financial support.

This book is dedicated to Olia and Leonardo, my wonderful family, who have assisted, energized and even sweetened the bitter part of this work with the happiness of our lives together.

Rotterdam, 8 July 2012

List of abbreviations

CA	Companies Act (UK)
CEO	Chief Executive Officer
CG	Corporate Governance
D&O	Directors & Officers (typically 'statutes') (US)
DGCL	Delaware General Corporation Law (US)
ECGI	European Corporate Governance Institute
EU	European Union
FSA	Financial Services Authority (UK)
GAAP	Generally Accepted Accounting Principles
GDP	Gross Domestic Product
HR	Dutch Supreme Court (*Hoge Raad*)
ICC	Italian Civil Code
IPO	Initial Public Offering
ISS	Institutional Shareholder Services
LR	Listing Rules (UK)
MBA	Master of Business Administration
M&A	Mergers and Aquisitions
MBCA	Model Business Corporation Act (US)
MOM	Majority of Minority
NED	Non-Executive Director
OECD	Organization for Economic Co-operation and Development
OK	Dutch Enterprise Chamber (*OndernemingsKamer*)
PBC	Private Benefits of Control
PFI	Participative Financial Instruments (Italy)
S&P	Standard and Poor's
SC	Special-purpose Committee (US)
SEC	Securities and Exchange Commission (US)
SEO	Seasoned Equity Offering
SER	Social Economic Council (Netherlands)
SFAS	Statement of Financial Accounting Standards
UK	United Kingdom
US	United States of America

Introduction

A Corporate governance: what we know and what we don't know

A.1 *Why corporate governance is important*

The governance of large, listed companies is a hot issue in public opinion.[1] Many people of the developed world are shareholders of a listed company: either they hold shares on their own, or they have their savings invested in financial institutions that act as shareholders. Although the vast majority of these people are unaware of the economic and legal implications of being a shareholder, they care about their money. They would not dare to invest in business ventures they hardly know anything about if they did not rely on the quality of corporate governance; neither would they trust financial institutions doing that job on their behalf, in the absence of 'good' corporate governance. Moreover, not only shareholders, but also people in general have an easy culprit to blame should anything go wrong with their money: once again, this is corporate governance. As a result, successes and failures of corporate governance are always on front pages of newspapers. This is particularly the case in this century, because of a series of financial scandals and a long-lasting financial crisis.

Corporate governance is also on top of the policymakers' agenda. In a sense, this may look rather obvious in light of the growing importance of corporations and of the investments channeled through them. Corporate governance has become a widespread social issue, whereas it was not only a few decades ago—perhaps with the exception of the United States (US) and the United Kingdom (UK). However, while this explains the attention of politicians and may also justify the growing interest of sociologists, it does not tell why corporate governance is a major concern for economic policy. Here the point is that corporate governance 'matters' for economic performance, which is in turn a key determinant of the well-being of society. In this perspective, policymakers

---

1 To be sure, corporate governance deals not only with listed companies. However, listed companies are the exclusive focus of this study.

are concerned with more than investors' welfare. The goal of the latter is to get the highest possible return on their investment; that of the former is to spur economic growth. In a capitalist economy, these issues are related to each other through finance. Finance is not just what allows investors to make money on their savings, but more importantly, what allows firms to raise the funds necessary to be established, to commit resources to production and its development, and to grow. Thus, policymakers do worry about investors' confidence in corporate governance. Most prominent international organizations (as the OECD and the World Bank) consider 'good' corporate governance a key recipe against underdevelopment.

Corporate finance seems to be, therefore, the fundamental reason of the importance of corporate governance. Corporate finance comes in two basic kinds. One is debt, which features a maturity (i.e., it has to be repaid) and midstream interests (i.e., scheduled payments of a predetermined amount). The other is equity, which features none of the above. In their capacity as providers of equity funds, shareholders are owners, not creditors: they sink their money in a business venture in the hope that it will be successful. When it is so, they may get conspicuous dividends or, alternatively, sell their shares for more than they invested in the first place. However, when the company is not successful, there is little, if anything, that they may claim from its liquidation.

This situation may well suit a sole proprietorship: the owner will take all the decisions on how to run the firm, and will bear all the wealth effects of these decisions on the capital that he has supplied the firm with.[2] On the contrary, the combination of ownership with dispersed provision of capital is a potentially pernicious one. Not only do shareholders have no guarantee of getting anything back at all, but they are also too many and too distant to be in control of how profits and losses are made on the funds they provide. The only plausible reason why they still invest in this situation is that they rely on how management decisions are taken by those in control. This is also how companies manage to raise funds from shareholders in exchange for no promise about the investment returns and its safety. Corporate governance is what makes all this possible. To this purpose, it addresses *separation of ownership and control* as the core problem.

A.2 *What we know (i.e.,* why *corporate law 'matters')*

Separation of ownership and control is the point where ordinary people's concerns meet the scientific debate. The problem was first studied by lawyers, and in an often-quoted passage, Adam Smith (1776) expressed his concern about the management of "other people's money" by directors of joint-stock

2 For convenience of exposition, any individual will be considered as male in gender throughout the present work. This has no bearing on shareholders, entrepreneurs, or corporate controllers being actually men or women.

companies who may have conflicting interests. In the eighteenth century, the proportions of separation of ownership and control were not judged to be worthy of further speculation. Things suddenly changed in the early twentieth century, at least in the United States of America. Adolf Berle and Gardiner Means (1932) denounced separation of ownership and control as a major problem of the corporate business. Separation of ownership and control had acquired significant proportions, and therefore was studied much more in depth. Analyzing the largest American companies in the 1930s, Berle and Means concluded that shareholders had simply surrendered control over the corporate enterprise to professional managers. Berle and Means did not just describe facts, they also claimed that this situation was a major threat to the legal principle according to which ownership and control should lie in the same hands. The modern study of corporate governance had just started.

Economists joined the debate only about 40 years later. By the 1970s, economic theory included a powerful tool for analyzing separation of ownership and control as a matter of delegation of tasks under asymmetric information. According to the agency theory, providers of services are regarded as agents of the people on whose behalf the service is performed – the principals. This allowed framing separation of ownership and control as a matter of division of labor: shareholders are specialized providers of capital, whereas managers are specialized providers of business administration skills. The problem of asymmetric information paralleled the traditional concerns of lawyers about the managers' conflict of interest with shareholders. By pointing to the underlying problem, the agency setting was able to address the same concerns with the force of mathematical analysis of behaviors. Michael Jensen and William Meckling (1976) demonstrated that separation of ownership and control was desirable (i.e., efficient) in spite of the management's ability to pursue their own interest at the shareholder's expenses, if the agent's incentives to provide the services were aptly aligned to the interest of the principals. Asymmetric information just made incentive alignment costly, and these costs – agency costs – were all that separation of ownership and control was about.

Efficiency had a stronger case than the lawyers' worries about the legal principles. Minimization of agency costs was not only a positive, rational explanation of why separation of ownership and control had occurred. It was also a powerful normative criterion on how to implement it in the best possible way. This approach also had an important point of tangency with the methodological developments in the US legal thought. With the publication of the first edition of Richard Posner's *Economic Analysis of Law* (1972), the law and economics approach had cleared its way from antitrust to virtually any other area of law: efficiency was imported as a paradigm also suitable for legal analysis. Corporate law and economics was still in its infancy, but it had already managed to bring an important contribution to the economics of corporate governance. Much before the agency approach was introduced in the study of separation of ownership and control, Henry Manne (1965) had already discovered one fundamental mechanism for aligning the managers' incentives with the interest of dispersed shareholders. That was the market for corporate control, where underperforming management is replaced by those who find the company's stock undervalued and may profitably take over inasmuch as they are able to improve performance.

This insight was rapidly merged with the agency theory of separation of ownership and control, albeit with an important variant. In the view of financial economists, minimization of agency costs was due to takeover *threat* more than to its *actual* occurrence. In other words, takeovers need to be hostile in order to keep managers on their toes while performing their duties to shareholders (Scharfstein 1988). During the 1980s, hostile takeovers became so popular in the US that hardly anybody could question the validity of this paradigm. Managers were indeed in control of firms that they did not own; but owners always had the ability to oust underperforming managers. The only way for managers to keep their position was to please shareholders with high stock returns; a low stock price would have easily triggered a hostile takeover. This simple market mechanism was sufficient to induce managers to behave as loyal and diligent shareholders' agents. To be sure, this relied on efficiency of stock market prices; back then, however, the majority of commentators believed in that efficiency (Gilson and Kraakman 1984).

Meanwhile, the second generation of Law and Economics scholars brought corporate law and economics to its maturity. The picture of separation of ownership and control was just too bright to think that law could do much to improve it. Quite the contrary, chances seemed high that legal intervention would just make corporate governance worse. After a debate of about ten years, *The Economic Structure of Corporate Law* – the first comprehensive economic analysis of corporate law – was published in 1991 (Easterbrook and Fischel 1991). Economic analysis was based on a straightforward agency perspective. As a result, the legal discipline of corporations was regarded mainly as a collection of default rules, aimed at saving the contracting costs between the principals (shareholders) and their agents (professional managers). Professors Easterbrook and Fischel advocated very few exceptions worthy of mandatory regulation, the most important of which being the pro-hibition of managers to fend off a hostile takeover. Other Law and Economics commentators had a somewhat less liberal view of corporate law, but the vast majority of them stuck to the agency framework dominating the economic literature. This framework is contractual in nature and, unless some problems in the contracting process are assumed, it hardly allows for very limited grounds for mandatory rules. However, the mainstream view was that effi-ciency of the stock market and hostility in the market for corporate control were sufficient reasons to make that assumption unwarranted.

In the late 1980s, the theory started to be challenged on empirical grounds. It was first shown that managers were not in control of every large corporate business even in the US, where a significant proportion of listed companies had indeed a controlling shareholder (Holderness and Sheehan 1988).

But even worse, by looking at the other side of the Atlantic, it turned out that controlling shareholders were the rule in the governance of listed companies, whereas managerial control was the exception nearly everywhere but in the UK (La Porta et al 1999). Separation of ownership and control was not substantial in continental Europe, where hostile takeovers were mainly disallowed by concentration of ownership.

Hostile takeovers started to disappear also from Anglo-American finance in the 1990s. Nonetheless, the UK and the US continued to feature extensive separation of ownership and control. Something was missing from the theoretical paradigm developed up until then. Shareholders were seemingly willing to hire professional managers as their agents, even in the absence of hostile takeovers; but they would hardly dare to do so outside the US and the UK. These countries needed to have something specially suitable to separation of ownership and control, and corporate law was considered that special feature (Shleifer and Vishny 1997).

Agency problems are always the same no matter the nationality. But corporate laws vary across countries, and they affect how agency problems are dealt with. Specifically, 'good' corporate laws can support investors' confidence in corporate governance. Even if shareholders do not get any enforceable promise of a return on their investment, corporate law provides sufficient guarantees that they would not be expropriated by professional managers. The same proposition does not hold when the quality of legal protection of shareholders is not high enough. 'Bad' corporate laws require that agents be more tightly monitored by the principals. This is how concentrated ownership emerges as the solution to the principal–agent problem.

The above argument seems to explain fairly well how corporate governance was dealt with differently in different countries. Four American economists showed that law 'matters' for separation of ownership and control depending on how well it protects non-controlling shareholders (La Porta et al 1998). The proof was based on regression analysis. The quality of law was assessed on the basis of an index of shareholder statutory rights as opposed to the powers of directors (considered as management representatives), and this variable had a very strong explanatory power of ownership concentration. The distribution of shareholder rights exhibited another important feature: Anglo-Saxon countries scored markedly higher than the others on this account. As a result, superiority of the common law tradition in shareholder protection sprang out as a powerful corollary of the 'law matters' thesis. All of this appeared in a milestone publication of the second half of the 1990s, *Law and Finance* (La Porta et al 1998), inaugurating a well-known series of articles by Andrei Shleifer and various co-authors.[3] After about fifteen years, the 'law matters' proposition is still at the core of the debate on positive analysis of corporate governance, and on its normative implications for corporate law.

---

3 The series is concluded by La Porta et al (2008), which also summarizes the main findings, extensions and limitations of this literature.

At least originally, the theoretical background of the 'law matters' thesis was not entirely clear. In a typical agency framework, the problem of asymmetric information between the principal and the agent is dealt with contractually. Unless the parties are unable to contract efficiently, law is bound to play a minimal role. Inefficiency of the corporate contract is difficult to argue on the basis of just asymmetric information, for the same contract is concluded between sophisticated players when companies go public. Unsophisticated shareholders only enter the play at a later stage. So how can corporate law possibly matter in this setting? The answer is that the same setting is incomplete, and so are (is) the (nexus of) contracts around which it is built.

The literature on incomplete contracts is actually grounded on this simple intuition: people cannot contract upon every possible future contingency affecting their relationships. This is not just because parties may have asymmetric information about these contingencies. More importantly, future contingencies are *uncertain*, and therefore none of the parties can costlessly foresee them at the outset (Hart and Moore 1988). One prominent consequence of uncertainty is that what is optimal today may be not optimal tomorrow. Given that future contingencies are limitedly foreseeable in contracts, the latter need to feature *flexibility*, to be managed through *organizations*, which are in their turn directed by *authority* (Williamson 1991). Corporate governance actually features all these elements. Unfortunately, this also means that contracting outcomes may turn out to be inefficient. The corporate contract cannot fully protect financiers – including shareholders – unless they get some authority, at least when their investment is endangered. When contracts are incomplete, authority is ultimately supported by institutions. In this perspective, the economics of institutions is the ultimate explanation of *why* law matters for protecting shareholders in corporate governance.

How law matters is another problem. It is sometimes believed that the 'law matters' thesis was revolutionary from the perspective of corporate law and economics, but it was not quite so. Before the publication of *Law and Finance*, no legal commentator I am aware of had ever claimed the opposite. Rather, the debate was about the right balance between enabling and mandatory provisions in corporate laws (Bebchuk 1989a). Law and economics scholars uncovered the efficiency rationale for mandatory regulation of the corporate contract some time before the importance of such regulation was highlighted by the economic theory. That rationale was the risk that management abused their powers due to the structural flexibility of corporate charters – a problem of contractual incompleteness. But the literature on contractual incompleteness was still in its infancy. As a result, law and economics scholars were still blaming agency costs as being responsible for the need of mandatory rules in corporate law, exactly when one of the founding fathers of the literature on incomplete contracts – Oliver Hart (1989) – denounced the limits of the principal–agent framework in explaining the economics of the firm.

After *Law and Finance*, the Law and Economics debate gained a comparative dimension that it did not have before. The account of comparative corporate law based on the index of shareholder rights became a standard reference for mainstream economics, but it was heavily criticized as superficial by the lawyers. Prominent scholars in corporate law and economics (e.g. Coffee 2001b) showed that, even in the US, the celebrated index of shareholder rights had little to do with how providers of equity capital are actually protected from expropriation. American shareholders had very few statutory powers to challenge directors' decisions, but they could count on a highly sophisticated system of private enforcement of fiduciary duties in courts. Although this was very pertinent to the common law tradition, and to be sure even more pertinent than the statutory rights considered in *Law and Finance*, the same argument was not applicable to the UK. There, directors appeared to be in a much weaker position relative to institutional investors, but this was due to a peculiar combination of ownership structure with statutory entitlements. Shareholder litigation was simply not an issue in the UK, and this confined judge-made law to a marginal role. Given that the patterns of separation of ownership and control were similar in these two countries, the part of the 'law matters' argument relating to legal families also seemed to be misguided. More accurate inquiries in comparative law and economics showed that functional comparison was the real issue: the problem of investor protection may be dealt with differently by different corporate laws, yet legal systems can deliver equivalent results (see lately Atanasov et al 2011).

Causality could run in the opposite direction. Comparative legal analysis has also shown that in no jurisdiction of continental Europe is the issue of legal protection of non-controlling shareholders neglected. These jurisdictions simply address different functional problems. The management–shareholders conflict of interest is a too parsimonious account of agency problems in corporate governance. Agency problems are also important in the relationship between controlling and minority shareholders. Corporate law in continental Europe had traditionally focused on the second problem more than on the first one. As a result, at least some European jurisdictions have created a legal environment more suitable for concentrated ownership. Alternatively, it was concentrated ownership to call for a particular attitude towards agency conflicts. The causal determinism of *Law and Finance* is unwarranted once the statistical correlation with the tradition of legal families is dismissed as irrelevant: whether corporate law comes before separation of ownership and control, or the other way around, which then becomes a chicken–egg problem. Corporate law is clearly inefficient when it fails to protect outside investors from the management and the controlling shareholders, because this would impair any form of separation of ownership and control. However, it cannot be argued that dispersed ownership is preferable to concentrated ownership. The superiority of corporate laws supporting dispersed ownership is likewise to be demonstrated.

Law and economics also went further in exploring the theoretical under-pinnings of the 'law matters' proposition. That investigation delivered two prominent results, both of which are based on integration of institutional analysis in the traditional principal–agent framework. The first result is that corporate law faces structural limits in protecting non-controlling shareholders. The most efficient laws that we could imagine may protect shareholders from outright expropriation, but not also from the management's failure to maximize profits. With a suggestive alliteration, Mark Roe (2003) has shown how corporate law can police *stealing*, but may hardly do anything about *shirking*. Other institutions are responsible for that. Provided that corporate law is doing its job in constraining shareholder expropriation, extralegal institutions will determine the degree of ownership concentration compatible with minimization of agency costs. This view has a problem with at least one institution: the market for corporate control. In fact, takeovers *do* police shirking *and* they are affected by the law. The point is that hostility in takeovers is often short-circuited by any possible device allowed by corporate law. This may be either the ownership structure supporting controlling shareholdings or the availability of takeover defenses to directors in dispersed ownership. The final result is that corporate control is not contestable. This contradicts both the goal of agency costs minimization and the irrelevance of the law in this respect. Here comes the importance of a second result of theoretical analysis.

Lucian Bebchuk (1999) has developed a theory of how failure of corporate law to protect non-controlling shareholders results in ownership concentration. The reason is not only, as was suggested in *Law and Finance*, that shareholders are less willing to buy non-controlling stakes in the absence of such a protection but, more importantly, corporate controllers are unwilling to deconcentrate ownership when they can divert a sizeable amount of resources from minority shareholders, for fear of being taken over and expropriated in their turn. This was framed as a more general problem of control rents, or *private benefits of control*, thereby including any benefit that corporate controllers may extract at the expenses of minority shareholders. Bebchuk's rent-protection theory explained not only why dispersed ownership structures were not practicable in those countries whose corporate laws allowed too much scope for private benefits of control; it also explained why hostile takeovers could be disallowed even in dispersed ownership structures, when the management was able to extract a moderate, but still relevant amount of control rents. Given the assumption that control rents are merely redistributive of ex-post firm value, but may induce behaviors that undermine its production ex-ante, both these mechanisms were considered inefficient in an incomplete contracts perspective. As such, the theory carried a very strong normative implication for corporate law: the priority of legal policy should be to constrain the extraction of private benefits of control.

Since then, private benefits of control have become a most popular way to interpret comparative corporate governance and the role of the law in affecting its patterns. The rent-protection theory was tested empirically. As far as both ownership concentration and stock market performance are concerned, cross-country estimates of private benefits of control exhibited higher explanatory power than the index of shareholder rights of *Law and Finance* (Nenova 2003; Dyck and Zingales 2004). On the one hand, this confirmed the general merits of the 'law matters' proposition: private benefits of control are just another way to look at shareholder protection. On the other hand, the study of private benefits also made clear to economists that the problem of shareholder protection is addressed functionally in corporate governance: different combinations of legal and extralegal institutions could determine comparable levels of private benefits of control. Unfortunately, the techniques employed only allow for private benefits that are *transferable* in the marketplace to be measured. At least one of the empirical studies on private benefits warned that our knowledge of the phenomenon to date is too limited to draw definitive conclusions. What can only be inferred from the empirical evidence is that not all private benefits are physic, and those that are not are likely to be affected by corporate laws and other institutional factors protecting investors. However, it cannot be excluded that other kinds of private benefits are also at play and may contribute to determining the different patterns of corporate governance that we observe around the world.

A.3 *What we still don't know (i.e.,* how *corporate law 'matters')*

The state of scientific knowledge about corporate governance leaves us with a number of open questions from both an empirical and a theoretical perspective. To start with, the standard account of private benefits of control, which synthesizes the predictions about how law matters in corporate governance, faces one important contradiction. There are some countries where the average size of private benefits is apparently low, and yet ownership is significantly more concentrated than in the UK and in the US.

Sweden is a case in point. Sweden features functionally good protection of non-controlling shareholders, although this seems to be more based on powerful social norms than on tough enforcement of corporate law. Unsurprisingly, the Swedish stock market is well developed; maybe more surprisingly, the frequency of controlling shareholders in Sweden is much higher than in the US, in spite of private benefits being on average nearly as low. According to Ronald Gilson (2006), the reason is that private benefits also come in a non-pecuniary kind, which can be neither measured nor policed by investor protection, but result anyway in ownership concentration. The effect of this kind of private benefit is not necessarily inefficient. Differently from the Italian case (where control benefits appear to be more pecuniary in kind, and then must be inadequately policed by corporate law and related institutions), the high frequency of controlling shareholders in Sweden may be interpreted as the outcome of agency costs minimization. Some businesses endogenously involve higher levels of non-pecuniary benefits, and ownership concentration is just the way to have them consumed efficiently.

While attempting to answer an important question, Professor Gilson's analysis raises two different ones. First, if non-pecuniary private benefits of control are truly endogenous to the business, why are they so important in Sweden but not so much, for instance, in the US and in the UK? Second, even assuming that pecuniary private benefits are equally low, how can we make sure that existing controlling shareholders maintain efficient levels of extraction of non-pecuniary private benefits over time? After all, these benefits have an opportunity cost in terms of shareholder value, which would rise when more efficient controllers were willing, but unable, to take over. Both the positive and the normative question are actually considered by Gilson, but he is ultimately unable to provide a satisfactory answer to either of them. One problem is that – contrary to what is often reported in the international comparisons – controlling shareholders are not just abnormally frequent in Sweden. Virtually any listed company has one, so that endogenous private benefits of control cannot be the only explanation. Another problem is that the category of private benefits not arising from outside shareholder expropriation may be under-specified: non-pecuniary private benefits may account for different kinds of control rents having different impact on the wealth of non-controlling shareholders.

If it is not even non-pecuniary benefits that explain ownership concentration, what can? Sofie Cools (2005) has suggested that the answer may be, once again, corporate law, if only we approach it from a different angle. Corporate law may not only determine ownership concentration in that it fails to protect non-controlling shareholders from the consequences of abuse of control powers. Paradoxically, it may also determine an identical result in that it fails to support the exercise of these powers, when they are not being abused by extraction of pecuniary private benefits. Ongoing exercise of corporate control in dispersed ownership structures requires legal support, indeed management could not stay safely in charge otherwise. In certain jurisdictions, directors cannot simply do without a controlling shareholder: they would constantly risk being voted down at the general meeting and, worse still, to be ousted by a takeover. Only when corporate law supports a distribution of powers that potentially favors the board of directors relative to the general meeting does managerial control become feasible. Actually, besides the policing of private benefits of control, this is exactly what happens in the US. In contrast, in most jurisdictions of continental Europe shareholders are just too powerful to allow for managerial control, regardless of how well they are protected from expropriation. One exception is the Netherlands, where shareholders are traditionally less powerful and, as expected, concentration of ownership is somewhat lower than in the rest of the continent.

Legal distribution of powers may be an important piece of the puzzle. It nicely tells us how separation of ownership and control may occur differently, all else being equal, but still does not tell us why. Others have tried to answer this question. For instance, Edward Rock and Michael Wachter (2001) have based their analysis of distribution of powers under US (Delaware) corporate law on managerial firm-specific investments. Departing from a straightforward agency perspective, they have analyzed the corporation as a response to pervasive contractual incompleteness. Their results are amazingly consistent with the state of American law.

In the US, outside shareholders are particularly well protected from expropriation by corporate controllers, whether these are managers or a controlling shareholder, but they may expect little else from corporate law. The default rule is that centralized management, as featured by the board of directors, has all of the remaining entitlements concerning decision-making. In this way the corporate structure copes with the limits of contracting, and therefore it features *power* as a way to deal with unforeseen contingencies. This provides managers with the incentives to specialize their skills to the corporate enterprise, as long as they can keep control over the firm's assets uncontested. Since managers are not expected to behave just like agents, shareholders are not entitled to get rid of them whenever they find it profitable. Still, how management is induced to provide shareholders with commensurate profits is not entirely clear in this framework. According to Professors Rock and Wachter, the answer is to be found in social norms as a fundamental guarantee of incentive-compatibility. Apparently, the state of knowledge about incomplete contracts does not allow for any better solution.

In the economics of incomplete contracts, the question of how ownership can be separated from control still awaits a final answer. Perhaps the most important achievement of this literature is that ownership should be bundled with control rights. This is the fundamental tenet of the property rights theory of the firm, which, however, is ultimately a theory of sole proprietorships. Economists have tried to explain incomplete financial contracting in spite of that. Philippe Aghion and Patrick Bolton (1992) have provided a very interesting theory of debt on that basis. These and other eminent economists have also tried with equity, but the results are not as satisfactory (see Hart 2001). The problem is that allocation of control rights to any constituency other than shareholders is extremely difficult to reconcile with the property rights theory. One way out of this is to assume that separation of ownership and control is not for real, but is in fact a separation between *de jure* and *de facto* authority (Aghion and Tirole 1997). This has been framed in several different models, whose bottom line is that shareholders are formally entitled to control rights but may refrain from exercising them against the management in a number of circumstances (Tirole 2006). The threat that these rights are exercised is a fundamental device for aligning managerial incentives with shareholder interest. Conversely, a credible commitment not to exercise them is the only way to preserve managerial incentives to make firm-specific investments. Unfortunately, this framework allows no way out of a tradeoff between shareholders' security benefits (stock returns) and managers' private benefits of control.

This tradeoff is currently a most serious challenge for the economic theory of separation of ownership and control and this is also the conclusion that research in corporate law and economics has reached. Private benefits of control are most probably the key to the solution. Luigi Zingales has nicely characterized them as evidence of an *appropriability* problem concerning the value of corporate control, which has not yet been completely understood by the theory. The principal–agent framework does not even feature this problem. The incomplete contract framework does, but is in trouble when it comes to solving the appropriability and the incentive-compatibility problems simultaneously. Professor Zingales has attempted, with Raghuram Rajan, to "search for new foundations" in a stakeholder theory of corporate governance, which allows for control rents to be appropriated through sources of power alternative to ownership (Zingales 2000; Rajan and Zingales 1998b). These sources are considered to be extralegal, but this is quite at odds with the positive attitude of corporate laws.

In reality, it seems that the law worries much more than economic theory about protection of control rents: either it allows managers to fend off hostile takeovers or provides controlling shareholders with equivalent devices to that purpose. Stakeholder protection is often the alleged reason, but incumbent controllers are always the ones who gain from these legal arrangements. Martin Hellwig (2000) has brilliantly made these points. Professor Hellwig is not worried that non-controlling shareholders stand to lose from entrenchment of corporate control. Inefficiency of this outcome is just the received wisdom, which he finds unconvincing. Whether or not entrenchment actually results in inefficient allocation of managerial and financial resources depends on the performance of the market for corporate control.

Another economist has approached the problem from a similar standpoint. Colin Mayer (1999) has explained entrenchment of corporate control on the basis of a special category of private benefits of control, which have nothing to do with those (either pecuniary or non-pecuniary) that are featured by traditional agency theories. He claims that these benefits, which he does not define, do not amount to reduction of wealth available to non-controlling shareholders, but simply account for entrepreneurial activities that markets are unable to reward. The same benefits are not entirely innocuous to outside shareholders, though. After some time, markets may become able to improve the allocation of corporate control, but may still be prevented from doing so by the size of existing control rents. This is akin to the appropriability problem described above. None of the authors that I have mentioned has wondered how the market for corporate control could solve this problem efficiently. One of the purposes of the present book is to answer this question with a comprehensive theory of corporate governance that matches the empirical evidence. We do not yet have such a theory.

B Purpose of research

The central research question of this inquiry is exactly the one which both legal and economic theory has been unable to answer so far: how corporate law matters for corporate governance and its efficiency. The question is two-sided. It includes a positive account – the impact of legal rules on corporate governance; but it also has a normative dimension – what are 'good' rules for corporate governance. I am addressing the question from a comparative law and economics perspective. This means that diverging corporate laws of several jurisdictions are analyzed based on their consequences on economic incentives of individuals, and they are assessed on the basis of economic efficiency of the resulting behaviors. The methodological implications of this approach, as applied to the study of corporate governance, will be discussed in the next section.

The research question is ambitious and it is clearly impossible to consider all the factors potentially affecting its answer. We need to identify the most relevant ones. To this purpose, the question is divided into a sequence of sub-questions. The answer to each of them provides the basis for selecting the relevant issues.

The first sub-question is: how does corporate governance work? We need a framework for analyzing the phenomenon before we can discuss the impact of its legal discipline. Based on the ongoing debate in the economic and legal analysis of corporate governance, I have chosen private benefits of control as such a framework.

The second sub-question is: how do private benefits of control affect the efficiency of corporate governance, or what are the consequences of private benefits of control on social welfare? Stakeholders other than shareholders and managers (hereinafter simply stakeholders) potentially enter the definition of social welfare, so whether they are affected by corporate governance needs to be assessed beforehand. Assuming, as I will argue, that this is not the case, the next question is: how do private benefits of control affect the joint welfare of the two remaining constituencies: corporate controllers and non-controlling shareholders? These two categories are defined broadly so as to fit both managerial control and shareholder control systems. I contend that the answer to the above question rests upon a qualitative distinction between three categories of private benefits having different welfare implications. In order to make discussion intuitive, I provisionally describe these three categories of private benefits as the 'good,' the 'bad,' and the 'ugly.'

The third sub-question is: how does corporate law affect each category of private benefits of control? This involves consideration of three major areas of regulation of corporate governance. The first is legal distribution of corporate powers, determining how 'good' private benefits can be appropriated by corporate controllers. The second is legal discipline of conflicted interest transactions, setting constraints on the extraction of 'bad' private benefits of control. The third is regulation of corporate control transactions, affecting the way in which 'ugly' benefits are minimized by the market for corporate control. With respect to each area, I formulate predictions on how different corporate laws make separation of ownership and control different from country to country, and on whether the outcomes are efficient. The positive account of these predictions is tested through the analysis of corporate governance and its regulation in a five-country case study. If the test is successful, the theory of private benefits of control underlying the predictions may be considered sufficiently robust to deliver normative implications for the economic policy of corporate law.

This is how this monograph will attempt to answer the research question.

B.1 How corporate governance works

In order to understand how corporate governance works one has to start from the empirical evidence. Internationally, the evidence shows two major patterns of separation of ownership and control: one is managerial control, where no shareholder is large enough to exert control and a professional management is in charge; the other is shareholder control, featuring one large shareholder, or a coalition of them, in control of firm management. Each pattern is chosen at two levels. At the firm level, the choice depends on the market conditions for the exchange of non-controlling stock. Under either pattern, control is rarely made contestable through deconcentration of ownership. At the country level, the choice depends on how institutions affect the market conditions. In some countries, managerial control is hardly featured; in others, shareholder control is very infrequent; few countries feature both patterns. There is apparently no set of institutions that rules contestability of control, no matter how this is separated from ownership.

Scientific interpretation of facts is based on theoretical assumptions, which may be accepted inasmuch as the theory matches the evidence. One standard hypothesis in theoretical analyses of corporate governance is that *protecting control and its rents is unimportant* at least for large, listed firms (Hart 1995). This is based on the idea that controllers perform towards non-controlling shareholders the duties of an agent. As far as private benefits of control are concerned, this hypothesis has one thesis and two corollaries. The thesis is that extraction of private benefits undermines separation of ownership and control and its efficiency. One corollary concerns the choice of the corporate governance pattern under this premise: this choice depends on the alignment of incentives of the controlling agent, which in turn depends on minimization of private benefits of control. The second corollary is about the range of feasible choices: ability to minimize private benefits of control depends on institutional and legal constraints on their extraction by the controlling agent. The first corollary is contradicted by the evidence on hostile takeovers, which would indeed align the agents' incentives, but which can be and often are short-circuited under different forms of separation of ownership and control. The second corollary is contradicted by the fact that managerial control seems not to be an option also in those institutional environments where the average level of extraction of private benefits from shareholder wealth is low.

The thesis itself cannot be falsified, however. This may be simply due to the fact that the hypothesis of irrelevance of control rents is not true in every circumstance. Therefore, I advance the opposite hypothesis: *protection of control and its rents is important in corporate governance*. This is based on the idea that controllers are not always acting as agents of shareholders, but can be also entrepreneurs who do not entirely own the firm's assets. Under this hypothesis, private benefits of control need to be featured in corporate governance so long as they do not undermine the incentive-compatibility of equity finance. This thesis brings about three major corollaries. First, separation of ownership and control requires willing sellers of the company's stock: entrepreneurial controllers would stop deconcentrating ownership as soon as this involves that control and its private benefits are endangered. Second, separation also requires willing buyers: the stock demand is negatively affected by the risk that private benefits are extracted at the non-controlling shareholders' expenses. Third, the range of feasible ownership structures is affected on two prongs by institutions and the law: on the one hand, this range depends on constrains placed on shareholder expropriation; on the other hand, it depends on opportunities given for protection of control rents.

The last hypothesis seems to fit empirical evidence better. It is consistent with the lack of contestability of corporate control that we observe in the real world. It is not contradicted by ownership concentration in those countries where expropriation of minority shareholders does not seem to be an issue. As such, it provides a good basis for answering the next sub-question.

B.2 *Private benefits of control and efficiency*

At first glance, stakeholders different from shareholders appear to be a major matter of concern for welfare analysis. When the principal–agent framework is rejected as incomplete, shareholders no longer enjoy a special position among the corporation's constituencies. Exercise of control, and extraction of rents from it, may harm stakeholders as well. This concern may be unwarranted. Private benefits of control are a problem for stakeholders if the latter are also to be compensated through rents for some specific investment of theirs. However, this hypothesis is rejected if corporate governance does not require stakeholders' investment to be firm-specific. Another problem may be that the controller-shareholders arrangements as to *their* firm-specific investments may generate externalities on stakeholders. This hypothesis is also rejected if the problem of externalities on stakeholders depends on how business is conducted, and not on how ownership is separated from control.

In the relationship between corporate controllers and non-controlling shareholders, welfare analysis of private benefits of control can be conducted based on the distinction between rents and quasi-rents. This distinction has a long-standing tradition, dating back to Alfred Marshall (1893). Quasi-rents are the prospective reward to inventiveness, whereas rents are the ongoing reward to incumbency. Two important strands of literature may be brought together in this way: one is the theory of entrepreneurship; the other is the theory of the firm. Since Ronald Coase's *The Nature of the Firm* (1937), these two theories have hardly communicated with each other. The loopholes of the incomplete contract theories of the firm, when it comes to separation of ownership and control, leave ample scope for integrating entrepreneurship into the analysis of corporate governance.

In contract theory, quasi-rents are non-contractable rewards to investments in relationship-specific assets. According to transaction costs economics, asset specificity depends on the identity of the investing party: firm-specific investments by any constituency are therefore characterized as "idiosyncratic" (Williamson 1979). According to the property rights theory, rewards on idiosyncrasy are instead appropriated just by the owners of the physical assets being specialized (Grossman and Hart 1986). Both approaches try to explain why firms exist. However, they do not entirely explain entrepreneurship, which involves the highly peculiar idiosyncrasy of inventiveness in management, but "for which ownership is never a condition" (Kirzner 1979: 94). Corporate governance may indeed feature entrepreneurship. This requires that quasi-rents be allocated as a reward of managerial talent, independently of ownership of the underlying assets. I define these quasi-rents as *idiosyncratic* private benefits of control; and I maintain as an assumption that they must be featured by separation of ownership and control in order for corporate governance to support entrepreneurship.

Idiosyncratic private benefits are initially harmless to non-controlling shareholders. These quasi-rents are of no value to anybody but the entrepreneur. What makes entrepreneurs important in the economy is exactly that they are able to foresee profit opportunities that markets are unable to price. In corporate governance, this means that the value of corporate control to the entrepreneur is higher than to anybody else. This situation is allocatively efficient and the private benefits at issue may thus be characterized as the 'good' ones. However, things may change over time. Eventually, the value of entrepreneurship may become exhausted and the company may do better under new management. Yet protection of idiosyncratic private benefits may still be sufficient reason for the incumbent to prevent the insurgent from taking over. Whether and to what extent idiosyncratic private benefits effectively undermine the efficient dynamics of control allocation is a fundamental question of this inquiry.

Other kinds of private benefits of control deserve a more severe judgment. To start with, they have no quasi-rent feature. This is exhausted by idiosyncratic private benefits, and so any other kind of such benefits are just rents. Separation of ownership and control allows for these rents to be extracted in two different ways. One is outright diversion of a firm's assets and profits from non-controlling shareholders. The other is distortion of management decisions aimed at maximizing consumption of control perquisites rather than the firm's profits. Based on Mayer (1999), I define the rents arising from the first kind of behavior as *diversionary* private benefits of control, and those arising from the second kind as *distortionary* private benefits of control.

Diversionary private benefits account for 'stealing' in its broadest characterization. The welfare assessment of stealing is not a novel subject in law and economics. Ex-post, stealing may look like a redistribution of resources, which already exist, so that – paradoxically – it may seem neutral to overall social welfare. This is not true for two reasons. The first is that any effort taken to implement or to prevent stealing is a waste of resources. In corporate governance there is a second and even more important reason for inefficiency: the risk that stealing is operated ex-post reduces investors' willingness to pay for non-controlling stock ex-ante, thereby raising the cost of equity capital all else being equal. A rational corporate controller would be willing to commit to a no-stealing policy at the outset, in order to maximize the proceeds from the sale of non-controlling stock. However, to the extent that this commitment is not credible, diversion is always implemented ex-post and less separation of ownership and control than would be optimal occurs ex-ante. In this perspective, diversionary private benefits are certainly the 'bad' ones.

Distortionary private benefits of control crudely account for bad management of the firm's resources. This is intuitively illustrated by a broad notion of 'shirking': a non-owner manager will always put a lower effort than he could into the management of the resources under his control, and consume some of them in the form of perquisites. In economics, this is understood as an opportunity cost – that is, the value of the next best use of the same resources. Under separation of ownership and control, extraction of perquisites will until it is worth far less to the controller than it costs to the owners as a whole. Therefore, distortionary private benefits are always extracted in an inefficient amount, whether they are considered in an ex-ante or in an ex-post perspective. Unfortunately, there is not much we can do about it. Separation of ownership and control can only generate second best outcomes. This is perhaps the most important result of the agency theory of corporate governance. Distortionary private benefits of control are nothing but an illustration of agency costs. In spite of their adverse effects on efficiency, they can only be characterized as 'ugly.'

The matter is more complicated in a dynamic perspective. Conditions for second best are bound to change and the market for corporate control is the place where these changes are handled. The prevailing interpretation of this dynamics is that diversionary and distortionary private benefits of control stand in a tradeoff relationship: the latter may be minimized by hostile takeovers on condition that prospective acquirers are entitled to appropriate the former to some extent. However, there are more hostile takeovers in law and finance textbooks than in the real world. One reason why this is the case is efficient protection of (idiosyncratic) control rents. In this situation, I wonder whether the market for corporate control could also be operated efficiently via friendly takeovers. I shall therefore discuss a scenario where idiosyncratic private benefits set a constraint on dynamic minimization of distortionary private benefits, and efficient allocation of corporate control may be achieved through side payments on condition that diversionary private benefits do not interfere with the process. As I will show, both the static and the dynamic conditions of this scenario require support by corporate law.

B.3 Corporate law's impact on private benefits of control

How the three categories of private benefits of control are dealt with in corporate governance depends on institutions, which determine the range of feasible contractual arrangements as to separation of ownership and control and the degree of efficiency that may be reached thereby. In order to assess the role of legal rules in this context, I posit that corporate law affects separation of ownership and control via its impact on each category of private benefits of control described above. This implies that how corporate law 'matters' for corporate governance can be summarized in the following three predictions.

B.3.1 Prediction 1: Law and investor protection

Law matters as a device supporting protection of non-controlling shareholders against *diversionary private benefits* that may be extracted by the corporate controller. Effective protection makes separation of ownership and control a workable way to finance business, whereas ineffective protection hampers it.

The prediction is not novel: it lies at the core of the standard 'law matters' argument.

B.3.2 Prediction 2: Law and support of corporate control

Law also matters for separation of ownership and control in that it protects the corporate controller's *idiosyncratic private benefits*. Corporate law may provide entitlements to firm control independently of corporate ownership. This affects the distribution of powers between the corporate controller and non-controlling owners. Once shareholders have been protected from expropriation of their investment, distribution of corporate powers determines the degree of separation of ownership and control that can be afforded by entrepreneurs concerned with their control rents.

The prediction is partly novel: although the importance of distribution of legal powers for separation of ownership and control has already been emphasized in the literature, no connection with the role of control rents in corporate governance has yet been made.

B.3.3 Prediction 3: Law and the market for corporate control

Law does not only matter statically, in that it supports the exercise of power by the corporate controller and constrains its abuse. It also matters dynamically, in the same two respects, by promoting the allocation of corporate control to the best managers while preventing non-controlling owners from being exploited through unfair control transactions. *Insufficient protection* of non-controlling shareholders leads to concentrated ownership structures where the efficiency of the market for corporate control is impaired by value diversion. However, particularly in the presence of idiosyncratic private benefits of control, *excessive* shareholder *protection* may prevent insurgents from compensating the incumbents' control rents through the proceeds of efficient control transactions. Eventually, this leads to excessive consumption of *distortionary private benefits* under too dispersed or too concentrated ownership structures.

The prediction is basically novel: both the consequences of managerial control rents on the takeover mechanism and the effects of minority shareholder protection on the acquirer's incentives have been dealt with in previous literature, but they have always been considered separately.

Depending on how we look at private benefits of control, these predictions are both positive and normative in character. They might be questioned on either count. In order to verify whether they provide a satisfactory answer to the research question, I am testing their positive contents against the evidence. This requires that corporate laws be compared between countries whose prevailing patterns of separation of ownership and control differ. For the reasons that I shall clarify momentarily, I will not perform a quantitative analysis, but a qualitative one. I am checking the effects that any regulatory factor having a bearing on each prediction produces on the corporate governance of a restricted sample of countries. These factors pertain to three different *functional* areas of corporate law, namely: (i) conflicted interest transactions; (ii) distribution of powers; (iii) corporate control transactions.

According to the mainstream view, only the first area of law really matters because it counters the expropriation of non-controlling shareholders. I have based the selection of the countries of the sample upon the falsification of this view. I have picked five countries that, for different reasons, cast some doubts on the validity of the standard account of how law 'matters.' These countries are Italy, the US, the UK, Sweden, and the Netherlands. Two of them – Sweden and the Netherlands – seem to reject the standard 'law matters' thesis in two opposite directions; they can be regarded as respectively a good law/concentrated ownership and a bad law/dispersed ownership combination. Another two countries – the US and the UK – seemingly confirm the view that dispersed ownership is supported by good law as to investor protection; however, the US and the UK protect investors by means of completely different, and sometimes opposite, legal arrangements. The last country – Italy – has been for over a decade the case in point for bad company law among developed countries. However, it is puzzling to observe that despite the significant improvements in investor protection over the past fifteen years, there is still no sign of evolution towards more dispersed ownership structures.

If the legal analysis based on the three above-mentioned predictions matches the corporate governance patterns observed in these five countries, the theory I am advocating has perhaps higher explanatory power than the mainstream view about corporate law and economics. Therefore, at least in the restricted domain of the sample of countries that I have chosen, I feel comfortable to extend the discussion to what corporate law should look like, based on the welfare analysis of private benefits of control.

C Methodology

This research has been carried out with a comparative law and economics approach. In spite of the long-standing tradition of economic analysis of law, the legitimacy of this approach is still questioned in some fields of legal analysis. Not in corporate law. This should already be clear from the foregoing illustration of the state of the art. General issues of legitimacy of economic analysis of corporate law are not worth discussing any further. Nevertheless, the approach being taken here has a number of specificities that deserve a brief illustration.

To start with, a prominent implication of the comparative feature is that the analysis of corporate laws is purely functional. The legal rules will be considered regardless of their *nomen juris*. They are selected on the basis of their ability to influence behaviors which are relevant to the subject-matter of this study: that is, those behaviors affecting separation of ownership and control via the extraction of control benefits of the three kinds described above. It follows that the strength of the legal analysis depends more on the quality of the selection than on its inclusiveness.

The comparative approach has also important implications on the economic side. I am not taking any *a priori* as regards the 'most important' rules in corporate law. Rather, I consider any of these rules potentially suitable to address the problem of private benefits of control. I am also considering any pattern of separation of ownership and control as a potentially efficient way to combine rewards to entrepreneurship with equity finance. This means that I am not making the assumption that an optimal model of corporate governance exists across the board. Likewise, I do not expect corporate law to be optimal in that it supports a single pattern of separation of ownership and control. Whether corporate law is efficient or not should rather depend on its ability to promote the choice of the optimal governance and ownership structure at the firm level. Empirical analyses have been unable so far to reject the hypothesis – first advanced by Harold Demsetz (1983) – that corporate governance is endogenous to the business being carried out. Others (e.g. Gilson 2006) have approached the comparative law and economics of corporate governance under this assumption. However, the results of this exercise are heavily affected by the underlying reliance on the agency paradigm. The latter may be ultimately irreconcilable with the endogeneity hypothesis.

The functional approach to both the analysis of legal rules and the interpretation of economic evidence also explains why the theoretical predictions concerning the role of private benefits of control, and the impact of corporate laws thereon, are not tested with a quantitative methodology. In spite of the popularity of the "numerical comparative law" (Siems 2005) inaugurated by La Porta et al (1998), this approach has a number of practical shortcomings and perhaps a structural one. Short of the problem of inferring causation from statistical correlations, the quantitative analysis has been much too coarse with regard to the legal comparison and also as far as the descriptive statistics on ownership and control patterns are concerned. While the latter problem could be cured, I doubt that separation of ownership and control can be described, let alone explained, on the basis of a single scale or index of corporate law's quality.

In order for legal comparison to be functional, all the rules potentially affecting the explanatory variables of corporate governance should ideally be considered. Having identified such variables in a tripartite account of private benefits of control surely helps to reduce the scales of measurement to a finite number. However, every jurisdiction is likely to affect each category of private benefits in a different fashion and the number of jurisdictions to be considered must be sufficiently large in order for statistical inference to make sense. The consequence of this on the definition of the indexes of comparison is twofold. On the one hand, we would need an algorithm to transform the qualitative impact of national rules on private benefits of control into quantitative ranking. On the other hand, if we want the sample of jurisdictions to be suitable for statistical inference, the amount of legal information to process for the qualitative analysis and its consistent reduction to numbers would be huge. Unfortunately, neither do we have one such algorithm, nor have a single researcher or a group of them yet acquired sufficient knowledge of corporate laws around the world to allow for its construction. For this reason, the legal and economic comparison of the present work is undertaken for just five jurisdictions. In this domain, the predictions of the theory are tested on a qualitative basis, depending on *how* – and not also on *how much* – each functional area of corporate law may affect the extraction of private benefits of control and, in turn, the separation of ownership and control.

A last methodological *caveat* is about the interdisciplinary of the analysis. This may seem straightforward, given the choice of a law and economics approach. However, in my opinion, making sense of interdisciplinarity also requires that the discussion be equally intelligible and interesting to economists and lawyers. Many papers in today's corporate law and economics do not have this feature. Either legal or economic analysis is overly technical, or some legal inquiries are so deeply embedded in the technicalities of the jurisdiction being analyzed (which is, most often, federal and/or state law in the US) that economists are hardly able to recognize what is relevant for the economics of corporate governance. The majority of economic analyses of corporate governance are based on highly formalized models featuring a very stylized account of legal rules. Lawyers seldom read more than the introduction and conclusion of those papers, and they stop reading even earlier when they do not recognize the actual contents of corporate law in the stylized description. Yet these two worlds have much to learn from each other, if only interdisciplinary communication could be put through.

The intuition of the thesis being argued in the present book comes from years of study of comparative corporate law at public policy institutions and lately at university. It has been remarkable to note that in the law of many corporate jurisdictions, the support of corporate control looks at least as important as the protection of shareholders from control abuse. In economics, this circumstance may be understood on the basis of highly formalized models addressing incentive alignment and allocation of bargaining power under uncertainty, and how institutions, including corporate law, shape the range of the feasible contracts in these respects. Besides the thesis, one novel element of this work is the attempt to bring together these two areas of knowledge. While I am taking stock of both in-depth legal analysis and formal economic models, I am just presenting the results of this investigation as a combination of *functional* legal disciplines and *informal* economic mechanisms. I refrain as much from the dogmatic illustration of legal institutions as from the use of mathematics in explaining individuals' behavior. In spite of what I had to go through to retrieve the underlying information, I believe that this style of presentation is the best way to interpret the interdisciplinary character of this research.

As with anything in economics, and most probably also in life, this approach comes at a price. The novel elements in the interpretation of corporate law and economics that I am advocating will be discussed by arguments of consistency between positive law and existing economic theory, but not also with the force of legal theory or mathematics. The legal categorization and the economic formalization of the framework that is going to be presented are very interesting topics for future research, respectively in law and in economics.

D Scope and limitations of this research

This book draws extensively on Pacces (2007), where I first attempted to develop the above framework for interpreting corporate governance and the role of law therein. Although the materials have been restructured, updated, and hopefully improved, this book still shares the structure, the focus, and the limitations of the original research on which it is based.

As far as the structure is concerned, the book is divided in eight chapters. Chapter 1 discusses the theory and the evidence about corporate governance. It aims to show what mainstream theory of the economics and the law of corporate governance has so far been unable to explain about separation of ownership and control. Chapters 2 and 3 introduce an alternative framework of analysis, based on three categories of private benefits of control and on how corporate law provides opportunities for and constraints to their extraction. The three predictions on how corporate law affects separation of ownership and control through regulation of private benefits are derived from this framework. These predictions are confronted with the five-country case study in Chapters 4 to 8. I will attempt to demonstrate the explanatory power of this theoretical framework through the analysis of three major areas of corporate law in these countries, suggesting what their bearing on the prevailing patterns of separation of ownership and control is likely to be. Chapter 4 deals with the legal distribution of powers between the management and the shareholders. Chapter 5 presents a functional framework to cope with self-dealing; how the law of the five countries compares with this framework is discussed in Chapter 6. Chapter 7 introduces the law and economics of friendly takeovers; this is the main way in which control transactions are operated and the only way to include private benefits of control in corporate governance. Chapter 8 discusses the regulation of control transactions in the five countries from this angle. As summarized in the concluding remarks, this analysis produces several policy implications for the regulation of corporate governance; these implications are tailored to the corporate laws of the five countries of the case study.

This book covers a wide range of issues in corporate governance, some of which – like the question of how far-reaching shareholder powers should be – are very topical these days. However, despite the high inclusiveness, this study is much focused. First, it seeks only to explain how corporate law functionally affects the core problem of corporate governance, namely separation of ownership and control. Second, this research is undertaken exclusively from the perspective of private benefits of control, which, for good or evil, are supposed to affect the incentives to control a firm owned by others. Third, the legal analysis only concerns the institutions of corporate governance having a likely impact on the three categories of private benefits of control that I have hypothesized, whether by allowing or by restricting their extraction. The focus on only three, albeit broad, functional areas of corporate law – distribution of power, self-dealing and takeovers – is an illustration of this approach. As will be shown, each of these three areas has an impact on separation of ownership and control via their effect on private benefits; often that impact can be improved in terms of efficiency of the corporate governance arrangements.

As a result of the tight focus of this inquiry, there are considerable omissions from it. The list of corporate governance institutions not being reviewed, or in some case not even mentioned in this work, would be longer than what can be afforded in this introduction. That being said, many of the limitations of this work stem from its focus on control and the legal institutions supporting it. Short of a basic dichotomy between managers and controlling shareholders, I will not be distinguishing between different categories of corporate controllers. Also the dynamics of decision-making within the board of directors will not be considered; neither will other topical issues, like the expertise of board members or the gender balance. The consequences of this focus affect even more visibly the broad category of non-controlling shareholders. Not only will the institutional investors receive no more attention than is needed to describe their interference (desirable and not) with control powers, but also I will make no distinction between different categories of institutional investors. On the legal side, one major omission is the political economy of corporate governance, particularly in as much as this affects the production of corporate laws in different, but all path-dependent, institutional environments. But here it is important to bear in mind that this work does not attempt to explain how certain patterns of separation of ownership and control have emerged in a particular country; much more modestly, I seek to identify the legal institutions that make certain patterns possible regardless of whether these are (were) established or not. As a consequence of this approach, one classic topic of corporate law and economics is excluded from this book, namely regulatory competition.

The reader will also notice that the financial crisis is hardly mentioned in this book, short of as an occasion for the enactment of certain legislation or policy documents. The reason of this omission is twofold. First, somewhat trivially, this research was designed before the financial crisis occurred. Second, and more importantly, the results of this research mainly concern the relationship between firm controllers and non-controlling shareholders; these results are basically unaffected by the financial crisis. If anything, the thesis that control matters and so does its legal protection is even reinforced by the revealed unreliability of financial markets in assessing performance in the short run. But apart from this very general observation, the welfare analysis of this book is much too narrow to allow the integration of the problem of financial stability in the study of the governance of a very peculiar kind of firm, like banks and comparable financial institutions.

1 Corporate governance

Theory and evidence[1]

1.1 The principal–agent approach to corporate governance

1.1.1 *Separation of ownership and control*

Economic theory of corporate governance approaches separation of ownership and control as a problem of separation of firm management from firm finance. While this is undoubtedly the core problem of corporate governance, most commentators take quite a narrow view of the matter, by stressing the latter term (finance) and overlooking the former (management). Managers and financiers of course need each other. A manager (or an entrepreneur) "needs the financiers' funds, since he either does not have enough capital of his own to invest or else wants to cash out his holdings" (Shleifer and Vishny 1997: 740). However, the focus of the corporate governance debate is rather on how managers are hired by financiers, and on what terms. As a result, no different from other long-term contractual relations, corporate governance is typically regarded as an agency problem: financiers act as the principals, hiring one or more agents to generate returns on their funds (Jensen and Meckling 1976).

In this perspective, the manager's position might look not much different from that of a high-rank employee. However, what distinguishes managers from the rest of the company's employees is their position on top of the firm hierarchy. Corporate managers are vested with enormous discretionary powers, for they bear ultimate responsibility of how the firm is managed. This discretion is the very essence of firm control. The conventional approach to corporate governance deals more with how this discretion is *constrained* than with how it is *exercised*. According to the mainstream economic theory of corporate governance, the special feature of management compared to the other constituencies of the corporate enterprise is their direct accountability

---

1 This chapter summarizes chapters 1–4 of Pacces (2007), where the theoretical, the empirical and the law and finance literature on corporate governance are discussed in greater detail (and many more references can be found).

to one kind of financier. Managers are essentially regarded as agents of the shareholders.[2]

Why should shareholders, and only shareholders, be the manager's principals? Shareholders are the firm's owners and, therefore, the residual claimants on the firm's assets. However, lacking both coordination and the necessary expertise, they do not know how to manage them in such a way as to maximize their value as an open-ended stream of profits. Managers are in charge of managing those assets, although they are not residual claimants unless to a limited extent. Either they lack the funds to own the firm's assets altogether or they simply do not want to commit a too large portion of their wealth to the company's affairs. Consequently, managers are induced to enjoy the assets under management rather than maximizing their value. Although there is quite an extensive debate about whether other providers of input (the so-called *stakeholders*) are also interested in the firm's residual (see Tirole 2006), the majority of economists and many legal scholars continue to believe that only shareholders should be. This is also the approach being followed here. The economic rationale for this position will be illustrated at the end of this chapter.

In the meantime, let us assume with the mainstream theory that the fundamental principal–agent relationship in corporate governance is established between managers and shareholders and, more in general, between those who decide about the firm's management without (entirely) owning its assets and those who (partly) own the firm's assets but do not participate in their management. This last definition is sufficiently general to also account for a manager whose ownership stake is so large as to qualify as *controlling shareholder*. As opposed to the latter, non-controlling shareholders are financiers holding a very special (and difficult) position. They provide funds to the firm, but what they receive in exchange is nothing but the promise to share in a future and uncertain stream of profit. The realization of this profit, however, is not entrusted to shareholders, or at least not to all of them. It is entrusted to somebody who may, or may not, be a shareholder himself. I shall henceforth refer to this individual as to the firm (or the corporate) *controller*.[3]

The nature of a shareholder claim on the firm's assets has also a special feature compared to a typical ownership claim. Normally, property rights over an asset confer the entitlement to both the asset management (control rights) and its profit stream (cash flow rights). The ownership of a corporate enterprise works quite differently. On the one hand, shareholders are entitled

---

2 I deal with the question why firms are not just financed with debt in Pacces (2007). See also Zingales (2000) and Mayer and Sussman (2001).

3 To be sure, the corporate controller need not be a single individual. The corporate practice shows many instances of plurality of corporate controllers. However, when there are two or more people exerting ultimate control over a publicly held corporation, they typically do it as a *coalition*. Throughout this work, I shall not deal with how these people manage to co-ordinate. Unless otherwise indicated, I shall always assume that a coalition of corporate controllers acts in fact as a single person.

to all the firm revenues that have not been assigned to any other provider of inputs. Having the status of owners of the enterprise, shareholders are *residual claimants*, so they are the ones with the strongest interest in the maximization of the firm's profits and the firm value (Fama and Jensen 1983b). On the other hand, they are not necessarily in control of the assets they own. Differently from the typical owner, shareholders who are not also the corporate controllers (non-controlling shareholders) do not have *residual rights of control*: that is, the rights to discretionally manage the firm's assets in circumstances not disciplined by any contract entered into by the firm. For the reasons and in the ways that I am just about to discuss, residual rights of control are held by the firm controller(s).

The typical problem of agency relationships is the conflict of interest of the agent when it comes to performing some task on the principal's behalf. Scope for exploiting the conflict of interest is provided by asymmetric information. The agent may pretend to be more skilled than he actually is, in order to be hired – or not to be replaced. Alternatively, he may cheat on the principal by underperforming his obligations, or not performing them at all, to the extent that he has some chances of not being caught. These two problems are respectively known as adverse selection and moral hazard. Delegation of management responsibilities is the source of both problems in corporate governance. The managers might easily abuse their superior knowledge at the principals' expenses, by staying in charge – or attempting to take over – when more capable managers are available, or by enjoying both pecuniary and non-pecuniary benefits of their position while failing to maximize shareholders' profits. These benefits are known as *Private Benefits of Control* (PBC).

Based on those conflicts of interest, two major conclusions are drawn. First, the ultimate goal of corporate governance should be to cope with agency problems in such a way as to guarantee maximization of shareholder value, because the latter corresponds with the sum of residual claims on the firm's assets – that is, the firm value. Secondly, the implementation of the above goal requires a discipline of managerial discretion, aimed at preventing managerial adverse selection and moral hazard. At its very core, the agency approach to corporate governance is based on the defense of shareholders' interest from managerial misbehavior.

1.1.2 *Agency problems under incomplete contracting*

1.1.2.1 *Two models of corporate control*

Agency costs are not sufficient to make corporate governance problematic (Hart 1995). In order for 'governance' to be a meaningful problem, there must be a contracting failure (Zingales 1998). Ideally, principals could write optimal contracts disciplining their agents' behaviors. In this situation, there would be no need to take decisions that were not foreseen (and thus accounted for) in the initial contract. In reality, corporate governance is all about such decisions. The reason behind it is that contracts are *incomplete*. Given that the contracts between managers and the owner of a company are imperfect, one may wonder whether an optimal corporate governance model exists instead. Although this view has enjoyed some popularity (e.g. Hansmann and Kraakman 2001), the idea that one single model of separation of ownership and control is the best does not seem to be borne out by the evidence.

Large firms in the developed world are characterized by two major patterns of corporate control. One is *managerial control* of a company where no shareholder has enough voting power to influence corporate decision-making systematically. This is the so-called 'public company', a model of corporate governance prevailing in Anglo-Saxon countries and infrequent in the rest of the world. Managers govern a public company without significant share ownership, since they enjoy considerable advantages in controlling how votes are cast by dispersed outside shareholders. The second and much more widespread model of corporate governance is *shareholder control*. It is based on a controlling shareholder (or more of them, acting as a coalition) exerting direct voting power through share ownership. The vast majority of corporate enterprises around the world are governed by a controlling shareholder (La Porta et al 1999). Even in the US and the UK, the public company model just applies to some of the largest firms, but not to all of them.

An issue often overlooked in the corporate governance literature, especially by US commentators, is that managerial control of a public company is just *one* model of corporate governance; also shareholder control should be accounted for. A related problem is that 'controlling' shareholders are not clearly distinguished from shareholders that are just 'large,' but do not really exert any control over the firm decision-making and, therefore, are still 'non-controlling' shareholders. The classification between corporate controllers and non-controlling shareholders that I have introduced is intended to cope with these problems. On the one hand, the notion of corporate controller points at the exercise of real authority in the firm decision-making (Aghion and Tirole 1997). As a result, it includes shareholders that are actually 'in control' while excluding shareholders that are just 'large.' On the other hand, the same notion is *neutral* to the two basic models of separation of ownership and control. 'Corporate controller' is in fact a suitable definition for either managers or a controlling shareholder having the last word over firm decision-making. Understanding corporate governance requires consideration for both models of corporate control, and not just for one of them.

Both under shareholder control and under managerial control there is delegation of residual rights of control from non-controlling shareholders to a corporate controller. This is motivated by the owners' wealth constraints, their liquidity needs and their risk aversion (the ultimate reason why their financial investments are diversified). It is not only entrepreneurs (and managers) that may not be rich enough or otherwise unwilling to own all of the firm's assets. Investors are the same, and that is the reason why large, publicly held companies have many small non-controlling shareholders. Ownership dispersion of large companies leads to the problem of shareholders' rational apathy. Within the incomplete contracts approach, this generates likewise a principal–agent problem. Professor Hart (1995: 127) has described it very clearly in the stylized case of a public company subject to managerial control:

> [Dispersed ownership] creates two . . . problems that [are] not relevant in the case of a private company. First, those who *own* the company, the shareholders, are too small and too numerous to exercise control on a day-to-day basis. Given this, they delegate day-to-day (residual rights of) control to a board of directors who in turn delegate it to management. . . . Second, dispersed shareholders have little or no incentive to monitor management. The reason is that monitoring is a public good: if one shareholder's monitoring leads to improved company performance, all shareholders benefit. Given that monitoring is costly, each shareholder will free ride in the hope that *other* shareholders will do the monitoring. Unfortunately, all shareholders think the same way and the net result is that no – or almost no – monitoring will take place.

Although it may be less intuitive, a similar reasoning applies to those companies where a controlling shareholder is in charge. Non-controlling shareholders are normally no less dispersed, and thus they are induced to delegate residual control rights to the controlling shareholder while abstaining from monitoring his behavior. In theory, the latter might be less of a problem compared to the case where managers are in charge with (almost) no shareholding, due to the large ownership stake that must be maintained to support the position of a controlling shareholder (Becht et al 2007). While a non-owner manager may waste too many resources in enjoying perquisites or building empires at the shareholders' expense, a controlling shareholder will refrain from doing so to the extent he loses more as an owner than he gains as a controller. Apparently, then, the exercise of corporate control by a large shareholder requires less monitoring by the other owners. In practice, however, the difference in incentives between the two models of corporate governance is more apparent than real (Hellwig 2000).

On the one hand, the ownership stake of controlling shareholders is always limited by their wealth constraints and risk diversification needs. Based on Jensen and Meckling's original insight (1976), standard theory holds that ownership concentration arises as a solution of a tradeoff between enhanced *monitoring* incentives of large owners and reduced *liquidity* of their investment. In that perspective, a controlling shareholder may even be preferable to a completely dispersed ownership structure, if only he could be subsidized to hold larger blocks (Bolton and Von Thadden 1998). However, the empirical evidence shows us a somewhat different picture. There are legal devices that allow separation of control rights from ownership claims. These devices – such as dual class shares, pyramidal group structures, or other instruments allowing departure from the 'one share–one vote' default rule governing corporate voting – help to satisfy liquidity preferences or constraints of the corporate controller. This of course dilutes the corporate controller's incentives as a residual claimant, by allowing control to be exercised and maintained with a limited ownership stake (Bebchuk et al 2000). For instance, one comparative study on corporate control patterns presents "examples in which the cash flow rights of the controlling family in some of the pyramid member firms are comparable to the stakes of the managers of the most diffusely held of US corporations" (Morck et al 2005: 678).

On the other hand, where managers are in charge with a tiny (or even no) ownership, their incentives can be nonetheless aligned with shareholder interest by putting them on an incentive scheme contingent on the realization of shareholder value (Shleifer and Vishny 1997). This mechanism has also an important limit. "[I]f managers have a strong interest in power, empire, and perks, a very large bribe may be required to persuade managers to give up these things" (Hart 1995: 128). Beyond a certain threshold, shareholders will prefer to share a smaller pie rather than to award managers the biggest part of a larger one.

The above results are consistent with the generality of Jensen and Meckling's analysis. Whatever the model of corporate governance (i.e., whatever the degree of separation of ownership and control), the incentives of the corporate controller can never be perfectly aligned with the interest of the non-controlling owners. Unfortunately, this framework does not completely explain the *choice* of ownership structure. In theory, this should just depend on minimization of agency costs across the board. In practice, however, agency costs minimization does not tell us why managerial control with dispersed outside ownership prevails in a few countries, whereas the governance of most publicly held companies around the world features controlling shareholders even with limited inside ownership. One possible solution to this puzzle is that the law makes a difference (La Porta et al 1998).

1.1.2.2 Law matters

The idea that law plays a role in corporate governance comes from the application of the agency theory to an incomplete contracts setting (Shleifer and Vishny 1997). Under asymmetric information, shareholders (the principals) cannot perfectly monitor the manager's (the agent's) behavior; therefore they are willing to buy stock only at a discount. The source of the discount is the agency cost. Agency costs could be minimized by an incentive-compatible contract between shareholders and the manager. If the corporate contracts were complete, minimization of agency costs would take place without the aid of legal rules, because it is in the interest of both managers and financiers. However, given contractual incompleteness, optimal shareholder protection cannot be specified ex-ante in detailed corporate contracts. What is optimal today might not be optimal tomorrow. For this reason managers are vested with discretionary authority in corporate governance. Minimization of agency costs requires that some external constraints on the managers' behavior be established by institutions, particularly by corporate law. Failure of corporate law to place sufficient constraints on the ability of managers to abuse their authority undermines shareholders' willingness to delegate the exercise of control rights. This, in turn, undermines separation of ownership and control.

Delegation of residual rights of control from the owners to a corporate controller still involves agency problems. Once he is in charge, the controlling agent could take advantage of his position by extracting private benefits, which ultimately come at the expenses of the principals' interest (shareholder value). Like in every principal–agent setting, it is asymmetric information that prevents dispersed shareholders from better disciplining the agent's behavior. However, provided that real discretion – in the form of exercise of residual control rights – is involved in that behavior, the problem must be dealt with differently from the traditional agency approach. Because control rights are 'residual' with respect to the feasible contracts, they cannot be disciplined contractually. As a result, agency problems arising from delegated exercise of control rights cannot be completely dealt with ex-ante. Rather, they need to be solved ex-post, when an inefficient misbehavior, which was not accounted for, materializes.

There are two possible ways to make sure that the corporate controller's discretion is disciplined in such a way as to prevent ex-post deviations from the goal of shareholder value maximization. The first way is to allow for a third-party intervention aimed at punishing outright abuses of firm control, thereby ruling out the most outrageous instances of corporate controller's misbehavior.[4] Clearly, the legal system, which was unimportant in a complete contracting framework, now plays a key role. Corporate law is supposed to regulate the company management in such a way as to prevent shareholder expropriation. This leads to the famous '*law matters*' proposition (La Porta et al 1998), which dominated the corporate governance debate for over a decade. I will discuss it at length in the following section on law and finance.[5]

The second way to make sure that shareholder value is maximized under contractual incompleteness is to have a change in control when the latter is being no longer exercised efficiently. Whether the corporate controller is induced to give up, or forced to do so, ultimately determines the way in which '*control matters*' in corporate governance (see Becht et al 2007). It might be less evident, but this also depends on the legal system and, specifically, on how entitlements to (residual) control rights are allocated by corporate law.

Crucially, under the incomplete contracting framework, both the constraints on the ongoing exercise of corporate control and its reallocation at certain points of the firm lifecycle not do completely depend on private ordering. Therefore, these factors may not be univocally determined across the board by

---

4 See Pacces (2011) for a comprehensive discussion.
5 See *infra* section 1.3.

agency costs minimization. Entitlements to control powers and the constraints provided for by the legal system (for instance, in the form of property rights) just make a difference. This allows the choice of ownership and control structure to vary from country to country, depending on different corporate laws. As we will see later on in this chapter, this is a result broadly consistent with the empirical evidence.

However, it is one thing to say that corporate law matters, but another to claim that corporate law matters only as far as the empowerment of non-controlling shareholders is concerned. A corporate controller may be a thief, but still the most talented manager available; alternatively, he might be utterly honest, but also very incompetent. Ideally, you would want the first manager to stay and refrain from stealing, whereas the second should simply part with control. Of course, shareholders would prefer to deal with neither a dishonest nor an incompetent manager; but the fact is that – when contracts are incomplete – these are two different issues. On the one hand, how the ongoing exercise of control rights is *regulated* by corporate law. On the other hand, how control rights are *allocated* through corporate law. Many misunderstandings in the economic and legal theory of corporate governance arise from confusing them.[6] This problem depends on the assumption that residual rights of control can only reside with the owners. This assumption depends, in turn, on the property rights theory of the firm (Grossman and Hart 1986; Hart and Moore 1990), according to which control should always be allocated to the owners of the firm's key physical assets – that is, in the case of a company, the shareholders.[7] Yet this assumption is unwarranted and even more importantly, it does not really match the positive structure of corporate law. I shall further speculate on this key point when I will introduce a broader framework for the economic analysis of corporate law in Chapter 3.

The mainstream theory of corporate governance maintains that the allocation and regulation of residual control rights are no separate issues. Both of them should empower the owners' position relative to that of the managers. Unfortunately, the theoretical implications of this reasoning are quite different from the outcomes that we observe in the real world.

1.1.3 *Optimal delegation of control rights*

Based on the standard framework, ultimate control rights can only be allocated to the company's owners. Corporate control is an issue not because it is actually *separated* from ownership, but rather, because it is *delegated* by shareholders to the management. When effective control of the corporation is merely delegated to an agent by non-controlling shareholders, the solution to the agency problem is apparently straightforward: ex-post misbehavior negatively

---

6 See illustratively, in the economic literature, Becht et al (2007) and, in the legal literature, Kraakman et al (2009).

7 Another way to get to the same result is the notion of pledgeable income. See Tirole (2006).

affecting shareholder value should be policed by (the threat of) withdrawing control rights from the agent (Hart 1995). The legal system is supposed to do little more than to empower shareholders in that fashion (Shleifer and Vishny 1997). In theory, under a credible threat of ouster, no rational corporate controller would ever misbehave. In the presence of asymmetric information (both actual and prospective managers always know more than shareholders about their own skills and effort), this would provide a second best solution of the moral hazard and adverse selection problems. On the one hand, the corporate controller will refrain from abusing his discretion for fear of being replaced with a more diligent or loyal manager. On the other hand, incompetent managers will ultimately have to yield to more efficient ones.

The weakness of this approach is that, in most situations characterizing corporate governance in the real world, the credibility of the threat of ouster is highly questionable. Ousting an inefficient corporate controller is not an option while non-controlling shareholders remain dispersed; rational apathy prevents small, individual shareholders from voting out a corporate controller they may be dissatisfied with. However, collective action problems, which affect the individual shareholder's incentives to monitor the corporate controller's misbehavior, could be coped with by legal or contractual mechanisms for coordinating outside shareholders. These mechanisms are very often available in corporate law, but in practice the power of non-controlling shareholders is very seldom enhanced by them. As we will see in the following chapters of this book, most prominent instances of these mechanisms (e.g. proxy voting and board composition arrangements) have proven generally ineffective to that purpose, and so far they seem to empower managers more than shareholders.[8]

Yet, collective action problems would be "overcome by someone who acquires a large stake in a company and takes it over" (Hart 1995: 127). Large shareholdings can be acquired in many different ways. Acquisitions solely aimed at ousting an incumbent controller against his will are called *hostile takeovers*. Therefore, how credible the threat of ouster is for policing the corporate controller's behavior could simply depend on the ease with which hostile takeovers can occur.

Since the very beginning of economic and legal research on this topic (Manne 1965), hostile takeovers have been considered a very important mechanism of corporate governance, if not the most important one (Scharfstein 1988). However, even one of the most prominent theorists of hostile takeovers recognized that "the takeover mechanism does not always work well" and that "in many cases the managers or the board of directors of a public company can pursue their own goals, possibly at the expenses of those of shareholders, with little or no outside interference" (Hart 1995: 127–8). Apparently, the reason is that (hostile) takeovers are often made so expensive

---

8 See particularly *infra* Chapter 4.

that the benefits they may provide to the acquirer are largely offset by the costs of the acquisition. "In practice the ease with which a takeover can occur depends on a variety of factors, including the range of defensive measures available to management, the attitudes of the courts, the existence of anti-takeover legislation, the ability of a successful bidder to expropriate minority shareholders, etc." (Hart 1995: 186–7).

1.1.4 Hostile takeovers: a myth?

1.1.4.1 Lack of contestability in the market for corporate control

I shall deal with both the economic and the legal impediments to the functioning of hostile takeovers at a later stage of this inquiry, after having introduced a more comprehensive framework for the analysis of the market for corporate control.[9] In anticipation of a more detailed analysis, let me just sketch out the major problems with hostility in takeovers.

To begin with, the empirical evidence shows that the hostile takeover might not yet be an extinct phenomenon, but it is an endangered species. At least in the US, hostile takeovers were very fashionable during the 1980s, but they have almost disappeared since beginning of the 1990s; and even in the 1980s, hostile takeovers may have been motivated more by restructuring of conglomerates than by the need to police managerial inefficiency (Holmström and Kaplan 2001). Maybe even more surprisingly, careful analysis of available information about M&A activity shows that most takeovers in the 1980s – and nearly all of them from the 1990s on – were not even 'hostile' or at least not in the way in which this term is normally understood (Schwert 2000). Similar results hold for the UK (Weir and Laing 2003).

Secondly, hostile takeovers are far from a general mechanism for policing the corporate controller's misbehavior (Burkart and Panunzi 2008). They are only possible in the absence of a controlling shareholder who owns (directly or indirectly) the majority of voting rights – no hostile takeover could ever succeed in such a situation. Controlling shareholders are very common outside the US and the UK. In most countries of the Wealthy West, corporate governance is based on shareholder control models where hostile takeovers are generally not possible. Even in those few situations in which they could happen, their actual occurrence is infrequent; therefore, hostile takeovers are unlikely to represent a general threat to the incumbent's control (Becht et al 2007). In Anglo-Saxon countries, where publicly held companies have typically no controlling shareholder, hostile takeovers can also be ruled out by the incumbent management's ability to resist ouster (Becht and Mayer 2001). We will see that this conclusion may hold whether or not takeover defenses are explicitly allowed by the legal system.[10]

---

9 See *infra* Chapters 4 and 7.
10 See *infra* Chapter 4 and Arlen and Talley (2003).

The above evidence is very difficult to reconcile with a theory of corporate governance based on delegation of residual rights of control from shareholders to an agent. One could hardly speak of delegation in the absence of a meaningful mechanism of withdrawing control rights from the agent (Hellwig 2000). One explanation of this puzzle – and, indeed, the most common one – is that the corporate controller's behavior aimed at ruling out hostile takeovers (so-called 'entrenchment') is *inefficient* (e.g. Morck et al 2005). This might be true when entrenchment arise ex-post, from the corporate controller's behavior *after* he has taken control of the company (Bebchuk 2002). However, inefficiency is much more difficult to argue when entrenchment is established ex-ante, and outside shareholders nonetheless entrust their money to controlling shareholders resistant to any possible hostile takeover or to managers powerfully entrenched via takeover defenses or equivalent devices (Coates 2004).

1.1.4.2　*Why contestability should be established at the outset*

This is the point where theory and practice of corporate governance exhibit the highest rate of discordance. Ex-ante, the controller's entrenchment can be accounted for or ruled out by the corporate charter, depending on whether takeover defenses or security-voting structures that shield the company from hostile takeovers are allowed. In theory, allowing for entrenchment devices should never be optimal ex-ante. As Professor Hart (1995: 187) put it:

> Before a company goes public, it is in the interest of the company's initial owner to design the security-voting structure in such a way that future management is subject to an appropriate amount of pressure from the market for corporate control, and to ensure that changes in management occur in the right situations.

That is, the security-voting structure that maximizes the likelihood of efficient takeovers (the changes in control "in the right situations") should also maximize the entrepreneur's proceeds from taking his company public. Under a reasonable set of assumptions, the security-voting structure providing optimal incentives to value-enhancing takeovers (thereby maximizing shareholder value ex-ante) is based on a single class of shares regulated by the 'one share–one vote' principle. In this situation, every share has the same chance of being decisive for taking over corporate control, and then, as in perfect competition, none of them (and no shareholder) is pivotal for the success of the acquisition (Grossman and Hart 1988).

For the same reason, takeover defenses should also be non-optimal, at least in theory (Easterbrook and Fischel 1991). Having them allowed (that is, not ruled out) by the corporate charter is roughly equivalent to awarding the corporate controller a super-voting share. Like security-voting structures deviating from the 'one share–one vote' model, takeover defenses then operate as a barrier to entry undermining competition in the market for corporate control. To the extent that the incumbent's consent is pivotal for the success of the acquisition, there is no guarantee that corporate control will be allocated to the most efficient manager. No different from deviations from 'one share–one vote', the cost of anti-takeover arrangements should be borne by the initial owner in the form of reduced proceeds from the stock placed with the investing public.

1.1.4.3 How contestability actually fails to be established

Nevertheless, firms that actually go public normally allow for various forms of entrenchment of corporate control. The security-voting structure of many companies listed outside the US and the UK departs from the 'one share–one vote' arrangement.[11] This result is easily achieved when (and to the extent that) dual class shares are allowed by the legal system. Alternatively, the 'one share–one vote' rule is circumvented through pyramidal groups, cross-ownership and other similar devices for separating voting rights from ownership claims (Faccio and Lang 2002). Even in the US, a significant proportion of public companies have dual class security-voting structures that insulate them from hostile takeovers (Gompers et al 2010); and, very often, corporate charters at the IPO stage allow for takeover defenses likewise shielding the incumbent management from the competitive pressure of the market for corporate control (Field and Karpoff 2002; Daines and Klausner 2001). The situation in the UK is only seemingly different (Brennan and Franks 1997). To be sure, US-style takeover defenses are not available to the management, and significant departures from 'one share–one vote' security-voting structures are uncommon among listed companies (Cheffins 2008). However, for a number of legal and extralegal reasons, incumbent managers enjoy a competitive advantage over insurgent shareholders, stock ownership being equal (Franks et al 2001). As a result, managers of UK public companies can also shield themselves from hostile takeovers, unless they perform very badly.[12]

1.1.5 Entrenchment and private benefits of control

A few theoretical contributions attempt to investigate the reasons underlying the departure from an otherwise optimal 'one share–one vote' security-voting structure.[13] Intuitively, such a departure can only make sense if the original owner expects to derive significant benefits from availing himself of superior voting stock or being otherwise entrenched – i.e., private benefits of control. Outside shareholders will pay much less for inferior voting stock (in general,

---

11 See Adams and Ferreira (2008) for an excellent survey.
12 See *infra* Chapters 4 and 8.
13 See Burkart and Lee (2008) for an excellent survey.

in the presence of entrenched control) than they would do should everybody hold the same class of voting shares (in general, under a more competitive control structure). On condition that private benefits of control arise out of expropriation of outside shareholders, such a strategy might be privately optimal (from the initial owner's standpoint) but socially inefficient (ex-post redistribution of shareholder value, in the form of private benefits of control, undermines ex-ante the incentives to its production). This is how deviations from 'one share–one vote' (as well as takeover defenses) are generally understood (Bebchuk et al 2000).

However, the lack of a comprehensive welfare analysis of private benefits of control in the economics of corporate governance is also recognized (Zingales 2000). Actually, private benefits of control need not reduce shareholder value. In terms of positive analysis, private benefits of control that do not directly reduce the wealth of outside shareholder are sufficient to explain a dual class security-voting structure as a strategy aimed at maximizing the initial owner's proceeds from going public (Zingales 1995). It is worth noting that, in one important model from where this implication is derived, "the level of private benefits has no efficiency consequences, but only distributional ones" (Dyck and Zingales 2004: 541). Based on a similar framework, some attempts have been made to demonstrate the ex-post inefficiency of securing control rents that ex-ante do not affect the production of a firm's surplus. This has been argued on grounds that the farther from 'one share–one vote' the security-voting structure is, the more the same rents reduce the likelihood of control transfers that would eventually increase firm value (Bebchuk and Zingales 2000).

To my knowledge, nobody has attempted to investigate that result any further and, more importantly, to combine it with an account of private benefits of control as an ex-ante incentive mechanism for the production of the firm's surplus.[14] As I am going to argue, this often-neglected perspective may tell us much about how entrepreneurship is featured in corporate governance, and the role played by corporate law in this regard. For this reason, I will attempt to introduce another category of private benefits of control as idiosyncratic control rents, on which I will elaborate in the next chapter. Given the state of economic research in corporate governance, all we know about idiosyncratic control rents is that, because they initially do not affect shareholders' profits, they must account for further, non-verifiable surplus to be divided. The entitlement to this surplus depends on the allocation of residual rights of control.

Determining how that surplus should be divided, and what the consequences of such a division are for the production of surplus ex-ante and

---

14 However, for a similar approach, see recently Chemmanur and Jiao (2012) on dual class shares (showing their optimality in the presence of near-term uncertainty) and Manso (2011) on the desirability of control tenure in the presence of innovation. A welfare analysis of PBC is absent from both models.

its enhancement ex-post, is one major goal of the present study. However, I will also strive to identify the legal factors that make this possible. Intuitively, these factors vary from country to country for the simple reason that corporate laws differ. This is after all the main intuition behind the 'law matters' argument. The emphasis on (residual) control rights that drives the present analysis suggests that investor protection may not be all that matters at law for separation of ownership and control. Seemingly, in the most developed countries, the prevailing ownership structure is affected not only by legal investor protection, but also by control considerations and the way in which control can be supported by corporate law.

1.2 Comparative corporate governance

1.2.1 Economic and legal comparison

One empirical investigation about how corporate law affects corporate governance requires two steps. The first one is *economic comparison* of patterns of corporate governance prevailing in different countries. Variation of corporate governance within a country can hardly depend on corporate law, which is very similar even in those countries – like the US – allowing for different jurisdictions.[15] On the contrary, regardless of the within-country variation, pronounced cross-country differences in national corporate laws might possibly be responsible for the systematic prevalence of one model of corporate governance over another.

The second step to be taken is *legal comparison*, which is in a sense an empirical work too. Rules that most significantly affect corporate governance in each country have to be selected and then compared with the possibly – and, most often, typically – different kind of corporate law arrangements that address the same problems in other countries (Zweigert and Kötz 1998). No matter whether those key problems of corporate governance are dealt with by identical or just opposite legal rules, their different solution with similar rules may indeed explain discrepancies in national patterns of corporate governance, whereas similar solutions – albeit with different rules – may provide the basis for understanding resemblances. In other words, legal comparison has to be performed functionally rather than nominally (Kraakman et al 2009).

Over the last fifteen years the corporate law and economics scholarship has embarked on both tasks. Comparative analysis of corporate governance has rapidly shown the weakness of the prevailing account of separation of ownership and control, based on a framework where managers only act as agents for shareholders. This is the standard principal–agent framework. The corporate governance paradigm typically arising out of that framework – the public company, governed by managers and not by controlling

---

15   See *infra* Chapter 4.

shareholders – has proven almost nonexistent outside most developed Anglo-Saxon countries and, to be sure, featured with some puzzling differences even in that restricted sample (see Holderness 2009). Comparative legal analysis has tried to restore that account, claiming that 'law matters' for shareholders to be willing to delegate control to corporate managers (La Porta et al 1998). Delegation of management responsibilities to an agent can only arise in the presence of a strong legal protection of the principals (the shareholders), and apparently Anglo-Saxon countries perform much better than the rest of the world in that respect. To date, however, these two kinds of comparison have only been performed quite poorly. Even more importantly, they have been very unsatisfactorily related to each other. The reason is threefold.

To begin with, the underlying theoretical background is highly incomplete. As I have shown in the foregoing section, the agency paradigm alone leaves too many theoretical questions unanswered as well as most facts of corporate governance in the real world unexplained. Both economic and legal comparison cannot but suffer from this problem, by showing inconsistencies, leading to inconclusiveness, or wondering about apparently inexplicable puzzles. The comparative picture shows that separation of ownership and control is featured more by disenfranchisement of outside shareholders than by their empowerment. Contrary to conventional wisdom, this result equally holds under managerial control and shareholder control systems (see Hellwig 2000). Whether managers or controlling shareholders are in charge, non-controlling shareholders are normally entitled to little interference with the firm management; very seldom do they manage to take over firm control against the incumbents' will. Most typically, as I will show in this section, control is insulated from the threat of hostile takeover nearly everywhere in the world. This picture has little to do with the standard characterization of corporate governance as a principal–agent relationship, which would involve – among other features – contestability of corporate control.

Secondly, while comparative corporate governance has provided us with a significantly improved understanding of how separation of ownership and control can mean different things in different countries, it has been unable so far to deliver a clear-cut description of how firms are actually governed around the world, as well as of their typical ownership structure (Becht and Mayer 2001). I will try to address this issue in the following pages, taking stock of the limited knowledge we have to date. However, a more precise picture of corporate governance around the world would require more empirical research.

Thirdly, comparative legal research in the field of corporate governance appears to have been carried out with either too much superficiality by the economists or with too much meticulousness by the lawyers. None of the two approaches is consistent with the goal of ascertaining the role of corporate law in comparative corporate governance. The first one does not comply with the *functional* criterion that makes comparison of legal rules meaningful. The second one does not meet the *relevance* requirement that makes the same comparison useful for understanding rather than just describing differences and similarities.

One important exception to this criticism is a landmark publication by a selection of leading scholars on corporate law worldwide: *The Anatomy of Corporate Law*. This rich, but concise book has now come to the second edition (Kraakman et al 2009). It provides a state-of-the-art illustration of corporate laws in the major jurisdictions in the world with a straightforward functional methodology. Intentionally, Kraakman et al (2009) refrain from taking a normative approach, that is, from formulating policy prescriptions on what corporate law should look like. They also stick to the mainstream principal–agent approach to show the effects of different legal arrangements. These are two major differences with the analysis being undertaken in this book. On the one hand, the theoretical framework is broader than agency costs; on the other, the analysis of law will be both positive and normative. Otherwise, this study draws extensively on Kraakman et al (2009) for the method, and sometimes the contents, of the legal comparison.[16]

1.2.2 Corporate control and its entrenchment: Europe and the US

This and the following two sections (1.2.3 and 1.2.4) summarize the second chapter of Pacces (2007) with the purpose of providing an overview of corporate ownership and control in a selection of developed countries. There are a few important warnings on the validity of the information that follows. To start, the background data are presented and discussed very succinctly. In reality, we do not know how listed companies are effectively controlled around the world. Particularly if we aim to compare different ownership and control patterns, we can only make general hypotheses about the implications of ownership concentration/dispersion on control. Pacces (2007) discusses this problem at length. Moreover, the following discussion is highly selective as far as both the countries and the data are concerned. I am mainly referring to the study edited by Fabrizio Barca and Marco Becht (2001). Pacces (2007) also discusses the limitations of this study and attempts to reconcile it with other empirical comparisons (e.g. Faccio and Lang 2002). Finally, the data on ownership concentration is roughly fifteen years old: they refer to the mid-1990s.[17] There are a number of reasons why reporting them is still a valuable exercise. First, detailed cross-country comparisons of ownership structures have not been undertaken since then. Second, the empirical literature still widely refers to these data (Laeven and Levine 2008) on grounds that patterns of ownership and control are relatively stable over time. Third, the circumstance that ownership and control structures prevailing in a certain country do not change that rapidly is

16 See *infra* from Chapter 4 onwards.
17 See Pacces (2007) and Barca and Becht (2001) for the country details.

confirmed by a few, more recent studies at the national level.[18] I will refer to those occasionally.

That being said the purpose of this section is to answer the following questions:

(i) What fraction of listed firms is governed by a controlling shareholder in each country (or at least a consistent lower bound on the effective figures)?
(ii) How much voting power do these shareholders control on average (when both indirect and coalitional holdings are traced as accurately as possible)?
(iii) How likely are informal coalitions to be formed between large shareholders or owner-managers in order to *entrench* corporate control?

1.2.2.1 How frequent is shareholder control?

The answers to the above questions can be derived from the following Figure 1.1 and Table 1.1. Figure 1.1 shows, for each country, the percentage

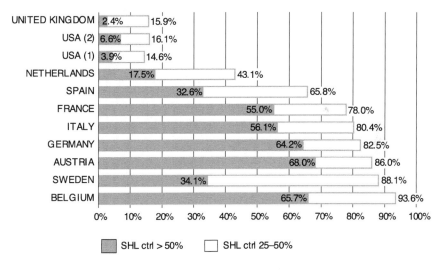

Figure 1.1 Incidence of shareholder control in Europe and in the US

Note: Fraction of listed firms governed by a controlling shareholder or by a formal coalition of shareholders (voting pacts). A firm has a controlling shareholder when at least one shareholder or a coalition of them holds more than 25% of voting power (the grey area refers to the percentage of firms with an absolute majority shareholder). Data refer mainly to 1995–6 (see Table 1.1 below).

Source: Pacces (2007).

---

18 See e.g. Van der Elst (2008) comparing ownership in Belgium, France, Italy, Spain and the UK; de Jong et al (2010) reporting data on the Netherlands; Henrekson and Jakobsson (2012) on Sweden; and Holderness (2009) on the US.

Table 1.1 Size of voting blocks by rank

	Year	No. of companies	Largest Voting Block		2nd Largest Voting Block		3rd Largest Voting Block	
			Mean %	Median %	Mean %	Median %	Mean %	Median %
Belgium	1995	135	56.1	55.8	6.6	10.2	4.5	4.7
Austria	1996	50	54.1	52.0	7.8	2.5	2.6	0
France[a]	1996	674	52.0	N/A	N/A	N/A	N/A	N/A
Italy	1996	214	51.9	54.5	7.7	5.0	3.5	2.7
Germany	1996	372	49.6	57.0	2.9	0	0.6	0
Netherlands[b]	1996	137	42.8	43.5	11.4	7.7	4.0	0
Spain[c]	1995	193	40.1	34.5	10.5	8.9	3.5	1.8
Sweden[d]	1998	304	37.7	35.0	11.2	8.7	5.6	4.8
USA (1)								
NYSE	1996	1,309	8.5	5.4	3.7	0	1.8	0
NASDAQ	1996	2,831	13.0	8.6	5.7	0	3.0	0
USA (2)	1996	1,130	15.8[e]	10.0	5.1	5.8	2.4	0
United Kingdom	1992	207	14.4	9.9	7.3	6.6	6.0	5.2

Notes: Descriptive statistics about the average (mean) and median size of voting blocks held by the three largest shareholders in each country. Zero values are not excluded and are assigned when no voting block above the disclosure threshold (5% for all countries except the UK – 3% – and Italy – 2%) is observed.
Source: Pacces (2007).

of firms under shareholder control. Since in Barca and Becht (2001) data for the US are not entirely based on official sources, they have been supplemented with elaborations on other data discussed in Pacces (2007): the latter are displayed as USA (2), whereas the original results are reported as USA (1). Control is inferred at two thresholds. The first (50% of voting rights) provides the most conservative, but also the most reliable estimate of shareholder control. The second (25% of voting rights) is still more conservative than the 20% threshold chosen by Faccio and Lang (2002).

Bearing in mind that the data refer to the mid-1990s, controlling shareholders dominate the corporate governance arena in the Old Continent by a typical rate of about 80% of listed companies when shareholder control is inferred at the 25% threshold. The opposite result holds for the US and the UK where shareholder control is very uncommon: it accounts for just about 15% of listed firms at the same 25% cut-off. By three out of four measures available for the US, controlling shareholders are slightly more frequent in the US than in Britain (see Holderness 2009 for a similar finding). Yet the frequency of controlling shareholders is incomparable with the figures for continental Europe. There is only one significant exception to the dichotomy between continental Europe and Anglo-American countries. This is the Netherlands, which geographically belongs to the European continent, but where only about 43% of listed firms appear to be managed under the authority of a controlling shareholder.[19]

Trends of ownership (voting power) concentration remain relatively stable whether we consider a 50% or a 25% threshold. Countries that have more shareholders with at least 25% of voting rights also have a higher proportion of absolute majority shareholders. Very noticeably, in most countries of continental Europe, the latter and far more expensive governance structure prevails: the majority of listed firms are governed by a shareholder featured with at least one half of voting rights.

There are two exceptions, both relating to otherwise very concentrated ownership structures, where only about one third of the firms appear to be governed by an absolute majority shareholder and at least as many firms have one shareholder whose voting power is between a half and a quarter of voting rights. One is Spain, where according to the country experts (Crespi-Cladera and Garcia-Cestona 2001) this is due to a takeover regulation: mandatory bid obligations arguably make the acquisition of a 50% stake particularly expensive. In addition, voting power concentration would be higher in Spain if also formal coalitions between shareholders had been taken into account. The other country seemingly supporting less majority shareholders, but still with several controlling minority shareholders, is Sweden. Sweden, however, is a peculiar case because of the extensive use of control enhancing mechanisms; not all deviations from 'one share–one vote' were likely tracked by Agnblad et

---

19 See Pacces (2007) for details on how this figure is calculated.

al (2001). Subsequent estimates of voting power concentration in Sweden showed that in 2000 nearly half of the listed companies had a largest shareholder controlling at least 50% of the voting rights (Holmén and Högfeldt 2009). Although the impact of control enhancement mechanisms seems to have decreased dramatically since then, the prominence of shareholder control in Sweden has not changed (Henrekson and Jakobsson 2012).

When we switch to the countries where ownership is more typically dispersed, shareholder control with a relative majority of the votes is instead *always* more popular than absolute shareholder control. This holds for the Netherlands, the US, and the UK; and it is particularly true for the latter. Indeed, the position of a controlling shareholder of a listed company is not very convenient in the UK. To be sure, the disfavor of British corporate governance towards controlling shareholders extends to all significant shareholders, and it used to be particularly severe when they controlled more than 30% of voting rights. Indeed, if one relies on less underestimated measures of American ownership concentration than in Barca and Becht (2001) (for instance those labeled as USA (2) in Figure 1.1), ownership appears to be the least concentrated in the UK also with respect to the frequency of large stakes ranging between 25% and 50% of voting rights.

1.2.2.2 The exercise of shareholder control in continental Europe

Table 1.1 aims to show two things. The first is how strong the largest shareholder is on average (i.e., how likely he is to be powerful enough to exert uncontestable control over the company management). The second is how strong other large shareholders are on average relative to the largest one (i.e., what the likelihood is that informal coalitions are formed to govern the company and to shield it from hostile takeovers). The three largest shareholders in each company are considered and we complement information about country averages with median values. By comparing this value with the average (sample mean) we are able to get an idea about how skewed are the country distributions of the largest shareholders. The further the sample mean is from the median value, the more skewed is the distribution. In addition, when the median is lower than the mean, there are more below-average than above-average firms; and the reverse is true in the opposite case. This tells us about the direction of skewedness.

It seems that the distributions of the largest voting blocks in continental Europe are not very skewed. Median values confirm that, apart from Spain, Sweden, and the Netherlands, the majority of firms listed in any country of the Old Continent have a controlling shareholder with more than 50% of voting rights. In the same countries, also the average size of the largest voting block is above (or just below) 50%, and there are more firms with above-average than below-average controlling shareholders.

Apparently, the typical controlling shareholder does not need much help in Austria, Belgium, France, Germany, and Italy: his position is normally uncontestable.[20] Neither would other shareholders be large enough to help. In fact, the average figures for the second and the third largest shareholders are very much lower than those of the largest one, and if we also look at median values, the vast majority of the firms have second and third largest shareholders below the average. Even though such shareholders have substantial stakes in the company, their relative weakness compared to the largest shareholder gives them little chance to be involved in corporate control. In these countries, shareholder coalitions not featuring a disclosed voting pact (which would bring them together in the definition of controlling blocks) seem to have just a residual importance, limited to those instances where the largest shareholder's voting power would not alone be sufficient to guarantee stability (i.e., non-contestability) of corporate control. This might hold, for instance, for that fraction of listed firms where each single shareholder accounts for less than 25% of voting rights, and therefore the three largest shareholders are likely to be closer to each other. But one should not forget that this fraction of listed companies is lower than 20% in all of the countries under consideration. Whatever is the actual, and still unexplored, role of shareholder coalitions in these countries, the near totality of listed firms exhibits very little contestability of corporate control, if any at all.[21]

The picture looks somewhat different in a few other countries of continental Europe, namely in Spain, Sweden, and the Netherlands. However, in all but the last country, the differences may be more apparent than real.

In Spain, the average size of the largest voting block is about 40%, and the median is five percentage points lower. That means that most listed firms have below-average voting power concentration. This is consistent with the previous observation about the relatively low frequency of absolute majority shareholders in Spain. However, one should not forget that for Spain, Barca and Becht (2001) underestimate shareholder control failing to account for formal voting pacts between shareholders. Actually, the relatively short distance between top-ranking voting blocks (as displayed in Table 1.1) suggests that shareholder coalitions may be an important feature of Spanish corporate governance – even though it is ultimately unclear whether they are formal or informal. Consistently, the country experts report that little contestability is observed among Spanish listed firms (Crespi-Cladera and Garcia-Cestona 2001).

In Sweden, the average size of the largest voting block seems to be even lower than 40% and again, the majority of listed firms appear to be (slightly) below average. However, these figures only account for the effect of dual class shares for enhancing voting power. Once indirect holdings through intermediate companies (typically organized in a pyramidal structure) are also accounted for, the picture of Swedish corporate governance becomes not much

---

20 With more recent data, Van der Elst (2008) shows that the situation has not changed much with respect to some of the countries under consideration.
21 For Italy, see Bianchi and Bianco (2006).

different from the rest of continental Europe. Two separate inquiries about concentration of both ownership and voting power in Sweden either show or suggest that the average largest block is about 50% and it is basically equal to the median value (i.e., about one half of listed firms have an absolute majority shareholder) (Cronqvist and Nilsson 2003; Holmén and Högfeldt 2009). This is achieved by extensive separation of voting rights from ownership claims, particularly through a combination of dual class shares with pyramidal ownership structures.

It should also be noticed that, in Sweden, control enhancement is much higher at the margin than on average. About one half of market capitalization at the Stockholm Stock Exchange used to be under the control of two major closed-end funds: *Investor* – controlled by the Wallenberg family – and *Industrivärden* – controlled by the *Svenska Handelsbanken* (SHB). In 2000, the integrated ownership of the two major corporate controllers in Sweden was 23 times lower than the stock market capitalization of the firms under control. If there was one single firm accounting for such a stock market capitalization, this would involve the ultimate ownership of the controlling shareholder being as low as 4.4%, but nonetheless sufficient to exert corporate control.[22] The levels of control enhancement reached their peak in 2000 and they were substantially reduced later on (the control/capital ratio became a more reasonable 5.9% in 2010) (Henrekson and Jakobsson 2012). Still, these figures should give an idea of the corporate governance pattern still having the highest relevance in the Swedish stock market.

Of course, in such a scenario, the voting power held by the second and the third largest shareholder is unimportant. In addition, the data in this regard are likely to be significantly *overestimated* relative to those concerning the largest voting block because direct and indirect holdings of the ultimate controlling shareholders are considered separately. Overall, the typical controlling shareholder of a Swedish listed company enjoys so much voting power in excess of ownership to be already insulated from a takeover threat. As a result, contestability of corporate control and shareholder coalitions appear to both be very exceptional in Sweden.

1.2.2.3 Dispersed ownership in the Netherlands

The situation in the Netherlands is even more different from continental Europe than it appears from the figures. The average size of the largest voting block is indeed quite high (about 43%) and roughly equal to the median value. But this is mainly due to the blocks held through trust offices (*administratiekantoor*) – the typical way in which voting rights used to be separated from ownership in the Netherlands.[23] Since the shares deposited in

---

22 In effect, this was even lower due to further control enhancement. See Holmén and Högfeldt 2009.

23 See *infra* Chapter 4, section 4.3.3. The popularity of this device has decreased dramatically in recent years (from 39% in 1992 to 15% in 2007). See de Jong et al (2010).

a trust office are mostly controlled by inside management while belonging to dispersed investors, ownership in the Netherlands seems to be more concentrated than it actually is. Once we look at the beneficial ownership of shares held by trust offices, the average largest stake gets as low as about 27% and the median is almost one third lower: that is to say, a half of Dutch listed firms have the largest owner accounting for no more than 18% of share capital. Only about a quarter of listed firms have a blockholder accounting for over 40% of share capital (de Jong et al 2001). Shares held through trust offices explain why *voting power* concentration is much higher (more than a half of listed firms have a voting block larger than 40%). The difference should be credited to managerial control.[24] More recent studies report that the frequency of large blockholders has decreased even further: in 2007 only 12% of the companies had an absolute majority shareholder; and only 11% had a shareholder with a stake of between 30% and 50% (de Jong et al 2010).

In this perspective, information about the second and the third largest voting block adds little to our knowledge. For the reasons that will be clarified by the analysis of corporate law in the Netherlands, the management of a Dutch publicly held company does not have much either to expect or to fear from shareholders, provided that they do not get too large; and Dutch corporate law allows for a number of techniques to prevent this from happening.[25] Coalitions might instead be of some help to support shareholder control, whenever the largest shareholder is not large enough to hold the management accountable. In theory, this might be an option for some of the companies. How many companies are actually controlled by a coalition of shareholders instead of by their management is ultimately an empirical question that can hardly be answered on the basis of aggregated data. The overall result would be unchanged anyway: contestability of corporate control is definitely *not* a feature of Dutch corporate governance in spite of the circumstance that managerial control is (today by far) the prevailing model in the Netherlands.

1.2.2.4 *Managerial control of Anglo-American firms*

Differently from continental Europe, controlling shareholders are rare in both the US and the UK. In these countries the average size of the largest voting block is significantly lower (accounting for about 15% of voting rights) and clearly insufficient, as such, to guarantee the unchallenged exercise of corporate control. In addition, the distribution of top voting blocks is highly skewed. Median values are about one third lower than the average. This means that in the majority of listed firms voting power is far more dispersed than on average. Similar results hold for ownership. Deviations from 'one share–one vote' are a negligible phenomenon in the UK and, even though they can be substantial in the US, they only account for about 6% of the firms listed on American

---

24 See Pacces (2007).
25 See *infra* Chapter 4, section 4.3.3.

stock markets (Gompers et al 2010). It is worth noting that the basic traits of this picture match the distribution of corporate ownership in the Netherlands, where the mean and median values of the largest stake are almost doubled but exhibit the same distance (about one third) from each other. In other words, the majority of listed firms have below-average ownership concentration.

The Anglo-American average largest shareholder is also very weak relative to *other* large shareholders. In at nearly one half of British listed companies, a coalition of the second and third largest shareholders would be sufficient to outvote the largest one. In the US, it seems that the size of voting blocks by rank declines somewhat more rapidly, especially if median values are considered, but not as rapidly as in continental Europe. The potential for coalition of moderately large shareholders is then quite an issue for the vast majority of Anglo-American listed firms, whereas it is so at most for a small minority of firms listed in continental Europe. Whether or not such a potential is exploited in practice, and how, is another question. The answer depends on contestability of corporate control.

The above picture about Anglo-American corporate governance yields three conventional – but far from undisputed – conclusions. The first is that in both the US and in the UK, the vast majority of listed firms are under managerial control, provided that no controlling shareholder is around. The second is that, differently from continental Europe (where a controlling shareholder typically holds a majority of share capital), corporate control is normally contestable in Britain and the US: allegedly, shareholders may anytime oust the management they are dissatisfied with, by coalescing and voting them out. The third is that, consequently, the basic corporate governance pattern is the same in the US and in the UK. Only the first conclusion is essentially correct, subject to one major qualification about the different impact of regulatory biases in the US and the UK. The second is apparently contradicted by empirical evidence on takeovers in Britain and the US. Finally, the standard belief that the US and the UK share a common pattern of corporate governance is manifestly wrong.

Corporate governance is indeed quite different between the US and the UK, and a better understanding of those differences helps to find out why corporate control of most Anglo-American firms is actually far from contestable. On the one hand, ownership concentration appears to be slightly higher in the US than in the UK, when only the position of the largest shareholder is considered. The potential for shareholder coalitions is instead higher in the UK than in the US. More importantly, regulation of corporate governance is substantially different. On the other hand, contestability of corporate control appears to play a minor role in both countries, where the overwhelming majority of takeovers ultimately take place with the consent of the incumbent management and, therefore, they are by no means hostile.[26]

26 On this point see more extensively Pacces (2007: 139–40).

Inside ownership and takeover defenses explain both the differences and the lack of contestability in British and American corporate governance. In a nutshell, the two are substitutes as far as takeover resistance is concerned (Franks et al 2001). An incumbent management may either be allowed to implement takeover defenses or hold on to enough shares to make potential takeovers unprofitable for the aggressor. The management of a typical US corporation does not need to resort to the latter strategy, for it is entitled to takeover defenses as long as it controls the board of directors – which it most often does (Macey 2008). The management of a public company in the UK has instead almost no choice except inside ownership to shield it from a hostile takeover, because straightforward takeover defenses are not available to the board of directors under British law. What is puzzling is how this situation did not result in concentrated ownership structures as in most part of the European continent. Authoritative commentators (e.g. Franks et al 2009) have identified a number of extralegal factors that fostered historically the deconcentration of ownership in the UK; these factors likely include the taxation of individual wealth (Cheffins 2008). Without denying the importance of these historical circumstances, an additional reason why, differently from the rest of Europe, the unavailability of takeover defenses does not prevent managerial control in the UK is that the UK systematically disfavors controlling shareholders in listed companies, by either regulation, best practice, or both. I shall elaborate on this point in Chapter 4.

Managerial ownership plays an important role in UK corporate governance, whereas it does not seem to be equally important in the US. In 1992, directors were the second most important category of owners in the UK, following institutional investors, and they accounted for an average aggregate stake of about 11% in established companies and 22% in recent IPOs (Goergen and Renneboog 2001). Comparable figures are not available for the US, but, according to the data reported in Barca and Becht (2001), US directors jointly hold *more* than 10% of voting rights in just 30% of the firms listed at the NASDAQ and in 10% of those listed at the NYSE. In addition, one should not forget that, in about 6% of US listed firms, directors have their voting power enhanced through dual class shares (which on average confer upon them more than 50% of voting rights) so that they are basically to be regarded as controlling shareholders (Gompers et al 2010).

The few economists that have realized this fundamental difference between the US and the UK claim that the underlying reason is essentially regulatory (Franks and Mayer 2002). Contrary to conventional wisdom, the legal discipline of corporate governance is in fact very different in the two countries (see also Armour and Skeel 2007). Two points have been especially highlighted by this strand of literature. The first is the special character of minority shareholder protection in the UK, which is achieved by disfavoring both the acquisition and the maintenance of a controlling position by large shareholders. The second is the very management-friendly regulation of takeover defenses in the US. I shall elaborate upon these and related differences from the fourth chapter of this book. For the moment, it should be sufficient to present the resulting patterns of corporate governance.

In both the US and the UK managerial control largely exceeds shareholder control, but this does not imply that corporate control is always contestable. Similarly to controlling shareholders in continental Europe, Anglo-American managers can entrench themselves. However, managerial entrenchment is achieved in two quite different manners in the US and in the UK. In Britain, managers entrench themselves by forming informal coalitions within the board of directors. In normal times, these coalitions hold enough voting power to reckon with outside shareholder interference and to resist a hostile takeover (see e.g. Crespi and Renneboog 2010). In fact, very few takeovers are hostile in the UK. During the 1990s, hostile takeovers accounted for less than 5% of changes in control in Britain (Weir and Laing 2003). As a result, board turnover is inversely related to inside ownership but basically unrelated to firm performance, apart from the cases of considerable underperformance (Franks et al 2001).

US managers can afford a much easier life because they do not need much voting power to exert or to maintain corporate control; all they need is to control the board of directors.[27] Under US law, board members can count on a number of advantages over outside shareholders, the most important being perhaps takeover defenses. These are implemented pre-bid by a majority of US listed firms, and can be employed post-bid (Daines and Klausner 2001). As a result, there seems to be no more hostility in US takeovers than "in the eyes of the beholder" (Schwert 2000). Also in the US board turnover is inversely related to inside ownership, but very noticeably, the same turnover appears to be more related to underperformance than in the UK (Franks et al 2001). Albeit far from hostile, US takeovers seem to support quite an efficient market for corporate control (Schwert 2000).

1.2.3 Comparative stock market performance

We have now a fairly good idea about how listed firms are owned and controlled in Europe and the US; but we do not know anything yet about how much equity finance is raised from the market in each system. In other words, we lack information about stock market performance.

Stock market performance means different things for different purposes. Performance indicators likewise differ depending on the phenomena they are intended to describe. For our purposes, we can just rely on the simplest proxy for each country's stock market performance, namely the stock market capitalization of national listed firms relative to the Gross Domestic Product (GDP). This gives an idea about the relative weight of equity finance in an economy. However, one important bias of this indication is worth noting.

---

27 See *infra* Chapter 4, section 4.3.1.

Stock market capitalization does not only account for external financial resources accruing to national listed firms, but also for the corporate controller's financial commitment and the firm's retained earnings (Hellwig 2000). The bias is clearly the more pronounced the higher the frequency of controlling shareholders and the larger their ownership stake.

Some economists (La Porta et al 1997) have attempted to calculate a performance index based on 'external' stock market capitalization. Although the idea is interesting, its implementation in practice is still much too rough. In theory, external stock market capitalization should be derived by subtracting the average proportion of share ownership in the hands of the corporate controllers. Because calculating such a proportion for different corporate governance systems is very difficult, the figures used so far in the literature are quite imprecise (Pacces 2007). More reliable estimates of how much stock is actually in the hands of corporate controllers are not yet available. Therefore, I prefer to rely on *total* stock market capitalization bearing in mind that this over-estimates the availability of equity finance where ownership structures are typically concentrated. Data are reported in Figure 1.2 below. They refer to a ten-year period in order to account for dependence of stock market performance on the economic cycle. I am using the same data as in Pacces (2007) although they are now almost 10 years old. This is with reasons. On the one hand, the period matches the observations regarding ownership concentration in the previous discussion. On the other hand, short of the economic trends, the patterns of stock market development are relatively stable over time.

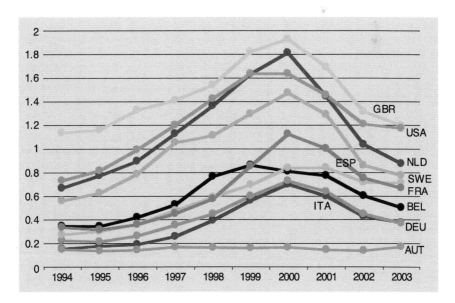

Figure 1.2 Stock market capitalization to GDP in Europe and in the US
Source: Pacces (2007).

Notwithstanding the controlling shareholders bias, the data show that stock markets are the most developed where corporate ownership is the most dispersed – namely, in the US and in the UK. This is not surprising. Dispersion of ownership naturally nurtures equity finance. Perhaps more surprisingly, the Dutch stock market appears to be almost as developed as the American one. In part, the result might be distorted by the higher proportion of controlling shareholders in the Netherlands. Still, arguably, Dutch listed firms have the highest access to external equity finance in continental Europe. Sweden has the second highest stock market capitalization to GDP in continental Europe. Even though controlling shareholders dominate Swedish corporate governance, the Swedish model is based on extensive separation of voting power from ownership stakes. In this regard, one should bear in mind that in 2000 more than one half of stock market capitalization was controlled with an average financial commitment lower than 5%. The very high development of the Swedish stock market should not be surprising in this perspective. The rest of continental Europe lags far behind the above-mentioned countries. Germany, Italy, and even more so Austria – which all have top-concentrated ownership structures – exhibit in particular the lowest rates of stock market capitalization to GDP.

1.2.4 Does the evidence match the theory?

The stylized picture of corporate governance in a selection of developed countries still contrasts the US and the UK with continental Europe. Anglo-American listed firms are typically widely held; the vast majority of them are under managerial control. Nearly all of their equity is placed with the investing public and so stock markets are highly developed. Both ownership and voting power are dispersed because deviations from the 'one share–one vote' rule are exceptional. As a result, in both the US and the UK corporate control is often assumed contestable, at least to the extent that the takeover defenses available to incumbent managers are not powerful enough to short-circuit contestability.

In the Old Continent, listed firms have typically a controlling shareholder (possibly a group of them acting as a coalition). Relatively little equity is placed with the investing public and stock markets are normally underdeveloped. Voting power is often held in excess of ownership, with both of them normally concentrated in the hands of controlling shareholders. As a result, corporate control is assumed only exceptionally contestable in continental Europe, at least inasmuch as the incumbent controller enjoys so much voting power to avoid being outvoted by an insurgent shareholder taking over.

This is already enough to question the standard view of corporate governance as a principal–agent relationship between inside management and outside shareholders. On the one hand, in the European continent, corporate control does not appear to be delegated to professional managers on behalf of the entire shareholder constituency, but if anything, just on behalf of a controlling shareholder (with the exclusion of non-controlling owners). On the other hand, even when managers are in charge – as it is most often the case in the US and the UK – outside shareholders may still be unable to exert an effective discipline on their supposed agents. Managers often succeed in insulating themselves from the threat of ouster, which of course undermines the ability of investors to hold them to account. Both circumstances are quite difficult to reconcile with a theoretical model based on delegation of corporate control from non-controlling shareholders.

After the previous review of the empirical evidence on comparative corporate governance, all we can say is that these two circumstances may be even more frequent than they appear at first glance. To begin with, we discovered that controlling shareholders play an important role in Anglo-American corporate governance too. In addition, departures from 'one share–one vote' are not so uncommon at least in the US, although they remain far less frequent than in continental Europe. Finally, managerial control does not automatically involve contestability, as it is often believed. In fact, controlling managers can be entrenched in the US and in the UK, too. In the US, they can shield themselves behind a wide array of takeover defenses. In the UK, they are likewise able to resist takeovers by forming powerful coalitions unless they seriously underperform or otherwise enter into a conflict with the institutional investors. As a result, hostile takeovers are highly exceptional not only in continental Europe, but also in Anglo-American corporate governance.

In continental Europe, controlling shareholders generally dominate the corporate governance arena. But there are exceptions. For instance, the majority of Dutch listed firms seem to be under managerial control; and the importance of managerial control has increased in recent years. Moreover, stock markets are not always underdeveloped relative to the US and the UK: this is true for some countries (like Italy), but not for others (most noticeably, Sweden and the Netherlands). Finally, also, systems based on controlling shareholders allow for different degrees of separation of ownership and control. The presence of a controlling shareholder normally implies a higher concentration of voting power, but this does not necessarily involve that concentration of ownership be as high. Although they are less popular today than in the past, the extensive deviations from 'one share–one vote' that characterize the Swedish corporate governance model provide a good example of how controlling shareholder systems can also feature significant separation of ownership from control.

The problem at this point is that the prevailing theoretical approach to corporate governance fails to explain all this. Non-negligible regularities such as the entrenchment of corporate control are not supported by the principal–agent model, if not of course as a source of inefficiency in the form of agency costs. Systematic differences like the two polar models of corporate governance discussed above – shareholder control and managerial control – are also a puzzle for the agency theory. However, particularly the circumstance that ownership and control structures are not randomly distributed across countries, but rather, dispersed ownership is quite unusual outside the US and the UK, suggests that institutions plays a role in the minimization of agency costs. In other words, when the law (or other complementary institutions) does not help to reduce agency costs ownership remains concentrated and access to equity finance is undermined. This is the fundamental intuition of the law and finance scholarship, which is the ideal reference point for the present investigation on how (corporate) law 'matters' for the shape and the efficiency of corporate governance.

1.3 Law and finance

1.3.1 *The measurement of corporate law*

1.3.1.1 *Theoretical background*

As we have seen, when contracts are incomplete, minimization of agency costs requires that some external constraints on the managers' behavior be established by institutions, particularly by corporate law. The theoretical underpinning of the 'law matters' proposition (La Porta et al 1998) is that when these legal constraints are insufficient to discipline the managers' conflicts of interest with the shareholders, separation of ownership and control will be impaired. On the one hand, shareholders fearing managerial misbehavior would be willing to pay less for the company's stock. When the discount becomes high enough, selling shares to the investing public would become unattractive for the entrepreneur, and therefore ownership could not further separate from control. On the other hand, in the absence of reliable legal protection of the shareholder interest, maintaining a large stake is the only way for the shareholders, including the controlling shareholder, to discipline management.

Consistent with the agency framework, the logic underlying the law and finance scholarship is that unconstrained opportunities for the managers to abscond with shareholders' money, or to place them to suboptimal use, make investors unwilling to sink equity capital in the firm. More technically, a too high risk of moral hazard and adverse selection going unchecked contractually limits the corporate controller's ability to raise equity via separation of ownership and control, making equity capital much costlier. 'Law matters' is an appealing way to say that failure of national corporate laws to protect non-controlling shareholders from expropriation is responsible for ownership concentration and for the underdevelopment of stock markets. To the extent that external equity funds are needed to finance uncertain growth opportunities available to the firm, this would ultimately lead to inefficient allocation of financial resources within an entire economy.[28]

---

28 The law and finance scholarship occupies a prominent position in the theory of legal origins (La Porta et al 2008), not only because it started the empirical inquiry on the effects of law

In this perspective, the 'law matters' proposition has an implicit normative flavor: it suggests that enhancing shareholder protection is efficient and should be the goal of corporate law. I will discuss this point in the following sections. Yet the main achievement of the law and finance scholarship is having *ranked* corporate laws on this basis and having shown that the effect of law on finance can be captured – statistically at least – by such rankings expressed in the form of legal indices. The first and still the best known of these indices – the 'Anti-director Rights Index' (La Porta et al 1998) – included only a few specific corporate law rules. But it was shown to significantly and substantially affect ownership concentration, the relative availability of external equity funds to firms situated in different countries of the world, and a number of other indicators of financial performance.[29]

A group of financial economists led by Professor Shleifer managed to prove empirically that different patterns and performances of corporate governance systems depend on a few representative items of corporate law and on the quality of their enforcement, which were both determined, in turn, by the historical tradition of the legal system. According to these findings, good law and good enforcement of shareholder rights characterize legal systems whose roots lie in the English common law, while the reverse holds true for systems based on the French civil law tradition. That should explain why Anglo-American firms have typically diffuse ownership and managers in control, whereas the lower quality of corporate law only allows for controlling shareholders and concentrated ownership in continental Europe.

The impact of these findings has been enormous, not only in the academic debate, but more importantly in policymaking. Many developed and developing countries have engaged in legal reforms with the goal to improve their score on the Anti-director Rights Index. Over a decade since the publication of *Law and Finance* (La Porta et al 1998), the indices have evolved and have been improved or replaced. They have become part of the investors' and the policymakers' thinking about regulation of corporate governance. Prominent examples of this influence are the Doing Business project of the World Bank, the EU Directive on Shareholders' Rights and, to a lesser extent, the OECD Principles of Corporate Governance.[30] A brief review of these

---

on economic performance, but also – and perhaps more importantly – because financial development is the most plausible channel through which efficient law affects economic growth. The empirical validity of this channel has been demonstrated by Rajan and Zingales (1998a) and subsequently tested, among others, by Levine et al (2000).

29 See particularly La Porta et al (1998) on ownership concentration and La Porta et al (1997) on stock market development. Other applications to different measures of financial performance are surveyed in La Porta et al (2008). For the extension of the law and finance argument to economic growth, see Levine (1999).

30 See e.g. World Bank, *Doing Business 2011: Making a Difference for Entrepreneurs*, 2011, available at www.doingbusiness.org. (All of the Doing Business reports since 2004, the data, and the methodological notes are downloadable from the World Bank website: www.doingbusiness.org).

indices and of their limitations is thus necessary to appreciate their actual relationship with the question, what is efficient corporate law?

1.3.1.2 Indices of corporate law's quality

La Porta et al (1998) reported many statistics on alternative sources of legal protection of shareholders. However, it was a particular combination of substantive rules in corporate law that had the strongest explanatory power in the econometric analysis. Such a combination apparently explained why ownership is dispersed in some countries and concentrated in some others; and similarly, why some countries have more developed stock markets than others (La Porta et al 1997). The combination at issue was based on a selection of six legal rules allowing shareholders to constrain managerial power as exercised via the board of directors (captured by the management as an assumption). The quality of law was measured by an index ranging from zero to six, where a score of 1 or 0 was assigned depending on whether a certain 'anti-director' rule was present or not in national corporate law. Legal systems whose origins lie in the common law tradition scored much better on the Anti-director Rights Index than those based on a civil law tradition, and in fact, the former have on average much lower ownership concentration and better developed stock markets than the latter. Thus, superiority of the Anglo-American legal origin in the regulation of corporate finance sprang out as a powerful corollary of the 'law matters' thesis.

In the original econometric setup, legal origins were an instrumental variable used to overcome concerns of reverse causality between law and financial performance. Because legal origins pre-existed the development of stock markets, they had to be exogenous in the statistical model. Short of the doubts of comparative lawyers about whether legal origins capture a meaningful legal pattern, it is worth noting that the authors themselves have ultimately come to the conclusion that legal origins are not a good instrument for assessing the relation between law and finance, but remain a causal determinant of this and other relations between law and economic outcomes (La Porta et al 2008: 298). Given our interest in the substantive elements of good corporate law, it is worth focusing on the construction of the indices rather than on the causal determinants of its scores.

There are a number of issues with this construction which have been variously emphasized during over a decade of debate on the Anti-director Rights Index (for a recent survey, see Siems and Deakin 2010). First, there are problems of *coding*. The same variable may be given inconsistent scores across jurisdictions, for instance because the distinction between default rules and/or the impact of case law is neglected. The second problem is the *selection* of the Index components, as it has been argued that the Anti-director Rights Index suffers from a strong 'US bias' and fails anyhow to identify the most important legal tools for investor protection. The third problem is *weighting*. Intuitively, the impact of different rules for investor protection varies, so it is arbitrary to put all of them on equal footing – as it would be arbitrary to assign any specific weights. The final issue can be understood as a combination of the above problems. Legal comparison should be performed *functionally*, this implying that the coding, selection and weighting of legal rules affecting investor protection in different jurisdictions can diverge substantially, although the effects may be similar.[31] This critique casts serious doubts on the possibility to measure the quality of legal rules, and particularly on the validity of the Anti-director Rights Index as a prototype of this measurement.

The problems with coding have been documented with respect to several countries (Spamann 2006; Cools 2005; Braendle 2006). Some countries received a score of 1 on shareholder rights which are only optional under corporate law, whereas some others scored 0 on shareholder rights that are not codified but are nonetheless plainly granted by courts. The most serious issue in coding is inconsistency as, for instance, default rules received different scores depending on the jurisdiction. Technically speaking, both case law and the distinction between mandatory, default, and optional rules are not accounted for in the definition of components of the Anti-director Rights Index, even though this distinction clearly matters for shareholder protection particularly when those who are in control can engage in opportunistic charter amendments (Bebchuk and Hamdani 2002).

Coding problems with the Anti-director Rights Index were ultimately addressed by the law and finance scholarship (Djankov et al 2008), although according to the critics they were never completely overcome (Spamann 2010). Other points of criticism are more radical. First, who tells that in every country shareholder protection depends on exactly the same rules to the same extent? And why should they be just those six rules? Could not an equivalent degree of protection be granted by a different, but neglected set of rules? And how should the importance of each rule in a given country be weighted within each set? These problems are much harder to cope with than coding, since they cast doubt on the very relevance of each component of the index as to investor protection. The six equally weighted components of the Anti-director Rights Index are the following: (i) the right of shareholders to mail their proxy vote to the firm; (ii) the individual right to participate in the general meeting without having shares blocked in advance; (iii) proportional shareholder representation in the board of directors (or so-called 'cumulative voting'); (iv) judicial venues against unfair conduct by directors actionable by shareholders accounting for no more than 10% of share capital; (v) preemptive rights in new issues of stock; (vi) the right to call an extraordinary general meeting granted to shareholders representing no more than 10% of share capital.

---

31 See the comprehensive qualitative study performed by Kraakman et al (2009), focusing more on the similarities than on the differences across corporate laws in addressing agency problems.

The relevance of the above rights as to shareholder protection was questioned even for the US, on whose typical corporate governance model the selection of rules was based (Paredes 2004). A few American scholars stressed that corporate lawyers would not consider any of the components of the Anti-director Rights Index among the principal tools of investor protection provided for by US law (see Coffee 2001b; Roe 2002). The criticism went even further in Europe. Not only rules other than those considered by La Porta and co-workers seemed to be actually responsible of the quality of outside shareholder protection, but some of the rules included in the Anti-director Rights Index were even going in the opposite direction (see Baums and Scott 2005 and Cools 2005).

One important example is proxy voting. This is allowed in many countries but does not always have to do with investor protection. In France and in Germany, for instance, proxy voting is regulated in such a way that it can only support incumbent controllers (Kraakman et al 2009). To be sure, proxy voting most often works to the advantage of insiders rather than of outside investors, and this is also the case in the US and in the UK.[32] Another example of a shareholder right that may turn out against outside investor protection is proportional representation on the board, or cumulative voting. This might be helpful for minority shareholders in concentrated ownership structures, but is counterproductive where ownership is dispersed and shareholder empowerment depends on the ability to coalesce and take full control of the board (Easterbrook and Fischel 1991). Similarly, preemptive rights are supposed to protect minority shareholders from dilution, but are irrelevant to this purpose in a dispersed ownership structure. Only in the UK do preemptive rights perform another function, namely supporting the bargaining power of institutional investors vis-à-vis the management when the company is short of funding (Franks et al 2001). Elsewhere the problem of investor dilution by controlling shareholders is addressed by functionally equivalent rules (Kraakman et al 2009).

Problems of this kind are probably impossible to overcome with an 'indexing' methodology unless indices are allowed extraordinary wideness and complexity. Taking stock of the decennial experience of the law and finance scholarship, a group of more legally oriented scholars have tried to construct broader and more sophisticated indices (see Siems and Deakin 2010). However, it is at least doubtful that more fine-grained indices, allowing for 60 instead of 6 components, can overcome the critique of lack of functional approach by comparative lawyers (Hertig 2010). Even if the selection of corporate law items effectively accounted for all the relevant tools of investor protection across different countries, the problem with weighting the items would remain. Still, the advantage of these more recent studies is not just that they are more sophisticated, but that they are less ambitious. They seek to describe

---

32 See *infra* Chapter 4.

patterns of legal evolution and their economic effects across countries and over time, instead of claiming that one model of investor protection is better than another. This approach remains instead the major weakness of the law and finance scholarship, despite the improvements in the methodology.

Professor Shleifer and his co-authors ultimately acknowledged the limitations of the Anti-director Rights Index, particularly its *ad hoc* character and the mistakes in coding. The more recent articles of the law and finance scholarship (La Porta et al 2006; Djankov et al 2008) sought to improve on these two issues by surveying, with the help of local lawyers, the legal response to key problems in a number of jurisdictions. However, short of a more precise problem definition, the methodology and the ambition of the law and finance approach remained unchanged. New measures of investor protection were crafted in order to address the two main venues of shareholder expropriation, namely security fraud and self-dealing. According to the authors, investors are concerned about expropriation even more than of their powers relative to the management, and thus legal tools aimed at countering expropriation illustrate better how law 'matters' for finance.

As a result, the Anti-director Rights Index was still revised for reason of continuity, but it was effectively replaced by two new indices of investor protection under securities law ('Disclosure in Prospectus' and 'Prospectus Liability,' in La Porta et al 2006) and a compounded index of protection from self-dealing under corporate law ('Anti-Self-Dealing Index' in Djankov et al 2008). These indices had stronger and sometimes even more statistically significant effects on stock market development and dispersion of corporate ownership. They continued to support the view that the common law tradition outperforms civil law countries as to the quality of investor protection and the availability of equity finance to the corporate enterprise. The impact of the new indices went beyond academia, as this time they were endorsed by the World Bank in the Doing Business project. This project has the great ambition to lead the improvement in the legal infrastructure worldwide. To this purpose, the World Bank calculates and publishes yearly a series of indices of quality of business law. Investor protection is one of these indices, and it is based – as are most of the other Doing Business indices – on the work of the law and finance scholarship.[33]

It must be acknowledged that the last indices developed by the law and finance scholarship follow a somewhat more functional approach to legal comparison. The two indexes of quality of securities law refer to categories of tools available to investors for preventing or challenging a standard securities fraud. The Anti-Self-Dealing Index is based on a number of ex-ante and ex-post remedies in the face of a stylized case of self-dealing. Unfortunately, not all the possible reactions of each legal system to either securities fraud or related-party transactions are accounted for, which still affects the precision of

---

33 See particularly the construction of the Investor Protection index within Doing Business (http://www.doingbusiness.org/methodology/protecting-investors).

the legal comparison. A second problem is that the weighting of each kind of reaction is standardized, although it is likely that the relative importance of each category of remedies varies from country to country.[34]

As far as the first problem is concerned, the statistical approach to legal comparison may overlook important issues. For instance, both American and comparative lawyers acknowledge that a major strength of investor protection under US securities law comes from a rather unique combination of class action suits with the lawyers' contingent fees (Coffee 2001b; Kraakman et al 2009). However, this issue is deliberately dismissed from the quantitative assessment of the quality of securities law on grounds that, statistically, it bears no significant relation with stock market development across countries (La Porta et al 2006). A similar point can be made about the Netherlands, whose collective enforcement tools are becoming increasingly popular among disgruntled investors worldwide. However, La Porta et al (2006) present the Netherlands as one typical case of under-enforcement of securities law.[35]

As far as the weighting is concerned, how effectively self-dealing is policed by the legal system is not just a matter of how many safeguards are available but rather, of how they are combined. For instance, in Djankov et al (2008), the Swedish score on the Anti-Self-Dealing Index was even lower than the Italian one (33% and 42% respectively, as opposed to 65% for the US and 95% for the UK) whereas the Netherlands scored as bad as many developing countries (20% – that is, less than a half of the world average). Based on the qualitative research that I will present in Chapter 6, both the Netherlands (by means of a special procedure and a specialized Court) and Sweden (by means of severe public enforcement supporting powerful social norms) functionally provided investors with good protection from expropriation. These findings match the perception of international investors. However, the Anti-Self-Dealing Index overlooks these circumstances. On the contrary, the index correctly assigns a low score to Italy for the years of reference because anti-self-dealing provisions used to be (and to some extent still are) under-enforced.[36]

The problem with weighting is well illustrated by the performance of the above countries on the Doing Business index of investor protection. This

---

34 See *infra* Chapter 6.
35 It must be acknowledged that the legal information underlying the indices in La Porta et al (2006) refer to 2000. The international relevance of the Netherlands for securities law enforcement is much more recent (see Kortmann and Bredenoord-Spoek 2011 and *infra* Chapter 6). Still, the gist of the law and finance approach is that legal investor protection is quite stable over time as it is strongly influenced by the legal origin. The Dutch case contradicts this argument on a number of counts, including the enforcement of securities law.
36 Djankov et al (2008) describe Italy in detail as a 'bad law' environment as opposed to the UK example of 'good law.' This corresponds with other comparative, but more qualitative analyses (Enriques and Volpin 2007). However, see Enriques (2009) for more recent developments in Italian law.

index is officially based on Djankov et al (2008), but the scores differ significantly. Specifically, as of 2006 (the reference year of Djankov et al 2008), the UK scores 80% instead of 95%; the US, 83% instead of 65%; Italy and Sweden, 57% instead of 42% and 33% respectively; the Netherlands, 47% instead of 20%. Given that both the source of legal information and the methodology of calculation is the same for both indices, there is no reason why the output should differ, particularly regarding the ranking of countries. The reason of difference is indeed a trivial one: the scores of sub-indices are aggregated with two different formulas in Djankov et al (2008) and in Doing Business. This is sufficient evidence that arbitrary weighting may have a very significant impact on the final scores.[37]

From the first attempts to measure the quality of corporate and securities law it can be concluded that the results of this exercise are considerably less objective than they look. Thus, they should be taken with a lot more caution. The second generation of comparative law and finance, which remains indeed a valuable exercise, seems to be going exactly in this direction (Siems and Deakin 2010). Particularly noticeable is a shift of focus from the aprioristic selection of legal institutions that are supposed to 'matter' for financial development to the study of how corporate and securities laws have actually evolved across countries, possibly to reflect converging legal patterns in investor protection.

The more recent approach acknowledges that indices, however sophisticated, can never replicate a fully-fledged functional comparison. Because the selection of legal variables must allow for some arbitrariness, these indices cannot reveal more than trends. For this reason, the time-series dimension is currently receiving more attention than the cross-country dimension. In this regard, it is worth noting that legal investor protection ceases to have statistically significant effects on financial development once the legal indices are allowed more complexity; some specifications even reveal that investor protection may be excessive and then undermine efficiency (Armour, et al 2009b). It remains to be established whether our ability to measure the quality of corporate law is simply too limited or whether there are factors other than legal investor protection which determine financial development and the prevalence of one ownership structure over another. We now turn to this question.

1.3.2 *The effects of corporate law*

1.3.2.1 *Law and ownership concentration*

The fundamental claim by the law and finance scholarship, that law 'matters', was based on the observation that separation of ownership and control is very

---

37 In this regard, it is also remarkable that the country scores were ultimately removed from the published version of Djankov et al (2008). As a matter of academic policy, however, Professor Shleifer has always made these data available on his homepage.

rare outside the Anglo-Saxon world (La Porta et al 1999). Controlling shareholders effectively dominate corporate governance worldwide. This is not necessarily an inefficient outcome under the agency approach to corporate governance. Because controlling shareholders have stronger incentives to monitor, it may be efficient to trade this advantage against lower liquidity and diversification of the controller's investment (see Bratton and McCahery, 2001). The problem, correctly identified by Shleifer and Vishny (1997), is when concentrated ownership is chosen because the law is too weak to support monitoring of management by dispersed shareholders. This intuition, which is theoretically valid, had to be significantly stylized in order to fit the empirical setup of law and finance and its progeny discussed earlier. This had important consequences for the definition of both the dependent and the independent variables of the law and finance regressions.

To begin with, the dependent variable – ownership concentration – was oversimplified in the whole series of articles based on the findings of La Porta et al (1999), which were the first to document the dominance of blockholders in the largest companies listed outside the US and the UK. However, the measure of ownership concentration in that study (mean ownership of the three largest shareholders in the ten largest listed companies) was much too coarse to allow for an effective description of the degree of separation of ownership and control in the countries of the sample. The problem is that controlling shareholders exist in virtually any corporate law jurisdiction, including the US and the UK, but their actual frequency across countries is difficult to estimate with a standardized methodology. In addition, not all blockholders are controlling shareholders. Although there are more accurate studies of comparative ownership and control,[38] some of which have been reviewed in the foregoing sections, a precise understanding of concentration of ownership and voting powers has not yet been synthesized in one single measure applicable worldwide. Perhaps for this reason, despite wide availability of data, previous comparative statistics on ownership and control have not been updated within and outside the law and finance scholarship.

As a result, all the articles of the law and finance series show effects of corporate law on ownership concentration that would be questionable even in the absence of controversy on the accuracy of the legal indices. For instance, in the US corporate ownership is considered as dispersed as in the UK, but recent studies document a much higher frequency of controlling shareholders in American companies (Holderness 2009). Likewise, the Netherlands is considered a country with highly concentrated ownership whereas Sweden is presented as a moderately concentrated ownership jurisdiction; in reality, the opposite is true.[39] Most importantly – as the law and finance scholarship explicitly recognized – there is nothing bad with ownership concentration *per se*; the problem is when ownership concentration *depends* on the law. Two

---

38   Prominent examples include Barca and Becht (2001) and Faccio and Lang (2002).
39   See *supra* section 1.2.2.

wrongs do not make a right. Because both ownership concentration and legal investor protection were not measured precisely, the message came through that ownership concentration mainly depended on the bad quality of corporate law. La Porta co-authors never denied the virtues of ownership concentration outside that perverse relationship; more simply, they ignored ownership concentration not determined by bad law.

The implications of this omission for the independent variable – the legal indices – have been recently emphasized by Bebchuk and Hamdani (2009). They have argued that legal investor protection (as well as the investor friendliness of corporate charters) cannot be assessed in the same fashion when the management is in control and when there is a controlling shareholder. The essential difference is that, while the management can be replaced – at least in principle – by a takeover, this is normally not the case for a controlling shareholder. On the other hand, while managers may care too little about maximizing shareholder value due to their limited ownership, the interest of controlling shareholders is better aligned with that of the other shareholders, unless controlling shareholders can engage in unconstrained self-dealing and/ or control-enhancing mechanisms. These aspects are all dealt with by different legal rules and enforcement mechanisms.

The essential point of this argument is that the law and finance scholarship managed, at best, to capture one half of the story. Particularly, the Antidirector Rights Index was well suited to a dispersed ownership structure, but its features are largely irrelevant in a concentrated ownership structure. The opposite conclusion holds for the more recent Anti-Self-Dealing Index, whose design is based on a stylized case of self-dealing by a controlling shareholder. But if the law and finance scholarship only included investor protection in one setting (say, concentrated ownership), how could they possibly claim that the same variable simultaneously affected the frequency of the other setting (dispersed ownership)? Despite all the reservations on the accuracy with which both independent and dependent variables are measured, indeed this ambiguity has an impact in the last findings of the law and finance scholarship. In Djankov et al (2008), for the first time a legal variable (the Anti-Self-Dealing Index) has no statistically significant effect on ownership concentration.[40]

The argument that the quality of corporate law needs to be verified for at least two different models of corporate governance – one with concentrated and one with dispersed ownership – can be carried further. Not only does investor protection mean different things depending on who is effectively in control, which implies that the legal discipline of *both* management and controlling shareholder matters for stock market development. Also, investor protection could be excessively demanding, in either the concentrated or the dispersed ownership setting, and induce companies to select an inefficient ownership structure or to forego separation of ownership and control altogether

---

40 Curiously, however, a different result is reported by La Porta et al (2008), where the Anti-Self-Dealing Index has a slightly significant effect on ownership concentration.

in order to avoid overly burdensome regulations. Although this proposition has never been tested empirically, it is in line with the recent findings that excessive investor protection may even impair stock market development (Armour et al 2009).

1.3.2.2 What is missing from the 'law matters' framework?

It would be premature to conclude that, if only the features of legal protection of outside shareholders were measured with more precision, this account of corporate law would explain the variation in corporate governance patterns around the world and particularly between continental Europe and the US/UK. The problem with the 'law matters' argument may be not technical, but conceptual: legal protection of outside shareholders may not be just the only institutional factor affecting the choice of corporate governance arrangements. Even aside from the weakness of comparative law analysis, the argument seems to be incomplete because it fails to explain a few facts of corporate governance in the real world, let alone their efficiency or inefficiency.

To begin with, there are some countries where, regardless of the scores on the various indices of the law and finance scholarship, investor protection appears to be functionally equivalent (Gilson 2006). Nonetheless, the ownership and control structures of publicly held companies differ significantly. For instance, in both Sweden and the US expropriation of minority shareholders does not appear to be a major problem. However, while the typical Swedish company has a controlling shareholder, the vast majority of US listed companies do not have one. Based on the theoretical framework underlying the law and finance literature, one could hardly explain that result. Neither, of course, could one say which system is the best.

Conversely, in some other countries, investor protection is achieved in completely different ways, for instance because corporate laws put different emphasis on litigation versus effective governance by non-controlling shareholders. Contrary to a long-lived misconception, the two countries where dispersed corporate ownership is most pervasive in the world – the US and the UK – actually provide outside shareholders with different modes and intensity of legal protection (Armour and Skeel 2007). Once again, how do these results possibly obtain? Even more importantly, is the British system any better than the American one, or it is just the other way round?

These and other observations have led many commentators, on both the economic and the legal side, to conclude that the impact of legal rules on corporate governance has been exaggerated. Alternative hypotheses thus emerged on the institutional determinants of corporate governance. There are too many to be reviewed here, but two of these hypotheses are particularly interesting for the potential implications on efficiency. The first hypothesis deals with the broader institutional determinants of private benefits of control; the second hypothesis concerns the politics of corporate governance, i.e. the constituencies in whose interest companies are supposed to be managed.

1.3.2.3 *Private benefits of control*

A broader and, in a sense, less rudimentary account of the 'law matters' story is based on the bearing of various institutions (including the law) on private benefits of control. As we know, private benefits of control are utilities enjoyed *exclusively* by the corporate controller, which can mean one or more controlling shareholders or the managers depending on the ownership structure. Because private benefits of control include different things, their extraction can be efficient or inefficient (Coates 2004). In the mainstream agency framework, however, private benefits of control can only be extracted at the expenses of non-controlling shareholders. This is always inefficient because it leads to either underproduction of the firm's surplus or to its outright diversion from investors (who then become less willing to invest). The agency view completely neglects the possibility that extraction of private benefits of control may be efficient, for instance because it supports unverifiable investments in entrepreneurship whose value could not be captured by investors otherwise. I will discuss this limitation in the following section (1.3.3).

Regardless of whether private benefits are efficient or inefficient, their presence in corporate governance naturally leads to concentrated ownership. However, this is not only because shareholders refrain from investing in listed companies for fear of being expropriated. More importantly, the entrepreneur who expects to enjoy high private benefits of control will not be willing to deconcentrate ownership beyond a certain extent, for this would involve leaving corporate control and its private value up for grabs (Bebchuk 1999). Therefore, the ultimate reason for ownership concentration is that protection of control rents requires that contestability of corporate control be ruled out at the outset. Now, assume that these private benefits of control depend on the controlling shareholder's inability to commit to a policy of no-investor-expropriation when it would be efficient to do so. Then gains from trading equity between the entrepreneur and outside investors are foregone because institutions, including corporate law, fail to police inefficient extraction of private benefits, which leads in turn to suboptimal separation of ownership and control (Gilson 2006). This is the point of tangency with the law and finance scholarship. However, the notion of private benefits of control can tell us more about the institutional determinants of corporate governance.

A few attempts have been made to quantify private benefits of control empirically, on a cross-country basis (Nenova 2003; Dyck and Zingales 2004). These studies capture pecuniary values realized or traded on the stock market which should account for the present value of expected diversion of cash flow from non-controlling shareholders. These studies have some methodological problems, making comparisons between developed countries particularly difficult (see e.g. Nicodano 1998; Nicodano and Sembenelli 2004). Nevertheless, even this rather crude proxy for the real size of private benefits of control appears to be more significantly related to ownership concentration than 'poor' legal protection of outside shareholders as measured by the Anti-director Rights Index. Since these indicators essentially point at expropriation of non-controlling shareholders from two different angles, this implies that corporate law – at least as measured by the law and finance scholarship – is *not* the only institutional factor that affects shareholder expropriation.[41]

The empirical analysis of private benefits of control reveals that the latter depends not only on the quality of legal investor protection and of its enforcement, but also on a number of other factors like social norms, product market competition, an independent financial press, and a high rate of tax compliance (Dyck and Zingales 2004). By enhancing the protection of shareholders' investment, these factors contribute to the minimization of agency costs. A remarkable result is that, once the effect of extralegal institutions is included in the regressions, the size of private benefits of control is no longer correlated with the origin of each country's legal system. That is to say, systems based on English common law fare no better in policing private benefits of control and in fostering dispersion of ownership. The only group of countries that have some statistically significant advantage in this regard is Scandinavia, where some peculiar extralegal institutions are likely to drive the result.

These findings have important implications for the 'law matters' argument. First, there is no one-size-fits-all model of legal investor protection promoting financial development. The statistical effects of corporate law on financial performance are best captured by a measure of private benefits of control, but the size of those is determined by combinations of legal and extralegal factors varying considerably across countries. A second implication is that, because abnormally high levels of private benefits of control do not allow ownership to separate from control, legal curbs on shareholder expropriation indeed 'matter' for financial development, although not necessarily according to the indices of the law and finance scholarship. The third implication is a puzzle. Moderately low levels of private benefits of control are observed both in countries with typically dispersed ownership (like the US) and in countries where ownership is typically concentrated (like Sweden). This suggests that, as soon as shareholder expropriation ceases to be the determinant of large private benefits of control, the relationship between investor protection and the ownership structure becomes ambiguous.

1.3.2.4 Political theory

The political hypothesis does not only claim that institutions other than corporate law matter for investor protection; but also, more importantly, that politics shapes corporate law and its evolution (Roe 2003). While corporate

41 To be sure, the last paper of the law and finance scholarship (Djankov et al 2008) finds that the measure of private benefits of control estimated by Dyck and Zingales (2004) is significantly determined by the Anti-Self-Dealing Index and it is strongly correlated with the legal origin.

law may and should indeed protect investors from expropriation, shareholders do not simply care about not being expropriated; they want the value of their investment to be maximized. Corporate law, especially if regarded as a mere anti-expropriation tool, seems to be far less important than politics in the second respect. On the one hand, social democracy brings stakeholders, like the employees, into corporate governance. If shareholders want to keep their primacy and have the firm managed in their interest, they need to be large enough to resist stakeholders' impact. On the other hand, this process creates vested interests resistant to legal changes that would involve redistribution of economic rents (Pagano and Volpin 2005). Specifically, established controlling shareholders and labor unions oppose dispersed ownership as much as managers of free-standing companies resist concentration of ownership.

This approach contends that ownership did not separate from control in continental Europe because stakeholders were entitled to various degrees of interference in corporate governance and they would have prevailed in the management of large companies in the absence of controlling shareholders. The same account suggests that the emphasis of courts and legislatures on shareholder value maximization, instead of protection of employees, enabled dispersion of ownership and managerial control in both the US and in the UK. In this perspective, politics matters more than law for corporate governance. At the end of the day, how friendly to shareholders the institutional environment is seems to depend on politics, first, and on the law only consequently.

Yet the idea that the regulation and the patterns of corporate governance are determined by politics, in particular by social democracy, seems to fly in the face of reality. Stakeholder involvement in corporate governance is compatible both with systems characterized almost exclusively by the presence of controlling shareholders (like Sweden and Germany) and with those supporting also managerial control (like the Netherlands). On the contrary, the absence of stakeholder involvement in corporate governance comes with ownership structures that are either very dispersed (as in the UK) or very concentrated (as in Italy). One may of course disagree on the precise meaning of stakeholder involvement and on how this should be measured in empirical analyses. But it seems fair to conclude that, while politics has undeniable influence on corporate governance, the choice of ownership structure may not be entirely determined by politics.

1.3.2.5 May law still matter?

The foregoing analysis suggests that, contrary to the claim by the law and finance scholarship, certain features of corporate and securities law do not unambiguously determine the shape of corporate governance, particularly the ownership structure. However, neither do other institutional factors like, for instance, politics and social norms. If anything, the empirical evidence shows important effects of all these factors, which, however, are not easy to disentangle.

Especially on historical grounds, some commentators have pushed the argument so far as to claim that law may not matter at all for separation of ownership and control (see e.g. Cheffins 2008). Particularly in the UK, separation of ownership and control had emerged in the absence of meaningful legal protections of outside shareholders (Franks et al 2005). These protections were subsequently bargained for by institutional investors. Also, in the US, separation of ownership and control seems to have preceded the establishment of strong shareholder rights (Coffee 2001b). Finally, in the beginning of the 20th century, there was more separation of ownership and control in continental Europe than in the US and in the UK, despite the allegedly low quality of investor protection outside the common law tradition (Rajan and Zingales 2003). The law and finance scholarship ultimately replied that none of these argument shows that law does not matter (La Porta et al 2008). Legal investor protection did arise in the US and the UK to support models of corporate governance based on dispersed ownership, and subsequently both the degree of investor protection and separation of ownership and control became significantly higher in the Anglo-Saxon world than in continental Europe. Whatever the historical factors behind separation of ownership and control, this separation would have evolved differently and perhaps even failed to persist, in the absence of legal support. Therefore, law does play a role.

What this role exactly is and under which conditions corporate law improves the efficiency of corporate governance outcomes, remains an open question. The final answer by the law and finance scholarship (La Porta et al 2008) is that legal origins determine whether the regulatory style is oriented to sustain markets (as in the common law tradition) or rather to replace them (as in the civil law tradition). Powerful legal tools for investor self-help naturally emerge only in the first situation, because in the other situation governments play a direct role in the production of goods and in its financing. At least when financial markets work without major crises, countries in the first situation outperform those in the second one. Without entering the controversy on the legal origin theory, there is one important truth in this kind of reasoning: legal systems are path-dependent (Bebchuk and Roe 1999). If this is the case, the impact of law on corporate governance always depends on a particular combination of legal and extralegal factors that make it almost impossible, at least statistically and on a cross-country basis, to show what determines what.

While this insight casts some doubts on the prospect of international convergence of corporate laws to a single model, it does not undermine the quest for efficient rules in corporate governance. The only problem is that these rules may 'matter' differently in different institutional contexts, for instance because one country guarantees good investor protection only in concentrated ownership structures and another one only in dispersed structures. This is after all the essence of the functional critique to the measurement of the quality of law. From a normative perspective, however, corporate law may still aim for the same goals and be *functionally* efficient to the extent that these goals are achieved. Protection of outside investors is certainly one of these goals. But it might not be the only one.

1.3.3 *What is efficient corporate law?*

1.3.3.1 *Why legal protection of outside shareholders is important, but it is not enough*

One limitation of the 'law matters' thesis is that it does not distinguish 'stealing' from 'shirking' in corporate governance (Roe 2002). Both are sources of agency costs that should be minimized through protection of outside shareholders. While appropriate legal rules can possibly contain the diversion of the firm's surplus once it is produced (stealing), no legal mechanism can substitute for the suboptimal exercise of business judgment over the production of the same surplus (shirking). Conversely, ownership concentration provides high-powered incentives to put effort in the firm's management, but does not limit the controlling shareholder's ability to divert cash flow from minority shareholders. As a result, an effective legal protection of non-controlling shareholders does not necessarily lead to dispersion of ownership; whereas ownership concentration alone provides no guarantee against minority shareholder expropriation. As Professor Roe (2002; 2003) has efficaciously pointed out, protection of investors from outright expropriation does not automatically explain separation of ownership and control.

Another issue is whether separation of ownership and control is desirable at all. This is the case according to the standard principal–agent approach to corporate governance, which supports efficient separation of management from risk-taking. In this perspective, all private benefits of control deriving from agency problems are unambiguously inefficient. It makes no difference whether they are obtained by outright expropriation of the company's cash flow (stealing) or, rather, by on-the-job consumption of the assets under management (shirking). Limiting the extraction of private benefits of control by the corporate controller and minimizing agency costs are in fact two sides of the same coin (Shleifer and Vishny 1997). This means that promotion of equity finance by the legal system requires not only behavioral constraints on shareholder expropriation by the management but, even more so, allocation of control rights to shareholders: shareholders should be entitled to replace the management when they are stealing or shirking too much (Becht et al 2007).

The only legal implication from this framework is that law should support hostile takeover (Easterbrook and Fischel 1991). That would be sufficient to support separation of ownership and control. Contestability of corporate control would ultimately make sure that no private benefits of control can be secured by the management, for this would immediately attract a takeover bid (Macey 2008). The mere threat of hostile takeovers encourages separation of ownership and control. Alternatively, inasmuch as corporate control can be shielded from hostile takeover, selling shares to the investing public may not be profitable enough for the entrepreneur to give up his private benefits of control, and ownership will likely remain concentrated (Bebchuk 1999).

Why then is the law and finance scholarship focused on expropriation of outside shareholders to identify efficient corporate law? The reason is that the hostile takeover mechanism does not really work in practice (Becht et al 2007). The threat of hostile takeover can be avoided essentially in two ways. The first is permissible takeover defenses that can be credibly operated by the management through their control of the board. The second is simply one or more controlling shareholders acting as a coalition to stop changes in control not previously agreed upon. Most companies around the world can and do avail themselves of these control entrenchment devices, often supplemented by legal rules that make hostile acquisitions costlier (as for instance, the mandatory bid). This explains why hostile takeovers have become too rare to constitute a credible threat, which makes investors dependent on other tools to secure a return from their investment (Shleifer and Vishny 1997).

Entrenchment of corporate control is allowed on different conditions by legal systems, but it is ultimately a matter of choice. From the entrepreneur's standpoint, insulating from hostile takeovers when going public must be preferable to committing to a policy of contestable control. Even in those jurisdictions, like the UK, making it difficult for listed companies to avoid exposure to hostile takeovers, entrepreneurs always have the choice to keep or take their company private. But the real question is what is so important about control to induce entrepreneurs to forego the profit of selling valuable equity to the investing public. The answer must be, in one way or another, the presence of private benefits of control (Hart 2001). As I mentioned, private benefits of control come in different forms, but those arising from investor expropriation are the greatest source of inefficiency because market mechanisms cannot correct a stealing problem without institutional support.

Unconstrained opportunities for expropriating outside shareholders imply that hostile takeovers be always ruled out by the corporate controller. Any different commitment would not be credible (Bebchuk 1999). Private benefits from stealing are perfectly transferable control rents, so why should an incumbent controller leave them up for grabs while he can always trade them for a control premium? This of course implies that investors will heavily discount non-controlling stock. As a result, separation of ownership and control will always occur to a limited extent, if not at all, in the presence of expropriation of non-controlling shareholders. The key finding of the law and finance scholarship is that a commitment that investors will not be expropriated must be supported by corporate law in order to be credible. For this reason a good quality of legal investor protection is a precondition for separation of ownership and control and a defining feature of efficient corporate law.

If that was the whole story of private benefits of control, however, we should observe dispersed ownership and contestable control in every jurisdiction that protects investors well. This is not the case. In the US, for instance, a sizeable number of listed companies have a controlling shareholder. More importantly, the vast majority of listed companies are under management control, but they are mainly incorporated in Delaware whose courts allow boards to fend off hostile takeovers. This circumstance is very hard to reconcile with a principal–agent paradigm, because an undisciplined management can consume perquisites and engage in value-destroying projects. In this situation, concentrated ownership and closer monitoring by a controlling shareholder should be preferable for efficiency. Another puzzling example is Sweden, where despite the perceived high quality of (legal and extralegal) investor protection, there is hardly any company with a fully dispersed ownership structure. It seems that even in those countries where shareholder investments are well protected from expropriation, corporate control remains an issue and both managers and controlling shareholders are unwilling to leave it up for grabs. This implies that there must be some other kind of private benefits of control, unrelated to expropriation, which managers and controlling shareholders care for.

Private benefits of control can also be extracted in the form of on-the-job consumption, or shirking in the broad sense. Differently from the benefits from stealing, however, it is always profitable for an entrepreneur to commit not to benefit from shirking in the future by opting for a contestable ownership and control structure (Grossman and Hart 1988). Once stealing is ruled out, committing to a no-shirking policy via exposure to hostile takeover should allow entrepreneurs to sell more equity for a higher price. The other outcomes we observe more frequently in the real word, namely managerial control with at least moderate anti-takeover protection or straightforward controlling shareholdings, are inconsistent with the standard principal–agent approach in the absence of expropriation of non-controlling shareholders.

1.3.3.2 *Private benefits of control and the legal support for entrepreneurship in corporate governance*

Law may not matter much for efficiency apart from preventing shareholder expropriation. Then the actual patterns of corporate governance that we observe around the world would be determined by how the remainder of agency costs (shirking) is dealt with by different, and typically non-legal, institutional factors. For instance, efficient corporate governance could be dependent on the political support for shareholder value maximization as opposed to the protection of different constituencies of firm's stakeholders. Another important factor affecting efficient separation of ownership and control could be the social norms embedded in each country's financial community which may, or may not, provide the same support.

While I do not doubt the importance of these and other non-legal institutions in shaping corporate governance, I believe that consideration for one important element of the theory of the firm is missing from the analysis, which is entrepreneurship.[42] This element operates at the firm level, which may explain the variety of corporate governance patterns within individual countries. This is an issue systematically neglected by the law and finance scholarship. Crucially, as I am going to show in the next chapters of this book, corporate law also affects the way in which entrepreneurship can be implemented in corporate governance. If that is the case, corporate law may fail to support entrepreneurship in certain ownership structure, which could explain why certain models of corporate governance have not emerged in some countries even in the absence of shareholder expropriation.

The reasons why entrepreneurship matters in corporate governance has nothing to do with agency costs (see Mayer 1999). Actually, when they perform some entrepreneurial function, managers or controlling shareholders are not acting as agents for shareholders. Rather, they foresee some potential from running the company that is not yet visible to anyone else, including the owners (Kirzner 1979). The value of this potential must be appropriable in order to generate incentives to uncover it. The problem is that entrepreneurship is a factor of production that cannot be fully rewarded contractually. Contracts are incomplete for exactly the same reason why entrepreneurship exists and it is valuable: the future is uncertain and therefore it is not possible to specify a perfectly state-contingent system of remuneration (Aghion and Bolton 1992). The implication of this circumstance for corporate governance is that private benefits of control do not only arise from misalignment of managerial incentives, but also from the need to combine entrepreneurship with separation of ownership and control. In this perspective, extraction of private benefits of control is efficient and may justify legal support for control powers (see e.g. Schnitzer 1995).

To see why this is the case one should consider the entrepreneurial talent of managers and/or controlling shareholders as a firm-specific investment under structural uncertainty about whether this investment will pay off.[43] It is a bet on the firm's success along some management strategy that nobody other than the entrepreneur in question is prepared to place. In the spirit of Williamson (1979), this investment for the firm's success by the manage-ment or the controlling shareholder would be both idiosyncratic (i.e., non-redeployable outside the relationship with the company) and unverifiable (i.e., non-contractible with the company's owners). Therefore also the reward of this investment should come in the form of idiosyncratic control rents. One way to look at those is the psychic benefits of control that only the entrepreneur can enjoy (see e.g. Gilson 2006). Because these benefits have no opportunity costs for investors, they are not a source of agency costs. How large idiosyncratic control rents are relative to the verifiable stream of profits that can be expected from a business venture (and therefore be contracted upon with investors) is a key determinant of the firm's optimal ownership structure.

---

42 This topic would deserve more elaboration than can be afforded here. Some of my earlier work (Pacces 2007; Pacces 2009) deals with it at length.
43 See Manso (2011) for a recent model with a very similar setup.

As argued by Demsetz (1983) and Demsetz and Lehn (1985), this approach implies that the ownership structure is endogenous. The more uncertain are the business prospects of the company, the higher will be the subjective value of entrepreneurship and the lower the future verifiable income that may be pledged to outside investors. Therefore, the amount of outside equity that can be traded is limited and ownership will remain relatively concentrated. Conversely, when the valuation of the company's outlook does not differ considerably between the entrepreneur and outside shareholders (i.e. the idiosyncratic private benefits of control are low), ownership can be more dispersed.

This mechanism has two prominent implications. First, because we are assuming no prospective expropriation of outside investors, the choice of ownership and control structure is certainly efficient ex-ante, but it might become inefficient ex-post, typically because the company value is no longer maximized under the entrepreneur's control (Gilson 2006). This problem can be solved by an appropriate design of the market for corporate control, which I will discuss in Chapter 7. The second implication is that protection of idiosyncratic investments in entrepreneurship requires control rights in order to prevent ex-post expropriation by outside investors, regardless of the ownership structure. When corporate law prevents shareholders from freely negotiating the allocation of control rights with the management, this may result in the selection of a suboptimal ownership structure. This issue deserves a little elaboration.

An entrepreneur concerned with his firm-specific investment cannot choose an ownership structure where control is contestable because that will not allow securing a control premium as a reward for (successful) entrepreneurship. This control premium will instead be auctioned to the best bidder by shareholders as a group, who will then appropriate the value of the entrepreneur's private benefits of control that motivated the initial investment. Obviously, no rational entrepreneur would be willing to invest in this situation. The consequence of this is not lack of entrepreneurship in corporate governance, but rather the choice of potentially suboptimal ownership structures. As I have already mentioned, and I will illustrate in more detail in the following chapters, it is always possible to shield corporate control from takeover. But corporate law sometimes makes this option prohibitively costly, or impossible, with certain ownership structures.

For instance, under Swedish law, securing control and its private benefits is only possible with concentration of voting power in the hands of a controlling shareholder. In the Netherlands and in the US, managerial control is also an option because takeover defenses are allowed along with a number of control-enhancing mechanisms available to the management as well as to controlling shareholders. As I will show, in the UK the control powers of managers essentially depend on a regulatory disfavor towards controlling shareholders, whose prominent illustration is the mandatory bid. Shareholder protection in Britain may go as far as to restrict even efficient extraction of private benefits of control (Mayer 1999), particularly when this extraction requires concentrated ownership. All else being equal, such an approach may undermine entrepreneurship in corporate governance.

Although it is counterintuitive, the bottom line is that efficient corporate law may not just need to protect investors from expropriation, but also to enable the exercise of control powers and the protection of a control premium in different ownership structures. The remainder of the book will discuss precisely this point. This intuition arises from the empirical observation that good quality of investor protection is not a sufficient condition for separation of ownership and control. This casts doubts on the validity of the mainstream agency approach to corporate governance. If we depart from that framework, there can indeed be too much investor protection, particularly when this is achieved by restricting the control powers of those – managers or controlling shareholders – who are supposed to be running the company. When this protection is too costly to opt out of under the applicable corporate law, a suboptimal ownership structures may be chosen just in order to protect control and its benefits from outside interference.

In the following chapters, I will argue that efficient corporate law should support freedom of contract on the allocation of control rights between investors and the controlling managers or shareholders. However, because this freedom should not result in expropriation of outside shareholders via self-dealing and similar conflicts of interest, mandatory rules (or a configuration of default rules aimed at supporting credible commitments) are still necessary to prevent the abuse of control powers.

1.4 Are stakeholders left in the cold?

1.4.1 *Abuse of power by the corporate controller*

In the foregoing analysis, I have suggested that the allocation of residual control rights to a corporate controller may be necessary to induce him to invest his entrepreneurial talent, notwithstanding separation of ownership and control. Elaborating on the economic and legal implications of this intuition is all that the remainder of this work will be about. For the moment, let us just assume that such allocation of control rights is necessary in order for the corporate governance of listed companies to feature entre-preneurship (which would be otherwise confined to debt, close-knit or even self-finance). While necessary, this may not be sufficient. We would still need to know whether this solution is acceptable to other providers of firm inputs, in the presence of opportunities for mismanagement by the corporate controller. Once he is in charge, the controller could wastefully play with the firm's assets (shirking), appropriate them fully or in part (stealing), or simply be incompetent but unwilling to give up the benefits from stealing and shirking (inefficient entrenchment). The next question is, therefore: Which category of investors is most likely to be endangered by managerial misbehavior?

1.4.2 *Shareholders vs. stakeholders: what is special about the corporate contract*

In standard corporate governance terminology, some providers of firm inputs (creditors, employees, and long-term suppliers) are labeled 'stakeholders.' Whatever they invest in the firm, this is at least partly hazardous (Becht et al 2007). In this respect, stakeholders are contrasted to shareholders. Shareholders are stakeholders themselves, but their investment is highly peculiar: it is a share of the company's equity; that is, of the firm's *own* capital. I am going to argue that some special protection of shareholder investments, setting non-contractual constraints on the exercise of entrepreneurial/managerial discretion, is required to make equity finance viable. Contrary to the view of those who believe that stakeholders should be entitled to the same degree of protection as shareholders (e.g. Blair and Stout 1999), I will show that this protection is not required also to induce stakeholders to invest. In any event, such a protection should not be an issue for corporate governance.

An entrepreneur-manager is not the only person who may be required to make firm-specific investments in the company. In the view that is being developed in this study, he is just the person whose investments may be the most indispensable, the 'magic' glue that makes a combination of assets within a firm unique (Rock and Wachter 2001). In the absence of full ownership, one such person is the least protected from ex-post expropriation of the return on his investments (Hart and Moore 1990). Because these investments are idiosyncratic (i.e. they have no value outside the relationship) they are rewarded by quasi-rents (Williamson 1979). If this kind of investor is unable to secure quasi-rents from their activity, underinvestment of firm-specific assets (including entrepreneurship) will ensue. This is the well-known hold-up problem (Klein et al 1978).

I have argued that the entrepreneurial talent is unverifiable. Hence its reward cannot be secured contractually, but only through idiosyncratic (quasi-)rents stemming from control rights. After residual rights of control are allocated to the entrepreneur-manager for this reason, we might have the glue but still lack enough assets to be combined. In other words, we need somebody else willing to provide the assets, and to have them specialized and managed at the controller's discretion (Zingales 1998). To this purpose, investors of both physical and human capital need some degree of protection from mismanagement. Such a protection could be detailed contractually, leading to a standard principal–agent relationship (à la Jensen and Meckling 1976). Alternatively, given that contracts are incomplete and that control rights have already been allocated to the entrepreneur-manager, this protection could be achieved by allowing for a lesser degree of asset specificity. The less specialized (locked-in) to the firm the assets are, the easier they are to redeploy outside the firm by a disgruntled investor (Williamson 1985). These are also way-outs of the hold-up problem.

Non-controlling owners, namely outside shareholders, are the firm's stakeholders facing the greatest difficulty to protect themselves in these circumstances. As far as the contractual protections are concerned, equity contracts are virtually empty at their core (Bratton and McCahery 2001). In exchange for the resources they provide, shareholders receive only a residual claim on the firm's assets together with a vague promise that the value of their claims will be maximized by the firm management. There is hardly any commitment by the managers backing such a promise. This outcome is efficient though: the pursuit of a prospective, open-ended stream of profits requires discretion (Fama and Jensen 1983a; 1983b). The only contractual safeguards available to shareholders are those aimed to align the exercise of managerial discretion with the shareholders' interest. In any case, these safeguards are negatively affecting either the overall prospective value of the residual claim (some potentially profitable business opportunities might be foregone if there are too many constraints on the manager's discretion) or the share of the residual claim available to shareholders (the larger the share of the residual claim they give to the manager, the smaller the share that is left for themselves). Because of these tradeoffs, the degree of alignment of managerial incentives that can be achieved contractually is always much less than perfect.

The weakness of the contractual safeguards available to shareholders is only partly due to the agency costs stemming from asymmetric information. It mainly depends on the particular problems of contractual incompleteness affecting the provision of equity capital. Lacking a general theory of why contracts are incomplete (Tirole 1999), I am not entitled to say whether one kind of contract is *more* incomplete than another.[44] However, I feel rather confident about claiming that equity contracts are at least *particularly* incomplete. This is not because shareholders' basic obligations ('provision of funds') are unspecified, but because the manager's ('making profits') are. And it could not be otherwise, because profit is – and must be – a residual variable.

What is 'residual' is not simply unspecified; it is non-specifiable. Either you specify in advance how much of the cake you want, and then ask the baker to provide some guarantees he will not produce less than that, or alternatively, you go for a share of what is left after all promised slices are handed over. But then you cannot get from the baker any meaningful guarantee that the cake would be as big as possible.[45] Apparently, shareholders prefer the second option; stakeholders the first one.

For shareholders, trying to avoid being locked-in their own firm-specific investment is also not an option. Equity investment is unavoidably characterized by a considerable degree of asset specificity, which is independent of shareholders' will. This might seem counterintuitive. Shares of equity

---

44 See Zingales (1998) for a forceful discussion of this point.

45 Still, you would like to have the baker interested in producing as much surplus cake as he can, unable to steal your share of it, and induced to change his job as soon as a more talented baker becomes available. This problem will be the subject-matter of Chapter 3.

capital are normally exchanged for cash in secondary markets. After all, what shareholders typically invest is the least specialized commodity of all: money. The first claim is not pertinent to shareholders as a group: 100% of the firm's shares could be sold, at most, in a highly illiquid market for firms (Williamson 1985). The second argument is also misguided. What matters for asset specificity is not what shareholders invest, but the entitlements that they receive in exchange for their investments. These entitlements do not include any right in whatever (money or anything else) shareholders provided to the firm, but only a residual claim on the firm's assets. An open mandate to specialize those assets is conferred upon the manager. This means that, once shareholder investment is placed under the corporate controller's management, it is committed either to the purchase of highly firm-specific assets or to be almost irreversibly combined with them (Rock and Wachter 2001).

Simply put, whatever shareholders invest, they are never entitled to get it back (Shleifer and Vishny 1997). Even if they had residual rights of control, they could only liquidate the firm's assets after they have been specialized, thereby losing most part of the value of their initial investment. The difference between the latter and the liquidation value of the shareholders' residual claim is a sunk cost. Therefore, the same difference is lost once the specialization of assets has taken place, no matter the allocation of residual rights of control. Conversely, allocation of residual rights of control matters a lot for the production of unverifiable surplus by an entrepreneur-manager: this surplus may never come to light without the protection afforded by residual rights of control (Aghion and Bolton 1992). Shareholders may be willing to give up residual rights of control when this is the only way they can commit themselves not to hold up the entrepreneur, after he has been successful.[46] But then the position of shareholders becomes extremely weak. They cannot prevent the manager from uselessly exploiting their investment, making it even more sunk than necessary (e.g. Shleifer and Vishny 1989). This is a part of a broader problem. Shareholders worry that managers misuse 'their' resources, in both bad and good states of the world, due to either opportunistic behavior or incompetence. To avoid this, shareholders desperately need protection of their residual claim. However, whenever shareholders want to incentivize entrepreneurship in a public company, they may have to give up both detailed contractual provisions and residual rights of control.

The position of all the other stakeholders is different. To begin with, stakeholders typically do not get a residual claim on the firm's assets. This simple circumstance makes the return on their investment easier to protect contractually (Easterbrook and Fischel 1991). This is indeed the traditional argument against stakeholder involvement in corporate governance. The virtue of this argument has only been questioned with the advent of the literature on contractual incompleteness. When all contracts are incomplete – the

---

46 See *infra* Chapter 3, section 3.2.

argument goes – there is no compelling reason to exclude stakeholders from what is left after the contractual obligations are fulfilled, that is from residual claimancy (Becht et al 2007). However, a second argument for drawing a distinction between stakeholders and shareholders is decisive. This argument explains also why only shareholders should be considered residual claimants, whereas the other stakeholders should not be.

Differently from shareholders, other stakeholders are able to set limits on how much their investment can be specialized by the firm's manager, thereby improving their ex-post bargaining power (Williamson 1985). For instance, creditors normally ask for easy-to-liquidate collateral while most promising young executives often ask their employers to pledge for an MBA. The reason why they can easily do this, without worrying too much about constraining managerial discretion over the assets they provide, is that they are not interested in the maximization of an open-ended stream of profits. Therefore, stakeholders' lower exposure to hold-up risk (relative to shareholders) and the absence of a residual claim on the firm's assets are just two sides of the same coin. Stakeholders simply *choose* not to have a residual claim in order to improve their bargaining position ex-post.

Stakeholders unhappy with what they get from their contracts can always give up their position and become shareholders. We do not necessarily have to assume a discontinuity here. Creditors, employees, or suppliers can and sometimes do take hybrid positions, particularly when a residual claim is necessary to induce them to accept further (discretionary) specialization of their assets, but when they still do not want to commit the whole of their investments to the firm. In a sense, we are back to the fundamental alternative between markets (consensus) and hierarchies (authority) that explains the firm's existence. In this regard, the analysis of hybrid stakeholder-shareholder positions would be a very interesting topic for a theory of business organizations.[47]

---

47 At least one stakeholder theory of the firm is worth mentioning briefly at this point. Building on the seminal work by Professor Hansmann (1996), who first discussed the different forms of firm ownership (including business corporations and also cooperatives), Professors Rajan and Zingales (1998b) have elaborated a stakeholder theory of the firm in which shareholders are still in charge. They argue that stakeholders protect their firm-specific investments in human capital by controlling access to a critical resource in the firm organization. In order to be given access to this critical resource, shareholders must be committed to rewarding stakeholder investments ex-post. Arguably, shareholders can do this by delegating control rights (which they need to have in the first place) to a "mediating hierarchy" (Blair and Stout 1999). In principle, this reasoning applies equally to employees and to entrepreneur-managers.

The problem with this approach is that no critical resource is bound to stay such forever. Rajan and Zingales (2001) account for this problem when they describe a dynamics of progressive empowerment of key employees within an organization, supported by competition in the generation of critical resources. In their framework, shareholders are committed to rewarding employees who make firm-specific investments by trading access to critical resources for increasing responsibilities within the corporate hierarchy. This, in

However, for the purposes of corporate governance, the two positions of shareholder and stakeholder should be considered separately. As stakeholders, providers of firm inputs can negotiate with the manager both limited asset specificity and detailed contractual protections. As shareholders, the same investors may be instead at the controlling manager's mercy. The whole of their investments as shareholders is potentially sunk; detailed contractual safeguards are not (and cannot be made) available; and they may have even to relinquish residual rights of control if they want to profit from the investment of entrepreneurship by the controlling manager.

Along these lines there is another category of investors that can be considered a relevant stakeholder in corporate governance. This is the management, to the extent that it performs an entrepreneurial function. Managerial skills may be characterized by a formidable degree of asset specificity; but differently from shareholder investments, their prospective value is not verifiable and thus a commensurate reward can only be granted via residual control rights. While this solution would not affect the position of other stakeholders, providing management with residual control rights is extremely risky for shareholders. In the absence of other protection of the shareholders' residual claim, nobody would be willing to supply the firm with equity funds, separation of ownership and control would be impaired, and entrepreneurial innovation would be confined to debt and self-finance.

For all the above reasons, I believe that shareholder protection from managerial misbehavior lies at the core of the corporate governance problem, whereas stakeholder protection does not. The management is no exception to this statement. Even considering entrepreneurs as stakeholders, I have argued that these people should be in control in order to avoid hold-up by (non-controlling) shareholders. Therefore, I shall continue to characterize corporate governance as a relationship between a corporate controller and non-controlling shareholders, leaving other stakeholders out of the play.

1.4.3 *Externalities of the corporate contract: are there any?*

Focusing on the relationship between the corporate controller and non-controlling shareholders, one risks overlooking an important problem. That relationship could produce negative externalities on stakeholders, since they are not at the "bargaining table" together with the entrepreneur-manager and the outside shareholders (Becht et al 2007). Negative externalities would lead, in turn, to both under-provision of stakeholders' investments and an

---

turn, provides employees with additional incentives to make themselves indispensable. However, shareholders cannot take such a commitment with an entrepreneur because an entrepreneur must be situated on top of the firm's hierarchy. When the company is auctioned to the best bidder, a valuable hierarchy may still protect the employees but not the entrepreneur who set it up. The entrepreneur should thus be able to protect his firm-specific investments via control rights.

overall reduction of social welfare. There are many examples of such externalities. For instance, increasing debt/equity ratio, or undertaking overly risky projects, may undermine the interest of outstanding creditors; managerial incompetence might lead to unemployment; reacting (or failure to react) to changed circumstances might drive efficient long-term suppliers out of business; development of hazardous activities or products can damage health and safety of either the customer or the members of an entire society.

While I do not question the importance of these and similar issues, I believe that corporate governance should not deal with them. The reason is straightforward: none of these externalities arise from separation of ownership and control, which is the core problem of corporate governance. Given that limited liability is also available to the entrepreneurial firm, I cannot see why a corporate controller, non-controlling shareholders, or both should be less concerned about stakeholders than about an entrepreneur with full ownership. Actually, when stakeholders are entitled to interfere with the management of a non-entrepreneurial firm, the reverse might become true. Most often, however, when ownership is separated from control, a higher consideration for stakeholders is just an excuse to preserve the corporate controller's freedom. Accountability to many constituencies is in fact accountability to none of them. Therefore, a standard argument against a "stakeholder society" is that it would leave management with too much discretion (Tirole 2006). As Professor Hellwig (2000: 128) put it, "the CEO of a corporation may defend himself in one year against shareholder interference by citing stakeholder interest, and in the next year announce layoffs in the name of shareholder value." Consideration for stakeholders in corporate governance then becomes instrumental to empowering management and disenfranchising shareholders. This might even be not too bad in some circumstances; but it has little to do with the protection of any stakeholder other than the management.

Conversely, it might be argued that stakeholder involvement in corporate governance is the price to pay for large-scale equity finance. After all, large publicly held corporations are likely to produce more dangerous externalities than small entrepreneurial firms. This is quite often argued in debates on public policy. A more refined version of the argument was provided by Professors Shleifer and Summers (1988). In their capacity as financiers, outside shareholders may want to redistribute wealth from stakeholders to themselves, and the market for corporate control may provide them with a succulent opportunity to do so. Shareholders of takeover targets may just gain from externalizing on stakeholders the negative effects of changes in control. This requires that takeovers be hostile. An owner-manager would be committed not to take advantage of the stakeholders with whom he has previously established a relationship, whereas outside shareholders simply would not care.

The argument has some virtue, but one major shortcoming: it neglects the stakeholders that are still to be born (Hellwig 2000). Takeovers are a dynamic, mainly entrepreneurial process. As such, they involve a 'creative destruction' of stakeholders. While takeovers are a powerful way to implement change, they are not the only possible source of change. Specific investments on the stakeholders side are no more exposed to hold-up in takeovers than they would be in the general case of alteration of labor, inputs, or product market conditions faced by sole proprietorship. Besides, there are many ways to restructure a company other than takeovers. Like other forms of restructuring, takeovers promote an overall reallocation of resources supplied by stakeholders; this is efficient ex-post so long as takeovers are motivated by maximization of the firm value. As a consequence of such changes, new stakeholders will emerge and some others will disappear, depending on which resources are valued the most. There will be winners and losers, but stakeholders as a class will hardly be worse off when shareholders as a class are better off.

Competition between actual and potential stakeholders should be taken into account in evaluating the effects of takeovers on stakeholders. This competition involves pecuniary externalities, like the entry of a new competitor in a market. Rents may have to be redistributed among market participants, which explains the resistance to change by the incumbents, but says nothing about whether social welfare will increase or decrease. The externalities of takeovers would instead be non-pecuniary if competition forced redistribution of *quasi*-rents from one class of stakeholders to another, thereby making the former unwilling to make firm-specific investments. As we have seen in the previous section, this applies to stakeholders only to the extent that the resources they provide to the firm have no alternative use. Employees, lenders, suppliers, and customers are rarely so much locked-in to the firm. If these stakeholders cannot get contractual protection against takeovers, they will likely refrain from specializing their human capital too much. Corporate governance adds little, if anything, to this outcome.

The situation is different for an entrepreneur-manager situated on top of the firm's hierarchy. Here the argument that takeovers may be abused by shareholders is more forceful and it equally applies to present and future management constituencies. Managerial human capital is automatically specialized (and thus non-redeployable) when it is committed to uncovering the unknown profit opportunities available to a certain firm. Contractual protection is also not an option because such opportunities are by definition only observable by an entrepreneur and they are not verifiable. Property rights could still help if the managerial human capital was bundled with the ownership of the firm's physical assets. Yet separation of ownership and control also rules out this arrangement. Somewhat paradoxically, the management may be asked to engineer an entrepreneurship process while being otherwise at the owners' mercy. If takeover gains were to be divided just between the shareholders of the target and those of the aggressor, neither incumbency nor insurgency could provide managers with a reward for firm-specific investments (which, therefore, they would never make in the first place). Entrepreneurship and separation of ownership from control would be incompatible with each other. Therefore, if there is a problem with takeovers, it does not concern the externalities that shareholders may impose on stakeholders, but the management's bargaining power relative to outside shareholders. However, to the extent that the two constituencies sit at the same 'bargaining table,' this can hardly be characterized as a problem of externalities.

In conclusion, separation of ownership and control does not seem to involve further externalities on the firm's stakeholders. For this reason, the problem of the adverse effects of corporate management on stakeholders should be dealt with by regulating the firm's activity, not the way in which this activity is governed or financed. In other words, whatever legal protection stakeholders may need, that should be neutral to corporate governance arrangements. Stakeholder protection should be pursued by other areas of law like, for instance, competition law, tort law, employment law, bankruptcy law, and so on.

2 Private benefits of control

2.1 Departing from the principal–agent approach

2.1.1 *How private benefits of control can help to understand corporate governance*

Based as it is exclusively on investor protection, the standard 'law matters' argument does not provide an explanation of separation of ownership and control across developed countries that is fully consistent with the empirical evidence. For this reason, authoritative commentators have claimed that law does not matter across the board for the shape and the relative efficiency of corporate governance around the world (Milhaupt and Pistor 2008). Although I am sympathetic to the criticism towards a one-size-fits-all approach to corporate governance, the comparative analysis may still suffer from the lack of an adequate theoretical paradigm. This chapter aims to cope with this problem and to revitalize the explanatory power of the 'law matters' proposition accordingly. On this basis, we will see in the following pages that law matters in at least two different, but complementary, respects in corporate governance.

As I argued, investor protection by the legal system is far from unimportant in corporate governance. Actually, it seems that dispersed ownership structures could not emerge and, even if they could, they would not be sustainable for long in the absence of this protection. However, ownership concentration also obtains in those institutional contexts where investor protection is apparently strong. To account for this one does not have to throw the baby out with the bath water. Rather, we may look for what else is needed, at the legal-institutional level, for ownership to be separated from control when investor protection is not an issue to worry about. For instance, managers may also need access to some protection, in order for entrepreneurship to be featured in the absence of full ownership of the company's assets. This double need of protection may be integrated in the discussion of one single feature of corporate governance which has always been kept in the background during the foregoing analysis, but that is going to be in the forefront from now on. This is private benefits of control (henceforth PBC). To this purpose, however, the notion of PBC needs to be broad enough to include all kinds of benefits accruing exclusively to the corporate controller by means of his staying in charge of the company management, and not just those which result in reduction of shareholder value (Coates 2004).

Once PBC are defined in such a fashion, they may account for both the corporate controller's motivation to undertake firm-specific investments and for expropriation of non-controlling shareholders. Consequently, one analysis of corporate governance based on PBC can provide us with three fundamental advantages compared to the standard, and much narrower, agency framework. The first advantage would be a theoretical framework of corporate governance that accounts for investor protection, but allows also for a non-contractable incentive mechanisms of managerial firm-specific investments to be considered (Rock and Wachter 2001). The second would be a positive theory of corporate law, which allows for both variety and regularities in each system where separation of ownership and control is implemented. Variety should depend on the amount of private benefits necessary to motivate the undertaking, in the corporate form, of a specific business venture characterized by high uncertainty. Regularities should depend on both opportunities for and constraints to the extraction of PBC provided for by corporate law, which would determine in turn the willingness of outside shareholders to provide equity capital and of corporate controllers to deconcentrate ownership (Mayer 1999). The third advantage of this approach would be to lay the foundations of a normative theory of corporate law, which tells how PBC should be regulated depending on a qualitative distinction between different categories of them and on their implications for economic efficiency.

2.1.2 Complicating the comparative taxonomy

An authoritative scholar in corporate law and economics (Gilson 2006) suggested that a qualitative distinction between different categories of private benefits of control may fare much better in explaining alternative corporate governance patterns than the standard 'law matters' account, according to which PBC just arise from the weakness of institutions and, specifically, from the failure of corporate law to police minority shareholder expropriation. The embarrassment with that thesis, in the face of the prevalence of controlling shareholders even in those systems that are credited with excellent investor protection, was summarized by Professor Gilson in a very efficacious sentence: "When the world seems more complicated than what our theory can explain, we probably do not yet understand the world" (Gilson 2006: 1650).

A broader account of private benefits of control in corporate governance may possibly provide a way to understand the world better. To this purpose, in the words of Professor Gilson, the "comparative taxonomy" has to be "complicated." Professor Gilson argues that the classical divide between controlling shareholder systems and widely held control structures is a too parsimonious account of corporate governance and it is most likely to be wrong. Controlling shareholders are not alike. They might be bad for corporate governance, but only when they arise as a response to inadequate investor protection. However, this is not the only reason why controlling shareholders are there. Their presence may indeed be efficient in corporate governance, when no expropriation of minority shareholders is involved. *Inefficient* controlling shareholders avail themselves of 'pecuniary' private benefits that necessarily come at the outside shareholders' expenses, thereby increasing agency costs, whereas *efficient* controlling shareholders reduce agency costs by exploiting a different kind of PBC that involves no cash flow diversion. According to Ronald Gilson, these benefits are 'non-pecuniary.'

The efficiency explanation of controlling shareholders should tell why they still prevail in European countries where expropriation of outside shareholders has never been a matter of concern (as, for instance, in Sweden), and they have not completely disappeared even in the US and the UK, which apparently feature investors with a high quality of legal protection. Non-pecuniary PBC are the key for understanding the puzzle. Their presence in the system is allegedly endogenous, and so is shareholder control, for they both depend on whether the nature of the business better suits a dispersed or a concentrated ownership structure.[1] Only pecuniary PBC depend on the quality of corporate law. Should this quality be assessed functionally rather than by synthetic indexes, the comparison would show that controlling shareholders persist in spite of their inefficiency when expropriation of minority shareholders is not adequately policed by the legal system, but dispersed ownership does not arise in spite of good investor protection when non-pecuniary PBC are high (Gilson 2006: 1652–1661).

Gilson's criticism of standard comparative institutional analysis highlights two fundamental points. The first one is that legal comparison has to be performed with a functional approach, and this is ultimately at odds with 'indexing' the overall quality of corporate law. The second one is that legal protection of outside shareholders, even when accurately accounted for, affects just one kind of PBC and, therefore, cannot explain alone why controlling shareholders prevail in some systems while managerial control prevails in some others. Complicating the comparative taxonomy requires then both a more precise assessment of how investor protection is, or is not, achieved by different corporate laws and what else – either legal or non-legal – determines ownership concentration.

That being said, there are still two problems with Gilson's analysis. The first is that not all 'non-pecuniary' benefits are harmless to outside shareholders. They may involve significant opportunity costs inasmuch as they lead to non-profit-maximizing corporate decisions. This is what I have previously referred to as 'shirking' (Roe 2002), which includes any possible instance of on-the-job consumption of personal benefits by the corporate controller (managerial

---

1 On the endogeneity of ownership structure, see Demsetz and Lehn (1985).

perquisites, misuse of free cash, empire building, etc.). Consistently with the standard agency framework, high non-pecuniary benefits of such a kind are only compatible with limited separation of ownership and control where the owner-manager bears a significant part of their opportunity costs. This is how efficient controlling shareholding is derived (Bratton and McCahery 2001). However, as Professor Gilson has acknowledged, efficiency may become compromised dynamically. The reason is that while non-pecuniary private benefits are idiosyncratic to the corporate controller, their opportunity costs may rise over time. At some point, it would be efficient that control changes hands. Yet idiosyncrasy of private benefits may prevent this from happening. On the one hand, the incumbent controller would not part with control unless his private benefits are fully compensated. On the other hand, the same private benefits cannot be compensated just because they are idiosyncratic, and this makes them unsuitable for exchange (Gilson 2006: 1667–1770).

The assumption that all non-pecuniary private benefits are idiosyncratic to the corporate controller is problematic, and it is most likely to be incorrect. If non-pecuniary PBC – like, e.g., consumption of managerial perquisites – have a negative balance with opportunity costs, this means that at least one corporate controller exists who can compensate the incumbent and still be better off by taking over and reducing on-the-job consumption to the efficient level. The reason why this may not happen is that *another* kind of PBC is involved, like for instance the personal pride of uncovering the success potential of the company, which the market is not yet able to price (Mayer 1999). Until the market is unable to set a price for change in control, that kind of private benefit has no alternative use and, therefore, no opportunity cost. Only *these* private benefits are truly *idiosyncratic*. By sticking to the traditional agency framework, Professor Gilson overlooks the distinction between non-pecuniary benefits arising from non-value-maximizing behavior and those rewarding firm-specific investments whose value is not yet acknowledged by the market, but may be possibly recognized in the future. In fact, the latter category of private benefits of control is incompatible with a principal–agent paradigm and can only make sense in an incomplete contract setting (Hart 2001).

A second, related problem with Professor Gilson's analysis is that he does not allow corporate law to play a role as far as non-pecuniary PBC are concerned. In his view, non-pecuniary private benefits are endogenous and, therefore, they can only evolve in connection with the controller's *tastes* (specifically, when corporate control is transferred to the founder's heirs). To be sure, this is consistent with the typical patterns of evolution of ownership structures that we observe in continental Europe.[2] Yet this is not true with respect to controlling shareholders situated in different institutional environments – e.g. in the US. Therefore, one may conjecture that non-pecuniary PBC can also evolve in connection with the controller's *pockets* (that is, by means of a change in

---

2 Mayer (1999) makes a similar point, although he gives more credit to the regulatory determinants of this outcome.

control) if corporate law allows for those benefits to be compensated by means of a control sale.

In order to understand how this may work, and the implications for corporate law, we need to further complicate the taxonomy of PBC. Corporate law may not only be concerned with curbing private benefits from shareholder expropriation. In addition corporate law may have to do, on the one hand, with protecting private benefits that are idiosyncratic to the corporate controller and, on the other hand, with having shirking and other perquisites minimized through control transactions whereby private benefits are exchanged for larger security benefits. This interpretation involves *three*, not just two, *categories* of PBC: those arising from stealing, those depending on shirking, and those idiosyncratic to the corporate controller.[3] Similarly to Gilson's, this framework also posits that the efficient ownership structure be ultimately endogenous. However, the tripartite account of PBC further implies that corporate law can distort the choice of ownership structure in two ways. On the one hand, when expropriation is not adequately policed; on the other, when it fails to support control and its idiosyncratic benefits.[4]

Idiosyncrasy of private benefits is the novel and crucial hypothesis being explored here. However, we need to depart from the agency paradigm and to fully embrace an incomplete contracts perspective in order to understand how idiosyncratic investments by the corporate controller, and their likewise idiosyncratic reward, can be of vital importance in corporate governance.

2.2 Private benefits of control: the 'good,' the 'bad,' and the 'ugly'

2.2.1 *The missing piece of the puzzle*

The empirical evidence shows that the two basic patterns of corporate governance prevailing around the world put either the top management or a controlling shareholder in ultimate control of the corporate assets. This evidence is at odds with the standard theoretical approach to separation of ownership and control, according to which shareholders as a group should eventually be able to exercise their control rights as owners. Control over the corporate assets does not appear to be even implicitly delegated by principals (the outside shareholders) to one or more agents (the corporate insiders). Quite to the contrary, outside shareholders seem to be involved in corporate finance just up to the point where the insiders' position is not endangered by the risk of shareholder insurgency (Hellwig 2000). In other

---

3 Few commentators have hypothesized three categories of PBC in corporate governance. See e.g. Mayer (1999); Coates (2004); Hart (2001). The taxonomy and the welfare analysis being employed in this work are closer to Mayer (1999).

4 For the idea that corporate law may matter for reason other than investor protection see e.g. Cools (2005).

words, corporate control is often entrenched.[5] In addition, thanks to legal devices separating either control or voting rights from ownership claims, corporate control is often exerted without a substantial financial interest in the firm's residual (Morck et al 2005).

Why then should a corporate controller bother about maximizing the firm's profit when this would benefit non-controlling shareholders more than himself? More importantly, why should outside shareholders accept to place their money under the corporate controller's management, the latter being so little interested in the firm's profits while so much insulated from the threat of ouster? To put it briefly: is corporate governance in the real world only about shareholder empowerment, at least as this is generally understood in both economic and legal theory?

As Professor Mayer (1999: 5) put it, "Faced with a threat to theory, the first reaction of economists is naturally to doubt the evidence. As one eminent theoretical economist said, 'I do not trust anything that works in practice unless it works in theory.'" However, there is one theoretical argument whose role in explaining separation of ownership and control has not yet been completely explored. "Concentration of control in the hands of a few investors who have little direct financial interest can be justified if they derive other benefits – what economists term 'private benefits'" (Mayer 1999: 5). Entrenchment of corporate control is required, in turn, to secure those benefits from ex-post expropriation by insurgent shareholders. Finally, the *quality* of those benefits matters. By definition, PBC are not shared with non-controlling shareholders (they would not be 'private' otherwise). However, they might or might not reduce the firm's surplus available to shareholders as a whole. Determining whether PBC always reduce firm value, or – alternatively – might also enhance it, is of fundamental importance in order to assess their efficiency.

2.2.2 *Private benefits cannot be just 'bad'*

2.2.2.1 *The theoretical account*

Apparently, the extraction of private benefits by the corporate controller cannot be but 'bad,' for it always comes at the outside shareholders' expense. Control benefits can arise from more or less directly 'stealing' the corporate assets, thereby *diverting* profits from non-controlling shareholders. Based on Mayer (1999), let us refer to these benefits from now on as *diversionary PBC*. When outright theft is effectively ruled out by the legal system, PBC can still harm non-controlling shareholders by *distorting* the management choices. The smaller the corporate controller's equity interest in the firm, the more he will tend to manage the corporate assets in such a way as to maximize his own

---

5 See *supra* Chapter 1, sections 1.1.4. and 1.2.2.

goals (empire building, luxury expenses, extravagant perquisites) rather than the firm's profits (Jensen and Meckling 1976). To this point, this behavior has been broadly referred to as 'shirking.' Henceforth, I shall call *distortionary PBC* any personal utility that a corporate controller may derive from failing to maximize shareholder value – i.e., shirking in the broadest possible meaning. Based on a straightforward agency approach, diversionary and distortionary benefits are the only two ways in which private benefits of control can be understood in corporate governance (Mayer 1999).

It is therefore quite difficult to imagine that rewarding the corporate controller with private benefits could possibly enhance the efficiency of corporate governance. Actually, the problem to solve seems to be quite the opposite. As Oliver Hart argues: "The crucial issue may be how the company's investors can design financial structure so as to *limit* management's ability to pursue its own goals at the expenses of investors" (Hart 1995: 126). This is the leading approach to PBC.[6]

Following this approach one important issue is foregone. Curbing private benefits of control might improve the position of outside investors, but it undermines the entrepreneurial incentives to undertake specific investments for the firm's success. We might assume that specialization of managerial skills is of limited importance in the case of large firms, where ownership is significantly separated from control due to the financing needs of large-scale investments.[7] However, if we take the view that the management of a corporate enterprise cannot always be dealt with as a matter of routine, rewarding the managerial talent (and entrepreneurship in general) can be a crucial issue regardless of the firm size. Then, private benefits of control cannot simply be dismissed as an impediment to the efficiency of corporate governance. What we are facing here is a *gap in the economic theory of corporate governance*. Professor Hart (1995: 208) was well aware of this problem:

> In future work, it would be desirable to incorporate the entrepreneurial incentives and private benefits [into a model of separation of ownership and control]. [For instance, it] would be interesting to see whether the optimal security-voting structure consists of a single class of shares that are widely held, together with a class of superior voting stock held by insiders. Such a result would appear to be consistent with empirical evidence.[8]

2.2.2.2 *The empirical evidence*

The empirical evidence about the different patterns of separation of ownership and control around the world actually calls for a reappraisal of PBC. As far as

6 See e.g. Shleifer and Vishny (1997). For the view that PBC extraction is not necessarily harmful for outside shareholders, see e.g. Holderness (2003).
7 Professor Hart (1995: 126–129) has made such an assumption.
8 This gap has not been filled. See Burkart and Lee (2008).

developed economies are concerned, data shows that private benefits are on average higher in continental Europe than in the US and the UK.[9] It is generally argued, on both theoretical and empirical grounds, that higher control benefits lead to a lesser degree of separation of ownership and control, as well as to more frequent occurrence of devices for separating voting rights from ownership claims – like dual class shares and pyramidal groups (Bebchuk et al 2000). However, while it is true that the governance of publicly held companies in continental Europe is typically characterized by the presence of a large, controlling shareholder (or a coalition of them) holding dispro-portionate voting power, the estimated average size of PBC in each country cannot explain a number of other differences.

A few points are worth emphasizing in this regard. For instance, a relatively low degree of separation of ownership and control in Scandinavian countries coexists with levels of private benefits being on average not much higher than in the US and the UK, but significantly lower than in other countries on the European continent, namely Italy (Gilson 2006). Dual class shares and pyra-mids are quite common in Sweden and Italy (regardless of the difference in the average size of PBC),[10] dual class shares (but not pyramids) are sometimes adopted by US companies,[11] while both dual class shares and pyramids are very little used in the UK.[12] Is this just a matter of *how large* PBC are? And, more importantly, are 'large' PBC always that bad? If private benefits of control were only to be considered as a curse for corporate governance, we would expect dramatic differences in economic performance between the Old Continent and Anglo-Saxon countries. This is not the case. Professor Mayer (1999: 7) made this point long ago:

> In the presence of significantly higher private benefits, the economic performance of continental European economies should have been mark-edly worse than that of the UK. At best they should have been subject to more empires, expenses, extravagance or worse to more cronyism, corrup-tion and crime. Anyone who follows league tables of economic perform-ance or just walks round the streets of Barcelona, Birmingham and Bonn can appreciate the problem with this thesis.

2.2.3 Maybe private benefits are 'ugly'

Comparative analyses of corporate governance have tried to solve the puzzle. According to Professors Bratton and McCahery (2001), private benefits are to be regarded as the price to pay for a more focused management of the corporate enterprise. PBC are then neither 'bad' nor 'good,' but just the second best

---

9 See Dyck and Zingales (2004) and Nenova (2003).
10 Compare Holmén and Högfeldt (2009) with Bianchi et al (2005).
11 See Gompers et al (2010) and Morck and Yeung (2005).
12 Cheffins (2008).

outcome of a tradeoff. From a first best perspective, they might be regarded as 'ugly,' but one could not tell whether corporate governance in the real world would be any better without them.

Large shareholding aligns the corporate controller's incentives with the interest of outside shareholders, but involves illiquidity and suboptimal diversification of financial investments (Bolton and von Thadden 1998). Private benefits arising from diversion of the firm's cash flow should be understood exactly as a solution to this tradeoff. They are intended to reward the corporate controller's financial commitment to the firm. However, provided that private benefits always reduce the share of the surplus available to non-controlling shareholders, they involve a higher cost of outside equity capital and a lesser degree of separation of ownership and control. Conversely, in the absence of (diversionary) private benefits, there would be no incentive to stable blockholding, ownership would be spread among a large number of dispersed investors, and senior managers would enjoy substantial freedom in pursuing their own goals at the shareholders' expenses (distortionary PBC).

On theoretical grounds, one could not say which of the above systems is the best. On the same grounds, the two systems are incompatible (Bratton and McCahery 2001: 12):

> A system either controls access to [diversionary] private benefits for the purpose of protecting liquid trading markets or does not control [those] private benefits, so as to nurture its blocks. The theory of the firm holds out no hospitable middle ground.

A tradeoff between diversionary and distortionary benefits of control provides at least one explanation of why corporate governance systems based on concentrated ownership (i.e., on controlling shareholdings) do not exhibit significant underperformance compared to those based on dispersed ownership (i.e., on managerial control). But this cannot be the whole story. Corporate control is not simply a matter of financial commitment, for it could possibly involve none at all. What about a penniless entrepreneur with some great ideas on a new product, on how to improve the production, distribution or marketing of existing ones, or simply on how to revamp a troubled corporate business? How could he possibly combine an adequate reward for his talent with the need to raise equity funds for financing a highly uncertain business venture, should PBC be necessarily diversionary or distortionary? Clearly, whenever corporate control has to be featured with entrepreneurship, its reward cannot entirely come at the expenses of non-controlling shareholders, for no equity finance could be raised otherwise.[13]

---

13 See Hart (2001) and Tirole (2006).

2.2.4 What if private benefits can also be 'good'?

Based on the above concern, a few economists (e.g. Zingales 2000) and lawyers (e.g. Coates 2004) have started to consider a third category of private benefits of control, which are neither diversionary nor distortionary. Let us call them, for the moment, the 'good PBC.' Their role in corporate governance should be precisely to foster entrepreneurship while allowing for separation of ownership and control. What exactly such benefits account for is still unclear in this literature. Prestige and personal satisfaction for the firm's success are typical, albeit not exhaustive, examples. None of them involves reduction of outside shareholders' wealth, in the form of either suboptimal profits due to extravagant expenses or expropriation of their residual claim. Therefore, the only way in which such benefits can affect non-controlling shareholders is by *indirectly* increasing the value of the firm's assets that they partly own (Holderness 2003).

"Non-pecuniary" pride or "psychic" benefits of control are most common definitions of the private benefits at issue (e.g. Gilson 2006). However, these are of little help for understanding the implications of 'non distortionary–non diversionary' private benefits for corporate governance. Colin Mayer's (1999: 10–12) definition as "a power for good" sheds more light on those implications:

> Desires to enhance family names and to pass on enterprises to offspring are powerful incentives to enterprise formation. . . . They do not directly benefit investors but they may encourage actions and activities that indirectly do so. . . . But they have also deficiencies. [They involve] continuing reliance on family as against professional managerial capitalism.

In the absence of private benefits, control is purchased by those who attach the highest value to the management of a corporate enterprise – those who are able to manage it the best. Control is auctioned on "perfectly functioning markets in corporate control," and they "ensure that at any point in time the value of exercising control is maximized" (Mayer 1999: 12). Conversely, the significance of private benefits as 'a power for good' implies that such a power is maintained over time, even when 'good' does no longer mean 'best' and parting with control would actually increase firm value. As Professor Mayer (1999: 12) put it, "Control rents remain with the original entrepreneurs and are transferred through subsequent generations of owners."

Even though they do not reduce shareholder wealth (and might possibly enhance it for some time) private benefits then undermine the efficient dynamics of control allocation. In fact, whatever their source (diversionary, distortionary, or 'a power for good'), control rents can only be secured through entrenchment of corporate control.[14] However, when private benefits involve neither distortion nor diversion of the firm's surplus, they fill in the gaps of market (contractual) incompleteness. In other words, they account for some value that would have *not* been produced otherwise. Such a value depends on firm-specific investments by the entrepreneur. In the jargon of contract theory, the same value is 'non-verifiable,' and therefore it cannot be contracted upon at the outset (Hart 1995). Ex-post, one might regret that private benefits provide no guarantee that firm (shareholder) value is always being maximized. But one should not forget that ex-ante, in the absence of those benefits, there would have been no firm (or, at least, not *that* one) and no value to maximize.[15] This point has been nicely summarized by Colin Mayer (1999: 13):

> {D}*ifferent forms of corporate control are associated with different types of economic activities.* Private benefits are required in the initial stage of development of corporations and economies before high financial returns are anticipated. . . . The value of private benefits comes from their ability to encourage investments that would otherwise be subject to capital market failures.

The crucial question is, then, what the investments to be encouraged are and how private benefits can actually encourage them. In order to answer this question, private benefits of control should be regarded as a solution to an *appropriability problem* (Zingales 2000) rather than as a matter of physic satisfaction. The founding reason for 'good' instances of private benefits in corporate governance is that, whenever firm control is separated from ownership, financial markets are unable to *price* further surplus brought about by the entrepreneurial talent. The entrepreneur would certainly prefer to get cash (or stock) in return for his effort and investments in producing that surplus. However, because the same surplus is unverifiable (markets would be able to price it otherwise), it cannot be divided contractually. An entitlement to unverifiable surplus can only be secured through (residual) control rights over the firm's assets – the right to sell the assets at a premium above market price.[16]

'Good' private benefits of control account exactly for that surplus. They are the idiosyncratic control rents that are needed in order to motivate the entrepreneur to undertake firm-specific investments for the firm's success.[17] They might well be initially a matter of pride or psychic satisfaction. Yet,

---

14 On the ex-ante/ex-post tradeoff that this involves, see very effectively Laffont and Tirole (1988).
15 On how, in corporate governance, ex-post inefficiency may be necessary to achieve the efficient outcome ex-ante, see Zingales (1998).
16 See *infra* Chapter 3, section 3.2.3.
17 On the idiosyncrasy of control rents, as related to the theory of entrepreneurship, see *supra* Chapter 1, section 1.3.3, and in more detail Pacces (2007; 2009).

when the firm proves successful, they will translate into appropriable surplus: the value of firm control. Such a value has to be intended as a *deferred compensation* for the investment of managerial talent, contingent on the firm's success.[18]

2.2.5 Implications of 'good' private benefits for corporate governance

In the above perspective, 'good' (i.e., neither distortionary, nor diversionary) instances of PBC get an important meaning. We are speaking about the entrepreneurial reward mechanism that standard theory of corporate governance fails to account for. To the extent that such a reward is established through idiosyncratic control rents, I shall henceforth refer to them as to *idiosyncratic private benefits of control*. Once we take those benefits into account, some apparently puzzling evidence about separation of ownership and control can be actually explained on efficiency grounds.

To begin with, entrenchment of corporate control may be needed to protect idiosyncratic control rents as a reward for the investment of non-verifiable managerial talent. In this perspective, entrenchment of the corporate controller should not necessarily be regarded as disenfranchisement of outside shareholders, but possibly as a matter of *(efficient) protection of control rents* from subsequent expropriation by shareholder insurgency (Bebchuk 2003a).

Secondly, to the extent specialization of managerial skills is very often (if not always) an issue for the firm's success, there is no compelling reason to believe that the incentive role of idiosyncratic PBC is limited, as Mayer (1999: 13) put it, to the "initial stages of development of corporations." If entrepreneurship is a continuing process of "creative destruction" (Schumpeter 1947), innovation and related uncertainty may be involved at *every* stage of development of a business, and then financial incentives could be insufficient to reward managerial skills. The importance of idiosyncratic control rents to keep motivating entrepreneurship in the corporate business varies, perhaps considerably, with the type of economic activity involved, but that is a difference in degree, not in kind.[19] The fact is that control of the vast majority of corporations around the world is held by managers or controlling shareholders with a limited (if not negligible) ownership stake and, nevertheless, it is often entrenched. Diversionary and distortionary PBC only partially account for this phenomenon. A more general explanation is that *corporate control has a value*. This value also depends on the amount of idiosyncratic private benefits necessary to motivate business undertakings.

18 Schnitzer (1995) was the first to model the importance of deferred compensation for non-contractable investments. See more recently Manso (2011).
19 See Demsetz and Lehn (1985) and more recently, for the implications on efficient entrenchment, Chemmanur and Jiao (2012).

This leads me to the third and conclusive point. Since *idiosyncratic PBC are not just psychic, they can be compensated in cash*. This should provide a way out of control allocations that become inefficient over time. Idiosyncratic PBC do account for the prospective value of corporate control, which is neither verifiable nor contractable ex-ante, but might become appropriable ex-post. As such, control rents need not be either enjoyed by the original entrepreneur or transferred to his descendants, they can also be cashed in through a control sale. This requires a prospective buyer willing to bid more for the firm control than it is worth to the incumbent controller. It also requires that the latter be entitled to 'sell' firm control, thereby cashing in his idiosyncratic PBC. Corporate control transactions do in fact satisfy these two requirements.

Corporate control is very seldom taken over against the incumbent's will. Most typically, it is bought and sold, with the incumbents getting some reward in return for their control rents.[20] *Golden parachutes* paid to outgoing management (Hartzell et al 2004) and *control premia* awarded to blockholders (Dyck and Zingales 2004) are prominent examples in this regard. Intuitively, the larger the control rents to be rewarded, the more control transactions that would increase shareholder value will have to be foregone due to the corporate controller's entrenchment.[21] This might seem unfortunate (inefficient) ex-post. However, one should not forget that those rents that now prevent some efficient control transfer from taking place were needed in the first place, in order to induce the corporate controller to create a surplus that markets were unable to finance. If we add this surplus to the welfare analysis, idiosyncratic PBC do not necessarily hamper efficient reallocations of corporate control.[22]

Similar conclusions of course do not hold for diversionary and distortionary PBC, whose welfare implications are completely different. Differently from their idiosyncratic companions, these kinds of PBC negatively affect the production of shareholder value (Hart 2001). And they do not even have redeeming virtues as far as the corporate controller's incentives are concerned. The only behaviors they can motivate are either *stealing* the corporate assets or *shirking* from their efficient management (Roe 2003). Being a matter of conflict of interest between the corporate controller and non-controlling shareholders, diversionary and distortionary PBC are consistent with the standard agency framework.

Within the agency framework, however, the corporate controller's misbehavior is not always characterized as extraction of private benefits. Rather principal–agent models focus on the two problems arising from asymmetric information, namely moral hazard and adverse selection. Diversionary and distortionary PBC are just a *consequence* of these two problems. This terminology is more suitable to the incomplete contracts perspective being adopted

20 See Manne (1965: 112–114) making precisely this point.
21 This also depends on the degree of separation between ownership and control (Bebchuk 1994).
22 See, in the same vein, Coates (2004).

here, since the very notion of PBC involves a non-contractability dimension. Under contractual incompleteness, diversionary and distortionary PBC (like stealing and shirking from which they are generated) cannot be entirely coped with ex-ante via mechanism design, but require institutions (and the law therein) to support efficient ex-post bargaining over the allocation of quasi-rents.

Diversionary and distortionary PBC may sound somewhat different from the traditional agency approach to corporate governance; but, conceptually, they still belong to standard theory. What makes an important addition to the economic theory, and to its implications for corporate law, is the introduction of a *third* category of PBC in this framework, namely idiosyncratic (quasi-) rents of control. In order for idiosyncratic PBC to motivate firm-specific investments by the corporate controller, they should amount at the outset to a constraint on any subsequent bargaining over the allocation of control. This is only possible to the extent that corporate law provides the right entitlements to protection of control rents. The important consequences of this reasoning for corporate law will become clearer shortly. But let us start by discussing the problems with the more conventional understanding of private benefits of control.

2.3 Private benefits from stealing: the 'bad' ones

2.3.1 Defining 'diversionary' private benefits of control

The most intuitive example of moral hazard in corporate governance is the corporate controller *stealing* money from helpless outside shareholders, by diverting some or all of the firm's assets placed under his management to his personal and exclusive benefit. This can be done in several possible ways. A typical instance is so-called 'tunneling' (Johnson et al 2000; Atanasov et al 2011). A manager is entitled to buy and sell the firm's assets to anybody he likes and for any consideration he wishes. In theory, he could sell a valuable asset to a company he owns entirely for a consideration well below market prices. That would be equivalent to diverting shareholder money directly to his pockets. Of course, in the presence of such opportunities for straight-out expropriation, not only equity investment, but also any other kind of outside finance would not be practicable. Stealing is the most dangerous (albeit not necessarily the most harmful) instance of a corporate controller's misbehavior, because it involves the deepest conflict of interests: in the absence of constraints, absconding with the money is *always* preferable to providing financiers with the return they would expect.

The corporate governance literature focuses on stealing as the most important source of PBC (La Porta et al 2000; Bebchuk 1999). However, PBC need not arise from stealing resources that shareholders are entitled to (Dyck and Zingales 2004). There are many sources of PBC arising from the management of the firm's assets, and they are all equally important. Stealing is a very peculiar one. On the one hand, stealing always reduces the ex-post firm value available to shareholders, thereby undermining their incentives to the equity investment ex-ante. On the other hand, stealing is a purely pecuniary transfer from shareholders to the manager, which does not affect the production of their aggregate wealth. Stealing is therefore a source of pecuniary PBC whose extraction by the corporate controller has *no redeeming virtue*. Stealing is always inefficient ex-ante (Fox and Heller 2006).

If stealing was the only instance of pecuniary PBC to be accounted for, it would be tempting to divide PBC into a pecuniary and a non-pecuniary kind. Indeed, this is how PBC are often categorized in corporate law and economics (Gilson 2006). However, not all ex-post pecuniary transfers to the corporate controller come from stealing and are consequently inefficient ex-ante. For instance, managers' golden parachutes and large shareholders' control premia need involve no stealing, but may be consciously awarded in return for firm-specific investments undertaken ex-ante by the corporate controller. In addition, some non-pecuniary benefits accruing to the managers' utility reduce shareholder wealth by a far larger amount than stealing (e.g. shirking, empire building), while others do not affect shareholder wealth at all (e.g. the idiosyncratic, namely non-verifiable and non-transferable, control rents) (Hart 2001). For these reasons, I do not think that the usual distinction between pecuniary and non-pecuniary PBC is particularly meaningful. Sticking to the PBC taxonomy that I have laid down in the previous section, I shall continue to refer to the benefits the corporate controller derives from stealing as to 'diversionary', rather than pecuniary, PBC.

2.3.2 Law and institutional constraints on shareholder expropriation

In theory, the stealing problem could be dealt with contractually. In practice, this is not generally possible because of contractual incompleteness. Particularly in the case of shareholders, detailing behavioral constraints as a contractual safeguard against stealing is often not an option. A provision against managerial stealing is not difficult to draft, but is extremely difficult to implement. Would it suffice to state in the corporate charter that the controller is not entitled to cash in any larger portion of the firm's (verifiable) surplus than that one contracted for as profit sharing? Of course, it would not. While that is exactly the result that shareholders would like to achieve, such a vague provision is clearly too easy to circumvent (Rock and Wachter 2001).

Related-party transactions are a case in point.[23] Performance of those transactions is a part of managerial discretion that shareholders themselves are not willing to constrain. Nonetheless, shareholders might claim some monitoring rights on most dangerous transactions and have them included in

---

23 See Kraakman et al (2009) for a comparison of how these transactions are regulated.

the corporate contract. Apart from its unavoidable agency costs, this solution would be an efficient way to minimize opportunities for stealing if provisions in the corporate charter were stable over time. Unfortunately, they are not. Neither can they be.

Equity investments are residual claims over an indefinite time horizon: the firm's lifetime. Rules of decision-making about the firm's management do affect the value of equity investments, but do not have the same characteristic: they might need to be changed over time (Hansmann 2006). Provisions intended to protect shareholders against stealing can be set up in the corporate charter (the equity contract) by means of rules of decision-making. Think, for instance, of a charter provision requiring unanimous shareholder consent to operate a merger (mergers allow for exquisite stealing opportunities). Such a provision of course constrains the exercise of managerial discretion. However, being agreed upon by both the entrepreneur and the outside shareholders, they were presumably efficient *at the time they were established* (no opportunity for a profitable merger was foreseeable at that time). When unforeseen business opportunities arise (like a profitable merger), provisions constraining their exploitation become suddenly outdated.

Then there are two possibilities. The first one is the typical long-term contract solution of the unforeseen contingencies problem. In this scenario, renegotiation of the original contract would be bargained for ex-post, and shareholders (who enjoy a veto power) would be entitled to capture a larger share of the gains from the new opportunity by making a take-it or leave-it offer to the manager: either you part with control (getting your share of the profits, but giving up the control rents) or no merger will take place. The problem is that ex-ante no manager would make firm-specific investments leaving such a hold-up opportunity available to shareholders.

The governance structure of the firm provides an alternative. The manager could have the terms of the original contract altered when this is required for exploiting a new business opportunity without being exploited himself. This situation matches the corporate practice in the real world, where we usually do not observe unanimity provisions in corporate charters. Instead, whoever controls a publicly held company (either inside management or a controlling shareholder) typically exerts a considerable influence over charter amendments (Hellwig 2000).

This particular feature of corporate governance, as opposed to the governance of market relationships, has two implications. The first is that the controller's residual rights of control may include the power to modify the rules of the game, at least some of them. The second implication is that even the rules of decision-making established in the equity contract may not be stable enough to prevent the corporate controller from abusing his power for stealing purposes (Rock and Wachter 2001). Shareholders protection against straight-out expropriation therefore requires an *external* set of constraints disciplining the exercise of control power. Since these constraints need to be stable over time, they can only be provided by institutions.

In each society, stealing is dealt with by a different mix of institutions. In more developed ones, law plays a prominent role in constraining expropriation (North 1990). The need for institutional constraints on diversionary PBC is the very essence of the standard 'law matters' argument (La Porta et al 1998). But then, a number of additional conditions must be fulfilled by the law in order for corporate governance to be efficient. We are gradually coming closer to a more comprehensive description of what this means.

2.4 Private benefits from shirking: the 'ugly' ones?

2.4.1 *How shirking differs from stealing*

Should legal rules (and their enforcement) be effective enough in constraining shareholder expropriation, the corporate controller could still harm shareholders in a subtler, but potentially much more detrimental way. Making profits requires *effort* by the manager. While the benefits of this effort are shared with shareholders (depending on the division of the residual claim between them and the manager), its costs are borne entirely by the manager. As a result, the manager will tend to shirk (Tirole 2001). Shirking in the broadest sense is the typical source of agency costs in the framework of Jensen and Meckling (1976).

In the classic specification of the principal–agent model, shirking would be dealt with no differently from stealing. Ex-ante, the original contract would both minimize the opportunities for stealing available to the corporate controller and maximize his incentives to put effort into the firm's management. However, the matter is more complicated when contracts are incomplete.

Stealing cannot be fully constrained through the corporate charter because the latter may be subject to opportunistic renegotiation by the holder of residual rights of control – who, as a positive matter, is the corporate controller. However, outside shareholders are not completely exposed to stealing by the corporate controller – why would they entrust him their money otherwise? Stealing affects the division of the firm's surplus *after* this is produced, so it is normally verifiable ex-post by a third party (e.g. a judge). This implies that stealing can be coped with by the legal system, and specifically by corporate law, provided that its rules and its enforcement are efficient in this respect (Rock and Wachter 2001).

Shirking is a completely different story. On the one hand, it affects not only the division, but the production of the firm's surplus. This, in turn, depends on the corporate controller's effort, which is only limitedly observable and intrinsically not verifiable. Therefore, although this is theoretically possible in some corporate law jurisdictions, questioning managerial shirking in courts hardly makes any economic sense (Kraakman et al 2009: 79–81). Only an appropriate set of incentives, both internal (the corporate contract) and external (market institutions) to the firm, can contain the manager's inclination to shirk without possibly eliminating it (Roe 2002). On the other hand, the perspective of a favorable renegotiation of the corporate contract with shareholders may provide the corporate controller with additional incentives to put effort into firm management (Schnitzer 1995). In a dynamic perspective, the manager's effort may improve his bargaining position in a future control transaction where valuable firm-specific investments are due to be rewarded through the proceeds of an efficiency-enhancing control sale (Almazan and Suarez 2003). Such a reward usually takes the form of golden parachutes or control premia. Hence, the problem of shirking ultimately overlaps with managerial reward in the form of idiosyncratic PBC. How the dynamic efficiency of control allocation is affected by this mechanism depends on the market for corporate control.

2.4.2 Defining 'distortionary' private benefits of control

Shirking is another source of private benefits of control. These benefits are non-pecuniary. They come from enjoying the firm's assets under management without stealing any of them. As a result, shirking does not involve diversion of the firm's cash flow. Even worse, it does involve suboptimal management of this cash flow and overall underproduction of the firm's surplus. Typical instances of such PBC are consumption of perquisites (such as plush carpets, company airplanes, and the like), expanding the firm beyond what is necessary (so-called 'empire building') and, more in general, misuse of free cash (selection of investment projects that enhance the controller's personal benefits, rather than shareholder profits) (Jensen 1986). They all involve *distorted management* (i.e., misallocation) of funds available to the firm, namely the cost of more profitable business opportunities being foregone. In economic terms, the cost of distorted allocation of corporate funds is an *opportunity cost* borne by shareholders.

Misallocation of funds is not necessarily a feature of non-pecuniary PBC. Some of them do not come from shirking, like – for instance – the pride due to still unobservable firm's success, or the development of synergies (implying less effort, without shirking) in the management of two different corporations (Holderness 2003). This kind of benefit is *idiosyncratic* to the corporate controller, and therefore the opportunity cost to shareholders is zero. For this reason, to avoid possible confusion arising from the notion of non-pecuniary private benefits of control, I shall continue to refer to the PBC from shirking as to 'distortionary' PBC.

2.4.3 The limits of institutions in constraining managerial shirking

Distortionary PBC are extremely difficult to handle. One might have to live with them, and they might be 'ugly' for that reason. As I mentioned, legal rules are of little help due to non-verifiability of effort in the management of a firm. To be sure, foregone business opportunities (the cost of shirking to shareholders) are normally not even observable by shareholders. The best way to deal with the problem is, therefore, the provision of *incentives* to the corporate controller. To some extent, this can be done through the corporate contract, by making managerial compensation contingent on the realization of a future, observable variable correlated with his effort (Zingales 1998). This variable is typically the firm performance. In a sense, this is equivalent to sharing the residual claim between shareholders and an owner-manager, and then – as Jensen and Meckling (1976) showed – it provides just a second best solution to the problem.

Consider an entrepreneur-manager who is risk averse, has a limited capacity to borrow and is wealth-constrained: indeed, these are the ultimate reasons for separating ownership from control. This manager cannot pay for the residual claim up front. Being unable to contract upon managerial behavior in detail, shareholders are willing to award the manager only a limited share of the firm's profits (Hart 2001). When the incentives provided in this way are not sufficient to have the firm run effectively by a non-owner manager, separation of ownership and control can only occur to a limited extent. The entrepreneur-manager will be able to raise a limited amount of funds from outside shareholders and will have to retain a significant share ownership. I shall elaborate later on the reasons underlying that choice. In any case, the degree of alignment of managerial incentives that can be reached contractually, through profit sharing, is always imperfect.

Other market institutions can improve the alignment of managerial incentives with shareholders' interest. The most important one is *product market competition* (Roe 2001). Perfect competition would be more than enough to keep managers on their toes. When managers do not catch up with competitors, sooner or later there will be no firm to manage. However, since competition is never perfect, this would happen later rather than sooner. In the meantime, managers would be relatively free to enjoy distortionary PBC while making shortsighted shareholders happy with their monopoly profits.

A similar argument applies to *capital market competition*. Any constraint on managerial misbehavior coming from the capital market requires that additional external finance be needed. Until investment projects can be financed with retained earnings (shareholders receive dividends at the corporate controller's discretion), this constraint is not likely to be effective.[24] What makes competition in both the product and the capital markets an imperfect, albeit important, constraint on mismanagement is that resources permanently committed to the firm (i.e., equity capital) are sunk costs. This circumstance will give managers slack, until there is some free cash to mismanage without risk of losing their job.

Debt could help making financial constraints binding on the corporate controller (Hart 1995). Equity finance has a comparative advantage over debt

24 Hellwig (2000). But see Hart (2001) for a theory of why companies pay dividends.

as far as agency costs are concerned (Jensen and Meckling 1976). However, the source of this advantage, namely the incentive effect of equity holding by the manager, decreases with separation of ownership and control. In contrast, no matter how much external finance is raised by the firm, debt keeps its major advantage over equity: it has to be repaid. This is particularly relevant under contractual incompleteness, for it involves that debt-financed resources are not sunk costs (Aghion and Bolton 1992). Should the manager fail to pay back the firm's creditors, they will ultimately force the firm into bankruptcy and the manager will lose his job. In addition – given the firm's financial needs – the more indebted the firm, the less outside equity is needed. *Ceteris paribus*, debt both reduces the amount of free cash flow available for mismanagement and increases the manager's share of the residual claim (i.e., his incentives to make profits).

As such, debt would look like a marvelous mechanism to reduce distortionary PBC. However, every firm has a limited indebtedness capacity (Becht et al 2007). When additional funds are needed, pushing the financial leverage is not always the solution. Beyond a certain leverage threshold, this would not even be an option because no more credit would be available. Financing risky investment projects with debt increases not only managerial discipline but also the expected bankruptcy costs to shareholders. From this perspective, debt can reduce the firm value. Highly leveraged firms tend to undertake overly risky projects (one instance is the so-called 'gambling for resurrection') and this tendency makes creditors unwilling to provide funds when the firm is already much indebted. Also in this situation, equity-holders may be reluctant to provide additional funds, since this would benefit outstanding creditors more than themselves. As a result, fewer funds are available to highly indebted firms for financing new profitable investment opportunities. This is the so-called 'debt-overhang' effect (Myers 1977). Finally, those who are in charge of deciding the firm's financial structure (the managers) do not like creditors breathing down their neck. Consequently, they will tend over time to free themselves from creditors as, in general, from the need to resort to the capital market for doing business (Hellwig 2000). Such freedom is possible as soon as retained earnings become sufficient to finance investments. This strategy is not necessarily inefficient. However, it implies that the disciplinary effect of debt over managerial misuse of free cash flow is not only limited in the first place, but also tends to shrink over time.

Taken together, equity ownership and related financial incentives, product and capital market competition, and the firm's financial structure do actually constrain shirking by the corporate controller. However, all those constraints are insufficient to rule out distortionary PBC. To some extent, this is unavoidable. In the Jensen and Meckling (1976) complete contracting model, the owner-manager always ends up pursuing some private interests to the outside shareholders' disadvantage, and this is reflected in the agency costs borne ex-ante by the owner-manager. However, when contracts are incomplete, not all ex-post inefficiencies can be foreseen (and priced) ex-ante. In other words, distortionary PBC are ultimately dependent on the exercise of managerial discretionary powers, and so they might exceed the amount originally foreseen in the corporate contract (Zingales 1998). Some further solution to the problem of misuse of free cash by the corporate controller must be therefore devised ex-post, in order to make equity finance viable ex-ante.

Given contractual incompleteness, the problem of managerial shirking finally collapses into a problem of (re)allocation of corporate control (Hellwig 2000). Managers should be replaced (or induced to part with control) when their shirking becomes excessive relative to the best management alternative available on the market. More in general, incumbent managers need to be replaced when they prove incompetent and a new manager could do a better job. In this perspective, the problems of managerial moral hazard and adverse selection affecting distortionary PBC are solved dynamically, provided that other institutions take care of the corporate controller's misbehavior when it comes to stealing (diversionary PBC). In other words, assuming that stealing is otherwise ruled out of the system, even a straightforward agency perspective would ultimately rely on ex-post replacement of underperforming managers for the efficiency of corporate governance.

Replacement of inefficient managers takes place in a very special market: the market for corporate control. What makes it even more crucial to corporate governance is that this is also the place where idiosyncratic PBC may be cashed in, thereby allowing for firm-specific investments by the corporate controller to be rewarded. However, this has nothing to do with agency theory.

2.5 Trading ownership for private benefits: the market for corporate control

2.5.1 *Coasian bargain and the efficient allocation of corporate control*

The market for corporate control is the place where firm control changes hands. The reason why it should help to constrain distortionary PBC is very intuitive. Provided that managerial shirking is inefficient (its opportunity costs to shareholders are larger than its gains to the manager), it should always be possible to arrange a control transfer to a more efficient manager in such a way as to make everybody better off. What is crucial to this purpose is that the incumbent controller is awarded a compensation for his control rents, which is large enough to offset his personal benefits from inferior management and to reward his initial firm-specific investments if there were any (Hellwig 2000). A similar reasoning applies to incompetence. Whenever a more talented manager shows up, the additional profits he would bring about should provide gains from trade sufficient to induce the incumbent manager to part with control. In this perspective, efficient control transactions are regarded as Pareto improvements. This is an application of the well-known Coase Theorem: no matter what the initial allocation of property rights is (i.e., residual rights of control), the efficient outcome (i.e., efficient allocation of the firm's control) will be reached by the parties (i.e., both incumbent and insurgent managers, and outside shareholders) dealing with each other.[25]

The Coase Theorem holds on condition that transaction costs are nil. Since transaction costs are positive in the real world, allocation of residual rights of control may indeed matter for the achievement of the efficient outcome. If shareholders have residual rights of control, managers will stay in charge on condition that they maximize shareholder value, but will be replaced otherwise. However, provided that they cannot buy from shareholders the entitlement to idiosyncratic control rents (for they have no contractible value ex-ante – i.e., transaction costs would be infinite), managers will always refrain from undertaking firm-specific investments that cannot be contracted upon whether this is efficient or not (Hart 2001). Conversely, if managers can be allocated residual control rights, they may have an incentive to undertake firm-specific investments even though these are not contractable. However, managers would then be shielded from shareholder interference (managers with residual control rights are entrenched by definition) and there is no guarantee that they will ever yield to a superior manager. Differently from the previous scenario, though, *the party with no entitlement can offer a side payment to the holder of control rights in order to achieve the efficient outcome*. In fact, shareholders can offer to compensate managers for their control rents as soon as they get contractable; that is, as soon as shareholders are willing to bid more for firm control than it is worth to the incumbent management.[26] This would just require that, under a new management, overall shareholder value increases by an amount larger than the incumbent's control rents (I am still assuming that stealing is otherwise ruled out of corporate governance). Based on this intuition, I believe that the Coase Theorem is the right starting point for analyzing the market for corporate control.

This is not how the market for corporate control is described by the mainstream literature on corporate governance. Most economists and lawyers do not only assume that the Coase Theorem breaks down in corporate control transactions.[27] They also posit that the only way to achieve the efficient outcome is to assign residual rights of control to shareholders who ultimately own the corporation, even though they have it run by professional managers on a daily basis (Shleifer and Vishny 1997). Standard theory of corporate governance considers firm-specific investment by corporate managers as 'unimportant' for the firm's success and leaves no room for protection of control rents (Hart 1995). Although I do not share this view (it does not really explain why a talented entrepreneur-manager should accept such a deal in the

---

25 See Coase (1960). Ronald Coase never stated his 'theorem' in his writings; George Stigler (1966) did. See also Stigler (1989) and Coase (1992).
26 For two different ways to formalize this intuition, see Almazan and Suarez (2003) and Schnitzer (1995).
27 See e.g. Hart (2001): Shleifer and Vishny (1997); Easterbrook and Fischel (1981).

first place, giving away his non-contractable talent for no reward), it is worthwhile analyzing it in some details, for it leads to the probably most celebrated and debated institution of corporate governance: the hostile takeover.[28]

2.5.2 *Why hostile takeover is not the answer*

The hostile takeover is, in theory, a terrific mechanism for replacing inefficient managers, since by definition it does not require that managers agree on being taken over. Its basic functioning is extremely simple. When the incumbent manager is availing himself of too many distortionary PBC, stock prices will go down and this will make it profitable for a more efficient manager to buy the firm out. This manager will be able to capture the efficiency gains by acquiring the firm's stock and replacing the old manager. In this perspective, hostile takeovers would actually suffice to keep incumbent managers constantly on their toes, thereby solving the problem of distortionary PBC. No manager would actually shirk, for if he did, he would immediately lose his job.

Even more importantly, hostile takeovers make sure control is always allocated to the best possible manager. Firm performance does not only depend on the manager's effort, but also on his capabilities. At least in theory, the set of incentives underlying hostile takeovers is such that the corporate controller is replaced whenever a slightly better manager is available. Apparently, hostile takeovers solve two major problems of corporate governance at the same time: on the one hand, they *discipline* managerial behavior (coping with the problem of moral hazard); on the other hand, they guarantee the efficient *allocation* of corporate control in a dynamic perspective (providing a solution to the adverse selection problem) (Jensen and Ruback 1983).

Unfortunately, hostile takeovers are not as helpful with respect to diversionary PBC whenever these are not effectively coped with by the legal system. Stealing could indeed be policed by hostile takeovers on condition that the acquirer buys *all* of the company's shares at *one single* price accounting for the current value of the firm.[29] Yet this is not required for the success of a takeover. On the contrary, such a requirement makes takeovers less likely to succeed.[30] This puts us in a bind. For hostile takeovers to police stealing, a strict principle of shareholder equal treatment should be implemented. However, this may end up frustrating any takeover attempt, whether it is hostile or not. Given that, the market for corporate control cannot work well whenever diversionary PBC are being extracted. Hostile takeovers may actually make the problem even worse. If anything, acquisitions that go

---

28 See Burkart and Panunzi (2008). The attention of academics to hostile takeovers dates back to Manne (1965). Manne, however, never advocated hostile takeovers; his approach to the market for corporate control is closer to Coasian bargain than it is commonly understood.

29 See e.g. Bebchuk (1985).

30 See Easterbrook and Fischel (1982b).

unchecked by the incumbent controllers are more likely to be motivated by looting purposes and, therefore, to result in an outcome highly detrimental to shareholders. Corporate governance simply needs to feature different solutions to the stealing problem.

Takeovers are considerably more problematic in the real world, where the mechanisms of acquisition are not as simple as in the stylized picture that I have just depicted. The actual functioning of hostile takeovers encounters a number of difficulties both ex-post (when control should be reallocated) and ex-ante (when separation of ownership and control is decided by the entrepreneur). The first kind of problems makes hostile takeovers much less effective in both disciplining shirking managers and replacing incompetent ones (Roe 2003). Ex-ante, hostile takeovers can even hinder separation of ownership and control, at least when protection of idiosyncratic control rents is an issue for the entrepreneur (Coates 2004).

To be workable, hostile takeovers require both a very high degree of separation of ownership and control and regulatory support. To begin with, the corporate controller's ownership needs to be insufficient to resist a hostile acquisition (or to make it unprofitable for the acquirer). In addition, non-controlling shareholders need not be in the position to hold out, since otherwise they will not let the acquirer cheaply buy their stock in order to replace the incumbent manager (Burkart and Panunzi 2008).

The first requirement is a matter of ownership and control structure. In models of corporate governance based on a controlling shareholder or on coalitions of owner–managers, hostile takeovers can be easily ruled out by means of devices allowing incumbents to exert disproportionate voting power (e.g., dual class shares in Sweden and many other European countries) or preventing insurgents from taking over unless they put together nearly all of the company's shares (e.g., rules disfavoring controlling shareholding at the London Stock Exchange).[31]

The second requirement is a matter of appropriation of takeover gains by the acquirer. This is what ultimately motivates the acquisition. Non-controlling shareholders may be able to claim a large fraction of those gains – if not all of them, pro-rata – either because they are large enough to hold out, or because they are alerted by the launch of a formal bid or by the incumbent management that the company is undervalued, or finally because either the incumbent management or the legal system make some or all of them entitled to capture takeover gains in the form of a premium on their shares (Kraakman et al 2009). When these factors are at work, a prospective acquirer may fail to recover the costs of the acquisition; therefore he will desist from the acquisition in the first place.

Even when favorable conditions were realized on the above two accounts, hostile takeover would still work far from perfectly. First, hostile takeovers are extremely costly. Even though they are dispersed, shareholders are not

---

31 See, for an excellent overview, Becht and Mayer (2001).

completely stupid: why should they sell their shares at current prices, letting the acquirer get all the gains from the takeover? Shareholders would rather demand a premium for tendering their shares. In fact they always do. The underlying theoretical problem is known as 'free riding.' Shareholders who do not tender will benefit from the efficiency gains brought about by the acquirer, so the latter has to 'bribe' them in order to succeed (Grossman and Hart 1980). In practice, the free rider problem makes takeover premia always substantial and this confines the disciplinary effect of hostile takeovers (if any) just to the major instances of underperformance (Shleifer and Vishny 1997; Franks et al 2001).

Second, hostile takeovers do not guarantee that only efficient control transfers take place. The acquirer might be more interested in enhancing his PBC (from both stealing and shirking) rather than the firm value (Shleifer and Vishny 1988; Jensen 1993). This is because, for succeeding in a hostile takeover, a prospective acquirer needs neither to buy all of the company's stock nor to pay for the incumbent's PBC. Notice that this problem is overcome not only when the acquirer is forced to bid for all of the company's shares at the same price (the underlying rationale for mandatory bids with equal treatment of outstanding shareholders), but also when the acquirer has to pay for the incumbent's PBC, on condition that stealing is otherwise ruled out by the legal system.[32] *Under this condition*, takeovers can only be profitable when the acquirer buys enough shares on the stock market (possibly all of the firm's outstanding shares) to compensate the incumbent's private benefits with the enhanced security benefits of a more efficient management. Given that taking over firm control requires the purchase of at least the incumbent's ownership stake, and anyway of enough shares to gain control of the board of directors, the acquirer would have no choice for recovering takeover expenses but to reduce the opportunity costs of shirking or otherwise increase shareholder value. Clearly, to the extent the incumbent's PBC need to be compensated upfront, this takeover mechanism allows for no hostility.

Third, hostile takeovers require that a huge amount of funds be raised to finance the stock acquisition. Even where capital markets are deep and liquid enough, takeovers need to bring about quite large efficiency gains to pay back the funds raised. However, as I have just pointed out, hostile acquisitions provide no guarantee in this respect. Changes in control by hostile takeover are not necessarily efficient, whereas – under certain conditions – negotiated control transfers (so-called 'friendly takeovers') are always such.

2.5.3 *Friendly takeovers and the protection of control rents*

The most important impediments to hostile takeovers are not in their *functioning* when ownership has already been separated from control. They are

---

32 See *infra* Chapter 7.

in its *tolerance* by an entrepreneur when separation is decided in order to access equity finance on a large scale (that is, when the company 'goes public' and its shares are listed on a stock exchange).

Hostile takeovers are based on contestability of control. The theory of contestable markets tells us that no monopoly rent can be maintained under perfect contestability (Baumol et al 1982). This is true also in the market for corporate control: once control is made (perfectly) contestable, there is no way for the corporate controller to secure private benefits (i.e., control rents) of any kind.

However, like monopoly rents in product market competition, control rents are not always a bad thing for corporate governance. In particular, protection of quasi-rents may be needed to foster entrepreneurial innovation (Marshall 1893). When those rents are substantial, *the entrepreneur might be unwilling to separate ownership from control if this necessarily involves being subject to hostile takeover*. True, going public may provide the entrepreneur with benefits sufficient to offset the loss of his idiosyncratic PBC. However, this is not always the case. To be sure, the empirical evidence on entrenchment of corporate control rather suggests that often this is *not* the case. Thus, we need to investigate whether the market for corporate control can also work through mechanisms other than hostile takeovers.

By introducing this topic with a reference to the Coase Theorem, I have already suggested that this is possible. A market for corporate control can be reconciled with the incumbent controller's entrenchment when takeovers are friendly, that is, when changes in control are operated with the incumbent's consent. Friendly takeovers guarantee that idiosyncratic PBC are safeguarded. Provided that the incumbent's firm-specific investments are rewarded, *friendly takeovers can also guarantee that control changes hands if (and only if) this is efficient*, thereby enhancing the overall efficiency of corporate governance. This is a crucial point I shall return to in the next chapter. But let me stress, once again, how the scope for *diversionary* PBC (i.e., stealing opportunities available to any corporate controller) must be curbed by the legal system for that result to hold.

The importance of effective legal policing of cash flow diversion for the efficiency of corporate governance is the realm, and indeed the fundamental strength, of the classical 'law matters' thesis (Djankov et al 2008). This argument tells us little about how *distortionary* PBC are dealt with, since in theory the only way legal rules can cope with them is by supporting shareholder insurgency, but in practice hostile takeovers and similar instances of outside shareholder interference can be (and actually are) excluded in different corporate governance system. The presence of idiosyncratic PBC offers an explanation, other than widespread expropriation, of why entrenchment is so frequent. What we still do not know is how incentive compatibility can be preserved under these conditions; that is, whether and how the protection of idiosyncratic control rents can be reconciled with the incentives of the corporate controller to maximize shareholder value.

2.6 Idiosyncratic private benefits: the 'good' ones

2.6.1 Costly shareholder intervention, managerial rent protection, and the over-monitoring theory

Although the implications of control rents for the overall efficiency of corporate governance have so far not yet been completely explored, economic theory has acknowledged the importance of their protection for fostering ex-ante firm-specific investment by an entrepreneur or a manager, notwithstanding separation of ownership and control.[33] It might be surprising – given that the same author prefers to consider the case where the manager's preferences are 'unimportant' for the firm's success – but perhaps the most lucid description of how managerial control rents may indeed have efficiency motivations, and how this could explain the disproportion between control rights and corporate ownership that most frequently we observe in practice, is provided by Professor Hart:

> In some companies it may be efficient to allocate control rights to managers in order to allow them to enjoy their private benefits, or to motivate them to undertake relationship-specific investments. Alternatively, the company's initial owner may 'sell' the private benefits to a large investor, along with voting control, so that the investor can consume the private benefits without risk of expropriation. If managers and investors are wealth-constrained and cannot afford to purchase a large equity stake (or if they are risk-averse), it may be necessary to depart from one share–one vote to achieve these outcomes.[34]

Building on the same insight, three European economists – Mike Burkart, Denis Gromb, and Fausto Panunzi (1997) – developed a theory of separation of ownership and control where delegation of control rights *cannot* be withdrawn by outside shareholders if not in certain states of the world, i.e. only when it is profitable for shareholders to do so.[35] This is supposed to happen when shareholders are much dispersed and ousting the incumbent management would not be worth the expense of a hostile takeover, unless the firm is managed very badly. In all remaining situations, the corporate controller has *full* (and not just *delegated*) *discretion*, namely unchallenged effective control over the firm's assets.

Moderately shielding the manager from the risk of outside shareholders' interference is ex-ante beneficial for both parties. The former will have incentive to undertake firm-specific investments, like searching for new

---

33 See Kirzner (1979: 94) and more recently Ricketts (2003: 81) for an entrepreneurship perspective. See also Hellwig (2000) for a corporate finance approach to the problem.
34 Hart (1995: 188).
35 See also Hart (2001) and Tirole (2006) with a similar approach (costly shareholder intervention).

business opportunities, without risk of being subsequently expropriated of his private benefits by insurgent shareholders taking over. The latter will have to reap some of the benefits of the manager's initiative in the form of profits, since below a certain threshold of stock returns shareholders would find it profitable to hold the manager up (thereby depriving him of *all* control rents). Ex-post, this arrangement also involves some costs. Shareholders will have to yield to the manager's preferences for (moderately) high-PBC investment projects, thereby foregoing more profitable alternatives (possibly brought about by a new manager) that would fail to compensate the incumbent manager for his initial investment. The basic intuition of this model is thus that "even if managerial discretion is ex-post detrimental to shareholders, it can be beneficial ex-ante as it favors firm-specific investments, like searching for new investment projects" (Burkart et al 1997: 693).

The above intuition is based on the property rights theory of the firm, and it tries to overcome its major shortcoming when it comes to separation of ownership and control:

> [The property rights literature] argues that parties without ownership may be discouraged from undertaking firm-specific investments because the owners of the assets can use their control rights to hold them up. This theory, however, cannot capture the separation of ownership and control because it equates these two concepts. Following Aghion and Tirole (1997), we suggest that control rights translate into effective control only when their holders have the incentives to exercise them. We argue that the ownership structure is a powerful technology to allocate effective control in a way that mitigates the holdup problem.[36]

The implications of this reasoning are highly peculiar. The authors point to a so-called *over-monitoring problem*. Managers would only undertake firm-specific investments that are not verifiable (and, therefore, not contractable) ex-ante on condition they can secure an adequate reward for such a behavior in the form of PBC. In other words, they need to feel safe from subsequent hold-up by outside shareholders. However, if managers are closely monitored by shareholders, the latter will always be able to deprive ex-post the former of their PBC, and unable to commit ex-ante to any different policy (provided that holding managers up is always worth the effort – i.e., profitable ex-post). As a result, managers would not take any unverifiable initiative when they are too closely monitored.

Monitoring is costly, and therefore not every shareholder is expected to implement it in the same way. A large shareholder is supposed to be a tighter monitor than small, dispersed ones (who are most likely to free ride). Given

---

36 Burkart et al (1997: 696). Their approach is based on the distinction between formal and real authority, which is a cornerstone of modern organizational theory (Aghion and Tirole 1997).

the monitoring costs, a dispersed ownership structure is a way to commit credibly to a policy of no-interference by outside shareholders, thereby promoting managerial incentive to undertake firm-specific investments. Hostile takeovers and similar instances of shareholder intervention work just on the side of this mechanism. The scope of managerial discretion (and the size of PBC that managers are entitled to) is negatively related to the incentives to informed intervention by shareholders (that is, ownership concentration) and positively related to its costs – which also depend on how weak legal protection of outside shareholders is. This leads to the conclusion – quite unconventional, indeed – that not only large shareholdings may overkill managerial initiative (and, more broadly, entrepreneurial innovation), but also 'excessive' legal protection of shareholders could lead to the same outcome, unless it is matched by an extremely dispersed ownership structure. Therefore, the over-monitoring problem might explain why takeover defenses and other managerial entrenchment devices, while inefficient ex-post, might prove efficient ex-ante.

While extremely insightful, this theory fails to explain a few facts of corporate governance in the real world. A major problem with the above framework is that one of its basic assumptions is highly unrealistic: that is, "perfect congruence of interests between large and small shareholders" (Burkart et al 1997: 697). Although this assumption has been removed in a subsequent paper by Professors Burkart and Panunzi, the underlying problem stays. Models of corporate governance based on the over-monitoring problem do not properly account for the role of controlling shareholders.[37]

Large investors, who are not also *controlling* shareholders, only monitor very mildly the firm management. Likewise, they can hardly be expected to challenge managerial control rents with a hold-up strategy. Those (moderately) large shareholders – typically, institutional or otherwise very wealthy investors – just strive for getting the highest possible monetary return on their investment. In case they do not, they would not interfere with firm control by withdrawing from their support to the incumbent management; they would simply withdraw from their investment.[38]

Alternatively, shareholders may get *so large* that they do not simply monitor the firm management; they *control* it. But then assuming that managers are still in charge of the firm's core decision-making, while subject to over-monitoring by a significantly large shareholder, becomes both a useless and a misleading fiction for describing corporate governance. It is useless, because making corporate managers accountable to a controlling shareholder – who takes the real decisions – is the ultimate reason for the acquisition of a controlling stake in the firm ownership, so that management over-monitoring

37 I have discussed the shortcomings of the overmonitoring theory in more detail in Pacces (2007).
38 See e.g. Coffee (1991), Stapledon (1996: 252–269), and more recently Edmans and Manso (2011).

can no longer be an issue (Shleifer and Vishny 1997). It is misleading, because what matters in that situation is not the managers' initiative, but rather the controlling shareholder's incentive to undertake firm-specific investments. As a result, the hold-up problem affects the relationship between controlling and non-controlling shareholders, rather than that between managers and large shareholders. It is highly questionable that this problem can also be interpreted as a matter of over-monitoring.

2.6.2 *Entrenchment and the manager's incentive-compatibility*

Over-monitoring could be the wrong way to look at the right problem. As Burkart and Panunzi (2001: 13) recognized, "In a firm with a manager-owner and otherwise dispersed small shareholders, neither lacking initiative nor excessive shareholder interference are essential issues." But, then, what protects the owner-manager's investment from subsequent hold-up by outside shareholders? The answer is the corporate controller's entrenchment.

Entrenchment is in fact a more powerful commitment device than dispersed ownership. While the latter makes holding up the incumbent management *more expensive* to shareholders (that is, too costly to be implemented, unless the firm is managed very badly), the former makes it just *impossible* (that is, too costly to be implemented *in any case*). Entrenchment is also a more general way to protect firm-specific investments by the corporate controller. It works under both dispersed and concentrated ownership structures (i.e., those 'with a manager-owner and otherwise dispersed small shareholders'), provided that the managers of a public company and the controlling shareholder of an otherwise publicly held corporation are both shielded from hostile takeovers.

Of course, allowing for straight entrenchment of corporate control is much riskier than committing to a 'soft' policy of management replacement through dispersed ownership. Once residual control rights are delegated to an absolutely entrenched corporate controller, there is practically no way for shareholders to withdraw from that delegation. Entrenchment involves a *definitive* assignment of residual rights of control, rather than their mere delegation. While this would wonderfully protect the corporate controller's firm-specific investments, thereby promoting entrepreneurial innovation and managerial initiative, apparently it would also expose non-controlling shareholders to an unacceptable hold-up risk. Facing no threat of ouster, an incumbent controller would appear to be able to appropriate the firm's *entire* surplus in the form of PBC, while failing to provide outside shareholders with *any* return on their investment.

If that was the case, we would not observe either entrenched controllers or outside equity finance in the governance of corporate enterprises. In fact, however, these two circumstances can occur simultaneously. Why do we have plenty of takeover-proof public companies around the world? The reason must be that corporate governance allows for factors preventing an entrenched corporate controller from just taking advantage of non-controlling shareholders (Roe 2003). Taken together, those factors should induce or force the corporate controller to cut back his PBC when they reduce shareholder wealth by either diverting their profits (stealing) or distorting its production (shirking, empire building, etc.), without depriving him of residual control rights – which would undermine his incentives to unverifiable firm-specific investments. Compared to over-monitoring models, this result is not based on the *size* of PBC allowed by limited shareholder oversight (with just *moderate entrenchment* consequences), but it is rather obtained by implementing *absolute entrenchment* with a different treatment of PBC, depending on their *quality*.

Let me recall the PBC taxonomy that I introduced at the beginning of this chapter. An ideal system of corporate governance would curb both diversionary and distortionary PBC (the 'bad' and the 'ugly' ones), so that entrenchment cannot be aimed at fostering those benefits at the shareholders' expenses. In the absence of diversionary and distortionary PBC, the hold-up potential remaining available to an entrenched controller would concern just the unverifiable part of the surplus, whose protection makes economic sense when there are non-contractable firm-specific investments at stake (Schnitzer 1995; Canoya et al 2000). As we know, idiosyncratic PBC (the 'good' ones) account exactly for that surplus and they ultimately justify entrenchment as efficient protection of control rents. Eliminating – or, more realistically, minimizing – the amount of diversionary and distortionary PBC that can be extracted by a corporate controller is then a precondition for entrenchment to work efficiently. Luckily, as I mentioned before, a number of factors are at play in corporate governance, which are intended to guarantee that result; even though – as we will see in later chapters – they are not always handled as they should be by the legal systems.

First, the typical controller's monetary compensation is partly contingent on the realization of profits accruing to the shareholder value. This is quite obvious when the corporate controller is a shareholder himself. But it is no less true in the case of a non-owner manager whose compensation depends on both current performance (think of 'pay-per-performance' incentive schemes, like stock option plans) and past track record (affecting his standing on the managerial labor markets, and thereby the amount of his fixed salary). In general, failing to provide non-controlling shareholders with a return on their investment will also negatively affect the corporate controller's monetary compensation (Hart 1995). His consumption of distortionary PBC will then have to be traded off against direct and indirect consequences on profit sharing.

Second, the compliance with the profit sharing rule originally contracted for is (or at least should be) guaranteed by a body of legal rules, commonly referred to as *fiduciary duties*, which ex-post prevent the corporate controller from outright expropriating non-controlling shareholders of their share of the realized surplus (Rock and Wachter 2001). Scope for expropriation unaccounted for in the corporate contract depends on contractual incompleteness, and that is the reason why law 'matters' for actively minimizing agency costs instead of merely enforcing contracts that have already achieved that result (Becht et al 2007). That being said, there is some confusion in economic theory about the role of legal rules in corporate governance, for economists often consider as relevant 'law' whatever enhances, in a legally enforceable manner, outside shareholders' powers relative to those of the corporate controller. Entering in this fashion, legal protection of outside shareholders can also be counterproductive for separation of ownership and control, to the extent that it threatens the corporate controllers' discretion and his incentives to undertake valuable firm-specific investments. This is actually an important result highlighted by the over-monitoring literature. However, legal protection of outside shareholders does not necessarily mean the right to interfere with the firm management. Quite to the contrary, many legal arrangements in corporate governance actually deal with how to short-circuit shareholder interference (Hellwig 2000). Fiduciary duties certainly do not involve any such interference. When properly implemented by the legal system, they do not allow non-controlling shareholders to hold the corporate controller up. However, fiduciary duties prevent the latter from expropriating the former in that they counter diversion of the firm's profits (i.e., stealing).

The above factors still leave some scope for shareholders being held up. Once again, this is due to contractual incompleteness. We already know from the basic principal–agent model that ownership (profit) sharing can never eliminate distortionary PBC. Neither can institutions, whether they are legal or extra-legal, fare any better in this respect. It is ultimately for this reason that I have characterized these private benefits as 'ugly': we have to leave with them. Entrenchment could, however, worsen this problem over time and raise the related agency costs. The opportunity cost of perquisites consumption or empire building increases whenever a more efficient manager shows up. This might be due to moral hazard (the next manager would be more diligent) or to an adverse selection problem (the next manager would be more competent). In this situation, an entrenched controller would hold on to his position while underperforming relative to a potential insurgent, thereby enlarging his distortionary PBC at the non-controlling shareholders' expense.[39] When non-controlling shareholders have committed not to withdraw control rights from the incumbent management, perhaps in order to promote firm-specific investments by the managers, they can no longer *force* a change in control even in the case of considerable underperformance. However, shareholders can *induce* such a change. And they actually do.

In dispersed ownership structures, incumbent managers often get sizeable severance payments (so-called 'golden parachutes') in return for their parting with control. In concentrated ownership structures, even larger control premiums are awarded when the controlling stake changes hand. In the two

---

39 This is the so-called management entrenchment hypothesis. See Burkart and Panunzi (2008) and Schnitzer (1995).

situations, maximizing deferred compensation from a future control sale should induce the corporate controller both to invest his managerial talent (and effort) ex-ante and to part with control when facing a significantly more efficient manager ex-post. Consistent with the incomplete contracts framework, both moral hazard and adverse selection problems are then solved dynamically by ex-post *bargaining* rather than by ex-ante *contracting* (Zingales 1998).

In this perspective, distortionary PBC look quite less 'ugly' than they appear at first glance. Contrary to the mainstream view, shareholders need not be entitled to hold the corporate controller up in order to counter their extraction. Actually, in the presence of idiosyncratic PBC, shareholders may deliberately choose to relinquish their control rights in order to promote managerial firm-specific investments. Intuitively this implies that shareholders will forego some efficient control transfers later on. This is because some ex-post inefficiency is necessary to preserve the right incentives for the corporate controller ex-ante (Schnitzer 1995). As in a famous movie, from which I took inspiration in labeling private benefits of control, the ugly is not necessarily enemy of the good.

In the next chapter, I will further investigate the entrenchment mechanism, in order to specify the conditions under which it can work efficiently. To this purpose, its motivations – in terms of different kinds of PBC that entrenchment is intended to protect – will be analyzed from both the outside shareholders' and the corporate controller's standpoint; positive implications will be derived for the corporate ownership structure; and, finally, both a positive theory and the normative goals of corporate law will be outlined on that basis. But I have already laid down the basic intuition: residual rights of control can be assigned from shareholders to a non-(entirely)-owner-manager while preserving the incentive-compatibility of corporate governance. For this outcome to hold, appropriate constraints should be set on the corporate controller's behavior. As I mentioned, these constraints could be possibly analyzed in a standard agency framework, allowing for law and other institutions to make the difference because of contractual incompleteness. This is actually how behavioral constraints on management and controlling shareholders are dealt with in mainstream law and economics. However, a full account of contractual incompleteness implies that a corporate controller may not always be an agent of shareholders. His position may need to be featured with residual control rights if we want to induce him to invest any non-verifiable, firm-specific entrepreneurial talent.

3 The law and economics of control powers

A theoretical framework

3.1 Corporate governance defined

The tripartite account of private benefits of control (PBC), which was introduced in the last chapter, can be the basis of a relatively novel framework for analyzing corporate governance. This framework may provide a better understanding of corporate governance and of its different patterns around the world. More importantly, a positive and a normative account of corporate law can be derived on this basis, at least from a law and economics standpoint. Both the positive and the normative accounts differ from the mainstream view. However, on the one hand, this approach seeks to respond to a number of questions that still await an answer from the law and economics literature.[1] On the other hand, the interpretation of corporate governance based on PBC yields a number of theoretical propositions that can be tested against the empirical evidence. I will undertake this test through a five-country case study. The development of this theory, and of the set-up for testing its propositions, is the subject-matter of this chapter.

I will start by discussing the leading definitions of corporate governance in the economic theory. So far I have preferred to focus on the underlying core problem – separation of ownership and control – to find out how corporate governance should deal with it. In order to preserve the functional character of the analysis, I shall still refrain from providing any definition of my own, for it would be over-inclusive or under-inclusive at any rate. Nevertheless, discussing the existing definitions and their shortcomings is a good way to both resume the main arguments of previous analysis and to introduce a new paradigm for interpreting corporate governance in the real world.

3.1.1 The limits of the agency costs perspective

Probably the most cited definition of corporate governance is that provided by Professors Shleifer and Vishny in their authoritative survey of the topic: "Corporate governance deals with the ways in which the suppliers of

1 See *supra* Chapter 1.

finance to corporations assure themselves of getting a return on their investment" (Shleifer and Vishny 1997: 737). Their approach to corporate governance is declaredly an agency perspective. However, they recognize that contracts are incomplete, and therefore financiers cannot reliably secure a given return on their investment contractually. The authors then conclude that *both* legal constraints on managerial misbehavior *and* residual rights of control are needed to protect outside shareholders, thereby minimizing agency costs and allowing equity funds to be raised efficiently by the corporate enterprises.

There are two problems with this view, which make it unsatisfactory from both a positive and a normative perspective. Starting from positive analysis, outside shareholders' powers in the actual governance of publicly held corporations hardly fit in with the above description, at least as far as control rights are concerned. Shleifer and Vishny (1997: 741) seem to be aware of this problem when they acknowledge: "There may be limits . . ., but the fact is that managers do have most of the residual rights of control." Nonetheless, they claim (1997: 750): "The principal reason that investors provide external financing to firms is that they receive control rights in exchange." And, later on (1997: 753): "If legal protection does not give enough control rights to small investors to induce them to part with their money, then perhaps investors can get more effective control by being large." Then, according to Shleifer and Vishny, the absence of large shareholders and separation of ownership and control thereby depend on how effectively outside shareholders' control rights are protected by the legal system. Joined by Rafael La Porta and Florencio Lopez-de-Silanes, they published their first article on the 'law matters' thesis – 'Legal Determinants of External Finance' – in the *Journal of Finance* (La Porta et al 1997).

3.1.2 Are shareholders 'stupid and impertinent'?

In a path-breaking essay, Martin Hellwig (2000) showed how promises of control for finance are in fact *not credible* even in most developed financial and legal systems. This observation holds irrespective of the kind of finance (debt vs. equity) and of what institutions (banks vs. markets) provide for its allocation. As far as equity finance is concerned, outside shareholder disenfranchisement is also independent of whether ownership is dispersed or concentrated. That is, large shareholders do not seem to make much difference in real-world corporate governance. As Professor Hellwig (2000: 111) put it, "In the United States [where ownership is most often dispersed] as in continental Europe [where ownership is typically concentrated], ongoing changes of [corporate charters] are used to buttress management independence from outside control and to dilute or void the control rights of outside shareholders." Then, the author paraphrases the famous words of a German banker of the early twentieth century:

> Shareholders are stupid and impertinent – stupid because they give their
> money to somebody else without any effective control over what this
> person is doing with it, and impertinent because they ask for a dividend
> as a reward for their stupidity.[2]

Hellwig (2000: 109) adds that the peak of shareholders' impertinence is
reached when "in opposition to management, they try to exert some control
after all." To my understanding, Hellwig did not actually mean to claim that
shareholders are stupid or impertinent. Rather, it seems that shareholders are
unwilling to make themselves understood by mainstream economics.

A second problem with Shleifer and Vishny's description of corporate
governance concerns its normative implications. The circumstance that the
whole of shareholders' investment is potentially placed at hazard involves that
outside shareholders should be granted *some form of protection*, not that they
should be protected via *residual rights of control* (Zingales 1998). Shareholders
sink their money in the firm, but do not decide how that money is invested
and to what extent the firm's assets are specialized – nor do they want to
(Williamson 1985). The entrepreneur-manager does, and to this purpose he
has to commit irreversibly his expertise to the venture. Investment of entrepreneurial talent is no easier to contract upon than the provision of equity
funds. Reward of the latter (profits) is at least verifiable ex-post, whereas compensation of the former typically includes some unverifiable component that
cannot be contracted upon. This is the efficiency rationale of private benefits
of control. Then in the presence of non-contractible investments it is the
entrepreneur, not shareholders, that needs residual rights of control.

Consider, for instance, a fishing enterprise.[3] To avoid expropriation,
shareholders need to make sure the fisherman can only profit from fishing and
sharing the catch with them according to the contract. Shareholders need,
therefore, effective protection of their share of the residual claim. Contrary to
conventional wisdom, they do not also need residual control rights (i.e., the
threat of ousting an underperforming fisherman) to this purpose. Eventually
the fisherman will have to supply shareholders with their share of the revenues, on condition that his reward is tied to that supply by contract and
straight-out expropriation is ruled out by law. Such a reward would be enough
for an agent, not for an entrepreneur.

Our fisherman will have also to rig the fleet, select the crews, and set the
fishing courses. Sometimes a mere delegation of control rights would suffice
to have all this done. However, this is not the case when firm-specific investments (for instance a very innovative approach to the above issues) are
involved. If rational entrepreneurs fear that their firm-specific investments are

---

2 Hellwig (2000: 109). The original quotation is (Baums and Scott 2005): "Aktionäre sind
   dumm und frech. Dumm, weil sie Aktien kaufen, und frech, weil sie dann auch noch
   Dividende haben wollen." Carl Fuerstenberg (1850–1933).
3 I have provided a more articulated example in Pacces (2009).

not protected from opportunism, they would not make such investments in the first place. To avoid being expropriated of firm-specific investments, particularly after the firm's goodwill has been established, our fisherman needs tenure. He needs to be entitled from the beginning to the unverifiable surplus generated by the investment of his talent. Protection of this surplus is not contractable, and therefore it requires residual rights of control being assigned, not merely delegated, from shareholders to the entrepreneur. In this perspective, shareholders who relinquish control rights to support entrepreneurship, but still expect a return from their investment, appear to be neither stupid nor impertinent.

3.1.3 *The incomplete contracts perspective reconsidered*

The above approach is ultimately at odds with Shleifer and Vishny's definition of corporate governance. However, it is consistent with an alternative definition of corporate governance offered by another leading economist. According to Luigi Zingales (1998: 498), corporate governance is "the complex set of constraints that shape the ex-post bargaining over the quasi-rents generated by a firm."

Compared to Shleifer and Vishny's, this is a much broader definition. The reader should recall, from Chapter 1, the meaning of quasi-rents as the excess value of the firm's assets over their market price, which is intended to reward non-redeployable (i.e., idiosyncratic) investments. As such, Professor Zingales' definition focuses on the division of non-contractable surplus rather than on the conflicts of interest affecting its production; that is, it deals more with contractual incompleteness (ex-post bargaining) than with agency costs (ex-ante contracting). In this perspective, the set of constraints (both legal and contractual) is not just intended to keep the interest of the firm's manager aligned with those of the input providers, but rather to discipline the ex-post division of the firm's surplus in such a way as to provide the incentives to maximize its overall production. Whatever allocation of residual control rights is necessary to achieve that goal, it implies that a third party who is entrusted the firm management "should not be in the position of a mere agent, who owes a duty of obedience to the principal, but should be granted the independence to act in the interest of the firm" (Zingales 1998: 501).

Professors Rajan and Zingales (1998b) have further argued that maximization of the firm's surplus can be achieved notwithstanding retention of residual control rights by shareholders, provided that the bargaining power over the division of the same surplus also stems from access to critical resources and that access is granted by suppliers of key human capital, including the entrepreneur. This would involve that shareholder value is not the only argument of the firm's objective function (Jensen 2001). Quite to the contrary, the firm should be managed in the interest of all providers of specialized assets – the so-called stakeholders (Rajan and Zingales 2001). Neither of these conclusions can be agreed upon.

On the one hand, human capital resources are not bound to stay critical forever. Since nobody likes the idea of finding himself exploited of his talent when it is no longer indispensable (he would rather refrain from investing it in the first place), at least one category of suppliers of human capital – the entrepreneurs – should be protected via residual rights of control in order to secure a non-contractable surplus.[4] Only to the extent that corporate law also makes such a kind of entitlement available to a non-owner, ownership will be allowed to separate from control also when entrepreneurship matters.

On the other hand, once shareholders are deprived of residual rights of control, they would refuse to commit their money to the firm's discretionary management in the absence of a meaningful residual claim on the firm's assets. Shareholders need then to be entitled to the firm's *entire* verifiable surplus. Any stakeholder claiming a share of the firm's profits in return for further specialization of his assets at the entrepreneur's discretion will have to acquire a shareholder-like claim (e.g., pay-per-performance, stock options plans, and the like). Anyway, the firm should be managed in the interest of shareholders. Corporate law and the corporate contract needs also to protect such an interest from the entrepreneur-manager's misbehavior in order for ownership to separate from control. Stakeholders' protection is better left to other areas of the law.[5]

Notwithstanding these disagreements about the allocation of residual control rights and the role of stakeholders in corporate governance, the view of the matter that is being presented here is very similar to that of Professor Zingales. The basic idea is that corporate governance should not be merely regarded as an agency problem, but rather as a matter of distribution of powers and constraints on their exercise.[6] Law seems to matter in both respects: as a source of legal entitlement to corporate control powers alternative to direct ownership of the firm's assets; and as a source of legal constraints on those powers that could not be reliably established by contract, and yet are needed to induce outside shareholders to place their money under the corporate controller's discretionary management. Only in the latter respect could corporate law possibly be considered as a way to reduce agency costs in a world of incomplete contracts, thereby fostering equity finance and separation of ownership and control. However, in taking this view, one should bear in mind that separation of ownership and control can only co-exist with entrepreneurship if the corporate controller is allowed to retain residual rights of control.

In the foregoing chapters, this result has been presented in rather speculative terms. The failure of mainstream theory to fully explain the variety that we observe in comparative corporate governance has been highlighted. It has been shown that the prevailing explanation of how law 'matters' in that respect is, at best, incomplete. Finally, it has been argued that the standard

4 See *supra* Chapter 1, section 1.4.2 (especially note 47).
5 See *supra* Chapter 1, section 1.4.3.
6 See in the legal literature Cools (2005).

account of private benefits of control is too parsimonious to capture the choice of separation of ownership and control at the firm level. What I have suggested so far is that the inconsistencies between the theory and the practice of corporate governance could be resolved if we only allowed the residual control rights to be allocated to a corporate controller regardless of his ownership stake. What I am now going to show is how control rights can be effectively allocated in such a fashion, when that should be the case (and why), and what the implications of all this are for corporate law.

3.2 Control matters

3.2.1 *Sources of power alternative to the firm's ownership*

Let us start from the property rights theory of the firm in economics and add one *legal* circumstance: that the corporate enterprise is featured with legal personality (Kraakman et al 2009). This is sometimes dismissed as a useless fiction in law and economics, but it is actually quite important to feature control over corporate assets as separated from ownership of the enterprise (Clark 1986). The firm's assets belong to the corporation, and thus who *controls* the corporation also controls its assets whether or not he *owns* the corporation. This is how *real* separation of ownership and control is *legally* possible. The next step is to assess whether it is also desirable from an economic standpoint.

In economic terms, corporate control is the ultimate authority over the allocation of non-contractable surplus (the so-called quasi-rents) generated by the firm's assets. Such an authority is supported by residual rights of control: that is, the power to decide upon any matter concerning the use of the firm's assets that have not been previously contracted upon with other providers of inputs. The key issue for corporate governance is, therefore, to determine to whom residual rights of control should be allocated: to the owners, or to somebody else?

The narrow set of assumptions of the property rights theory of the firm does not allow for *real* separation of ownership and control (Hart 1989). Control should be allocated to the party most indispensable to the production process (the entrepreneur) and he should *own* the firm's assets altogether. This solution is necessary to promote the entrepreneur's firm-specific investments, where the firm value ultimately comes from. However, when this individual is wealth-constrained, risk-averse, and has a limited capacity to borrow, equity finance may be needed and the problem becomes more complicated. Apparently, the problem can be solved by allowing *delegation of authority* from the corporate owners (the shareholders) to some professional managers. *Management*, but not also *formal control*, should then be separated from ultimate ownership of the firm's assets (Hart 1995). Unfortunately, this solution does not allow for firm-specific investments to be undertaken by the managers. Managers cannot play any entrepreneurial role under the property right theory of the firm.

Recent advances in economic theory have shown that ownership is not the only possible source of power over the ex-post allocation of the firm's quasi-rents and, therefore, not the only possible source of authority within a firm. In many circumstances of today's real world, ownership seems not even to be the most important one (like, for instance, in many high-tech enterprises) (Rajan and Zingales 2000). According to Professors Rajan and Zingales, a broader definition of the source of authority is the right to provide *access to a critical resource* (Rajan and Zingales 1998b). As long as some of these resources cannot be 'owned,' this leads to a source of power alternative to ownership.

Human capital is the case in point. By having to grant access to a human capital resource in every single period, *provided the same resource remains irreplaceable*, the individual gains power within the organization (Rajan and Zingales 2001). This, in turn, provides him with incentives to specialize over time, which are even more powerful than those coming from ownership. This approach has two major implications: (a) there can be multiple sources of power in the organization of the firm, challenging the owner's residual rights of control; (b) the firm's control need not necessarily arise from ownership of its key physical assets.

While the first implication seems to yield quite promising results for the analysis of the employment relationships within a firm (leading eventually to a 'new' theory of business organizations), the second one could finally explain why firm control matters so much, and yet it can be separated from ownership (leading eventually to a 'new' theory of entrepreneurship and corporate governance) (Zingales 2000). Unfortunately, neither of the two above theories has yet been developed in any comprehensive fashion. Given the importance of firm control for understanding corporate governance, we cannot escape from dealing with the second matter here.

3.2.2 Featuring a non-owner entrepreneur

The intuition that control need not arise from ownership is of fundamental importance. Eventually, some degree of separation between ownership and control will be needed for the firm's growth, but this does not necessarily involve that entrepreneurship become suddenly 'unimportant' (Hart 1995: 126).[7] In the perspective sketched out above, the entrepreneur could in fact retain control, even without ownership, until he keeps power over the access to the critical resource around which the firm is built. However, as I am going to show, this power would be merely temporary, and therefore it does not guarantee that specific investments in human capital are made ex-ante by a non-owner entrepreneur.

To make the discussion more intuitive, I shall refer to this firm-specific critical resource as to entrepreneurial/managerial talent. There are two

---

7 But see Hart (2001) for an attempt to integrate private benefits of control in financial contracting.

requirements for the exploitation of this resource: discretion and reward. *Discretion* is needed to transform the subjective talent into objective firm value, without having to incur a huge amount of transaction costs contracting for complementary resources. *Reward* is needed as an incentive for the entrepreneur to concentrate efforts on managing the firm at his best, namely to invest and specialize his human capital over time without risk of being subsequently held up. To this purpose, reward has to be contingent on the firm's success and must be open-ended. Since the exercise of discretion cannot be contracted for by definition, its prospective reward is likewise non-contractable.

With full ownership, a talented entrepreneur gets both discretion (residual rights of control) and an open-ended prospective reward (residual claim). Without ownership he risks getting none of them. To be sure, discretion can be granted to the entrepreneur even without ownership, but just at the owner's will and on a *temporary* basis. This is what is ultimately meant by delegation of firm control. However, delegation also involves that the entrepreneur has no ex-post bargaining power to secure any share of the surplus not previously contracted for (his prospective reward). As a result, no entrepreneurial talent will be invested in the first place. Let us see why.

At the beginning, it is in the owners' interest to let the entrepreneur do his job. This will hold until the owners believe sufficient results are achieved and can be maintained *without* the entrepreneur's contribution (or they simply realize there will never be any such result). Afterwards, they can easily get rid of the entrepreneur, since by then they will own a valuable (or an almost bankrupt) firm, while he will own just his exploited talent which is no longer needed for the firm's success.[8] Of course, no entrepreneur would ever accept to play such a game. *Mutatis mutandis*, there is no reason why this should be different for a talented manager to be hired at a later stage of the firm's lifecycle.

Therefore, in a world of incomplete contracts, the entrepreneur-manager cannot be merely regarded as an agent who ultimately owns the firm's physical assets. Discretion is misplaced when you cannot secure enough benefits from its exercise (Zingales 1998). When entrepreneurial discretion is delegated by the owners, its reward can neither be contracted upon ex-ante nor bargained for ex-post. On the one hand, entrepreneurial initiative is surrounded by too much uncertainty for being fully priced ex-ante. Ex-ante, the entrepreneur himself does not *know* whether he will be successful and to what extent – although, as we will see shortly, he may have some subjective *beliefs* on the above matters. On the other hand, without residual control rights, there seems to be no way for the entrepreneur to secure a reward ex-post, namely when the initiative has proven successful, access to the entrepreneurial resource is no longer critical, and then somebody else can take over. At least in this context, delegated discretion is in fact no discretion at all.

---

8 For a theory of debt built on this approach see Aghion and Bolton (1992).

In order to adequately combine entrepreneurial discretion and reward, our non-owner entrepreneur should be in charge. Delegation of control, if any, should be *irrevocable* without the entrepreneur's consent. In particular, his discretion needs to cover the decision on whether, when, and at what price control over the assets should be transferred back to the owners (Schnitzer 1995). This means *entrenchment of corporate control*. Entrenchment of the controlling position is the way in which the entrepreneur-manager can secure a reward of his specific investments through ex-post bargaining power over an eventual control sale (Almazan and Suarez 2003).

The constraint on the identity of the transferee is intended to make sure that, whenever control is transferred, the source of the entrepreneur's reward comes from the owners, thereby inducing the entrepreneur to increase the value of the residual claim on the firm's assets. However, this is clearly not enough to rule out the entrepreneur's misbehavior. On the one hand, there is no guarantee that the entrepreneur will *ever* part with control and not, rather, keep staying in charge while maximizing something else than the firm's profits (a typical agency problem). On the other hand, even if control was ever transferred, the entrepreneur would be entitled to claim the whole of the firm's surplus from now powerless owners (a typical hold-up problem). Of course, no owner would ever be willing to sign such a contract.

3.2.3 Shared ownership and private benefits of control

A possible way out of this impasse would be a rule setting ex-ante the pro-rata sharing of the firm's surplus between the entrepreneur and the owners. This could be achieved by granting the controlling entrepreneur compensation fully contingent on the future realization of the firm's profits (think, for instance, to a stock options plan). Notice that this solution corresponds to the award of a share of the owners' residual claim. Thus, it is roughly equivalent to shared ownership, provided the entrepreneur's stake is always sold back to the owners whenever control returns to them.

In theory, one should be able to find a sharing rule apt to induce both the entrepreneur and the owners to invest ex-ante. Ex-post, such a compensation scheme would provide the entrepreneur with the incentive to both maximize the firm's profits and walk away with his reward once he cannot increase any further the value of his share of the residual claim. Since we are implicitly assuming no further surplus is to be divided, this solution would leave no room for ex-post bargaining (Zingales 1998).

This approach has a major shortcoming, which makes it just a partial solution to the problem. It is in fact a complete contracting approach (Myerson 1983). It should be noted that the way in which the award of a residual claim to the entrepreneur affects his incentive to invest his talent is *independent* of the allocation of residual rights of control. Owners could keep staying in control of the firm's assets while taking a credible commitment not to remove the entrepreneur until they can profitably take over and pay him the stipulated share of firm value realized so far. As a result, similar to the standard principal–agent approach to corporate governance, control does not really matter. This would work perfectly if the entrepreneur's capabilities and effort were entirely *observable* through firm performance. The latter being a *verifiable* variable, a long-term profit sharing contract (so-called 'pay-per-performance') would provide the optimal solution. However, firm performance is typically a *noisy* signal of the manager's investment (Laffont and Tirole 1988). There is always a part of managerial skills that is neither observable ex-ante nor verifiable ex-post, and therefore is not contractable.

More precisely, the exercise of managerial skills might uncover some business opportunities that become observable over time, but get verifiable only at a later stage. In the meantime, the same opportunities are up for grabs (Schnitzer 1995). In the absence of alternative property rights protection (e.g., through the patent system), the reward of entrepreneurial innovation cannot be secured through a share of the residual claim on the firm's assets. Such an innovation will eventually become observable but not yet verifiable, and consequently it will not be reflected in objective firm value – the stock price (Laffont and Tirole 1988). Rewarding innovation requires that the entrepreneur retain not just a pro-rata residual claim, but residual rights of control on the firm's assets. Indeed, the unverifiable part of entrepreneurial talent is a source of control (quasi) rents.[9] When the entrepreneur loses control over the firm's assets, those rents are likewise lost. Therefore, if the entrepreneur is unable to safeguard his controlling position over time, he will not be willing to make specific investments whose results are not promptly verifiable.[10]

In the previous chapter, the above control rents have been characterized as idiosyncratic private benefits of control. By definition, any effort intended to pursue such a kind of PBC is *not* reducing the verifiable part of firm value, but is not yet increasing it either. Initially, idiosyncratic PBC are only accruing to the entrepreneur's (subjective) expected utility as a byproduct of the firm's success. One could think, for instance, to the pride of establishing a successful and outliving firm (Mayer 1999). For the moment, I am assuming the entrepreneur cannot reap any different kind of private benefits from the firm's control. This is not true because diversionary and distortionary PBC are also at play in corporate governance. I shall include consideration for these other instances of PBC in the next section.

---

9 In the spirit of Burkart et al (1997), Schnitzer (1995) characterizes these as information rents depending on managerial skill. This difference does not affect the substance of the reasoning.

10 Another way to look at the problem is that management exposed to the threat of ouster tends to be short-termist (Laffont and Tirole 1988). For a more recent approach to the problems of entrepreneurship and non-contractible rewards in corporate governance, see Manso (2011).

There are two possible ways for the entrepreneur to cash in the value of his idiosyncratic PBC. One is to work hard for the transformation of idiosyncratic PBC into objective (i.e., verifiable) firm's revenues, thereby increasing the value of his share of the residual claim. The second, more promising way is to sell control back to the owners, as soon as they can hire a new manager with better skills at producing verifiable value by controlling the firm's assets. Alternatively, the entrepreneur could sell control to the same manager after the latter has bought out the ownership of the firm – which comes closer to how takeovers actually work. The implementation of any of these strategies requires residual rights of control.

Idiosyncratic PBC may ultimately result in a sizeable increase of firm value. However, without residual rights of control, idiosyncratic PBC cannot be appropriated by the entrepreneur. If the owners have residual rights of control, they can fire the entrepreneur anytime by just paying the current value of his share of the residual claim; the entrepreneur would lack the bargaining power to obtain anything more than that. This means that eventually the owners (or the talented manager they will hire) will be able to exploit the business opportunities uncovered by the entrepreneur (observable but not verifiable), without having to pay any premium in return for his PBC. While this would be ex-post efficient (control would always end up being allocated to the best manager), it would not be efficient also ex-ante. Without the possibility to secure PBC, less business opportunities (or none at all) would be uncovered by the entrepreneur. In other words, the unavailability of residual rights of control to the entrepreneur tends to kill entrepreneurial innovation.

Allocating residual rights of control to the entrepreneur could solve the problem in a number of situations (see Manso 2011). But this solution may also have adverse effects. The controlling entrepreneur could entrench himself and hold up the owners in any subsequent control transaction. An inefficient outcome might then arise: the entrepreneur might be unwilling to part with control, unless he gets not only the idiosyncratic value of his PBC but also the extra surplus from the change in control. This could lead to a suboptimal frequency of efficient transfers of control (or even to none of them).

From the entrepreneur's standpoint, however, the advantages of a hold-up strategy must be traded off against its negative effects on the cashable value of his share of the residual claim. Given that the entrepreneur now has bargaining power over the control transfer, that share must not be sold at current value, but can be sold at a premium on condition that the transfer takes place.[11] Since I am assuming that the controlling entrepreneur knows he cannot enrich himself by any amount larger than his (idiosyncratic) PBC, while I am hypothesizing the owners can further increase firm value by appointing a new manager, the division of the extra surplus will be bargained for between the parties, and the transfer will take place anyway. In this scenario, the only

---

11 This effect is emphasized by Almazan and Suarez (2003) although their bargaining model only includes (the current value of) managerial compensation (pay-per-performance).

transfers that do not take place are those whose surplus does not exceed the incumbent's PBC (Schnitzer 1995). To the extent that the latter are due to incorrect beliefs of the entrepreneur about his own managerial capabilities, some efficient control transfers would always be foregone. This is, however, the price to pay for fostering entrepreneurial innovation.

This overly simplified scenario will be qualified in the following discussion. However, the basic intuition holds: when residual rights of control are allocated to an incumbent entrepreneur retaining an equity interest in the firm, the only changes in control that do not take place are those whose transaction surplus does not exceed the value of the entrepreneur's PBC.

3.3 Management entrenchment and a workable market for corporate control

3.3.1 Is entrenchment always inefficient?

The above mechanism for promoting entrepreneurial incentives, notwithstanding separation of ownership and control, is based on the corporate controller's ability to entrench himself. Entrenchment implies that corporate control be not contestable. As a result, the market for corporate control cannot allow for hostile takeovers. However, this does not mean that the market for corporate control cannot work in some other way.

Takeovers need not be hostile. They can also be friendly. Hostile takeover is the exception in corporate practice, whereas friendly takeover is the rule (Hellwig 2000). Compared to hostile takeover, allocation of corporate control through friendly takeover is based on the *opposite* regime of residual rights of control. When residual rights of control are assigned to the corporate controller instead of to outside shareholders, the former is entitled to protect his idiosyncratic control rents: control cannot be transferred without his consent (Coates 2004). This arrangement eliminates the major disadvantage of separation of ownership and control from the entrepreneur-manager's standpoint: the risk of being subsequently taken over against his will and expropriated of his control rents.

The outside shareholders' point of view should also be taken into account. In a traditional agency perspective, non-controlling shareholders worry about the distortionary and diversionary PBC that a corporate controller could extract at their expense. The analysis of hostile takeovers in the previous chapter already shows two important results concerning diversionary PBC. First, hostile takeovers are not very helpful to police the extraction of diversionary PBC, since the aggressor might simply be a better thief than the incumbent is (the so-called 'looting' argument). Second, hostile takeovers disallowed in the presence of stealing opportunities available to the incumbent management: no good thief would ever leave his treasure up for grabs once he sits on it (the so-called 'inefficient rent-protection' argument). Since no regret for hostile takeovers seem to be justified just by the presence of diversionary

PBC, let me set them aside for the moment. The following analysis will show that diversionary PBC bear no different relationship with friendly takeovers and thus they should be policed in some other way.

What about distortionary PBC? Once the corporate controller is entrenched, he might just play with the firm's assets. Outside shareholders might then regret hostile takeovers. Indeed, one might doubt that a market for corporate control based on friendly takeover could play any role in both inducing managerial effort (*disciplinary* function of hostile takeover, policing moral hazard) and replacing inefficient managers with more capable ones (*allocative* function of hostile takeover, dealing with adverse selection). Apparently the outcome could be quite the reverse: incumbent managers would hold on to their positions, keeping (if not increasing) their private benefits from misuse of free cash while refusing to surrender control to a more efficient manager (Jensen 1986).

This is the so-called 'management entrenchment hypothesis' (Becht et al 2007). According to the standard view of corporate governance, when the corporate controller is entitled to protection from hostile takeover, shareholders lose twice. First, their shares are worth less because of excessive distortionary PBC being enjoyed by the corporate controller. Second, they forego the opportunity of profitable tender offers by more efficient managers willing to take over.

I am going to show that both conclusions are premature. Counterintuitive as it might appear, the corporate controller's entrenchment can result in a constrained-efficient outcome.[12] In other words, entrenchment of corporate control is the most efficient result in terms of both incentives for managerial effort and dynamic allocation of corporate control that can be reconciled with the protection of idiosyncratic control rents. This protection is a necessary condition whenever there is a need for entrepreneurship in corporate governance.

3.3.2 An alternative to hostile takeovers: cashing in idiosyncratic private benefits of control

When the corporate controller is able to entrench himself, what prevents efficient control transfers from taking place is the amount of PBC: they have to be compensated for the incumbent manager to part with control. However, this may be less problematic than it appears at first glance. As I suggested in the last chapter, the market for corporate control can also be understood as an application of the Coase Theorem although this is not how the mainstream theory tends to approach it. Here comes the importance of that insight. Shareholders (or directly a manager who buys the company's stock) could offer the incumbent manager a *side payment* to compensate his loss of PBC due to

12 For the view that corporate governance outcomes are generally constrained-efficient see Zingales (1998).

the control transfer. To the extent that the latter brings about gains from trade sufficient to offset the incumbent's PBC, efficient reallocation of corporate control will take place also when hostile takeovers are ruled out and friendly takeovers are the only way to implement changes in control.

Intuitively, in this scenario, some efficient control transfers would be foregone. They would be at least those ones whose efficiency gains are not sufficient to compensate the incumbent's PBC (Almazan and Suarez 2003). This is not necessarily inefficient. After all, ex-post protection of control rents is what induces the entrepreneur-manager to invest his talent ex-ante. In a dynamic perspective, what determines the efficiency of the outcome, in terms of both managerial effort and allocation of control, is rather the evolution of the firm's ownership structure. As we will see, this depends on both the amount and the kind of PBC involved.

As in the hostile takeover scenario, I am not considering *diversionary* PBC here. Provided that stealing is a purely pecuniary transfer, it would not hinder efficient control transactions in a friendly takeover regime. However, in the absence of legal constraints on expropriation by the corporate controller, stealing would make those transactions unattractive to outside shareholders: the higher the firm value, the more can be stolen from non-controlling shareholders. In addition, no different from the case of hostile takeover, diversionary PBC would also allow for inefficient control transactions to take place: control could easily end up being allocated to the *best thief* instead of the best manager (Bebchuk et al 2000). Looting may actually occur whether or not hostile takeovers are allowed; it needs to be policed otherwise (Easterbrook and Fischel 1982a). Therefore, scope for diversionary PBC does not only limit the entrepreneur's ability to raise equity finance ex-ante; it also compromises the efficient allocation of corporate control ex-post. One might recognize the standard 'law matters' argument here. In the absence of appropriate constraints on shareholders expropriation, ownership cannot easily separate from control. This proposition holds true regardless of the character of takeovers.

The above-mentioned constraints need to arise from an external set of rules, which – consistently with the 'law matters' thesis – are mostly legal in character. As far as stealing is concerned, Coasian bargaining could not lead to any improvement in the allocation of corporate control: provided that diversionary PBC are already a pecuniary transfer from shareholders to any corporate controller, side payments would of course be of no help. To see how these payments affect the functioning of the market for corporate control I will therefore assume, from now on, that stealing purposes are ruled out of control transactions and, consequently, control transfer can only be efficiency enhancing (or, at worst, neutral in this respect).

Side payments are extremely helpful as far as *idiosyncratic* PBC (which cannot be transferred, by definition) are concerned. When the efficiency gains from the acquisition are sufficiently large, shareholders can 'bribe' the manager to give up control and its rents, and still be better off. As I have already mentioned, the reason why the manager should accept the bribe is that the acquisition would also increase the value of his share of the residual claim more than he would ever be able to do. This can be illustrated by the example of anticipated vesting of stock options plans. In the hypothesized situation, 'selling' the residual claim by having all stock options vesting, accepting the bribe, and parting with control, is the most profitable option for a manager facing a significantly more skilled colleague (Almazan and Suarez 2003).

This simple mechanism still does not guarantee that incumbent managers will maximize their effort in firm management. Because profit sharing is never sufficient to perfectly align managerial incentives with shareholder interest, managers will always shirk to a certain extent. A side payment from shareholders will make sure that the incumbent manager yields to a more efficient one when the latter is able to compensate the former for the loss of his position: the incumbent manager will get his full reward without need to work anymore. However, this ex-post side payment would provide no incentive to work harder. Until the incumbent manager stays in charge, it seems that he would prefer enjoying *distortionary* PBC to enhancing firm value.

3.3.3 Severance payments as a way to reduce managerial shirking

The disciplinary function of hostile takeovers on managerial shirking is based on the stick: the threat of ouster. Friendly takeovers may achieve a similar result, yet based on the carrot: the prospective increase in deferred compensation for the controlling position. A process of dynamic allocation of corporate control based on negotiated transfer can also help to reduce distortionary PBC. To this purpose, the incumbent manager always needs to be granted a reward for his initial investment (idiosyncratic PBC) in case of change in control. On top of this, the expected proceeds of an eventual control sale should be allowed to *increase* further with managerial effort. Both conditions can be fulfilled through an appropriate setting of side payments from shareholders to the incumbent manager, in case of control transfer.[13] These payments are in fact very common in corporate practice. I am referring to severance payments, better known as the managers' *golden parachutes*.

To see how golden parachutes can reduce managerial shirking, "one has to start from the observation that money in the company is still not money in the manager's pockets" (Hellwig 2000: 119). Distortionary PBC (misuse of free cash) are worth less to the manager than they cost to shareholders (foregone profitable opportunities). For this gap to be reduced, the manager needs to be

---

13 The earliest theoretical work in this spirit is Almazan and Suarez (2003). Manso (2011) has more recently and more comprehensively integrated the problem of rewarding innovation in the compensation and term structure of management contracts. Both models advocate a combined use of tenure and side payments to induce effort without frustrating the incentives to innovate.

entitled to a larger share of the firm's surplus. Contrary to the standard agency framework, increasing the manager's share of the residual claim *is not* the only way to achieve this result. Also entrenchment can raise the diligent manager's prospective reward, when it is combined with a severance payment high enough to compensate him for the initial investment of his talent (idiosyncratic PBC), but sufficiently low to induce further effort (foregoing some distortionary PBC) (Almazan and Suarez 2003). Such a combination would provide *only* the manager who does not shirk with the opportunity to exploit his bargaining power in a subsequent control sale. Eventually, a diligent manager would be entitled to appropriate a larger share of firm value through bargaining over the proceeds of an efficient control sale. Conversely, the same opportunity would *not* be available to a manager who shirks after having invested his talent. On condition that the severance payment is properly set up in advance, he would simply take his golden parachute and leave.

Assume that a severance payment is set up ex-ante in the corporate contract as to cover both the idiosyncratic PBC and the manager's share of the profits corresponding to his minimal effort. This is equivalent to granting the incumbent manager a put option on his share of the residual claim conditional on a takeover bid (once again, the example of anticipated vesting of a stock options plan should do). If the manager does not put more effort in the firm management, he will leave when shareholders offer him the severance payment. This will happen as soon as the efficiency gains brought about by a subsequent manager are just sufficient to offset the incumbent's idiosyncratic PBC; the lower bound on pay-per-performance does not affect shareholders' decision because it is a sunk cost. Provided that a shirking manager would not get anything more than his severance if he stays, he will certainly leave.

The matter stands differently if the manager puts more effort into the firm management. This will raise the value of his share of the residual claim and he will therefore be committed *not* to accept the severance payment originally contracted for. He would profit more by staying (e.g. keeping his stock options plan unchanged) than by leaving (e.g. having his stock options vesting in advance and liquidated at a discount). To induce him to part with control when a better manager shows up, *renegotiation of the severance payment* must occur. This means that, by not shirking, a manager will be committed to claiming a larger share of the surplus involved by an eventual control transaction. Prospectively, renegotiation of the severance payment provides an additional, deferred compensation of managerial effort.[14]

Obviously, the higher the effort, the higher must be the trade surplus that makes the control transfer acceptable to the incumbent manager while leaving both shareholders and the acquirer better off. Since the probability of finding a considerably better manager is always lower than that of

14 See also Manso (2011).

finding a slightly better one, the incentive effect of the deferred compensation will decrease with the manager's effort. As a result, no different from pay-per-performance, renegotiation of severance payments can never eliminate managerial shirking.

The crucial point here is that *moderate* unobservability of managerial effort is more cheaply dealt with through a renegotiable severance payment rather than through plain pay-per-performance; only the former strategy allows idiosyncratic control rents to enter the compensation package explicitly (Almazan and Suarez 2003). In addition, renegotiation of severance payments is better at coping with contractual incompleteness. Being both open-ended and independent of profit sharing with shareholders, the incumbent's deferred compensation makes sure that shirking does not increase over time with free cash available for mismanagement. Whatever the increase in the amenities potential brought about by retained earnings, renegotiated severance payments supply the manager with countervailing incentives to additional effort. The larger the free cash flow available to the firm, the more attractive it gets as a target for a (friendly) takeover and the richer the renegotiated golden parachute that the incumbent manager will be entitled to bargain for provided that he is not shirking.[15]

An incentive mechanism based on a combination of entrenchment with severance payments is not always optimal.[16] To begin with, severance payments are *costly* to shareholders. To induce further effort by the manager, shareholders must be willing to forego ex-ante the gains of future profitable takeovers up to the amount of the manager's idiosyncratic PBC. According to our definition, idiosyncratic PBC represent the unobservable value of managerial talent, and therefore they are not contractable. The value of control rents claimed by the manager need then to be accepted by shareholders on a take-it or leave-it basis. Additional costs are incurred ex-post. The extra surplus of efficient control transfers that take place will have to be shared with the manager. Intuitively, when the overall costs of a severance payment mechanism become too high, shareholders might be unwilling to accept the deal.

In addition, the probability of an efficient takeover does not only decrease with the incumbent manager's effort. It is also inversely related to the value of his idiosyncratic PBC: the higher these are, the larger must be the efficiency gains necessary to have a feasible control transaction. This circumstance harms shareholders in two ways. When idiosyncratic PBC are high, not only will a larger number of profitable control transactions be foregone, but also the incumbent manager – facing a lower probability of a favorable renegotiation of his severance payment – will tend to shirk more. High PBC therefore make

---

15 Although this is a straightforward implication of the model by Almazan and Suarez (2003), this point was made by Hellwig (2000).

16 Almazan and Suarez (2003) consider this an optimal solution only when control rents are sufficiently low and performance is a very noisy signal of effort. The findings of Manso (2011) are comparable.

severance payments both costlier to shareholders and less effective in inducing a diligent behavior by the managers.[17]

3.4 High control rents and the need of a controlling shareholder

3.4.1 Entrenchment without severance payments

When idiosyncratic PBC are high and the probability of an efficient takeover is relatively low, the combination of managerial entrenchment with a severance payment would be too costly for shareholders to sustain. Since I am still assuming that idiosyncratic PBC are significant, contestable control would still not be an option. Without entrenchment, an entrepreneur-manager would be unable to secure an adequate reward for his initial investment, and therefore he would be reluctant to separate ownership from control or to invest in the first place. In contrast, entrenchment without severance payment is hardly acceptable to shareholders. On the one hand, in the absence of side payments, control would not be transferred even to a significantly more efficient manager. On the other hand, in the absence of deferred compensation, the incumbent manager would extract too many distortionary PBC to the shareholders' disadvantage. Therefore, an alternative mechanism must be devised to achieve the best possible result in terms of corporate control allocation and managerial effort, despite the high level of idiosyncratic control rents.

In this situation, corporate governance would bear a *lower degree of separation of ownership and control*. Whether or not severance payments are available, control rents have to be cashed in by an entrenched entrepreneur-manager for control to be eventually transferred. Being aware of this, shareholders are reluctant to provide equity finance in the presence of high control rents. Because of those rents, they will have to forego many profitable control transactions. Therefore, idiosyncratic PBC *always* make outside shareholders willing to pay a discounted price for the company's equity.[18] The discount can be offset by the promise of a side payment, which would directly compensate the manager for the loss of control rents in the event of a takeover. This is precisely the function of severance payments discussed in the previous section. However, this particular case holds until

---

17 Another possibility (explicitly considered by Almazan and Suarez 2003; see also Canoya et al 2000) is to give managers a severance payment *without* entrenchment. This solution has a long-standing tradition (e.g. Knoeber 1986). The reason why this solution is not considered here is that it cannot solve the problem of non-contractability of firm-specific investments, particularly as far as entrepreneurship is concerned (Schnitzer 1995). The most recent literature, however, see the problem in terms of overall cost of motivating exploration as opposed to exploitation by the management: in some situations golden parachutes could be optimal also without entrenchment (Manso 2011).

18 This holds irrespective of the nature of control rents. See Pagano and Röell (1998).

idiosyncratic PBC claimed by the entrepreneur-manager becomes too large for being compensated up front.

For any given level of idiosyncratic PBC, shareholder willingness to pay for the firm's stock decreases with the share of the residual claim retained by the entrepreneur-manager. Intuitively, idiosyncratic PBC must be low enough to make it always preferable for shareholders to directly 'bribe' the entrepreneur-manager with a severance payment, instead of buying less stock from him at a discount. That is to say, the severance payment claimed by a manager relinquishing his entire ownership stake should be *lower* than the highest possible discount on the trading of a limited amount of shares between the owner-manager and outside shareholders.[19] This would mean that, notwithstanding the costs of the severance payment, separation of ownership and control still involves gains from trade. Otherwise, only a limited amount of the firm's stock can be traded between the manager and outside shareholders.

3.4.2 Why a limited separation of ownership and control

The reason why shareholder willingness to pay for the firm's stock decreases with separation of ownership and control is twofold, and it is related to both idiosyncratic and distortionary PBC. First of all, in the absence of renegotiable severance payments, the higher the corporate controller's ownership, the higher the likelihood that control will be effectively transferred when the efficiency gains brought about by a subsequent manager are larger than the incumbent's PBC. Indeed, the higher the ownership stake involved in a control transaction, the more gains from trade will be available for being divided between the incumbent and the insurgent. Neither party actually cares about the impact of the control transaction on outside shareholders (Bebchuk 1994; Zingales 1995). Secondly, when a severance payment *cannot* be set ex-ante as to compensate idiosyncratic PBC, the perspective of bargaining over the proceeds of an eventual control sale would not induce any further effort by the manager. Consequently, to avoid excessive shirking (i.e., distortionary PBC), the manager's ownership must be increased. Again, a larger share of the manager's residual claim substitutes for the incentives that would be provided by a mechanism based on renegotiable severance payments.

Notice that what makes share ownership preferable to severance payments for inducing efficient behavior by the corporate controller is the *significant* unobservability of managerial effort. This circumstance can be due to high noisiness of performance as a proxy of managerial effort, which characterizes certain industries and/or business development stages (Demsetz 1983). This implies that *both* idiosyncratic control rents claimed by the entrepreneur-manager *and* the discount rate requested by outside shareholders be higher.

---

19 See Pacces (2009) for an explicit treatment of this tradeoff.

When these effects are strong enough, compensating the control rents upfront via a severance payment becomes simply too expensive. In addition, in those situations where managerial skills and effort are hardly observable via the firm short-term performance, a state-contingent contract (e.g., pay-per-performance with no tenure) would not be optimal (Aghion and Bolton 1992)

Therefore, share ownership provides in many respects a better alignment of the corporate controller's incentives with the interest of outside shareholders, making shareholders willing to pay a higher price for the company's stock. However, share ownership is costly for the entrepreneur-manager to maintain, for he will have to forego the benefits of liquidity and risk diversification, not to mention the investment projects beyond his self-financing capacity (Bolton and Von Thadden 1998). Thus, provided that corporate control can remain unchallenged, the entrepreneur-manager will always prefer to sell shares to the investing public *until the discount requested by outside shareholders becomes so large to make further selling unattractive.* When the stock price falls below the value of the expected stream of verifiable profits that it represents, the corporate controller will be better off keeping his share of the firm's ownership (Maug 2001). In this situation, the discount on outside stock will *already* be equal to the manager's idiosyncratic PBC. An equivalent way to look at this difference is the premium on the corporate controller's stock (the so-called control premium), which cannot be lower than idiosyncratic PBC in equilibrium. That means, in turn, that further separation of ownership and control cannot be efficiently achieved through a severance payment. As a result, ownership will separate from control only to a limited extent.

3.4.3 Endogenous dynamics of the firm's ownership structure

Idiosyncratic PBC are typically high when the prospective revenues of the firm are surrounded by a deep uncertainty. In this situation, shareholders are likely to require a higher discount rate on the firm's stock price, while higher specificity of human capital investments by the entrepreneur-manager calls for higher control rents. Both effects go in the same direction, namely *against* separation of ownership and control (Demsetz 1983). As a result, the corporate controller has to be an owner-manager to a certain extent. This implies that the firm's *ownership structure must feature a controlling shareholder.*

The ownership stake retained by the controlling shareholder is not determined by control considerations. Here I am taking the corporate controller's entrenchment as given, assuming that there are sizeable idiosyncratic control rents to protect in this fashion.[20] Entrenchment of corporate control also needs to be supported by the legal system, but I am not yet considering this problem. In this setting, the entrepreneur-manager should also be able to maintain his controlling position with a very tiny share of the corporate

---

20 A few models of the decision to go public make similar assumptions. See Zingales (1995) and Boot et al (2006).

ownership.[21] However, outside shareholders will not go for this deal when it would be too expensive to compensate entrenchment of corporate control with a severance payment accounting for the manager's idiosyncratic PBC. Shareholders would rather require that a significant share ownership be associated to the controller's entrenchment. This block of shares (control block) will trade at premium (control premium) to account for the controlling shareholder's PBC. In this perspective, the firm's ownership structure is determined *endogenously*. It is the outcome that maximizes firm value for both the corporate controller and the outside shareholders, given the amount of idiosyncratic PBC (Demsetz and Lehn 1985).

This outcome is clearly efficient ex-ante. Neither more nor less separation of ownership and control could improve both parties' aggregate wealth. To see whether this holds true also ex-post, one has to investigate the dynamics of ownership structure and control allocation.

As Professor Zingales (1995) demonstrated, when the controlling shareholder is able to entrench himself, separation of ownership and control is a strategy for maximizing the incumbent's proceeds from an eventual control sale. The underlying intuition is straightforward. The price of outside shares includes the expected gains from a profitable takeover, provided that non-controlling shareholders will be able to free ride on them (Grossman and Hart 1980). Therefore, by selling shares to the investing public, the corporate controller is able to appropriate part of those anticipated gains. The remainder of the gains will be impounded in the ownership stake retained by the controlling shareholder – the control block – and are due to be shared between the incumbent and the insurgent when the control sale will actually take place.

For an efficient change in control to take place, the size of control block needs to be large enough to allow for a value increase offsetting the difference between the incumbent's and the insurgent's PBC (Bebchuk 1994). However, the lower that size, the higher the gains that can be extracted from the investing public in anticipation of future takeovers (Zingales 1995). Thus, the structure of the corporate controller's incentives leads to an overall reduction of the private surplus available for efficient changes in control. By minimizing his ownership stake, the incumbent controller prefers to forego moderately efficient control transfers in order to maximize his anticipated revenues from the most efficient ones only. This can result in excessive separation of ownership and control and, in turn, to a suboptimal frequency of efficient control transfers (Bebchuk and Zingales 2000).

The dynamic inefficiency of ownership structures based on a controlling shareholder holds true on condition that *all* the parties involved share the

---

21 This option is available to the corporate controller in many legal systems, which allow dual class shares. However, also in those systems, the potential for separation of ownership and control is not fully exploited by publicly held companies (La Porta et al 1999). This observation is consistent with the theoretical argument developed in the text.

same information.[22] In the real world, we observe less separation of ownership and control than this theory would predict: the potential for departure from 'one share–one vote' is never fully exploited (La Porta et al 1999). I speculate that this may be due to asymmetric information, which should set a lower bound to the above mechanism of inefficient separation of ownership and control. Under asymmetric information, shareholders do not know how large the corporate controller's PBC are. Therefore, a pooling equilibrium should emerge where the expected gains from future takeovers are *discounted* by the same rate. Provided that the corporate controller stays entrenched – which is typically true for a controlling shareholder – the discount factor will be increasing with the degree of separation of ownership and control. For any level of the incumbent's PBC, this would limit the amount of the surplus that can be extracted ahead of future control sales. The inefficiency arising from separation of ownership and control in the presence of high control rents should be reduced accordingly.

It is worth noting, though, that this inefficiency is never entirely eliminated. Idiosyncratic PBC unavoidably draw a wedge between the controlling shareholder's interest (having *only* those changes in control that maximize *his* share of the surplus) and that of outside equity holders (having control *always* transferred when this is efficient). However, if this difference is due to the necessity to promote the *initial* investment of unobservable entrepreneurial talent, it will shrink *over time* as long as such a talent gets easier to recognize and to reward through the firm performance. To the extent this is eventually reflected in a lower discount on outside stock price, it would make further separation of ownership and control profitable for both the corporate controller and outside shareholders, and therefore efficiency-enhancing.

There are two ways to reduce outside shareholders discount efficiently. One is to limit the scope for shirking, the other is to reduce directly the control premium. The first option implies that the corporate controller take credible commitments to put additional effort into the firm management. By adopting such a strategy, the controlling shareholder would trade some benefits from shirking (distortionary PBC) for a larger share of the anticipated gains from an eventual control sale. The overall size of the control premium would be unchanged, but the corporate controller would be able to sell more shares to the investing public, thereby reducing his ownership stake.[23] Fewer efficient changes in control would take place, but the overall firm value would slightly increase with separation of ownership and control.

The implementation of the above strategy requires that managerial effort becomes over time easier to observe through the firm performance and,

---

22 Bebchuk and Zingales (2000) assume symmetric information. In addition, in their model PBC do no play any incentive role (although PBC extraction *per se* has only distributional consequences). Their findings are affected by these restrictive assumptions.

23 In other words, the per-share value of the control premium would be higher. That will reduce the likelihood of efficient changes in control. See Pacces (2009).

therefore, easier to contract upon. In such a scenario, a more promising enhancement of the efficiency of ownership structure comes from a straightforward reduction of idiosyncratic PBC (that is, of the control premium). Improved observability of managerial effort may reduce not only the inefficiencies of shirking, but even more so the value of idiosyncratic control rents necessary to induce the initial investment of entrepreneurial talent.

Ceteris paribus, a lower control premium would raise the probability of efficient control transfers, thereby inducing outside shareholders to pay a higher price for the firm's stock. Reduction of control rents is of course not an option for the *incumbent* controller, whose idiosyncratic PBC are determined ex-ante as a reward of his unobservable initial investment. However, the role of unobservable investments and related control rents in promoting the firm's success is likely to become less important in subsequent stages of the firm's lifecycle. When there is less uncertainty on future firm performance, a lower amount of idiosyncratic PBC will be required for having the firm run by the *next manager*.

Reduction of the control premium cannot then arise from incumbency; but it is likely to emerge from insurgency. This reduction is the natural outcome of a process of dynamic allocation of corporate control based on negotiated transfers (that is, friendly takeovers). In the absence of radical changes in the firm's core business and provided that stealing purposes are ruled out of control transactions, as I am still assuming, successive takeovers are likely to bring about increases in the verifiable stream of profits that will offset the decreases in idiosyncratic PBC. Not only is this a sufficient condition for the incumbent to cash in a control premium from the insurgent, it also involves that the control premium will decrease in future changes in control. With the resulting increase in the likelihood of next efficient takeovers, a higher degree of separation of ownership and control will become gradually workable. Eventually, the control premium might become low enough to be immediately compensated via a managerial severance payment. Ownership would then be allowed to completely separate from control.

3.4.4 One final note about shareholder expropriation: the market for 'lemons'

Throughout the foregoing analysis, I have been assuming that no scope for expropriation of non-controlling shareholders is allowed by the legal system. Unfortunately, this assumption hardly ever holds in the real world. To be sure, diversion of profits from outside shareholders' pockets is a major problem in most systems of corporate governance. This problem is certainly more acute in developing and emerging economies, but it does not spare even those countries that are economically most developed. Even within that restricted sample, dishonesty of the corporate controller(s) enters in different fashions: either as a widespread pattern of ordinary misbehavior (affecting *every* publicly held company in the same way, or at least perceived as such by the investing public); or as occasional, and therefore unanticipated corporate scandals of big proportions (Enriques 2003).

Realistically, the enforcement of the best fiduciary standards that we could imagine for corporate law will never be so rigorous to rule out the latter. Nevertheless, a good system of fiduciary duties in corporate law should be effective enough to police the former (Easterbrook and Fischel 1991). Only on that condition will corporate scandals be regarded by investors as exceptional events (like the Enron and WorldCom cases in the US), instead of as the peak of an endemic disease of corporate governance (like the Parmalat case in Italy). The conclusions of the standard 'law matters' argument will hold otherwise. Ownership will only moderately (and, presumably, to a suboptimal extent) separate from control, and the bad quality of legal protection of non-controlling shareholders will be responsible for the underdevelopment of equity finance.

What I am claiming here is that – contrary to conventional wisdom (Becht et al 2007) – the functioning of the market for corporate control under alternative arrangements (hostile vs. friendly takeovers) does not affect the above result. This holds true unless we posit a tradeoff between shareholder protection and efficient allocation of corporate control (Burkart and Panunzi 2008; Kraakman et al 2009). As I will argue, we are not necessarily confined to this tradeoff. This approach has two major implications. On the one hand, it allows for a *separate treatment* of the problem of corporate control allocation and of that of diversionary PBC. On the other hand, it leaves unprejudiced one of the fundamental conclusions of the corporate law and economics scholarship. When legal protection of non-controlling shareholders from the extraction of diversionary PBC is weak, the efficiency of the market for corporate control will anyway be impaired (Bebchuk 1999).

Having diversionary PBC curbed by an effective system of fiduciary duties is in fact a *precondition* not only for separation of ownership and control, but also for the efficient functioning of the market for corporate control (Roe 2003). None of the conclusions that I have presented in the previous sections would hold in the presence of diversionary PBC. Corporate control would still be entrenched, but the resulting ownership structure would provide no guarantee of being efficient. Entrenchment would be aimed at protecting stealing opportunities or, at best, at preventing further looting from occurring. Not much scope would be left for fostering entrepreneurship. Being unable to distinguish thieves and looters from honest entrepreneurs and managers, shareholders will assume that all corporate controllers are just something in between (Black 2001). Shareholders will offer lower prices for the firm's stock and, as a result, most talented entrepreneurs and managers will exit the market for corporate control or even refrain from entering the stock market in the first place. Both the stock market and the market for firm control will be regarded as "markets for lemons" (Akerlof 1970). Then ownership could not separate from control, if not in those few cases where non-legal commitments not to expropriate minority shareholders can be taken. This would impair both equity finance available to large firms and the pursuit of growth opportunities by Small and Medium Enterprises (SMEs). That is quite likely to be the situation characterizing, for instance, the Italian economy.[24]

3.5 Institutional analysis revisited

3.5.1 *The dual role of legal rules in promoting separation of ownership and control*

So far I have implicitly assumed absolute freedom of the corporate contract in determining the allocation of control rights between the entrepreneur-manager and outside shareholders, whatever the firm's ownership structure. This assumption was an extreme oversimplification because it neglects the role of the institutional environment and of corporate law therein in determining the corporate governance arrangements. In fact, allocation of residual rights of control is highly dependent on the legal entitlements respectively available to the corporate controller and the outside shareholders under the pertinent corporate law jurisdiction. However, the 'freedom of contract' assumption has proven extremely useful to understand the basic mechanisms underlying separation of ownership and control. That is, first, what should induce a corporate controller to profitably manage a firm that he does not own completely; and, second, what makes sure that outside shareholders are willing to invest their money in a firm that they do not control?

I have argued that the answers to these questions depends on the role played by private benefits of controlling a corporation (PBC). Indeed, the taxonomy of PBC being adopted in the present study appears to be sufficiently inclusive to account for the major determinants of separation of ownership and control. Some PBC (idiosyncratic control rents) are needed to create firm value from the investment of unobservable managerial talent, and in that case they must be protected through residual rights of control. Some others (benefits from shirking and stealing) reduce firm value to the shareholders' disadvantage and thus they must be restrained by means of either incentives (e.g., raising the controller's ownership stake) or external constraints (e.g., legal rules constraining shareholders expropriation). What should induce the corporate controller to manage the firm in the shareholders' interest is a ban on their expropriation (minimizing the scope for diversionary PBC), incentives based on profit sharing (optimizing the extraction of distortionary PBC) and, whenever entrepreneurship is important, the perspective of eventually cashing in idiosyncratic PBC through the surplus brought about by an efficient change in control (thereby policing both moral hazard and adverse selection in a dynamic setting). Given the firm's financial needs, the choice as to separation

---

24 See Bianchi et al (2005) where the problem is discussed at length.

of ownership and control will depend on how the above categories of PBC interact with each other and how they are consequently dealt with.

Private ordering does not explain everything about institutions. Institutional choice does not take place in a vacuum, but only within the range of feasible choices determined by the institutional environment. Likewise, the available patterns of separation of ownership and control are determined by the legal system. Protection of outside shareholders from the corporate controller abusing his power (i.e., stealing) is a precondition for separation of ownership and control. However, the legal discipline of diversionary PBC is just one part of the story. It deals with how to prevent expropriation of non-controlling shareholders in order to make them willing to invest in the corporate firm. This is the typical way in which law 'matters' in standard law and economics of corporate governance. According to this view, legal protection of non-controlling shareholders is coupled with their entitlement to residual rights of control as owners of the firm. Provided that legal protection is intended to restore outside shareholders' control rights *notwithstanding* delegation of the *de facto* control to a non-owner manager, this approach does not question the role of the legal system in allocating residual rights of control.

This is clearly different from the view of corporate governance that is being developed here. Whenever protection of control rents is necessary to promote firm-specific investments by the entrepreneur-manager, residual rights of control cannot simply be delegated, but need to be assigned from the beginning to whoever is in charge of managing the firm. Therefore, outside shareholders have to be granted a different kind of protection. Within this framework, legal rules play a *dual role* in corporate governance. They matter not only in a dimension that is *restrictive* of control powers, so as to protect outside shareholders from the corporate controller's misbehavior. They also matter in an *enabling* dimension, in that they allow the corporate charter to allocate definitive entitlements to residual rights of control independently of corporate ownership.

The way in which ownership *can* be separated from control is determined by the above two sets of legal rules. This separation would occur to a limited extent in the absence of adequate legal protection of outside shareholders (La Porta et al 1998). However, a similar result would hold when the legal entitlements available to the corporate controller do not allow the entrepreneur-manager to secure idiosyncratic control rents without a significant share ownership (see Cools 2005).

As such, the revised 'law matters' thesis enters as a positive statement: the legal system shapes the *opportunities* for separation of ownership and control available to the firms. On condition that the scope for diversionary PBC is minimized, the *efficient* degree of separation of ownership and control depends on a number of firm-level variables: the firm's financial needs as opposed to the entrepreneur's wealth constraints and degree of risk aversion; the uncertainty about the prospects of the firm's success and the related extent of idiosyncratic PBC; the unobservable features of managerial effort and the scope for distortionary PBC. In this perspective, the revised 'law matters' argument also has an extremely important normative dimension: the legal system *should allow individual companies* to select the efficient degree of separation of ownership and control.

3.5.2 Efficient vs. inefficient protection of control rents

Comparative corporate governance shows that perfect contestability of corporate control may be more in the finance textbooks than in the real world.[25] Consistently with the view of corporate governance presented in the foregoing analysis, I posit that this is due to imperfect observability of entrepreneurial and managerial talents. When the investment of these talents cannot be adequately rewarded through the price of outside stock sold to the investing public, motivating unobservable effort by an entrepreneur-manager under dispersed ownership structures requires that a non-contractable deferred compensation be secured by means of residual control rights. In this perspective, legal protection of outside shareholders' control rights, perhaps in the form of an unconditional right to oust underperforming management, does not explain separation of ownership and control. In some situations, such an approach might lead to quite the opposite result.

In the agency framework from where the standard 'law matters' argument was originally derived, control rents that do not reduce shareholder wealth do not exist. PBC can only be 'bad' for corporate governance. On the same account, Professor Bebchuk (1999) has developed a formal "Rent-Protection Theory of Corporate Governance." This theory has demonstrated one of the basic claims of the present work: when PBC of *any* kind are high enough, contestable control cannot emerge as a stable equilibrium. According to Professor Bebchuk, this circumstance is also responsible for *suboptimal* separation of ownership and control. Ownership concentration is a privately optimal strategy to secure PBC by short-circuiting contestability. However, if under a more dispersed ownership structure shareholder value would increase by a higher amount than those PBC, the same strategy would also be socially inefficient.

The above results are derived on the assumption that control rents are transferable. Then no controller would dilute his ownership stake in such a way as to leave control rents up for grabs. He would rather keep a controlling stake large enough to claim adequate compensation of the private benefits transferred with firm control. As such, the theory and its normative implications are mostly applicable to diversionary PBC. Unless the legal system is effective in constraining shareholder expropriation (thereby providing a credible commitment device against diversionary PBC), concentrated ownership would be the only possible outcome even though a higher degree of

---

25 See *supra* Chapter 1, sections 1.1.4 and 1.2.2.

separation of ownership and control would be efficient. In the end, Professor Bebchuk's contention provides an alternative formulation of the 'law matters' thesis, from the corporate controller's standpoint instead of that of outside shareholders.

Professor Bebchuk's rent-protection theory does not consider that PBC can also be 'good' for corporate governance. Yet control rents also include idiosyncratic PBC, and they are different from the diversionary kind in a number of respects. First, while diversionary PBC are based on unproductive transfers of the firm's cash flow, idiosyncratic PBC represent the unobservable value of entrepreneurship. Therefore, their effect on the firm's ownership structure *is not* unambiguously inefficient. Second, idiosyncratic control rents (like, for instance, the founder's pride of managing 'his' business creation) are never up for grabs, for they depend on the identity of the corporate controller: they are not transferable by definition (Gilson 2006). In case of hostile takeover, they would be simply lost. Idiosyncratic control rents thus do not fit within Bebchuk's rent-protection theory, but they result in a similar outcome. Whenever idiosyncratic rents are significant, contestability of corporate control cannot emerge. This is not because PBC would be 'up for grabs' otherwise. Rather, because there is no way to price them ex-ante, they need to be cashed in ex-post by selling the control of the firm. Therefore, in the presence of high idiosyncratic PBC, ownership cannot entirely separate from control.

Similarities between diversionary and idiosyncratic PBC end with a positive analysis. Both categories of PBC lead to ownership concentration. On normative grounds, however, *only* diversionary PBC are unambiguously inefficient since they distort the choice of ownership structure with no redeeming virtue. Conversely, one could not say whether a pattern of rent-protection based on idiosyncratic PBC is efficient or not without including the latter in the welfare assessment (Coates 2004). In conclusion, consideration for idiosyncratic PBC must be added to the 'law matters' framework. An adequate discipline of diversionary PBC by the legal system is a necessary, but not also a sufficient condition for efficient separation of ownership and control.

3.5.3 *The dark side of the 'law matters' argument*

High idiosyncratic control rents also entail limited separation of ownership and control, but that is not necessarily inefficient. The economic theory of PBC is still very much underdeveloped in this regard. In the little literature existing on the relation between idiosyncratic control rents and ownership structure, PBC with neither stealing nor shirking implications have no efficiency consequences, but only distributional ones (Zingales 1995). They imply that control is never sold piecemeal, but rather through a strategy aimed at cashing in the highest possible share of the surplus from a negotiated control sale.

Whether or not this leads to an efficient outcome depends on the role played by idiosyncratic control rents in corporate governance. I posit that they are motivating the investment of unobservable managerial talent, thereby fostering entrepreneurial innovation, and are therefore efficient ex-ante. However, the outcome seems to be different ex-post because idiosyncratic PBC involve that some efficient changes in control will be foregone (Mayer 1999; Gilson 2006). This may not necessarily be the case, at least in a dynamic perspective. I have conjectured that – in the absence of major business innovations – unobservability of managerial talent shrinks over the firm's lifecycle and so does the amount of idiosyncratic PBC required to induce any subsequent manager to invest his talent. In each change in control, production of a larger verifiable income should substitute for idiosyncratic control rents and consequently allow for more outside stock to be sold at higher prices. Over time, this would not only improve the process of allocation of corporate control, but also lead to a higher degree of separation of ownership and control.

The dynamic evolution of idiosyncratic PBC can contribute to explaining why patterns of separation of ownership and control vary both geographically and in time. This evolution is a market dynamics driven by ex-post exploitation of gains from trade by all the parties involved, subject to the ex-ante constraint of protection of idiosyncratic control rents by the incumbent. Therefore, it is constrained-efficient. For such a result to hold, the law needs not only to guarantee protection of outside shareholders from expropriation by the corporate controller, but controllers who are concerned with entrepreneurship also need the ability to secure idiosyncratic control rents regardless of their ownership stake. Otherwise, they would stop diluting their ownership stake as soon as this involves the risk of being taken over.

The scope of entrenchment devices available to secure the entrepreneur-manager's residual rights of control is determined by the legal system. Protection of corporate control from hostile takeover may require private ownership (no listing on a stock exchange), majority ownership, minority ownership, or no ownership at all. This depends on the *entitlements to control rights* provided for by corporate law and available to the person who is in charge of corporate management. These entitlements affect the degree of separation of ownership and control that a corporate controller can afford without risk of being subsequently expropriated of his control rents. Legal entitlements to control rights consequently affect the selection of the firm's ownership structure; their inadequacy (or worse, unavailability) might impair the efficiency of that structure.

The idea that every firm has an optimal ownership structure, which is determined endogenously depending on the firm's characteristics, has a long-standing tradition (Demsetz 1983; Demsetz and Lehn 1985). These studies also pointed out the importance of control rents in determining ownership concentration, due to 'noisiness' of the business environment and imperfect foreseeability of factors affecting the firm's success. My definition of idiosyncratic PBC – depending on unobservability of managerial talent – makes no different a point. What this work attempts to demonstrate further is that corporate law influences the process of ownership dispersion, and possibly undermines its efficiency, also by requiring that a significant ownership stake be maintained in order to protect idiosyncratic control rents.

This is the dark and largely unexplored side of the 'law matters' argument. Efficiency of corporate governance may not only depend on agency costs being minimized, but also on residual rights of control being allocated in such a way as to promote the investment of unobservable managerial talent. If this is true – as appropriate consideration for entrepreneurship in corporate governance suggests it should be – legal entitlements to control rights should be independent of the firm's ownership structure for efficient separation of ownership and control to emerge. What matters for separation of ownership and control – possibly as much as a strict legal discipline of diversionary PBC – is then the possibility to distribute control rights freely between shareholders and the corporate controller.

3.6 Reframing corporate law and economics

3.6.1 A different framework for analyzing legal rules (and their efficiency)

The last conclusion suggests that both *power* and *law* matter, in two complementary respects, for corporate governance. In the foregoing discussion I have explained how this is consistent with a theoretical analysis of separation of ownership and control that goes beyond the traditional agency framework, and how, once contractual incompleteness is fully accounted for, power and law are no longer independent of each other. Specifically, law does not only matter as a *constraint* on the corporate controller's power, but also as a *support* of the same power. Although the way power is supported on legal grounds (entitlements to residual rights of control) is different from the way it is constrained (duties owed to the non-controlling shareholders), the dual role of legal rules in corporate governance ultimately involves a tradeoff. Economic analysis then supports the view of some legal scholars that corporate law is to be regarded as a solution of a discretion–accountability tradeoff (Dooley 1992; Bainbridge 2002). The analysis of this tradeoff, from both a positive and a normative Law and Economics perspective, will be the subject-matter of the following chapters.

Positive analysis will speculate on how corporate law influences the models of corporate governance prevailing in different countries of the Wealthy West of the world. The foregoing analysis of the economics of corporate governance has shown on what basis the efficient structure of corporate ownership *should* be selected and should then evolve endogenously. However, the legal system determines to what extent that process *can* take place. On the one hand, legal rules need to prevent the corporate controller from expropriating non-controlling shareholders by disciplining the extraction of diversionary PBC. Unconstrained opportunities for stealing would in fact undermine separation of ownership and control. On the other hand, separation of ownership and control need also to be supported by legal entitlements to discretionary management and control safeguards. In this respect, law shapes the actual patterns of corporate governance by vesting ultimate decision-making power in one or more controlling shareholder (through the shareholders' meeting), or in the corporate managers (through the board of directors).

The flip side of the coin is that both opportunities for expropriation of non-controlling shareholders and entrenchment devices available to the corporate controller influence, in turn, the evolution of control allocation over time. Through the comparison of some representative systems of corporate governance, I will therefore investigate the corporate law's role in determining the following: (a) whether the interest of non-controlling shareholders is adequately protected from expropriation; and (b) how control can be exerted by an entrepreneur-manager, how it is maintained and, ultimately, transferred. Alternative solutions of the discretion–accountability tradeoff will be analyzed accordingly.

One might then wonder whether there is an optimal solution of the above tradeoff; that is, is there an *optimal regulation of corporate governance*? This is the question underlying an efficiency-based normative analysis of corporate law. Such a question ought not to be confused with another issue: whether or not there is an *optimal model of corporate finance, ownership, and governance*. If there was such an optimal model, we would also expect one optimal regulation across the board. However, economic theory to date cannot say whether dispersed corporate ownership is preferable to concentrated ownership (Becht et al 2007). The most credited answer to this dilemma is that different models suit different needs (Milhaupt and Pistor 2008).

This does not exclude, however, that corporate law can be optimized in at least one way: namely, by providing *alternative legal solutions* that allow for the efficient selection of the corporate governance model. In this perspective, I will investigate what legal instruments should be made available to firms for them to select the model of ownership and control most suitable to their needs. The normative analysis will be likewise based on the comparison of some representative corporate law jurisdictions.

Is this framework of analysis consistent with the empirical evidence? Two important steps need be taken in order to answer this question. First, one should check whether the underlying assumptions are not contradicted by the evidence. Second, once we feel confident enough about the strength of our assumptions, we might be able to investigate whether the effects of alternative legal arrangements on corporate governance are consistent with what our theory predicts. To this purpose, I shall first outline the theoretical predictions, and then identify a methodology for testing both their positive and normative implications for corporate law.

3.6.2 *The main hypothesis of the framework*

The above framework for analyzing the impact of corporate law on corporate governance and its efficiency rests on a very strong assumption. The assumption is that, whatever the degree of separation of ownership and control, *entrepreneurship matters* and has to be rewarded in the form of control rents so long as it cannot be 'priced' by financial markets. This assumption would be rejected by empirical evidence if one optimal ownership structure existed across businesses, regardless of the investments in human capital required from entrepreneurs and managers. Conversely, if every firm has *its own* optimal structure of ownership, this should allow consideration for firm-specific factors including entrepreneurship. If we focus on entrepreneurship, the optimal ownership structure will depend on the amount of control rents necessary to reward idiosyncratic investments by the corporate controller; that is to say, the control rents necessary to motivate business undertakings that cannot be just self-financed out of debt and personal funds, but also require some degree of external equity.

I have operationalized this intuition through the concept of *idiosyncratic PBC*, claiming that their existence and amount is specific to the combination of entrepreneurial talent with the firm's assets. In this perspective, idiosyncratic PBC become a determinant of the *efficient* degree of separation of ownership and control. Whenever high idiosyncratic PBC are required to motivate very uncertain undertakings, equity finance should be relatively more expensive and this should lead, in turn, to higher ownership concentration typically featured with a controlling shareholder in charge of fundamental decision-making. The opposite outcome (ownership dispersion and managerial control) is supposed to emerge when managing the business does no longer require a high degree of innovativeness and inventiveness and, therefore, idiosyncratic PBC are low or even nil. In this perspective, the firm's ownership structure is supposed to be *endogenous*. That is, as Professors Demsetz and Lehn showed, ownership concentration is not systematically related to firm performance. Endogeneity of ownership structure then underlies, not only conceptually but also empirically, the existence of idiosyncratic PBC.

Demsetz and Lehn's proposition and results (1985) were challenged by subsequent studies on the empirical relationship between ownership structure and firm performance.[26] Earlier work, mainly based on the analysis of US listed companies, found empirical support for the argument that firm performance initially increases but then rapidly decreases in ownership concentration (Morck et al 1988). This account would clearly reject the basic assumption of nonexistence of an optimal ownership structure across businesses, because moderately dispersed ownership with contestable control (where managers are in charge) would be *always* superior to concentrated ownership with entrenched control (where a controlling shareholder is in

---

26 See Shleifer and Vishny (1997) for a survey.

charge). However, albeit still very popular especially among American economists, this view is not supported by more recent empirical analyses (Becht et al 2007).

Improved knowledge of the nuances of corporate governance, as well as more sophisticated econometrics, have shown that finding an unbiased, systematic relationship between corporate ownership and performance is far from easy. At best, the empirical evidence available to date is inconclusive. This is especially true when the relationship is investigated cross-country – as it tends to be in the recent empirical work (Morck et al 2005). Different patterns of corporate ownership and control apparently bear no relationship with firm performance when (most) countries of Western Europe are compared (Faccio and Lang 2002), whereas they show a negative effect of control by large shareholders in East Asia (Claessens et al 2002) and a positive effect of ownership stakes retained by controlling shareholders in a sample of 27 wealthy economies (La Porta et al 2002). Although those results are not necessarily in contradiction with each other, they do not show any univocal path either.

In addition, the same results have to be taken with extreme caution. Whether performed on a within-country or a cross-country basis, all of the available studies on the empirical relation between ownership structure and firm performance suffer from one or more of the following biases: (a) definition of ownership structure; (b) definition of corporate control; (c) reverse causality.[27]

If the empirical analysis does not reject the hypothesis that the ownership structure is endogenous, and then that concentrated ownership can be as efficient as dispersed ownership, casual empiricism mildly supports this view. As I mentioned in the previous chapter, at least within most developed economies, corporate governance systems where dispersed ownership prevails (the US and the UK) do not significantly outperform those typically based on a more concentrated ownership structure (the developed countries of continental Europe). However, this does not mean that we live in the best of all possible worlds. In fact, I claim that legal regulation of corporate governance, interplayed with other institutional factors, creates *biases* that might prevent the efficient ownership structure from being chosen by individual companies.

3.6.3 Ownership and performance: testing the wrong hypotheses?

Specifically, law may produce both *shortcomings* and *constraints* that undermine the selection of the efficient ownership structure. Shortcomings may lead to 'excessive' ownership concentration due to weak protection of outside shareholders from expropriation by the corporate controller (that is, too much scope for diversionary PBC). Constraints may lead to both 'excessive concentration' and 'excessive dispersion', depending on whether entitlements to corporate control (that is, to idiosyncratic PBC) are only available to a

---

27 See respectively Bianchi et al (2005), Becht et al (2007), and Demsetz and Lehn (1985).

controlling shareholder or, alternatively, to a management-controlled board of directors. Empirical analyses so far have only attempted to integrate the first problem into the study of the relationship between corporate ownership and performance (e.g. La Porta et al 1997; Djankov et al 2008), while completely neglecting the second one. This might provide a further explanation of why the empirical evidence on this matter is inconclusive.[28]

Failure to account for idiosyncratic PBC in the empirical analyses of ownership structure is not surprising. As we already know, those PBC are *not* in the theory of corporate governance, or at least not in the mainstream one. Therefore, the empirical work available to date may be testing the wrong hypotheses. Adequately testing the empirical relationship between ownership structure and corporate performance would require that the role of idiosyncratic PBC be taken into account.

Although this would be interesting, I am not venturing into this unknown territory. Rather, the remainder of this work will try to assess how corporate laws affect the selection of the ownership and control structure of the firm, depending on their ability to curb the potential for diversionary PBC and to support the exploitation of idiosyncratic PBC. This kind of legal analysis is going to provide support for a theory of corporate governance based on interaction of the three categories of PBC that are assumed to be at play. As will be shown, two of them (the diversionary and the idiosyncratic kinds) are directly affected by regulation, whereas the third one (distortionary PBC) is dealt with indirectly through the market for corporate control whose features are also determined by regulation. On the normative side, this approach has major policy implications, which will be illustrated. To this purpose, I shall always maintain that the optimal ownership structure depends on the amount of idiosyncratic PBC that is necessary to motivate business, and it is therefore endogenous. Adequately testing this proposition within the above framework is a matter for future research.

3.6.4 *Testable propositions*

The foregoing discussion brings about some key propositions about how corporate law affects separation of ownership and control. They initially enter just as cause–effect relationships and, thus, as a number of positive statements. Adding consideration for the efficient degree of separation of ownership and control makes then possible to uncover their normative implications. As I showed, efficient separation of ownership and control requires credible commitments being taken not to expropriate non-controlling shareholders of their share of the pie (curbing diversionary PBC), prospective reward being secured by the corporate controller in return for his firm-specific investments (protecting idiosyncratic PBC), and corporate control being transferred when

28 For a more general critique of empirical work on legal institutions, see Klick (2010).

a more efficient manager is available (cashing in idiosyncratic PBC as a more profitable alternative to inefficient exploitation of distortionary PBC).

If one of the above conditions is not satisfied, separation of ownership and control may take place to an inefficient degree. Too much scope for diversionary PBC can only lead to less separation than would be desirable (outside shareholders are less willing to invest when they face the risk of being robbed). Inability to secure idiosyncratic PBC from subsequent expropriation by a prospective raider normally restricts the opportunities for separating ownership from control.[29] But it may also lead to a system where high idiosyncratic PBC (and most innovative businesses) are incompatible with the stock market, for instance because maintaining concentrated ownership in the governance of a listed firm would be too costly. Finally, difficulties to cash in idiosyncratic PBC through control sales that nurture the evolution of the firm's ownership and control structure undermine the efficient dynamics of corporate control allocation. Similarly to the previous case, this may lead either to excessive ownership concentration or to excessive ownership dispersion.

It should be noticed that the notion of 'excessive' ownership concentration (or dispersion) refers to an optimal ownership structure that is not known at the outset, for it is endogenous by assumption. My point here is simply that inadequate treatment of the above kinds of PBC is likely to determine a departure from the efficient outcome, although it does not do so necessarily. That being said, I posit that inadequate treatment of PBC mainly depends on legal regulation of corporate governance. From this contention, three fundamental predictions arise about the role of corporate law for separation of ownership and control. They consist of both positive statements and normative implications.

3.7 Three predictions on how corporate law affects separation of ownership and control

3.7.1 *Protecting investors (law and diversionary private benefits of control)*

Prediction 1

Law matters as a device supporting protection of non-controlling shareholders against *diversionary private benefits* that may be extracted by the corporate controller. Effective protection makes separation of ownership and control a workable way to finance business, whereas ineffective protection hampers it.

The prediction is not novel: it lies at the core of the standard 'law matters' argument.

---

29 See e.g. Coates (2004).

3.7.1.1 *Theoretical background*

Legal protection of non-controlling shareholders from expropriation of their investment is a *precondition* for a model of corporate finance based on separation of ownership and control.[30] In the absence of such a protection of outside providers of equity finance, the corporate controller will hardly be able to take credible commitments that non-controlling owners will be dealt with fairly. The reason is that corporate contracts are incomplete and the corporate controller can influence the process of its adaptation to changed circumstances. As a result, households will be ultimately unwilling to invest their savings in corporate stock, for fear of being subsequently expropriated, whereas entrepreneurs will refrain from selling their firm's shares for lack of adequate consideration.

3.7.1.2 *Positive implications*

Weak protection of non-controlling shareholders from expropriation by the corporate controller determines a high level of diversionary PBC in the system. High diversionary PBC have three major consequences for corporate governance:

1   They make access to equity finance costlier (La Porta et al 1997).
2   For listed firms, they involve concentration of ownership in the hands of the corporate controller (La Porta et al 1998).
3   They undermine the efficient functioning of the market for corporate control (Bebchuk et al 2000).

3.7.1.3 *Normative implications*

There is no such thing as a 'good purpose' for expropriation. Diversionary PBC are always 'bad' (i.e., inefficient) for corporate governance. Nonetheless, policing diversionary PBC through the legal system is costly and that explains why the normative goal cannot be to eliminate them outright, but it should be rather to *minimize their amount in a cost-efficient manner*. The costs involved by an anti-expropriation legal policy are both direct and indirect. The *direct* ones arise from setting up a system of legal controls and providing for its enforcement. Of course, such a system should make corporate finance cheaper, not costlier.[31]

Indirect costs of curbing diversionary PBC are the most difficult to handle. Absolute prevention of mismanagement ultimately involves a close scrutiny of

---

30 To be sure, other institutional factors matter to counter expropriation. Historically, they may have played an even more important role than the law. See e.g. Cheffins (2008) and Franks et al (2009).
31 See Becker (1968) for a general approach to efficient enforcement.

management. Inasmuch as this undermines managerial discretion, such a scrutiny would neither be in the interest of the corporate controller nor of non-controlling shareholders. Investors too do not like the merits of corporate decision-making to be systematically reviewed by a judge and, more in general, by anybody other than the market. Therefore, although virtually all corporate transactions may involve expropriation by the corporate controller, only the most dangerous should be subject to legal (judicial or procedural) controls, mostly with a hands-off approach aimed at detecting cash flow diversion without interfering with business judgment. The efficient policing of diversionary PBC is based on the optimal solution of a discretion–accountability tradeoff.

3.7.2 Supporting control (law and idiosyncratic private benefits of control)

Prediction 2

Law also matters for separation of ownership and control in that it protects the corporate controller's *idiosyncratic private benefits*. Corporate law is a source of entitlements to firm control independent of corporate ownership, affecting the distribution of powers between the corporate controller and non-controlling owners. Once shareholders have been protected from expropriation of their investment, distribution of corporate powers determines the degree of separation of ownership and control that can be afforded by entrepreneurs concerned with their control rents.

The prediction is partly novel: although the importance of distribution of legal powers for separation of ownership and control has been highlighted by the literature, no connection with the role of control rents in corporate governance has yet been made.[32]

3.7.2.1 Theoretical background

Low diversionary PBC are a necessary, but not sufficient, condition for separation of ownership and control. Idiosyncratic PBC must also be considered. Their protection is necessary to motivate the undertaking of highly uncertain business requiring unobservable and unverifiable firm-specific investments. Having these investments combined with separation of ownership and control requires that entitlements to control rents be available to a corporate controller who is not also the corporate owner. These entitlements need to be stable over time (for otherwise control rents risk being eventually expropriated by the owners taking over), and thus must be legal in character. They determine

---

32 Compare Cools (2005) on the importance of distribution of legal powers with Zingales (2000) and Hart (2001) on the role of private benefits of control in corporate governance.

a range of alternative distributions of legal powers between the corporate controller and the corporate owners.

Legal devices aimed at empowering corporate controllers, freeing them from non-controlling shareholders' interference, basically comes in two forms: (a) separation of voting rights from ownership claims; and (b) separation of control rights from voting rights (Becht and Mayer 2001). The former devices, typically but not exclusively dual class shares, allow for *shareholder control* being exerted by dominating the general meeting in spite of a limited ownership stake; they may also support *managerial control* when voting rights can be stripped outright from share ownership. The latter devices make control available to the corporate managers, featuring boards of directors with little need for support by the general meeting of shareholders and with the power to influence the initiation if not the passing of resolutions favored by the incumbent management.

When corporate law falls short of providing legal entitlements to corporate control independently of share ownership, separation of ownership and control can only take place to a limited extent, no matter how low the potential for the extraction of diversionary PBC is. This might impair the selection of the efficient ownership structure by individual companies.

3.7.2.2 *Positive implications*

There might be little separation of ownership and control also in those systems where diversionary PBC are low. I hypothesize this is due to legal entitlements to corporate control being too closely linked to share ownership. The following results are therefore expected:

1   Listed firm will be governed by controlling shareholders whenever legal devices for separating control rights from voting rights are not available.
2   Ownership will be relatively less concentrated, and stock markets relatively more developed, to the extent that controlling shareholders are allowed to partly separate voting rights from ownership claims.
3   The investing public will not allow the (legal) potential for separation of voting rights from ownership claims to be fully exploited under a shareholder control structure.
4   Fully dispersed ownership structures with managerial control can only arise where separation of control rights from voting rights is allowed by corporate law.

3.7.2.3 *Normative implications*

Since we do not know what the optimal ownership structure is, we cannot say whether corporate law should favor shareholder control or managerial control, or whether corporate ownership should be more or less concentrated. This matter should be left for firms to decide. In order to be efficient, such a decision should be taken when corporate controllers and outside shareholders contract with each other, namely when firms resort to the market for equity capital by going public (Initial Public Offerings – IPOs), raising additional funds from the stock market (Seasoned Equity Offerings – SEOs), reducing their market capitalization (stock repurchase), or going private. In those situations, the share ownership that the corporate controller *is willing* to maintain relative to outside shareholders will depend on how favorable the stock price is (taking the amount of idiosyncratic PBC into account). The share ownership that he *has to* maintain in order to keep firm control undisputed will depend instead on corporate law. When these two levels are incompatible, the efficient choice of ownership structure can be impaired.

Most often, ownership will be more concentrated than desirable because the majority of corporate law systems are biased towards shareholder control of publicly held firms. But also the reverse outcome can occur (i.e., ownership more dispersed than desirable) when regulation of listed companies is biased towards managerial control. An optimal regulation of corporate governance should avoid both kinds of biases. In particular, corporate law should provide for alternative arrangements suitable for both *shareholder control* with different degrees of ownership concentration and *managerial control* featured with outright dispersed ownership, in order for the optimal ownership structure to be selected by publicly held companies.

As we will see in the following chapters, not all of these arrangements are equally efficient. Some of them (for instance, dual class shares and anti-takeover provisions explicitly included in the corporate charter) must typically be implemented ex-ante, when equity funds are raised from outside investors, and therefore the resulting ownership and control structure is likely to be efficiently priced by the stock market. Some others (for instance, pyramidal groups and midstream introduction of anti-takeover devices) can be more easily implemented ex-post, altering the balance between control rights and ownership claims originally 'sold' to the market; therefore, these arrangements are more likely to come at the expense of outstanding, non-controlling shareholders.

3.7.3 Promoting a market for corporate control (law and distortionary private benefits of control)

Prediction 3

Law does not only matter statically, in that it supports the exercise of power by the corporate controller and constrains its abuse. It also matters dynamically, in that it promotes the allocation of corporate control to the best managers while preventing non-controlling owners from being exploited through unfair control transactions. *Insufficient protection* of non-controlling shareholders leads to concentrated ownership structures where the efficiency of the market for corporate control is impaired by value diversion. However, *excessive shareholder protection* may prevent insurgents from compensating the incumbents' control rents through the proceeds of efficient control transactions. Eventually, this could lead to excessive consumption of *distortionary private benefits* under too dispersed or too concentrated ownership structures.

The prediction is basically novel: both the consequences of managerial control rents on the takeover mechanism and the effects of minority shareholder protection on the acquirer's incentives have been dealt with in previous literature, but they have always been considered separately.[33]

3.7.3.1 *Theoretical background*

Whether corporate governance is based on shareholder control or on managerial control, the corporate controller often ends up being entrenched. Here I am assuming that this depends on non-trivial idiosyncratic PBC although the presence of high diversionary PBC would lead to the same result. While protecting the manager's firm-specific investments is ex-ante beneficial for corporate governance, his entrenchment might impair the efficient allocation of corporate control ex-post. Over time, more and more *distortionary* PBC may be enjoyed by an entrenched corporate controller through misuse of free cash, thereby compromising the efficient management of the firm. The market for corporate control provides a dynamic solution to this problem by re-allocating corporate control when its exercise is no longer efficient. However, this is not necessarily based on (the threat of) hostile takeover, which would not be compatible with the protection of idiosyncratic control rents, but rather on a system of friendly takeovers where idiosyncratic PBC are cashed in through the surplus of an *efficient* control sale. Distortionary PBC are minimized as a result of this operation of the market for corporate control.

Cashing in the incumbent's control rents is crucial for the efficiency of this takeover mechanism. Provided that takeovers are friendly (and therefore at least the incumbent's ownership stake needs to be transferred), they only make sense when their gains to the acquirer are large enough to offset both the incumbent's PBC and the cost of the stock purchased. On condition that expropriation of non-controlling shareholders is adequately policed, those gains can only arise from increased value of corporate stock under the new management. How much of those gains can be appropriated by a

---

33 See Burkart and Panunzi (2008) in economic theory and Kraakman et al. (2009) in comparative corporate law.

prospective acquirer – and, therefore, the likelihood of an efficient change in control – depends on both the amount and the price of the stock purchased for the acquisition. The role of corporate law in this mechanism is therefore not only that of protecting non-controlling shareholders from exploitation (in the form of 'looting' or similar instances of expropriation), but also that of preventing outside shareholders from free riding on the incumbent's control premium as well as on the acquirer's takeover gains.

3.7.3.2 *Positive implications*

A theory of the market for corporate control that accounts for the role of idiosyncratic PBC in corporate governance leads to the following expectations:

1   Regardless of whether a controlling shareholder or the management is in charge, hostile takeovers are the exception, while friendly takeovers are the rule.
2   A necessary, but not sufficient, condition for an active market for corporate control is that diversionary PBC are also policed by regulation of corporate control transactions.
3   Takeovers may improve the allocation of corporate control depending on the ease with which idiosyncratic PBC can be cashed in by a less efficient incumbent. Rules providing for the equal treatment of outstanding shareholders (such as a mandatory bid rule) undermine that ease and thus the efficiency of the market for corporate control;
4   Limited appropriability of takeover gains by the acquirer likewise reduces the frequency of efficient changes in control.
5   Although this may look counterintuitive, excessive protection of non-controlling shareholders in takeovers reduces the chances that distortionary PBC are policed by the market for corporate control. Ownership may be stuck in either too concentrated structures or too dispersed ones.
6   Differential treatment of the corporate controller and non-controlling shareholders in takeovers (favoring both cashing in of idiosyncratic PBC by the incumbent and appropriation of takeover gains by the acquirer) makes it easier to re-concentrate ownership when this is needed. However, an easier operation of the market for corporate control will not necessarily lead to dispersed ownership structures. Dispersion of ownership depends on the availability of entitlements supporting managerial control.[34] If controlling shareholders cannot profitably transfer control to a professional management, they (and their heirs) will be eventually building empires or otherwise enjoying distortionary PBC.

---

34 See Prediction 2 above.

3.7.3.3 Normative implications

The normative implications of the above reasoning are straightforward. An efficient discipline of the market for corporate control should not be exclusively concerned with contestability. Reasonable minds may disagree on whether contestability of corporate control is a desirable feature of corporate governance, but certainly it cannot be *imposed* by regulation. Even in those environments where customarily dispersed ownership is more favorable to contestable control, this option appears to be neglected by the vast majority of publicly held companies. Quite the contrary, very often they deliberately choose to *exclude* contestability.

Albeit not based on contestability, an efficient market for corporate control should be a prominent goal of corporate law. The legal discipline should then move its focus towards *friendly* takeovers, with the aim of promoting the occurrence of the efficient ones while preventing the inefficient ones from taking place. When takeovers are friendly, the above two goals are not incompatible with each other. Avoidance of value-decreasing takeovers can be guaranteed simply by extending the legal policing of diversionary PBC to corporate control transactions. This would make sure that non-controlling shareholders could not be expropriated of the current value of their shares by collusion between the seller and the purchaser of corporate control. Then takeovers can only be efficient, provided that *both* the incumbent's equity interest in the firm *and* his PBC are bought out: the acquirer cannot perform worse than the incumbent simultaneously on both accounts, otherwise he would lose.[35] However, if he performs better, he risks being unable to reap the gains of his performance, since non-controlling shareholders will free ride. We might then observe far less takeovers than would be desirable.

The role of corporate law is crucial for avoiding that outcome. To this purpose, the costs of acquisition of corporate control should be minimized, and the gains to the prospective acquirer enhanced. An efficient regulation of corporate control transactions should provide for *differential treatment* of the corporate controller and non-controlling shareholders. The former should be exclusively entitled to cash in his idiosyncratic PBC in a negotiated control sale; whereas it should be possible to induce the latter to tender at a limited premium over market price, under the credible threat of being squeezed out on the same terms when they do not tender. Both categories would get their share of the transaction surplus. More importantly, all of the remaining gains would be left to the acquirer. Any legal impediment to the above mechanism should be removed.

---

35 The acquisition could be motivated by higher idiosyncratic PBC. However, this is unlikely in the absence of major business innovations. Even then, the idiosyncratic value will sooner or later have to be cashed in through the security benefits of the next acquisition. I posit that most often the acquisition will be motivated by an expected increase in the stock price offsetting a decrease in the amount of idiosyncratic PBC (see section 3.4.3 above).

3.8 Comparative corporate law

3.8.1 The regulatory objects to be compared

The three predictions that I have just outlined are aimed at carrying further the basic 'law matters' insight that, since La Porta et al (1998), has informed the economic and the legal debate on corporate governance. These predictions depart from the standard account of separation of ownership and control in that they posit that investor protection is not all that matters, at least as far as corporate law is concerned. In order to support separation of ownership and control, the law needs also to feature control entitlements available for both concentrated and dispersed ownership structures, and to provide for the smooth functioning of a market for corporate control where control rents can be cashed in through negotiated transactions. On the one hand, most entrepreneurs would not accept separating ownership from control when this involves giving up their idiosyncratic PBC. On the other hand, non-controlling shareholders would not just be content with good legal policing of diversionary PBC, should the market for corporate control fail to police distortionary PBC and allow firm control to change hands when this is efficient.

Testing this view against the empirical evidence requires that corporate laws be compared across different countries which, according to the empirical evidence, are characterized by different patterns of corporate governance. However, not only the 'taxonomy' of those patterns has been by now sufficiently 'complicated' to overcome the simplistic dichotomy between concentrated and dispersed ownership (Gilson 2006). Also the following approach to the legal analysis will be sophisticated enough to allow departure from the standard methodology of comparison set by La Porta et al. Sticking to the fundamental tenets of comparative law, the bearing of national corporate laws on the above three predictions will be analyzed in a purely *functional* perspective (see Kraakman et al 2009). Now having clear in mind what the underlying economic problems are, we should know exactly what to look for: not just legal rules that almost *look the same* in different systems, but legal rules that *affect equivalent phenomena* within each national context.

Let me refer to those phenomena as 'regulatory objects.' There are three main regulatory objects to be compared in order to check whether corporate law actually affects corporate governance according to the predictions formulated in the previous section. Any of these objects may possibly call into play completely different categories of legal rules within each country. In fact, as we will see in the next chapters, very often they do. The objects at issue can be outlined as follows:

(a) Entitlements to corporate control (that is, the legal distribution of corporate powers).
(b) Safeguards against non-controlling shareholder expropriation (that is, the legal discipline of conflicted interest transactions).

(c) Support for a market for corporate control (that is, the regulation of corporate control transactions).

It would be nice to apply this methodology of comparison to as many countries as possible; or at least, to all of the countries that exhibit comparable levels of economic development and reliability of the rule of law.[36] However, functional legal comparison is particularly burdensome. Numerical comparisons of the kind of La Porta et al (1998) are based on a highly simplified account of corporate laws, which easily allows for indexing the quality of legal rules. As such, "numerical comparative law" (Siems 2005) only requires collecting information about *single* categories of legal rules in different countries. It is not surprising that this kind of comparison of corporate laws has been performed for as many as 72 countries (Djankov et al 2008).

Functional comparison is more demanding. For each country, it requires that the *entire* corporate law system be understood in order to find out which rules *actually* have a bearing on comparing the regulatory objects (Zweigert and Kotz 1998). This approach may be ultimately irreconcilable with econometrics, particularly given our limited knowledge of comparative corporate law. Despite valuable attempts to code corporate laws more precisely and more extensively in recent years (e.g. Armour, et al 2009; Spamann 2010), there does not yet seem to be a group of researchers with such an understanding of corporate law systems around the world that is sufficiently deep to allow for meaningful comparisons and sufficiently broad to allow for statistical inference.[37] Therefore, I will stick to a narrower case study methodology.

3.8.2 A five-country case study

I have selected five countries for the purpose of the comparative legal analysis of the following chapters. The selection is based on a falsification criterion. I have picked five countries that, for different reasons, cast some doubt on the validity of the standard 'law matters' account – that is, investor protection by the legal system being the major determinant of both ownership concentration and stock market development. The analysis will show that what investor protection (or lack thereof) fails to explain is instead consistent with the above-mentioned three predictions about how corporate law functionally affects corporate governance. These countries are Italy, the US, the UK, Sweden, and the Netherlands.

3.8.2.1 Italy

Among the top-developed countries, Italy has been the case in point of the standard 'law matters' argument (e.g. Roe 2003). Its stock market is

36 This would make the inference of economic effects from legal rules more plausible.
37 See *supra* Chapter 1, section 1.3.

considerably underdeveloped relative to the rest of the Wealthy West; and ownership of publicly held corporations is highly concentrated. Traditionally, this picture is coupled with weak legal protection of outside shareholders. According to La Porta et al (1998), the bad quality of Italian corporate law is reflected in the very low score it gets on the Anti-director Rights Index (one out of six). Even those who disagree on the methodology of numerical comparative law nonetheless share the view that the poor standards of investor protection are responsible for the backwardness of Italian equity markets and corporate governance (Gilson 2006). This account is mostly correct.

And yet, there are some puzzles. The quality of investor protection in Italy has significantly improved since 1998, when a major reform of the regulation of listed companies was undertaken.[38] The improvement is also reflected in the more recent law and finance scholarship (La Porta et al 2006; Djankov et al 2008), particularly in the Revised Anti-director Rights Index (now two out of six) and the new indexes for the quality of securities law and legal policing of self-dealing. Nevertheless, this has hardly brought any change in the basic patterns of corporate governance (Culpepper 2007). Ownership of Italian listed firms is still very concentrated and stock market capitalization continues to lag far behind the rest of developed countries (Bianchi and Bianco 2006). There are two possible explanations for this. One is that there are discontinuities in investor protection. Improvements in the law of Italian listed companies might not have been enough to effectively cope with the problem of expropriation of non-controlling shareholders.[39] The second is that there may be something else going on. On the one hand, Italian corporate law may not support managerial control, while on the other hand, it may not allow for a smooth functioning of a market for corporate control.

3.8.2.2 *The US and the UK*

The US and the UK stand on the opposite side of the standard 'law matters' argument. These two countries have probably the most dispersed ownership structures and the highest rate of stock market development in the world and they exhibit an impressively high frequency of listed firms under managerial control (Barca and Becht 2001). They both have 'good' quality of corporate law as assessed in terms of investor protection (Djankov et al 2008). This holds equally true if we abandon a simple indexing methodology in favor of a more functional approach to comparison (Franks and Mayer 2002). Functional legal comparison shows, however, that the two systems achieve that result through completely different, and somewhat opposite, legal strategies. On

---

38 Legislative Decree No. 58/1998 ("Testo unico delle disposizioni in materia di intermediazione finanziaria"). For more recent developments in the Italian corporate and
financial legislation see Enriques (2009).

39 Particularly on enforcement issues, see Enriques (2009).

the one hand, good standards of investor protection are met by means of a different legal policing of self-dealing by the corporate controllers (Pacces 2011). The discipline of conflicts of interest is 'transaction-based' (i.e., ultimately relying on judicial scrutiny of the most dangerous transactions) in the US, whereas it is more 'governance-based' (i.e., depending on empowerment of non-controlling shareholders) in the UK (Kraakman et al 2009). On the other hand, the legal discipline of corporate control is very friendly to the management in the US, whereas it is quite unfriendly to controlling shareholders in the UK (Armour and Skeel 2007).

Formerly identical, and today still relatively similar, scores on the indexes elaborated by the law and finance scholarship (La Porta et al 1998; Djankov et al 2008) seem, then, a much too coarse explanation of the causes of Anglo-American corporate governance. Among other historical and institutional factors (Bank and Cheffins 2008; Franks et al 2009), what is more likely to explain the rise of dispersed ownership in so different legal environments is instead an *analogous* legal support for managerial control coupled with *equivalent* levels of outside shareholders' legal protection. Neither of these issues is accounted for by numerical legal comparison. Nor could they be, since both managerial support and investor protection are based on different combinations of legal rules in the US and in the UK.

3.8.2.3 Sweden and the Netherlands

Finally, at least two countries in well-developed continental Europe plainly contradict the standard account of the law and finance scholarship. One is Sweden, whose functionally excellent degree of investor protection does not come with managerial control or dispersion of voting power in listed companies (Gilson 2006). The other is the Netherlands, whose allegedly 'bad' quality of corporate law has not inhibited the emergence of managerial capitalism (de Jong et al 2010).

The Swedish case is often referred to as the most compelling evidence *against* the 'law matters' thesis. Sweden is featured with a fairly good developed stock market but with one of the highest rates of voting power concentration in the developed world (Henrekson and Jakobsson 2012). Managerial control is basically unheard of and separation of ownership and control is achieved by means of extraordinary deviations from 'one share–one vote' security-voting structures, which are normally considered as a clue to 'bad' quality of corporate law (Bebchuk et al 2000). Numerical comparative law then credits Sweden with an intermediate degree of legal protection of minority shareholders (Djankov et al 2008). Nobody doubts, however, that this account seriously underestimates investor protection in Sweden. There is in fact no single anecdotal evidence of cash flow diversion from non-controlling shareholders ever reported for Swedish companies (Holmén and Högfeldt 2004). According to national and international commentators, expropriation of minority shareholders is simply not an issue in Swedish corporate governance (e.g.

Angblad et al 2001). One conventional explanation of the Swedish case is powerful social norms (Coffee 2001a). However, the following chapters will show that the strength of moral constraints upon stealing – that surely helps – is in fact supported by legal institutions in the background, which make sure that any cheating would be promptly realized and severely punished. But then, why does Sweden not allow for managers being in charge of large publicly held corporations? I will argue that, consistent with the theoretical paradigm developed in this chapter, the answer could lie in a legal distribution of corporate power that does not support managerial control.

The Netherlands exhibits an exceptionally high degree of stock market development and perhaps the highest rate of ownership dispersion in continental Europe. However, surprisingly, the numerical assessment of the quality of Dutch corporate law is very low. According to those measures, outside shareholder protection in the Netherlands is almost as weak as in Italy and, as far as legal policing of self-dealing is concerned, even much weaker (Djankov et al 2008). However, this assessment is incorrect. Non-controlling shareholders are actually quite well protected from expropriation in the Netherlands (Timmerman and Doorman 2002; Bekkum et al 2010). As I will show, both a special procedure and a specialized Court are provided for this purpose by Dutch corporate law.

The latter feature of Dutch corporate governance has not received much attention by economists, who generally prefer to stress the weakness of the shareholder position when it comes to interfering with the firm management. It is for this reason that Dutch commentators often agree that corporate law's quality is 'bad' in the Netherlands (see e.g. Roosenboom and van der Goot 2003). However, such a weakness has little to do with the potential for cash flow diversion by corporate controllers and may instead be responsible for the emergence of managerial capitalism. As I have argued, investor protection may not be sufficient to achieve dispersion of ownership. Differently from Sweden, Dutch corporate law does not only police expropriation but also supports managerial control by shielding the firm management from interference by non-controlling shareholders. However, some of the ways in which such support is created give rise to rigidities that hinder the smooth functioning of the market for corporate control and, consequently, the transition from shareholder control to managerial control.

These few observations suggest it might be worth investigating the law of those five countries more in depth than the law and finance scholarship has done so far. In the remainder of this book I will illustrate how this five-country case study supports the predictions of the framework developed in this chapter and how, based on this theory, corporate laws could be improved in each of the countries at issue.

4 Legal distribution of corporate powers

4.1 Introducing the legal analysis

The framework of analysis of the economics of corporate governance employed in this book is based on three kinds of private benefits of control (PBC). The first has to do with 'stealing': that is, diverting profits from non-controlling shareholders (diversionary PBC). The second one has to do with rewarding the corporate controller of his firm-specific investments, when these are substantial (I have called such a reward idiosyncratic PBC). The third kind has to do with 'shirking': that is, misusing free cash with either over-investment or under-investment implications (distortionary PBC). This threefold account of PBC generates three predictions about how corporate law affects separation of ownership and control and its efficiency. They were amply discussed in the previous chapter, but it is nonetheless useful to summarize them below.

To begin with, *outside investors need to be protected*. Separation of ownership and control would always be less than optimal, and possibly undermined, when regulation of conflicted interest transactions is not effective at curbing diversionary PBC. Second, *control needs to be supported*. Separation of ownership and control is also affected by availability of legal entitlements to exert control and, where necessary, to protect its rents (idiosyncratic PBC) independently of the ownership structure. Finally, *a market for corporate control needs to be promoted*. Either too much or too little separation of ownership and control may emerge over time. This may lead to excessive exploitation of distortionary PBC by the corporate controller, whenever selling corporate control to a more efficient manager is not a preferable alternative to 'playing' with the firm's assets.

The previous analysis suggests that comparative empirical evidence about some developed countries tends to reject the mainstream view that corporate law affects separation of ownership and control *only* on the first prong; that is, that ownership is dispersed in those countries where legal protection of non-controlling shareholders is 'strong' and concentrated where it is 'weak' (the standard 'law matters' argument). On this basis, I have selected five countries for a more in-depth investigation. Two of them – Sweden and the Netherlands – plainly reject the standard 'law matters' thesis in two opposite directions (respectively as good law/concentrated ownership and bad law/

dispersed ownership combinations). Another two – the US and the UK – seem to support it, albeit by means of completely different legal arrangements. The last one – Italy – provides perhaps one of the strongest supports for the 'law matters' thesis among developed countries, and yet something else seems to be going on there too. The analysis of this and the following chapters is aimed both at uncovering the legal shortcomings in the prevailing account of the economics of corporate law and at performing a qualitative empirical test of the alternative explanation that I have suggested. This test is based on comparative law.

As I have already mentioned, the problem with the standard explanation of the role of corporate law in corporate governance is basically twofold. On the one hand, legal protection of minority shareholders from expropriation might be inaccurately measured – and it is actually doubtful whether it could ever be 'measured' by an index. On the other hand, such a protection might not be the only way in which corporate law matters for separation of ownership and control. The evidence about our five-country sample shows that these two concerns may not be unsound.

As far as 'measurement' problems are concerned, the final developments in the law and finance scholarship have acknowledged that investor protection is actually dealt with very differently in the US and in the UK. Surprisingly, however, 'American' corporate law scored significantly worse on investor protection than British law (Djankov et al 2008).[1] Nonetheless the two countries exhibit very similar patterns of elevated separation of ownership and control as well as of stock market development. The Netherlands is still characterized as a legal system where shareholder protection is 'weak', and yet Dutch corporations are featured with perhaps the highest average degree of separation of ownership and control within continental Europe. In addition, between the mid-1990s and the mid-2000s the stock market capitalization relative to gross domestic product (GDP) was nearly as high in the Netherlands as it was in the US.[2] Swedish law apparently provides minority shareholders with some intermediate degree of legal protection; and yet stock market capitalization relative to GDP is slightly below the figures for the above three countries – even though the typical Swedish ownership structure is highly concentrated. Finally, the Italian case of weak legal protection of minority shareholders being *the* determinant of high ownership concentration and stock market underdevelopment appears to not be as strong as it used to be in the past (Bianchi and Bianco 2006; Enriques 2009).

---

1 The country scores were ultimately removed from the published version of Djankov et al (2008). As a matter of academic policy, however, Professor Shleifer has always made these data available on his homepage Formally there is no such thing as an 'American corporate law.' At least for listed companies, US corporate law is typically the law of Delaware (Bebchuk and Cohen 2003). Federal securities law, also applies to a number of corporate governance issues (e.g. proxy voting). For a recent discussion of the origin and reasons of Delaware's primacy in the production of corporate law, see Carney et al (2010).
2 See *supra* Chapter 1, Figure 1.2.

Even if the measurement problems were fixed, the empirical analysis would still leave us with some puzzling evidence very hard to reconcile with the standard 'law matters' argument. The US and the UK actually display different styles and intensities of investor protection by corporate law but, at the same time, Anglo-American ownership structures are dispersed more often than not and the stock markets are probably the most developed in the world. Under both Swedish and Dutch corporate law, non-controlling shareholders actually enjoy high standards of protection from expropriation of their investment. This may possibly explain the development of their stock markets, but still Sweden and the Netherlands are characterized by two different patterns of corporate governance. In Italy, significant improvement in investor protection over the past few years have hardly brought any change in either the ownership structures or in the trend of stock market development.

I shall start from dealing with the second problem in this chapter. The reason for this choice is straightforward. I believe that what is missing from the agency theory of corporate governance, and consequently from the standard 'law matters' argument, is appropriate consideration for idiosyncratic control rents. How these control rents can be protected in corporate governance – i.e., under what ownership structure such a protection is allowed – depends on the legal distribution of corporate powers, regarded as a source of legal entitlements to corporate control. Understanding that distribution in each legal system is also a precondition for an accurate analysis of outside investor protection. Only when you know how power is exerted can you meaningfully say how its abuse should be prevented. For this reason, the investigation about the legal constraints on expropriation of non-controlling shareholders will have to be postponed to the next two chapters. In Chapters 5 and 6, I shall finally discuss how the protection of the corporate controller's powers (and of his idiosyncratic PBC, when they are relevant) can be ultimately reconciled with an efficient dynamics of the market for corporate control.

4.2 Legal distribution of powers

4.2.1 *What does distribution of powers mean?*

Supreme decisions about how to 'run' a company are taken by two categories of players: the directors and the shareholders. Corporate law features directors with both the authority over the firm's centralized management and the responsibility for the exercise of this authority (Bainbridge 2008). Responsibility is most often established towards the shareholders that provide the firm with their own capital, even though in some systems other stakeholders also enter the play. These are typically the company's employees and, especially in the presence of the risk of bankruptcy, its creditors. However, neither shareholders nor stakeholders are entitled to exert *direct* authority over the firm management, thereby bypassing the directors (Rock and Wachter 2001).

That would be against one of the basic tenets of corporate law's structure: the company's *centralized management* (Kraakman et al 2009).

Shareholders and stakeholders who are granted governance rights by corporate law may only *indirectly* influence the exercise of that authority, either by vetoing directors' decisions when their support is required or by removing incumbent directors and having them replaced by new ones. The last option always favors shareholders over stakeholders. Even under the more stakeholder-oriented corporate laws, at least the majority of directors are appointed by or without the opposition of shareholders (Kraakman et al 2009). The most important source of ultimate authority within the corporation thus remains *shareholder ownership*, often referred to as 'shareholder franchise', which is another fundamental tenet of the corporate law's structure (Easterbrook and Fischel 1991). Creditors' almost fully taking over the shareholder franchise in bankruptcy is no exception to this principle: when a company is bankrupt, the creditors' position in fact resembles that of the shareholders (Aghion and Bolton 1992).

The fundamental question about the balance of power in corporate law concerns, then, directors and shareholders. Stakeholders are only apparently a separate source of authority. In no system of corporate law can directors manage the company's affairs just by relying on stakeholders support. However, directors may be much less in need of shareholder support when stakeholders also have a say in corporate governance (Hellwig 2000). As it turns out, having two bosses can mean being accountable to neither of them. Similarly, stakeholders involvement in corporate governance does not actually establish a different balance of power. It merely tilts the existing balance between directors and shareholders in favor of the former (Roe 2003). Shareholders may react to this, making sure that only directors they trust are appointed and can manage the firm without their opposition; or they may simply give up, leaving directors more powerful than ever. Which of these two outcomes occurs does not seem to depend on stakeholders effective involvement in corporate governance. However, the legal support for stakeholder involvement typically affects how directors are empowered vis-à-vis shareholders.

4.2.2 *Organization and competence: the company's organs*

Essentially, corporate law affects the distribution of powers between directors and shareholders in two ways. On the one hand, it sets the *organizational* rules (how each category of players decides) for implementing both centralized management and the shareholder franchise. On the other hand, it provides for an allocation of tasks (who decides what; that is, *competence*) consistent with the same principles.[3] There is clearly some tension between the two goals of

---

3 This is the typical legal approach to distribution of powers in company law. See e.g. Hamilton (2000: 228–253) for the US, Davies (2008: 365–473) for the UK, and Baums (2000) for continental Europe.

centralized management and shareholder franchise, which is ultimately a major concern for corporate law. Where should centralized management end and shareholder franchise begin? This is sometimes called the 'discretion–accountability' tradeoff in corporate law (Bainbridge 2002; Dooley 1992). The combination of organizational and competence rules in corporate law tries to solve this tradeoff by providing both the legal entitlements to corporate control and the constraints on its exercise.

Although the tradeoff is the same, and the legal instruments by which it is solved (organization and competence rules) may look similar, entitlements and constraints serve completely different purposes. Corporate law's entitlements are meant to support the corporate controller's powers, for instance allowing idiosyncratic PBC to keep on motivating entrepreneurship notwithstanding separation of ownership and control.[4] Legal constraints make credible the commitment not to abuse such a power, thereby preventing diversionary PBC from frustrating the provision of external finance by non-controlling shareholders. This distinction is one major result of the analysis carried out in the foregoing chapter. Most misunderstandings in the economic and the legal theory of corporate governance arise from confusing the above two problems. Also, many regulatory biases arise from having legal entitlements dealt with as a matter of investor protection instead of as a matter of control support. The reason why I am dealing only with legal entitlements to corporate control here is not mere convenience of exposition. At the end of the day, the matter *should be* dealt with separately from investor protection.

4.2.2.1 Voting at the director's and the shareholder's level

Let us start with organization. Corporate laws provide that directors and shareholders have a typical organizational form: the board structure for directors, and the general meeting for shareholders. In almost any of the countries considered here, a board structure is compulsory unless companies are private and cannot be listed on a stock exchange (Kraakman et al 2009: 66–72). Italy is the only country in our sample where single directors are in theory also allowed in publicly held companies, but this happens very seldom in practice. In every system, shareholder action affecting corporate control takes place through the general meeting. Shareholders are also featured with individual and collective rights of action outside the general meeting (for instance, the right to sue directors), but they are established just for investor protection purposes and therefore will only be dealt with in the next two chapters.

Decisions within both the board of directors and the general meeting are normally governed by a majority principle: decisions are upheld when they receive support by the majority of the votes. The matter basically stands as

---

4 See Cools (2005) although she is not considering the role of private benefits of control.

simply as far as the board of directors is concerned.[5] Directors must attend board meetings in person and their failure to participate in the board's activity is a typical ground for liability. However, most directors, particularly those with executive tasks, have high-powered incentives to participate in decision-making. They have equal voting rights ('one head-one vote'), even though special rights may be granted to the chairman just to avoid impasse. Majorities do not require additional rules to be either calculated or achieved, even though quorums are usually set up to avoid practical circumvention of the board requirement (e.g. Hamilton 2000). To cut a long story short, decisions are taken with a certain ease by directors.

The matter gets more complicated when it comes to the general meeting (Baums 2000). Shareholders are not required to attend either in person or by proxy (which is generally allowed), and the vast majority of them do not have sufficient incentives to participate in the meeting anyhow (Easterbrook and Fischel 1983). Corporate shareholders have unequal voting rights, basically depending on share ownership ('one share–one vote'), but also in excess (multiple voting shares) or in reduction of it (limited voting or non-voting shares) where and to the extent this is allowed (Adams and Ferreira 2008). Everywhere the majority at the general meeting means in fact a minority of outstanding shareholders, and having decisions taken by shareholders might be either very easy or relatively difficult, depending on whether quorums are established, how majorities are calculated and how voting is implemented (Cools 2005). This varies considerably from country to country (Kraakman et al 2009: 58–63, 89–94). To put it briefly, regulation of shareholder voting is more favorable to directors in the US, in the Netherlands and – with qualifications – in the UK; whereas it definitively favors shareholders in Sweden and in Italy. The legal discipline of shareholder voting is a key feature of the distribution of corporate powers and it is mainly (albeit not only) an organizational issue.

4.2.2.2 Board structure

Another set of organizational rules deserves attention too. Directors' powers may be scarcely affected by board voting, but they are ostensibly very much affected by the board structure.[6] Corporate laws know basically two kinds of such a structure. The first is a one-tier board whose members are at least formally elected by the general meeting, in all or in major part. This used to be the only option in Italy before a recent reform, and still is such in Sweden, the US, and the UK. The alternative arrangement is a two-tier board, where only members of one tier are possibly elected by the general meeting, or at least without its opposition; whereas the members of the lower tier are always appointed by the upper one. Within our sample of countries, this arrangement

---

5 See Kraakman et al (2009: 56–58), noting the increasing importance of committees and independent directors for board decision-making.
6 See for a recent survey Adams et al (2010).

is very peculiarly implemented by Dutch corporate law (which makes it compulsory for certain listed firms and optional for all of them) and it has become an option in Italy (Ventoruzzo 2004); another prominent example of a mandatory two-tier structure is offered by German corporate law (Kraakman et al 2009: 100–1).

In two-tier board structures, the lower tier is directly in charge of the firm's (top) management ('management board') while the upper one is entrusted the management's supervision ('supervisory board'). Indeed, the rationale underlying this board structure is exactly separation of supervisory tasks from active management, given that the two functions are necessarily performed within the same board in a one-tier structure. Most often, two-tier structures are provided for by corporate law in order for supervision to be performed not only on shareholders', but also on stakeholders' behalf (Kemperink 2004). This is what happens, for instance, in the Netherlands and in Germany. However, two-tier boards are neither a necessary nor a sufficient condition for stakeholder involvement in corporate governance: consideration for stakeholders is implemented within a one-tier board structure under Swedish corporate law (Skog and Fäger 2007). Opting into a two-tier board structure brings about no stakeholder involvement under Italian corporate law.[7] As far as shareholders are concerned, it is theoretically unclear why a separate supervisory board should make directors more accountable to the shareholder interest (Boot and Macey 2004). In fact, it seems that two-tier structures only take powers *away* from the general meeting of shareholders (such as, for instance, that of approving the annual accounts), including a fundamental one: that of appointing *all* directors. Other things being equal, two-tier boards empower directors relative to shareholders, not the other way around (Cools 2005).

Other things are never equal, although sometimes economists have to assume they are. To begin with, the above result about board structures has to be coordinated with the organizational rules affecting shareholder voting. A weak general meeting, of course, complements a two-tier board structure in strengthening directors' power relative to shareholders'. This has been long the case in the Netherlands (de Jong et al 2001), although the situation is changing (Bekkum et al 2010). However, director primacy does not require a two-tier board structure. In the US, the weakness of the general meeting suffices (Bainbridge 2002). And a two-tier structure does not always allow for director primacy. For instance in Germany, a case I am not considering here, the general meeting of shareholders is still too strong for that result to occur (Cools 2005). It seems then that, like stakeholder involvement, the importance of board structure in corporate governance has been exaggerated by the literature (see Becht et al 2007 for a survey). Other factors appear to make the difference in the distribution of corporate powers. The legal discipline of shareholder voting – determining the strength or the weakness of the general

---

7 See art. 2409-octies et seq. Italian Civil Code (henceforth ICC).

meeting relative to the board of directors, *whatever* its structure – is one such factor and, contrary to what many believe, it allows for a considerable degree of variety across countries.

How shareholders cast their votes is definitely not the only issue. Equally important is how shareholder voting is called for, and the matters upon which a vote is needed. These are no longer organizational issue. They are in fact a question of competence.

4.2.2.3 Competences: board vs. the shareholders general meeting

The lower bound on directors' competence is their authority over the firm's centralized management: there are a number of matters which do not bear shareholder interference (Rock and Wachter 2001). The upper bound is directors being replaceable and, anyway, periodically up for election: directors cannot stay in charge forever, unless shareholders (at least formally) consent (Kraakman et al 2009: 56–63). Many factors affect the actual width of this range, wherein directors' authority is basically unfettered. Equally importantly, other factors determine the actual degree of shareholder involvement in corporate governance *outside* that range. The fewer matters that have to be decided upon shareholder voting, the higher will be the directors' power relative to the shareholders'. The case becomes extreme when even director appointment (and replacement) does not completely depend on shareholder voting.[8]

Directors' powers can be enhanced in a much subtler way, no matter of how many corporate matters ostensibly require that a decision be taken by shareholders. Directors may be in fact the only ones who can bring those matters to shareholder attention (Bebchuk 2007). For instance, in the US, charter amendments need to be endorsed by shareholders but can only be proposed by directors. Shareholders who want their own amendments to be passed will have no choice but to first replace opposing directors with people they trust. But there comes a trick. Directors may also enjoy privileged initiative rights in choosing nominees to the election – as they actually do in the US and in the Netherlands. As a result, director replacement through voting may not be an option, unless one shareholder (or a coalition of them) gets strong enough to challenge directors' nominations.[9] Disgruntled shareholders would then have only one way to get rid of incumbent directors: taking over the company.

4.2.2.4 Takeover defenses

Once the issues regarding subject-matters and initiative have been set up, takeover resistance becomes the last piece of the competence puzzle.

8 See the discussion of the Netherlands below in this chapter.
9 For the US see Bebchuk (2003b).

Entitlements to takeover resistance may reside either with shareholders or with directors (Kraakman et al 2009). The distribution of powers between the two categories of players is affected accordingly. When takeover defenses need to be authorized by the general meeting of shareholders (as in Italy and in the UK) directors' positions become suddenly very weak: unless they enjoy strong support from one or more large shareholders (or they are large shareholders themselves), they will be basically at the insurgents' mercy. As we will see, directors deprived of takeover defenses might nonetheless be granted some unintended 'secret weapons' by takeover regulation, listing rules, or the general corporate law, to the extent they can make insurgency costlier or less profitable. But, sure enough, when the board of directors is basically free to decide about the implementation of takeover defenses (as in the Netherlands and in the US) it may become virtually impossible for disgruntled shareholders to have directors replaced against their will.

Takeover defenses have to be put in perspective. Of course, they may dramatically tilt the balance of corporate powers in favor of directors (e.g. Becht et al 2007). But – in the economists' jargon – takeover defenses can only empower directors at the margin. That is, directors need to *already* be powerful enough to exert corporate control without much shareholder interference. This is what we observe under both American and Dutch corporate law, where organization and competence rules empower directors also when control is unchallenged, but they have nonetheless to look after the firm management (Cools 2005). In such a situation, takeover defenses complement directors' empowerment. Being in a prime position in the ongoing exercise of corporate control would seem, however, insufficient when directors are unable to defend their otherwise powerful position from takeover. This is the puzzling case of the UK. However, the combined effect of mandatory bid, regulatory disfavor towards controlling shareholders, and limited squeeze-out rights available to a successful insurgent shareholder is often overlooked in interpreting British corporate governance.[10] In fact, all these factors together allow directors in the UK to entrench themselves even in the absence of formal takeover defenses (Crespi and Renneboog 2010).

Conversely, the mere ability to resist a takeover becomes useless when directors are not so powerful relative to shareholders, and so both their position and decisions have to be endorsed by outstanding shareholders *on a regular basis*. Unsurprisingly, in the past, the liberal attitude of Swedish corporate law towards takeover defenses did not minimally contribute to directors' empowerment relative to shareholders (Agnblad et al 2001). Neither are opportunities for takeover resistance likely to make a difference in Italy. Takeover defenses might be very important to reinforce directors' empowerment. However, by themselves, they cannot turn around a balance of powers that is already favorable to shareholders.

10 For a prominent exception, see Franks et al (2001).

4.2.3 *Why economics is not enough to support corporate power*

Surprising as it may appear, the distribution of powers in corporate govern-ance is very seldom regarded as a legal problem, but rather as an economic one. Since Berle and Means (1932: 70), directors' empowerment within the corporate structure has always been explained as a consequence of ownership dispersion. Shareholders of large listed companies are too many and too little to bother interfering with the firm management. Economists have formalized this situation as a collective action problem leading individual shareholders to a characteristic state of mind, which is normally referred to as 'rational apathy.' As a result, directors are only in theory fostering shareholders interest. In practice, they are 'captured' by the same managers they are intended to super-vise, since shareholders are too distant and too passive to care about choosing their own representatives.[11] Most legal scholars on both sides of the Atlantic have bought this account at face value. In law and economics, the basic prob-lem of corporate governance is how to make directors less dependent on inside management and more accountable to outside shareholders.[12] Indeed, this is the story that we all learned and that we still teach to our students.

There is, however, too little wonder about the facts of corporate governance that that story leaves unexplained. Crudely speaking, why do some legal systems like the American, the Dutch, and (at least to some extent) the British continue to empower directors relative to shareholders precisely when the latter are most weak due to ownership dispersion? Even more strangely, why do shareholders seem to be more willing to invest in the stock market exactly in those countries whose corporate law is most supportive of directors' power? Conversely, why do other systems that prefer to empower shareholders instead of directors (like Swedish and Italian corporate law) end up with concentrated ownership structures and relatively thinner stock markets? Are we sure that what matters is the economic distribution of power and not, rather, the legal one? In fact, the least that can be said is that the two issues are equally impor-tant and closely related (Cools 2005). Assessing whether they are determined by one another and the direction of causality is certainly more complicated.

A few commentators have gained over time some moderate awareness of this problem. On the legal side, Professor Roe (1994) had already suggested long ago that some regulatory factors were indeed responsible for shareholder weakness in the US, even though such a weakness was anyway achieved through dispersion of ownership. The point is that ownership dispersion did not arise by chance in the US. Financial regulation preventing both banking and non-banking institutions from holding controlling stakes in non-financial companies, just when the financial needs of large business became too high to

---

11 See Hart (1995) and on the legal side Macey (2008). Authoritative economists, like Tirole (2006) disagree on grounds that the law is too far away from this outcome and thus the explanation must be more nuanced (e.g. Aghion and Tirole 1997).

12 See e.g. Easterbrook and Fischel (1991), Shleifer and Vishny (1997), and Kraakman et al 2009.

be sustained by otherwise wealthy families, led to the "strong managers–weak owners" situation that still characterize today's corporate America. Professor Black (1990) complemented Roe's analysis with similar arguments. Even though both accounts have more to do with securities regulation than with corporate law, the patterns of corporate governance regulation are 'path-dependent' (Roe 1998; Bebchuk and Roe 1999). At the beginning, political support against powerful financiers (emerging as a backlash to the crisis of the 1930s) only indirectly empowered directors; but then directors became the only interest group able to influence corporate legislation and case-law – as they probably did. As a result, the trend in American directors' empowerment is not likely to be reversed until some other backlash occurs.

Mark Roe (2003) subsequently extended this approach to the comparative analysis, developing a broader 'political' theory of corporate governance. Whether directors or shareholders are empowered in corporate governance is ultimately regarded as a political issue, because law (and especially corporate law) can do little in this respect. Politics determines whether ownership dispersion is induced in the first place, thereby empowering directors. But where the political conditions are not such as to make ownership dispersion affordable for shareholders – for instance, because support for stakeholders is too strong – only concentrated ownership structures can emerge and persist over time, leaving no scope for directors' autonomy. The opportunity to address the question whether directors' empowerment also needs support by legal entitlements was completely missed.

Professor Roe's conservative position on that account is far from unique. Within the general disagreement upon the determinants of corporate ownership structures, almost nobody dares to question the basic Berle and Means insight that managers are empowered just by ownership dispersion. To my knowledge, there are just two exceptions on the legal side and one on the economic side. Among legal scholars, Lucian Bebchuk (2005: 842) made the point that the weakness of American shareholders is not a necessary consequence of dispersion of ownership, but it is "at least in part due to legal rules that insulate management from shareholder intervention." However, he also claimed that further empowerment of shareholders relative to directors would not alter the "existing patterns of ownership," and it would indeed be very advisable for the efficiency of US corporate law.

By taking a comparative approach, Sofie Cools (2005) has carried the argument even further, possibly reversing its policy implications. Dispersion of ownership is itself not sufficient to bring about managerial control because the latter *also* needs to be supported by an appropriate distribution of legal powers between the board of directors and the general meeting of shareholders. This should explain why powerful directors are in charge of American corporate governance, *and then* ownership is dispersed; whereas shareholders have the lion's share of legal powers in most countries of continental Europe, *and then* ownership is concentrated. Ownership structure thus follows the balance of power established by corporate law, not the other way around.

Comparative analysis shows that shareholder empowerment is incompatible with dispersion of ownership, while director empowerment prevents controlling shareholders from taking the lead.

This approach can possibly explain why managerial capitalism has never become ascendant in most countries of continental Europe, but not why controlling shareholders are significantly present in the governance of US listed companies. In addition, the peculiarities of other systems where corporate ownership is often dispersed (as in the Netherlands and in the UK) were not accounted for. But still, the crucial importance of the legal distribution of corporate powers was finally brought to light.

Neither Lucian Bebchuk nor Sofie Cools realized that a similar point was being made by two economists. Professors Becht and Mayer (2001: 5) explicitly claimed that "regulation visibly affects the relationship between ownership and control." At first glance, this proposition may recall the never-ending debate about whether over- or under-regulation is the problem of corporate governance (Becht et al 2007). But in fact it has very little to do with it. Becht and Mayer's contention was rather that regulation (whether there is too much or too little of it) anyway creates biases, and the *direction* of such biases is what really matters. Regulatory biases allocate powers between different agents. They can empower dominant shareholders ('private control bias'), or alternatively prevent or discourage them from exerting ongoing corporate control ('market control bias') to such an extent as to practically shield the managers from their interference ('management control bias'). Nearly all of those biases arise from corporate law, in that it provides – or does not prohibit – devices for separating voting rights from cash flow rights (which empower shareholders), or control rights from voting rights (which empower the managers).

Although they do not explicitly refer to the legal distribution of powers between shareholders and directors, Becht and Mayer simply look at it from a different angle. In fact, 'private control bias' means nothing but shareholder empowerment (again, what we observe in Italy, Sweden, and in many other countries of continental Europe); whereas a 'management control bias' is achieved by either depriving shareholders of some of their entitlements (as in the UK) or directly providing directors with additional ones (as in the US or in the Netherlands). The 'market control bias' appears to be confined in a theoretical limbo with almost no practical relevance (Becht and Mayer 2001: 37). What comparative empirical evidence shows is shareholder control or management control, none of which is ever contestable on the market except in exceptional circumstances. Undeniably, each control pattern is supported by corporate law with a consistent distribution of powers.

4.2.4 How does distribution of powers affect corporate governance?

Having the traditional account of directors' power – dispersion of ownership – dismissed as a matter secondary (and possibly just consequential) to the legal distribution of powers may sound overly exaggerated to many readers. It is. The foregoing review of the legal and the economic thought in point shows something different, namely that managerial control and dispersion of ownership do not simply arise from one another. For that result to emerge, directors' autonomy from shareholders needs also to be supported by a favorable distribution of legal powers. However, managerial control is not just a necessary consequence of directors being favored in the legal balance of corporate powers. Whatever that balance is, directors could not be in charge in the presence of a controlling shareholder. Indeed, even those countries whose corporate law appears to be the most supportive of directors' managing powers (the US, the UK, and the Netherlands) allow for the presence of controlling shareholders – notwithstanding shareholder control being sometimes disfavored. I will further speculate on both the causes and the consequences of corporate law's non-neutrality between shareholder and managerial control later in this chapter. But it should be rather clear by now that corporate control patterns are affected by *both* the legal distribution of powers *and* the ownership structure. Therefore, the two issues must be considered together.

A crucial point for any corporate controller is the power to appoint and to remove directors. This clearly holds for a controlling shareholder. A necessary condition for his being in charge of decision-making is that at least the majority of directors owe their position to his good wishes. The achievement of that result is relatively easy for a shareholder featured with a large share of voting rights. He can easily control resolutions of the general meeting, provided that the vast majority of non-controlling shareholders would never show up there (due to rational apathy), and the few that possibly would are not even together large enough to outvote the controlling shareholder. Regulation can indeed make life more complicated for controlling shareholders, perhaps by constraining his entitlements to appoint and remove members of the board of directors.[13] However, in none of the jurisdictions under consideration (nor, I believe, anywhere else in the world), a controlling shareholder is unable to have his own representatives appointed to the board. Even under the hurdles of the traditional Dutch 'structure regime' – which have been somewhat reduced in recent times – a controlling shareholder might have obstructed the process of board members cooptation or anyway threaten disloyal directors with withholding his support (which they would eventually need) at the general meeting.[14] The dominant position of the controlling shareholders obviously extends to all of the other issues of corporate life (like charter amendments, mergers, and so on) that need to be endorsed by the general meeting.

The managers' position is structurally weaker. Managers do not typically hold large portions of the firm's stock. So let us assume for a moment that they hold none. How can they possibly succeed in having themselves and/or the

---

13 See the discussion on the UK below.
14 See the discussion on the Netherlands below.

people they trust appointed to the board of directors? One option is obviously to place themselves under the authority of a controlling shareholder. As we have just seen, this is indeed the *only* option when there is a controlling shareholder. But what if there is none? Then, Berle and Means had predicted that directors would be automatically in charge and that they would be *de facto* selected by the inside management.[15] However, Berle and Means were wrong in that they posited managerial control being just the consequence of a shareholder power vacuum. Filling in that vacuum is indeed far from automatic. Managers might be unchallenged by a controlling shareholder, but they still need to find a way for having trusted directors (or themselves) appointed to the board and making sure that they are not removed the day after. More often than not, this would require that ongoing support by the general meeting be obtained (unless directors are *not* appointed by the general meeting, as it used to be for some Dutch corporations). The same support is anyway needed to exert corporate control in those instances where any decision has to be approved by the general meeting. Curiously enough, very few commentators – on both the economic and the legal side – have ever wondered how this is actually achieved.

At least as far as I understand the comparative picture, proxy voting is the key word. Proxy voting is a terrific way to exploit shareholders' rational apathy to the managers' advantage, even though this is definitely not the way in which proxy voting is commonly understood. It might seem that proxy voting serves to enhance shareholder democracy, by allowing otherwise rationally apathetic owners to participate in corporate decision-making (Kraakman et al 2009). Upon this account proxy voting was included in the first investor protection index by La Porta et al (1998). However, in the real-world corporate governance there is no such thing as a shareholder democracy. Somebody has to be in charge. And, in this case, this is the one who collects the proxies, not those who send them in (Eisenberg 1989).

In three out of the five countries considered here – the US, the UK, and the Netherlands – managerial control is more frequent than shareholder control.[16] In all of them, corporate law allows directors to collect or otherwise hold proxies from dispersed shareholders *at the company's expenses*. Although this is achieved by different legal arrangements in Anglo-American corporate governance and in the Netherlands (where management control over shareholders' votes does not exactly depend on proxy voting), the result is anyway that shareholder voting is reduced to little more than a formality (see Hellwig

---

15 "In the typical large corporation . . . control does not rest upon legal status. In these companies control is more often *factual* . . . . Such control . . . may be maintained over a long period of years, and as a corporation becomes larger and its ownership more widespread, it tends towards a position of impregnability comparable to that of legal control, a position from which it can be dislodged only by a virtual revolution." Berle and Means (1932: 79–80).

16 See *supra* Chapter 1.

2000). It is in fact directors who cast shareholder votes, subject to the very loose condition that – rationally apathetic! – shareholders do not object. Therefore, it is corporate law and not just dispersion of ownership that enables directors to enjoy ongoing support at the general meeting. This explains not only how directors manage to be appointed (and re-appointed) to the board, but also how they have the upper hand in having other resolutions passed by the general meeting whenever they favor these.

Both in Italy and in Sweden, proxy voting cannot systematically work to the directors' advantage; nor are there other ways for directors to get support at the general meeting unless, of course, they are sponsored by a controlling share-holder. To be sure, proxy solicitation was introduced more than a decade ago in Italian corporate law and it is available under Swedish legislation too. However, in none of these systems are directors (or other constituencies) entitled to collect proxies at the company's expense.[17] In such a situation, directors would risk being voted out at every general meeting and would have practically no way to implement decisions that require shareholder support. Soliciting proxies at their own expense would be clearly too a high price to pay for exerting corporate control. And it is in fact no surprise that such a burdensome regulation of proxy voting has proven unfruitful to both directors and shareholders, at least in Italy. As far as directors are concerned, that simply excludes any possible autonomy from the general meeting. The ultimate reason why managerial control has never emerged as a corporate governance pattern in Italy and in Sweden seems to be then one of *technical infeasibility*. There – as in many other countries, I suppose – corporate law does not allow directors to exert corporate control without the support of a controlling shareholder.

For the sake of brevity and intuitiveness, I have oversimplified the matter. Many more factors are indeed at play in determining the distribution of cor-porate powers. However, the basic intuition holds. Directors' legal empower-ment is a precondition for the emergence of managerial control. Where directors are not entitled to exploit shareholders' rational apathy through a favorable discipline of voting at the general meeting, a controlling shareholder shall be practically the only option for corporate governance. This proposition is only based upon consideration for shareholder voting, thereby including just one part – albeit the fundamental one – of the organizational discipline of the general meeting. It has therefore to be supplemented with other important organization and competence features of corporate law that affect the distribution of power between the board of directors and the general meeting of shareholders. Adequate consideration for all those features requires a rather in-depth investigation that cannot be performed cross-country. By the country analysis that follows, I shall be able to uncover consistent paths of either director or shareholder empowerment in corporate law.

---

17   To be sure the new Swedish Company law allows companies to bear the expenses of voting by mail (Skog and Fäger 2007). However, this option cannot likely be used by directors in order to support their own reappointment. See the discussion on Sweden below.

4.3 Legal underpinnings of managerial control

4.3.1 Directors autonomy in the US

In the US, directors are quite well known for being the most powerful category of players in corporate governance, perhaps immediately followed by corporate lawyers (Paredes 2004). The (intuitively legal) reasons underlying the latter belief will become clear in the following chapters. As far as directors are concerned, their power basically depends on the ability of the board to control the outcomes of the general meeting, provided that shareholders remain dispersed, and to entrench its members, should shareholders ever dare to coalesce their power.[18] It is in fact a combination of organizational rules (shareholder voting procedures) and competence rules (initiation rights and takeover defenses) that makes corporate directors so powerful in the US. While the former set of rules allows directors to exert ongoing control over the firm management, the latter makes sure they can keep such control uncontested.

4.3.1.1 Directors appointment: the US proxy voting system

Once directors are in charge (let us suppose they were appointed before the firm went public) their basic concern is being re-elected. The default rule in US corporate law is that directors are elected by a plurality, not strictly by a majority, of the votes cast at the general meeting provided that a quorum is present in person or represented by proxy.[19] Directors must normally be up for election *every year*. There is one important exception to this rule, when the board is 'classified' (or 'staggered'); among other things, this implies that each

---

18 This has been brilliantly illustrated by Professor Bebchuk in a series of articles, including *inter alia*: Bebchuk et al (2002), Bebchuk (2003b), Bebchuk (2005). Cools (2005) takes stock of Bebchuk's work for analyzing the matter from a different and, in a sense, opposite angle.

19 Under Delaware law, the default quorum of general meetings is the majority of the shares entitled to vote; it cannot be lower than one-third. DGCL § 216. Other jurisdictions are more flexible (see e.g. MBCA § 7.25). In the election of directors, the general rule is plurality voting. See DGCL § 216 and MBCA § 7.28. This was efficaciously illustrated by Joseph Grundfest (see Bebchuk 2003c):

> What is interesting is the way Delaware law works, and every state law of which I'm aware works, is that a director needs to be elected by a plurality. That means that if a million shares count as a quorum, and if 999,999 ballots strike your name out and say no, you, as the director, owning only one share, and you vote for yourself, congratulations, you win. You have the plurality.

An amendment of Delaware law in 2006 made opting in to majority voting somewhat easier. Plurality is still the default rule, but this may be changed through a shareholder bylaw that directors cannot repeal. See DGCL § 216. Since 2006 a large number of companies, including about two-thirds of S&P 500 companies, have opted in to majority voting (Yermack 2010).

director's term of office is extended up to three years.[20] Staggered boards will be discussed later, though, since in the US they are more a takeover defense than a device for facilitating director re-appointment. Proxy solicitation is instead one such device.[21]

Every year directors solicit proxies from dispersed shareholders by sending them a form that carries their own nominations to the board. Individual shareholders may return the proxy form with their signed approval, totally or partially deny their consent, abstain, or they may simply not return the form. What shareholders cannot do is to vote for other candidates. This is not possible unless an independent proxy solicitation is promoted *in opposition* to the board or shareholders propose alternative nominees by showing up *in person* at the general meeting – which they will never do as long as they are dispersed (Donald 2004). Opposition would involve a contested vote (i.e., a so-called proxy fight) which, for the reasons that will be clarified shortly, occurs very infrequently in the US (and almost never in the rest of the world) (Kraakman et al 2009). Traditionally, in the US, corporate elections are uncontested and incumbent directors are routinely reappointed under the loose condition that a sufficient number of shareholders return their proxy (Blair and Stout 1999).

Since returning the proxy does not cost shareholders more than a signature (postage is also paid for), many individual investors and most institutional ones always return their proxies unless they have something to object to the incumbent management. Traditionally, dissident shareholders (both individual and institutional) would sell their shares rather than voice their opposition (Easterbrook and Fischel 1991). Meeting the quorum in an uncontested election is, then, not a problem. In addition, shareholders are not likely to do more than to sign the form (thereby conferring a vast amount of discretion upon soliciting directors) because any other course of action would involve additional decision-making costs they are normally not willing to bear. Even shareholder failure to support directors would not change the outcome of the general meeting provided that alternative candidates cannot be voted for. Because directors are traditionally elected by a plurality of the votes, a "mere abstention or a vote against a proposed candidate will not be sufficient to prevent her election" (Cools 2005: 746). To be sure, even each director's group of votes for his own share ownership would suffice to make a plurality, provided that enough shares are represented by proxy to count as a quorum. Proxy voting is therefore a rather complicated mechanism through which American directors are quite easily re-appointed. It should be noticed that

20 DGCL § 141 and MBCA § 8.06.
21 Most shareholders of a publicly held corporation would not vote if not by proxy. Proxy voting is a distinctive feature of US corporate governance. It is regulated at both the state and the federal level. By and large, state law governs the "substantive aspects" of proxy voting, whereas federal law takes care of the procedure of proxy solicitation under § 14(a) of the Securities Exchange Act of 1934 (Bainbridge 2002: 439–517).

proxy voting also costs nothing to the directors: US corporate law places upon the company the heavy burden of expenses of proxy solicitations promoted by the incumbent board.[22]

In recent years, the emergence of activist shareholders and a number of changes in the attitude of institutional investors as well as in the regulations seem to have altered the above picture (Yermack 2010). Partly thanks to advisory services like those provided by ISS-Riskmetrics, institutional investors have started to withhold their votes from the election of certain directors. This development has paralleled the pressure to opt out of the plurality rule, particularly after Delaware had clarified the possibility to do so via a shareholder bylaw (Ventoruzzo 2011). As a result, listed companies have increasingly adopted majority rules in elections and refrained from appointing directors not supported by a clear majority of shareholders (Kahan and Rock 2011). Other regulatory measures have enhanced shareholders, say, in corporate elections. As of 2010, the NYSE has repealed an old rule conferring upon stockbrokers the power to vote the shares of their depositors at elections in the absence of specific instructions; as a matter of routine brokers used to rubberstamp the board's proposals.

In addition, the Dodd-Frank Act 2010 had explicitly conferred upon the Securities and Exchange Commission (SEC) the authority to introduce proxy access, namely the ability of shareholders to make nominations that the board would be obliged to include in the annual proxy materials.[23] However, the SEC Rule 14a-11 introducing mandatory proxy access never came into force because the US Court of Appeals for the DC circuit struck it down.[24] In the end, only SEC Rule 14a-8(i)(8) remained in place, allowing shareholders to introduce proxy access by making a binding proposal to that effect. It is worth noting that Delaware had introduced a similar option one year before the Dodd-Frank Act came into force (Ventoruzzo 2011). Perhaps because of the uncertainties regarding the application of federal law this option was not used in practice. Whether and to what extent individual companies will effectively opt in to proxy access via SEC Rule 14a-8(i)(8) is not yet known at the time of writing.

The proxy access debate has been heated for many years.[25] To be sure, even if more shareholder involvement in elections was always welcome, which is itself controversial (Macey 2008), the merits of proxy access would be unclear. Shareholders can achieve many of the intended goals of proxy access in cheaper and more effective manners (Kahan and Rock 2011). If that is the case, the most important change that has occurred over the last few years is the ability

---

22 Rosenfeld v. Fairchild Engine and Airplane Corp., 128 N.E.2d 291 (N.Y.1955).
23 On the remainder of corporate governance provisions included in the Dodd-Frank Act 2010 see, critically, Bainbridge (2011).
24 Business Roundtable and Chamber of Commerce of the United States of America v. Securities and Exchange Commission, No 10-1305 (DC Cir 22 July 2011).
25 Compare e.g. Bebchuk (2003b) with Bainbridge (2006).

of shareholders to signal their discomfort by withholding their vote. While this is an important means of communication between shareholders and management, vote withholding is typically insufficient to prevent the board from appointing their candidates (Ventoruzzo 2011). Directors experiencing significant withholding of votes may be induced to step down or individually choose to do so, perhaps with conspicuous severance payments. However, the norm that directors cannot be replaced in US corporate governance remains unchanged in the absence of proxy access established as a default if not a mandatory rule (Bebchuk and Hirst 2010). This is not likely to happen very soon in the US.

4.3.1.2 Decisions by the general meeting of shareholders

Proxy voting is not only a way for directors to be re-appointed to office. Proxy voting also helps to have resolutions passed by the general meeting when the law or the charter requires that certain decisions be upheld by shareholders. Here the matter is more complicated because this kind of resolutions must always be voted by majority and not by plurality.[26] In addition, motions involving charter amendments or other so-called 'fundamental' corporate transactions need to be endorsed by the majority of the votes carried by *outstanding* shares, no matter how many of them are represented at the general meeting.[27] Directors, then, always run the risk of being unable to summon enough favorable votes through proxy solicitation to have their decision affirmed by the general meeting. However, they do not also run the risk of being outvoted by a *different* proposal, for American shareholders practically have no power to place motions on the agenda of the general meeting whose endorsement would be binding on directors (Cools 2005: 741–742). This statement suffers only two exceptions: director removal, which will be discussed in the next subsection; and bylaws amendment, which can be adopted unilaterally by shareholders or the board of directors but are always subordinated to the corporate charter. As regards the other issues that might be brought to the attention of the general meeting of shareholders, a few qualifications are in order.

Major structural changes like charter amendments, mergers, substantial sale of assets, and dissolution can only be initiated by the board of directors, who therefore enjoy a veto right on such matters (Bebchuk 2005). In theory, shareholders can also veto directors' proposals by refusing to return the majority of proxy votes with their approval (Kraakman et al 2009: 186). In

26 Plurality is the default rule only for directors' election. In general, resolutions are passed by the majority of the votes cast at the meeting, provided that a quorum is present in person or by proxy. Compare DGCL § 216 (abstentions count as NO) with MBCA § 7.25 (abstentions are ignored).

27 DGCL §§ 242, 251, 271 (majority of outstanding shares); MBCA §§ 10.03, 11.04, 12.02 (majority of the shares entitled to vote).

practice, this might possibly depend on rational apathy (when accounting for more than 50% of voting rights), but it is seldom due to a knowledgeable dissent unless the directors' proposal is noticeably outrageous.[28] Only in the last case may the proposal find such a widespread opposition that it has no chance of being passed. The introduction of classified (staggered) boards by charter amendment is one prominent example in this regard (Bebchuk 2003a). Dissent could otherwise be summoned by a proxy contest. This option is often mentioned in legal textbooks under the name of 'issue contest' to have it distinguished from the typical instance of a proxy fight, the 'control contest', where directors' election is in question (Bebchuk and Kahn 1990). However, since in that case all expenses of proxy solicitations against a board proposal have to be definitively borne by their promoters, issue contests are basically unheard of in American corporate practice. In conclusion, directors have the exclusive right to initiate a structural change, whereas dispersed shareholders have little power to vote it down.

For any other matter, US directors usually do not need shareholder support (Bainbridge 2008). Perhaps the most cited provision of Delaware corporate law is that the corporation "shall be managed by or under the direction of a board of directors."[29] By such a statement, shareholder involvement is basically ruled out of corporate governance to the extent it is not restored by specific statutory or charter provisions. Neither the former nor the latter – whose amendments, as we have just seen, are in the end under directors' control – provide for much further involvement of shareholders in corporate decision-making (Bebchuk 2007). Nonetheless, regulation provides shareholders with at least one way to make their voice heard by directors, even though directors are not compelled to listen. This is the 'shareholder proposal' under Rule 14a-8 of the Federal Proxy Regulations.[30]

Under a number of relatively tolerant eligibility and procedural requirements, shareholders are entitled to place items on the agenda of the general meeting and to have them included, with a brief supporting statement, in the proxy material circulated by the board of directors *at the company's expense*. Piggybacking is the basic advantage of a shareholder proposal compared to an issue contest. However, while an 'expensive' issue contest might at least lead to a (negative) resolution binding directors against their will, 'cheap' shareholder proposals are usually not binding regardless of how large the support that they receive at the general meeting is.[31] This is due to one fundamental ground for excluding the proposal: that is, it being 'improper'

---

28 For a review of the empirical evidence that shareholders still tend to vote with the management, see Yermack (2010).
29 DGCL § 141(a).
30 See SEC Rule 14a-8, promulgated under § 14(a) of the Securities Exchange Act of 1934.
31 There are important exceptions. For instance, SEC Rule 14a-8(i)(8) – discussed above – allows shareholders to introduce a proxy access via a binding shareholder proposal (bylaw amendment).

under state law (Cools 2005: 742). Since state corporate laws commit most power of initiating shareholder action to the board of directors, the SEC has recognized that proposals of a mandatory resolution may be regarded as improper and thus recommended that they be framed in a precatory form.[32] As a result, directors often feel free to ignore resolutions arising out of a shareholder proposal, including one of the most popular: removing board classification (Bebchuk and Hirst 2010).

4.3.1.3 *Directors removal: staggered boards*

Little wonder that such a powerful directorship should be easily brought to an end. In theory, directors can be removed anytime in the US, with or without cause.[33] In practice, however, something like that hardly ever happens in the US. Midterm removal is constrained by the ability of shareholders to summon a special meeting to this purpose – which is excluded under Delaware law, unless otherwise provided for in the charter.[34] In addition, director removal without cause is just the *default* provision.[35] Yet directors can only be removed *with cause* when a classified board structure is adopted, and this happens to be true for the *majority* of US publicly held corporations.[36] Board classification involves that board members are divided into up to three classes. Every year, only one class of directors is up for election, so that board members' term of office is 'staggered.' Since midterm removal is practically excluded, directors of a typical staggered board stay in charge for three years. At first glance, this may seem just a postponement of their destiny. However, staggering also prevents shareholders from replacing *all* board members at once. As such, staggered boards can be a source of board entrenchment against hostile takeovers. This outcome may not necessarily be bad for some companies, particularly if they have chosen it.

Incumbency provides US directors with all the advantages that I have just reviewed. Still, they may lose the annual elections in a contested vote aimed at replacing them. There are two possibilities. One is to have incumbent directors outvoted in a proxy contest. The other one is to have them replaced by a shareholder taking over firm control. Staggered boards ensure that an insurgent shareholder has to win two consecutive proxy contests to gain control of the majority of the board; under US corporate law, only after an

---

32 Note to SEC Rule 14a-8(i)(1).
33 At common law, directors could only be removed for cause. However, this has been superseded by statutory law. See DGCL § 141; MBCA § 8.08.
34 DGCL § 211(d) allows for special meetings to be called only by the board and any other person explicitly authorized by the articles or bylaws. MBCA § 7.02(a)(1) also empowers the holders of at least 10% of the voting shares to call a special meeting.
35 Options available to the corporate charters slightly differ across US jurisdictions. Compare MBCA § 8.08 with DGCL § 141(k).
36 Bebchuk and Cohen (2005). See also Bebchuk and Hirst (2010: 344) for updated information.

insurgent has succeeded might he have a chance of being reimbursed of the huge proxy solicitation expenses (Bainbridge 2002). Takeovers would seem to be a fairly better option, if directors were not entitled to resist hostile bids – which in fact they are. Having either voting power or share ownership (or both) coalesced against directors is, then, far from easy in the US.

Proxy contests used to be very popular among academics in the past, and that contributed to the widespread belief that proxy voting could work to the shareholders' advantage. Then Professor Manne (1965: 114) famously described proxy fights as "the most expensive, the most uncertain, and the least used of the various techniques" for control acquisition and advocated takeovers as the really important tool of both managerial discipline and efficient control allocation in the US. In fact, he only advocated the merits of fully-fledged acquisitions over proxy contests, without making a case for hostile takeovers – which he regarded as inferior to negotiated mergers.[37] But this is not the point. Hostile takeovers were extremely popular in the US during the 1980s, in the face of the economic and legal hurdles that proxy contests were actually confronted with. Afterwards, things changed slightly as far as proxy contests are concerned and most significantly with regard to hostile takeovers.[38] Today, proxy fights seem to have somehow resurrected in connection with initially hostile bids. The liberal attitude of Delaware courts and of many other states' legislation towards takeover defenses has made hostile bids almost impossible to succeed without first taking control of the board and of his exclusive entitlements (Bainbridge 2002). However, even a combination of a hostile bid with a proxy contest would be ultimately frustrated by a staggered board. This is how most hostile bids in the US only manage to go through, ultimately, as friendly deals.

A proxy contest alone is a quite inconvenient option for insurgent shareholders: they risk losing too much when they are unsuccessful and gaining too little when they are successful (Bebchuk and Kahan 1990). In the former case, they will have to bear all the expenses of the proxy solicitation. In the latter, they will be reimbursed if both the (new) board and the general meeting so decide. But, still, what is in it for them? Should they manage the firm any better than the earlier directors, all the other shareholders will free ride (Grossman and Hart 1980). Taking from the firm's profit any larger share than their pro-rata would involve a breach of fiduciary duties. As we will see, there duties are quite well enforced in the US. Takeovers work differently. If there is no impediment, a successful insurgent will not only take control of the board, but also become the owner of the company (technically, by having it merged in another one that he owns entirely). By this strategy, a would-be acquirer seeks to appropriate a significant part, if not all, of the takeover gains.

---

37 "[Friendly] mergers seem in many instances to be the most efficient of the three devices for corporate takeovers." Manne (1965: 119).
38 Hostile takeovers have basically disappeared from the US since then. See Holmström and Kaplan (2001).

Impediments to this strategy are created by making the acquisition of a large stake in the company unsuitable for takeover or just unprofitable to the prospective bidder. Takeover defenses are aimed exactly at that purpose.

4.3.1.4 *Takeover defenses in the US*

A comprehensive review of defensive techniques and their statutory and case-law regulation in the US would be too lengthy to be undertaken here.[39] However, one would not exaggerate by saying that in many situations an incumbent board can 'just say no' to any unwanted takeover bid. Even though neither Delaware courts – the most director-friendly and, at any rate, the most important corporate jurisdiction in the US – nor state anti-takeover statutes have ever put it so bluntly, this is how many commentators depict the state of American law regarding takeover defenses.[40]

Let us consider just the most notorious weapon within the wide directors' arsenal: the 'poison pill.' The pill's official name is 'shareholder rights plan.' Basically, the plan entitles *existing shareholders* to purchase stock either of the target or of the bidding company (after a merger has been performed) for a consideration well below market price (say, a half of it), thereby diluting both voting power and cash flow rights of the aggressor. "Boards can adopt this pill without a shareholder vote and at any time, even *after* a hostile bid has been launched (the 'shadow pill' or 'morning after pill') if they do not already have one at that time" (Cools 2005: 748). Pills can be more or less poisonous, but takeovers can hardly succeed once the shareholder rights plan has been implemented and until those rights are not redeemed. Only the board of directors has the authority to redeem the pill (Bainbridge 2002).

One extreme form of pill, unredeemable by anybody but the *incumbent* directors ('dead hand' or 'no hand' pill), was invalidated by Delaware case-law.[41] Apart from that, Delaware courts are of the opinion that directors are under no duty to redeem the pill in the face of a hostile bid. In the implementation of defensive tactics, they enjoy the protection of the 'business judgment rule' (that basically shield directors' discretionary authority from judicial review), provided that the presumptive requirements of directors' fiduciary duties are met.[42] In a nutshell, this involves that takeover resistance is allowed under the business judgment rule if, after a reasonable investigation by the board of directors, it proves commensurate to the threat posed to

---

39 See Bainbridge (2002) for an overview.

40 See e.g. Bebchuk et al (2002); Gordon (2002); and Kahan and Rock (2002).

41 Carmody v. Toll Bros., Inc., 723 A.2d 1180 (Del.Ch.1998); Mentor Graphics Corp. v. Quickturn Design Sys., Inc., 728 A.2d 25 (Del.Ch.1998); Quickturn Design Sys., Inc. v. Shapiro, 721 A.2d 1281 (Del.Sup.1998).

42 In the takeover context, the operation of the business judgment rule is somewhat 'special.' See Hamilton (2000: 460–463).

the corporation (the *Unocal* standard).[43] Such a threat may simply consist of shareholders being potentially misled in the decision whether to tender their shares (the *Time* ruling, often referred to as 'just say no' rule).[44] The proportionality test for enjoying protection of the business judgment rule is therefore satisfied within a quite extensive 'range of reasonableness' (the *QVC* ruling).[45] Such a test anyway excludes 'draconian' defensive provisions (those which are 'preclusive' of any change in control – *Unitrin*);[46] and it is replaced by a more stringent standard when the company is *already* put up for sale (in which case the board should behave like a neutral auctioneer – *Revlon*).[47]

What apparently Delaware judges only care about is that shareholders are not deprived forever of a takeover premium: that is, that the market for corporate control is not definitively set aside by board entrenchment.[48] Provided that a control sale is always possible either now or in the future, the courts have shown little objection so far to the board deciding if, when, and on what terms it should be implemented.[49] Takeover defenses have thus to be regarded as a device for having takeovers most often (if not always) negotiated with incumbent directors, who retain a great deal of discretion on redeeming poison pills and similar impediments to a change in control.[50]

A prospective bidder would still be able to bypass directors' resistance by taking control of the board and redeeming the poison pill himself. This could be done by a proxy contest immediately followed by a takeover bid (Bebchuk and Hart 2001). Staggered boards are there just to make this strategy overly burdensome and often impracticable. An insurgent shareholder would have to win two elections before he can gain the majority of the board seats and redeem the pill. In the meantime, he would have to keep his bid open to outstanding shareholders. Even without considering the risk of losing one or both of the elections – which would involve bearing all the expenses of the procedure – it is quite clear that a staggered board has a "powerful antitakeover force" (Bebchuk et al 2002). Nor would any insurgent shareholder ever be able to de-stagger it, since charter amendments can only be initiated by the board itself.[51]

---

43 Unocal Corp. v. Mesa Petroleum Co., 493 A.2d 946 (Del.Sup.1985).
44 Paramount Communications, Inc. v. Time, Inc., 571 A.2d 1140 (Del.Sup.1989).
45 Paramount Communications, Inc. v. QVC Network, Inc., 637 A.2d 34 (Del.Sup.1994).
46 Unitrin, Inc. v. American General Corp., 651 A.2d 1361 (Del.Sup.1995).
47 Revlon, Inc. v. MacAndrews and Forbes Holdings, Inc., 506 A.2d 173 (Del.Sup.1986).
48 As Professor Gordon (2002: 820) put it, 'just say no' should be distinguished from 'just say never,' which is not legal in Delaware. 'Just say no' is "perhaps better characterized as 'just say later'."
49 Bainbridge (2002: 705–738). This approach has been confirmed recently in Air Products and Chemicals, Inc. v. Airgas, Inc., C.A. No. 5249-CC (Del.Ch. Feb 15, 2011).
50 The propriety of takeover resistance by the board of directors has been a long-standing matter of debate in the US law and economics scholarship. See, illustratively, Easterbrook and Fischel (1991: 162–211). But see also Gilson (1982) and Bebchuk (1982).
51 During the recent battle for the control of Airgas, shareholders sought to de-stagger a board via a bylaw amendment (aimed at shortening the term of office). While the Chancery

In conclusion, the power of US directors can be both unfettered on an ongoing basis and unchallengeable by means of a takeover. Corporate law supports this outcome. Individual companies would be free to opt out, in all or in part, of this default regime. However, the circumstance that very few companies opt out of antitakeover devices (Daines and Klausner 2001) while some do opt in to these (Listokin 2009) suggests that entrenchment has some value for US companies.

4.3.2 *The disfavor for controlling shareholders in the UK*

For some time legal and economic commentators considered the American and the British systems of corporate governance relatively similar to each other,[52] but economists on both sides of the Atlantic later realized that this is not entirely the case.[53] Comparative lawyers also remedied the misconception by uncovering fundamental differences between corporate law in the US and in the UK.[54] For our purposes, it is sufficient to say that regulation of corporate governance is far more shareholder-friendly in the UK than in the US. However, as far as publicly held companies are concerned, this proposition holds rather for non-controlling shareholders than for shareholders 'as a class.' Since both theory and practice show that shareholder interference with firm management can only be an issue when corporate control is at stake (that is, non-controlling shareholders are rationally apathetic), British law is *not neutral* between shareholder control and managerial control.[55] Regulatory disfavor for controlling shareholders may be ultimately responsible for directors' empowerment in British publicly held firms. Non-controlling shareholders seem to have a great power in the UK, but they have hardly any incentive to exercise it – at least for control purposes. In Britain, directors are still the most favored category of players in corporate governance but, differently from the US, they need also to be 'non-controlling' shareholders to some extent, for otherwise they would have no way to resist an unwanted takeover attempt.[56]

Court upheld the bylaw in Airgas, Inc. v. Air Products and Chemicals, Inc., C.A. No. 5817-CC (Del.Ch. Oct 8, 2010), the Supreme Court reversed that ruling and invalidated the bylaw as conflicting with the charter. Airgas, Inc. v. Air Products and Chemicals, Inc., C.A. No. 5817-CC (Del.Sup. Nov 23, 2010).

52 See e.g. La Porta et al (1998); Hansmann and Kraakman (2001).

53 See Djankov et al (2008) and Franks and Mayer (2002).

54 See Kraakman et al (2009) and, specifically on takeover regulation, Armour and Skeel (2007).

55 This proposition is highly controversial. I have argued that UK investor protection is not neutral in Pacces (2011). See also Becht and Mayer (2001).

56 See Franks et al (2001) on the importance of insider ownership for management entrenchment in the UK.

4.3.2.1 *Director appointment and removal: the silent role of British institutional investors*

As in the US, reappointment of British directors is basically obtained through the proxy voting system (see Davies 2008). British law allows directors to solicit proxies from outstanding shareholders at the company's expenses. To be sure, they might not even need it. Uncontroversial resolutions can be taken at the general meeting by a show of hands. When proxies are not counted, the majority of the *people* present at the meeting win. Directors voting as shareholders normally count as such a majority, since fewer outside shareholders ever show up at the general meeting and quorum requirements are basically nonexistent under company law of the UK.[57] The importance of voting on a show of hands should not be exaggerated, though. Voting in a pool can always be demanded at the general meeting, and then the weight of both share ownership and proxy votes would be restored.[58] Unless the issues to be decided at the meeting are contentious, directors would not worry much anyway because they still hold on their own shares and on outside shareholders' proxies.

Proxy voting *normally* confers upon directors enough voting power to count as a majority or even as a super-majority when it is required by the law or the charter to have a resolution passed by the general meeting. However, this does not also involve that directors will *always* manage to pass any resolution they wish. Differently from those of their American colleagues, both the position and propositions of British directors can be contested.[59] In fact, however, very seldom are they. The credible threat of being outvoted is sufficient for directors to refrain from any action that would not receive support by outside shareholders and (here is the most important difference from the US!) may also lead to their replacement (see Black and Coffee 1994).

Removing directors is much easier in the UK than in the US. This might seem counterintuitive at first glance. British company law does not set any mandatory term of office, even though the UK Corporate Governance Code recommends a period no longer than three years which becomes one year for the FTSE 350 companies (Hopt 2011).[60] British boards may be staggered as the American ones and often they are. Finally, it is unclear whether proxy contestants would be entitled to any reimbursement even in the case of success – and, at any rate, proxy contests are unheard of in British corporate governance (Kraakman et al 2009). A limited handful of company law rules

---

57 In the UK the default quorum for the validity of general meetings is ridiculous: two people present either in person or by proxy, § 318 of CA 2006.
58 See Davies (2008: 460–463).
59 Differently from the US, proxies must be three-way in the UK (i.e., they have to provide shareholders with equal opportunity to vote *for* and *against* proposed resolutions; or to *abstain* altogether). See Davies (2008: 456) and LR 9.3.6.
60 FTSE 350 companies are the 350 largest companies by market capitalization having their primary listing in London.

apparently suffices to offset all this. One key mandatory provision of the 2006 Companies Act is § 168 (formerly § 303 of the 1985 Companies Act). This rule stipulates that directors can be removed at *any time* and *without cause* by a resolution of the general meeting of shareholders. Under British law, shareholders accounting for at least 10% of voting rights can always summon an extraordinary meeting for this purpose.[61] Alternatively, shareholders accounting for 5% or more of the voting rights may piggyback the circulation of proxy materials for the annual meeting, and no restriction is established as to the contents of the shareholder proposal.[62] However, because of mismatch between the special notice requirements of a removal resolution and the timing of piggybacking, in practice this has not been an option to replace directors cheaply.[63] Provided that the expense of soliciting suffrages for directors' removal cannot be spared anyhow, it is doubtful whether it would be any convenience for disgruntled shareholders to wait for the annual meeting when they can get rid of directors earlier.

Indeed, the crucial question is a different one. Who will do the deed and put together sufficient votes to oust incumbent directors, given the collective action problem faced by shareholders? In practice, it seems that directors are hardly ever removed by a shareholder resolution in the UK. This is consistent with the standard account of rational apathy of non-controlling shareholders. And yet, directors resign. They do it not only after a takeover – a situation that will be considered shortly – but also in the case of considerable underperformance or mischief (Franks et al 2001). It is exactly in these rather extreme situations that directors no longer enjoy the *silent support of institutional investors*. One should mention here that institutional investors are the largest shareholders of the typical British listed company, and that on average they jointly account for more than 20% of each firm's share capital (Goergen and Renneboog 2001). Together, they are powerful enough to give a hard time to directors. In practice, such a struggle would be in the interest of no one. Institutional investors would lose their time and money, and directors their most valuable asset – reputation. Institutional action therefore takes place behind closed doors (Black and Coffee 1994). Major investors in the firm talk to its non-executive directors; executives that no longer enjoy institutional support are then induced to resign by the board; and finally, the board itself fills in the vacancies and has the replacements endorsed by the next annual meeting (Stapledon 1996). This mechanism works entirely through 'moral suasion,' but always 'in the shadow of the law.' It is in fact § 168 (formerly § 303) of the Companies Act that makes the removal threat so credible that it never needs to be actually implemented (Cheffins 2008).

---

61 § 303 CA 2006.
62 § 314 CA 2006.
63 The picture has not changed substantially with the 2006 Companies Act. See Davies (2008: 449).

The reader should be cautioned that the above situation is rather the exception than the rule. Institutional investors usually do not interfere with how the firm is managed until the value of their investment is seriously endangered. All over the world, institutional investors acknowledge that choosing the management team is beyond their task and expertise. Indeed, the market should do the job (Macey 2008).[64] This is no different in the UK, where in fact, as we have just seen, it is still the board that replaces the executives whom institutions are dissatisfied with. Normally, British institutions sign in their proxy to the incumbent board and that is sufficient to have its members routinely re-elected at the annual meeting. Other shareholders are collectively too dispersed and individually too small to outvote directors; unless, of course, they are or they become controlling shareholders. I shall turn to this in a moment.

4.3.2.2 *Passing shareholder resolutions at the general meeting*

It is worth nothing that, similarly to the US, the proxy voting system in the UK also allows directors to have resolutions passed by the general meeting that do not concern their election. This is even more important for governing a British listed firm than an American one, since the statutory competences of the general meeting are wider (even though not as much as in most countries of continental Europe), and they can be enlarged at will by the charter and its subsequent amendments (Kraakman et al 2009). One prominent example in this regard is the approval of significant transactions involving one or more director's conflict of interest – an issue that will be deeply investigated in the next two chapters. The position of British directors is, then, apparently weaker than that of their American colleagues, for they risk being unable to control the firm if they cannot get shareholder support for some matters requiring endorsement by the general meeting. The picture might look even worse if one considers that, under British company law, some of these resolutions also require a three-quarters super-majority and directors have by no means exclusive initiation rights (Davies 2008).

Difficulties are more apparent than real. Shareholders may indeed initiate any resolution they wish, but when this overrides directors' competence a three-quarters majority is *always* required. However, majorities are established with reference to the votes cast;[65] and – as I mentioned – the meetings whereby resolutions are approved have in fact no meaningful quorum whoever initiates them.[66] When ownership is dispersed, the majority of the votes are cast by proxy and only directors are entitled to solicit proxies cheaply. Unsurprisingly, then, only directors can have a super-majority resolution

64 But on shareholder activism see, recently, Becht et al (2009) and Yermack (2010).
65 § 283 of CA 2006. The complicated distinction between extraordinary and special resolutions was abolished by the 2006 Act (which maintained only the latter category).
66 § 318 of CA 2006.

passed when there is no controlling shareholder and, as in the US, proxy voting is the reason.

On both sides of the Atlantic board-initiated resolutions can be possibly voted down. In the UK, this would require institutional shareholders withdrawing their consent from the board and positively *voting* against its proposals. As a matter of fact, this only happens in two situations: when institutions realize that they have been cheated; and when the outcome of the resolution would be against the policy matters they have agreed upon for protecting their own rights as shareholders (Stapledon 1996). This explains why British boards never manage to have pre-emption rights waived or dual class shares, pyramiding, and pre-bid takeover defenses introduced for enhancing their control power (and, to be sure, they do not even dare to do these things) (Cheffins 2008).

4.3.2.3 *Takeover resistance and the regulatory burden of being a controlling shareholder*

Directors' empowerment in the UK ultimately depends on the absence of a controlling shareholder. Not only does this mean that when a controlling shareholder is already in place directors must defer to his authority, it also involves that the UK directors' position is constantly endangered by the risk that a controlling shareholder emerges and takes over the firm.

Differently from their American colleagues, British directors are not entitled to any defensive strategy. In essence, pre-bid defenses have been ruled out by the opposition of institutional investors (Cheffins 2008). The City Panel on Takeovers and Mergers provides for the rest, by prohibiting directors from engaging in defensive tactics other than seeking a competitive bid after a tender offer has been made – unless shareholders approve resistance, which they would hardly do if they are offered a significant takeover premium.[67] Therefore, it could seem that the legal system is very favorable to hostile takeovers in the UK and that managers can do little to prevent shareholder insurgency (Becht et al 2007). Surprisingly, however, over 90% of takeovers in the UK are friendly, that is, they are implemented with the board's consent (Weir and Laing 2003). In addition, empirical evidence suggests that board members can entrench themselves by forming informal voting coalitions to resist an unwanted takeover (Crespi and Renneboog 2010).

The question is how is this *legally* possible? The answer probably lies in an often-overlooked regulatory bias against controlling shareholders.[68] Being unable to resist takeovers on their own, British directors can still exploit such a bias to their advantage. Regulation of listed companies in the UK includes rules affecting any owner (or a group of owners acting in concert) who either

---

67 Rule 21 of the City Code on Takeovers and Mergers (September 2011).
68 Few commentators acknowledge the existence of such a bias. See e.g. Becht and Mayer 2001.

qualifies as 'substantial shareholder' in that he controls the exercise of at least 10% of votes,[69] or else wishes to acquire more than 30% of voting power. On the one hand, a controlling shareholder's relationship with the firm has to be at 'arm's length,' meaning that – among other things – he shall not be entitled to appoint more than a *minority* of board members nor shall he be able to remove other members unless a majority of independent directors consent.[70] On the other hand, any attempt to acquire more than 30% of voting rights triggers a mandatory bid for all outstanding shares at the highest price paid within the twelve-month period before the threshold is surpassed.[71] None of these constraints is established by the Companies Act. They are nonetheless binding on listed firms, either via the rules of the City Panel on Takeovers and Mergers or because of the significant pressure by institutional investors not to depart from the letter of the UK Corporate Governance Code (Arcot et al 2010; Armour 2010). Misdisclosure concerning the application of the code can be sanctioned by the Financial Services Authority (FSA).[72]

Being a controlling shareholder can be quite inconvenient in the UK. In spite of the large stake in the company ownership, a controlling shareholder may be ultimately unable to control the board decision-making. This used to be a straightforward implication of the Listing Rules for holdings larger than 30%,[73] which in a sense explains the rarity of controlling shareholders larger than 30% in the UK (Goergen and Renneboog 2001). The current regulation of listed firms in Britain does not explicitly rule out control by a dominant shareholder. However, in practice, any shareholder accounting for more than 10% of voting rights would face hurdles in exerting control. First, the Listing Rules compel this 'substantial' shareholder to seek independent approval of all significant related-party transactions by the general meeting.[74] Second, as

---

69 See LR, Appendix 1, Relevant definitions.
70 Becht and Mayer (2001) and Wymeersch (2003) first made this point referring to the former LR 3.12 (2003), which was subsequently repealed. So formally the Listing Rules do no longer require that the board operates independently of a controlling shareholder. This requirement is now only included in the UK Corporate Governance Code (recommending that, except for smaller companies, the majority of the board be independent of a "significant shareholder" – see provisions B.1.1 and B.1.2). Formally the code is not binding and operates on a comply-or-explain basis. But as I illustrate in Pacces (2011), a recent case study (EasyJet) shows that a dominant shareholder may have to refrain from taking control of the board in order to show the institutional investors that he complies with the code.
    It is currently debated whether the former LR 3.12 should be reinstated and/or strengthened at least for premium listed companies (see the FSA Consultation Paper 12/2). The London Stock Exchange requires that all companies applying for listing show that they can operate independently of controlling shareholders. To this purpose, newly listed companies must have a relationship agreement in place in which the controlling shareholder commits to the 'arm's length' requirement.
71 Rule 9 of the City Code on Takeovers and Mergers (September 2011).
72 See LR 9.8.6.
73 See the former LR 3.13 (2003).
74 Substantial shareholders and their associates qualify as 'related-party,' and trigger the application of LR 11 (independent shareholder approval of all significant transactions).

I mentioned, the Corporate Governance Code recommends that such a shareholder refrains from appointing more than a minority of board members; and it may be embarrassing for a controlling shareholder to explain non-compliance in the presence of significant holdings by institutional investors.[75] Finally, a large shareholder should be very careful in seeking to increase his impact on decision-making because crossing the 30% threshold would trigger the mandatory bid. Taken together, these inconveniencies attached to a would-be controlling position make takeovers unattractive, at least unless the incumbent board cooperates.

A way out of the above hurdles would be to take the company private after a takeover, because then the arm's length requirements of board composition would have no reason to apply. This implies that minority shareholders who do not tender their shares need to be squeezed out. Here, however, the cooperation of the board of directors is required. The Companies Act provides for two major options as far as going private transactions are concerned. The first option is the so-called scheme of arrangement, whereby takeovers are followed by a peculiar cash merger transaction upon agreement with the incumbent board and endorsement by a super-majority of minority share-holders.[76] Classical squeeze-outs can instead be implemented unilaterally. However, this option is only available when at least 90% of the firm's stock is put together.[77] Traditionally, the vast majority of takeover bids in the UK are conditional on that result being achieved (Franks et al 2001). This may explain how directors would manage to frustrate a fully hostile bid by holding onto their shares (that jointly account, on average, for 11% of voting power) and recommending outside shareholders to do the same.[78] In many, if not most, British listed firms, boards enjoy a *de facto* veto power on minority squeeze-out. And the regulatory hurdles faced by a controlling shareholder in the UK often make squeeze-out a necessary condition for the success of a takeover.

In conclusion, British directors are also able to exercise ongoing control over the firm management and to moderately entrench themselves in the face of a hostile takeover. This is due to the distribution of powers in corporate governance, but – differently from the US – such a distribution does not empower directors directly. A subtle combination of laws, regulations and best practices supports the board of directors indirectly by disfavoring controlling shareholders.

4.3.3 *Bypassing shareholders in the Netherlands*

The regulatory structure of Dutch corporate law is completely different from what we have just seen for the US and the UK. Comparative analyses often

---

75　See Pacces (2011).
76　See Davies (2008: 1061–79) and CA 2006 §§ 895–899.
77　See Davies (2008: 1046–56) and CA 2006 §§ 979–982.
78　See in a similar vein Goergen and Renneboog (2001) and Crespi and Renneboog (2010).

avoid discussing it because it can become very complicated. However, the resulting distribution of powers between the board of directors and the general meeting of shareholders in the Netherlands provide for no less empowerment of directors than under Anglo-American law, and to be sure for even more than that. I will therefore attempt to portray the Dutch distribution of legal powers skipping all not strictly necessary complications.

4.3.3.1 The hypocrisy of stakeholder protection and the evolution of Dutch corporate law

To begin with, in the Netherlands, the general meeting of shareholders does not have supreme authority over corporate decision-making (Bekkum et al 2010). Although this is practically true also in Britain and in the US, it has never been put this way by the courts who, if anything, always state the opposite as a matter of principle (Bebchuk 2005; Armour et al 2003). In the Netherlands, instead, the very essence of shareholder franchise is bluntly put into question.[79] This is quite exceptional for the continental Europe jurisdictions being considered here. The recurrent explanation of the peculiarities of Dutch corporate law is a high, and possibly extreme, consideration for stakeholders – basically, for one category of them: the employees (De Jong and Röell 2005).

Compared to other stakeholder-oriented corporate societies (most prominently, Germany and Sweden), the Dutch attitude appears to have historically featured the least shareholder-friendly jurisdiction in Europe (and yet – relative to GDP – one of the highest stock market capitalization in the world). As it often turns out, however, it is highly questionable whether this has led to any actual empowerment of employees in corporate governance (Hellwig 2000). Rather, it seems that stakeholder protection has been just the Trojan horse of *directors'* empowerment. In recent times, Dutch scholars and policymakers have started to realize this. As a result, corporate law was changed in 2004 on exactly those points that we have under consideration (Bekkum et al 2010). Yet distribution of powers is probably the most path-dependent feature of corporate law. Changes that allegedly brought to an end the most controversial peculiarities of Dutch law are in fact unlikely to reverse the path. This is fortunate, for that path has made the Netherlands perhaps the only country in continental Europe that allows a majority of publicly held companies to be under managerial control. Historically, this might possibly have to do with the Dutch people having 'invented' the corporate enterprise and the stock market in the sixteenth century (De Jong and Röell 2005). In what follows, I will show that, at least nowadays, it mainly depends upon the law.

---

79 This is the long-standing position of the Dutch Supreme Court (*Hoge Raad* – HR). See HR 21 January 1955, NJ 1959, 43 and more recently HR 13 July 2007, JOR 2007, 178 (Abn-Amro).

Three key features determine the basic distribution of power under Dutch corporate law. The first has mainly to do with competence: who is entitled to appoint and remove directors. The second one is a matter of organization: how shareholder votes are cast. The third one is – as usual – takeover resistance. In many firms listed in the Netherlands shareholders used to have almost no say in directors' appointment (and removal), not even formally. 'Almost no say' turns into a modest 'little say' after the reform. Other traditional peculiarities of Dutch corporate law are the entitlement of directors to have outside shares voted according to their wishes (through the institution of an *administratiekantoor*) and to implement both pre-bid and post-bid takeover defenses that are possibly even stronger that those upheld by US law (see e.g. Kabir et al 1997). In a nutshell, the evolution of Dutch corporate law has reduced, but not yet eliminated, its peculiarities concerning director appointment and removal. It has also introduced regulatory support for proxy voting, although this technique remains little used in the Netherlands. On the other hand, takeover defenses have been basically unaffected by regulatory changes. The Netherlands opted out of the board neutrality rule introduced by the EU Takeover Directive as of 2006.[80] In addition, case-law has been quite supportive of the board's ability to fend off hostile takeovers (Bekkum et al 2010). This stands in sharp contrast with the empirical evidence, showing that Dutch listed companies have recently decreased the number of takeover defenses probably under the pressure of increasingly important institutional investors (de Jong et al 2010).

4.3.3.2 The Dutch 'structure regime'

Issues of competence under Dutch corporate law are deeply embedded within the discipline of the board structure, which is traditionally two-tier in the Netherlands even though this is not always compulsory. After the entry into force of the so-called One-Tier Board Act (expected by 1 July 2013)[81] all companies will be able to opt in to a one-tier board regime. However, for the time being only one – Unilever – has done it (Hopt 2011). The two-tier structure consists of a supervisory board ('*raad van commissarissen*') and a management board ('*raad van bestuur*'). However, contrary to that one would expect, it is competence and not board structure that matters the most. Beyond the board structure, Dutch law provides for a *mandatory* discipline of corporate governance where all key decisions used to be taken by (supervisory) directors; this still includes the decisions concerning their own appointment.

---

80 Directive 2004/25/EC of the European Parliament and of the Council of 21 April 2004 on takeover bids (hereinafter Takeover Directive). Art. 9 of the Directive lays down shareholder approval of defensive tactics, unless member states choose to make the provision optional for individual companies.

81 Because of the many amendments proposed to the Bill, the date of implementation has been postponed. At the time of writing, it is not known when the new legislation will precisely come into force. See the NautaDutilh Newsletter, *One-Tier Board Act: The Current Status*, 12 June 2012.

This discipline is called the 'structure regime' (*structuurregime*) (Schuit et al 2002; Bekkum et al 2010).

The structure regime is: (a) *compulsory* when the company is 'large' enough to meet some requirements in terms of net assets and number of employees (the latter also triggering a mandatory work council); (b) *mitigated* for multi-national groups whose parent or operative companies are established outside the Netherlands, provided that the majority of the group work force is also employed outside the Netherlands; (c) *optional* for any company, provided that there is a work council. Traditionally, the structure regime involved the transfer of certain decision rights (approval of significant transactions initiated by the management board and adoption of the annual accounts) from the shareholder meeting to the supervisory board. After the reform, most of these rights have been reallocated to the general meeting. More importantly, under the unmitigated structure regime shareholders used to have almost no power in the appointment of directors to either board. Nowadays they can influence that process to the extent that they are large enough to toughly bargain with the members of the supervisory board. When the structure regime is not adopted, shareholders get back their right to appoint directors. This applies to either board when the structure is two-tier, but the company is also free to adopt a one-tier structure. Shareholder rights are also restored under the mitigated regime, but – until the One-Tier Board Act enters into force – the board structure must be two-tier. As of 1997, 61% of Dutch listed firms had adopted the structure regime, and almost one quarter of them (16% of listed firms) had done it voluntarily; the mitigated regime accounted for just 3% of listed firms (de Jong et al 2001). However, the popularity of the structure regime has decreased in recent years. Today, many 'large' listed companies that operate as a holding of an international group manage to avoid the rigidities of the structure regime (Bekkum et al 2010).

In the structure regime, only the supervisory board can appoint directors to the management board. No interference by shareholders is allowed. So the key question is *who appoints the members of the supervisory board*. Before the reform of 2004 the answer was the supervisory board itself, by a system of so-called "controlled co-optation" (Kemperink 2004). In the international literature, that mechanism used to be compared to the reciprocal appointment of the Pope and the Bishops (Becht and Mayer 2001). To be sure, cooptation was subject to some control by both the work council and the general meeting, which could potentially result in a veto right. On the one hand, both organs were entitled to make non-binding recommendations to the supervisory board. On the other hand, they could object to the people appointed by the supervisory board. However, any objection could be resisted by the supervisory board unless it was upheld by the judiciary – namely, by the Enterprise Chamber of the Amsterdam Court of Appeals.[82] For this reason, veto rights

82 The Enterprise Chamber of the Amsterdam Court of Appeals (*OndernemingsKamer* – OK) is a special court in charge of dealing with key corporate matters in the Netherlands. Most

were actually granted to either the shareholders or the work council only on grounds that the supervisory board would have been 'improperly constituted.'[83]

This has changed more in form than in substance after the 2004 reform. Today the supervisory board is still entitled to *exclusive* nomination rights at least as far as the majority of its members are concerned (a minority is subject to the *binding* recommendations of the work council). However, nominations of the supervisory board have to be endorsed by shareholders and they can be overruled by the majority of the votes cast at the general meeting, even without a quorum. The problem is that shareholders are by no means entitled to present their *own* candidates for the election. As it turns out, this double-veto regime enables only a controlling shareholder to bargain upon the composition of the supervisory board. When they are dispersed, Dutch shareholders are not less apathetic than Anglo-American ones. Then they are equally likely to rubberstamp the supervisory board's nominations. Different rules apply to midterm removal of members of the supervisory board, who can now be collectively dismissed anytime for reasons of lack of confidence. Removal resolutions need to be upheld by a majority representing at least one third of outstanding shares, but still they bring no nomination right to shareholders. The Enterprise Chamber will take care of the temporary replacements. Provisions concerning both nomination rights and collective dismissal of the supervisory board are mandatory, whereas the article of incorporation may determine a different mechanism of appointment and even reintroduce the controlled cooptation.

As a result, on condition that ownership stays dispersed, members of the supervisory board are still quite easily reappointed and very unlikely to be removed by the general meeting under the structure regime. Even though supervisors cannot directly intervene in the firm management, they retain the exclusive power to appoint directors to the management board and to remove them from office. Plain deference of the management board to the supervisory board cannot but follow.[84] Even though the two boards

importantly, it is in charge of administering the objections of shareholders and employees to the nominations of the supervisory board and the inquiry procedure (*Enquêterecht*) into the management of the company (Kemperink 2004). It is worth noting that shareholders and trade unions may also challenge the position of supervisory board members on grounds of mismanagement, to the extent they can activate the inquiry procedure and seek any of the court's remedies thereby (shareholders accounting for at least 10% of share capital always have this right).

83 SER (Social Economic Council) 27 Sept. 1983, De NV 1983, 233; OK (Enterprise Chamber) 2 February 1989, NJ 1990, 86.

84 Indeed, this is the natural line of command arising from the appointment rules. It should also be noticed that, in the absence of a controlling shareholder, at least the majority of each board cannot but be captured by the incumbent management. Thus, in a sense, the members of the supervisory board will also ultimately defer to the managing directors. So long as the two boards get along well with each other, directors will be insulated from shareholder interference; whereas, in case of disagreement, directors in both boards run the risk that shareholders coalesce and take over. This situation is no different from the past. See Becht et al (2007).

have to be formally independent of each other, in practice they are both still insulated from shareholder interference. In the structure regime lies one of the legal roots of managerial capitalism in the Netherlands. As we are going to see, it is not the only one and nowadays it is neither necessary nor desirable.

4.3.3.3 *Voting trust foundations and priority shares*

The highly peculiar use of voting trusts in Dutch corporate governance has been perhaps even more important than the structure regime, although this is sometimes overlooked in the international comparisons. Shares of a publicly held company can be placed with a foundation (*stichting*) that issues depository receipts (*certificaten*) in exchange. The foundation operates as a trust office (*administratiekantoor*) whose most important task is the exercise of voting rights (Meinema 2003). Those rights are stripped from the depository receipts held by beneficial owners – the shareholders. Once the shares are transferred to the trust office, shareholders basically lose their voting rights and are left just with their cash flow rights. Depository receipts are traded on the stock market instead of the underlying shares. Even though shareholders are formally the beneficial owners, the foundation is typically formed by the corporation and so the trust office is most often friendly to the management. The *administratiekantoor* then routinely supports directors' decisions at the general meeting, whether or *not* the firm is subject to the structure regime (de Jong et al 2006). That explains how directors have managed to gain voting power from dispersed shareholders in the Netherlands, even in the absence of legal support for an Anglo-Saxon style proxy voting system. In 1996 nearly 40% of Dutch listed firms had shares placed with such a trust office; the latter held more than a quarter of voting rights in over 35% of the companies. Since few large shareholders seem to stand behind an *administratiekantoor*, this is a remarkable tool for managerial control which is reported to have the highest incidence in the Netherlands compared with the rest of continental Europe (Bekkum et al 2010).

In recent years, probably due to pressure by foreign institutional investors, there has been a significant drop in the use of depository receipts by listed companies, namely from 39% to 15% in 2007 (de Jong et al 2010). On the other hand, this technique has not been substantially affected by legal reform. Receipt holders are now formally entitled to cast their vote without exchanging their certificates for shares (which would be limited by the trust deed, usually to 1% of outstanding share capital), by simply requesting voting proxies from the trust office. The board of the *administratiekantoor* can refuse to issue the proxies when there is a risk of takeover or when this would be otherwise against the company's interest (Bekkum et al 2010). Clearly, however, dispersed shareholders are not likely to make any such request *unless* a takeover is in the making. Even if they did, Dutch boards may today avail themselves of mass solicitation of proxy votes at the company's expense – an option that was technically unavailable a few years ago. Whatever attenuation (if any at all) the reform has brought to the management's ability to collect voting power from the *administratiekantoor*, this might be more than offset by the availability of a very board-oriented proxy voting system.[85]

Managerial control of voting rights is of course of fundamental importance outside the structure regime, where the general meeting of shareholders retains full power to appoint and to remove directors in either a one-tier or a two-tier structure. However, it is also important within the structure regime where some, but not all, of the general meeting powers are transferred to the supervisory board. Prominent examples include charter amendments, mergers, divisions, and – after the 2004 reform – the sale of all or of a substantial part of the company's assets. Anyway, these decisions need to be endorsed by the general meeting. Voting power held by the trust office might be either unavailable or insufficient to have those resolutions passed: charters may require a quorum, a qualified majority, or both (Schuit et al 2002). Proxy solicitation could be an option, in theory, but it has been introduced too recently and it is still little used. In fact, Dutch corporate law traditionally provides for another instrument of directors empowerment: the so-called 'priority shares.'

Non-voting shares and customary differentiation of voting rights through dual class shares are, in principle, not featured by Dutch law (Schuit et al 2002; Chirinko et al 2004). Priority shares carry in fact no excess voting rights. They do carry, however, special initiation and veto rights, as well as the entitlement to have resolutions of the general meeting passed with a simple majority and no quorum. On the contrary, proposals *not* made by the holder of priority shares can only be endorsed by a two-third majority accounting for at least 50% of outstanding shares. For that reason, priority shares are also called 'oligarchic devices' (de Jong and Röell 2005). Needless to say, they confer an enormous power upon their holder who can thereby easily dominate the general meeting. This would be true both for directors and for a controlling shareholder. Directors would count on their indirect voting power (they do not need to hold many shares on their own, particularly when *certificaten* are outstanding), on rational apathy of otherwise dispersed shareholders, and on the privileges of the priority for having resolutions passed (and never opposed) by the general meeting. A controlling shareholder would have his own shares on top of that. In addition, special initiation rights of priority shares can be extended to binding nominations of the board members, on condition that the company is not subject to the structure regime. This explains how directors can also control corporations that adopt the 'regular' regime and, possibly, even a one-tier board structure.

---

85 But see Bekkum et al (2010) for the technical difficulties that still exist.

4.3.3.4 *Takeover defenses in the Netherlands*

There is often confusion about whether all of the above devices serve ongoing control purposes or are, rather, takeover defenses (e.g. Rosenboom and Van der Goot 2003). Surely, both effects are at play, but the former normally outweigh the latter. Structure regime, voting trusts, and priority shares certainly make takeovers more difficult, but not always impossible, to a rider who manages to acquire more than 50% of outstanding shares. Having those devices labeled as takeover defenses is indeed common practice in both Dutch and international literature (Becht et al 2007), but it is ultimately misleading.

Dutch law in fact allows for takeover defenses *strictu senso*. They might be implemented by the board either before or after a takeover attempt. One rather typical technique is based on so-called 'preference shares', which can be issued at *nominal* value with *only 25%* of the amount being paid up (Schuit et al 2002). Like US-style poison pills, Dutch preference shares are therefore a relatively cheap way to dilute any insurgent shareholder's voting power, since they carry the same voting rights as common stock and they are issued to a management-friendly foundation (a *stichting,* different from the *administratiekantoor*). Since Dutch law allows the issuance of preference shares to be delegated to the management board for a five-year period, many firms have such a takeover defense constantly in place (de Jong et al 2001). For those that do not have this, the board seems to be nonetheless entitled to post-bid resistance. The legality of takeover resistance, under relatively loose conditions of proportionality of action taken by the board, is a genuine product of judge-made law (Timmerman 2004); it has been implicitly endorsed by the Dutch legislature by opting out of article 9 (board neutrality rule) of the EU Takeover Directive. The case-law on takeover resistance started with a famous struggle between the management of Gucci and Louis Vuitton, bringing the unusual matter of hostile takeovers to the attention of the Dutch judiciary (Meinema 2003). Takeover resistance is upheld under the general standard of compliance with the "elementary principles of good business judgment," which is comparable to – albeit different from – the US business judgment rule (Bekkum et al 2010). The key issue is whether the board can make a good faith argument that the takeover threat was against the best interest of the target and all its constituents (which includes its shareholders, but also its employees, creditors and other relevant parties).

The Dutch case-law on takeover resistance has grown considerably in recent years. The guiding principles that defenses have to be necessary, proportional and temporary have been laid down by the Supreme Court in *Rodamco*,[86] a decision that according to some commentators (e.g. Bekkum et al 2010) resembles the Unocal standard set by Delaware courts. In a number of high-profile cases (*Abn-Amro, Stork, ASMI*) the Enterprise Chamber has tried

---

86 HR 18 April 2003, JOR 2003, 110.

to develop a somewhat more investor-friendly approach.[87] However, this has not been supported by the Supreme Court who has ruled against the Enterprise Chamber in some of these cases, confirming the importance of boards' autonomy in protecting the interest of the company's stakeholders.[88]

In conclusion, the Dutch boards are entitled to exert ongoing control over the firm management and to oppose a takeover bid, if they so wish, thanks to a favorable distribution of power provided for by corporate law.

4.4 When shareholder control is the only option (and why)

4.4.1 *The legal distribution of corporate powers in Sweden and in Italy*

The foregoing discussion of legal institutions supporting managerial control should tell how difficult it is to provide control entitlements when the controller is not a major shareholder. Having a controlling shareholder in charge is much easier. It suffices that he is there and has his rights as the major owner of the company enforced. We will see that the reverse is not true. Therefore, the classical Berle and Means argument is turned on its head. Dispersed ownership alone does not bring about managerial control and, rather, may never arise when corporate law does not support managerial control. When directors are not entitled to fill in the power vacuum left by the absence of a controlling shareholder, the vacuum will not be created in the first place. This is likely to be the typical situation in most countries of continental Europe. Let us focus on just two of them, which exhibit similar patterns of family capitalism albeit with a very different importance of equity finance (Barca and Becht 2001). They are Sweden, whose stock market capitalization relative to GDP comes close to the Anglo-American figures; and Italy, which has one of the least developed stock markets among the top economies.

4.4.1.1 *Why directors need a controlling shareholder*

The legal distribution of corporate powers in Sweden and Italy is quite similar on most fundamental aspects, which allows treating them jointly.[89]

---

87 See OK 17 January 2007, JOR 2007, 42 (Stork); OK 3 May 2007, JOR 2007, 143 (Abn-Amro); OK 6 August 2009, LJN: BJ4688 (ASMI).

88 See HR 13 July 2007, NJ 2007, 434 (Abn-Amro); HR 9 July 2010, NJ 2010, 544 (ASMI).

89 Both Italian and Swedish corporate laws were reformed quite recently. In Sweden, the Companies Act of 1975 was replaced in 2006. The changes have not been substantial, at least as far as the matters dealt with here are concerned, and they were mainly aimed at further empowering shareholders (Skog and Fäger 2007). The new rules do not affect the primacy of controlling shareholders in Sweden, and still leave no scope for managerial control.

The process of corporate law reform in Italy begun in 1998 and was concluded not long ago (Enriques 2009). A major reform took place in 2004 when the Italian Civil Code (ICC)

In both countries, board members are elected by the general meeting. Employees are granted board representation in Sweden, but this does not affect the distribution of powers since the majority of the board always need to be appointed by the general meeting (Skog and Fäger 2007). Directors are elected by majority in Italy and by plurality in Sweden, and appointment resolutions can be freed from quorum requirements.[90] The crucial point is, however, that incumbent directors cannot be sure they will be re-appointed, unless they own a sufficient number of shares to this purpose or they enjoy the protection of a controlling shareholder. Even more importantly, when none of these conditions is fulfilled, they run the risk of being replaced anytime and – at the very latest – at the next annual meeting (see Cools 2005).

Under both Swedish and Italian law, directors can be removed without cause and a special meeting to this purpose can be summoned by shareholders representing at least 10% of outstanding shares.[91] Therefore, terms of office only matter for liability damages, not for tenure (and they are limited anyway by the law, the charter, and self-regulation). In addition, annual meetings where directors are not up for election are nonetheless very dangerous for them. This is certainly true in Sweden, where individual shareholders have full access to the agenda of the general meeting (Karnell 1981). But also in Italy, directors can be removed 'anytime' by the general meeting, where shareholders' access to the agenda is traditionally more limited.[92]

One may object that the above situation is no different from at least one of the board-oriented jurisdictions that we have just reviewed, namely the UK. And yet, Italian and Swedish directors are powerless without the support of a controlling shareholder, whereas they would not be in the UK. The underlying reason is very simple. Neither in Italy nor in Sweden can proxy voting be solicited by the board of directors at the company's expense – whereas it can in the UK. To be sure, nothing today prevents Swedish and Italian directors from soliciting proxies, provided they hold some shares (they have to do it in their capacity as shareholders, at least in Italy) and they are willing to bear all the expenses. Both Italian and Swedish laws provide for proxy solicitation, since 1998 and 2006 respectively, but they do not allow any involvement of the company with the related expenses. Unsurprisingly, such a device has hardly ever been used in Italy either to support the incumbent board or to

---

was amended to introduce a new discipline of joint stock (public or private) companies and limited liability (private) companies. Other reforms were enacted as a reaction to the Parmalat debacle.

90 Art. 2368(1) ICC (majority voting) and art. 2369(3) ICC (no quorum in second call); Karnell (1981).

91 Art. 2367 ICC; Skog (1994).

92 Art. 2383 ICC (directors can be removed without cause); art. 2366 ICC (directors are in control of the meetings' agenda) – but, in this regard, see *infra*, next subsection.

challenge its position.[93] And it is doubtful whether it will ever become popular in Sweden.

Italian and Swedish boards are therefore unable to exercise control over the firm management on an ongoing basis, for the obvious reason that they cannot make sure they *stay* in charge unless a controlling shareholder supports them. This has neither to do with takeovers nor with their resistance, which will be dealt with shortly. The problem is rather that the board, in itself, has almost no way to avoid being outvoted at the general meeting. Directors would be in fact at the mercy of whoever can cast the majority of the votes at the general meeting. He (or they) may account for whatever small fraction of outstanding shares, provided that directors account for less and nobody else shows up at the meeting. Why should the board ever be outvoted by an insignificant ownership stake? For a number of both rational and psychological reasons. For instance, envy, greed, blackmail, or even a shareholder willing to be the company's one-day king. Actually, shareholders might even show up at the meeting just for taking a chance on this!

This is of course a parody to describe a nonsensical situation. Corporate control is quite a serious issue that cannot be left to the temper of small, individual shareholders. Sooner or later a controlling shareholder would come up to take care of the matter. But it is exactly for that reason that controlling shareholders would hardly disappear in the first place. When directors are ultimately powerless – as they are under both Italian and Swedish corporate law – managerial control cannot emerge in corporate governance.

4.4.1.2 *Shareholder control over the agenda of the general meeting*

Further discussion of board freedom from (and influence on) shareholder resolutions may add very little to the above conclusion. To what extent directors can do without the general meeting of shareholders, or have a favorable resolution passed therein, is basically unimportant when the very process of their election and removal is out of their control. Yet, here lies quite a significant difference between Italian and Swedish law that is worth mentioning.

The general meeting of shareholders retains supreme authority over the firm decision-making under Swedish corporate law (Karnell 1981; Skog 1994). Many board decisions have to be upheld by shareholders; and every year the general meeting has to decide whether directors are individually discharged from liability. Shareholder resolutions can be voted on almost any subject – unless they are explicitly reserved for a decision by the board or the managing director – and they are binding on directors. Finally, individual

---

93 There has been at least one exception in Italy, where a proxy fight was initiated (but then withdrawn) in the midst of a takeover battle. See Arena Holding, *Documento di Offerta Pubblica di Acquisto Obbligatoria su Azioni Ordinarie Roncadin*, 2004 (filed with the *Consob*, available at www.consob.it).

shareholders can have any matter added to the agenda of the general meeting, provided the request is not too late to be included in the notice. These features have not been changed by the new Companies Act of 2006 whereby, if anything, the position of the general meeting of shareholders has been strengthened even further (Skog and Fäger 2007).

Italian shareholders are weaker even though, paradoxically, directors are no more powerful. To begin with, default powers have always resided with the board under Italian corporate law. The board of directors has exclusive competence over the firm management and shareholders are not allowed to interfere.[94] This principle was somewhat controversial before the 2004 reform – and anyway it could be derogated by the charter – but it is now explicitly stated in the law as a mandatory rule.[95] As in the US, this basically implies that the shareholders who wish to have any management strategy, or even a single decision implemented, would need to replace the members of an opposing board of directors first. Differently from the US, though, directors are quite easily removed under Italian corporate law. The introduction of three options as regards the board does not change this (Ventoruzzo 2004). Italian boards still cannot do without a controlling shareholder.

Whatever the board structure, directors also enjoy exclusive initiation rights on many matters falling within the competence of the general meeting – like mergers, divisions, waiver of pre-emption rights, and the approval of the annual accounts under one-tier board structures. Yet, in the absence of a workable proxy voting system, there is no chance that directors will ever have any resolution passed without the support of a controlling shareholder.[96] Italian boards also have a very strong competitive advantage in setting the agenda of the general meeting, which used to be their exclusive responsibility.[97] This rule has always had one important exception: when

94 Before the 2004 reform, this principle was indirectly derived from the discipline of the general meeting. Art. 2364 ICC provided for a limited number of tasks of the general meeting, which, however, could be expanded almost at will by the articles of association. After the reform, this is no longer an option.

95 Art. 2380-*bis* ICC now clearly states that "the management of the firm resides exclusively with directors." This holds irrespective of the board structure. The new version of art. 2364 ICC still allows the articles of association to require shareholder authorization for certain board decisions, but the general meeting is now prevented from withdrawing delegation of any management task from directors.

96 Voting at the general meeting is governed by a complicated set of rules under Italian law. See e.g. Ventoruzzo (2004) for a clear illustration of quorums and majorities.

97 Art. 2366 ICC. This has changed lately with the introduction of a general right to place items on the meetings agenda by shareholders of listed companies who account for at least 2.5% of share capital. Art. 126-*bis* Legislative Decree No. 58/1998 (as amended by art. 5 of the Act No. 262/2005 – so-called 'Savings Act'). However, shareholder proposals are not allowed on any issue upon which the board has exclusive initiation rights (this is consistent with the limitations of shareholders' power to summon a special meeting – art. 2367(3) ICC). In addition, in the absence of the possibility to recover the expenses of a proxy solicitation, shareholder proposals are unlikely to ever be passed by the general meeting, if ever put forward at all.

shareholders are entitled to summon a general meeting, they also set its agenda. In practice, a general meeting is only summoned by minority share-holders in opposition to a controlling shareholder. Whatever hostility there may be in this game, directors are hardly those who play it.

Hostile takeovers are very rare in Italy, and basically unheard of in Sweden. This does not only depend on the overwhelming presence of controlling shareholders, but also on the law.

4.4.2 Takeover resistance by a controlling shareholder

In both Italy and Sweden, takeover defenses have to be considered in a different perspective. Since managerial control is technically unfeasible on an ongoing basis, takeover defenses cannot serve the purpose of protecting *directors* from shareholder insurgency. While a controlling shareholder would do a much better job on this account, takeover defenses would not help directors to do without a controlling shareholder. Directors' resisting a takeover actually makes little sense when their position depends on the good wishes of the general meeting of shareholders who may remove directors at any time. Takeover defenses may instead serve the purpose of protecting a *controlling shareholder* from any insurgency that might result in his being outvoted at the general meeting. Needless to say, differently from directors, a controlling shareholder does not *need* takeover defenses for this purpose. Holding 50% (plus one) of outstanding voting shares will always do. But this is quite a burdensome solution, for it limits the firm's access to equity finance to an amount depending on the corporate controller's wealth constraints, liquidity preferences, and risk aversion; and it likewise limits the firm's growth prospects by the amount of internal cash flow reinvestment. Therefore, even in a corporate governance structure based on shareholder control, takeover defenses are of fundamental importance to ease the above constraints – at least, to some limited extent (see Coates 2004).

The typology of takeover defenses also changes within this perspective. Anti-takeover devices no longer need to be based on separation of control rights from voting rights, as in the case of board resistance. On the one hand, in many European jurisdictions such a separation would be ultimately impossible to reconcile with the leading principle of shareholder primacy. On the other hand, featuring board resistance against a takeover is far from necessary when a controlling shareholder is in charge. The battle would indeed be for the control of the general meeting not of the board of directors. At the general meeting, it is only voting power that matters. Unsurprisingly, then, the typical way of implementing takeover resistance in continental Europe is having *voting*, and not *control* rights, separated from ownership claims – clearly to the advantage of the controlling shareholder (Becht and Mayer 2001). The board of directors indeed plays a minor role in this game, if any at all.

Quite surprisingly, it is exactly that role that is most extensively regulated. Regulators seem to care for board passivity in the face of a takeover more than of the controlling shareholder's behavior.[98] This is possibly justified on grounds that the controlling shareholder may not yet be completely entrenched when a takeover bid is made. Still, directors will do what the controlling shareholder compels them to do. Under shareholder control, board resistance is not practically restrained by a simple requirement that any defensive tactic be upheld by the general meeting. Yet, this is the tendency of many European jurisdictions, lately supported by the EU takeover law.[99]

Under Italian law, for instance, post-bid defenses are only valid if approved by 30% of voting rights at the general meeting. Short of the possibility for individual companies to opt out, which is unique to the Italian law, this is illustrative of the law of those European member states that did not opt out article 9 of the Takeover Directive.[100] One may easily recognize the influence of the London City Panel here.[101] However, such a provision is of very little use in continental Europe, where controlling shareholders typically account for more than 30% of voting rights. To be sure, the Takeover Directive also goes a little further, attempting to 'break through' the voting power of controlling shareholders when it exceeds his ownership stake.[102] However, since this rule has nothing to do with distribution of powers within the corporation, it will be dealt with in the chapter where the market for corporate control is discussed.

Because something always escapes regulation, Italian companies may have additional leeway in adopting takeover defenses. The corporate law reform of 2004 has increased flexibility in this respect. Italy already had a (mandatory) board neutrality rule back then, but the reform introduced the possibility to adopt something similar to US-style takeover defenses. A new kind of securities, named 'Participative Financial Instruments' (PFI), could in fact be employed in that fashion (Enriques 2006). Holders of PFI can be granted special appointment rights to board membership and likewise special veto rights on resolutions by the general meeting.[103] According to the mainstream view, appointment rights cannot concern more than a minority of board members. Thus, let us briefly consider veto rights. Holding just one of those PFIs, a controlling shareholder could for instance block a merger. This would be enough to frustrate a 'classical' takeover attempt. Of course, this is just one of the possible examples. Upon authorization by the charter or any subsequent amendment thereof, directors are entitled to issue PFIs without significant limitations – they do not even need to be paid-up. Post-bid issuance would

---

98　The implementation of the Takeover Directive is illustrative of this point. The vast majority of member states have chosen to opt in art. 9 (board neutrality rule) and to opt out art. 11 (breakthrough rule). See European Commission, *Report on the implementation of the Directive on Takeover Bids*, SEC(2007)268, 2007, available at www.ec.europa.eu.

99　See art. 9 of the Takeover Directive.

100　See Davies et al (2010). Major opt-out member states are Germany and the Netherlands.

101　Rule 21 of the City Code on Takeovers and Mergers (September 2011).

102　See art. 11 of the Takeover Directive.

103　Art. 2348(2) and art. 2351(5) ICC.

probably be subject to a special authorization by the general meeting, but pre-bid issuance would not. No doubt that this is not sufficient to tilt the balance of powers in favor of directors because they could not use PFIs for having all of them appointed to the board. But it is not unlikely that a controlling shareholder may wish to avail himself of PFIs for anti-takeover purposes, when he is not already completely entrenched by means of his voting power.

4.4.3 Pyramids and dual class shares

A controlling shareholder would not need much of pre-bid or post-bid takeover defenses if not in peculiar situations. Normally, he would already be entrenched by means of devices that *permanently* enhance his voting power relative to his ownership stake – thereby supporting *both* the exercise of ongoing control *and* takeover resistance (Morck et al 2005). Dual class shares and pyramidal groups are the most typical of such devices. They might be used individually or in combination both with each other and with other ancillary devices that, for the sake of brevity, I am not considering here.

Similarly to other countries of continental Europe, corporate governance in Sweden and Italy features a wide resort to both pyramids and dual class shares. In a nutshell, the former are more characteristic of large Italian listed firms, while the latter are more popular among all Swedish publicly held companies.[104] This depends only in part by their direct regulation in corporate law. The amount of voting power that can be leveraged in excess of the corporate controller's ownership stake also depends on outside investors' willingness to uphold such leverage through the stock price.[105] On the one hand, this is inversely related to the likelihood being expropriated by the controlling shareholder. On the other hand, outside investors' willingness to pay for comparatively weakened voting rights is ultimately dependent on the likelihood of a value-increasing change in control. I shall discuss how corporate law affects these two problems in the following chapters. How and to what extent voting and cash flow rights can be separated from a strictly legal perspective will be the subject matter of the following subsections.

4.4.3.1 Multiple and limited voting shares

Under Swedish corporate law (basically unaffected on this point by the 2006 reform), there are little restrictions to the usage of dual class shares. Basic restrictions are the prohibition of non-voting shares and an upper bound on voting rights that can be granted to super-voting shares: since the mid-forties, multiple voting rights cannot exceed a ratio of ten to one (Karnell 1981). This

---

104 Barca and Becht (2001). But this is changing in both countries. See Bianchi and Bianco (2006) and Henrekson and Jakobsson (2012).
105 See *supra* Chapter 3.

still allows a controlling shareholder to achieve an enormous degree of separation of ownership and control: 5% of cash flow rights would be sufficient to control 50% of voting rights. In practice, such an extreme separation is never implemented through dual class shares – although similar results are sometimes achieved through the joint use of dual class shares and pyramidal groups (Holmén and Högfeldt 2009). Former empirical analyses (Agnblad et al 2001) showed that in the late 1990s over 60% of Swedish listed firms employed dual class shares, and this allowed controlling shareholders to exercise on average 1.47 voting rights for any unit of direct ownership (the average figure could rise up to about 2 when the effect of pyramids was also considered). More recent studies (Henrekson and Jakobsson 2012) show that the leverage of control enhancement mechanisms has decreased significantly over the past few years, most likely because of the influence of foreign institutional investors. However, as the present analysis would predict, this has not determined any change in the Swedish corporate governance model, particularly no transition to managerial control.

The situation is remarkably different in Italy, where dual class shares have never been very popular among listed firms (they have almost disappeared in recent times) and their effect on leveraging of voting power is negligible both on average and for individual firms (Bianchi et al 2005). This has certainly to do with regulation. In Italy, multiple voting shares are prohibited. Before the 2004 reform, only two kinds of differentiation were allowed: either non-voting shares ('azioni di risparmio') or preference shares carrying voting rights limited to the extraordinary general meeting ('azioni privilegiate'). In addition, non-voting and limited voting shares could jointly account for no more than 50% of outstanding share capital.[106] A controlling shareholder had therefore limited possibilities for enhancing his voting power through dual class shares. In addition, these possibilities have only been exploited to a limited extent. One might think that there is not much difference between downwards and upwards deviations from the 'one-share-one-vote' rule, but this is not completely true. Compared to a shareholder whose voting rights are indirectly weakened, a shareholder deprived outright of voting rights might have no chance to share in any takeover premium. All the more so as the holder of non-voting shares might face a higher risk of being expropriated of his cash flow rights. This should explain why non-voting or very limited voting shares do not enjoy much popularity among investors, especially where – as in Italy – opportunities for expropriation of minority shareholders are still not very effectively constrained by the law.

The above situation has changed little after the 2004 reform (see Ventoruzzo 2004). The two major constraints on dual class shares (prohibition of multiple voting shares and the 50% bound on the proportion of limited voting shares) have been maintained. Enhanced possibilities of variation of

106 Art. 2351 ICC and art. 145 Legislative Decree No. 58/1998 (before the reform).

voting rights and some minor improvements in the protection of cash flow rights might possibly increase the popularity of limited voting shares among investors in Italian companies. But it is quite doubtful that they will ever be used for enhancing the corporate controller's voting power to any significant extent. And yet, such a power is enhanced in Italy too. As of 1996, the average voting leverage of a controlling shareholder was about 1.2 voting rights for each unit of integrated (i.e., direct plus indirect) ownership (Bianchi et al 2001). The figure is significantly lower than the Swedish average for the same period, but is still not negligible. Provided that dual class shares do not play almost any role in this story, and other control enhancement mechanisms are prohibited in Italy, pyramids were basically the only responsible option. However, it is worth noting that the popularity of pyramids is gradually decreasing in favor of more articulated forms of coalitional control (see Bianchi and Bianco 2006).

4.4.3.2 *Pyramidal groups*

Pyramids are tricky. On the one hand, they could be the only option for having ownership separated from control when a controlling shareholder is (or must be) in charge and other devices for leveraging voting power are impractical or unavailable (Bebchuk 2003a). On the other hand, they might lead (as they often do) to undesirable outcomes for non-controlling shareholder at both the bottom and the intermediate layers of the pyramid (Bebchuk et al 2000). The latter contention requires some greater precision.

Pyramidal (voting) power is enhanced by two factors: the number of company layers and the proportion of minority shareholders at each layer. The ownership stake of the corporate controller is concentrated at the apex of the pyramid, whereas it can be much diluted at the bottom. By definition, the controller controls every layer. Investors of course care about the ultimate controller's financial commitment in each company, since the less is such a commitment the more his decisions might end up driven by the pursuit of distortionary PBC (say, empire building) and diversionary PBC (say, tunneling) (Almeida and Wolfenzon 2006). Let us assume for the moment that stealing problems are effectively policed by corporate law, perhaps in one of the ways that will be illustrated in the next chapter. Under a shareholder control structure, distortionary PBC are only policed through share ownership, which also affects the likelihood that an efficient change in control will take place in the future. Consequently, the corporate controller will not be allowed to dilute indefinitely his ownership stake through pyramiding, for investors at each layer will apply a discount on the outside stock price until further dilution is no more profitable to the controller than retention of (indirect) cash flow rights (Holmén and Högfeldt 2004). When also the risk of diversionary PBC is accounted for, and it is high enough, the discount might actually get so large that no pyramiding can take place: no investor would dare to buy stock at the bottom of a pyramid, knowing that nearly all of the profits will be diverted to its apex!

Nevertheless, non-controlling shareholders may still be tricked by pyramiding. Outside investors can only constrain the corporate controller's behavior when new stock is first sold to them. But assume that a further layer is added at the *bottom* of the pyramid. Minority shareholders of the newly set company (NewCo) will not be affected: they will buy stock at a discount consistent with the ultimate controller's ownership stake. On the contrary, minority shareholders at *any* intermediate layer of the pyramid will simply see the value of their investment diminished by the potential for empire building added by the NewCo – and they cannot do anything about it.

According to some commentators (Holmén and Högfeldt 2009) this could be one major problem of Swedish corporate governance despite the absence of tunneling. The above strategy would be more difficult to implement in Italy, since investors might refuse to buy stock in the NewCo of an already long control chain for fear of being expropriated. But something even worse could happen in Italy. One or more layers could be added on *top* of the pyramid, thereby diluting the controller's ownership stake in any lower layer. Minority shareholders of existing layers cannot but be harmed by such a strategy; but, again, they are powerless. In contrast, new outside investors are more easily found on top rather than at the bottom of a pyramid. This is therefore a terrific strategy for expanding equity finance in a group enterprise, without risk of losing its control. In fact, it was implemented for at least one of the largest Italian listed groups: Telecom Italia, the formerly state-owned public utility company.

However, it should be noted that Italian corporate law basically supports no alternative for corporate governance. As in Sweden, legal entitlements supporting managerial control are not available. Differently from Sweden, however, dual class shares are more severely regulated and practically of no use for achieving a significant leverage of voting power. Italian entrepreneurs have just two options to secure corporate control: either they maintain – by themselves or through a voting coalition – a direct ownership stake of about 50%, thereby giving up large-scale equity finance; or they set up a pyramidal group structure. Perhaps surprisingly, only the largest Italian listed firms have chosen the second option while the vast majority of them have a controlling shareholder holding more than 50% of direct ownership (Bianchi et al 2005).

This should tell why the Italian stock market is still so underdeveloped. Administrative costs of pyramiding cannot be the only explanation, nor can it be group taxation, which is neutral under Italian law.[107] Pyramiding appears to be only available to the largest and most reputable companies, to the extent

---

107 Mork et al (2005) analyze these as the two key factors determining the frequency of pyramids in a given country.

that they manage to overcome corporate law's shortcomings regarding investor protection against expropriation. Other firms cannot avail themselves of equally effective, but far less expensive and dangerous devices, like multiple voting shares, since Italian corporate law prohibits these. In Sweden, there is none of the above two problems. Expropriation of minority shareholders has never been a matter of concern there. And, as far as separation of voting from cash flow rights is concerned, at least Swedish controllers may choose between pyramids and multiple voting shares for the arrangement which suits their firm best.[108]

4.4.3.3 *One advantage of dual class shares over pyramids*

The problem of successive implementation (or extension) that affects pyramiding does not apply to dual class shares with equal severity. One would just wish that corporate controllers were unable to impose a change in the capital structure to non-controlling shareholders without having to bear the effects of outside investors' discount. This is straightforward in the absence of conversion. New limited voting rights will have to be placed with outside investors, who will only buy them at a discount. When multiple voting shares are issued to ease the controller's financial constraint, they would ultimately have to replace a portfolio of common stock carrying comparatively weakened voting rights; this likewise leads to a discounted sale.

However, midstream implementation of dual class capital structure can also be operated through conversion of existing common stock. These are so-called dual class recapitalizations, which may be unilaterally implemented by coercing non-controlling shareholders (Gilson 1987; Gordon 1988). After a long-standing debate, regulation of listed firms in the US has coped with this problem (Rock 2002). In Europe, dual class recapitalizations are less of a problem (Ferrarini 2006). On the one hand, regulation of share capital prevents corporate controllers from diluting minority shareholders outright. On the other hand, midstream alteration of the security voting structure is financially less attractive for controlling shareholders than for the management – and managerial control is very infrequent in Europe.

In conclusion, dual class shares are preferable to pyramids as far as midstream implementation is concerned. If anything, regulation should address remaining problems on this account, instead of biasing the choice of disproportional voting structures in favor of pyramidal groups. The European legislator has so far taken the opposite course of action, if anything, with the Takeover Directive, despite the ambiguous case for 'one share–one vote' regulations both theoretically (Burkart and Lee 2008) and empirically (Adams and Ferreira 2008).

---

108 See Holmén and Högfeldt (2009), noting that the choice may be distorted by tax considerations. See also Henrekson and Jakobson (2012).

4.5 Are managerial control and shareholder control compatible?

4.5.1 Board empowerment and controlling shareholders

The foregoing discussion has uncovered two very important results. On the one hand, some corporate law systems – the American, the British, and the Dutch – provide for enough empowerment of the board of directors to make managerial control of publicly held corporations viable. On the other hand, other corporate laws – the Italian and the Swedish – do not provide for entitlements supporting managerial control, and then shareholder control is basically the only option for corporate governance. Whether this also allows ownership to be significantly separated from control depends, in turn, on the availability of legal devices for exercising voting rights in excess of the corporate controller's cash flow rights.

It seems that some corporate laws favor managerial control over shareholder control, whereas some others display exactly the opposite attitude. This was also suggested by the one analysis of legal distribution of corporate powers as "the real difference between the US and continental Europe" (Cools 2005). This conclusion is only partially correct. The analysis performed throughout this chapter shows that, in fact, managerial control is not feasible in some European jurisdictions – and this may hold for many other countries of continental Europe. But the same analysis does not also show that, where managerial control is feasible, shareholder control is necessarily disfavored by the legal system. Indeed, the fundamental question is whether the availability of legal entitlements to managerial control is compatible with the presence of a controlling shareholder. That is, whether individual companies can effectively *choose* the ownership structure that is more efficient for them.

The answer is a qualified yes. To my knowledge, there is no corporate governance system in the entire world where shareholder control has been completely displaced by managerial capitalism. On that account, the famous Berle and Means (1932) prophecy was most visibly wrong. There are a considerable number of controlling shareholders in the US (Holderness 2009). Controlling shareholders have not disappeared from the Netherlands or even from the UK. From a legal point of view, this is not surprising. A controlling shareholder is always in the position to hold board members (and thereby the firm management) strictly accountable to himself. Whatever the power they are entitled to, a controlling shareholder will ultimately be able to allow only directors he trusts to sit on the board. This is basically the reason why directors are so afraid of hostile takeovers when they are in charge, because a controlling shareholder would emerge from takeover. Legally speaking, allowing directors to resist takeovers – a precondition for managerial control – does not necessarily imply that the powers of an *existing* controlling shareholder be weakened, but only that his unwelcome *emergence* could be frustrated. Normally, jurisdictions that feature managerial control follow this second path. But sometimes – as in the UK – they rather follow the first one. In this case, the presence of entitlements to managerial control ultimately depends on shareholder control being disfavored.

4.5.2 How easily a controlling shareholder can be in charge in the US

There is no such thing as a regulatory disfavor for controlling shareholders in the US.[109] Once he holds a large enough voting block, an American controlling shareholder will have no problem at governing any corporation. He would only need to show up at the general meeting and to vote his shares. Showing up in person is sufficient to break the board's monopoly over directors' nominations and, normally, to win the elections by plurality (see Donald 2004). Then any autonomy of the board would be ended. Directors alone cannot challenge the controlling shareholder's voting power, when this is significant enough to have all board members elected (and replaced) at his will. If necessary, it would be the controlling shareholder to solicit proxies from outside investors, not directors against him because they would have no chance to win. This explains how a controlling shareholder has nearly always himself, or somebody he controls, appointed to the board (Gadhoum et al 2005). In addition, the voting power of a controlling shareholder can be enhanced almost without limits through the use of dual class shares.

In the US, dual class shares used to be restricted by the listing rules of the major stock exchanges, but the restriction was removed in the late 1980s (Bainbridge 2002). Today, about 6% of US publicly held companies (meaning a few hundred) employ dual class shares (Gompers et al 2010) and this may account for between one-half and one-third of family controlled firms, depending on how shareholder control is inferred. When a controlling shareholder avails himself of multiple voting shares he will hardly need any other takeover defense. In the absence of multiple voting shares, the wide array of takeover defenses available under US law anyway allows a controlling shareholder to make his position unchallenged with a relatively tiny share ownership (provided, of course, that it is sufficient to control the board). This should also explain why pyramids are basically unheard of in American corporate governance. Although the mainstream explanation lies in both fiscal and regulatory disfavor of pyramidal groups in the US (Morck and Yeung 2005), pyramids have never been much needed in the first place. In fact, American corporate law provides controlling shareholders with several other means of empowerment.

---

109 Black (1990) and Roe (1994) have argued the opposite, but this is controversial (see e.g. Holderness 2009). For a more nuanced distinction between the US and the UK approaches to corporate governance, see Kraakman et al (2009: 82–83).

4.5.3 Imperfect neutrality of legal distribution of corporate powers in the Netherlands

Dutch law is not as neutral to corporate control structure as US law. Before the reform, the structure regime undoubtedly favored directors over a controlling shareholder. Yet, a significant proportion of the companies subject to the structure regime were controlled by a shareholder. This probably required the corporate controller being *de facto* in control of one or more positions on the supervisory board. Anyway, even a 'structure' Dutch company would have been very difficult to govern with the opposition of a controlling shareholder. That is, in the end, some harmony between the management and the general meeting of shareholders should have been the only possible equilibrium.[110] After the recent reforms, the regulatory bias against controlling shareholders is much attenuated in the Netherlands and it might have possibly disappeared altogether. Today, a controlling shareholder may veto any nomination to the supervisory board and can dismiss all of its members at will. It is therefore quite difficult to imagine that, in the long run, either the management board or the supervisory board can be constituted of members who do not enjoy the trust of an existing controlling shareholder. This would not hold as simply as when a controlling shareholder suddenly materializes after a takeover. We will discuss this particular case in the last chapter.

Other 'oligarchic devices' that characterize corporate law in the Netherlands are perfectly neutral between shareholder control and managerial control. A voting trust foundation (*administratiekantoor*) can also be set up by a shareholder, and priority shares can be held by a controlling shareholder as well as by the company's directors. Similarly, Dutch-style 'poison pills' (i.e., preference shares) can also be employed to defend the position of a controlling shareholder anytime he is in control of the management board. Even more importantly, none of the above devices is compulsory. Individual companies adopt them if they so wish. Indeed their use – particularly combined – has been decreasing over the last few decades (de Jong et al 2010). When a controlling shareholder is present, these devices might work as a good substitute for dual class shares – whose issuance is confronted with a number of hurdles under Dutch law – or pyramids – which are rare in Dutch corporate governance. For instance, a controlling shareholder would not need to retain a large ownership stake when he has priority shares that allow him to have the general meeting passing favorable resolutions by a simple majority of the votes cast and endorsing no unfavorable resolution without a two-thirds majority and a quorum of 50% of share capital. Similar results can be possibly obtained by stripping voting rights from outside shareholders and placing them with an *administratiekantoor* deferring to the controlling shareholder instead of to the company management.

110 See de Jong et al (2010) along these lines.

In conclusion, it seems that a controlling shareholder would have few difficulties in governing a Dutch corporation on an ongoing basis. In the 1990s, shareholder control accounted for about 40% of publicly held firms in the Netherlands. This proportion decreased considerably in recent years, but still in 2005 nearly one-quater of Dutch listed companies had a largest shareholder accounting for 30% or more of the capital (de Jong et al 2010).

4.5.4 Impediments to shareholder control in the UK

Controlling shareholders have a much harder life in the UK. Substantially, shareholders face hurdles in controlling the majority of the board because of a particularly unfavorable combination of rules and best practices disciplining the governance of listed companies. The Listing Rules used to presume the status of controlling shareholder in the presence of a concentration of voting rights exceeding 30%, which likewise triggered a number of restrictions in the exercise of governance rights. It is therefore unsurprising that, as of 1992, only about 9% of British listed firms had a shareholder accounting for more than 30% of voting rights, and the percentage goes down to 2.4% for firms controlled by an absolute majority shareholder (Goergen and Renneboog 2001). These figures are lower than in the US and possibly the lowest in the world. Regulation is most likely to be responsible.

The British discipline of listed companies is far more shareholder-friendly than US law. However, differently from most jurisdictions of continental Europe, shareholders in the UK are not simply protected *as a class* – which would ultimately empower controlling shareholders. British shareholders can in fact exercise their extensive governance rights as against the directors' on condition that they hold *non-controlling* positions. Since minority shareholders do not actively exercise any control rights they might be entitled to, such a special protection indirectly empowers management-controlled boards (whose directors are entitled to fill in the power's vacuum through the proxy voting system). The only losers in this game appear to be both existing and would-be controlling shareholders.

Regulatory disfavor for controlling shareholders in listed companies clearly does not imply that they are completely ruled out of corporate governance. However, publicly held companies under shareholder control might be less than they should be in the UK. A British entrepreneur basically faces the following alternative: either he takes his firm public, and then he must be ready to have firm control handed over to professional management or anyway exerted with a very limited ownership stake; or he keeps it private, but then he has to give up the opportunity of both liquidating his investment and raising equity funds on a large scale. The first alternative would be only profitable for the entrepreneur on condition that idiosyncratic PBC are not too high. In other words, the corporate governance system in the UK may not allow for highly innovative and uncertain businesses to be financed through the stock market, for that kind of business would require a rather concentrated ownership structure whose control is difficult to implement under the regulation and the best practices applying to listed firms in the UK. Professor Mayer (1999) emphasized this circumstance:

> The UK . . . goes further than virtually any other system in restricting private benefits. The advantage is that we live in a society in which there is less concentration of power, more protection of minorities and small investors, and less risk of banking failure. The drawback is that there is less incentive to invest in activities that markets are inadequate to sustain.

The high peculiarity of legal distribution of corporate powers in Britain could also be responsible for the limited (and practically nonexistent) use of devices for separating voting rights from cash flow rights. On the one hand, these devices would not help to circumvent the status of a substantial shareholder because this is established in terms of influence and, ultimately, of voting rights. On the other hand, institutional investors have always been in the position to oppose these devices, particularly at the IPO stage, in their capacity as the most important financiers of British public companies and as the holders of the last word over charter amendments and directors' tenure.

In conclusion, the ownership structure of publicly held firms in the UK may be more dispersed than desirable due to a traditional regulatory bias against controlling shareholders. The related inefficiencies could be corrected dynamically, however, in the market of corporate control. In the last chapter of this book, I shall discuss how an overly restrictive takeover regulation may also prevent that goal from being achieved.

4.6 Policy implications

Normative implications are implicit in the above discussion only if the reader recalls how the prescriptions about the 'optimal' corporate governance regulation were derived from Prediction 2 in the previous chapter. These implications are briefly summed up below.

4.6.1 *Providing entitlements to support managerial control*

The legal distribution of corporate power affects the range of ownership structures that can be implemented under a certain corporate law. Since we do not know what the efficient ownership structure is, and this is likely to vary from business to business under the endogeneity assumption that drives the present work, that range should be as wide as possible.[111] However – as we have just seen – *regulation very often creates biases that may distort the firm's choice of ownership structure*. In particular, a dispersed ownership structure may fail to

---

111 See *supra*, Chapter 3.

be implemented in the absence of legal entitlements to managerial control. An entrepreneur/manager will have to stop diluting his ownership stake as soon as he risks being unable to exercise and defend firm control just by holding on to one or more positions on the board of directors. For similar reasons, firm control may never be handed over to professional management where managers are not able to run the firm without the support of a controlling shareholder. No entrepreneur/manager would ever leave firm control up for grabs. When he cannot 'sell' it to professional management, he will have no choice but to keep it for himself of for another controlling shareholder willing to pay him enough for taking over. This might be unfortunate, since the business may be ripe for a more dispersed ownership structure if only the founder could cash in his idiosyncratic PBC, by selling his ownership stake to the market and corporate control to the management.

The above situation characterizes most countries of continental Europe and, arguably, of the entire world. Publicly held firms are often likely to be stuck in ownership structures that are more concentrated than desirable. That ultimately means a shortage of equity finance that negatively affects the pursuit of growth opportunities, and might result in fewer firms actually going public when the benefits of listing are so tiny that they are systematically outweighed by its costs (Coates 2004; Boot et al 2006). The foregoing analysis is important because it uncovers one *legal* reason that may underlie such a situation, which does not depend on *insufficient* investor *protection* (a matter that will be dealt with in the next two chapters) but, rather, on *insufficient empowerment* of corporate controllers. I conjecture that, in many corporate law systems, managers simply cannot be in charge and, as a result, ownership must be concentrated in order to support controlling powers even when such a concentration is inefficient. The previous discussion has shown that this is most probably true for Sweden and for Italy.

In Italy something else should also be at play. The standard explanation of the very high ownership concentration that features Italian corporate governance lies in weak investor protection (Gilson 2006; Djankov et al 2008). The analysis of the following chapters will confirm that this problem is still in place. But I suspect that, even if the investor protection problem was suddenly fixed, the prevailing ownership structure would not change much – in fact, it has not despite the significant improvements in investor protection. Under Italian corporate law, managerial control is technically unfeasible since the board members have no entitlement to influence the outcomes of the general meeting of shareholders as regards their own appointment and removal. What is lacking is basically a board-controlled proxy voting system, since – especially after the 2004 reform – Italian directors could be otherwise very powerful relative to both dispersed shareholders and to the insurgency of a controlling shareholder.

On this account, the situation is much worse in Sweden, where directors can be completely deprived of authority and placed – as they normally are – at the mercy of the general meeting of shareholders. That should explain why, in a country where weak investor protection has never been an issue, ownership is still very concentrated and managerial capitalism has always been unheard of. Allowing for a change in that corporate governance path would require much more than the mere introduction of a rule entitling the board to solicit voting proxies at the company's expenses. In fact, the entire system of competence rules should also be adapted to director control, and ultimately include the possibility of board-initiated takeover defenses.

4.6.2 Pyramids and dual class shares: should they be regulated?

To be sure, in Swedish corporate governance, it is not exactly corporate ownership to be concentrated but, rather, voting power. In the recent past, Sweden exhibited one of the highest rates of divergence between voting rights and cash flow rights in worldwide corporate governance (Agnblad et al 2001). This probably explains how the Swedish stock market managed to be among the most developed in the world. The degree of disproportionality between voting rights and ownership has decreased recently, but this has paralleled an increase in the frequency of transactions going private (Henrekson and Jakobsson 2012). Good investor protection has traditionally allowed Swedish controlling shareholders to widely dilute their ownership stake by raising considerable amounts of equity finance from the stock market. Corporate law has allowed them to do it without losing the majority of voting rights. The permissive regulation of dual class shares in Swedish law seems to be, then, a key factor that lead to the stock market development. Pyramids have certainly also contributed to that result, even though – as we know – their effects on the efficiency of corporate governance are at best ambiguous and at worst counterproductive.

As is often the case for extremely complex phenomena, the welfare analysis of pyramids is still very much underdeveloped. Nevertheless, authoritative commentators argue that they should be regulated, if not even prohibited (Bebchuk et al 2000). No doubt, they are very dangerous in those legal systems where the risk of expropriation of minority shareholders is substantial (Bertrand et al 2002). Even in that case, having pyramids prohibited outright seems to be a much too coarse solution compared to a comprehensive policing of conflicted interest transactions.[112]

Anyway, minority shareholder expropriation is apparently not a problem in Sweden. Still, pyramids could be used as a vehicle for misusing free cash (in the form of empire building) instead of returning it to non-controlling shareholders (Holmén and Högfeldt 2009). I believe that the market for corporate control could do better in coping with this problem, on condition that cashing in the control premium is a more profitable alternative than playing with the

---

112 See most recently (on the corporate governance of Israeli companies organized as pyramids) Ronald J. Gilson and Alan Schwartz, *Report Concerning Recommendations of the Committee on Enhancing Competitiveness*, 1 December 2011 (on file with author).

firm's assets for a controlling shareholder. Unfortunately, this condition is not always satisfied in Sweden. The ultimate reason is that managerial control, which could bring about further equity finance without need of pyramidal structures, is not supported by corporate law.

Then we are in a bind. Short of promoting a more efficient dispersion of ownership, a restrictive regulation of pyramids (for instance, through an appropriate fiscal policy) might just undermine separation of ownership and control when legal entitlements to managerial control are unavailable. One reason why this did not happen in the US (where pyramids have always been disfavored) is that managers and controlling shareholders hardly *need* pyramidal groups to control American listed companies and to shield them from hostile takeovers. This suggests that, at least in other countries, the case against pyramids is not yet strong enough to yield to a draconian prohibition. On the one hand, contestability of corporate control cannot be imposed by regulation. Many entrenchment devices are difficult to regulate, and some may turn out to be definitely "unregulable" (Arlen and Talley 2003). On the other hand, although control tends to be naturally uncontested, entrenchment devices may not be equally efficient under different circumstances. Regulation undoubtedly distorts their choice. On the contrary, we cannot rule out that the market would select the most efficient arrangement if freed of unwarranted legal constraints. Pyramids may be spontaneously superseded as soon as more efficient alternatives to separation of ownership and control become available.

The above reasoning applies even more forcefully to Italy, where multiple voting shares are not allowed and pyramids are the only way to have owner-ship substantially separated from control. Italian law performs comparatively worse than Swedish law on the dual class shares account. Allowing multiple voting shares should not worry policymakers too much, when this is supple-mented by a substantial improvement in how non-controlling shareholders are protected from expropriation and by some minor changes in corporate law that would also make managerial control an option for Italian corporate gov-ernance. As the US experience shows, the market would ultimately make sure that dual class shares are not overused when alternatives as to both shareholder control and managerial control are present. In addition, even where manage-rial control is not an option (as in Sweden), multiple voting shares present fewer problems than pyramids. Both can feature shareholder control with a higher degree of separation from ownership, thereby nurturing large-scale equity finance and the firm's growth. The advantage of dual class shares is that they can hardly result in unfair surprises for minority shareholders.[113]

---

113 This conclusion parallels the findings, of a study commissioned by the European Commission in 2007 (Institutional Shareholder Services, Shearman and Sterling, and ECGI, *Report on the proportionality principle in the European Union*, 18 May 2007). Based on these findings, the European Commission suspended its plan to introduce mandatory one-share-one-vote regulations. The academic background of this study can be found in Burkart and Lee (2008) and Adams and Ferreira (2008).

4.6.3 No bias is good: corporate law's neutrality as to the ownership structure

From a purely theoretical perspective, ownership can be either more or less concentrated than desirable. The first situation tends to prevail around the world, and supposedly characterizes corporate governance in continental Europe as opposed to the UK and the US. This stylized picture is, at best, imprecise. Public companies having no controlling shareholder are in fact rare on a worldwide basis, but they are by no means confined to Anglo-Saxon countries. As far as Europe is concerned, managerial control seems to account for the majority of listed firms as also in the Netherlands. The foregoing analysis has shown how this depends on the legal distribution of corporate powers more than upon any influence of the common law tradition (see La Porta et al 2008 for the contrary view). Normally, in continental Europe, this distribution is so biased towards shareholders as a class that it fails to support directors' autonomy from the general meeting. This provides no legal grounds for transition from controlling shareholdings to managerial control. In that respect, Italy and Sweden should be regarded as illustrative of a more general problem. However, the US and the UK are definitely not the only legal models supporting dispersed ownership.

The foregoing analysis also shows that the distribution of powers can be biased in the opposite direction, that is, it may fail to support shareholder control. If there is a country where this is likely to happen, it is the UK. Under British laws and the legacy of former regulations currently embedded into codes of best practices, directors' empowerment supporting managerial control ultimately comes at the expense of controlling shareholders. There is therefore a fair chance that, in the UK, ownership might be more dispersed than desirable, due to the non-neutrality of the distribution of corporate powers. As the US experience shows, disfavoring shareholder control is not necessary for the emergence of managerial capitalism. The combination of British law with the Corporate Governance Code should become, then, more neutral between shareholder control and managerial control.

At first glance, the first candidate for reform would be the arm's length obligations that a dominant shareholder faces in dealing with the board. These obligations are currently established by the Listing Rules and the Corporate Governance Code (the latter on a comply-or-explain basis). However, on the one hand, this would expose management of British listed companies – who are otherwise defenseless in the face of a hostile takeover – to the insurgency of controlling shareholders; on the other hand, this might have adverse effects on protection of minority shareholders. As in other European countries, a solution like that would probably result in too little scope for managerial control. The matter is far more complicated and it cannot be addressed piecemeal. At the end of the day, the regulatory distortion of corporate governance choices has to do with confusion between issues of (minority) investor protection and issues concerning the empowerment of corporate controllers. Such confusion is responsible for most misunderstandings in the standard interpretation of corporate governance. The British regulation of listed firms is the living proof of how those misunderstandings can translate into regulatory biases that possibly undermine the efficiency of corporate governance.

It could be that British investors enjoy 'excessive' legal protection. I find this interpretation not entirely convincing. Rather, it seems to me that strong investor protection – which is not necessarily too bad – is implemented in the wrong fashion in the UK. Outside shareholders are not just *protected*; they are *empowered* by British regulation (see Pacces 2011). Yet, in corporate governance, shareholder protection should be dealt with separately from distribution of powers. As I am going to show in the following chapters, this is possible. It requires that the role of the judiciary be directed, and that of institutional investors be limited, to constraining expropriation. In the same vein, the optimal regulation of corporate control transactions should rely not on either a mandatory bid or a prohibition of takeover resistance in order to protect non-controlling shareholders. The law of the UK has none of these features, and – as I will show – this makes British corporate governance suboptimal in spite of its otherwise good performance.

At least as far as distribution of powers is concerned, the Netherlands and the US appear to be the winners of our five-country tournament. In these countries, the legal distribution of corporate powers is basically *neutral* between shareholder control and managerial control. In other words, American and Dutch corporate laws allow for a wide range of entitlements to corporate control. In either country, this range is large enough to support both directors' autonomy from the general meeting and a controlling shareholder being in charge with as much ownership dispersion as the market can bear. Individual companies can, then, choose the ownership structure that suits them best.

Dutch law is not perfectly neutral though. The structure regime cannot yet be opted out by a significant number of companies listed in the Netherlands, even those that will be enabled to choose a one-tier board in the near future. Although the structure regime is not sufficient to rule out shareholder control, especially after the 2004 reform has partly restored shareholder powers in directors' appointment, it is nonetheless not particularly suitable for a controlling shareholder. It could easily be repealed, since also directors do not strictly need it for their empowerment and – as it is often the case – stakeholder protection is little more than an excuse for vested interests that could be satisfied otherwise. At any rate, the Dutch structure regime does not much distort the initial choice of the ownership structure as it affects its subsequent evolution. The remaining rigidities of the structure regime are only likely to make changes in control more difficult. I shall discuss this particular problem in the last chapter of this book.

5   How to cope with self-dealing

5.1 Investor protection: stealing and shirking compared

5.1.1 *Policing investor protection*

Separation of ownership and control requires both willing sellers and willing buyers of the company's stock. In the previous chapter, the supply side (the sellers' point of view) has been analyzed. It has been shown how the corporate controller should be willing to dilute his ownership stake, provided that his position and idiosyncratic private benefits of control (PBC) are not endangered. The range of legal entitlements available to this purpose determines how far ownership *can* be separated from control. However, the demand side (the buyers' point of view) is crucial for the *actual* choice of the ownership structure within that range. On condition that the corporate controller retains residual control rights, how much stock he is willing to sell to the investing public will depend on the price he can get for the shares sold. Outside shareholders' willingness to pay is affected, in turn, by two major concerns: their not being expropriated of the investment and their expected return on the same investment being maximized.

In other words, what worries outside shareholders is both 'stealing' and 'shirking' by the corporate controller, interpreted in their broadest sense. The next question is how stealing and shirking can be policed in such a way as to make shareholders willing to invest. In principle, this should be primarily the corporate controller's concern, for it ultimately affects the price he can get for the shares sold to the investing public. However, as we have seen, contractual incompleteness undermines his ability to *commit credibly* to a 'no-stealing, no-shirking' policy. Neither can he give up residual control rights to this purpose, for he would then be no longer able to protect his (idiosyncratic) control rents. Another solution needs to be worked out in order to exploit the gains from trade arising from efficient policing of both diversionary and distortionary PBC. Intuitively, such a solution cannot be left to private ordering, or at least not entirely. This is basically *why* institutions, and the law, matter for investor protection.

Which institutions matter, and *how*, is another question. On the one hand, institutions have to make sure that the corporate controller will not misuse his power to divert cash flow from outside shareholders ('stealing') when he has the opportunity to do so. Law is the best candidate for this job: the legal discipline of conflicted interest transactions is a major device for curbing *diversionary* PBC. But, on the other hand, institutions also need to support investors' expectations that the value of their investment will be ultimately maximized by the corporate controller (i.e., that he will not 'shirk'). Economic analysis suggests that law can do little to obtain this result directly (e.g. Roe 2002). However, the law can contribute to achieving this goal indirectly, promoting an efficient market for corporate control. Another area in which law matters is thus regulation of corporate control transactions, whereby private benefits can be profitably exchanged for enhanced security benefits which should lead to dynamic minimization of *distortionary* PBC.

This chapter will show how legal regulation of corporate governance should be mostly concerned with the stealing problem, but very little with shirking – as, in fact, corporate law seem to be in most jurisdictions. The next chapter will analyze the five jurisdictions of our sample in this perspective. It will be shown that this provides the basis of a positive theory of corporate law and fruitful guidelines on how to improve its efficiency. The impact of regulation of corporate control transactions on the dynamic efficiency of corporate governance will be analyzed in the last two chapters of this study.

5.1.2 Separating stealing from shirking

Treating stealing separately from shirking yields two important implications for the legal policing of investor protection. The first one is a different approach to the discretion–accountability tradeoff – our ultimate yardstick for evaluating regulation of corporate governance.[1] In this respect, discretion in the exercise of corporate control and the problem of managerial shirking are two sides of the same coin. Easing the entrepreneur's financial constraints entails a reduction of the relative weight of his financial commitment, and then requires more accountability to the financiers (Tirole 2006). Parties should be free to work out by themselves the solution to this discretion–accountability tradeoff, choosing the pattern of separation of ownership and control that maximizes the joint value of cash flow rights sold to the market and of control rights retained by the corporate controller. The market for corporate control will correct for inefficiencies arising over time due to contractual incompleteness, by providing incentives to sell control to a more efficient manager instead of expanding the inefficient consumption of distortionary PBC – i.e., shirking. Both mechanisms are based on the *carrot* rather than on the stick: in the first situation, the entrepreneur's desire to cash out his

---

1 See also Bainbridge (2008).

holdings or to expand his business without having to surrender control and its rents; in the second one, the corporate controller's opportunity to cash in his idiosyncratic PBC when a more efficient manager takes over. Law should just provide the right entitlements for corporate control to be exercised and transferred in such a way.

Stealing is a completely different story. Ex-post, stealing is worth to the thief almost as much as it costs to the victim. Intuitively, then, the only 'carrot-deal' shareholders could ever offer to the corporate controller is the following: 'Please, do not steal: we will give you as much as you want.' The *stick* is therefore the only option for curbing diversionary PBC ex-ante. Differently from shirking, stealing cannot be dealt with as a matter of choice between alternative ownership structures. Whatever that structure, stealing has to be prevented ex-ante and severely punished ex-post. Law cannot protect investors from expropriation by simply allowing them to *choose* how much stock they are willing to buy from an entrenched controller. They might end up buying none. Law has rather to provide investors with reliable constraints on the corporate controller's ability to steal from their pockets, whatever his ownership stake. The corporate controller's discretion needs be constrained to this purpose. How and to what extent this should be done are the key policy issues. This is also a discretion–accountability tradeoff whose solution, however, is not implemented by different patterns of separation of ownership and control, but is a *precondition* for the latter to occur at any rate (Black 2001; Gilson 2006; Djankov et al 2008).

The second implication of separating shirking from stealing in corporate governance is that the anti-expropriation policy needs ultimately to be implemented by means of mandatory rules.[2] The reason why parties cannot be expected to 'work it out themselves' when it comes to stealing is that commitments not to steal the residual claim on the firm's assets are not credible when they are taken by those who retain residual rights of control over the same assets. Since corporate contracts are incomplete, in those contingencies which have not been contracted upon, whoever controls the assets has the power to appropriate them and basically no incentive to refrain from doing it (Rock and Wachter 2001). Within our framework, this situation always characterizes the corporate controller.

In more practical terms, contractual safeguards against stealing can never be detailed enough to rule out opportunities of expropriation. This is not simply a matter of including a strict 'no-stealing' provision in the corporate charter – anybody would agree to that. The problem is rather how to have such a provision implemented within an open mandate to discretionary management. In the absence of external constraints, the corporate controller is easily entitled to abuse his discretion for stealing purposes. This could only be constrained contractually by means of very *detailed* and *unchangeable* charter

---

2 See, in a similar vein, Eisenberg (1989).

provisions, limiting the corporate controller's discretion as to day-to-day control over the firm's assets. Provisions of such a kind should be based on actual or virtual unanimity rules, which would need to be extended broadly across the charter to avoid circumvention. Unsurprisingly, provisions like unanimity or high super-majority requirements are practically unheard of in the charters of publicly held corporations (Kraakman et al 2009). Companies going public do not seem willing to give up flexibility in prospective charter amendments in order to deter opportunistic latecomer terms (Hansmann 2006). For good or evil the corporate controller's discretion typically includes the ability to exert significant influence over the amendment of the charter (most clearly so when he is a controlling shareholder), and this is the ultimate reason why contractual commitment not to steal may not be entirely credible in corporate governance.

5.1.3 *The debate on mandatory rules in corporate law*

In advocating the case for mandatory regulation of 'stealing' in corporate governance, I am taking a narrower approach to the more general debate about whether corporate law should be mandatory or enabling – a most controversial issue in corporate law and economics.[3] As I am going to show, this approach provides more fruitful grounds for answering the question. The question about the mandatory/enabling balance in corporate law is misguided when one insists on bundling problems of shareholder expropriation with those of incentive alignment in the exercise of corporate control (that is, confusing stealing and shirking). No surprise, then, that law and economics scholars have not yet found agreement on such a matter.

In the standard debate, the rationale for mandatory rules in corporate law is twofold (Gordon 1989). On the one hand, charter terms might be ex-ante inefficiently priced by investors. On the other hand, the same terms might be modified ex-post without the investors' knowledgeable consent. Supporters of regulation argue that freedom of contract would not be sufficient to protect shareholders from both one-sided charter provisions and opportunistic amendments, provided that (non-controlling) shareholders are ill informed and rationally apathetic.[4] Supporters of de-regulation contend that shareholders also include market professionals, or are at least assisted by them, and this should ultimately make sure that charter provisions are adequately priced by the stock market, and that opportunistic amendments are ultimately voted down by shareholders.[5] However, it is better to separately analyze the two problems of efficient pricing of the corporate contract and of its midstream amendments, since only the latter seems to provide a rationale

---

3 See the symposium "Contractual Freedom in Corporate Law" (published in *Columbia Law Review*, vol. 89, 1395–1774).
4 Bebchuk (1989b); but see also Bebchuk and Hamdani (2002).
5 Romano (1989); but see also Macey (2008).

for mandatory regulation of the corporate charter; and this rationale is limited to the stealing case.

5.1.3.1 Pricing of contract terms

The problem of efficient pricing of contract terms that are not bargained for is not peculiar to corporate law. This is germane to the more general debate on standard form contracts entered into by consumers on a take-it-or-leave-it basis. Like consumers, investors are not expected to screen the quality of the standardized contract they enter into when they buy corporate stock. To be sure, individual investors do not even *feel* they sign any contract with the issuer of the securities in their portfolio, whereas, for instance, no consumer would deny having signed a contract with his Internet Services Provider – even though he hardly knows what is written in it. Yet, paradoxical as it may appear, investors in financial markets are in a better position relative to consumers of goods or services.

Individual investors do not deal directly with securities issuers but, rather, with market professionals acting as intermediaries (Pacces 2000). The latter have high-powered incentives to get stock prices right. Individual investors certainly do not go through corporate charters and corporate governance arrangements, but they buy and sell stock through securities firms that must do it at their own risk when they 'make the price.' Securities dealers, underwriters, and financial institutions provide investors with a professional pricing of contract terms that is normally unavailable to consumers of other goods and services (Gilson and Kraakman 1984). Investors' being unaware of the quality of charter terms is, therefore, not a good rationale for mandatory rules in corporate law, which ultimately disciplines contractual arrangements between relatively sophisticated players (like, for instance, the promoters and the underwriters of an IPO). This is not to say that investors do not need protection, but only that unfair charter terms is the wrong problem for investor protection. Investors might indeed be duped by the corporate disclosures and the securities professionals they must rely upon for participating in the financial market. However, this has little to do with exploitation of unfair charter terms, and then with corporate law. It is in fact a matter of securities regulation. In many respects, the actual degree of shareholder protection from extraction of diversionary PBC also depends on securities regulation (Rock 2002). But its connection with the protective stance of corporate law has to be put in the right perspective. This connection will be clarified throughout this chapter.

5.1.3.2 Opportunistic amendments

The argument concerning opportunistic amendments has more virtue. We know from the foregoing chapter that, under both managerial and shareholder control, the corporate controller is typically featured with the power to significantly influence, if not to determine, the process of charter amendment. Shareholder weakness in this regard does not simply arise out of their being ill informed, and thus cannot be cured just by the intervention of market professionals. Non-controlling shareholders simply lack the *power* to constrain the corporate controller's opportunistic behavior, since they are not vested with residual rights of control. Apparently, then, both stealing and shirking are good candidates for mandatory regulation when the risk of opportunistic amendments of the corporate contract is being considered.

In practice, however, the two problems appear to be dealt with differently by corporate laws. Take takeover resistance as an example of potential shirking. Although, especially in legal terms, the problem of entrenchment is considered different from plain shirking (Eisenberg 1989), entrenchment may be as well motivated by the corporate controller's desire to maintain on-the-job consumption of perquisites – and, to be sure, this is just how entrenchment is explained by the agency theory (Bebchuk 2003a). It is worth noting that the corporate controller's ability to have the charter amended is not as much legally constrained by his being interested in defending his controlling position as it would be by his interest in diverting shareholder money. Charter amendments formally upheld by a shareholder vote can be nullified by courts on grounds they are motivated by diversionary purposes, whereas they have little chances to be overridden based on allegation that they serve entrenchment purposes (Kraakman et al 2009). Even in those jurisdictions where takeover resistance is severely regulated, corporate controllers may always retain enough voting power to be entrenched or to legitimately amend the charter for purpose of entrenchment; and often they do. Whereas, in those jurisdictions with a more liberal attitude towards takeover defenses, corporate charters could always be drafted in such a way as to rule out anti-takeover devices unless they are approved by outside shareholders; and yet, most often the charters choose not to do so (Daines and Klausner 2001). The ease with which takeover resistance can be implemented by the corporate controller depends only apparently on the law; in the end, it is a matter of choice.

Supporters of de-regulation might be right, then, when they claim that little involvement of outside shareholders in the exercise and the allocation of corporate control is not the unintended consequence of the corporate structure, but the desired outcome of the contracting process (Romano 1989). The reason why outside shareholders have almost no say in the firm governance – and yet they still invest – is not that they like to be fooled by managerial consumption of perquisites. They know from the very beginning that some shirking is to be expected, but nonetheless they have *chosen* not to interfere with how and to what extent profits will be made by corporate management. This explains, in turn, why corporate law also does not *force* non-controlling shareholders to interfere. That is, there are no mandatory rules requiring that shareholders actually participate in decision-making for the corporate enterprise to be managed and its charter to be adapted to changed circumstances. As we know from the previous chapter, the requirement of shareholder voting can be – and most often is – reduced to little more than a formality in the practice of publicly held companies. Indeed, corporate charters can be made more or less easy to amend without the involvement of non-controlling shareholders, but this will depend on the amount of discretion that outside shareholders are willing to provide the corporate controller with at the outset. That choice being ultimately made by sophisticated players, interested in maximizing the revenues of placing the company's stock with the market, there appears to be little reason to have the same choice overridden by mandatory rules.

5.1.3.3 *The rubberstamp problem*

The above reasoning fits the shirking problem very well, but is inapplicable to the stealing case. Shareholders may be willing to buy stock at a discount accounting for a moderate risk of shirking (given the ownership structure and the controller's incentive scheme set up ex-ante), knowing that at some point the corporate controller will prefer to sell control to a more efficient manager rather than to expand his shirking. But the same discount would erode the entire value of the firm's stock, should stealing also be allowed. In other words, unconstrained stealing opportunities make financial exchange impracticable (Shleifer and Vishny 1997). Since no corporate controller would refrain from a 'take the money and run' strategy when this involves no penalty, no money would be provided by shareholders in the first place.

It is illusory to believe that the corporate controller would be able to commit to a no-stealing policy *anyway*, simply by means of the corporate contract, should any legal system ever make optional the anti-expropriation rules of corporate law (Coffee 1989). Here lies the major weakness of the deregulators' position. This position has been authoritatively articulated by Professor Romano (1989: 1601):

> Critics of the enabling regimes suppose that shareholders would vote to permit managers to steal corporate assets by rescinding the duty of loyalty. This is said to demonstrate a need for mandatory rules. But the hypothetical, eliminating the duty of loyalty, is too incredible to be seriously entertained: what sane shareholders would agree to license theft? . . . If investors are so poorly informed or foolish to vote to transfer their wealth to managers without compensation, we have far deeper problems than refining corporation codes. How can we have confidence that investors will make the fundamental allocative investment decisions required in a capitalist economy? Or better yet, to participate in a democracy?

The above reasoning has one important flaw: it assumes actual participation of outside shareholders to corporate decision-making through their voting at the general meeting. On that basis, mandatory rules in corporate law would be a trivial issue (Easterbrook and Fischel 1991) because they would do nothing more than mimick the standard outcome of a market bargain: 'I provide you with the money you need on condition that you are bound not to steal any of it.' Permissible deviations from such a scheme are unimportant, for they would never be implemented with the shareholder consent. However, we know from the previous chapter that charter amendments do not always require the *actual* consent of non-controlling shareholders. When a controlling shareholder is in charge with a substantial share of voting rights, not even their *formal* consent might be necessary. Anyway, also when ultimate control powers reside with the management (or likewise when a controlling shareholder has not enough voting power to have the charter amended at his own will) outside shareholder consent does not provide enough guarantees against opportunistic amendments put forward by the corporate controller (Eisenberg 1989a).

Of course, no single shareholder would ever support, either in person or by proxy, any explicit 'license to steal' (Romano 1989). But there are one million ways to induce outside shareholders to rubberstamp management proposals having equivalent purposes. Think, for instance, to a proposal of lowering the fiduciary standards of certain intra-group transactions, on grounds that this is needed to catch up with competitors. The alleged motivation might be truthful, and that could justify widening managerial *discretion*. Nevertheless, reduced *accountability* in transactions involving potential conflicts of interest may easily lead to outrageous instances of tunneling (Johnson et al 2000; Atanasov et al 2011). How can we expect investors to evaluate how changed circumstances affect the discretion–accountability tradeoff, and to cast their vote accordingly? This would be far more ambitious than claiming that shareholders are not foolish. In fact, such an expectation could even contradict the terms of the original agreement between shareholders and the corporate controller. The latter is vested with the authority to manage the firm and to adapt its governance to changed circumstances, possibly also by driving the amendment of the corporate charter. Shareholders will not interfere with this activity and will vote with the management when required.

Even though – according to Professor Romano – the rubberstamp strategy is suboptimal in the presence of uncertainty as to whether management resolutions are beneficial or detrimental to shareholder value, this is the outcome supported by the empirical evidence. With absolutely negligible exceptions, shareholders tend to vote with the firm management (de Jong et al 2006; Yermack 2010). While shareholders would not vote in favor of a resolution unambiguously detrimental of their own interest (which is then very unlikely to be ever put forward), they would not invest their money in the absence of a meaningful guarantee that the corporate controller cannot misuse his discretion (which they normally support with their vote) for stealing purposes. Such a guarantee cannot but come from institutions that are out of the corporate controller's reach (Rock and Wachter 2001).

5.1.3.4 *Mandatory rules as a credible commitment*

That corporate law should feature mandatory rules for purpose of commitment may seem straightforward. However, Professor Hansmann (2006) has recently advocated a different solution. First, he contends that, at least in the US, corporate laws only consist of default rules that could always be derogated by the corporate charter. Then he argues that, in practice, corporate charters are less flexible than is commonly understood, and therefore adaptation of the corporate contract to new circumstances should be realized by modification of corporate law's default rules. In his view, this explains why US companies hardly depart from default arrangements, which thus become both a source of commitment and a device for delegating to the state the process of charter amendment.

Professor Hansmann makes an interesting point, which would be worth investigating in depth in the future. Recent empirical studies confirm that default rules are sticky (Listokin 2009). But the story seems to be more complicated. On the one hand, even in the US corporate laws have a mandatory core. Hansmann's argument is that they could always be opted-out, by the choice of a more flexible statutory form or by reincorporation in a more liberal jurisdiction. Although American companies theoretically have this freedom, the fact is that they almost never use it in practice. Virtually all of the companies listed in the US choose to remain subject to the few, but fundamental, mandatory rules of the statutory form of business corporations. This is most often the Delaware General Corporation Law. On the other hand, the distinction between default and mandatory rules could still be meaningful. The majority of US listed firms are incorporated in Delaware. By so doing, companies do not simply 'buy' a package of default rules. Actually, the rules on director removal and the security-voting structure often depart from the statutory defaults. The argument that default rules favoring management are difficult to opt out of in the US (Bebchuk and Hamdani 2002) does not explain why they are ever opted in. Empirical evidence seems to suggest that shareholders often neglect to use the opportunities they have to strengthen their position relative to the management (Listokin 2010). However, quite unambiguously, the majority of American companies seem to choose Delaware law because that comes with the administration of fiduciary duties by a highly sophisticated judiciary – the Chancery and the Supreme Court of Delaware.[6]

In the end, we do not yet know enough about how flexibility and commitment can be efficiently balanced in the corporate charter. The solutions vary considerably across jurisdictions (Kraakman et al 2009: 186–189). In principle, a combination of default rules with very strict requirements for charter amendment should provide a sufficient source of commitment to investor protection. But that may end up being less flexible than a system of

---

6 See Coffee (1989); Rock (1997); Fisch (2000); Paredes (2004); and lately, in critical terms, Carney et al (2010).

mandatory rules administered by an expert judiciary. For this reason, I shall maintain the superiority of mandatory rules in guaranteeing commitment to investor protection in the reminder of this analysis. How to fine-tune alternative solutions based on default and menu rules is a question for future research (see Ayres 2006 for an agenda).

5.1.4 Conflicts of interest in a theory of private benefits of control

The important conclusion of the foregoing discussion is that policing 'stealing' by the corporate controller requires credible commitments and these are best established by mandatory rules. The notion of stealing not only underlies the economic rationale of this proposition, but also defines the boundaries of its validity. The reason why one cannot entirely rely on private ordering when it comes to corporate governance is that the corporate controller is vested with enormous discretion in managing the firm's assets, which would allow for exquisite opportunities for stealing. However, shareholders of a publicly held corporation do not want this discretion to be undermined by contract or, even worse, by the law. They simply do not want it to be abused to their own disadvantage. This is more easily said than done. The practical problem is that both 'stealing' and 'abuse of discretion' are very vague concepts, and they are almost of no use to operationalize a legal strategy against the extraction of diversionary PBC in corporate governance.

Perhaps a more fruitful way to look at the matter, more conventional at least from a legal perspective, is via the notion of *conflict of interest*. After all, what non-controlling shareholders are afraid of is the corporate controller's managing the firm in his exclusive interest rather than for the purpose of maximizing shareholder value (Fox and Heller 2006). The problem is that the potential conflicts of interest of a corporate controller include *more* than just stealing. As we know, once the corporate controller is in charge, he may not only wish to appropriate a part of the firm's residual that shareholders are entitled to (e.g. by siphoning off some of the firm's assets). The controller may also wish to derive non-monetary personal benefits (such as leisure) from the management of the firm's assets at the expenses of their productivity, and to keep on enjoying those benefits in the face of more efficient controllers available in the managerial labor market. Legally speaking, these are all equally relevant categories of conflict of interest between a corporate controller (management or controlling shareholder) and non-controlling shareholders. Also from an economic standpoint, all the above-mentioned behaviors are a matter of concern for non-controlling shareholders. The crucial difference is that they are not necessarily to be dealt with by means of legal rules, let alone by means of mandatory ones (see Black 2001).

The reader may recall from the critical discussion of the agency approach to separation of ownership and control that conflicts of interest are another way to look at the discrepancy between private benefits and securities benefits in corporate governance – that is, the problem of PBC. Our framework of analysis of corporate governance, based on a qualitative distinction between different categories of PBC, turns out to be very helpful in identifying the instances of conflict of interest that are eligible for mandatory regulation, and those that are not.

Like PBC, conflicts of interest come in three basic kinds. One is outright shirking or, broadly speaking, misdirection of managerial effort – what has been labeled so far as distortionary PBC. This is the most dangerous conflict of interest because it costs shareholders far more than the gains to the corporate controller. And yet, just because of this reason, shirking is the conflict more easily policed by means of non-legal *incentives*, both static (profit sharing) and dynamic (market for corporate control), which are supposed to align the corporate controller's interest with that of shareholders. So far this has been argued mostly on economic grounds. The following discussion will show that corporate laws are actually ill equipped to deal with the corporate controllers' failure to maximize shareholder value. Functionally, corporate law copes much better with stealing than with shirking (Roe 2002). In the next chapter, it will be shown that the absence of overreaching regulation of shirking in corporate governance is not just desirable from a normative perspective; it is also part of a positive theory of corporate law.

Another conflict of interest is due to the corporate controller's concern with staying in charge. Under standard agency theory, this is a byproduct of managerial on-the-job consumption (i.e., shirking) (Jensen 1986). However, the legal scholarship prefers to treat this as a separate instance of conflict of interest, which becomes relevant in actual or potential takeover situations: the so-called 'positional' conflict of interest (Eisenberg 1989a). The corporate controller's concern with his own position (entrenchment of corporate control) is a key feature of our framework based on a tripartite account of PBC. However, this is just *potentially* dangerous. When only idiosyncratic PBC motivate entrenchment, and they are still too high to be compensated through the proceeds of a control sale, the existing allocation of corporate control will be efficient. On the contrary, inefficiency arises when the prospective securities benefits of a control transfer are higher than the idiosyncratic value of control, and yet the former are foregone due to *shirking, stealing*, or both. The question of whether the positional conflict of interest should be regulated by corporate law, and to what extent this regulation should be mandatory, is therefore more complicated. The answer provided so far, on economic grounds, is that this has little to do with regulation of the corporate contract, which is left intentionally incomplete in this respect, and rather concerns the provision of the right entitlements to both the incumbent and the insurgent controllers. No different from the case of shirking in a static setting, there is no compelling reason to constrain the parties' freedom to exchange those entitlements in a takeover context, on condition that the exchange does not lead to stealing corporate assets from non-controlling shareholders. The theoretical underpinning of this proposition, and how it matches the regulation of corporate control transactions in Europe and in the US, will be dealt with in the last two chapters of this book.

This leaves us with just one subset of conflicts of interest between the corporate controller and non-controlling shareholders. In the wording of an authoritative commentator, "all agents have a potential interest in diverting the principal's assets to their own use through unfair self-dealing. This is the problem of *traditional conflicts of interest*" (Eisenberg 1989a: 1471). Although, according to the view presented here, corporate controllers are sometimes more entrepreneurs than mere agents of shareholders, the problem of diversion of assets is, if anything, even more severe than in a standard principal–agent setting. The reason is that virtually no agent is ever vested with the same discretion in managing 'other people's money' as the controllers of a publicly held company. This results in unique opportunities for diverting profits, if not property, from the owners.

Once the notion of conflict of interest in corporate governance is narrowed down to the diversion of corporate assets, the problem of diversionary PBC can be framed in more precise legal terms than just 'stealing.' The problem arises whenever the corporate controller has the opportunity to use his discretionary powers over the corporate assets for having the firm's cash flow diverted to his own pockets (e.g. Black 2001). Compared to the shirking and the positional conflicts that I have just reviewed, this traditional conflict is perhaps not the worst kind of conflict of interest (shareholders cannot lose more than the controller gains), but it is certainly the sharpest (the controller gets as much as he manages to steal from shareholders). Ex-post, stealing is simply a matter of distribution, which may thus seem to be neutral to the aggregate wealth of controllers and shareholders. Not only is such a view incorrect (any resource devoted to stealing or to its prevention is a pure waste), but redistribution is exactly what makes stealing so worrisome to shareholders ex-ante. Opportunities for stealing may undermine any incentive compatibility of the corporate structure. Unconstrained opportunities of such a kind would make shareholders unwilling to place their money under the corporate controller's management at the outset, since they would know they are not going to get anything back. That explains in turn the urge to have this, but just this, traditional conflict of interest policed by legal constraints on the controller's ability to divert resources from shareholders' pockets. For this reason, I shall consider only opportunities for diverting corporate assets and cash flow as relevant sources of conflict of interest in the remainder of this chapter.

5.2 Efficient regulation of self-dealing

5.2.1 *Non-pro-rata distributions and conflicted interest transactions*

5.2.1.1 *Related-party transactions*

The prototypical instance of 'diversionary' conflict of interest is the so-called 'self-dealing' by the corporate controller. Self-dealing means that the corporate controller's is transacting with himself in the company's name. The risk involved by such a kind of transaction is very intuitive: a corporate controller vested with discretionary powers will naturally tend to set the transaction terms in such a way as to foster his own interest at the expenses of that of the company (and thus, of non-controlling shareholders). Self-dealing transactions may easily result in diversion of corporate assets, whenever the consideration of the exchange departs from market prices. By and large, either a below-market price sale or an above-market price purchase may amount to outright stealing from the shareholders' to the corporate controller's pockets.

Unfortunately, this very basic case of self-dealing is not the only possible instance of conflicted interest transaction that may result in stealing by the corporate controller. To be sure, it is not even the most important one. Managers or controlling shareholders being explicitly on both sides of a corporate transaction is no longer as common as it used to be in the nineteenth century, at least in most developed countries (see Kraakman et al 2009). However, the same danger is involved by a much broader set of transactions (Atanasov et al 2011), which are formally third-party transactions, but where the corporate controller is *personally* interested in the welfare of the third party. The third party in question may be a family member of the corporate controller, an affiliate of his, or an entity (e.g., a corporation, or a partnership) in which he has a larger financial stake than in the company he controls. Clearly, as far as the interest in diverting corporate assets is concerned, it makes little difference whether the beneficiary is the corporate controller himself or any of the persons mentioned above, who are all 'related' to the personal interests of the corporate controller. As a matter of fact, this kind of third-party transactions shares the key features of traditional self-dealing. The corporate controller is free to set the terms of the transaction and he is interested in favoring the related party over the corporation that he controls (but that he does not own entirely), inasmuch as the interest in the wealth of the related party exceeds his stake in the company. For this reason, self-dealing is nowadays more broadly characterized as related-party transactions.

Related-party transactions do not need to involve directly either the corporate controller or the corporation he controls. A transaction between two differently related parties may indeed be characterized by the same traditional conflict of interest on the corporate controller's side, provided that interest is related to the company's interest and the other to the corporate controller's interest. The case in point is a transaction between one of the company's subsidiaries and another company or a partnership wherein the corporate controller of the former has a significant financial interest. The picture could be complicated much further. This is not our goal, though. What is worth noting is that diversion of corporate assets can be implemented through a very broad range of transactional techniques, provided that just two conditions are fulfilled. The first is that the corporate controller has unfettered discretion over the transaction and its financial terms. The second is that the transaction is affecting, at least potentially, the welfare of the corporation and of his corporate controller in two opposite ways: whatever the parties formally involved, the transaction is such that it may ultimately impoverish the corporation while enriching, at the end of the day, its controller.

The legal notion of shareholder ownership defines the entitlement of the company owners to share in the residual claim on the corporate assets. In functional terms, the prominent consequence of this principle is that all distributions of the firm's surplus (i.e., what is left after all the inputs of production are rewarded according to the contracts entered into by the company) must be made pro-rata, either in the form of midstream dividends or of final liquidation of assets upon the company's dissolution (Rock and Wachter 2001). Related-party transactions are perhaps the most dangerous challenge to this pro-rata rule, since they may easily feature 'tunneling' of the company's funds (which are subject to the pro-rata rule) to the corporate controller's individual property (which of course is not).

Easily does not mean certainly. I have defined related-party transactions in such broad terms that it would be foolish to believe that they are always characterized by cash flow diversion. In fact, these transactions are a significant part of every company's operation. The problem is not related-party transactions themselves, but rather the non-pro-rata distributions that they may, or may not, involve (Enriques 2000). Focusing on related-party transactions is just a way to operationalize a meaningful ban of non-pro-rata distributions. While avoiding non-pro-rata distributions is a fundamental task of corporate law, and – as I argue – the only task that should be implemented by means of mandatory rules, unfortunately this goal cannot be simply achieved by prohibiting related-party transactions altogether. The important consequences of this hurdle will be clarified shortly.

5.2.1.2 *Other conflicted interest transactions*

The domain of potentially non-pro-rata behaviors includes more than just related-party transactions. As far as outright diversion of assets and cash flow is concerned, at least three more categories of transactions are to be considered. One is *managerial compensation*. In the absence of a controlling shareholder, this is a very peculiar kind of self-dealing. Directors normally set their own compensation on behalf of the company. The situation is equally dangerous when there is a controlling shareholder, and he sits on the board of the company or of any of its subsidiaries. The problem of the corporate controller's compensation is, however, even more complicated than that of related-party transactions, for it overlaps with the question of rewarding managerial effort. Since one major focus of this inquiry, if not the most important one, is concerned with non-contractability of managerial compensation under separation of ownership and control, the potential distortions in contracting over the corporate controller's reward (e.g. salary, stock option plans, and the like) are not dealt with here. To avoid confusion between the problems of entrepreneurial reward and non-pro-rata distributions in corporate governance,

I simply assume that the contractable part of managerial compensation is always determined by an incentive-compatible mechanism set up in the corporate charter.[7] What the features of this mechanism are or should be, and whether they would need any support by corporate law in order to avoid the risk of non-pro-rata distributions via managerial compensation, is a matter for separate inquiry (see e.g. Bebchuk and Fried 2004).

For similar reason, this discussion does not deal with two other instances of generic misappropriation, which do not result in the corporation directly or indirectly transacting with a corporate controller's related party, but rather depend on the corporation or its shareholders being *excluded* from transacting with unrelated third parties (Davies 2002). The first is the appropriation by the corporate controller, typically through a related entity that he may own entirely, of investment opportunities that may be as profitably exploited by the corporation. Even though this misbehavior does not exactly consist of diversion of corporate assets, it would ultimately result in diversion of cash flow potential from the company. As a result, the problem can be handled within a framework not very different from that which I am going to present for the discipline of related-party transactions. However, in many legal systems, this problem is dealt with by a separate doctrine: that of so-called *"corporate opportunities"* (e.g. Bainbridge 2002). Reviewing the doctrine of corporate opportunities in a comparative fashion would lead us away from the focus of this investigation: that is, how diversionary PBC are most typically extracted by corporate controllers, and what corporate law should do about it.

The second instance of exclusionary misappropriation by the corporate controllers is the so-called *"insider trading"* (see Bainbridge 2000). As a matter of fact, by virtue of his being in charge of ultimate decision-making about the company management, the corporate controller has access to privileged information ahead of actual and potential non-controlling shareholders. Trading the company's stock on the basis of this information may lead to easy profits at the expenses of outside shareholders. However, whether this trading actually amounts to non-pro-rata distribution of the company's residual is debatable. After all, differently from other conflicted interested transactions, the aggregate amount of this residual (the shareholder value) is unaffected by insider trading – the corporate controller's profits are just determined by a timely exchange of the company's stock. According to traditional corporate law and economics, this is sufficient to conclude that insider trading is just a matter of distribution of the firm value, having no efficiency consequences (Manne 1966). This view is apparently contradicted by subsequent theoretical analyses, and – in positive terms – by the fact that insider trading is prohibited in virtually any jurisdiction. The matter is still very much debated,[8] but the traditional argument against the prohibition of insider trading at least

---

7 Other commentators who analyze corporate governance under this assumption are *inter alia* Kahan and Rock (2002); Klausner (2004); and Macey (2008).
8 See e.g. Manne (2005) and Macey (2008).

gives us a good reason to avoid embarking on such a debate here. Insider trading is neutral to the corporate wealth, even though it might not be neutral to the aggregated wealth of the company's investors. The two issues are of course related, but, in principle, the efficiency of the placement of company's stock with the investing public, and of its exchange thereafter, is dealt with by a different set of legal rules, namely securities regulation. Here I do not deal with the non-pro-rata distributions affecting shareholder's wealth directly, but only with those which result in cash flow diversion from the company *and then* from outside shareholders. This is mainly, albeit not only, a matter of corporate law.

In addition, non-pro-rata distributions may be implemented even more subtly by the corporate controller, without diverting any asset or cash flow from the company's property. What may suffice to achieve the same purpose is – in the wording of two commentators – *"diversion of claims"* (Fox and Heller 2006: 16). This diversion is typically implemented through some form of corporate restructuring: share issues, mergers or divisions, spin-offs, winding-up, and the like. The result is that the original ownership claim of a non-controlling shareholder may be diluted through these restructurings, in favor of the corporate controller or of one related party of his, with nothing being formally diverted from the corporate assets, investment opportunities, or cash flow potential. At first glance, it might then seem wise to dismiss this problem from our inquiry based on the same argument that has just been made with reference to insider trading – claim diversion affects shareholders individually, not the company as a whole. But that would be a mistake. Virtually everywhere in the world, corporate restructuring is in fact a key part of corporate law, not of securities regulation. This is with good reason.

Corporate restructuring (or – in the typical corporate law and economics terminology – "fundamental changes") is first a matter of distribution of corporate powers (Kraakman et al 2009). Normally (albeit not always) restructuring involves some modification of the corporate contract, if not its termination. We have just seen in the previous chapter that, at least formally, corporate laws give shareholders much more authority in the field of charter amendments than in the ordinary management of the company's affairs; even though, in practice, the corporate controllers end up being vested with significant discretion also when it comes to these, so to say, 'extraordinary' affairs. That being said, conflicts of interest in this field must be put in context. On the one hand, they are comparable to those affecting related-party transactions in the ordinary course of business; the basic difference being that stealing may arise indirectly, from diversion of ownership claims instead of the assets over which ownership is established (Atanasov et al 2011). On the other hand, the conflicts of interest involved by corporate restructuring are much broader, and their exploitation by the corporate controller (i.e., actual diversion of claims) does not necessarily lead to stealing (i.e., actual diversion of assets).

One may recall from the foregoing illustration of the theory of corporate governance that differential treatment of controlling and non-controlling shareholders is a crucial issue for interpreting the role of PBC when ownership is separated from control. Dilution is but a way to discriminate between the two categories of shareholders. Because PBC can be good or bad, also dilution may be not only a way to expropriate outside shareholders of the value of their investment (diversionary PBC), but also a way for the corporate controller to cash in the value of the idiosyncratic PBC that motivated his entrepreneurial investment at the outset. Takeovers are customarily implemented through some form of corporate restructuring. This may or may not involve looting through dilution of minority shareholders, which is equivalent to asset diversion and should therefore be policed no differently from self-dealing. But takeovers may also need to involve some dilution of the interest of non-controlling shareholders (Grossman and Hart 1980) in order to feature the adequate rewards for both the insurgent and (in the normal case of friendly takeovers) the incumbent controller. It would make no sense to consider these two aspects of dilution separately. Their discussion is therefore postponed to the last two chapters, where corporate control transactions will be analyzed. Corporate restructuring taking place in the absence of changes in control would deserve a special investigation and, therefore, they are left out of this discussion.[9]

5.2.2 *False positives and false negatives in the discipline of related-party transactions*

In order to protect shareholder ownership in the absence of control rights, corporate law should ideally feature a ban on non-pro-rata distributions. In practical terms, such a general prohibition – which, by the way, is present in every jurisdiction – would be useless in the absence of more detailed constraints on the corporate controller's discretion. By reviewing the transactions involving the most severe conflicts of interest when it comes to non-pro-rata distributions I have identified the domain of these constraints, and chosen to focus on the most paradigmatic – and dangerous – example of transactions which may lead to expropriation of non-controlling shareholders: self-dealing or, more precisely, related-party transactions. In order to avoid circumvention, the definition of related-party transactions has to be as broad as possible. However, the broader the definition of potentially conflicted interested transactions, the higher the risk that the same transactions do not actually involve any non-pro-rata distribution, and instead constitute legitimate exercise of the managerial discretion entrusted to the corporate controller. Therefore, after having identified the operational domain of a legal policy against the extraction of diversionary PBC, one has to be extremely careful in setting the appropriate constraints on the corporate controller's behavior.

9 See Kraakman et al (2009: 183–224).

The law and economics approach features a standard paradigm for assessing the efficiency of constraints on human behavior, which may result in a socially undesirable outcome, but whose connection with the same outcome is ambiguous either ex-ante, ex-post, or – very often – in both situations.[10] Murder is a case in point. Ex-ante, we may for instance observe that John, a policeman, carries a gun when he is off duty and goes to visit his friend Bob. Ex-post, we will know that Bob was shot and he died. Let us assume that society wants murderers to be severely punished in order for murder to be deterred. We might be tempted to achieve this result by convicting John for a lifetime sentence, after having inferred from the above information that he intentionally murdered Bob. And it could seem even better to punish John ex-ante, for carrying a gun when he is off duty, thinking that this would prevent the murder from occurring. However, any of the above solutions would be regarded as a stretch of the imagination, if not completely mistaken, in the light of the following, additional information, which for the moment we assume is real, but was not proven at the trial. Bob managed to call John during a fight with a thief who had broken into his house. Then John rushed to Bob's place to help, but he arrived just too late – Bob had already been killed and the thief had disappeared forever.

This very stylized example shows how ambiguous the behavior of people under suspicion can be with regard to the conduct that society wants to be banned. In the light of the last-mentioned circumstances, convicting John would amount to finding an innocent person guilty. This is conventionally known as 'Type I error' or 'false positive' – the proposition 'John is a murderer' is considered true while it is actually false. Of course, depending on how the ambiguity of John's behavior is dealt with, the reverse kind of error is also possible. In fact, nobody knows the real circumstances in which Bob was killed and, short of being 'real,' the above story about Bob's phone call might have just been invented by John to escape conviction. If courts believe any of John's stories at face value, the risk will be high that he is found innocent while being guilty. This would be a 'Type II error', or a 'false negative' – the proposition 'John is *not* a murderer' is considered true while it is actually false.[11]

The Type I/Type II errors paradigm is perfectly suitable to the assessment of legal policing of related-party transactions. When the legal discipline of

---

10 The paradigm is known as Type I/Type II errors (or false positives/false negatives), and it is normally employed for the study of adjudication of the law (with special reference to the burden of proof). See Cooter and Ulen (2011) and Posner (2011).

11 The Type I/Type II errors paradigm is derived from statistical inference. Assume that the goal is to test a certain hypothesis (e.g. that the accused is guilty). This implies rejecting the opposite hypothesis (that the accused is innocent), considered as the default state of nature, which is conventionally referred to as the 'null hypothesis.' A Type I error occurs when the null hypothesis is rejected when it is actually true – the test of the hypothesis of interest is falsely positive: an innocent person is convicted. A Type II error occurs when the null hypothesis is accepted when it is actually false – the test of the hypothesis of interest is falsely negative: a guilty person is acquitted. For the application of this paradigm to self-dealing see Enriques (2000).

self-dealing is very strict, it will be relatively easy to infer non-pro-rata distribution (the socially undesirable outcome) from a related-party transaction (the ambiguous behavior). As a result, few non-pro-rata distributions may escape the legal policy against shareholder expropriation – i.e., there is a limited risk of false negatives – and it is fair to conclude that extraction of diversionary PBC would be highly deterred. The flip side of the coin is that the corporate controller might have to forego profitable investment opportunities featured by related-party transactions, for fear that he will be held liable for these transactions, notwithstanding that they have neither diversionary purpose nor do they involve any non-pro-rata distribution. In other words, a very strict policy against self-dealing leads to a high risk of false positives. Managerial discretion may be 'over-killed' and the maximization of overall shareholder value would be undermined consequently. It goes without saying that a very lax policy against self-dealing would lead to just the opposite result. The corporate controller's ability to make profits through the exercise of managerial discretion would not suffer many restrictions in the face of conflicts of interest (little risk of false positives), but the risk will be high that he would divert those profits to himself instead of dividing them pro-rata with non-controlling shareholders (false negatives problem).

In policing self-dealing, there is no way to avoid the tradeoff between Type I and Type II errors. From an economic perspective, it is just possible to optimize this tradeoff (see Easterbrook and Fischel 1991). Given the foregoing discussion of the theory of corporate governance, the optimization criterion should be shareholder value. It makes little sense to constrain the corporate controller's ability to enter into related-party transactions, when the potential gains of these transactions to shareholders as a group exceed the expected value of diversion. But it would be equally inefficient to allow related-party transactions when the potential benefits to the corporation are more than offset by the non-pro-rata distributions involved. Finding the right balance between managerial discretion and the constraints against non-pro-rata distribution is the crucial question of a legal discipline of self-dealing.

In a broader perspective, this is a part of the more general *discretion–accountability tradeoff* that characterizes the problem of corporate governance (Bainbridge 2002), and probably the part where legal rules and their enforcement are mostly relevant. However, the advantage of the approach being followed here is that the issue of shareholder expropriation is separated, at least conceptually, from that of the firm governance. On the one hand, this allows decision-making powers to be allocated independently of the protection of non-controlling shareholders, in such a way as to feature both entrepreneurial discretion and its prospective reward, notwithstanding separation of ownership and control. On the other hand, a precondition for control rights to be allocated to an entrepreneur/manager in the absence of full ownership is that these rights do not include the power to expropriate non-controlling shareholders of their part of the residual claim on the corporate assets and cash flow. The problem of Type I and Type II errors in policing self-dealing should then be managed in such a way by corporate law as to make credible the corporate controller's commitment that he will not abuse his powers to violate the pro-rata principle of distribution to shareholders. However, this policy should also be devised in such a way as to minimize interference with the exercise of the corporate controller's discretion (Rock and Wachter 2001).

5.2.3 *Three elements of a legal strategy towards related-party transactions*

There are several possible techniques to discipline related-party transactions. Perhaps the most intuitive one is to prohibit them outright. It should be evident from the foregoing discussion that this is not a practicable solution. Related-party transactions are not just evil. Their prohibition would lead to an enormous risk of false positives in the policing of non-pro-rata distributions. To be sure, this would not even suffice to avoid the risk of false negatives (Kraakman et al 2009). One should neither underestimate the fantasy of corporate controllers (and of their legal counsels) in devising related-party transactions in the face of their formal prohibition, nor overestimate the limited amount of resources that both shareholders and public authorities may efficiently commit to the enforcement of this prohibition. Therefore, modern corporate laws no longer include sweeping prohibitions of related-party transactions and contain, at the very most, just selective prohibitions. Normally, the transactions at issue tend to be both relatively easy to detect and to feature little risk of profitable business being foregone because of their prohibition. The typical example is credit transactions between the company and one or more of its directors, which are prohibited *per se* in a number of jurisdictions. Indeed, even in that restricted domain, whether outright prohibition of self-dealing is an efficient solution may be questioned. It is probably for this reason that the relevance of prohibitions of such a kind in positive corporate law is negligible (see Kraakman et al 2009: 169–73).

Regulation of related-party transactions in corporate governance is a more complicated matter. In the next few pages, I am going to describe in purely functional terms the solutions that may be featured by corporate law to cope with it. In the next chapter, the options of legal intervention will be compared with the policies actually implemented in the five jurisdictions of our sample: the US, the UK, Sweden, Italy, and the Netherlands. In the end, we will be able to assess the efficiency of each policy based on the theoretical framework developed thus far.

The functional terms of a legal policy against diversionary PBC have been nicely illustrated by Professor Gilson (2006). Basically, three requirements must be fulfilled for the same policy to have some bite. First, a *substantive standard* must be specified in order to assess whether conflicted interest transactions actually feature non-pro-rata distributions. Even if that standard were set in such a way as to catch all transactions involving non-pro-rata distributions, and only those, effectiveness of legal constraints on expropriation of non-controlling shareholders would still require two additional features. On the one hand, those who are supposed to enforce the standards need to know of the violations. This also implies that *disclosure* of conflicted interest transactions, which are subject to the substantive standard, should be featured. On the other hand, both the disclosure requirements and the substantive standard should be enforced. An effective *enforcement process* is then another essential requirement of a discipline of related-party transactions.

A rather common mistake in the analysis of the legal discipline of self-dealing is to consider the strength of the above factors as the end of story (see, authoritatively, Djankov et al 2008). However, this would tell us, at most, about the *effectiveness* of legal constraints against non-pro-rata distributions. Even though we all would like corporate governance not to feature any kind of asset or cash flow diversion, this should not come at the expenses of the *efficiency* of constraints on self-dealing. Therefore, the quality of each require-ment of an effective regulation of conflicted interest transactions must be ulti-mately assessed on the basis of the Type I and Type II errors which they may lead to, depending on how they are implemented by the legal system. Efficiency requires that, at the margin, the expected harm to shareholders depending on profitable business being foregone (false positive) be equal to the expected harm depending on additional diversion being allowed (false negative). In this perspective, I am going to analyze each of the three func-tional requirements of a legal discipline of conflicted interest transaction. One should bear in mind that all these requirements in fact form a system within each jurisdictional and institutional context, and therefore it is quite a stretch to consider them separately. However, the comparative-functional approach being followed in this inquiry leaves us with no alternative. The important synergies between the three requirements in question will be uncovered in the country-by-country analysis in the next chapter.

That being said, I shall start from disclosure. An optimal substantive standard, even when an efficient enforcement process backs it, would have no possibility of being implemented without knowledge of violations.

5.3 Showing conflicts of interest: disclosure

5.3.1 *Corporate law and securities regulation at a meeting point*

The debate in the aftermath of the Great Depression in the US made famous Justice Brandeis' advocacy of the disclosure strategy: "Sunlight is the best disinfectant; electric light is the best policeman" (Brandeis 1914: 92). To be sure, both the importance and the regulatory implications of disclosure by publicly held companies are not confined to the domain of conflicted interest transactions. This is too big an issue to be discussed here. It mainly concerns the placement of securities – including stock – with the investors, and their trading afterwards. Both stages require information about the company management to be disclosed before that stock can be knowledgeably purchased on the primary or the secondary market (see Paredes 2003). On that basis, disclosure is arguably a matter of securities regulation and not of corporate law.

However, when it comes to disclosure of conflicts of interest, the distinction between securities regulation and corporate law is not as clear-cut as in other fields of the legal discipline of corporate governance. From a law and economics perspective, the main goal of securities regulation is to have stock (and other corporate securities) priced efficiently. Intuitively, this requires that reliable information about the corporate assets, their management, and related profit opportunities be adequately disseminated in the market, for it to be impounded in stock prices. What mechanism of dissemination should be considered 'adequate' for purposes of efficiency, fairness, or both, is perhaps the most debated issue between financial economists and legal scholars, very often even within their own group. This is exactly the kind of debate that I am not going to address here.

Corporate law has in fact a different set of goals. The one we are considering here is setting efficient constraints to the corporate controller's ability to expropriate non-controlling shareholders. Disclosure of conflicts of interest, which is required for this purpose, is also necessary for stock prices to be determined accurately (Mahoney 1995). It is for this reason that such a disclosure is relevant in both corporate law and securities regulation (Kraakman et al 2009). However, the kind of reaction that corporate law expects from outside investors, when they are confronted with disclosure of conflicted interest transactions, is significantly different from that expected by securities regulation. From a corporate law perspective, non-controlling shareholders are expected to check, directly or indirectly, conflicted transactions in order to prevent or punish non-pro-rata distributions. From the perspective of securities regulation, investors are expected to decide whether to buy or sell corporate stock depending on the risk that they will be expropriated by the corporate controller. In terms of business organization theory, the latter reaction can be characterized as an 'exit' strategy, whereas the former involves a more proactive role, and then the exercise of 'voice' (Hirschman 1970).

Especially in the field of related-party transactions, these two strategies are clearly complementary. Investors' willingness to pay for corporate stock will not just depend on their knowledge of conflicted interest transactions (a matter for securities regulation), but even more so on the likelihood that they do not result in non-pro-rata distributions (a question of corporate law). Shareholders' ability to deter non-pro-rata distributions will in turn depend not just on the mechanisms (including disclosure), which are formally in place for the scrutiny of conflicted interest transactions (corporate law), but also on a broader knowledge of how these mechanisms are implemented in the actual governance of the company (securities regulation). Therefore, in order for a policy against non-pro-rata distributions to be effective, corporate law and securities regulation need to rely upon each other. This would achieve simultaneously the goal of efficient pricing of corporate stock and of efficient raising of equity funds from non-controlling shareholders, under two conditions: first, that efficient constraints are set forth on the corporate controller's ability to divert resources from the company; second, that outside investors are timely and reliably informed about the quality of these constraints.[12] In the light of the previous discussion of distribution of powers, and of the consequent ability of the corporate controllers to opportunistically alter the terms of the corporate contract, both corporate law and securities regulation should be mandatory as to the disclosure and discipline of related-party transactions.

5.3.2 Ex-ante and ex-post disclosure

Mandatory disclosure of conflicts of interest can be established both before and after related-party transactions are entered into. In both cases, the precise nature and the extent of the conflicts should be disclosed, together with how the conflicts are being handled, in order for the diversionary potential of the transaction to be knowledgeably assessed. It may seem then that this disclosure is only useful when it takes place ex-ante (Djankov et al 2008). After all, non-controlling shareholders are helpless if they know of the risk of asset diversion only after the suspected transaction has been concluded, which implies that their money could be gone already. This is not entirely true.

To start with, ex-post disclosure is always useful as a complement of ex-ante disclosure. Some non-pro-rata distributions will always escape the substantive discipline of conflicted interest transaction or its enforcement. Then there are two possibilities. If the terms of the transaction are fully disclosed ex-post, shareholders as a group may have the chance to have it scrutinized later and, should any non-pro-rata distribution be uncovered, this would be offset by damage compensation to the company. If, as is more likely to be the case, disclosure is either incomplete or misleading, shareholders as individual investors may have the chance to recover damages when it turns out that they bought the stock at inflated prices. Of course, the likelihood of each of these scenarios depends on how shareholders' rights can be enforced under both corporate law and securities regulation (Kraakman et al 2009). But, provided that an efficient enforcement process is in place, ex-post disclosure of conflicts of interest will increase deterrence of non-pro-rata distributions.

The above argument can be extended to the case in which only ex-post disclosure is available. Under certain conditions, ex-post disclosure can even work as a substitute of ex-ante disclosure. The conditions under which ex-post disclosure can suffice for an efficient policing of non-pro-rata distributions are

---

12 On both aspects see Rock and Wachter (2001) and Rock (2002).

determined by the corporate jurisdiction's choices as to the enforce-ment process. Relying just on ex-post disclosure basically implies that extraction of diversionary PBC by the corporate controller must be policed just by means of deterrence of harmful behavior, with little – if any – prevention of the wrongful conduct (see Shavell 1993). The implications of this choice will be discussed in more detail with other issues regarding enforcement. But it is important to bear in mind that also ex-post disclosure of conflicted interest transactions may fulfill the requirements of an effective policing of self-dealing.

5.3.3 *False positives and false negatives of mandatory disclosure*

It could seem that mandatory disclosure of conflicts of interests and of how they are handled by the corporate controller involves little risk of false positives, whereas it is normally the case that too lax disclosure requirements would lead to high frequency of false negatives. This kind of reasoning underlies the view that more disclosure is always better for society. Such a view is generally incorrect (see e.g. Easterbrook and Fischel 1991) and it turns out to be even more misguided in the case of conflicted interested transactions. Disclosure is in fact costly for both the originator and the recipient of information. To be sure, the costs to the originator (the company) may seem a little thing compared to the risk of asset diversion. But this overlooks a number of important factors.

On the one hand, too burdensome disclosure requirements may prevent the corporate controller from entering related-party transactions also in the absence of non-pro-rata implications. For instance, having to notify outside shareholders individually of any conflict of interest may undermine the exploitation of synergies through intra-group transactions, at least to the extent that the costs of disclosure exceeds the gains at stake. On the other hand, depending on how the related issues of standard setting and enforcement are dealt with by the legal system, corporate disclosures may increase as such the exposure of the corporate controller, and of the company management, to the risk of legal liability, market sanctions, and shaming (see e.g. Romano 1991 and Langevoort 2001). This could look desirable for enhancing deterrence of tunneling. However, this perspective overlooks the tendency of the investing public, and of market players acting on its behalf, to infer non-pro-rata distributions from the knowledge of just a potential conflict of interest. No different from the example of Bob's murder, this may be too hasty a conclusion, which may suffice nonetheless to deter related-party transactions that would ultimately benefit non-controlling shareholders. This is enough to conclude that disclosure requirements may also lead to Type I errors.

One final reason why more disclosure is not always better disclosure is that its recipients need to understand it properly (Paredes 2003). More informa-tion about the corporate controller's conflict of interest does not necessarily imply a closer scrutiny of conflicted interest transactions. Investors are rationally apathetic not only as far as participating in the company management is concerned, but also when it comes to self-help. The difference from the management of corporate affairs is that investors seem to be as reluctant to interfere with the judgment of business strategies as eager to prevent corporate controllers from absconding with their money. However, it is not worthwhile to process a huge load of information about the corporate controller's conflicts of interest, and to acquire the expertise to do it knowledgeably, in order to protect a few thousand euros of investment. For disclosure to be of any use, it has to be tailored to the needs, skills, and incentives of those who are supposed to scrutinize conflicted interested transactions on the basis of the disclosed information. Then individual, non-controlling shareholders cannot be reasonably expected to perform any thorough scrutiny on their own. Information is quite likely to be both too much and too little for this purpose. The amount of information *disclosed* may be too much, compared to what the typical investor can and will rationally handle. The amount of information actually *processed* may be too little, compared to what is needed to ascertain the diversionary potential of suspected transactions.

Disclosure requirements should, then, be more concerned with the recipients of information than with its overall amount. Knowledgeable assessment of conflicted interest transactions requires a professional expertise which individual investors cannot be given credit for. In order for disclosure to achieve the goal that "those with the power to enforce the standards know of violations" (Gilson 2006: 1653), some form of professional intermediation is required. That is to say, monitoring of the corporate controller's conflicts of interest cannot be undertaken by non-controlling shareholders individually, but must be in fact *delegated monitoring* (Paredes 2004).

On the one hand, this implies that the information required by disclosure regulation has to be selected to fit the delegated monitors' needs, and not shareholders'. On the other hand, this brings into the framework a specific agency problem: who monitors the monitor? Differently from the corporate controllers, delegated monitors (like, e.g., institutional investors, independent directors, and – under certain circumstances – corporate lawyers) can be plainly considered as agents of shareholders because they are not supposed to play any entrepreneurial role in corporate governance. The welfare assessment of disclosure requirements then faces an additional complication. Provided that information formally addressed to shareholders is ultimately filtered by delegated monitors, misalignment of their incentives with the shareholder interest may lead either to false positives or to false negatives in policing related-party transactions. Whether Type I or Type II errors are more likely to occur will not just depend on what information the corporate controller is compelled to disclose, and to whom, but also on the contents of delegated monitoring and the set of incentives underlying its implementation. The former is defined by the substantive standard for reviewing conflicted interest transactions; whereas the latter depends on the enforcement process.

5.4 Taming conflicts of interest: standards

5.4.1 *Why related-party transactions cannot be simply 'at arm's length'*

At first glance, setting a standard for the assessment of the diversionary potential of self-dealing may seem as easy as prohibiting non-pro-rata distributions. In order for conflicted interest transactions to respect the Eighth Commandment ("Thou shalt not steal"), it would be sufficient that they are entered into in terms which are comparable to those of an ordinary market transaction with a third party, unrelated to the interests of the corporate controller. This benchmark is customarily referred to as "arm's length transaction" – a typical English expression to depict a transaction between perfect strangers. The arm's length requirement is often invoked by the corporate governance scholarship (e.g. Djankov et al 2008) for assessing the merits of a conflicted interest transaction. It might be unfortunate, but the fact is that determining whether a conflicted interested transaction is (or was) in fact concluded at arm's length is virtually impossible. The approach to corporate governance developed in this book helps to explain why.

The difficulty with related-party transactions is that allegedly they may have plenty of business purpose other than the extraction of diversionary PBC (McCahery and Vermeulen 2005). But what may the business purpose be of transactions with, say, a subsidiary, a special purpose entity, a partnership, or simply a natural person in whose wealth the corporate controller happens to be significantly interested? In the neoclassical theory of perfect competition, all markets are characterized by homogeneous goods, so that there is apparently no reason why any corporate transaction should *not* be concluded at arm's length. The model of perfect competition also does not feature entrepreneurship for this reason – entrepreneurs would have to be homogeneous too! However, there is neither homogeneity nor perfect competition in the real world. The reason why neither the model of perfect competition nor the assumption upon which the model is built holds is that we live in a world of uncertainty. In modern economic theory, uncertainty brings two fundamental challenges to the neoclassical model. The first is that the identity of the entrepreneur/manager matters, because each of them is willing to establish and manage a certain firm just in order to tackle uncertainty (Knight 1921). The second is that the firm itself is not to be regarded as a standard profit-maximizing 'black box,' but rather as a rather unique web of relationships designed in such a way as to cope with uncertainty (Coase 1937). These two insights are very seldom brought together, but one of the goals of the present inquiry is exactly to merge them in a more comprehensive theory of corporate governance.

The bottom line is that non-homogeneous entrepreneurs/managers are also the designers of a web of non-homogeneous relationships. Such a design lies at the core of their decisions under uncertainty, that is, at the core of entrepreneurial discretion. Relationships differ from arm's length transactions because they involve some degree of idiosyncrasy (i.e., the parties' identity is not a matter of indifference). Idiosyncrasy of transactions inside the firm is of course higher than that of transactions outside the firm. However, the underlying rationale is the same in both cases: relationships may reduce exposure of the parties' investments to uncertainty (Klein et al 1978). The consequence is twofold (see Williamson 1991). On the one hand, the merits of idiosyncrasy in market relationships bear no more second-guessing than the basic choice as to 'make-or-buy.' On the other hand, the terms of transaction within idiosyncratic relationships cannot possibly be compared with those of any transaction between perfect strangers, since arm's length is by definition incompatible with idiosyncrasy. There is no reason to consider related-party transactions as separated from the idiosyncratic relationship they may be part of, for there lays the only legitimate business purpose that they may have in corporate governance (Bainbridge 2002).

In this perspective, any attempt to determine whether a related-party transaction was actually concluded at arm's length would be quite a stretch. But it would be even worse to allow for a judgment whether it was worthwhile for the company to enter into a certain transaction with a corporate controller's related party *instead* of at arm's length. In fact, both kinds of assessments are made ex-post, when most consequences of the transaction are known, and they amount to a review of a decision that was taken ex-ante, when the same consequences were uncertain (Easterbrook and Fischel 1991). In other words, both judgments are made with hindsight bias, which deny any virtue to idiosyncrasy as long as it turns out to under-perform ordinary market transactions. It goes without saying that, if such a review was allowed, no corporate controller would dare to take decisions under uncertainty because he would have to share the profits with outside shareholders while bearing all of the losses that the decision may involve (Eisenberg 1993). The presence of a conflict of interest is not sufficient reason to dismiss this argument. It only suggests that it should be handled with particular care.

Entering into a related-party transaction is a part of the mandate to discretionary management conferred upon the corporate controller. In principle, this implies that the merits of the transaction cannot be reviewed under any substantive standard; there is no benchmark that qualifies. However, we definitely want the diversionary potential of the transaction to be assessed against the no-stealing benchmark. The only possible way out of this bind is to set prohibition of non-pro-rata distributions as a substantive standard governing the corporate controller's *conduct*, but to have related-party transactions *reviewed* under a non-substantive standard. Given that these transactions are challenged only when they turn out to be unprofitable, a substantive review of the underlying conflict of interest would allow for a very high risk of Type I errors due to the second-guessing of entrepreneurial judgment with hindsight bias.[13] This is the reason why the standard of review of related-party transactions should disregard the merits of the decision, and just have regard to its process.

5.4.2 Fiduciary duties and judicial abstention from business judgment

5.4.2.1 Standards of conduct and standards of review

The distinction between standards of conduct and standards of review has a long-standing tradition in the legal studies of corporate governance. A standard of conduct (Eisenberg 1993: 437) "states how an actor should conduct a given activity or play a given role"; a standard of review "states the test a court should apply when it reviews an actor's conduct" to determine whether he complied with the standard of conduct. According to Professor Eisenberg, one fundamental feature of corporate law is that "standards of conduct pervasively diverge from standards of review" (Eisenberg 1993: 438). The reason is uncertainty and its consequences in terms of institutional design, which may involve deference to a corporate organ inasmuch as it is in charge of deciding in conditions of uncertainty. As a result, the standards on whose basis liability is imposed on corporate directors differ from those upon which, for instance, doctors or lawyers are held liable of malpractice or, more generally, an agent is considered to have breached the fiduciary duties he owes to his principal (see also Rock and Wachter 2001: 1665–1666).

The standards governing all of these actors' conduct look very similar. In fact they are all categorized under the same heading: *fiduciary duties*. Both corporate and non-corporate actors are expected to abide by a duty of loyalty and a duty of care in conducting business with their counterparties. In the general case, which may be characterized as a principal–agent relationship, the standard of review is whether actors were actually disloyal or negligent. Corporate directors, however, are held liable on a different basis. What matters is not whether their conduct was *actually* negligent or disloyal, but whether a breach of duties of care or loyalty can be *inferred* from non-compliance with different standards of review. The standards in question mostly concern the very process of decision-making, and not its contents or the actions they result in (Eisenberg 1993).

Legal scholars are often puzzled by this peculiarity of corporate law.[14] From a law and economics perspective, or at least from that being followed in this work, this may seem somewhat less puzzling, provided that corporate controllers (and so directors, whenever they act in this capacity) are not

---

13 Unfortunately, the flip side of the coin is that the absence of judicial review of situations involving a conflict of interest may easily lead to Type II errors (see Paredes 2004: 1083–1085).

14 See e.g. Manning (1984); Gevurtz (1994); Arkes and Schipani (1994).

considered to be agents, either of shareholders or of anybody else. Although in corporate law the divergence of standard of conduct and standard of review has a much broader scope of application than just related-party transactions, it is worth discussing it in some detail, for it explains how the problem of false positives and false negatives is dealt with in the scrutiny of the corporate controller's decision-making.

5.4.2.2 The business judgment rule

Let us start from the risk of false positives. Although the problem is similar when the duty of loyalty is in question, this is best understood with reference to the duty of care. Non-controlling shareholders of course want the corporate controllers to take care in managing the corporate affairs. In the economist's jargon, they want him to put effort in it, and not to shirk. Yet, at the same time, non-controlling shareholders – no matter how large and committed they are – are unable not only to observe managerial effort, but also to infer effort from the quality of management (Black 2001). On the one hand, shareholders are not entrepreneurs; neither do they wish to act as they were. On the other hand, every business decision is rather unique. At the end of the day, what determines one entrepreneur's success is his ability to identify business opportunities which no other person would have bet a dime on. This is indeed a crucial point, which makes the difference from a standard principal–agent setting. People can hardly observe their lawyers' or doctors' effort, but that can be verified ex-post with reference to an objective standard of conduct. The ultimate reason why it makes sense to put lawyers or doctors under a duty of care is that negligence may be assessed with reference to how another lawyer or doctor would have acted under a similar set of circumstances. This is also the reason why it makes almost no sense to review the entrepreneur's behavior in the same fashion. Other entrepreneurs' behaving differently in similar circumstances tells us very little about one entrepreneur's diligence. In fact, this is in the very nature of entrepreneurship.

Nearly every business decision may look negligent, or incompetent, in hindsight when it turns out badly.[15] Other people would easily claim that they would have never gone for it. Yet, in a different state of the world, they would as easily regret they did not have that idea first. The same decision would have been regarded as very clever if it turned out to be profitable. One might claim that negligence must not be assessed ex-post, but ex-ante, on the basis of probability calculus; and this is actually how fault liability is analyzed in Law and Economics (Cooter and Ulen 2011). However, entrepreneurs do not deal with risk, but with uncertainty. This implies that outcomes can hardly be predicted, let alone be assigned a probability, before they materialize (Knight 1921; Keynes 1937). In essence, reviewing an entrepreneur's choice

---

15 This problem is known as hindsight bias. See Eisenberg (1997) for the corporate law implications.

under a negligence standard is a category mistake that tends to generate false positives. Unsuccessful entrepreneurs may too easily be found negligent, no matter how much effort they put into the management of the company (Rock and Wachter 2001).

Intelligent judges understand this story pretty well (see Easterbrook and Fischel 1991). They know that shareholders will only complain about business judgment in hindsight despite being unwilling to interfere with it at the outset. Giving them an easy case in finding the corporate controller liable would result in the following game: heads – we all win; tails – the corporate controller loses. That is why judges tend to show so much deference to decisions taken by the company management. It is not just that judges acknowledge their being incompetent in second-guessing business judgment, as it is argued sometimes.[16] After all, judges cannot be expected to be any more competent in reviewing a doctor's practice. The reason is rather that, differently from the case of the doctor's or of any other agent's judgment, business judgment allows for no ex-post revision that would make sense also ex-ante. While both doctors and patients would agree on doctors' care being reviewed under some negligence standard, there is no such revision that shareholders and a corporate controller would ever settle for at the outset. In corporate law, this results in a principle of judicial abstention from reviewing managerial decisions, which is often referred to as the 'business judgment rule.' Although this is a doctrine of American judge-made law, similar principles are present under different headings and with different modes of implementation in virtually every jurisdiction. This is unsurprising, given that the underlying rationale is purely functional (Kraakman et al 2009: 79–80).

But why then are directors, at least formally, always subject to a duty of care by corporate laws? If the corporate controller's diligence in managing the corporate assets is a real standard of conduct, what is the corresponding standard of review? Should the business judgment rule be just the end of story, it would make little sense, if any, to speak about any judicial review of directors' conduct. The problem is that absolute judicial abstention from reviewing managerial choices would result in an extraordinary risk of false negatives. Apparently, this could still be regarded as a matter of inefficient effort – in legal terms, negligence. Albeit popular, this view is mostly incorrect. If the business judgment rule involves any problem of false negatives in reviewing the corporate controller's conduct, this does not concern compliance with the duty of care, but with the duty of loyalty.

5.4.2.3 *The extreme case of waste*

It is often argued that, in the absence of a duty of care, managing directors could simply *waste* shareholder's money. In fact, there is little evidence that

---

16 Dodge v. Ford Motor Co., 170 N.W. 668, 684 (Mich.1919).

they ever do, at least unless they have some other purpose (Rock and Wachter 2001). We know that managers having a limited ownership stake will naturally tend to shirk. But they can be reasonably expected to do it in a smarter way than just wasting corporate assets (that is, with a reward somewhat higher than the mere pleasure of wasting other people's money). On-the-job consumption of managerial perquisites and empire-building are two prominent examples (Jensen 1986). I have just explained why corporate laws cannot but abstain from policing these subtler forms of shirking, inasmuch as they have a potential business purpose. However, plain instances of waste are usually granted no protection under the business judgment rule (Bainbridge 2002). Why? The answer might seem pretty obvious to legal scholars, who would disagree on the contention that law can and should do little about managerial shirking (e.g. Hamilton 2000). On the contrary, an economist would be just puzzled by knowing that law worries more about waste, having apparently so little individual motivation, than about misdirection of managerial effort, which instead has plenty of it.

Waste *must* have a reason, and this has probably very little to do with laziness or even recklessness. If a professional manager allows that some of the assets under his management are wasted with no apparent purpose, something else must be at play. Judges are then worried with good reason. However, they can only argue that waste and similarly grossly negligent behaviors are incompatible with any rational exercise of business judgment, and they are therefore to be regarded as a breach of the duty of care (Rock and Wachter 2001). Most likely, judges will suspect that apparently inexplicable waste actually conceals some form of siphoning-off of corporate assets, however suspicions are no sufficient grounds for adjudicating a case. Imposing liability on the basis of waste, instead of fraud, is thus a practical way to cope with the false negatives of the business judgment rule, whenever none of the corporate controller's conflicts of interest is uncovered at trial, and yet conflict of interest is the most likely explanation of why shareholder wealth is dissipated.[17] At the end of the day, the false negatives problem does not actually concern violation of the duty of care, but of the duty of loyalty. This brings us back to the very core of our discussion: the standard of review of conflicted interest transactions.

5.4.3 Review of related-party transactions under the duty of loyalty

Legally speaking, conflicted interest transactions are regarded as a potential breach of the duty of loyalty. Most legal textbooks, in both the civil and the common law tradition, claim that the business judgment rule or equivalent

---

17 "[R]arest of all – and indeed, like Nessie, possibly non-existent – would be the case of disinterested business people making non-fraudulent deals (non-negligently) that meet the legal standard of waste!" Steiner v. Meyerson, 1995 WL 441999 at *5 (Del.Ch.1995).

doctrines do not apply in these cases. Judges seem to be willing to review business judgment in the presence of a conflict of interest of the decision-maker.[18] While formally correct, such a perspective may be misleading. I have already argued on economic grounds that conflict of interest is not a sufficient reason to consider related-party transactions outside the scope of managerial discretion. The basic standard of conduct – discretion in business judgment – is therefore not in question, but it must be coordinated with another equally important one: '*Thou shalt not steal.*' Accordingly, when it comes to the duty of loyalty, the standard of review of the corporate controller's decision-making should not be truly different, but simply more elaborated than a plain business judgment rule. The principle of judicial abstention from second-guessing business judgment should still apply to related-party transactions, but only on condition that the decision-making process has been emancipated from conflicts of interest (Bainbridge 2002). In this perspective, the duty of loyalty is no exception to the business judgment rule. However, while the business judgment rule protects the integrity of entrepreneur's decision-making, it should "create no license to steal."[19]

Comparative corporate law (Kraakman et al 2009) shows that related-party transactions are hardly reviewed by courts, so long as an independent assessment has been made that they do not involve diversion of assets or cash flow to either the corporate controller or an affiliate of his. However, courts do not abstain from reviewing related-party transactions when this independent assessment is lacking, or is unreliable. This is basically the choice corporate controllers are facing when they decide to enter into a related-party transaction: either the decision is meaningfully freed from the underlying conflict of interest, or the consequences of this conflict of interest may have to be scrutinized in the courts. Thus, another way to look at the matter is that conflicted interest transactions require an additional, independent assessment in order to enjoy the protection of the business judgment rule. In theory, this assessment is limited to the diversionary potential of the transaction, and therefore – no different from the operation of the duty of care – it should not involve any interference with business judgment.

This is more easily said than done. On the one hand – as I will show momentarily – the requirement of independent assessment has a number of qualifications, which are very difficult to fulfill in practice. On the other hand, whenever the assessment cannot be considered actually independent, judges will have to take up the role of independent reviewers. However unwilling they are to second-guess business judgment, they will have to review the transaction under an objective, substantive standard. The balance between

---

18 The attitude of the judiciary towards the review of business judgment tainted by conflicts of interest varies considerably across jurisdictions (Kraakman et al 2009). Delaware courts are perhaps the most interventionist.

19 Coffee (1989: 1650) citing Irwin v. West End Development Company, 342 F.Supp. 687 (D.C.Colo.1972).

Type I and Type II errors in the regulation of related-party transactions ultimately depends on this delicate balance between judicial abstention and judicial intervention in the review of corporate decision-making.

In conclusion, efficient policing of non-pro-rata distributions requires that related-party transactions be reviewed under a standard of either procedural or substantive fairness. The requirement of procedural fairness is met by virtue of independent assessment of the diversionary potential of the transaction. The requirement of substantive fairness has to be checked instead by the court, on the basis of the evidence provided by the plaintiff and the defendant at trial. In theory, the two requirements should be mutually exclusive. Substantive fairness should be presumed in the presence of procedural fairness; and procedural fairness should be unnecessary once the substantive fairness has been ascertained. The imperfections of the real world make this division merely suggestive. Based on the previous discussion, one may prefer the procedural standard in that it apparently minimizes the risk of false positives (Eastrebrook and Fischel 1991); but one may still wish that a residual check on substantive fairness is performed by courts in order to cope with the problem of false negatives (Kraakman et al 2009). In any event, the bearing of each standard on Type I and Type II errors cannot be predicted across the board, for it depends on how procedural and substantive fairness are actually enforced.

5.5 Conflicts of interest in action: enforcement

The general theory of enforcement in Law and Economics is simply too broad to be comprehensively reviewed here.[20] Therefore, the following discussion will be limited to two prominent aspects of enforcement of a discipline of related-party transactions. They are: (i) whether this discipline should be enforced *before*, or *after* related-party transactions are entered into (ex-ante vs. ex-post enforcement); and (ii) who should take the initiative of activating the enforcement process (institutional competence, including the choice between private and public enforcement).

5.5.1 Deterrence and the basic mechanisms of enforcement

5.5.1.1 Enforcing disclosure

The first step of the enforcement process is about disclosure. Extensive, but ineffective, disclosure requirements would be of no use and this would compromise the enforcement of the entire discipline of conflicted interested transactions. It would seem pretty obvious to conclude that under-enforcement of disclosure just leads to Type II errors. However, the matter stands differently

---

20 For an overview, see Shavell (2004); Garoupa (1997); Polinsky and Shavell (2000); Shavell (1993).

depending on whether it is ex-ante or ex-post disclosure. The purpose of ex-ante disclosure is to enable a thorough scrutiny of related-party transactions. Insufficient disclosure ex-ante undermines the procedural fairness of the transactions, and therefore it is best analyzed together with the enforcement of the standard of review. Ex-post disclosure works differently. Its purpose is rather to inform non-controlling shareholders that a number of conflicted interest transactions were entered into, and of how the conflicts of interest were managed by the corporate controller. Perfect enforcement of ex-post disclosure would enable outside investors to withdraw from their investment (or to refrain from entering it) anytime they are dissatisfied about how conflicts of interest are handled by the corporate controller.

Perfect enforcement is just a myth, or – in more technical terms – a purely theoretical reference point for the analysis of substantive rules. The reason why ex-post disclosure requirements may have a bite on non-pro-rata distributions is that failure to comply enables investors, or some other player on their behalf, to take some action that results in punishment of non-transparent corporate controllers. Expected punishment – the argument runs – will deter corporate controllers from untruthful or misleading disclosures, and this will result, in turn, in deterrence of non-pro-rata distributions: nobody is going to steal when he is actually forced to disclose his stealing ex-post.[21] However, implementing punishment is costly to both individuals and society. For this reason, short of being perfect, enforcement is just carried out up to the optimal level – i.e., where the expected reward of punishment is equal to the expected costs at the margin (Becker 1968). There are basically three kinds of punishment that may be triggered by violation of ex-post disclosure requirements. The first is legal liability; the second is ouster; the third is shaming. Liability and ouster directly depend on legal rules; shaming apparently does not, but there is reason to believe that it may only work – so to say – 'in the shadow of the law' (see e.g. Black and Coffee 1994).

5.5.1.2 Optimal deterrence: liability, ouster, shaming

Liability – which, for simplicity, I assume can only result in monetary sanctions – is imposed by the initiative of private parties or of public agencies. In the field of corporate disclosure there is apparently little reason to rely on private initiative. Because of collective action problems and the investor's rational ignorance (the typical investor has little knowledge of disclosure requirements, not to speak about information about their infringements), the cost to an individual of bringing a suit far exceeds the expected benefit of damage compensation (which would be commensurate to the size of his investment). The case for publicly enforced civil liability and/or administrative fines would seem, then, to be very strong. Although a public agency has

---

21 "People who are forced to undress in public will presumably pay some attention to their figures" Loss (1983: 36).

low-powered incentives and high administrative costs borne by taxpayers who may, or may not, participate in the stock market, public enforcement is a way to overcome the shareholders' collective action problem that undermines deterrence of private enforcement. This is only partly correct, for there are other ways to cope with the shareholders' collective action problem when it comes to constraining the corporate controller's ability to extract diversionary PBC. In light of these alternatives, public enforcement may not necessarily turn out to be the most efficient solution.[22]

Outside shareholders may have a suit brought by an agent representing them. This might solve the collective action problem in a cheaper and possibly even more effective fashion than public enforcement, at least to the extent that the agent's incentives are aligned with the interest of outside shareholders (Coffee 1985). The case for public enforcement of disclosure requirements would no longer look as strong, once a private litigator – acting on behalf of non-controlling shareholders – has sufficient incentive to know about disclosure regulation and the way in which the company management have dealt with it. The merits of this solution in terms of Type I and Type II errors depend on the principal–agent problem underlying delegated enforcement. Delegated enforcement is in fact one particular aspect of delegated monitoring. I shall come to this shortly.

The framework for analyzing the (threat of) ouster as a mechanism for policing insufficient disclosure is quite similar. However, the case for public enforcement is somewhat weaker here because ouster by a public authority implies overreaching private mechanisms of appointment and dismissal of the company management. In addition, in most situations, the deterrent effect of ouster adds up to the deterrence of monetary liability.[23] This reduces *ceteris paribus* the risk of false negatives. However, it also determines a more serious problem of false positives. Private enforcement of ouster would only apparently fare better. The problem is that it is practically impossible to empower shareholders to oust the management only when the latter is not transparent, or is dishonest (Pacces 2011). On the one hand, the threat would hardly be credible when it is limited to situations where ouster provides shareholders with little reward. On the other hand, normally shareholders have the power to oust the management or they do not have it. As we know from the foregoing chapters, it might not be entirely desirable that non-controlling shareholders

---

22 The debate on the relative merits of public and private enforcement in corporate governance is still open. Compare Armour, Black et al (2009) with Jackson and Roe (2009).

23 In the absence of errors in adjudication, liability under-deters (Cooter and Ulen 2011). When errors are introduced, the net effect of false negatives and false positives on deterrence is ambiguous (Enriques 2000). Ouster usually does not spare liability, unless it is implemented before the harm materializes. However, ouster always disrupts the value of specific investments made by the ousted. When this value is substantial – as it is assumed to be in the present work – the threat of ouster considerably increases deterrence. This argument does not hold in endgame situations (Gulati 1999).

have this power, for they might be induced to use it to appropriate the corporate controllers' idiosyncratic PBC. The bottom line is that, when a large enough non-controlling shareholder has the power and the incentive to oust management at his will, disclosure of conflicts of interest may not be much of a problem. However, the exercise of managerial discretion would be indeed problematic, at least to the extent that delegated monitoring by large, non-controlling shareholders extends beyond constraining the extraction of diversionary PBC (see Burkart et al 1997). If the goal is to police non-pro-rata distributions, this is a clear example of how private enforcement can boost the risk of false positives.

Shaming is a non-legal mechanism of enforcement (Skeel 2001). It works by complementing – if not even substituting – deterrence of legal sanctions with that of social sanctions. By virtue of shaming, the author of misconduct may end up being excluded from the social circle he belongs to. The economic implications of this mechanism are not always clear-cut. However, as far as corporate managers are concerned, there is little doubt that shaming is an issue of high economic importance (Paredes 2004; Blair and Stout 2001). The manager's reputation is in fact his most valuable asset on the labor market. Losing that reputation would ultimately imply that he has to change his job. To be sure, the deterrent effect of shaming depends on two crucial factors. On the one hand, social norms in the institutional context have to be such that the expected social sanction of misbehavior is credible (Coffee 2001a). It is illusory to take this for granted even in the restricted sample of developed economies we are considering, as we are not speaking about ferocious criminals but, rather, about somebody who ultimately turns out to be 'smart' enough to take the money and run (Enriques 2003). On the other hand, shaming in modern societies has most often to be backed by some form of legal sanction. In corporate governance, shaming will induce compliance with an established set of norms only when their violation produces some manifest consequence (like, e.g., ouster or liability), which would in turn trigger the social sanction. Like investors, the management society need to know of violations – and the problem of keeping managers up to their professional standards cannot be equated to that of policing littering in a close neighborhood. This has both positive and negative consequences. Shaming is a relatively inexpensive way to increase deterrence, thereby reducing the risk of false negatives. However, it can also turn out to be a multiplier of false positives, depending on how the matter is dealt with at the legal level.

5.5.1.3 *The gatekeepers' contribution*

It is worth noting that the enforcement of disclosure regulation in the securities market features a much broader range of techniques than the three that have just been reviewed (see Kraakman et al 2009). One of them is especially relevant as far as conflicted interest transactions are concerned. This is the so-called "gatekeeper strategy" (Kraakman 1986). Gatekeepers – like accountants, securities analysts, rating agencies, and underwriters – enjoy a special position in policing some instances of corporate misbehavior. By virtue of either regulation or financial economics, they control access of the corporation to the securities market. Therefore, they can enforce securities regulation by withdrawing support from the companies that fail to comply with it. The requirement of this "third-party enforcement strategy" is that gatekeepers face a sanction when they fail to prevent violators from entering, or staying on, the market. The sanction is either loss of reputation, legal liability, or both.

Efficient gatekeeping is indeed a crucial issue of securities regulation (Coffee 2006a). It is not by coincidence that 'gatekeeper failure' is often invoked as one major explanation of the corporate scandals of the beginning of this century (Coffee 2004a). The matter is very much related to the enforcement of the legal discipline of related-party transactions, but in just one respect: disclosure. Gatekeepers' failing to check the quality of disclosure as to both the corporate controller's conflicts of interest and the way in which they have been handled may have – as we have experienced – disastrous consequences. However, disclosure is only one element of a legal policy towards self-dealing. Disclosure would be of no help in the absence of professional assessment of the diversionary potential of the transaction. In theory, this assessment may also be enforced through a gatekeeper strategy. In practice, however, normally it is not.[24] Neither would it be desirable to have the merits of related-party transactions reviewed by, say, an accounting firm as a precondition for their viability. As a result, third-party enforcement of the discipline of conflicted interested transactions is only relevant as far as their disclosure to investors is concerned.[25] This being only tangentially related to corporate law, I shall put aside gatekeepers in the following discussion. Contrariwise, both the ex-ante and the ex-post review of related-party transactions is strictly a matter of corporate law. While gatekeeping affects the preconditions of this review (namely, the 'knowledge of violations'), third-party enforcement does (and should) play no role in this field.

---

24 This requires a little bit of explanation. In the wake of the financial scandals of the beginning of this century, most jurisdictions in the world have enhanced the role and responsibilities of gatekeepers, also with respect to the discipline of related-party transactions. Specifically, auditing firms have to review (normally ex-post, but sometimes also ex-ante) disclosure of conflicted interest transactions and of the internal procedures for managing the underlying conflicts. See e.g. Enriques and Gatti (2007). Auditing firms may prevent companies from circulating misleading statements about related-party transactions, but not from entering into them. As a result, related-party transactions are not policed by a gatekeeper strategy, only their disclosure is.

25 The key question in this respect is what exposure of gatekeepers to liability deters misdisclosure most efficiently? For a taste of the debate compare Partnoy (2001); Hamdani (2004); Coffee (2004b); Partnoy (2004).

5.5.1.4 Enforcing the standard of review

The liability-ouster-shaming paradigm can be easily extended to the enforcement of the standard of review of related-party transactions. We know that, in functional terms, this standard has both a procedural and a substantive fairness component. Violation of either component should result in liability, ouster, or shaming of the corporate controllers for the latter to be deterred from non-pro-rata distributions. However, as in the case of disclosure, activation of each of these remedies requires that the shareholders' collective action problem be overcome. The case for public enforcement appears to be much weaker here, at least from the point of view of society. While opacity of a corporate controller produces significant externalities on the well-functioning of the stock market, non-pro-rata distributions affect shareholders of one single company or of a group of them at most. It is probably for this reason that corporate law is typically enforced by private parties, whereas securities regulation is normally enforced both privately and publicly (Kraakman et al 2009).

That being said, private enforcement of related-party transactions' standard of review requires some special mechanism for aggregating shareholders' common interest in the operation of an exponential entity. I shall refer to the latter as shareholder representative, or agent, for expositional convenience. The remainder of the discussion will be concerned with this mechanism of delegated enforcement of the legal discipline of conflicted interest transactions.

5.5.2 Delegation of ex-post enforcement: shareholder litigation

5.5.2.1 The collective action problem

No individual shareholder would ever sue the corporate controller unless he expects the reward from such an action to offset the costs of litigation (see Cooter and Ulen 2011). None of the three remedies under consideration is likely to bring individual shareholders such a reward. To be sure, liability may look like a good candidate for the individual investor's reward, since he would be granted damage compensation anytime the corporate controller is found liable. But there are two problems with this approach. The first is that non-pro-rata distributions do not harm outside shareholders directly because resources are diverted from the company's assets, not from shareholders' pockets. This argument may seem of no use to an economist, but the fact is that this distinction is so important at law that individual shareholders do not even have standing to sue in some jurisdictions; and, where they do, they cannot claim damages unless on behalf of the corporation (see Kraakman et al 2009). The second problem is even more important, and applies as well to claims brought on the individual investor's account under securities regulation (e.g. in the case of insufficient disclosure). Whatever is the damage determined by the corporate controller's misbehavior, individual shareholders would only be entitled to recover a part of it, depending on their stake in the company's value. This leads to a well-known free rider problem (Baums and Scott 2005). The best strategy for the individual shareholder is to wait for other investors bearing the costs of litigation, which in the end would benefit non-controlling shareholders as a group. Since any rational shareholder would go for this strategy, this is the best guarantee of impunity that a fraudulent corporate controller could ever strive for.

The problem would be solved if shareholders managed to coordinate in such a way that both costs and reward of litigation are divided pro-rata. Coordination is also costly, and it is not likely to take place spontaneously in a group of thousands of investors. It is for this reason that the mechanisms of aggregation of both shareholder interests and shareholder action require some institutional background. There are basically two kinds of institutions supporting shareholder litigation: one is shareholder associations; the other is corporate lawyers. Both institutions feature the aggregation of shareholder interest and an action that is supposed to represent the interest of shareholders as a group. Therefore, both involve principal–agent problems. However, the characteristics of the problem are significantly different.

5.5.2.2 *Shareholder associations vs. corporate lawyers*

Shareholder associations are these days a very popular way to aggregate investors' claims in liability suits brought under corporate law or securities regulation (Schaefer 2000). Yet they suffer from one major inconvenience as regards the exercise of decision-making: accountability to the shareholder interest. Like consumer associations, shareholder associations may possibly form a powerful interest group.[26] However, whether they actually represent the interest of the underlying constituency is doubtful because the same constituency is featured by an extremely large number of members. In appointing the association's representatives and monitoring their performance, shareholders face the same collective action problem that prevents them from challenging non-pro-rata distributions in court. There is little reason why shareholder association should fare any better in this respect.

Under certain conditions, however, shareholder associations may reduce the risk of false negatives in reviewing related-party transactions without correspondingly increasing the risk of false positives. These conditions require that shareholder representatives have a personal gain from bringing a successful case to trial, but that they also get a penalty when the case brought turns out not to be meritorious. In the absence of regulation of shareholder associations, the fulfillment of the above conditions depends on the importance of concern for reputation in the institutional environment where the association is established.

---

26 On the theory of interest groups in general see den Hertog (2012).

Differently from shareholder associations, corporate lawyers have no mission to bring legal suits on behalf of a vast group of shareholders. However, they can be given a specific incentive to do so (Coffee 1985). This can be achieved by a two-sided strategy. On the one hand, their remuneration should be set on a contingent basis, so that lawyers get a percentage of damage compensation awarded to disgruntled shareholders in case they are successful, but get nothing otherwise. On the other hand, lawyers should be entitled to represent the entire class of investors that claim damage compensation, so that in case of success their reward will be commensurate to the damages awarded to shareholders as a group, not as individuals. Such an incentive scheme may allow for enormously generous lawyer's compensation, thereby inducing law firms not only to prosecute non-pro-rata distributions with much more determination than any disgruntled (non-controlling) shareholder, but also to screen the entire stock market in search of substantive or procedural violations of the rules that may result in a successful case (Romano 1991).

The combination of contingent fees and class action suits creates what has been defined as an "entrepreneurial system of private enforcement" (Coffee 1987). This does not come without drawbacks. Compared with shareholder associations, class action lawyers have much higher-powered incentives. However, these incentives are imperfectly aligned with the shareholder interest (see e.g. Macey 2008). The incentive scheme in question features high reward for meritorious cases, but almost no penalty for non-meritorious ones. The only penalty that lawyers may face is their bearing the litigation costs when the case is lost. The company and its controller risk losing much more, in both financial and reputational terms, from the very moment in which the case is brought to trial. Therefore, parties would tend to settle when there is any uncertainty about the outcome of the case, no matter of whether the latter is founded or unfounded. Lawyers – who get a substantial part of the money settled for – would be the only winners in this game.[27] In the absence of further regulation, the risk of false positives brought about by class action lawyers can be substantial. This could be too high a price to pay in order to cope with the false negatives problem (Coffee 2006b).

5.5.2.3 *Institutional investors*

Compared to liability, ouster allows for no mechanism of incentive manipulation. The ousting shareholder must be simply large enough to benefit more from ouster than from any other strategy, of course net of the related costs. In principle, there seems to be little reason why a non-controlling shareholder should prefer ousting a dishonest corporate controller than withdrawing from his investment in the company (Rock 1991). However, this view overlooks an

---

27 This implication is purely distributional and does not matter for efficiency. The problem is that the empirical evidence is ambiguous as to whether class action deter efficiently. See e.g. Choi (2004).

important problem. When a non-controlling shareholder like an institutional investor has a significant stake in the company, it might end up being locked-in in his own investment (Coffee 1991). Assume that one institutional investor becomes aware of non-pro-rata distributions before any other market participant. Selling, say, 10% of the company's stock straight away would not save any losses, but just anticipate their realization – the stock price would fall at any rate.[28] Filing a legal suit against the company or its directors is also no option, for it would add to the stock devaluation the expected costs of both litigation and loss of reputation: whatever the outcome of the case is, these costs would be a deadweight loss to the investor's portfolio.

In this perspective, ouster of dishonest controllers turns out to be the only possible strategy for institutional investors with a large financial commitment to the company (Stapledon 1996). In order to minimize its costs, it ought to be implemented as silently and quickly as possible. Under these conditions, the threat of ouster is credible and may suffice to deter corporate controllers from non-pro-rata distributions at the outset. However, as I mentioned earlier, threat of ouster may also lead to false positives to the extent it is not (and cannot be) confined to the policing of self-dealing. Shareholders may also use their power to hold up the corporate controller. Perhaps one way to avoid this outcome is to have ouster implemented by an agent who is not directly concerned about profitability of the company management, but who would ultimately lose his job when he fails to prevent or to punish non-pro-rata distributions: the outside director (Gilson and Kraakman 1991). This is how delegated enforcement ex-post connects with delegated monitoring ex-ante.

5.5.3 Delegated monitoring ex-ante: independent directors

5.5.3.1 Shareholders as independent reviewers?

Ex-ante enforcement of a discipline of related-party transactions aims at preventing non-pro-rata distributions, rather than deterring them through the threat of liability, ouster, or shaming. Compared to ex-post punishment, preventing extraction of diversionary PBC requires a tighter monitoring of related-party transactions. In order for non-pro-rata distributions to be effectively prevented, conflicts of interest must both be disclosed at the outset, in their full scope and implications, and systematically reviewed by means of a procedure that guarantees independent assessment of the diversionary potential of the transaction. Whether this enforcement methodology is efficient ultimately depends on its bearing on the balance between false positives and false negatives in policing non-pro-rata distributions. The classic argument that enforcement is normally more expensive ex-ante than ex-post (Shavell

---

28 For a view of how an institutional investor can effectively exert governance through (the threat of) exit see Edmans and Manso (2011). This strategy would be unhelpful against self-dealing.

1993) has, instead, not much relevance here, provided that disclosure and independent monitoring are required not only for preventing non-pro-rata distributions ex-ante, but also for having related-party transactions reviewed ex-post on the basis of procedural fairness. Whether one likes it or not, these two requirements have proven so far necessary to combine a discipline of conflicted interest transactions with protection of integrity of business judgment (see Enriques 2000).

There are several ways to implement the independent assessment of related-party transactions (Kraakman et al 2009). Perhaps the most intuitive is having the transaction previously approved by shareholders. But this is tricky. The illusion of shareholder sovereignty over the management of the company may easily lead to the conclusion that conflicted transactions may enjoy full protection of the business judgment rule once they have been approved by a majority of shareholders. In at least two situations this conclusion would turn out to be a terrible mistake. First, shareholders approving the transaction may not be independent from the corporate controller – even worse, a controlling shareholder may hold a sufficient majority to have any related-party transaction approved. Second, shareholders may not be adequately informed to assess the diversionary potential of the transaction. In both situations, shareholder approval would lead to false negatives. Ideally, the problem would be solved if shareholders qualify for transaction approval only inasmuch that they are insulated from the sphere of influence of the corporate controller, and they are provided with the optimal amount of information to assess its diversionary potential. In practice, however, the requirements for a truly independent shareholder approval are so burdensome that a corporate controller would rather refrain from entering a related-party transaction, unless there is a very big deal at stake. Even in the latter case, there would be the risk that a non-controlling shareholder will attempt to hold him up. This may lead to a serious false positives problem. There is hardly a way out of this bind. From a normative perspective, independent shareholder review of the corporate controller's conflicts of interest should just be limited to the most significant related-party transactions – i.e. those that may result in either outrageous tunneling, or in terrific profit opportunities.

5.5.3.2 *Proximity vs. objectivity in corporate boards*

Independent assessment of related-party transactions would apparently fare much better at the board level. It is perhaps for this reason that the issue of independent directors is so popular in both theory and policy of corporate governance around the world. However, as I mentioned earlier in this book, there is much confusion about the role that boards of directors should play in corporate governance, and this leads, in turn, to disagreements as to both the meaning of independent directorships and their overall desirability (Hertig 2005). Independent directors are normally characterized as general monitors of the corporate controller's performance in managing the firm. In this perspective, they are supposed to care about a much broader range of conflicts of interest than just diversion of corporate assets or cash flow. According to the standard view (Becht et al 2007), independent directors should police not only stealing, but also shirking and the corporate controller's tendency to entrench himself (the so-called 'positional' conflict of interest). The economic literature casts a number of doubts on the ability of independent directors to do all these things together (Hermalin and Weisbach 2003). Also the empirical literature has so far been unable to deliver clear-cut results as to the overall effects of board independence on firm performance: it seems that the number of independent directors in the board improves firm performance in some situations, whereas it has no significant effect in some others.[29] All in all, there seems to be a structural tradeoff between a director's independence and his sharing information with the corporate controller (Adams and Ferreira 2007). A director can either participate in managerial decision-making (thereby contributing to its quality) or be a tough monitor of the underlying conflicts of interest; but he cannot be expected to perform both tasks at the same time.[30]

The narrower approach being taken here to the problem of conflicts of interest may help to identify the proper role for independent directors. Directors that are supposed to contribute to shareholder wealth maximization – thereby policing shirking and entrenchment by the corporate controller – would not stay independent for long, even under the heroic assumption that they were at some point of their appointment process. *Proximity* is required for a knowledgeable participation in business judgment, but it is ultimately irreconcilable with *independence* (Boot and Macey 2004). However, there is little need of proximity for a knowledgeable policing of stealing. Directors being comprehensively informed about the corporate controller's conflicts of interest may simply be required by regulation for the procedural fairness of related-party transactions. This information flow would not compromise directors' independence to the extent that it does not allow interference with the decisions on how the company should be managed, and by whom. Independent directors turn out to be very useful for corporate governance, but only on condition that their role is limited to the assessment of the diversionary potential of conflicted interest transactions (Pacces 2011).

In this perspective, it is also easier to set forth the requirements for a truly independent assessment. Literal 'independence' of directors from the corporate controller will not automatically result in independence of judgment, when it comes to the diversionary potential of conflicted interest transactions. A director may be independent in that he has neither direct nor indirect financial involvement with the corporate controller or with any of his natural or corporate affiliates. This is just a necessary condition for an independent

---

29 Compare Romano (2001); Bhagat and Black (1999); Bhagat and Black (2002).
30 But see Ravina and Sapienza (2010) finding that independent directors do nearly as well as insiders in trading the company's stock (which implies that they have information).

scrutiny of related-party transactions, but is far from sufficient (McCahery and Vermeulen 2005). The director in question will still be under the influence of the corporate controller in one major respect: his reappointment, and to some extent also his staying in office, basically depend on the corporate controller's will. The reader may recall from the previous chapter that a prominent feature of corporate control is the ability to appoint (and dismiss) at least the majority of directors. In the absence of mandatory employee representation, it is the corporate controller that ultimately determines who will sit on the board, with what responsibilities, and for how long. This holds regardless of the board structure and of whether the company is governed by a controlling shareholder or by its management. It turns out that, at least in those jurisdictions that require employee representatives to sit in the board, the only directors who are actually independent of the corporate controller are those appointed by a non-shareholder constituency. However, they are not eligible for policing the extraction of diversionary PBC, provided that, by definition, the latter come at the expense of shareholders and not of other stakeholders.

If we want independent directors to carefully scrutinize the diversionary potential of conflicted interest transactions, they must be both *accountable* to shareholders and appointed *independently* of the corporate controller. Formally independent directors, who are appointed by the board itself or, even worse, by a controlling shareholder, cannot be entirely relied upon. True, they must have some concern for their own reputation of both honesty and professionalism, for nobody would take them seriously otherwise (Kraakman et al 2009). But they must also have some deference to the corporate controller, for nobody would take the risk of appointing them otherwise. For independent directors, a strategy balanced between these two concerns might be to *quietly* resign as soon as they realize that some diversion of assets is going on (Langevoort 2001). We would definitely expect more. We would expect that asset diversion be *loudly* stopped by independent directors, in such a way as to also activate shaming, if not ouster, of dishonest corporate controllers. So long as independent directors are appointed with the corporate controller's consent, this is very unlikely to happen (Macey 2008). Independent directors should then be appointed by somebody else, equally interested in maximization of shareholder value but with exactly the opposite interest in diversion of the same value. Non-controlling shareholders seem to be the only possible option. However, the appointment of minority representatives to the board, in the function of independent directors, raises different problems depending on the prevailing ownership structure. They will be discussed in the country-by-country analysis of the following chapter.

5.5.3.3 *Credible commitments: legally enforceable self-regulation*

One last point about independent directors is that they are a product of self-regulation (Becht et al 2007). Corporate laws only knew of 'disinterested' directors in the discipline of conflicted interest transactions, and in most jurisdictions – with the noticeable exception of the US – any director with no conflict of interest in the specific transaction qualified for the 'disinterested' label (Kraakman et al 2009). The spontaneous emergence of directorships supposed to be independent to a broader extent makes this institution a promising venue for the economic analysis of regulation of related-party transactions. But one crucial point must be clarified at the outset. Corporate controllers can only take a credible commitment that non-controlling shareholders will be dealt with fairly by placing themselves under some binding constraints. So far, it has been maintained that this requires mandatory rules.[31] Even more than charter provisions, self-regulation itself is in principle insufficient for credible commitment. Not only may a corporate controller unilaterally renegotiate compliance at a later stage, more importantly, a company may pretend to comply when it actually does not.

The evolution of self-regulation in corporate governance has tried to cope with these problems (Wymeersch 2005; Hopt 2011). On the one hand, once a code of corporate governance has been voluntarily adhered to, the implementation of its provisions is most often regulated by the so-called 'comply-or-explain' principle – which makes straight departures from the code provisions unlikely and at least formal compliance somewhat binding (Arcot et al 2010). On the other hand, at least in some jurisdictions, untruthful or misleading statements as to the compliance with the code being adhered to are regarded as infringements of securities regulation – which makes actual compliance with the code legally enforceable. In the following discussion, the provisions of corporate governance codes concerning independence of directors will be regarded as sources of credible commitment for the corporate controller only to the extent that – no different from mandatory rules of law – the same provisions are both *binding* and *enforced*.

---

31 Default rules may perform as well when they are difficult to opt out. See *supra*, section 5.1.3.

6 Regulation of related-party transactions

A comparative analysis

6.1 Introduction

This chapter discusses the functional framework of regulation of related-party transactions as applied to the five jurisdictions of our sample. This implies that the analysis will be structured according to the disclosure-standard-enforcement paradigm developed in the previous chapter, regardless of how the discipline of related-party transactions is described in the legal literature on corporate law and securities regulation of each country. However, differently from the previous chapter, the country-by-country approach will now enable us to take into account the institutional complementarities between the three fundamental aspects of the discipline.

The quality of legal rules and of their enforcement is going to be assessed on the basis of the false positives/false negatives criterion introduced in the previous chapter. The goal of this assessment is twofold. On the one hand, I will attempt to put the problem of protection of non-controlling shareholders in the right perspective. The legal analysis will confirm that ownership concentration and stock market underdevelopment obtains when the discipline of related-party transactions does not have enough 'bite' (false negatives problem). But it will also show that this is just one side of the story. The standard 'law matters' argument is still partly consistent with Italian law (whose investor protection features have significantly improved in the past years), but has very limited explanatory power as far as the other jurisdictions of the sample are concerned. For instance, controlling shareholders prevail in Sweden in spite of a nearly optimal balance between false positives and false negatives in the policing of minority shareholders expropriation. The British approach to related-party transactions is based on rebalancing the distribution of powers in favor of non-controlling shareholders; but the resulting false positives problem ultimately leads to controlling shareholders being disfavored.

On the other hand, the following discussion will demonstrate that the framework developed in the foregoing chapter provides a sound basis for both a positive and a normative legal analysis. For instance – contrary to the received wisdom – Dutch law turns out to feature quite high standards of shareholder protection from expropriation, whereas the excellent shareholder protection in Sweden has an important, but too often neglected, legal background. On the normative side, the Type I/Type II errors paradigm suggests that all of the discipline of related-party transactions considered here could be improved by separating the scrutiny of conflicts of interest from interference with business judgment. The functional question of whether the discipline is better enforced ex-ante or ex-post makes independent directorship a promising venue for inquiry in this regard, provided that their role is coordinated with the peculiarities of each jurisdiction. This casts some doubts on the prospects for convergence in the discipline of related-party transactions. More importantly, the present approach highlights the structural weakness of a much too coarse "numerical comparative law" (Siems 2005) as well as of clumsy harmonization attempts at the EU level, at least when it comes to shareholder protection.

6.2 Regulation of related-party transactions in the US

The United States is considered one of the countries providing outside shareholders with a very high level of protection from the corporate controller's misbehavior – if not the highest level in the world. This perception is based on a rather unique combination of rules and enforcement of federal (securities) regulation and state (corporate) laws, and of institutional factors that are both legal and non-legal (Paredes 2004). Whatever the relative importance of each of these determinants is, the fact is that US firms have access to vibrant stock markets, which apparently provide them with the equity finance necessary to exploit opportunities for growth. We know that outside shareholder protection is not a sufficient condition for this result to hold; but we also know that it is absolutely necessary. How the corporate America has achieved such high standards in policing non-pro-rata distributions, and at what price in terms of overall efficiency of corporate governance, is now going to be discussed. This is nicely illustrated by the discipline of related-party transactions and the problem of false positives and false negatives that it may involve.

In the US, this discipline has a number of special players: the Securities and Exchange Commission (SEC) – the oldest, and perhaps still the most aggressive, securities regulator in the world; Delaware courts – the leading jurisdiction in American corporate law; corporate lawyers – after executive directors, perhaps the second most important player in US corporate governance; and the financial press – the ultimate activator of reputational constraints in corporate America. How each of them fits our functional framework will be clarified in the following discussion.

6.2.1 Ex-post disclosure: federal securities regulation

Investor protection in the US relies heavily on disclosure (Kraakman et al 2009). When it comes to related-party transactions, conflicts of interest must be disclosed both ex-ante and ex-post. Disclosure ex-ante is relevant for the application of the standard of review under the corporate law of the state of incorporation; I shall come to this in a moment. Ex-post disclosure is mandated by securities regulation at the federal level.[1] Traditionally, in the US, related-party transactions had to be disclosed *individually*, in the periodic disclosures filed with the SEC, provided that they satisfied the requirement of materiality.[2] The same transactions also had to be reported in the annual accounts, following the strict requirements of the Generally Accepted Accounting Principles (GAAP).[3] In the aftermath of Enron and of the other financial scandals of the beginning of this century, these requirements have been supplemented with the obligation of real-time disclosure: material conflicted interest transactions must now be reported within two days.[4]

Disclosure of related-party transactions in the US is demanding, and therefore burdensome – no different from the rest of information regulation in the securities field. However, on the one hand, the requirement of materiality is established just to cope with the risk of false positives – which would be high when direct and indirect costs of disclosure exceed the value of the transaction. On the other hand, mandatory disclosure activates a number of mechanisms to cope with the risk of false negatives. This has not much to do with individual investors negatively reacting to information about the corporate controller's conflicts of interest. In spite of extensive disclosure (or maybe just because of that), most investors do not even know of them; and those who do know would hardly care (Paredes 2003). Much more important is that a dishonest corporate controller will never disclose non-pro-rata distributions concerning related-party transactions (Mahoney 1995). Extraction of diversionary private benefits of control (PBC) is therefore deterred more by the consequences of *violation* of mandatory disclosure (that is, false/misleading information, or omission of material facts), than by its *compliance*. These consequences are criminal and civil liability of either executive directors or controlling shareholders, depending on who is *actually* in charge (Lowenfels and Bromberg 1997). This in turn activates shaming in the managerial profession much before a verdict is delivered and a sentence pronounced.

This is basically how securities regulation contributes to the deterrence of non-pro-rata distributions in the US. Whether this is more likely to be over-deterrence or under-deterrence depends on interaction with enforcement and

---

1 This is based on two fundamental Securities Acts (Securities Act of 1933 and Securities Exchange Act of 1934) and on the SEC Regulations enacted thereon.

2 SEC Regulation S-K, Item 404 (disclosure in the annual filings of all company transactions directly or indirectly concluded with the management or their related parties, provided that they exceed $120,000 in value).

3 Statement of Financial Accounting Standards (SFAS) 57 – Related Party Disclosure.

4 § 16(a) of the Securities and Exchange Act of 1934, as amended by § 403 of the Sarbanes-Oxley Act of 2002. As a result, related-party transactions must not only be reported in the annual Form 10-K, but also filed in real time with a Form 8-K (provided, of course, that they are material).

the other substantive rules. The crucial point is that, not only in the discipline of related-party transactions, US securities regulation works as a "lobster trap" (Rock 2002). Corporate controllers of companies placing stock with American investors are thereby committed to high-quality disclosure, which in turn implies abiding by the restrictions on transactions suspected of diversionary implications, under the penalty of severe monetary and non-monetary sanctions.

While mandating disclosure of conflicted interest transactions, securities regulation does not set the criteria for assessing their diversionary potential or implications. That is the domain of corporate law. As I mentioned earlier in this work, corporate law in the US is basically the law of Delaware. This is the outcome of US states competition for corporate charters (see Carney et al 2010). As in the previous chapters, I shall refrain from entering the debate about the determinants and the implications of regulatory competition in American corporate law. Nevertheless, Delaware's primacy in the production of corporate law is a matter of concern, since one major reason for this primacy seems to be the superior ability of Delaware's judiciary to cope with the problem of Type I and Type II errors in policing non-pro-rata distributions and, more in general, with the discretion–accountability tradeoff in corporate governance. The design of the standard of review of related-party transactions is an exemplary illustration of this point.

6.2.2 Substantive standards: corporate law and its refinements by Delaware courts

6.2.2.1 Fiduciary duties of the board of directors

At early common law, corporate directors were subject to the agent's fiduciary duties. This implied that they faced liability in case of negligent behavior, and that director's conflicted interest transactions were *per se* voidable by the corporation as breach of the duty of loyalty. At the same time, controlling shareholders owed no fiduciary duties to non-controlling shareholders – so that, basically, no discipline of conflicts of interest was applicable to the former. This is history, and none of the above-mentioned rules applies any longer (Bainbridge 2002). The evolution of judge-made corporate law intro-duced the business judgment rule as a general standard of review of directors' conduct, thereby short-circuiting – in the corporate field – the interpretation of the equitable principle of the fiduciary's due care as a substantive negli-gence standard.[5] The standard became, at most, that of so-called 'process due

---

5 The so-called business judgment rule is a very old principle. See, e.g., Dodge v. Ford Motor, 170 N.W. 668 (Mich.1919); Leslie v. Lorillard, 18 N.E. 363 (N.Y.1888). The leading cases in modern corporate law are: Shlensky v. Wrigley, 237 N.E.2d 776 (Ill.App.1968); Kamin v. American Express, 383 N.Y.S.2d 807 (Sup.Ct.1976), aff'd, 387 N.Y.S.2d 993 (App.Div.1976). In Delaware, see Aronson v. Lewis, 473 A.2d 805 (Del.Sup.1984). However, "Delaware courts

care,' which basically requires that a decision is taken by the board on the basis of information reasonably available under the circumstances – no matter of the consequences of the decision in hindsight.[6]

The requirement of process due care is the essence of one of the most debated rulings of the Supreme Court of Delaware: Smith v. Van Gorkom.[7] Even this very mild requirement was subsequently short-circuited by the adoption of statutory provisions (so-called 'D&O' statutes) that allowed the corporation to indemnify directors and officers in case of fault liability, or to provide them with insurance for the same event.[8] This is how the business judgment rule has become *de facto* a principle of judicial abstention from reviewing directors' diligence in decision-making (Easterbrook and Fischel 1991). Board decisions can only be challenged in court by claiming that the business judgment rule is inapplicable to the particular case. In practice, such decisions hardly ever result in out-of-pocket liability for director's failure to exercise due care (Black et al 2006).

It may seem, then, quite difficult for a plaintiff to hold a director liable. However, the business judgment rule is not an irrefutable presumption of correctness of board decisions. A plaintiff could always demonstrate that the decision was irrational, or that there was none at all.[9] Delaware courts would never uphold a non-decision, nor one "that cannot be attributed to a rational business purpose."[10] Albeit very important (for the reasons that will be clarified in a moment), the irrationality exception to the business judgment rule still gives the plaintiff a hard life. More importantly, the protection of the business judgment rule cannot be invoked in a case of illegality and fraud. This implies that in the presence of conflicts of interest, such a protection is available only on condition that the decision is 'procedurally fair' (Bainbridge 2002).

Procedural fairness requires full and frank disclosure of the directors' conflict of interest and the approval of the conflicted decision by an informed and disinterested body: either a majority of independent directors, or a majority of independent shareholders.[11] Therefore, what is left of the old

---

often have not been as clear as they might be about the effect of the business judgment rule." Bainbridge (2002: 249). The business judgment rule has been 'codified' in the last version of the Model Business Corporation Act (hereinafter MBCA), in § 8.30; whereas the Delaware General Corporation Law (hereinafter DGCL) is absolutely silent on the matter.

6 The requirement of process due care is a peculiar feature of Delaware case-law. See Brehm v. Eisner, 746 A.2d 244 (Del.Sup.2000). In other US jurisdictions, directors are subject to much less stringent standards. See, e.g., MBCA § 8.30(c). See also Hamilton (2000).

7 Smith v. Van Gorkom, 488 A.2d 858 (Del.Sup.1985).

8 See, most prominently, DGCL § 102(b)(7) and DGCL § 145.

9 Aronson v. Lewis, 473 A.2d 805, 813 (Del.Sup.1984) (requirement of exercise of judgment); Sinclair Oil Corp. v. Levien, 280 A.2d 717, 720 (Del.Sup.1971) (requirement of a rational business purpose).

10 Brehm v. Eisner, 746 A.2d 244, 264 n. 66 (Del.Sup.2000).

11 See DGCL § 144 and MBCA Subchapter F (§§ 8.60–8.63), which superseded the former § 8.31 of the Model Act 1984. Former MBCA § 8.31 was based on DGCL § 144, and many

prohibition of self-dealing is that related-party transactions are allowed to the extent they are fair. They may be procedurally fair, and then they will enjoy the protection of the business judgment rule. Alternatively, they may fail to meet the conditions of procedural fairness, and then courts will uphold them if they are substantively fair.

A crucial issue is who has to prove what at trial. Once the plaintiff has demonstrated that the decision was not procedurally fair (i.e., that it was not reviewed and approved independently), it will be up to the defendant to show that the terms of the transaction were substantively fair (i.e., that the transaction did not involve diversion of assets or cash flow).[12] This is going to be as hard as demonstrating the adequacy of consideration in the absence of an objective benchmark – a rather typical situation when transactions are concluded with related parties instead of at arm's length.[13] As a result, liability is normally imposed on corporate controllers who fail to meet the standard of procedural fairness in conflicted interest transactions.

Under the business judgment rule, the reverse test is in principle not allowed. When the requirements of procedural fairness are fulfilled, the plaintiff should be prevented from any allegation that the transaction was not substantively fair, however difficult it is to prove this. While this is the law of some states, Delaware courts went further.[14] Not only is the immunization effect of the business judgment rule overcome upon a showing of waste (here comes the importance of the irrationality exception), but also, procedural fairness itself does not prevent Delaware courts from exercising a 'smell test' on the substantive fairness of the transactions (Enriques 2000). As a result, if the plaintiff manages to demonstrate that the transaction, albeit meeting the standard of procedural fairness, is highly suspected of being fraudulent, it will be subject to judicial review.[15] This is no repudiation of the

---

states have kept the old model provisions in their corporate statutes. Subchapter F is much more complicated, and it is intended to preempt common law by setting forward binding statutory definitions and safe harbors.

12　Marciano v. Nakash, 535 A.2d 400 (Del.Sup.1987).

13　See *supra*, Chapter 5, section 5.4.1.

14　Subchapter F of the MBCA preempts common law with immunizing safe harbors, whereas DGCL § 144 does not. Therefore, under Delaware law (and, to be sure, in a number of other American states as well), approval of related-party transactions by disinterested directors or shareholders has no immunization effect; it only shifts to the plaintiff the burden of proving that the business judgment rule is inapplicable.

15　This is well illustrated by Fliegler v. Lawrence, 361 A.2d 218, 222 (Del.Sup.1976):

DGCL § 144 does not provide a "broad immunity." "It merely removes an 'interested director' cloud when its terms are met and provides against invalidation of an agreement 'solely' because such a director or officer is involved. Nothing in the statute sanctions unfairness [to the plaintiff] or removes the transaction from judicial scrutiny."

In Kahn v. Lynch Communication Systems, 638 A.2d 1110 (Del.Sup.1994), the Supreme Court explicitly stated that ratification by disinterested shareholders or directors only has "the effect of shifting the burden of proof of unfairness to the plaintiff."

business judgment doctrine, but only a refinement. Delaware judges still defer to business judgment in the presence of disinterested approval of related-party transactions, but do not want this to generate a 'license to steal.' This has important effects on the balance between false positives and false negatives in the discipline of related-party transactions.

6.2.2.2 *Fiduciary duties of the controlling shareholder*

The practical approach of American case-law to the policing of non-pro-rata distributions is even better illustrated in the presence of a controlling shareholder. The extension of fiduciary duties to controlling shareholders is a rather unique feature of US law (Kraakman et al 2009), which has already taken place in the first half of the twentieth century.[16] Courts were prompt to recognize the obvious circumstance that a controlling shareholder has the power to elect the entire board of directors, and therefore that the latter lacked any possible independence absent proof to the contrary (Bainbridge 2002). This involves the presence of an inherent conflict of interest whenever a board decision may adversely affect minority shareholders. On this basis, the courts of Massachusetts refused to grant this kind of decision the protection of the business judgment rule, and imposed upon both directors and the controlling shareholder a general duty of equal treatment of minority shareholders.[17] The negative consequences of such a principle on the corporate controller's discretion (especially in the takeover context) are quite intuitive; they will be discussed in more detail in the next two chapters. However, this ruling has never been applied outside closely held corporations (Easterbrook and Fischel 1991). More importantly, it has never become the law of Delaware.[18]

Delaware courts have taken a more focused approach to the matter, which is essentially limited to self-dealing. Controlling shareholding is itself no exception to the business judgment rule, but only a reason to be more careful about related-party transactions.[19] A controlling shareholder will have to show the substantive fairness of transactions concluded with him or any related party of his, unless he can prove that the same transactions received

16 See, e.g., Southern Pac. Co. v. Bogert, 250 U.S. 483, 39 S.Ct. 533, 63 L.Ed. 1099 (1919); Pepper v. Litton, 308 U.S. 295, 60 S.Ct. 238, 84 L.Ed. 281 (1939).
17 Donaue v. Rodd Electrotype Co., 367 Mass. 578, 328 N.E.2d 505 (Mass.1975).
18 *Donaue* was explicitly rejected by the Supreme Court of Delaware in Nixon v. Blackwell, 626 A.2d 1366 (Del.Sup.1993).
19 The typical conflict of interest of a controlling shareholder takes place in parent–subsidiary transactions. The Supreme Court of Delaware identified two standards potentially applicable to such transactions: the business judgment rule (a rebuttable presumption of good faith) and the intrinsic fairness test (which places on the controlling person the burden of proving objective fairness of the transaction to minority shareholders). Under Delaware law, the intrinsic fairness test is applicable *only* when the controlling shareholder is in the position to extract non-pro-rata benefits, namely benefits "to the exclusion and at the expenses of the subsidiary." Sinclair Oil Co. v. Levien, 280 A.2d 717, 720 (Del. Sup.1971).

truly independent (i.e., both informed and disinterested) approval. The only corporate bodies that qualify for such an approval are either directors appointed without the votes of the controlling shareholders or – more in general – a 'majority of the minority shareholders.'[20] Finally, it is worth noting that Delaware courts take a case-by-case approach to the identification of controlling shareholders differently from other bodies of law or recommendations which rely instead on presumptive threshold of voting control (Bainbridge 2002).

This is apparently an ideal system of substantive regulation of related-party transactions. However, any judgment upon the US discipline would be premature until its enforcement is considered. Enforcement can take place at either the ex-post or the ex-ante stage. Perhaps differently from anywhere else in the world, one major driver of ex-post enforcement in the US is an "entrepreneurial system" of private litigation dominated by corporate lawyers (Coffee 1987). At least when it comes to violations of securities regulation, this is coupled with the action of one of the most aggressive public enforcers in the world: the Securities and Exchange Commission (Jackson and Roe 2009). Finally, the combination of public and private law enforcement activates shaming through the forceful action of the American financial press (Zingales 2005). From the very first moment a public investigation and/or a private suit are initiated, the corporate controller's reputation is seriously endangered. This may suggest two conclusions. On the one hand, enforcement of the discipline of related-party transactions makes constraints on non-pro-rata distributions quite effective in US corporate governance. On the other hand, the same enforcement is highly exposed to the risk of false positives, which may undermine the overall efficiency of the US discipline. As it turns out, both conclusions are correct, albeit with some qualifications.

6.2.3 Enforcement of shareholder protection against self-dealing

6.2.3.1 Securities litigation: class action suits

It is relatively easy for a company whose stock is traded in the US to end up being involved in securities litigation (Kraakman et al 2009). The wide reach

---

20 "A party alleging domination and control of a majority of a company's board of directors, and thus the company itself, bears the burden of proving such control by showing a *lack of independence on the part of a majority of the directors*." Odyssey Partners, L.P. v. Fleming Companies, Inc., 735 A.2d 386, 487 (Del.Ch.1999) – emphasis added. "Approval of the transaction by an independent committee of directors or an *informed majority of minority shareholders* shifts the burden of proof on the issue of fairness from the controlling or dominating shareholder to the challenging shareholder-plaintiff. Nevertheless, even when an interested *cash-out merger* transaction receives the informed approval of a majority of minority stockholders or an independent committee of disinterested directors, an entire fairness analysis is the only proper standard of review." Kahn v. Lynch Communication Systems, 638 A.2d 1110, 1117 (Del.Sup.1994) – emphases added.

of the major antifraud provision under US securities law – the famous Rule 10b-5 promulgated under the Securities Exchange Act of 1934 – is as well known by corporate lawyers as by the law and economics scholarship, which is often critical about it.[21] A detailed analysis of anti-fraud provisions under US securities law is outside the scope of the present inquiry. Here it is sufficient to point out that Rule 10b-5 provides individual investors with private standing to sue triggered by reliance on misleading, material information in the purchase or sale of securities.[22] Inadequate disclosures of related-party transactions clearly qualify, but indeed even the most honest statement concerning the corporate controller's conflicts of interest may be charged with being misleading until a federal court dismisses the petition as unfounded. Very often, such a petition would be filed as soon as anything goes wrong with the company's stock price for whatever reason (e.g. Garry et al 2004). Why? Because corporate lawyers would take over, being motivated by their own financial interest rather than by maximization of shareholder value.

The perverse combination of class action and contingent fees makes this result hold. In the US, a legal suit can be brought on behalf of the entire class of investors without need of an explicit mandate by all of them. As a result, a few disgruntled shareholders are sufficient to have a go. The contingent fee arrangement gives lawyers the incentive to actually *solicit* class actions whenever there are the slightest grounds for that; it also provides shareholders with the incentive to yield to solicitation.[23] Shareholders apparently risk

---

21 See e.g. Macey (2008). SEC Rule 10b-5 was promulgated under § 10(b) of the Securities and Exchange Act 1934. What makes Rule 10b-5 a nightmare for corporate managers (and the heaven of securities lawyers) is the so-called 'fraud-on-the-market' doctrine elaborated by the federal courts. See Basic Inc. v. Levinson, 485 U.S. 224, 108 S.Ct. 978, 99 L.Ed.2d 194 (1988). By and large, this exposes wrongdoers not only to the tough enforcement by the SEC, but also to private legal suits for massive damage compensation. Civil actions for breach of Rule 10b-5 are typically brought as class actions wherein any investor who traded in the presence of false or misleading information is considered as injured, independently of actual reliance on information in the decision of whether to trade or not the affected securities. The fraud-on-the-market doctrine has attracted lots of criticism. For a discussion of how both case-law and the literature have evolved (especially by taking the insights of behavioral finance into account), see Ribstein (2006).

22 Rule 10b-5 provides grounds for civil liability in the presence of the following elements: (1) a *misstatements* or an *omission* of facts; (2) *materiality* of information as to the decision whether to make or dispose of an investment; (3) *scienter* (i.e., knowledge of wrongness or illegality of the conduct – but the courts normally consider recklessness or an extreme departure from the applicable standard of care as sufficient); (4) *injury* of the plaintiff due to *reliance* on the misstatement or omission. The fraud-on-the-market theory is based on the assumption that market prices are informationally efficient (Gilson and Kraakman 1984). The underlying information is therefore presumed to be relied upon by rational investors. As a result, the causation test for the imposition of liability is trivialized.

23 The contingent fee arrangement makes the plaintiff's lawyers the key decision-makers in a class action. Under this arrangement, the lawyers get a percentage of the entire damage compensation to be awarded to the class in case of success, but nothing otherwise. See Rubinfeld and Scotchmer (1998).

nothing but being awarded damage compensation; and lawyers too can only profit from this strategy. This last point is tricky, since in theory American lawyers anyway bear the litigation expenses under a contingent fee scheme and they will get nothing if the case is lost. In practice, however, securities class actions are normally settled before going to trial, and almost none of them are concluded with a court judgment. Regardless of the merits of the suit, the company will always prefer an early settlement to an expensive discovery procedure and – even more so – to the adverse consequences of a jury trial on its reputation in both the financial and the products market (Paredes 2004). As a result, the lawyers being awarded very generous fees – as a part of the settlement – are the only winners of this game. A few shareholders, if any of them, do realize that this money is ultimately coming out of their pockets and that they are getting just a part of it back in the form of damage compensation.

This is of course an oversimplification. In fact, there are a number of safeguards against frivolous suits in American civil procedure, even though it is doubtful that they are sufficient to prevent the outcome sketched out above; these safeguards are even stricter in securities law (Hamilton 2000). In addition, the company is not the only defendant in a securities class action. Also directors and controlling shareholders are typically named as defendants, even though they cannot be reasonably expected to be the 'deep pocket' where the money of the settlement will ultimately come from. Finally, and most importantly, the question of who gets compensation and who pays for it is the wrong one from an economic standpoint. Ex-post, compensation is just a matter of distribution, although it affects incentives ex-ante. At the end of the day, what matters for efficiency is whether liability optimally deters misbehavior ex-ante. In this perspective, high reward of the lawyer's effort is in itself not a bad thing, if that is necessary to achieve deterrence of non-pro-rata distributions by corporate controllers (Coffee 2006b).

In the US, deterrence is most likely to arise from the threat of securities litigation. If anything, it is likely that there would be too much of it.[24] This holds irrespective of the limited personal wealth of wrongdoers (who would be ruined anyway by a class action suit). Rather, it depends on the circumstance that civil liability is just one part of the expected sanction (Paredes 2004; Kraakman et al 2009). Securities fraud is also a federal criminal offence, and it is regarded as a serious malfeasance by the American society. Traditionally, Americans do not want to 'mess with the feds' and the news of a SEC investigation – which is expected to follow the filing of a class action suit, if it was not already initiated – would suffice for the manager's reputation to be compromised by the national press, even in case of subsequent acquittal in both administrative and criminal proceedings.[25] It is because of a so powerful

---

24 This prediction is far from uncontroversial. So far, the empirical evidence has not borne out the theoretical hypothesis that securities class actions lead to over-deterrence, but has not rejected it either. See Choi (2004).

25 On the consequences of financial misrepresentation to managers see e.g. Karpoff et al (2008).

combination of enforcement mechanisms that US securities regulation may lead to over-deterrence of related-party transactions. Given the high exposure to the risk of false positives, honest corporate controllers may choose to forego efficient business opportunities whenever a potential conflict of interest could result in grounds for litigation – with the unavoidable follow-up of a public inquiry. Still, even this powerful enforcement machinery cannot entirely deter "spectacular, one-shot appropriations, of the 'take the money and run' sort" (Easterbrook and Fischel 1991: 103). This machinery did not prevent Enron; neither, arguably, could anything else have prevented it.

6.2.3.2 *Corporate litigation: derivative suits*

The balance between false positives and false negatives is somewhat more even in corporate litigation. Although the lawyers' incentive scheme is very similar to securities litigation, there are important differences. To start with, a shareholder suit is not formally a class action. It is more precisely a 'derivative' suit that the individual shareholder may bring on behalf of the corporation against its directors or controlling shareholder (Hamilton 2000). The prominent consequence of the derivative character of the suit is that only the corporation, and not the plaintiff shareholder, is entitled to damage compensation. This makes little difference for the corporate lawyer working on a contingency basis, provided that his expected reward is still commensurate to the damages indirectly suffered by shareholders as a group.

A more important difference is that a derivative suit has to be brought in the courts of the company's state of incorporation. For the majority of listed companies this means Delaware courts (Bebchuk and Cohen 2003). Whatever are the merits of state competition for corporate charters in the US, one rather uncontroversial result is that Delaware leads the process through its highly specialized judiciary.[26] On the one hand, this has lead to the development of the very sophisticated standards of review of related-party transactions, which we have just discussed. On the other hand, the technical skills of Delaware judges make frivolous suits very unlikely to go to trial. Indeed, both class actions and derivative suits may be dismissed by the court upon a summary judgment of the claim being not meritorious. However, this assessment can be reasonably expected to be much more accurate when it is made by a very specialized judiciary, whose prestige (perhaps the strongest motivation of judges) ultimately depends on its ability to adjudicate corporate law's cases. On top of that, derivative litigation has a further procedural hurdle: the 'demand requirement.'

Since the cause of action of corporate lawsuits ultimately belongs to the corporation, shareholders may not bring derivative suits unless they first make demand on the board or demand is 'excused' (Bainbridge 2002). In practice the demand requirement makes derivative suits relatively rare in the US

26 See e.g. Fisch (2000); but see also, critically, Carney et al (2010).

(Paredes 2004). Because directors are naturally reluctant to sue their colleagues (and even more so the controlling shareholder who appointed them), corporate lawsuits most often take place after a change in control or in bankruptcy proceedings. This result parallels what we observe in European jurisdictions (Kraakman et al 2009). Therefore, contrary to what one would expect, even in the US derivative suits raise little concern of false positives – at least, not as much as securities class actions. However, differently from other jurisdictions, derivative suits contribute to minimizing the risk of false negatives. The ultimate reason of this very special balance between Type I and Type II errors when it comes to the controller's exposure to liability under corporate law is the proficiency of Delaware courts.

A well-counseled shareholder will *not* make demand on the board knowing that chances are high that it will be refused. Then the crucial issue is when demand is excused.[27] Under Delaware law, futility of demand is based on a bifurcated test: *either* directors are tainted by a conflict of interest (in that they are not *independent* of the corporate controller) *or* they failed to exercise 'process due care' in deciding the challenged transactions.[28] These are basically the same conditions under which the business judgment rule is set aside. What suffices for demand to be excused is that a 'reasonable doubt' exists that one of these conditions holds (Bainbridge 2002). Once the plaintiff's petition passes this test, chances will be high that the case is settled – and, again, the lawyers will get the most out of the settlement. But the corporate controller has another option. He can set up a Special Litigation Committee, which will decide whether to continue the lawsuit is in the best interest of the corporation. When the members of the committee are independent and disinterested, their decision will be protected by the business judgment rule.

In many American states, a negative decision by the committee would just bring litigation to an end.[29] Not in Delaware, or at least not necessarily.[30]

---

27 Demand is excused when it is 'futile,' and so it is when directors: (1) have a conflict of interest in the challenged transaction; (2) were not reasonably informed when they approved it; or (3) the transaction was so egregious that it could not possibly have any rational business purpose. Marx v. Akers, 644 N.Y.S.2d 121, 666 N.E.2d 1034 (N.Y.1996).

28 Aronson v. Lewis, 473 A.2d 805, 814 (Del.Sup.1984). In Levine v. Smith, 591 A.2d 194, 205 (Del.Sup.1991), the court made clear that the test is a bifurcated one, so that satisfying either prong is sufficient for demand to be excused on grounds of futility.

29 See, e.g., Auerbach v. Bennett, 419 N.Y.S.2d 920 (N.Y.1979) (decision by the SLC to terminate litigation is protected by the business judgment rule, unless it is tainted by conflict of interest or inappropriateness of procedure).

30 This depends on whether demand on the board was required or excused in the first place. When demand is required, Delaware courts will grant decisions of the SLC the protection of the business judgment rule. Conversely, when demand is excused (which means that it was properly brought without making demand on the board), the court will be more skeptical about the judgment by the SLC. See Zapata Corp. v. Macdonaldo, 430 A.2d 779 (Del.Sup.1981) (the court will review both the *procedure* and the *merits* of the decision by the SLC to terminate litigation, in order to check whether termination can be deemed to be in the best interest of the company).

Delaware judges are in fact rather skeptical about 'independent' directors. Not only are they willing to review conflicted interest transactions that – notwithstanding formally independent approval – "stink bad enough" (Enriques 2000), but they will also not uphold decisions of the Special Litigation Committee just because its members have no apparent conflict of interest. They have in fact a *structural* conflict because they are appointed by the defendants to derivative litigation – like, in general, independent directors appointed by the corporate controller.[31] Therefore, in both litigation and substantive review of self-dealing, Delaware courts do take a 'hands-in' approach whenever the board judgment does not provide sufficient guarantees of being actually independent. This is also how derivative litigation ends up being a serious threat to the corporate controller's misbehavior. After securities litigation, this is perhaps the most important tool against investor expropriation in US corporate governance.

6.2.3.3 *Monitoring conflicts of interest: independent directors*

Delaware law's attitude towards independent directors highlights a major weakness of US corporate governance when it comes to the legal policy against non-pro-rata distributions. This policy is highly, if not exclusively, based on the deterrent effect of securities and corporate litigation, which in turn creates an almost unavoidable false positives problem. The problem would be less severe if independent directors could be relied upon. Ideally, independent directors should enforce the discipline of related-party transactions ex-ante rather than ex-post, by preventing more than deterring non-pro-rata distributions based on their professional judgment and the information they must be provided with by the corporate controller.

The above mechanism would confine both securities and corporate litigation to a residual role. On the one hand, independent directors' review of disclosures concerning conflicted interest transactions could provide a safe harbor for class action suits, or just make them harder to file. On the other hand, Delaware courts would easily stop being skeptical about the exercise of business judgment by independent directors, if only judges could trust their not being deferent to the corporate controller who appointed them. Even such an ideal system would never work in the absence of an institutional background. Corporate and securities law would still have to feature credible and severe

---

31 "The question naturally arises whether a 'there but for the grace of God go I' empathy might not play a role." Zapata Corp. v. Macdonaldo, 430 A.2d 779, 787 (Del.Sup.1981). This line of reasoning was endorsed by the federal Circuit Judge Ralph Winter in Joy v. North, 692 F.2d 880, 888 (2d Cir.1982), cert. denied, 460 U.S. 1051 (1983):

> It is not cynical to expect that such committees will tend to view derivative actions against the other directors with skepticism. Indeed, if the involved directors expected any result other than recommendation of termination at least as to them, they would probably never establish the committee.

punishment of misconduct, but the focus of substantive regulation could switch to the 'real' independence of director's oversight.

After Enron, this is apparently the direction that US law has taken. The Sarbanes-Oxley Act 2002, which would be impossible to discuss here in any detail, has undoubtedly intended to strengthen the role of independent directors in American corporate governance.[32] However, this effort and the others which followed or are in the making are still very much misdirected. The reason is twofold. On the one hand, regulators seem to insist more on the quantity of independent directors in the board than on the quality of their independence. On the other hand, the legal policy towards independent directors seems aimed at increasing their exposure to legal liability more than their accountability to non-controlling shareholders.

The Sarbanes-Oxley Act has notoriously compelled listed firms to set up an audit committee composed solely of independent directors, and the SEC – to say it with an understatement – 'encouraged' the stock exchanges to carry the matter of independent directorships further. So the New York Stock Exchange (NYSE) did: NYSE-listed companies must have a 'majority of independent directors' on their boards.[33] Listing rules are formally binding on the companies that wish to be listed on the NYSE, although the enforcement powers of the Stock Exchange are not comparable to those of the SEC.[34] But the crucial point is that neither in securities law nor in the Stock Exchange regulations is the independence requirement established with reference to appointment by the corporate controller, but only in terms of lack of financial or family involvement with the latter.[35]

One equally important point is that the Sarbanes-Oxley Act has overburdened independent directors of legal responsibilities, with the clear intention of making them an easy target of litigation (Ribstein 2006). While this works no differently than in the past in the presence of conflicts of interest, it has not resulted in outside, formally 'independent,' directors being subject to any stricter duty of care then their executive colleagues (Black et al 2006). Legal and economic commentators tend to agree that this would be neither feasible nor desirable. Companies will just have to pay more expensive D&O insurance policies, if they do not want

---

32   But see, critically, Ribstein (2002) and Romano (2005).
33   See § 303A.1 of the Listed Company Manual of the NYSE, approved by the SEC on November 4, 2003.
34   The limited enforceability of Stock Exchange regulations in the US is an old story. See Rock (2002). The Listed Company Manual of the NYSE compels the CEOs of listed companies to file an annual statement of compliance and to promptly notify in writing any material non-compliance with § 303A (NYSE Company Manual § 303A.12). In addition to the traditional sanction of delisting (which is hardly considered as a credible threat), the NYSE can now issue a public reprimand letter in case of violation (NYSE Company Manual § 303A.13). This is significantly different from the 'comply-or-explain' approach adopted by the European Corporate Governance Codes. See Kraakman et al (2009).
35   See § 301 of the Sarbanes-Oxley Act 2002; § 303A.2 of NYSE Company Manual.

good candidates to be strongly discouraged from serving as independent directors (Macey 2008).

The legal policy towards independent directors should be different; it should be based on accountability rather than liability (Boot and Macey 2004). To be sure, this kind of approach has been suggested in the US, at both the academic and the policy level. Professor Bebchuk (2003b) has long advocated empowering shareholders by giving them proxy access in corporate elections. This position was partly endorsed by the SEC in a series of proposals to amend regulation of the proxy machinery, until SEC Rule 14a-11 – introducing mandatory proxy access – was recently struck down in court.[36] As was discussed previously, the adoption of such a rule would have been unfortunate because of its mandatory character; whereas a number of developments in shareholder activism may lead individual companies to adopt a more balanced approach.

I shall discuss Bebchuk's position in more detail with regard to the Italian case, where the appointment of independent directors seems to be a major issue for preventing non-pro-rata distributions. As far as the US is concerned, adopting proxy access is anyway an option for shareholders. This option was first introduced by the Delaware mini-reform of 2006 and it is now clearly integrated in the federal discipline of shareholder proposals (SEC Rule 14a-8(i)(8)). In addition, after the changes that occurred in recent years (Yermack 2010), the board may still be in control of corporate elections but, on the one hand, it has been possible for shareholders to opt-in majority voting and, on the other hand, this has also enabled shareholders to *induce* disfavored directors to resign in uncontested elections, by simply withholding their vote. The importance of these changes has induced some commentators (Kahan and Rock 2011) to doubt whether proxy access makes so much difference in terms of investor protection. The same commentators acknowledge, however, that proxy access has the advantage of allowing the appointment of a *dissident* director, who in turn can be useful for monitoring conflicts of interest in the boardroom (Macey 2008).

Although, at the present stage, US corporate law does not provide for the independent appointment of outside directors, the outcome of the proxy access debate could be a first step towards a non-revolutionary rebalancing of the discretion–accountability tradeoff in this direction. Independent director appointment should be handled very carefully, however, in such a way as to preserve the corporate controller's managerial powers while constraining their abuse. It is for this reason that non-controlling shareholders should only be able to elect non-executive directors, who account for a minority of the board and whose tasks are strictly limited to the oversight of non-pro-rata distributions (Pacces 2011). Whether this will be actually an outcome of SEC Rule 14a-8(i)(8) is an interesting question for empirical research.

---

36 See *supra*, Chapter 4, section 4.3.1.

While in the US the independent appointment of directors is a question of fine-tuning an effective legal policy against diversionary PBC, independent directorship is a much more urgent matter in the other countries in our sample. None of them, and arguably no other corporate jurisdiction in the world, can rely on an "entrepreneurial system of private enforcement" of shareholder protection comparable to that of the US (Coffee 2001a).

6.3 The legal discipline of conflicts of interest in Europe

6.3.1 A European problem?

There are two good reasons to treat shareholder protection in the European countries of our sample under the same heading, but separately from the US. The first is that corporate law and securities regulation in European countries are not as elaborated as in the US in dealing with related-party transactions, and – even more importantly – exposure to the risk of legal liability is not the reason why European corporate controllers should refrain from non-pro-rata distributions (Kraakman et al 2009). In fact, this exposure is negligible, if not nil, in both continental Europe and – maybe surprisingly – in the UK. The second reason is that the establishment of an effective legal policy against diversionary PBC has become more and more a European problem; or, at least, it is perceived as such.

After the Ahold and Parmalat debacles demonstrated that corporate scandals were definitely not just an 'American thing,' the legal policy towards self-dealing has taken highest priority in the European regulators' agenda, at both the national and the EU level (McCahery and Vermeulen 2005; Hopt 2005). Most countries have taken some legislative or regulatory measure in this field (Enriques and Volpin 2007). The European legislator suddenly awoke from years and years of silence and embarked on the very ambitious project of setting Pan-European rules for both securities regulation and corporate law. A European Action Plan of both 'hard' and 'soft' legislation was approved and implemented by the Commission (see Baums 2007).

However, the outcome of this extensive legislative activity has not been very much up to expectations (Enriques and Gatti 2007). At the national level, the legislature's activism seems to have just followed the wake of 'me too' reforms, which mostly led to cosmetic changes (Hertig 2005). One major exception is perhaps Italy, whose regulation of related-party transactions lagged far behind both European and non-European developed countries. Anyway, it is at least controversial that the three major reforms of Italian corporate and securities law, which occurred in the past decade, determined any substantial improvement of corporate governance – Parmalat, perhaps the worst of European scandals, just occurred in between the second and the third one (see Enriques 2009). The picture is no rosier at the European level. As it turns out, the only substantial changes that the European

Commission managed to get through were already decided, or in the making, at the national level. While this was useful to overcome the moderate resistance of national vested interests, the European legislator has achieved little more. The adoption of the Takeover Directive is one major failure of European harmonization that I will discuss in the next chapters, but it is not the only one. According to Professor Enriques (2006), the overall effect of European legislation on national company laws has been rather trivial.

This is not unfortunate. The following discussion will briefly illustrate how Member States have found over time their own way to police non-pro-rata distribution, or – like Italy – are in the process of finding it. Anything of course can be improved, but legal and non-legal institutions need to evolve along their own path. As regards the discipline of related-party transactions, there is perhaps one issue on which the attention of national regulators converges. This is independent directors. The reason why European harmonization seems to have failed also in this respect is that the matter has to be put in perspective; and every legal system turns out to have its own. Still, in the recent Green Paper on Corporate Governance, the European Commission has included the issue whether the protection of minority shareholders from expropriation should require further action at the EU level.[37] One of the options being considered is the appointment of experts outside the influence of management *and* controlling shareholders to assess the merits of related party transactions. Although the outcome of this debate is yet to be seen, it seems unlikely that a one-size-fits-all solution can improve the efficiency of regulation of self-dealing across the board.

6.3.2 *Institutional monitoring in the UK*

6.3.2.1 *A peculiar approach to conflicts of interest*

It is now generally acknowledged that the British discipline of related-party transactions is significantly different from the American one (Kraakman et al 2009). On the one hand, the substantive rules are somewhat stricter than in the US. On the other hand, and more importantly, their enforcement is not based on private litigation but, rather, on a combination of public enforcement and (threat of) ouster by institutional investors. As a result, the balance between false positives and false negatives is ultimately determined by the bite of these enforcement mechanisms more than by the strictness of substantive standards. Overall, this bite is quite high, and the consequent risk of false positives is mitigated by the peculiar forms and the limited extent of institutional investor's activism in the UK (Stapledon 1996).

---

37 See European Commission, *Green Paper: The EU corporate governance framework*, COM(2011) 164 final, 5 April 2011.

As it was illustrated in Chapter 4, institutional activism in the UK takes place 'behind closed doors,' and it is basically limited to situations of director's severe underperformance or mischief. It is not in the institutional investors' interest to do more than induce directors to resign in these situations. At the same time, it is shareholder legal empowerment under British company law that makes the threat of ouster so credible that it hardly needs to be implemented (Armour 2010). This has more to do with distribution of legal powers than with the discipline of related-party transactions. To be sure, there is some evidence that this may be changing. On the one hand, some British institutions have become willing to take a more proactive role (Becht et al 2009). On the other hand, the company law's reforms seem to go in the direction of enhancing shareholders' ability to hold directors liable (Davies 2008). Provided that the corporate controller's discretion already suffers a number of constraints in the UK, this trend may increase the risk of false positives in policing non-pro-rata distributions.

6.3.2.2 *Board and shareholder approval*

Like their American colleagues, British judges traditionally refused to second-guess business judgment.[38] However, since no distinction between standards of conduct and standard of review has ever been elaborated in the British jurisprudence, the courts of the UK always risk reviewing the merits of director's conduct when they are requested to enforce the far-reaching number of duties that directors owe to the company (Davies 2002). Judges have hardly done this in the past. A director's duty of care used to be considered a subjective standard of diligence (whose assessment was based on the director's *actual* skill), which added little to the director's duty to act in (likewise subjective) good faith – i.e., in what *he* considered to be the best interests of the company. This has changed over time. In the recent codification of directors' equitable duties in the Companies Act of 2006, a number of objective elements have been injected into both duties, thereby allowing, at least in theory, judicial review of directors' skill and diligence.[39]

Related-party transactions are a completely different story. In principle, directors – like any fiduciary – are not entitled to profit from any transaction in which they have a conflict of interest ('no-conflict rule') (Davies 2008). Transactions violating the no-conflict rule are not binding on the company, and directors' profits must be disgorged. This could sound like a ban on conflicted interest transactions, but it is not. When the conflict of interest is disclosed and shareholders nonetheless approve or subsequently ratify the transaction, neither nullification nor disgorgement applies. This used to be

---

38 See e.g. Carlen v. Drury [1812] 1 Ves and B 154 ("the court could not undertake the management of every brewhouse and playhouse in the kingdom"); Burland v. Earle [1902] 3 All ER 420; Hogg v. Cramphorn Ltd. [1967] Ch 254.

39 See §§ 170–181 of the Companies Act of 2006 (CA 2006).

quite a burdensome discipline of conflicted transactions, although many British companies managed to opt out of it.[40] Under today's company law, most 'routine' related-party transactions can be authorized by the board of directors provided that full disclosure of the conflict of interest is made. Before the Companies Act of 2006, there was no need of disinterested approval and the interested director was entitled to vote. In the presence of full disclosure, it was only possible to attack the transaction on the basis of the duty of good faith. As of now, votes of interested directors no longer count for a valid board approval.[41]

Shareholder approval is still pivotal in the British discipline of conflicted interest transactions. First, it cannot be entirely opted out as company law makes it compulsory for certain transactions, most notably substantial property transactions.[42] Second, significant related-party transactions entered into by quoted companies are anyway subject to the different, and in a sense stricter, procedure of shareholder approval prescribed by the Listing Rules of the Financial Services Authority.[43] Third, only shareholder approval (or ratification) can safely relieve directors from liability, at least in those circumstances in which ratification is allowed. This may suggest that the British approach to non-pro-rata distributions leaves little margins for false negatives, but possibly allows for a high risk of false positives. This conclusion is essentially correct, but requires two major qualifications. One is about the controlling shareholders and how their behavior is policed in spite of their being in control of the general meeting. The other one concerns the limited standing to sue derivatively of non-controlling shareholders and how directors are nonetheless prevented from engaging in diversionary conduct.[44]

6.3.2.3 *Shareholder empowerment and the limited scope for litigation in the UK*

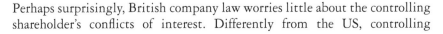

Perhaps surprisingly, British company law worries little about the controlling shareholder's conflicts of interest. Differently from the US, controlling

---

40 This was the result of three tiers of rules: (1) the equitable no-conflict rule; (2) art. 85 of Table A of CA 1985, which contained the default waiver of the equitable rule (on condition that the conflict of interest was disclosed); (3) § 317 of the CA 1985, which mandated disclosure of conflicts of interest to the board, but not also abstention of the interested director from voting. CA 2006 §§ 175–177 have largely simplified the matter, explicitly allowing board authorization of most conflicted interest transactions.

41 See § 175 of CA 2006.

42 See §§ 190–196 of CA 2006.

43 See Listing Rules (LR) § 11 (Related Party Transactions).

44 Minority shareholders in the UK can avail themselves of an additional, powerful statutory remedy against oppression by the majority shareholder: the 'unfair prejudice' remedy. See §§ 994–998 of CA 2006. However, for a number of reasons that cannot be discussed here, the standard interpretation is that this remedy is only available for closely held companies. See Davies (2008). The following discussion only deals with the remedies available to shareholders of public companies.

shareholders owe no fiduciary duty to minority shareholders in the UK (Davies 2008). Shareholders are always entitled to vote in their own interest. In theory, this should allow for exquisite opportunities for non-pro-rata distributions, given the ease with which controlling shareholders can have related-party transactions approved by the general meeting. However, this has never been a real problem in British corporate governance. To be sure, even though both interested directors and interested controlling shareholders used to face no limitation in casting their vote at the general meeting, courts have always maintained that breach of the duty of loyalty was not ratifiable.[45] In addition, in the presence of non-ratifiable breaches, the procedural hurdles of derivative litigation in the UK – which are going to be touched upon shortly – are not applicable provided that the wrongdoer is in control of the company (Davies 2008). Finally, the Listing Rules – which are strictly enforced by both the FSA and institutional investors – do not allow either directors or 'substantial' shareholders (i.e., those who control 10% or more of the voting rights) to vote on significant transactions with their related parties.[46]

And yet, none of these rules provide the ultimate explanation of why controlling shareholders do not only refrain from 'stealing,' but are also very rare among British listed companies. As discussed in Chapter 4, one explanation for this is that the Listing Rules (today in combination with the UK Corporate Governance Code) provide that these companies should anyway be capable of carrying on business independently of a controlling shareholder, which means *inter alia* that the latter cannot be in control of the board of directors without seriously upsetting the institutional investors.[47] Therefore, no differently from where managers are in control, non-pro-rata distributions by controlling shareholders are ultimately policed by institutional investors via their influence on the board of directors. The new provisions of the Companies Act of 2006 add little to this result. They require that the votes of interested directors or controlling shareholders be disregarded both in ratification decisions and in decisions whether to sue directors for breach of duty.[48]

In the vast majority of listed companies, where executive directors are in charge and there is no controlling shareholder, board and/or shareholder approval raise little concern of false negatives. Entering into related-party

---

45 Cook v. Deeks [1916] 1 AC 554, PC (shareholders cannot ratify fraud or illegality). See also Smith v. Croft (No 2) [1988] Ch 114 (individual shareholders may not sue for breaches that can be ratified by a majority of shareholders independent of the wrongdoer). British common law has not otherwise attempted to constrain decision-making powers of controlling shareholders, if not in just one long-standing exception (Allen v. Gold Reefs of West Africa Ltd. [1900] 1 Ch 656).

46 Based on LR § 11.1.7, related parties and their associates cannot vote on the shareholder resolution approving the transaction. According to LR § 11.1.4 a substantial shareholder qualifies as related party. 'Substantial shareholder' is defined in LR, Appendix 1, Relevant definitions.

47 See in this regards the Easy Jet case discussed in Pacces (2011).

48 See § 239(4) and §§ 261–263 of CA 2006.

transactions requires that extensive disclosures be made to the competent body, before it approves them, and in the annual accounts, after they have been approved (Kraakman et al 2009). Failure to disclose may trigger either criminal liability, a proceeding by the FSA, or both. A feature of British law when it comes to self-dealing is the availability of a number of venues for public enforcement. A certain proportion of shareholders may request, for instance, the Secretary of State to institute a proceeding of investigation of the company's documents, or to appoint an inspector for reviewing the company's affairs, when they suspect a director's misconduct.[49] However, the empirical evidence shows that public enforcement levels are negligible in the UK (Armour 2009a).

More importantly, non-transparent directors would never be forgiven by institutional investors and likewise by the business community of the London Stock Exchange.[50] More than any form of legal liability, directors fear ouster from that community. While the former would be forthcoming, and it is uncertain at any rate, the latter is immediate and not appealable. As a result, transactions featuring non-pro-rata distributions are very unlikely to be put forward because they will never pass the direct or indirect scrutiny of institutional investors. On the contrary, institutions are unlikely to exercise their *de facto* veto power on related-party transactions that potentially have business purpose: ex-ante, it is in their interest to defer to business judgment. Neither would they challenge these transactions ex-post, when they turn out badly. In the UK, shareholder ability to sue derivatively has been limited for over a century by the Foss v. Harbottle ruling, which gives standing against directors only to the company and its competent bodies, unless a fraud on the minority has been committed *and* the wrongdoer is in control of the company.[51] This principle has been heavily debated but never overruled, until the Companies Act of 2006 stepped in to regulate the issue explicitly. Derivative suits are now allowed when there is a *prima facie* case of breach of *any* of the directors' duties, subject to permission by the court and unless the transaction has been ratified by disinterested shareholders.[52]

The formal strengthening of shareholders' ability to hold directors liable has not altered the peculiar equilibrium of distribution of powers in UK corporate governance. Institutional investors do not like to sue (Stapledon 1996). When they are too committed to the company for a plain 'exit' strategy,

---

49 See, especially, the powers conferred upon the Secretary of State by § 432 (appointment of inspectors) and § 447 (investigation of company documents) of CA 1985. This part of the Companies Act has not been repealed by the CA 2006, which only amended the discipline of company investigations by enhancing the powers of the Secretary of State by moderately changing the investigation procedure. See CA 2006, Part 32, §§ 1035–1039.

50 On the reputational constraints faced by the business community of the City of London, see Armour and Skeel (2007) and Cheffins (2008).

51 Foss v. Harbottle [1843] 2 Hare 461.

52 See §§ 260–264 of CA 2006. Formally, this is not intended to overrule Foss v. Harbottle, but only to provide a statutory basis for derivative suits. See Davies (2008).

they would prefer having directors they are dissatisfied with ousted from the board. Other non-controlling shareholders, particularly the activist share-holders like hedge funds, might behave more aggressively. However, private enforcement is conspicuously absent from UK corporate governance (Armour 2009a). Shareholder litigation is severely constrained by the absence of effective procedures for collective redress and the combination of a ban on contingent fees with a loser-pays rule for the allocation of litigation expenses. The virtual absence of shareholder litigation fits the UK system of corporate governance well. If directors' liability had more bite, this would increase the risk of false positives. The policy of non-pro-rata distributions in the UK is instead governance-based as opposed to the litigation-based approach of the US (Kraakman et al 2009). As I mentioned, there is a strong case for institutions to evolve towards a more efficient equilibrium along their own path instead of by legal transplant. This makes monitoring by independent directors, rather than directors' liability, a most promising venue for improving the discipline of related-party transactions in the UK.

6.3.2.4 *Institutional monitoring and independent directors*

Independent directors as an instrument for governance (as opposed to a safe harbor for the corporate controller's liability) are a British, not an American invention. British law keeps on maintaining the self-regulatory character of this institution, but there is no reason to doubt that it is a source of credible commitment for corporate controllers. Provisions of the UK Combined Code are both binding and enforced according to our earlier classification. They are subject to the 'comply-or-explain' principle – which makes explicit departures very unlikely to be accepted by institutional investors; and they are attached to the Listing Rules – which makes truthful disclosure subject to oversight by the FSA.[53]

Among other things, the UK Code requires that at least a half of the board members – plus the chairman – be non-executive directors (NEDs) determined by the board to be independent. Independence requirements exclude representation of significant shareholders, so that controlling shareholders are effectively unable to appoint the majority of board members unless the company is characterized as being small.[54] This contributes to the bias against shareholder control in the UK, which has been illustrated in Chapter 4. On the other hand, the notion of independence does not exclude non-executives who are *de facto* appointed by directors in control of the proxy machinery. Although institutional investors must not object for an insider's nominations to be viable, this circumstance is no guarantee of 'real' independence from managerial control (see Macey 2008).

---

53 But see Arcot et al (2010) on compliance with the Code being more in form than in substance.

54 See UK Corporate Governance Code § B.1.1 and B.1.2.

Would such independence be any more desirable, or just feasible, given the tradeoff between proximity and monitoring in the boardroom (Boot and Macey 2004)? Probably it would not if we refer to the majority of the board. But the answer may change when a minority of the board, featured with specific monitoring tasks and no possible interference with business judgment, is considered. In the British tradition of a unitary board, this solution may only be implemented through a special committee composed exclusively of directors appointed by non-controlling shareholders. The next step would be to place institutional investors in the driving seat.[55] This may be problematic, provided that institutions seem to be quite reluctant to take any explicit involvement in the appointment of NEDs, while they usually monitor their nomination in the background; but a change in attitude may be in the making (Cheffins 2008).

Reserving a number of separate director's seats for election by non-controlling shareholders would not be a dramatic change. On condition that their role is limited to policing the controller's conflicts of interest, it would probably improve accountability without undermining discretion in corporate control. This provision would have to be supplemented either by a special indemnification of the costs incurred for soliciting shareholders' suffrages for the independent partition of the board, or by allowing institutional investors to piggyback the circulation of proxy materials not only for directors' removal, but also for their appointment. It goes without saying that – differently from the current state of British law in this respect – both appointment and removal powers of non-controlling shareholders should be mandatory, but strictly limited to the committee that we want to be actually independent from the executive management or from the controlling shareholders.

6.3.3 *Shareholder protection in the Netherlands: a neglected story of judicial oversight*

6.3.3.1 *The source of misunderstanding of the Dutch case*

The Dutch case is an interesting one. The received wisdom about corporate law in the Netherlands is that it protects non-controlling shareholders very little. Accordingly, when it comes to investor protection, the standard characterization of the Dutch jurisdiction in the international comparisons is 'low quality' (La Porta et al 1998). This characterization is at odds with the high degree of stock market development in the Netherlands, and is in fact misguided. The economists have been misled in their quantitative analyses, at both the national and the international level; whereas Dutch law is often neglected by comparative lawyers, who prefer to focus on jurisdictions considered to be more representative of the civil law tradition.

---

55 See Pacces (2011) on how this goal may be accomplished.

The reason of misinterpretation of the Dutch case is twofold. On the one hand, shareholder protection from non-pro-rata distributions is normally confused with shareholder empowerment in corporate governance (see e.g. Chirinko et al 2004). In Chapter 4, I have illustrated how the legal distribution of governance powers in the Netherlands does not actually favor shareholders, thereby allowing public companies to be under managerial control. But this has not necessarily to do with whether and how non-controlling shareholders are protected from expropriation. In fact, the only jurisdiction of our sample in which these two issues are connected with each other is the UK. On the other hand, the Dutch 'law on the books' seems not only to give shareholders little powers, but also to protect them insufficiently from the corporate controller's misbehavior. According to the coding by Djankov et al (2008),[56] both directors and controlling shareholders face little risk of liability for non-pro-rata distributions; neither judicial nor independent review of conflicted interest transactions is provided for; and disclosure of conflicts of interest is as little required ex-ante as poorly enforced ex-post. Upon a more careful investigation, however, none of the above statements proves to be true.

One fundamental tenet of legal comparison is that the analysis must be freed from reliance on *any* national legal category, and performed just in functional terms (Zweigert and Kötz 1998). True, Dutch corporate law does not allow shareholders to sue derivatively, confining the enforcement of directors' duties to situations where a change in control, or bankruptcy, has occurred. Standing to sue for directors' liability resides essentially with the supervisory board whose members – despite formal requirements of independence – naturally defer to the corporate controller who has *de facto* the last word on their appointment. In addition, controlling shareholders owe no fiduciary duties to non-controlling shareholders (Timmerman and Doorman 2002).

To be sure, most of the above categories have little meaning in the formal structure of Dutch corporate law, which does not acknowledge the primacy of shareholder interest in corporate governance and, consequently, does not distinguish between controlling and non-controlling shareholder. In principle, shareholder control should not be admitted for firms incorporated in the Netherlands. Some economists are inclined to believe that the prevalence of substance over form is a feature of the common law tradition (La Porta et al 2008). This is inaccurate: it is in fact a (functional) feature of case-law (Merryman 1969). As it turns out, in a civil law jurisdiction like the Netherlands, protection of non-controlling shareholders have been mostly elaborated by judge-made law, on the basis of the interpretation of corporate law's general clauses, of a dedicated procedure for enforcing legality in corporate governance, and of a specialized jurisdiction in charge of administering this procedure.

---

56 It is worth noting that the country scores on the Anti-Self-Dealing index are no longer reported in the published version of Djankov et al (2008). They are available on Professor Shleifer's website.

6.3.3.2 *The role of the judiciary and the mechanisms of private enforcement*

The so-called 'inquiry procedure' (*enquêterecht*) is the most important tool of shareholder protection under Dutch corporate law (Timmerman and Doorman 2002). To be sure, its formal scope of application is both wider and narrower: wider, because the instrument is also available for stakeholders' and public enforcement; narrower, because the most part of corporate litigation must follow the standard civil procedure. The aim of the inquiry procedure is to restore legality in the relationship between corporate stakeholders, which implies a judgment as to whether legality has been breached in the first place. For this reason, the most important limitation of this procedure is that it cannot lead to imposition of liability, but only to implementation of injunctions, corrective remedies, and pronunciation of declaratory judgment on whose basis liability can subsequently be sought for in a separate trial (Bekkum et al 2010).

In practice, the scope of application of the *enquêterecht* is very broad, and almost every situation that may be characterized as corporate mismanagement qualifies (Timmerman and Doorman 2002). This is potentially dangerous because it could lead to courts second-guessing the exercise of managerial discretion. According to Dutch law, mismanagement is to be assessed on the basis of a general criterion of reasonableness and fairness (Bekkum et al 2010). Although Dutch law has not formally elaborated any business judgment rule, the Enterprise Chamber of the Amsterdam Court of Appeals has developed a similar standard of review. Compliance with the "elementary principle of responsible entrepreneurship" is sufficient for courts to abstain from reviewing of business judgment.[57]

The Enterprise Chamber has exclusive jurisdiction on the *enquêterecht* and a number of other corporate matters; it is a judiciary highly specialized in corporate affairs. Its judgments are subject to review by the Dutch Supreme Court, which has played an important role in correcting the Enterprise Chamber's tendency to step into the corporate controller's shoes too much. It is now quite settled that corporate management is subject to "limited assessment" by the courts, having regard more to the process of decision-making than to the merits of decisions (Timmerman 2004). Conversely, conflicted interest transactions allow for almost no excuse in the absence of independent approval. Courts will check whether the statutory principle of equal treatment of shareholders is respected on a substantive basis, unless non-controlling shareholders have approved the transaction knowing of the conflict of interest, or alternatively the transaction has been decided by the supervisory board independently of the corporate controller.[58] The notion of corporate

---

57 This principle was first formulated by the Enterprise Chamber in OK 21 June 1979, NJ 1980, 71. See also the Supreme Court in HR 6 June 1996, NJ 1996, 695.

58 See OK 1 March 2001, JOR 2001, 131 (special information rights for minority shareholders in the presence of conflicts of interest); and HR 10 January 1990, NJ 1990, 466 (procedural obligations of the management and the supervisory board).

control is likewise assessed on a substantive basis, so that the conflict of inter-est is identified upon the members of the managing/supervisory board or upon a controlling shareholder, depending on who is ultimately in charge.[59] None of these judicial standards is written down in the Dutch civil code.[60]

A detailed discussion of the inquiry procedure is outside the scope of this brief discussion (see Jitta 2004 for more details). However, it is important to point out that only shareholders who individually or jointly account for 10% of share capital or hold 225,000 Euro in par value (and a few other persons or public institutions indicated in the law or in the articles of association) have standing to request an *enquêterecht*. In addition, damage compensation is not included in the remedies that can be granted by the Enterprise Chamber. In principle, although all the expenses of the procedure are borne by the corporation, there is little reason why any non-controlling shareholder should ever go for it. This is particularly problematic if we consider that institutional investors – which are normally reluctant to litigate – have been traditionally very passive in Dutch corporate governance.[61]

However, two fundamental ingredients of Dutch corporate law's enforcement must be added to the picture. First, a declaratory judgment of mismanagement by the Enterprise Chamber can form the basis for a success-ful suit for damages before the competent district court (Schuit et al 2002); such a suit may be brought either by the company for breach of director's duties (after a new management constituency has been appointed following the *enquêterecht*), or by individual shareholders under the general law of torts (e.g., for inadequate disclosure of conflicted interest transactions in the com-pany's financial accounts). Second, both the application for the inquiry procedure and a subsequent suit for damages can be filed in the form of share-holders' representative action, where standing or representative powers are conferred upon associations whose constitution is intended to protect a collective interest suitable for bundling. Shareholder associations are the case in point.

Dutch representative actions are not to be confused with class actions in the US (see Bekkum et al 2010). It is exactly for this reason that they provide similar incentives to private enforcement. Contingent fees are not allowed in the Netherlands, so it is up to shareholder associations, not to corporate lawyers, to aggregate the interest of non-controlling shareholders. Shareholder associations have only standing for requesting a declaratory judgment, after which, in theory, shareholders must proceed individually with their liability claims. In practice, disgruntled investors grant shareholder associations the power of attorney for the second stage, in which they are usually allowed to

---

59 See OK 8 October 1998, NJ 1999, 348 (conflicts of interest of the majority shareholder).
60 But see Bekkum et al (2010) for how these standards are derived from the principles of reasonableness and fairness in the Dutch civil code, particularly Article 8, Book 2.
61 de Jong and Röell (2005). But the attitude has been changing in recent times. See de Jong et al (2010).

collect some additional fees *conditional* – but as in the UK, not contingent – on success. As a result, most claims brought by shareholder associations in the Netherlands are settled for generous shareholder compensations before going to trial. Since mid-2005, the Amsterdam Court of Appeals may declare, under a number of conditions, the settlement binding also on shareholders not participating in the representative action.[62]

This procedure used to be little known outside the Netherlands, but is becoming more and more popular in the international literature and legal practice. The main Dutch shareholder association (*Vereniging van Effectenbezitters* – VEB) has already established a remarkable record of accomplishment in securities litigation. For instance, the suit against Ahold N.V. and its former management was already settled for sizeable compensation before the 2005 reform came into force. Because after 2005 the Dutch court can make the settlement binding on the entire class of investors, the Dutch jurisdiction has recently attracted some international litigation even without connection to Dutch investors (Kortman and Bredenoord-Spoek 2011).

6.3.3.3 *Independent directors and the corporate governance code*

Based on the foregoing discussion, it can hardly be denied that investor protection has a considerable bite in the Netherlands. Whether this also results in efficient policing of non-pro-rata distributions is, however, an open question. The inquiry procedure is very burdensome for the company, and its increasing popularity may lead to false positives. At the same time, deterrence by ex-post enforcement of liability and/or ouster – especially when the initiative is entrusted to shareholder associations – does not always provide sufficient guarantees against the risk of false negatives. In the wake of the Ahold scandal, the Dutch government decided therefore to follow a different path in order to strengthen the policing of non-pro-rata distributions.

In 2004 a new Corporate Governance Code (the so-called 'Tabaksblat Code') came into force. This code mainly relied on the independence of the supervisory board for monitoring corporate management and disciplining related-party transactions. The code was updated in 2008, when a new edition was published.[63] Similarly to the UK, the Dutch code has a statutory basis. The

---

62 See the 'Act on Collective Settlement of Mass Damages,' which came into force on 27 July 2005. Disgruntled shareholders have limited possibilities to opt out. See Bekkum et al (2010).

63 The Corporate Governance Committee (so-called 'Tabaksblat Committee') was established upon invitation by the Dutch Ministries of Finance and of Economic Affairs, and published the Dutch Corporate Governance Code on 9 December 2003. The Code was given a statutory basis by the Dutch Parliament on 30 December 2004. In 2005 a Monitoring Committee on the Corporate Governance Code was established with the task of reporting on implementation of the Code, as well as on national and international developments in CG. The Tabaksblat Code replaced the Forty Recommendations issued by the so-called 'Peters Report' in 1997. Both the current Dutch Corporate governance Code (2008 edition)

Dutch civil code requires that a statement about compliance with the code is published together with the company's annual accounts, explaining the reasons of non-compliance (Bekkum et al 2010). The Dutch legislation is less insistent than the British one on the enforcement of the 'comply-or-explain' principle by the securities regulator (Wymeersch 2005). However, according to the Monitoring Commission on Corporate Governance, the vast majority of Dutch listed firms comply on average with over 90% of the code.

As far as the contents of the code are concerned, most of the remarks made with reference to the UK Corporate Governance Code are applicable. The Dutch Code requires independence of *all* the members of the supervisory board (Hopt 2011). Independence is determined with regard to financial and family involvement with members of the managing board, and with respect to shareholders accounting for more than 10% of share capital. However, the peculiar rules governing the appointment to the two-tier board in the Netherlands are not given proper account. As a result, the independence requirements of the supervisory board are unrealistic. The supervisory board cannot be reasonably expected to be independent of the corporate controller, inasmuch as it is in charge of electing the managing board (see e.g. Hooghiemstra and van Manen 2004). Things may change if companies grad-ually move towards a one-tier board structure,[64] but for the time being it is illusory to believe that shareholders representatives in the supervisory board will not be *de facto* selected by the management or by the controlling share-holder, depending on the ownership structure. As a result, monitoring of con-flicted interest transaction by the supervisory board cannot be entirely relied upon (McCahery and Vermeulen 2005). The setup of the code, unchanged in this respect by the 2008 update, has another inconsistency with economic analysis. It assigns the supervisory board two contradictory tasks: monitoring and advice, which are very difficult to reconcile (Boot and Macey 2004; Adams and Ferreira 2007).

The direction of a desirable reform of Dutch corporate governance is twofold. On the one hand, the supervisory board should only be concerned with monitoring non-pro-rata distributions; unless a one-tier structure is chosen, in which case the monitoring role should be performed by an independent committee. The remainder of the board's tasks should be performed by the management board. On the other hand, the members of the supervisory board should be elected by non-controlling shareholders. A necessary condition for this solution to be workable is that the supervisory board is no longer in charge of appointing executive directors to the managing board.

and the reports of the Monitoring Commission on its implementation are available at www.commissiecorporategovernance.nl.
64 See *supra* Chapter 4 for the ongoing reform allowing this.

6.3.4 *Legal underpinnings of shareholder protection in Sweden*

6.3.4.1 *Legal rules, social norms, or just both of them?*

The Swedish case is also very interesting in comparative corporate governance, but for a different and, in a sense, opposite reason compared to the Netherlands: while the Dutch case has been little studied, the Swedish case seems to be overstated.

Apparently, Sweden poses a big challenge to the 'law matters' thesis: both stock market development and separation of ownership and control are very high in Sweden, in the face of shareholder protection appearing to be just average in legal terms. Comparative economists tend nowadays to consider Sweden as the exception that confirms the rule: common law jurisdictions still outperform civil law ones in investor protection, with the exception of Scandinavian countries where some other extralegal factor seems to contribute to investor's confidence (Djankov et al 2008). Swedish financial economists tend to subscribe to this position, and have tried to demonstrate it on empirical grounds (Holmén and Högfeldt 2004). Comparative lawyers have been more speculative. On the one hand, they have suggested that social norms, more than corporate law and its enforcement, may be the driver of investor protection in Sweden (Coffee 2001a). On the other hand, they have tried to explain the persistence of shareholder control in spite of good investor protection by introducing – as I am doing – a qualitative distinction of private benefits of control (Gilson 2006).

Unfortunately, Swedish corporate lawyers have hardly joined this debate.[65] Had they done that, they would have probably told the following facts about Swedish corporate law. First, that distribution of powers is based on shareholder supremacy, which implies that corporate management cannot do without a controlling shareholder. Second, that minority shareholders are as weakly involved in decision-making as strongly protected from non-pro-rata distributions. Third, that legal enforcement and the power of social norms work in tandem to achieve this result.

The argument that social norms may substitute for low quality of law and its enforcement has two major weaknesses. The first and obvious one is that, as such, social norms are beyond control by policymakers: there is little one can do with them, unless there is some way to shape their content through the legal system. This leads to the second and subtler criticism: in the absence of legal support, the norms of a society may be disrupted by exposure to a different set of norms. Globalization and competition, which are otherwise beneficial for the efficiency of corporate governance, may be responsible for this disruption. Sweden used to be very concerned about this risk, and traditionally limited the ability of foreigners to acquire a significant stake in national companies. These constrains were against European law, and today

---

65 But see Skog and Fäger (2007) for a good overview of the Swedish company law.

they are history. Yet, not even a single instance of shareholder expropriation has ever been reported in Sweden (Agnblad et al 2001). Swedish social norms have turned out to be strong enough to also prevent outsiders – who supposedly do not share the same social concerns as Swedish people – from engaging in extraction of diversionary PBC. The only possible explanation for this is that in Sweden – as probably anywhere else – social norms provide a source of credible commitment inasmuch as they are operated 'in the shadow of the law.'

6.3.4.2 *Public and private enforcement of legal rules in the background*

The legal policing of non-pro-rata distribution in Sweden relies extensively upon disclosure of conflicts of interest by both directors and controlling shareholders. Conflicted interest transaction must be reported in detail in the company's periodic disclosures. On the contrary, there is no requirement to disclose conflicts of interest ex-ante; neither is any procedure established for management of these conflicts by the company's organs. Basically, the entire discipline of related-party transactions in Sweden is based on ex-post enforcement.

Swedish people hardly consider the hypothesis that a corporate controller may violate this discipline, or fail to disclose his interest in the transaction. Sweden has a close-knit business community, made up of people who have built their reputation over a number of family generations. These families still control most of Swedish corporations, although to a lesser extent than in the past (Henrekson and Jakobsson 2012). They would have much to lose from violating the rules of the game (Holmén and Högfeldt 2009). The power of social norms is that they may provide an ideal balance between false positives and false negatives in enforcement. If they are relied upon by the community, there will be no risk of false positives on the assumption that everybody sticks to them. But this equilibrium depends on false negatives being likewise ruled out. For the reasons I have just mentioned, here the law must step in. The ultimate reason why shareholders can be confident about compliance with the norms of fair dealing is that they expect wrongdoing to be deterred. While the threat of social sanctions would suffice in most cases, law has to take care of residual risk of misbehavior to preserve the same threat's credibility.

The efficacy of corporate law and its enforcement in Sweden is such that hardly any punishment has to be implemented. As far as the substantive law is concerned (Skog and Fäger 2007), conflicts of interest need not only be disclosed ex-post; but they also cannot result in non-pro-rata distributions at any rate. Both directors and the CEO (the 'managing director') cannot deal with any matter where they, or their related parties, have a considerable interest that may be in conflict with that of the company. As a rule, shareholders can instead vote on any resolution even when they have a material interest; but they cannot vote on related-party transactions and on their discharge from liability as directors. More important, however, is the general principle that all distributions to shareholders must be made pro-rata, and that any act violating this principle is voidable. Neither the board nor a controlling shareholder may pass a resolution giving 'undue advantage' to one or more shareholders to the detriment of the company or of other shareholders. On top of nullification, violation of this general clause may trigger both criminal and civil liability.

As far as private enforcement is concerned, minority shareholders have both an individual and a derivative cause of action, depending on whether the company or individual shareholders have been harmed (Skog and Fäger 2007). By and large, director's liability is to be sought for through a derivative suit, which requires at least 10% of share capital to be initiated and pursued in spite of opposition by the shareholder meeting. A claim for shareholders' liability for discriminatory treatment is instead, normally, an individual action (Dotevall 2003). In fact, both actions are hardly ever brought in Sweden. Nevertheless, there is little doubt they could be brought quite easily. Maybe derivative suits were not so much of a threat before civil procedure was amended to account for aggregation of collective claims; but individual actions have always been so. On the one hand, Swedish shareholders are entitled to piggyback a criminal proceeding against the wrongdoer. On the other hand, legal costs of private litigation were traditionally very low in Sweden, and every natural person used to be entitled to public legal aid. This has changed, but the overwhelming majority of the population is nonetheless covered by private insurance of legal costs (see Broman and Granström 2003).

In 2003, Sweden was one of the first European countries to introduce collective actions. In corporate and securities law, both derivative and individual shareholder litigation qualifies. The action – which is more precisely a 'representative' action, for it requires actual opt-in by the class members – may be brought by an individual shareholder, a governmental authority, or a shareholder association (Mattil and Desoutter 2008). Opting-in individuals do not bear any expenses, and lawyer's contingent fee arrangement may be allowed upon the plaintiff's special request to the court. *Aktiespararna*, the main shareholder association in Sweden, may count on over 40 years of tradition and about 100,000 members (out of a population of a few million people) to make this a credible threat for prospective wrongdoers.

6.3.4.3 *The Swedish Code of Corporate Governance*

Being aware that non-pro-rata distributions were not a problem in Sweden, the national legislature took a very mild approach to legal reform in the wake of the financial scandals on both sides of the Atlantic. A Commission on Business Confidence (*Förtroendekommissionen*) was established in 2002, but just minor modifications of company law were advocated.[66] Most of them were already decided and came into force with the new Companies Act of 2006, in

---

66 Förtroendekommissionen, *Final Report*, Summary in English, SOU 2004:47, 43–74 (on file with author). The report used to be available at www.sou.gov.se, but it has been removed.

which regulation of conflicts of interest is basically unchanged. The Swedish legislature rather went for promoting self-regulation. A Swedish Code of Corporate Governance was first approved in 2005 and then revised in 2008 and 2010. Its adherence is required by the listing rules of the Stockholm Stock Exchange and is based on a 'comply-or-explain' principle. Listing rules have no statutory basis in Sweden. However, the listing authority has a number of enforcement powers, ranging from fines to delisting (Petersson and Sandberg Thomsen 2011). In the Swedish institutional environment, this means that the Code is both binding and enforced.

In practice, the Code's provisions amount to little more than fine-tuning of Swedish corporate governance. The major innovation is independent directors. Independence is required on both a financial and a family-ties basis with respect to the company management, and it applies to the majority of directors elected by shareholders excluding the CEO, who is the only executive who can be allowed to sit on the board. More importantly, two of these independent directors must also be independent of the controlling shareholder, and cannot be selected by him. Under these rules, the controlling shareholder can still arrange the board size and composition in such a way as to control decision-making. Still, the two independent directors will be in the position to provide a reliable check on conflicts of interests. This is probably the most balanced solution of the discretion–accountability tradeoff that we have reviewed so far.

6.3.5 Shareholder protection in Italy: a tortuous and slow path toward improvement

6.3.5.1 A tradition of weak protection of minority shareholders

For an Italian, it is embarrassing to write about the national corporate law's discipline of conflicted interest transactions. Short of being neglected or overstated, the Italian case is notorious, and with good reason. The story is almost as old as comparative corporate governance and, over the past 15 years, it has been told by economists and lawyers on the two sides of the Atlantic in nearly the same terms (see e.g. Djankov et al 2008; Ferrarini and Giudici 2005). Both rules and enforcement of corporate law in Italy do not supply minority shareholders with sufficient protection from expropriation, and this is the reason why ownership is so little separated from control and the Italian stock market is still underdeveloped compared to the other countries of the developed world.

Since then, the problem has been addressed by an outstanding number of legal reforms at the national level. Apparently, however, none of them has brought about any significant change in Italian corporate governance (Bianchi et al 2005). As a result, Italy is still the case in point of 'bad law' when it comes to shareholder protection (Gilson 2006). It is fair to say that, among most developed countries' jurisdictions, Italian law still provides the weakest safeguards against the extraction of diversionary PBC by corporate controllers.[67] However, it would be unfair to conclude that process of corporate law's reform in Italy was just cosmetic, driven by the national vested interests, and essentially misguided. All of this has been authoritatively argued by Professor Enriques (2005), and can be agreed upon with respect to a number of specific issues. Yet it is undeniable that, overall, Italian corporate law is now on the right track as far as the substantive discipline of conflicted interest transactions is concerned (Enriques 2009). Even though, perhaps the most important ingredient of an efficient policy against non-pro-rata distributions is still missing from the Italian system. In the words of Ronald Gilson, this is "an effective enforcement process" (Gilson 2006: 1653).

Traditionally, Italian minority shareholders used to be both powerless as to corporate decision-making and helpless in protecting themselves from expropriation. This situation led to the award of one of the lowest scores on the Anti-director Rights Index of La Porta et al (1998), which bundled governance rights with protection against self-dealing. In the light of our more sophisticated framework, the case was even worse, for it determined a perverse combination of false positives and false negatives in the discipline of corporate transactions. Minority shareholders had very few judicial venues for challenging decisions taken or upheld by the controlling shareholder. They could either individually attack resolutions of the general meeting on grounds that they violated the law or the articles of association,[68] or put together at least 10% of share capital and file a petition with the court for investigation on allegedly "serious" mismanagement.[69] In practice, both venues used to be pursued with reference to the approval of annual accounts. This had as little bearing on the policing of self-dealing (of which non-controlling shareholders had no chance of being informed), as much of the effects resulted in blackmail for different purposes. None of these actions was obviously appealing for small investors in listed firms, whereas they could amount to a serious nuisance in the presence of non-controlling blockholders.

With the clear intention of bringing Italian law up to the international standards set by La Porta et al (1998), the law of listed corporations was changed in 1998.[70] Among others, the most remarkable innovations were the introduction of a derivative suit for directors' liability, mandatory minority representation on the board of auditors, and a lower threshold for requesting a court investigation on serious irregularities.[71] The goal was to also make the

---

67 See Dyck and Zingales (2004) for the last available international comparison of the size of PBC.
68 See art. 2377 of the Italian Civil Code (hereinafter ICC) before the Corporate Law Reform of 2004.
69 See art. 2409 ICC before the Legislative Decree No. 58/1998 and the Corporate Law Reform of 2004.
70 See Legislative Decree No. 58/1998 ("Testo unico delle disposizioni in materia di intermediazione finanziaria").
71 See, respectively, art 129, art. 148(2), and art. 128(2) of Legislative Decree No. 58/1998 (original formulations). Arts. 128 and 129 are now replaced by arts. 2408, 2409, and

board of directors accountable to minority shareholders, at least as far as its members' legal obligations of due care and loyalty were concerned.

This did not succeed. Despite the broad definition of directors' duties in the Italian Civil Code, judges have traditionally shown a deferential attitude to the board decisions (Enriques 2002). Most surprisingly, this deference is not just concerned with exercise of business judgment, but extends also to situations in which directors and, even more so, the controlling shareholder has a conflict of interest. Judges were content just with *formal* compliance with the rules disciplining conflicts of interest on both sides. In practice, they would only check whether conflicted interest transactions were passed by the board or the general meeting with the determinant vote of either the interested director or the interested shareholder.[72] In addition, the requirement for shareholders' standing to sue (5% of share capital) was much too strict to determine a serious threat of litigation, and this was coupled with the absence of contingent fees or equivalent devices for aggregating shareholder claims in any incentive-compatible manner. On top of this, derivative litigation is unsuitable for challenging the controlling shareholder's conflicts of interest at the general meeting; investors had basically no way to recover damages from controlling shareholders in the face of most outrageous instances of tunneling. As a result, both directors and controlling shareholder continued to face a real threat of being sued for damages just in case of bankruptcy. It is worth noting that also litigation for the Parmalat debacle was handled in this way.

6.3.5.2 Corporate law reforms in Italy: catching up slowly?

That was just the start of the reform process in Italy. The Italian Securities Authority (*Consob*) continued by recommending a comprehensive ex-post disclosure of conflicts of interest as well as of the procedure by which they are handled. This remained a dead letter, so since 2003 ongoing disclosure of related-party transactions is mandatory in nearly the same terms as under US law. This provision has become more effective after the *Consob* issued a special Regulation on related-party transaction in 2012.[73] Failure to disclose triggers both directors' and the company's liability under securities regulation.

In 2004, a general reform of Italian corporate law came into force.[74] As far as self-dealing is concerned, two major innovations are worth noting. On the one hand, the discipline of directors' conflicts of interest was changed. Formal

---

2393-bis ICC. Art. 149(2) has been redrafted, with substantial modifications, by the Act No. 262/2005 and the Legislative Decree No. 303/2006.

72 See art. 2391 and art. 2373 ICC (before the 2004 reform).

73 Consob Reg. No. 17221/2010. See also Art. 71-bis Consob Reg. No. 11971/1999.

74 The general discipline of joint-stock companies contained in Book 5 of the Italian Civil Code was entirely replaced by the Legislative Decree No. 6/2003. References to the ICC are made to the legislation currently in force, unless otherwise indicated.

abstention from approving the conflicted transaction is no longer required, and it is not sufficient for the validity of the transaction. The transaction must be approved by a majority of disinterested directors on an informed basis. Directors – and, depending on the board structure, members of the board of auditors, of the audit committee, or of the supervisory board – face liability for failure both to disclose their own conflicts and to monitor those of their colleagues.[75] At the same time, the normative criterion for assessing both the directors' and the monitor's liability has been changed from the diligence standard of the agent (the reasonable care of the *bonus pater familias*) to a more even standard of professional competence, which is more consistent with the tenets of the business judgment rule.[76]

On the other hand, a completely new discipline was introduced for intra-group transactions.[77] In controlling shareholding systems, these transactions are perhaps the most dangerous source of tunneling, and the traditional approach of Italian law to the shareholder's conflicts of interest was ill equipped in coping with them. That far, case-law had just managed to stop most outrageous instances of abuse by controlling shareholders, because of the narrow interpretation of both the relevance of conflicts of interest at the general meeting and of individual shareholder's right to claim individual damages from directors.[78] After the reform, shareholders can individually sue both the subsidiary and the parent company when their stock has been devalued by intra-group transactions, unless the damage is compensated by the overall results of the group management.[79] Directors and controlling shareholders are jointly and severally liable to the extent that either they participated in the decision, violating the principles of 'fair business judgment,' or they anyway benefited from it. Apart from the obvious risk of false positives involved by the notion of 'fair business judgment,'[80] this is anyway the first step of Italian corporate law towards preventing controlling shareholders from non-pro-rata distributions. However, the actual deterrence of both this provision and the new regime of directors' liability for related-party transactions depends on the enforcement mechanisms – which, as we are about to see, are still very weak under Italian corporate law.

---

75 Art. 2391 ICC.
76 Compare the current formulation of art. 2392 ICC (due diligence is determined on the basis of directors' specific tasks and competences) with that of former art. 2392 (directors' diligence is tested against the general standard applicable to the agent).
77 See art. 2497 *seq.* ICC and its discussion by Ventoruzzo (2004).
78 See art. 2373 (conflicts of interest at the general meeting) and art. 2395 (directors' liability towards individual shareholders and third parties) ICC before the reform.
79 Art. 2497 ICC.
80 Italian judges have never elaborated a doctrine comparable to the business judgment rule. Their traditional deference to the decisions of corporate controllers appears to be rather the result of a formalistic application of statutory law. This is particularly evident from how trial courts have handled so far the cases of self-interested transactions and conflicted resolutions of the general meeting brought to their attention. See Enriques (2002).

The Parmalat scandal (Coffee 2005; Ferrarini and Giudici 2005) exploded just on the eve of the corporate law reform coming into force. Obviously, it was impossible to draw any conclusion about the new rules. Yet, the facts of the Parmalat case highlighted a number of weaknesses of the legal and institutional framework that were still to be addressed in Italy. Some of them were concerned with regulation of the securities industry and gatekeeper failure – two universal problems of the financial scandals at the turn of the century, which however are not dealt with here. Surprisingly, the attention of the public opinion and the political debate were instead concentrated on the alleged responsibilities of the Central Bank and of its Governor. But, in the end, it was clear in both the national and the international scientific debate that the problem was different, and – in a sense – very 'Italian.'

As two commentators and I argued elsewhere (Pardolesi et al 2004), one – if not *the* – major failure of Parmalat's governance was in the internal monitoring. Parmalat was one of the largest 'family firms' in Europe, and all the corporate organs were under control of the management, which in turn was controlled by the major shareholder, Mr. Calisto Tanzi. External monitoring could fare no better in this situation because it was likewise dependent on Parmalat's controlling shareholder, both for business and information. As a result – differently from the financial scandals of other countries – Parmalat was not a sophisticated case of earnings manipulation, but after all a rather naïve story of long-standing, but ongoing, diversion of both shareholders' and bondholders' money, which came to light when it was just too late. The problem with Parmalat is that the controlling shareholder exaggerated. The ultimate reason why Parmalat deserves more attention than the other scandals is that, while the latter can be at most characterized as an epidemic consequence of the international stock market's bubble burst in 2000, Parmalat is a paradigmatic example of an endemic problem in Italy: that of systematic extraction of diversionary PBC by controlling shareholders.

The Italian government was distracted for a long time by misdirection of the political debate and managed to come up with a rigorous legislation (a so-called 'Savings Act') only two years later.[81] One crucial point was minority representation on the board of auditors, a rule that turned out to be systematically circumvented by listed firms (including Parmalat). The new legislation requires that the votes of shareholders, which determined the majority representation on the board of auditors, be excluded from the election of minority representatives.[82] This rule applies not only to the board of auditors, but likewise to any monitoring body in the company's governance structure. Here is how, finally, minority shareholders are put in the driving seat as far as the election of truly independent internal monitors is concerned. Unfortunately, the

---

81 Act No. 262/2005 (so-called 'Savings Act'), subsequently amended by Legislative Decree No. 303/2006.

82 Art. 148(2) of Legislative Decree No. 58/1998, as amended by art. 2(1) of the Act No. 262/2005 and art. 3(14) of the Legislative Decree No. 303/2006.

new rules are both undershooting and overshooting the target of an efficient balance between false positives and false negatives in the discipline of related-party transactions.

Since 2004, Italian joint stock companies may choose among three alternative board structures (Ventoruzzo 2004): the traditional unitary structure with a board of auditors basically in charge of monitoring legality of management; a two-tier structure with a supervisory board in charge of a broader monitoring of the management board, and of the appointment of its members; and a new one-tier structure wherein a sort of Anglo-Saxon style audit committee is established to provide the monitoring. The members of each monitoring body must comply with statutory requirements of independence, none of which, however, is established with respect to the controlling shareholder. To be sure, independence of directors (let alone of the members of the board of auditors) from controlling shareholders has been required for a long time by the Corporate Governance Code, on a 'comply-or-explain' basis. However, since the code used to have no statutory authority, this provision was not legally enforceable and could be *de facto* not applied. Parmalat formally complied with the code while having its CFO as one 'independent' director.

The Savings Act attempted to fix these problems. On the one hand, it moved the issue of independent monitoring at the statutory level, and it solved it by mandating *actual* minority appointment of at least one member of the monitoring body, *whatever* the board structure.[83] On the other hand, it supplied enforcement of the 'comply-or-explain' principle of the Code with two statutory safeguards: one is the company's obligation to publish a yearly statement about compliance, coupled with the monitoring body's responsibility as to its correspondence with the company's practice;[84] the other was oversight by the *Consob*, which could impose fines in case of untruthful statements.[85] However, the latter provision was repealed in early 2007, casting serious doubts as to what extent the Italian Code can still be considered actually enforced.[86]

---

83 Compare the current and former art. 148 of Legislative Decree No. 58/1998. The crucial difference is that, while minority representation on the board of auditors was originally to be dealt with by the charter, it is now to be directly regulated by the *Consob*, under explicit constraint of exclusion of the corporate controller's votes and with the aim of having minorities *effectively* represented. See Ventoruzzo (2011). The same provision is applicable to the other board structures (per art. 148(4-*bis*) in the two-tier structure and per art. 147-*ter*(3) in the one-tier structure).

84 Art. 124-*bis* of Legislative Decree No. 58/1998, as introduced by art. 14(2) of the Act No. 262/2005.

85 Art. 124-*ter* of Legislative Decree No. 58/1998, as introduced by art. 14(2) of the Act No. 262/2005.

86 Art. 124-*ter* of Legislative Decree No. 58/1998, as amended by art. 3(11) of the Legislative Decree No. 303/2006 (the *Consob* is no longer in charge of monitoring truthfulness of company's statements of compliance with the Code).

A more serious problem is that Italian legislation went much beyond the policing of conflicts of interest in regulating corporate governance. In order to promote a more effective independent monitoring, it required the same mechanism of minority representation (based on the exclusion of the controlling shareholder's votes) not only for the monitoring body in each governance structure, but also for up to two members of the board of directors in the traditional structure.[87] Although one commentator (Ventoruzzo 2011) has applauded the virtues of this solution, which is rather unique in Europe as in the rest of the world, the outcome may be unfortunate for two reasons. First, it creates scope for regulatory arbitrage between the alternative board structures. Secondly, and more importantly, it makes worse the balance between discretion and accountability in the traditional board structure.

The advantage of the traditional Italian model, which provides a rather unique board structure, is that monitoring of conflicts of interest is naturally separated from involvement in discretionary management. In fact, the two matters are ideally dealt with by separate organs – respectively the board of auditors and the board of directors. This separation is exactly what I have been advocating throughout this discussion in order to achieve the right balance between false negatives and false positives. To be effective against non-pro-rata distributions, this solution requires that the board of auditors be in charge of approving related-party transactions on the basis of a mandatory flow of information about the corporate controller's conflicts of interest; and that its members are entirely elected by non-controlling shareholders. Although the requirement of approval by independent directors was recently introduced by the *Consob* in the Regulation of related-party transactions, the definition of director's independence in that context bears no relationship with the appointment of minority representatives.[88] On the other hand, minority representation on the board of directors does not add much to the monitoring of conflicts of interest (Macey 2008), whereas it may compromise the operation of the board because of outsiders' interference with discretionary management (Pacces 2011). In sum, the current state of Italian law still falls short of efficiently coping with the problem of self-dealing.

---

87 Art. 147-*ter* of Legislative Decree No. 58/1998, as amended by art. 1 of the Act No. 262/2005 and art. 3(13) of the Legislative Decree No. 303/2006. Notice that the combined provisions of art. 147-*ter* and art. 148 apply differently to different board structures. In the traditional one, minority representation is required in *both* the board of directors and the board of auditors. In the new one-tier structure, the potential overlap between art 147-*ter* and art. 148 is solved by having minority representation just in the audit committee (art. 147-*ter*(3) and art. 148(4-*ter*)). In the two-tier structure, minority representation just applies to the supervisory board (art. 148(4-*bis*)).

88 See Consob Reg. No. 17221/2010.

6.3.5.3 *Two venues for fine-tuning: independent directors and*
private enforcement

There are two fundamental requirements for independent directors' appointment, to whatever board, by non-controlling shareholders. One is – as Professor Bebchuk (2003b) put it – "shareholder access to the ballot." As we know, this is more of a problem in the US than in Italy, where especially after the recent reforms shareholders face little difficulties in proposing their own nominees at the elections. The important difference is the role of proxy voting, which is necessary for the exercise of managerial control whereas it is hardly of any use in controlling shareholders. In the US, access to the ballot essentially means shareholder access to the proxy machinery controlled by the incumbent board. That is the proposal that the SEC has not managed to push through, but – as Bebchuk (2003b: 64) pointed out – it is far from sufficient for independent nominee prevailing over the incumbent board. "To have a meaningful chance of success, nominees will have to incur expenses to make their case effective to shareholders. . . . A group of shareholders holding, say, five percent of the shares might be unwilling to bear significant costs even if they believe that election of their nominee would enhance shareholder value."

There is then a second requirement for the election of minority representatives: reimbursement of campaign expenses. In Italy, this is even more important than in the US, where a proxy campaign is launched every year by the board at the company's expense, and shareholders might be entitled to piggyback it – even though they still face a number of restrictions in this respect. Facing a controlling shareholder, Italian investors may have to launch *their own* campaign to win the elections. Italian law does not currently allow for any reimbursement of expenses incurred by proxy solicitation, not even if successful. It may therefore be insufficient to require – as the Savings Act did – that minority representatives be elected through list voting, and that a percentage of share capital ranging between 0.5% and 4.5% be sufficient to present a candidate.[89] Although Professor Ventoruzzo (2011) reports that the system has so far worked smoothly, good candidates may still face difficulties to prevail over nuisance nominee belonging to the controlling shareholder's sphere of influence. If we want institutional investors to lead the selection and promotion of good candidates for monitoring the corporate controller's conflicts of interest, non-controlling shareholders should be entitled to indemnification of the expenses incurred for a successful proxy solicitation.

The solution I am advocating is different from Professor Bebchuk's (2003b). First, success and not just "substantial shareholder support" should trigger reimbursement. Secondly, and more importantly, I am not advocating this solution across the board and definitely not for overreaching the board's control over the agenda of the shareholder meeting (see instead Bebchuk

---

89 Art. 147-*ter*(1) of Legislative Decree No. 58/1998, as amended by art. 1 of the Act No. 262/2005 and art. 3(13) of the Legislative Decree No. 303/2006.

2005). The reimbursement policy should be limited to corporate elections, and specifically to the appointment of the monitoring body's members under each board structure. In Italy, the number of seats reserved to minority appointment should be inversely related to the degree of interference allowed with the managing body – which is the highest in the two-tier structure. Reservation of seats to non-controlling shareholders may finally make proxy solicitation only a threat by institutional investors, which is credible inasmuch as the expenses would be reimbursed if successful, but is basically inexpensive for the company to the extent that other shareholders would spontaneously refrain from putting would-be losers up for election.

That being said, Italian law has another major weakness, which is judicial enforcement. Professor Enriques (2002) showed how corporate law's adjudication by Italian judges is so much tainted by formalism that it normally results in deference to the controller's decision-making, even in the presence of conflicts of interest. Although this is often regarded as a typical problem of civil law jurisdiction, especially by comparative economists (Djankov et al 2008), we learned from the foregoing review of both Dutch and Swedish law that this is not necessarily the case. The different outcome in Italy is most probably determined by the weakness of social norms (experience tells that little shaming is still attached to 'take the money and run' behaviors in financial markets) and the absence of a specialized judiciary comparable to Delaware courts.

To be sure, a specialized corporate jurisdiction may not only cope with the problem of formalism in adjudication, but also with the promotion of social concern for fairness in corporate governance. On the one hand, reputation and prestige of a specialized judiciary depends much more on the ability to cope with exercise of corporate control and its abuses than on the judge's general skill in jurisprudence. On the other hand, corporate law's judges are natural entrepreneurs of social norm. It is, for instance, quite a settled point that in the US – one environment otherwise characterized by relatively weak social norms – Delaware judges play a fundamental role in shaping the norms of corporate governance, by drafting their opinions more in the form of "corporate law sermons" than just like plain adjudication of rights and responsibilities (Rock 1997). Of course, such a role can only be played in combination with other institutional factors like, importantly, an independent financial press. As it turns out, all of this is lacking in Italian corporate governance. Italy has missed the opportunity to create a specialized judiciary for corporate and securities law. This was initially a part of the Italian corporate law's reform, but the proposal failed miserably under the opposition of both the judges' and the attorneys' constituencies.[90]

---

90 The Reform of Corporate Law was preceded by a committee study, which explicitly advocated the institution of specialized jurisdictions for corporate law in each regional district. The Reform Committee, led by Professor Mirone, released its final proposal of legislative delegation (*'Schema di legge delegata'*) in February 2000. The proposal included

The outlook of private litigation as a deterrent against non-pro-rata distributions may be just slightly rosier. For a long time Italian law did not provide incentive-compatible mechanisms for aggregating disgruntled shareholders' claims. The 5% threshold for activating derivative suits in listed companies was much too high to make this an effective tool for counteracting the corporate controller's opportunism; even though a lower threshold would probably not address the right problem (free riding), but just raise a different one (nuisance suits). Individual causes of action, which have been increased under both corporate and securities law, did not fare much better because of similar shareholder collective action problems.

However, a change is in the making. On the one hand, the legislature has managed to win one battle against the lawyers' vested interests: contingent fee arrangements are legal in Italy since mid-2006.[91] On the other hand, after a long-standing debate, collective actions have been introduced into Italian law effective 2010.[92] They differ significantly from US-style class actions. Italian law provides consumer and investor associations with standing to sue on behalf of their associates. The representative associations need not be for profit and the court decision (or settlement) is not binding on non-members unless they opt in. In principle, representative associations could hire lawyers on a contingent fee arrangement, but the loser-pays rule for allocation of litigation expenses may prevent this from happening in practice (Consolo 2009).

What the consequences of these recent developments will be for Italian corporate governance is hard to predict. The problem is that litigation is ulti-mately policed by rational expectations about judicial outcomes. In the absence of a specialized and skillful judiciary, the enhanced bite of shareholder litigation may result in much higher risk of false positives, with false nega-tives remaining essentially unaffected. As other commentators and I argued elsewhere, the problem of Italian institutions with the extraction of diversion-ary PBC by corporate controllers is manifold, and cannot be addressed piece-meal (Bianchi et al 2005). A tighter independent monitoring, a better skilled judiciary, more room for private enforcement, and the development of a social concern for corporate governance are all equally important ingredients of an efficient policing of self-dealing in Italy (see also Enriques 2009).

---

the statutory basis for the institution of specialized jurisdictions. The legislative delegation subsequently adopted by the following legislature (Act No. 366/2001) did not include these provisions. As a result, the Legislative Decree No. 5/2003 had no authority to amend the rules on jurisdiction, and only supplied minor changes to the procedural rules of corporate and securities litigation.

91 The government repealed the long-standing prohibition of attorneys' contingent fees in the civil code (art. 2233(3) ICC) with the Decree No. 233/2006 (converted into law by Act No. 248/2006).

92 Art 140-*bis* of the Italian Consumer Code.

7 Takeovers

Law and economics

7.1 Introduction

7.1.1 *The importance of takeovers and of their regulation in corporate governance*

This and the following chapter deal with one crucial issue of this book: the market for corporate control and the regulation of the paradigmatic transactions whereby it is operated, namely takeovers. In the foregoing chapters, two necessary legal conditions for separation of ownership and control have been discussed: (i) the availability of legal entitlements to idiosyncratic private benefits of control (PBC) for the corporate controller, which makes entrepreneurs willing sellers of corporate stock; and (ii) the legal constraints on the extraction of diversionary PBC by the corporate controller, which makes non-controlling shareholders willing buyers. We have seen that entrepreneurship in corporate governance requires that a person be in control of corporate assets that he does not own entirely; we have called this person an entrepreneur-manager. At the same time, the person in control needs to take a credible commitment that the proceeds of corporate management will be shared pro-rata with non-controlling shareholders. Failure of corporate law to provide both a sufficiently broad range of entitlements to corporate control and an efficient set of constraints on non-pro-rata distributions may result in too much or too little separation of ownership and control.

The conditions above are only sufficient for static efficiency. In the presence of uncertainty, contracts are incomplete and this explains the importance of power allocations and the need of legal constraints on the exercise of power. But, in addition to that, an allocation of control powers that is efficient today may no longer be efficient tomorrow. The players of the corporate governance game have thus no choice but to postpone all decisions about control reallocation until the moment when new, unforeseen contingencies will materialize. This does not mean that they dismiss the matter as unimportant. Quite the contrary, the players' decision to enter the game at the outset depends on their expectations on whether, how, and in what terms control reallocations will take place eventually. Once the two conditions for static efficiency are satisfied, the efficiency of corporate governance still depends on the dynamics of control allocation. The importance of control transactions and of their legal discipline stems precisely from this circumstance.

Why this is the case may not be intuitive. Thus, even at risk of repeating myself, let me recall a few key points about how corporate governance works according to the framework presented here. Suppose that corporate law features both an ideal system of corporate powers and a perfect ban on non-pro-rata distributions. Diversionary PBC ('stealing') would be disallowed and the parties to the corporate contract would choose the form and degree of separation of ownership and control that maximize the joint value of quasi-rents on both the entrepreneur's and shareholders' investments. Whenever entrepreneurship matters in corporate governance – which is the situation being considered in this study – these rents are respectively the idiosyncratic PBC (the profits 'in the entrepreneur's head') and the shareholders' profits (the expected earnings on corporate stock). In the absence of constraints on the exercise and maintenance of control powers, separation of ownership and control would be determined by the weight of idiosyncratic PBC relative to the expected stream of verifiable profits. The latter – which may be considered as stock demand – is decreasing in the amount of separation due to the problem traditionally characterized as agency cost (distortionary PBC). The former set a lower bound on the entrepreneur's willingness to sell – stock supply – because the discount on outside stock cannot be lower than idiosyncratic PBC. These two variables converge to the static equilibrium.[1]

The value of the two PBC parameters underlying the equilibrium may change over time. Distortionary PBC are an opportunity cost to outside shareholders and this cost will rise as soon as a more diligent or a more competent manager appears on the market, which would make the current allocation of corporate control inefficient. In such situation, control should definitely change hands. However, the presence of idiosyncratic PBC determines a tradeoff between ex-ante and ex-post efficiency. Protection of the incumbent's control rents is necessary for the entrepreneur to establish the firm and take it public at the outset. However, one would wish to disregard this protection ex-post, as soon as a slightly better corporate controller shows up.

Here comes the fatal attraction of hostile takeovers. However, hostile takeovers are not an option if we want entrepreneurship to be supported in corporate governance. The alternative solution is having takeovers agreed upon, that is, friendly takeovers. Friendly takeovers allow the incumbent's control rents to be compensated by the insurgent. Unfortunately, this implies that the higher the incumbent's idiosyncratic PBC, the higher discontinuity in the controllers' efficiency will be required for a value-increasing change in control to be feasible. Departure from the conditions of first best is the highest

---

1 See *supra* Chapter 3, section 3.4.2.

in the absence of idiosyncratic PBC on the insurgent's side. However, while this might be the case for highly mature businesses, which can be managed as a matter of routine (Hart 1995), normally it is unlikely that the role of entrepreneurship will be exhausted in just one takeover stage. More likely, the disappearance of control rents could be the asymptotical tendency of a multiple-stage takeover process in the indefinite time horizon of a firm's lifecycle. In this perspective, idiosyncratic PBC would be decreasing at each takeover stage.

It is fair to assume that insurgent controllers will be normally featured with idiosyncratic PBC too. The crucial question is how large the insurgent's PBC are relative to the incumbent's. Given the idiosyncrasy of entrepreneurial talent, it is hard to assume that the control rents of incumbents and insurgents are in general of equal size. This is unfortunate because control rents of equal size would eliminate the discontinuity in efficient changes in control. In theory, the insurgent's control rents could be even higher than the incumbent's. This may result in changes in control being entirely driven by the entrepreneurs' subjective expectations rather than by objective increases of shareholder value. In practice, this situation is unlikely to occur because such expectations need to be mostly self-financed (Mayer 1999) and the financial needs of taking over a publicly held company are incomparable with those of starting up an entrepreneurial firm. Positive, but decreasing, idiosyncratic PBC as the 'entrepreneurial' motivation of takeovers is therefore the most reasonable assumption. As a result, idiosyncratic PBC are insufficient to determine a change in control when this would undermine shareholder value. Takeovers will occur only when the insurgent can enhance firm value in the form of verifiable stock earnings *and* bring some further profit opportunities in the form of residual idiosyncratic PBC. These two components must generate sufficient surplus to compensate the incumbent's rents while leaving some reward for insurgency.

The above condition results in a constrained-efficient equilibrium in between each takeover stage, where the constraint is always the compensation of the incumbent's idiosyncratic PBC. In a comparative statics perspective, this preserves ex-ante efficiency at the cost of some ex-post inefficiency. However, in a dynamic perspective, the equilibrium evolves through the shrinking of control rents at every stage, which is efficient even though there is no guarantee that the process will ever lead to a first best outcome. Because the latter would require no control rents at all, the first best is probably unattainable in a world of uncertainty. In other words, the envisaged dynamics of control allocation can lead at most to a second best. The achievement of this second best outcome should be the ultimate goal of corporate governance.

Both controllers and non-controlling shareholders rely as much on the condition for dynamic efficiency as on those for static efficiency when they decide whether to separate ownership from control. Controllers will not just be content with securing control power and control rents, but also wish to have those rents cashed in eventually. Investors will indeed require protection from expropriation before they buy non-controlling stock, but they also wish that the prospective value of their investment is maximized. These two expectations are based on a smooth process of changes in control, whereas cashing in idiosyncratic PBC goes hand in hand with the reduction of distortionary PBC. An efficient market for corporate control will allow shareholder value to progressively increase its weight relative to control rents, thereby making separation of ownership and control more attractive ex-ante as it is bound to evolve efficiently. On the contrary, impediments to the takeover process will leave corporate control stuck in suboptimal allocations; in this scenario, inefficient consumption of progressively costlier distortionary PBC will become the only way to extract control rents and separation of ownership and control will remain either too high or too low compared to what would be efficient.

Impediments to efficient reallocations of corporate control may arise from different sources. The first one is the incentive-compatibility constraint of the takeover process that we have just reviewed: in order to preserve the entrepreneur's incentive to go public ex-ante, some efficient changes in control need to be foregone ex-post to allow compensation of the incumbent's control rents. The second source is the distribution of takeover gains. Due to contractual incompleteness, this distribution depends on the bargaining power of the parties involved. However, the same distribution also affects the incentive to undertake a takeover. The introduction of a third player in the game – the acquirer – is therefore problematic. On the one hand, the prospective acquirer's incentives are a key determinant of takeovers. On the other hand, the acquirer seems to have little chance to participate in the takeover gains because he has neither residual rights of control nor any significant share of the residual claim on the firm's assets.

The third source of impediment is regulation. The problem is two-sided. As I am going to show, the distribution of takeover gains is a matter that cannot always be solved by private ordering, for this would undermine the efficient dynamics of control allocation and, in turn, efficient separation of ownership and control. Thus, takeover regulation is necessary. However, regulation may – on the one hand – violate the above-mentioned incentive-compatibility constraint (for instance, by forcing exposure to hostile takeovers) and reduce the range of choices available for separation of ownership and control. On the other hand, regulation may fail to define the right boundaries of bargaining in the takeover game, thereby frustrating either the insurgent's incentives to initiate a takeover or the incumbent's incentives to part with control. The typical reason for this failure is inefficient legal protection of the third category of players – outside shareholders. Contrary to the conventional wisdom, *excessive* shareholder protection is most often the cause of distortion, although a similar problem may arise when protection is insufficient. The crucial point is that shareholder protection in takeovers is important, but it must be put in the right perspective.

This chapter will attempt to identify the right perspective for a functional law and economics analysis of takeover regulation. As will be shown in the next chapter, the solutions adopted in the majority of the jurisdictions in our sample are not based on the same perspective. Efficiency of the European markets for corporate control may be undermined for this reason.

7.1.2 *The novelty of the analysis*

The economics of takeovers is a most debated topic in corporate law and economics (Becht et al 2007; Burkart and Panunzi 2008). However, both the theory and its regulatory implications are extremely controversial – probably the most controversial issue in the analysis of corporate governance. The problem of distribution of takeover gains and the need for some regulatory intervention are both generally acknowledged (e.g. Kraakman et al 2009). However, little emphasis has so far been put on the divergence between ex-ante and ex-post efficiency. This is because the problem of entrepreneurs' incentives to go public and its implications on the takeover mechanism is typically neglected in the mainstream literature (but see Coates 2004). By considering the controller's idiosyncratic PBC, I am going to present a different approach to the problems analyzed in both the economic and the legal literature. Intuitively, the conclusions will differ from the mainstream. However, the approach I am advocating is consistent with the empirical evidence on both the structure of corporate governance and the takeover process.

As far as the first point is concerned (governance structure), the scenario which is going to be analyzed is that of friendly takeovers. While this rules out any 'disciplinary' function of the takeover threat (Jensen 1986), the empirical evidence in this respect questions the very essence of the agency approach to corporate governance. Changes in control only exceptionally can and do take place through hostile takeovers (Schwert 2000); and little discipline is involved by takeover threat even when hostile takeovers are theoretically possible (Franks et al 2001). Regarding the second point (takeover process), the ability of corporate controllers to block a takeover and the significant wealth effects of successful takeovers on target shareholders (Martynova and Renneboog 2008) suggest that takeovers are best analyzed as the outcome of a Coasian bargain for the division of transaction surplus. However, the involvement of a third party (the acquirer) and the presence of high transaction costs (due to both uncertainty and asymmetric information) make the outcome of private contracting on the division of transaction surplus unreliable for efficiency. Legal entitlements should therefore be allocated between the parties in such a way as to guarantee that control transactions take place if and only if they are efficient (Cooter and Ulen 2011).

While nobody would question that this should be the ultimate goal of takeover regulation, the legal and economic research in this field has reached the conclusion that the above result is not attainable if not at the risk of making outside shareholders worse off (Burkart and Panunzi 2008). That is to say, there is a tradeoff between an efficient market for corporate control and shareholder protection. By approaching the matter in terms of Coasian bargain, I claim that the tradeoff is different and it depends on the necessity to allow a control premium to reward the incumbent controller's investments ex-ante (idiosyncratic PBC). Given that part of the takeover gains are allocated to that purpose, the remainder should serve the function of allowing efficient changes in control. As a result, the two goals of promoting an active takeover market and protecting investors can be pursued independently by corporate law. On the one hand, takeovers decreasing shareholder value should be disallowed. On the other hand, the acquirer should be entitled to reap all the gains necessary to allow for value-increasing takeovers.

As I am going to show, when changes in control are correctly bargained for, there is no need to sacrifice the acquirer's gains to shareholder protection. Although this has been the prevailing position among European policy-makers (see Kraakman et al 2009), it is misguided at least from an economic standpoint. What mainstream economic theory concedes to this position is that reducing the likelihood of efficient takeovers is the price to pay for protecting shareholders from inefficient control transactions. I will show that this claim is also unwarranted, at least to the extent that diversionary PBC are efficiently policed by corporate law and complementary institutions. The latter claim is based on confusion between different categories of PBC. According to the framework presented here, they have different nature, and therefore they deserve different treatments. Before revisiting the economic theory of takeovers in this perspective, a brief introduction to the players' incentives in bargaining for a change in control is in order.

7.2 The basic structure of the takeover game

7.2.1 *Sale of office vs. sale of corporate control*

Corporate controllers typically do not like the idea of being taken over (Shleifer and Vishny 1989; Easterbrook and Fischel 1991). However, this depends on their being removed from office without consideration. Corporate controllers have nothing to fear about takeovers when they are tenured. Given the importance of idiosyncratic PBC in corporate governance, we can live with the fact that normally they are. And yet, the empirical evidence does not only show that corporate controllers are often entrenched, but also that they part with control now and then. The reason why controllers accept this is that, under certain conditions, it is in *their own interest* to have the firm they control taken over (Schnitzer 1995). For this to hold true, controllers just need to be compensated for their controlling position. As I mentioned throughout this work, this compensation may take the form of either a severance payment or a control premium, depending on whether the company is under managerial control or shareholder control. Compensation of the incumbent's rents may be regarded as a first application of Coasian bargaining to corporate control transactions.

Whether the Coase Theorem holds with respect to the efficiency of bargaining is another question. The answer depends on what kind of PBC the incumbent's compensation accounts for (Coates 2004). Let us maintain that diversionary PBC are ruled out by means of the various legal techniques that have been discussed in the previous two chapters. Because we know that even the most efficient regulation of non-pro-rata distributions is unable to achieve this ideal result, this assumption will be removed at a later stage. Idiosyncratic PBC deserve full compensation because of their role of promoting entrepreneurship at the outset. Then we are left with distortionary PBC, which have potentially adverse effects on the efficiency of control transactions, and therefore call for some legal constraints on private contracting.

In Chapter 3, the optimality of allocation of residual rights of control to a non-owner entrepreneur was derived on the basis of efficient rent protection. This has an important drawback. If the corporate controller faced no restriction on the identity of the transferee, he would have all the bargaining power in control transactions. Then, his best strategy would be to put his office up for auction. Control would be allocated to the highest bid for the company management, not for the company's shares. Whatever the resulting distribution of the transaction surplus (an issue which we are not considering yet), the crucial problem is that this surplus may be extracted at the expense of powerless shareholders. The change in control may be determined not just by a prospective increase in the firm value, but also by the insurgent's higher willingness to pay for on-the-job consumption of managerial perquisites (distortionary PBC) (Jensen 1986). It is for this reason that 'going over shareholder's heads' was disallowed by assumption in our previous discussion of the optimal allocation of residual rights of control. The corporate controller is free to decide whether and in what terms to part with control, but he can only transfer the latter to a shareholder. This assumption is reflected in the paramount prohibition of the sale of the manager's office in virtually any corporate jurisdiction; and it corresponds with the fact that control can only be transferred with a block of shares in the presence of a controlling shareholder. Control can only change hands by means of a transfer of corporate ownership; and that is the economic rationale (Easterbrook and Fischel 1991).

Having this fundamental principle functionally upheld by corporate law has two important consequences: on the one hand, it brings non-controlling shareholders back into play; on the other hand, it provides the basis for having inefficient takeovers ruled out.

7.2.2 Value-increasing takeovers and free riding by shareholders

Takeovers are a terrific source of empowerment for shareholders. Once it is established that takeovers must be implemented through stock acquisition, shareholders stand to gain either directly (because they have to sell the stock) or indirectly (because – diversionary PBC being ruled out – they will benefit pro-rata from the increased market value of the controlling block). This result is far from intuitive, but it is strongly supported by the empirical evidence: the wealth effect of takeovers is unambiguously and substantially positive for the non-controlling shareholders of the target, both for free-standing firms and for companies with a controlling shareholder (Burkart and Panunzi 2008).

To illustrate how the outcome above can occur, let us proceed as follows. First, let us assume for the moment that takeovers can only increase firm value; how value-decreasing takeovers are effectively ruled out will be explained shortly. This allows us to focus just on the problem of distribution of a positive transaction surplus. Secondly, the problem of surplus distribution is handled differently under managerial and shareholder control, so we describe the two scenarios separately. Non-controlling shareholders stand to gain in both cases, and the following discussion will show how this may be due to the same reason: free riding on the acquirer's skill and effort (Grossman and Hart 1980).

Under managerial control, both the incumbent management and shareholders have veto power on the acquisition: the first because I am assuming he is tenured; the second because they have to tender a sufficient number of shares to the acquirer for the takeover to succeed. In a completely dispersed ownership structure, a tender offer is the cheapest way to purchase a controlling stake. However, let us postpone the discussion of the economics of tender offers until the next pages. What is important to highlight here is that this situation allows bargaining power to be transferred from the management to non-controlling shareholders. Ultimately, this may lead to takeover gains being not appropriable by the prospective acquirer, who will then refrain from initiating a takeover in the first place. This outcome, which is in the interest of none of the parties involved, is determined by high transaction costs faced by dispersed shareholders. The following discussion will show that the Coase Theorem may not hold for this reason, and that efficient bargaining for corporate control may require further legal intervention.

Managers are committed to be tough negotiators up to the point in which their control rents are rewarded (Almazan and Suarez 2003). Skilled managers will go for renegotiation of their golden parachutes provided that this leaves the acquirer with sufficient gains to have the takeover initiated in the first place; they know that they will simply get nothing otherwise. The agreement between the incumbent and the insurgent on how to split the surplus is potentially endangered by the need to involve outside shareholders, which places them in the position to claim a premium for tendering their shares. However, this would not be much of a problem if there was just one single non-controlling shareholder: he would simply tender his shares for any price above his outside option, which is the current market price. This means that, in equilibrium, our hypothetical shareholder would make no profit and all efficient takeovers would succeed provided that their gains are sufficient to compensate the incumbent's rents and the insurgent's costs of engineering the acquisition. The other players would let the acquirer appropriate the residual surplus, for they would get nothing otherwise.

Such a single-minded shareholder hardly exists in a publicly held company. In the face of a takeover bid, a myriad of dispersed shareholders is confronted with two strategies. The first is tendering at any bid price above market value. The second is holding on to their shares. What makes the latter strategy attractive is that non-controlling shareholders who do not tender will free ride on the higher firm value brought about by the insurgent management, provided that the takeover succeeds – i.e., that other shareholders will tender (Burkart and Panunzi 2008). The source of shareholders' bargaining power is therefore not their veto power, but their ability to free ride. Notice that free riding may obtain in *every* situation in which there is more than one non-controlling shareholder. However, for this to result in bargaining power, a further condition is required: shareholders must be committed to stand firm for a share of the transaction surplus. That is, they must be in a position to holdout.

Holdout and free riding are sometimes confused, but indeed the two situations stand in a cause–effect relationship (Cohen 1998). A free rider's strategy is just to sit and wait while others do the job. A free rider will only turn into a holdout when this strategy makes the production of transaction surplus impossible or unprofitable. Then the producer – in our case, the insurgent controller – will have to buy him out. This is exactly what happens in the acquisition of a free-standing firm. A sufficient number of shares must be tendered for the takeover to succeed and gains to be generated. However, any shareholder would like to holdout hoping that others will tender and let them free ride on these gains. When there are many, atomistic shareholders, they will all think the same and none of them will tender for less than the entire bargaining surplus. As a result, the only takeover bids that can succeed in theory are those depriving the acquirer of all gains in favor of target shareholders (Grossman and Hart 1980). While this outcome is consistent with the empirical evidence on wealth effects of actual takeovers, it still cannot explain why would-be acquirers initiate takeovers in the first place. There must be some mechanism for preserving the acquirer's gains in spite of shareholder holdout. The problem will be addressed in the discussion of economics of tender offers.

The source of shareholders' commitment to holdout is their inability to coordinate due to transaction costs (Burkart and Panunzi 2004). If they managed to coordinate in a hypothetical bargaining table with the acquirer, they would settle for some split of the takeover gains. A similar result obtains in the presence of moderately large shareholders, to the extent that they are and perceive themselves as being pivotal for the success of the acquisition. Shareholders' holdout potential is instead eliminated in the presence of a controlling shareholder. The reason is twofold. On the one hand, since control is transferred between controlling shareholders without necessity of a tender offer, control transactions need not involve minority shareholders – unless takeover regulation gives them a special entitlement to participate (see Kraakman et al 2009). On the other hand, the controlling shareholder is not credibly committed to holdout. So long as his control rents are compensated, he will accept any division of the residual surplus that makes the takeover viable (Bebchuk 1994).

When control transactions are concluded between controlling shareholders, minority shareholders can still free ride on the acquirer's gains. This is of course much less of a problem compared to the acquisition of a free-standing firm, since the acquirer will still be able to make profits on the control block. Yet, free riding by minority shareholders (which explains how they do also gain in this scenario) is certainly unpleasant for the acquirer. The latter would indeed wish to buy out minority shareholders after gaining firm control. A tender offer is not an option for it would again place shareholders in a holdout position (Bebchuk 1994). One may think that, compared to the previous scenario, this is just a problem of distribution with no efficiency consequence – after all, changes in control take place independently of minority shareholders (Burkart and Panunzi 2004). However, if we reason by backwards induction, the free riding problem may lead to a situation in which takeover gains would be sufficient to compensate the incumbent, but the acquirer's share of them would not; in spite of their efficiency, such transactions will not be entered into in the first place.

In conclusion, the problem of the acquirer's gains differs in degree, not in kind, between managerial and shareholder control structures. In both situations, non-controlling shareholders can free ride on value-increasing takeovers. Therefore, the problem must also be addressed in the analysis of control transactions that apparently only involve controlling shareholders. Once again, the Coase Theorem does not hold because of transaction costs faced by outside shareholders: while it would be efficient to split the takeover gains with the acquirer, minority shareholders are unable to coordinate and are committed to rule out a number of value-increasing takeovers with their free riding.

7.2.3 A narrow set of conditions for value-decreasing takeovers

Takeovers need not be (shareholder) value-increasing.[2] Indeed, control could be transferred to a less diligent and skillful manager or, even worse, to a looter. This would be clearly inefficient. It might seem somewhat counter-intuitive, but this is more of a problem in hostile takeovers than in friendly ones. As I showed in Chapter 3, the character of takeovers bears no consequence on the risk of looting. I shall then keep on assuming, for the moment, that

2 Here I am not considering the issue of whether stakeholders should also enter the definition of efficiency. I have already discussed this problem in Chapter 1, section 1.4, where I concluded that stakeholder protection should not interfere with the normative goals of corporate governance.

diversionary PBC are ruled out. The friendly character of the takeover process, which is being analyzed here, provides instead an important advantage as far as distortionary PBC are concerned. This is due to the circumstance that execution of a friendly takeover requires the incumbent's idiosyncratic rents to be compensated and a significant ownership stake to be acquired.

The first source of restriction on inefficient sales of corporate control is the principle that takeovers require acquisition of an ownership stake sufficient to grant control. The significance of corporate ownership acquired for this purpose makes changes in control unlikely to be motivated only by an increase in distortionary PBC. The reason is that, no matter of how much these PBC are worth to the corporate controller, they have by definition a larger opportunity cost in terms of shareholder value.

Let us consider managerial control first. The insurgent will have to acquire a controlling stake in a company where there is none. As a result, he will bear the opportunity costs of distorted managerial choices to a much greater extent than the incumbent. The amenity of managerial perquisites to the insurgent should be very large for further extraction of distortionary PBC to be worthwhile. It is therefore fair to assume that distortionary PBC will hardly increase in this scenario, and that they are more probably bound to decrease. The situation is different when control is transferred between controlling shareholders. On the one hand, the problem of distortionary PBC is less severe in such ownership structures. On the other hand, the insurgent needs to acquire an ownership stake no larger than the incumbent's. Distortionary PBC can therefore increase if they are worth more to the former than to the latter. In both settings, the acquisition of a significant ownership stake limits the scope for increase in distortionary PBC, but provides no definitive guarantee against inefficient changes of control.

An additional restriction on takeover bargaining provides this guarantee: the need to negotiate changes in control with the incumbent. The reason is that takeovers do not only require the acquisition of a controlling stake, but also that the current value of corporate control (idiosyncratic PBC) be paid upfront. The last circumstance narrows the scope of the acquirer's gains further. In order for him to gain by increasing consumption of distortionary PBC, both the opportunity costs on the controlling stake and the price paid for the incumbent's idiosyncratic PBC must be offset. This is not possible under the assumptions being made here. On the one hand, idiosyncratic PBC must equal the (expected) value of distortionary PBC in the sale of non-controlling stock equilibrium;[3] on the other hand, idiosyncratic PBC are assumed to decrease in every change in control. Under these assumptions, it will always be more profitable for the acquirer to go for an increase in the value of corporate stock after the completion of a takeover rather than for an increase in consumption of managerial perquisites. This is straightforward

---

3 See *supra* Chapter 3, section 3.4.2.

when control of a free-standing firm is acquired. Little compensation of the incumbent's control rents would be sufficient to induce the emerging, controlling shareholder to sell his ownership stake at a premium back to the market – which can only be possible to the extent that distortionary PBC are not expected to increase. A similar outcome can be expected under shareholder control. Here the rent compensation would be much higher (the size of control premia is incomparable to the severance payments that managers receive when they leave) and therefore the increase in distortionary PBC cannot be ruled out. However, further separation of ownership and control would still dominate the strategy of expanding consumption of distortionary PBC so long as – as I assume – idiosyncratic PBC are decreasing.

The above conclusion requires a number of qualifications. The first is about takeover practice. The acquisition of a controlling stake is normally an intermediate step, whereas: (i) the funds for financing the takeover are raised *before* the acquisition; and (ii) the ultimate changes in the ownership structure are implemented through mergers, stock issue or repurchase, and other securities transactions *after* the acquisition. Although the sequence of events may vary depending on the transaction (and the ownership) structure, the above scheme of concentration/deconcentration of ownership is an intrinsic feature of the takeover process, which affects the underlying incentives regardless of the technicalities of control transactions.

The second qualification is the objection that 'the acquirer' is normally not a (natural) person, but another listed company. Therefore, takeovers may not harm shareholders of the target firm, but still be against the interest of the acquirer's minority shareholder – for instance, because of empire building by the acquirer's controller (Jensen 1986). This is correct, but given the limited scope of this inquiry, we just consider the governance of one company at once. I am, then, going to keep the assumption that the acquirer is either a person or, even if it is a company, its entering a takeover is not tainted by the problem of distortionary PBC. After all, an acquiring company misusing its free cash flow will eventually be acquired in its turn (Hellwig 2000).

The third qualification is that I am implicitly assuming that the acquirer makes some profit from taking over, so that reaping these gains in the form of increased shareholder value (either of the control block or of a stock sale on the market) is always preferable than extracting them in the form of distortionary PBC. Given the problem of free riding by shareholders, this cannot be taken for granted, and the acquirer's reward is actually the fundamental problem of takeovers that we are going to discuss in the following pages. However, it is worth noting that inability to reap this kind of gain does not affect the probability of inefficient transactions, but only lowers (and possibly brings to zero) the probability of efficient ones. When value-increasing takeovers are not an option for this reason, distortionary PBC will increase not because the firm is acquired, but just because it cannot be acquired. Then the incumbent has no alternative to enjoying, at the non-controlling shareholders' expense, on-the-job consumption and other distortionary PBC.

The fourth qualification is the fundamental assumption of the entire reasoning: the absence of shareholder value diversion of any kind. In the presence of diversionary PBC, there is no guarantee that control transactions are efficient (Bebchuk et al 2000; Burkart et al 2000). On the one hand, they may be simply motivated by the insurgent's higher ability to implement non-pro-rata distributions than the incumbent's. On the other hand, the incentive-compatibility constraint on extraction of distortionary PBC does not hold any longer: their opportunity cost to the new controller could just be compensated by increased diversion. As two commentators put it, "there is a potential interaction between the failure to make pro-rata distributions and the failure to maximize residuals" (Fox and Heller 2006: 19).

The flip side of the coin is that the presence of diversionary PBC may also ease the occurrence of efficient changes in control. When diversion is allowed, it is no longer necessary to assume that the acquirer makes profits through the acquisition (and the potential resale) of the company's stock for efficient takeovers to be viable. Actually, when the prospective increase in the firm value cannot be appropriated through capital gains in stock trading, an appropriate increase in the level of diversion could provide the acquirer with sufficient incentives to perform the acquisition. This provides a solution to the free riding problem (Grossman and Hart 1980).

The next question is, then: is shareholder value diversion that bad, after all? From an ex-post perspective, diversion is just a matter of redistribution, which, however, provides the advantage of easing the achievement of allocative efficiency. This may legitimate the view that diversionary PBC are a good way to promote an active market for corporate control. Hence the tradeoff with shareholder protection obtains, perhaps in the most extreme formulation (Burkart and Panunzi 2008). Unbounded diversion from minority shareholders is efficient only on the condition that overall value-decreasing takeovers are disallowed. A milder version of this statement is that – provided that value-decreasing takeovers may not be disallowed – some 'optimal' amount of diversion maximizes the probability of efficient takeovers while minimizing the probability of inefficient ones (Burkart and Panunzi 2004).

Neither statement is correct. To start with, diversion – or, more precisely, allowing diversion to increase in takeovers – is not necessary for promoting an active market for corporate control. There are other ways to cope with the problem of the acquirer's gains (shareholders' free riding) when diversionary PBC are ruled out. More importantly, unconstrained extraction of diversionary PBC is disruptive ex-ante. Being unable to distinguish thieves and looters from honest controllers, investors will regard both the stock market (where ownership is supposed to first be separated from control) and the market for corporate control (where incoming inefficiencies should be corrected) as 'markets for lemons,' which the best controllers will either exit or refrain from entering in the first place. Therefore, an upper bound on the extraction of diversionary PBC must be set in any case. If incremental diversion is necessary for takeovers to succeed, this implies that eventually there will be none. From the perspective of the overall efficiency of corporate governance, a solution of the free rider problem based on value diversion is thus unnecessary, undesirable, and ultimately ineffective.

The above result obtains because two different problems are inappropriately bundled together: one is shareholder protection from expropriation, and its intrinsic limitations; the other is shareholders' free riding on takeover gains. As we are going to see, the two problems should be treated separately. One would actually wish that diversionary PBC could be brought to zero in corporate governance. The reason why this is in fact not an option has nothing to do with the efficiency of takeovers, but rather depends on the problem of Type I/Type II errors in policing non-pro-rata distributions which we have reviewed in the previous chapter. This, and nothing else, is what forces us to live with only an upper bound on value diversion. However, this bound should be low enough to exclude any possible increase in diversion following a takeover. When this condition holds, the basic mechanism of friendly takeovers that I have just described cannot result in inefficient changes in control due to increase in either diversionary or distortionary PBC. Intuitively, law plays a crucial role in this respect, on the basis of mechanisms similar to those reviewed in the previous two chapters. But law plays an even more important role in allowing efficient takeovers to succeed.

7.3 Law and economics of (friendly) takeovers

The economic theory of takeovers is one of the most fascinating parts of modern microeconomics, and it would be nice to review it comprehensively. This would take us away from the focus of the present inquiry. Rather, what I am going to take stock of are the most important insights of this theory in order to deliver a paradigm of legal analysis consistent with the framework developed so far. This implies, first, that the efficiency of corporate controller's resistance to hostile takeovers will never be put in question; nor would be his ability to implement such a resistance via the legal tools available in the pertinent jurisdiction. Secondly, I will not further discuss shareholder protection from *ongoing* expropriation by the corporate controller. The rationale and conditions under which such protection is efficient have already been illustrated in the previous chapters together with the legal instruments for implementing investor protection.

Because this necessarily leaves some scope for shareholder expropriation, I shall discuss at the very end of this chapter how legal constraints should prevent takeovers from allowing *additional* non-pro-rata distributions. In the meantime, I am going to assume that an upper bound is set by the legal system on the ongoing extraction of diversionary PBC so as to make it *invariant* with the controller's identity. This involves that takeovers can only be value-increasing under a relatively small set of conditions and that diversionary PBC do not affect the probability of takeover, but only the degree of separation of ownership and control that is allowed in the first place. Essentially, this is equivalent to maintaining the assumption that diversionary PBC are ruled out.

7.3.1 *Changes in control in dispersed ownership structures*

The literature on takeovers mainly analyzes the case of listed companies where no controlling shareholder exists (see Burkart and Panunzi 2004). While this analysis is applicable to a minority of real-world situations, it nonetheless captures the most important problems underlying the takeover process. I am now going to illustrate how the assumptions of efficient entrenchment by the corporate controller and of absence of diversion of shareholder value changes the predictions of this analysis and delivers somewhat different normative implications for takeover regulation.

7.3.1.1 *Two dramatic scenarios: free riding and pressure to tender*

At first glance, the theory of takeovers seems only to deliver two opposite, and equally dramatic, scenarios. The first is based on the free riding problem. Professors Grossman and Hart (1980) have famously demonstrated that, when there are an infinite number of dispersed shareholders, no takeover bid can succeed for less than the post-acquisition stock price. Since in this situation no prospective acquirer can make any profit, or even recover the costs of engineering a takeover, there is no reason why takeover bids should be made in the first place. The economic theory of takeovers starts from this paradox and studies the ways to get round it.

For a law and economics scholar, it is most tempting to approach the matter in the paradigmatic case of holdout: that is, what lawyers usually refer to as 'eminent domain', 'compulsory purchase,' or simply 'expropriation' (see Bainbridge 2002). This is basically what the state does when the presence of several potential holdouts may undermine the conclusion of wealth-increasing transactions: the typical example is the sale of multiple parcels of land for the construction of a highway – perhaps one of the best illustrations of how the Coase Theorem may fail to hold (Cooter and Ulen 2011). The only drawback of the compulsory acquisition approach is that, compared to voluntary exchange, overreaching property rights provides no guarantee of efficiency. This may be even more dangerous in the context of private contracting. If we apply this approach to takeovers, the free riding paradox is easily turned on its head. In order to avoid holdout, shareholders may be simply compelled to sell. However, this may lead to a situation in which they sell at any price. Intuitively, this situation would remove any constraint about the takeover's efficiency; in our previous discussion, this constraint depended on the insurgent's inability to acquire the firm below its current value. The reason why shareholders may be induced to sell their stock at whatever price is the so-called "pressure to tender" (Bebchuk 1987).

I have assumed so far that the acquisition of corporate control when there is no controlling shareholder requires that a tender offer be made to outside shareholders. This is because, under the standard assumption of atomistic shareholders, transaction costs of the acquisition would be infinite otherwise (and they would anyway be much higher when shareholders are in a finite number of a sufficiently large magnitude). But tender offers are not alike and, once we introduce compulsory acquisition, they may be structured in such a way as to force any shareholder to sell. Specifically, the bidder may just make a take-it-or-leave-it offer for a number of shares sufficient to gain control (say, 50% of the voting shares) and be committed to buy out non-tendering shareholders only at a lower price (Kraakman et al 2009). Tendering becomes then "individually rational as a hedge against the unfavorable minority position, even though each shareholder prefers the bid to fail" (Burkart and Panunzi 2004: 750). Such a bid – known as a 'two-tier bid' – is inherently coercive. Competition among bidders may force the bid to be no lower than the market price: a negative takeover premium is ruled out, as a risk-free profit opportunity cannot occur in equilibrium under the 'no arbitrage' condition of market efficiency in weak form (see Gilson and Kraakman 1984). However, an inefficient bidder will still be able to acquire the firm below its value by rationing shareholders who tender and buying out the remainder at a lower price.

Although the example of two-tier bids is not very realistic, for they are ruled out by a number of legal mechanisms that will be reviewed later, this is useful to show how easily the free riding problem can be turned on its head through compulsory acquisition. The reason is always the same: shareholders are unable to coordinate for the common good. Atomistic shareholders know that they are not pivotal for the success of the acquisition, and then they behave opportunistically in any case. When they can free ride, for they stand to gain from the acquisition, they want to be those who *do not tender* despite the takeover's efficiency. When their free riding would be just ironic, for they stand to lose from the acquisition, shareholders want to be those who *do tender* in spite of the takeover's inefficiency.

As Professor Bebchuk (1987) has notably illustrated, the problem of pressure to tender is not confined to two-tier bids. The source of pressure to tender is not only the structure of the bid, but more in general the bidder's ability to impose a loss on minority shareholders after he has gained control. Even in the previous scenario, it was the right of a successful acquirer to compel shareholders to sell that generated pressure to tender at any higher price. This entitlement is known as 'freeze-out' or 'squeeze-out' right, and its regulation varies across different jurisdictions, particularly between Europe and the US (Kraakman et al 2009). Let us assume, from now on, that this right is triggered by the mere acquisition of control; we will compare this assumption with freeze-out regulations in the next chapter. Under this assumption, pressure to tender may obtain also when tender offers are unrestricted. These are the most common takeover bids (so-called 'any-or-all'), where the bidder is committed to purchase at equal price all of the shares which are tendered, provided that he gets control. Intuitively, all shares will be tendered and purchased at the bid price so long as minority shareholders can be squeezed out at a lower price. In equilibrium, none of them actually would, and therefore the unrestricted character of the bid makes it impossible for the acquirer to buy shares below the bid price (Burkart and Panunzi 2004). If we maintain the condition that takeover premium be always non-negative, no acquirer may profit from destroying (verifiable) firm value in spite of the coercive character of the bid so long as shareholders cannot be rationed.

However, coercion still has a potential drawback: it may allow inefficient acquisition of firms whose stock is undervalued. When the stock price underestimates the firm value, a bid equal to or slightly above the market price may be value-decreasing but nonetheless succeed due to pressure to tender (Bebchuk 1989c). One solution could be to allow the incumbent management to frustrate the bid. Apart from the shortcomings of this solution in terms of agency costs (which will be discussed later), the problem is that it may be insufficient because the management and the bidder can collude. Then we need to exclude coercion without placing shareholders back in the position to hold out. In a relatively recent contribution to the takeover literature, a combination of law and finance professors have demonstrated that this is possible. Amihud et al (2004) showed that when regulation requires that the squeeze-out price be equal to the bid price, all value-increasing takeovers occur because shareholders can no longer free ride. On the other hand, to the extent that *neither* the bid *nor* the freeze-out can take place below the current market price, coercion is disallowed and no value-decreasing takeover can occur. This important result has only one shortcoming: it allows for no positive takeover premium, a circumstance contradicted by the empirical evidence.

7.3.1.2 Is squeeze-out the optimal exclusionary mechanism?

I am going to elaborate on the squeeze-out rule advocated by Amihud et al (2004) in the next subsection. Other strands of literature do not consider squeeze-out at the bid price sufficient to avoid pressure to tender or necessary to overcome the free rider problem. According to Bebchuk (1987), dispersed shareholders are *structurally* under pressure to tender regardless of whether compulsory acquisition of non-tendering shareholders makes the bid coercive or not. The reason is that shareholders will anyway fear that the emerging controlling shareholder may engage in non-pro-rata distributions at a later stage. Therefore, when there is a positive probability that the bidder is a looter, shareholders can be under pressure to tender even when the squeeze-out price is set equal to the bid price or squeeze-out is simply not allowed.

Looting is ruled out by our assumption of zero diversionary PBC. But it is interesting to note that compulsory acquisition of minority shareholder is no longer necessary to overcome the free riding problem if diversion of shareholder value is allowed (Burkart and Panunzi 2004). Diversion is just an alternative way to generate pressure to tender. This is indeed the second paradoxical result of the celebrated model by Grossman and Hart (1980). In order to allow value-increasing takeovers, shareholders should let prospective acquirers dilute their property rights, so that they will no longer be able to free ride on the acquirer's gains. One way to do it is to write in the corporate contract that a successful acquirer may divert the post-takeover value from minority shareholders, that is, he may loot the company. Under this condition, shareholders are committed not to free ride and they will always tender their shares. One important constraint for the efficiency of this mechanism is that takeover bids cannot be lower than the *value* of the firm under the current management, and not just than the current market *price*. Because in this way value-decreasing takeovers are ruled out, Grossman and Hart demonstrated that the maximum level of value diversion (theoretically infinite) is optimal. Anyway, shareholders tender at a price equal to the current firm value, the acquirer reaps all of the takeover gains, and all efficient changes in control are operated without need to squeeze out minority shareholders.

There are a number of objections to this solution. To start with, it is unlawful, and we know that this is with good reason. Although actual diversion is unnecessary for takeovers to work in the framework of Grossman and Hart (diversion never occurs in equilibrium), the possibility of diversion generates a severe externality on corporate governance: should efficient takeovers fail to occur for any reason, the incentive-compatibility of separation of ownership and control would be undermined. Second, under the more realistic assumption that diversion may take place to a limited extent due to imperfections of legal rules and their enforcement, both efficient and inefficient takeovers might get out of control. On the one hand, some efficient transactions will be foregone due to residual shareholders' ability to free ride. On the other hand, the straight condition that takeovers cannot be value-decreasing becomes impossible to enforce with certainty. The latter is indeed a general problem with the attempt to regulate pressure to tender, and it depends on both the pre-takeover and post-takeover value of the firm being unverifiable by courts. Third, the model of Grossman and Hart shares the same contradiction of the alternative exclusionary mechanism based on freeze-out of minority shareholders: neither of them allows for a positive takeover premium in equilibrium, whereas the latter is always substantial in the real world.

It seems then that the two fundamental problems of the takeover process put us in a theoretical bind. Free riding may actually explain why shareholders get positive takeover premia by holding out, but this is ultimately irreconcilable with the fact that takeovers are initiated by a third player – the acquirer – who needs to gain something. Turning, by regulation, free riding into pressure to tender may allow the acquirer to reap his gains, but it cannot explain how shareholders manage to get positive takeover premia. The problem with pressure to tender is that it may result in value-decreasing changes in control. However, compared to dilution (diversion) of shareholder value, the squeeze-out mechanism provides the important advantage of being legally feasible and manageable by courts in such a way as to promote efficient takeovers, while avoiding inefficient ones, simply by setting constraints on the combination of verifiable variables. These variables are the bid, the squeeze-out, and the market price. In addition, the theoretical framework of the present study allows squeeze-out to generate a positive takeover premium in a dynamic setting.

This approach places the following analysis out of the mainstream approach to takeovers. As I mentioned, the state of the art in the legal and economic analysis is that there is a tradeoff between takeover efficiency and shareholder protection (Burkart and Panunzi 2008). This is solved by different combinations of free riding and pressure to tender both in economic models and in regulatory policies. Regulation will be addressed after the presentation of a different theoretical approach. As far as theory is concerned, the most popular modifications of the Grossman–Hart framework are worth mentioning to conclude this selective survey, for they at least partially solve the free riding problem without exclusion or dilution of minority shareholders.

First, free riding is imperfect in the real world, where the number of outside shareholders is large, but finite, and this allows for some gains to be captured by the acquirer (Holmström and Nalebuff 1992). Second, the acquirer may get around the free rider problem by capturing some gains *before* making a takeover bid. There are several ways to pursue this strategy, and they are all based on asymmetric information – a problem that was not relevant so far, since shareholders can free ride or may be under pressure to tender independently of asymmetric information. One is to finance the takeover with debt backed by the assets of the target firm (so-called 'leveraged buyout'), thereby forcing a discount on the bid price higher than the risk premium paid by the bidder (Burkart and Panunzi 2004). Another is to acquire secretly a stake (so-called 'toehold') in the target firm before the tender offer, thereby allowing the bidder to profit from the capital gain (Shleifer and Vishny 1986a). However, the extent to which both strategies are feasible is usually constrained by takeover regulation. Without going into detail, this may be justified by further inefficiency in the takeover outcomes brought about by asymmetric information. In any case, these mechanisms only allow for a partial solution of the free riding problem and, under certain conditions, they may generate inefficient pressure to tender (Burkart and Panunzi 2004).

Building on their earlier work, Professors Bebchuk and Hart (2001) have suggested an elegant solution based on a particular combination of a proxy contest with a takeover bid. Shareholders should be entitled to vote on the acquisition proposal before deciding whether to tender their shares. If approval of the offer by a majority of shareholders is a necessary and sufficient condition for the bid to succeed, both the free riding and the pressure to tender problems are eliminated and all gains accrue to the acquirer. It is also possible to make this approval a necessary condition for the bid's success, thereby allowing for shareholders to profit from the option to tender or free ride. The authors show that, under asymmetric information, all value-decreasing takeovers are anyway ruled out by this mechanism, while efficient takeovers occur with a very high probability even when shareholders are able to capture a takeover premium.

In contrast, minority shareholders' squeeze-out is "a simple and elegant solution of the free rider problem" (Yarrow 1985). The solution advocated by Bebchuk and Hart may be equally elegant, but is not as simple: it is difficult, if not impossible, to have it implemented by takeover regulation without fundamentally altering the distribution of powers in corporate law. A related, but more important point of criticism is that this solution relies on shareholders' ability to make efficient decisions in spite of information asymmetry. This reflects Professor Bebchuk's more general contention that non-controlling shareholders should be credited with sufficient information to participate in corporate decision-making (Bebchuk 2007). What this work attempts to demonstrate is that neither this information, nor shareholder involvement in decision-making which it may result in, are necessary or desirable for the efficiency of corporate governance. Takeovers are no exception to this claim.

7.3.1.3 *Bidding competition and management resistance: a change in perspective*

One important feature of the takeover mechanism has been neglected so far. That is actual and potential competition among bidders. Several empirical studies, surveyed by Burkart and Panunzi (2008), show that bidders' competition result in higher takeover premia. Of course, free riding must be excluded for this result to hold. Let us assume, for the moment, that this is achieved by the squeeze-out rule mentioned in the previous subsection, since it outperforms alternative solutions in a static setting. It will be shown that the same rule is utmost efficient in a dynamic setting.

Even in the absence of free riding, bidders' competition reduces the likelihood of efficient takeovers because it erodes the acquirer's gains in favor of target shareholders. Competition is in fact not in the bidder's interest for it naturally drives up the price of the acquisition. Worse still, it may result in overbidding. This is known as the 'winner's curse' problem. By and large, since the costs of screening the market in search of takeover targets are sunk, competition at the bidding stage may just force the first bidder to acquire the company at an inflated price. To the extent that this results in inability to recover the initial investment in screening, prospective acquirers will refrain from entering the takeover market (Easterbrook and Fischel 1982b).

There are a number of strategies to get round this problem. One of them is to pre-empt competitive bidding by immediately offering target shareholders a substantial premium. This strategy is supported by the empirical evidence, which shows that takeover bids are either uncontested, or alternatively competition proceeds by sizeable increases over the last preceding bid

(Burkart and Panunzi 2008). Under the reasonable assumptions of costly bid revision and/or costly investigation of potential targets, this proves to be an optimal bidding strategy that allows takeover premium to be limited to the acquirer's advantage and for some, but not all, efficient takeovers to take place. In this scenario, a positive takeover premium stems from potential rather than actual competition.

This perspective neglects the role of the incumbent controller in takeovers. To be sure, in the corporate law and economics scholarship, bidding competition has been related to the problem of managerial entrenchment but mainly to argue that this is a pernicious combination (Easterbrook and Fischel 1991). Apparently, promoting competition among bidders is a wonderful strategy for managers to frustrate any takeover attempt. All they need to do is to be sufficiently committed to takeover resistance, allegedly for the sake of securing the highest possible takeover premium for shareholders, as to make winner's curse the most likely (or just the only possible) scenario. On this basis Judge Easterbrook and Professor Fishel have famously argued in favor of *absolute* board passivity in the face of a takeover bid (Easterbrook and Fischel 1981).

This position has never been upheld by US case-law or agreed upon by the rest of the law and economics scholarship.[4] Some commentators have even argued that concern for managerial entrenchment is unwarranted, given that the anticipated vesting of stock option plans and otherwise conspicuous golden parachutes align managers' incentives with shareholder interest in value-increasing acquisitions (Kahan and Rock 2002). I am going to carry this fundamental intuition further. Short of being a matter of concern, managerial entrenchment is supported by empirical evidence and can be theoretically efficient.[5] If we include the possibility of severance payments, the incumbent management is not interested in having takeover attempts frustrated by disruptive bidding competition. Rather, the management is interested in having this competition under control in order to maximize the chances that value-increasing takeovers allow for their rents to be cashed in. Coupled with the appropriate freeze-out rule, this incentive scheme is consistent with both positive takeover premia and changes in control taking place if and only if they are beneficial for all the parties involved (i.e., they are efficient).

Some legal constraints must be set on managerial entrenchment as a precondition for this result to hold. Because in takeovers the Coase Theorem does not hold true in its strongest formulation, the bargaining game must be somewhat regulated (see e.g. Bebchuk 2002). A rather obvious corollary of

---

4 "It has been suggested that a board's response to a takeover threat should be a passive one. . . . . However, that clearly is not the law of Delaware, and as the proponents of this rule of passivity readily concede, it has not been adopted either by courts or state legislatures." Unocal Corp. v. Mesa Petroleum Co., 493 A.2d 946, 949 (note 10) (Del.Sup.1985). In the literature, see most prominently Gilson (1982) and Bebchuk (1982).

5 See *supra* Chapter 3.

the prohibition of the sale of the manager's office is that the incumbent management cannot profit from the bidding competition in its exclusive interest. If that was allowed, the management could simply induce bidders to compete on the severance payments instead of on the bid price. Since this may result in value-decreasing takeovers, both this pattern of competition and collusion between management and the bidder must be prevented by the legal system. This basically implies that managers can negotiate their golden parachutes only once. Bidding competition cannot be restricted by the incumbent management and may only result in a higher takeover premium for the shareholders.

Let us assume that the incumbent's control rents are fully compensated anyway: this is in fact a precondition for any takeover to occur on friendly terms. Then the management faces some weak incentive to foster competition among bidders. On the one hand, higher takeover premia will result in a higher value of the managers' share of the residual claim; on the other hand, managers may gain a reputation of tough negotiators in the shareholders' interest. This is, however, a little thing compared to the interest that managers have in avoiding a takeover's failure because of excessive competition. The problem is that managers do not have this competition completely under their control; neither is it desirable that they do.

The mere rumor that a takeover is in the making is good news for the target's stock. Especially if we assume that takeovers cannot be value-decreasing (we will shortly go back to the conditions that guarantee this outcome), the market infers from the willingness to bid for firm control that some gains are to be captured. Professionally informed traders – the real drivers of stock market prices (Gilson and Kraakman 1984) – will easily bet on a successful takeover by taking a long position (i.e., buying on cash, margins, or options) on the potential target's stock. According to Gomes (2001), this provides a sufficient condition for arbitrage to generate a positive takeover premium. The argument is that arbitrageurs may get in the position to holdout by acquiring sufficient stock to prevent the prospective acquirer from squeezing out non-tendering shareholders; the bid would thus fail unless arbitrageurs are offered a significant takeover premium. The mere presence of noise trading should allow this strategy to be profitable. Since we are still assuming that the threshold for operating a freeze-out is equal to that necessary to gain control, this mechanism may not always fulfill the conditions for an effective holdout strategy. Still, the same mechanism allows professionally informed traders to drive up profitably the market price thanks to the presence of noise, and this implies that also the bid price is bound to increase.

This scenario is very dangerous for the success of a takeover. So long as market professionals believe that the stock price is underestimating the post-takeover value, no takeover bid can possibly succeed unless the freeze-out price makes the offer coercive. As we know, a rule setting the freeze-out price equal to the bid does not allow for coercion (it just eliminates free riding), but it is necessary to rule out value-decreasing takeovers. In this situation, market professionals may also engage in competitive bidding, just with the purpose to capture as much as possible of the would-be acquirer's gains. This process may just end in the winner's curse, in which either the market or the bid price do not allow the acquirer to reap any gains from the acquisition and force him to make a loss from having initiated it. The only alternative to prospective acquirers refraining from entering such a game in the first place is the expectation that the above process is not endless, but may be terminated with the incumbent management's cooperation. In a friendly takeover, managers have an important advantage over market participants: they have inside information about the deal. Prohibition of insider trading does not allow them to participate directly in the formation of the stock price. However, they may influence it indirectly by disseminating new information to market participants (Gilson 1982).

I am assuming that control rents are fully compensated at this stage and that the management cannot extract further compensation from bidders' competition. The management has then no interest to allow redistribution of takeover gains from the bidder to shareholders; managers who are able to extract a compensation for their position would just like the bid to go through. Managers may prevent disruptive competition from exhausting the acquirer's gains by injecting new information in the form of a bid recommendation. However, this recommendation needs to be credible. The insider's information advantage is substantial, but limited due to information spillovers about the deal (Gilson and Kraakman 1984). Recommending any bid would be of no use if the underlying information is already used up. Market professionals would still profit from buying against noise traders. Management recommendations can only stop the price increase when they provide truly new information that reduces, and possibly eliminates, the noise. In other words, management can only exploit the information gap with professionally informed traders. The gap is likely to be sufficiently large to keep the stock price below the post-takeover value, thereby allowing the bidder to gain from the acquisition. But it is also likely to be sufficiently small to allow (professional) outside shareholders to get a positive takeover premium. In this perspective the takeover premium does not depend on free riding or competition among bidders, but rather on information spillovers in the dynamics of the market mechanism.

This interpretation is consistent with a number of empirical observations. First, management recommendations do have an impact on the outcome of takeovers (Burkart and Panunzi 2008). Recommended bids most often succeed, even though sometimes they attract competing bids. This illustrates the management's power to influence the takeover process, but also its limits. For this reason bidders often choose to pre-empt potential competition by immediately offering a takeover premium or otherwise revise their bid substantially upwards in order to win actual competition. This second observation may lead to many efficient takeovers being foregone in the absence of incumbent management's participation in the process. A third observation is indeed decisive to support our interpretation: the vast majority of takeovers that are initially characterized as hostile are concluded as negotiated deals (Schwert 2000). Compared to plainly friendly deals, initially hostile bids exhibit lower rates of success but higher bidding competition and takeover premia. To be sure, the direction of causality is uncertain. Takeover resistance may be the cause or the effect of these facts. If it was the cause, this would support the hypothesis of self-interested management entrenchment. But this hypothesis is contradicted by the evidence about the bidder's stock returns, which are unaffected by the perceived hostility of the takeover. Management involvement in the negotiations is then more likely to be the *effect* of a tough acquisition process, which is intended to keep both competition and takeover premia sufficiently low to preserve the acquirer's gains.

Professor Schwert (2000: 2639) concluded upon this evidence that "hostility seem[s] to reflect strategic choices made by the bidder or the target firm to maximize their respective gains from a potential transaction." I only add to this conclusion that the target management's and the bidder's interest converge on allowing mutually profitable transactions to succeed in spite of adverse fluctuations in stock price and/or bidding competition. This result is derived from the unparalleled illustration of "the mechanisms of market efficiency" by Gilson and Kraakman (1984) nearly three decades ago. It is therefore unsurprising that also Professor Gilson (1982) advocates a proactive role for target management in governing the information flow of the takeover process. His residual preoccupation about conflicts of interest between managers and shareholders is unwarranted in the present framework, because I am assuming that control rents are necessary to motivate entrepreneurship, that they must be compensated in a takeover, and that further rent extraction is disallowed. Still, incumbent managers may make profits at the shareholders' expense when they can disseminate false information about the merits of a takeover attempt. However, this behavior has little to do with takeover regulation, and I am assuming that it is restricted by the anti-fraud provisions of general securities regulation.[6]

The final question about this mechanism is whether it is efficient. To answer, we need to go back to the exclusionary mechanism of minority shareholders after a successful takeover. A rule setting the squeeze-out price equal to the bid price would make sure that shareholders cannot free ride and that they are not under pressure to tender to a value-decreasing bidder. To be sure, this also requires that the bid price be not lower than the current market price, for the firm could be acquired for less than its verifiable value otherwise. Imposing this condition in a static setting does no harm. However, once the target's stock price is allowed to fluctuate in a dynamic setting, the necessity to disallow negative takeover premia to prevent value-decreasing takeovers implies that some efficient transactions be ruled out. The reason is that the

---

6 See *supra* Chapter 6, section 6.2.1.

stock price will always be slightly higher than the pre-takeover value of the company, because takeover bids cannot be coercive and, therefore, they are bound to be value-increasing. As Amihud et al (2004) show, this is the reason why the squeeze-out rule that they advocate is constraint-efficient: the constraint does not depend on the possibility of a positive takeover premium, but on the impossibility of a negative one. The last circumstance implies that a bid below market price is bound to fail even when the insurgent is a better manager then the incumbent. Takeover regulation cannot avoid this inefficiency because, differently from the pre-takeover price, the pre-takeover value is not verifiable.

This is not the only constraint on the efficiency of takeovers under this mechanism. Another limit depends on the necessity for the insurgent to compensate the incumbent's rents; this may also be unavoidable for ex-ante efficiency whenever entrepreneurship is at stake. Positive takeover premia are apparently a source of further constraint, since they reduce the gains available to prospective acquirers. But it should be noticed that this would not be a problem if only takeover gains were perfectly divisible: management involvement in the takeover process would always split the pie in such a way as to allow efficient takeovers to succeed, no matter of how little the pie is. That moderately efficient takeovers do not occur in the real world seems to depend not on the inefficiency of the takeover process (or of its regulation), but on the frictions affecting the functioning of stock markets. The latter are characterized by "an equilibrium degree of disequilibrium" (Grossman and Stiglitz 1980). On the other hand, information spillovers and imperfect divisibility of financial assets constrain the incumbent manager's ability to preserve the acquirer's gains, and result in the sizeable takeover premia that we all observe. That being said, a rule setting the squeeze-out price equal to the higher between the bid and the market price is the most efficient regulatory solution given all the above constraints. I have complemented this important finding by Amihud et al (2004) by incorporating – as they suggest – "an active role for management in the takeover process" and providing an explanation of takeover premia that is broader than bidding competition.

7.3.2 Changes in control in the presence of a controlling shareholder

7.3.2.1 Efficient and inefficient sales of corporate control

The economic analysis of changes in control in the presence of controlling shareholders is quite different, and somewhat less developed, compared to that of takeovers of free-standing firms. In a sense, this scenario is less interesting for an economist because a sale of corporate control between controlling shareholders does not require that a tender offer be made to non-controlling shareholders facing collective action problems. This perspective, however, neglects that such tender offer might be in the interest of the acquirer not because it is strictly necessary for the takeover's success, but because it allows further gains to be captured. If we follow this line of reasoning, the possibility to buy out minority shareholders at a convenient price may not only increase the takeover's profitability for prospective acquirers, but also allow for a larger number of value-increasing takeovers to be viable. As I mentioned, this is a matter of efficiency and not just distribution.

What prevents acquirers from making a tender offer for non-controlling shares is not that this is unnecessary, but that this would not allow them to make any further profits. In both dispersed and concentrated ownership structures, non-controlling shareholders know that they can free ride on the acquirer's improvement in firm value. Therefore, they will holdout anyway when confronted with a tender offer, unless some compulsory acquisition mechanism is in place. The observation that, in the presence of a controlling shareholder, changes in control can and do occur in spite of this holdout potential very often overlooks that more changes in control would take place if this potential were excluded; and that this would be efficient.

One fundamental contribution to the analysis of the control transactions at issue is provided by Professor Bebchuk (1994) who, in a milestone publication, made a number of key points. First, sales of control are decided between the incumbent and the insurgent controlling shareholder based on their own interest in the control block, which may differ from the overall maximization of shareholder value. The reason is twofold: on the one hand, their participation in the security benefits (the residual claim on the firm's assets) is limited to the cash flow rights attached to the control block; on the other hand, the control block allows them to fully enjoy private benefits of control. The second point is that the transaction surplus is determined by the difference in the sum of private benefits and security benefits between the insurgent and the incumbent controller: a change in control will occur if and only if this difference is positive and sufficient to offset the cost of the acquisition. The third point is that the existence of such a surplus does not imply efficiency nor does efficiency imply a surplus. A change in control may occur when the acquirer's incremental private benefits are large enough to offset a decrease in the security benefits of control (positive transaction surplus), but the increase in private benefits is smaller than the overall decrease in firm value (inefficient takeover). Conversely, a change in control may fail to occur when the acquirer's private benefits are so much lower than the incumbent's that they cannot be compensated by the increase in security benefits (negative transaction surplus), although the overall firm value would increase thereby (efficient takeover). As a result, in the absence of regulatory intervention, both value-decreasing takeovers may be imposed on minority shareholders and value-increasing takeovers may fail to take place.

None of the above conclusions can be questioned. But this is definitively not the only possible approach to sales of control by controlling shareholders and, I believe, it is incomplete. To be sure, Professor Bebchuk does not make any assumption about the (in)efficiency of PBC. The problem is that he does not make any distinction among them either, so that all private benefits are alike in his framework. I maintain that this treatment of private benefits is incorrect. Indeed, once private benefits are allowed different consideration depending on their nature, the analysis of sales of control blocks yields significantly different results.

To start with, as I have shown, value-decreasing takeovers may occur only under a very narrow set of conditions when the control block is transferred for a consideration above the stock's market price. The existence of a control premium in block transactions is unambiguously supported by the empirical evidence, and I posit that idiosyncratic PBC – which *do not* affect shareholder value – are a sufficient condition for this to happen.[7] I have also assumed that idiosyncratic PBC decrease at every change in control because of their nature of reward of unverifiable entrepreneurial talent whose relevance may be asymptotically decreasing along the firm's lifecycle. Under this reasonable set of assumptions, the necessity of having the incumbent's control rents compensated by the insurgent makes sure that also distortionary PBC cannot increase (that is, firm value cannot decrease). This holds true on condition that at least as much of the control block is purchased for a price above the non-controlling stock's current value and shareholder value diversion is disallowed (or it has already reached the upper bound set by the legal system). Therefore, no different from takeovers in dispersed ownership structures, a necessary condition for value-decreasing sales of the control block being ruled out is the absence of diversionary PBC (or an appropriate upper bound on their extraction). This is also a sufficient condition to the extent that the company's stock cannot be otherwise purchased below its current value. This holds by definition when minority shareholders are not involved in the transaction, for they stand to free ride; but it may require further regulatory constraints once it is established that – as I am going to argue – compelling them to sell may be efficient and thus should be allowed.

That sales of control blocks are very seldom, if ever, value-decreasing when diversionary PBC are sufficiently low is confirmed by the empirical evidence (Burkart and Panunzi 2008). In the US, block trades are associated on average with abnormal price increases, thereby suggesting that gains are generated via improved security benefits rather than further extraction of private benefits (Holderness 2003). However, the other side of Bebchuk's argument remains. Unregulated sales of control blocks may result in many value-increasing transactions being foregone. Here the reason is different, and in a sense opposite, to that determining the risk of inefficient transactions: short of being determinant for the change in control, the insurgent's private benefits are insufficient to generate a transaction surplus in spite of the takeover's efficiency. As Professor Bebchuk (1994) acknowledges, this is due to minority

---

7 Notice, however, that the average control premium varies considerably across jurisdictions. This is evidence that also other kinds of PBC are at play. See Dyck and Zingales (2004).

shareholders' ability to free ride on future management improvements, which in turn makes it impossible for the controller to buy their shares at the current market value and sell them at a premium to the acquirer (who would then fully enjoy the residual security benefits). It is worth noting that, in this situation, any regulatory arrangement that strengthened shareholder protection could not but make efficient takeovers even *more unlikely* to succeed (Kraakman et al 2009); I shall come back to this important remark later. According to Professor Bebchuk, however, the opposite solution to weaken minority shareholders' position by allowing the controlling shareholder to freeze them out would be no improvement because of the courts' inability to set the freeze-out compensation equal to the pre-takeover value. By erring in either direction – the argument runs – courts would both allow inefficient takeovers to succeed and prevent efficient ones from taking place.

7.3.2.2 *Optimal squeeze-out after the sale of a control block*

Professor Bebchuk's argument proves too much. Although the pre-takeover value is indeed unverifiable, an efficient freeze-out of minority shareholders does not require that this value be actually ascertained. Under certain conditions, reliance on market prices is enough (Easterbrook and Fischel 1991). The first of these conditions is that the freeze-out may only be operated in conjunction with a tender offer and that both of them take place after, and not before, the sale of the control block is decided – that is, the operation is performed by the acquirer and not by the seller of corporate control. On the one hand, this makes an otherwise unnecessary tender offer for non-controlling shares an attractive option for the acquirer, provided that it is backed by compulsory acquisition of non-tendering shareholders. On the other hand, this arrangement generates two new pieces of information, which provide the basis for setting the 'right' squeeze-out price. The first is the bid price, which reflects the buyer's willingness to pay for non-controlling shares. Notice that this differs from the price paid for controlling shares, which also includes the control premium, but cannot be lower than the pre-takeover value when diversionary PBC are disallowed and the company's stock is not undervalued by market price. Actually, if minority shareholders could free ride, the opposite would be true. Conversely, if non-tendering shareholders can be squeezed-out at the bid price, we have to cope with the possibility of negative takeover premia. A negative takeover premium may lead to both acquisition of non-controlling stock below its value and to inefficient changes in control. Here comes the importance of the second piece of information: the stock market price *after* the sale of the control block is announced.

The post-announcement stock price has important properties, which, however, require that a preliminary constraint is set with reference to the pre-takeover price. The reader should recall that any constraint on the squeeze-out price is a lower bound to the bid price. No different from the case of the acquisition of free-standing firms, we need to impose the pre-takeover price as a lower bound to the squeeze-out price in order to prevent inefficient outcomes. This is necessary to avoid that value-decreasing sales of the control block are subsidized by a coercive bid for the rest of the company's stock, which would enable its acquisition below market price. However, this is not sufficient to rule out value-decreasing acquisitions. They may still be possible when the non-controlling stock is undervalued, and may be nonetheless acquired at the pre-takeover price via a tender offer backed by compulsory purchase of non-tendered shares. Here the problem is different from the case of free-standing firms, given that the bidder has no incentive to offer a takeover premium; he does not need to make the bid sufficiently attractive to gain control, for he has got it already. But the solution, if anything, is even simpler if we set the post-announcement price as a further constraint on the squeeze-out price. This would involve that the bid for non-controlling shares also cannot be lower than the post-takeover price whenever this exceeds the pre-takeover price.[8]

This requirement is only binding on condition that the market price rises after the sale of the controlling block is announced; but then, it is sufficient to rule out value-decreasing takeovers. In fact, the constraint implies that a tender offer for non-controlling shares may only succeed for a price equal to (or slightly above) the post-announcement price. Making such tender offer is profitable for the acquirer if and only if he can further increase the firm value.

It may seem that minority shareholders can still free ride under this squeeze-out arrangement. Apparently, the post-announcement price is determined by them, and not by the acquirer. This is not correct. After gaining control, the acquirer is confronted with two options. One is making a tender offer to minority shareholders, which would enable him to buy them out at the higher between the pre-takeover and the post-takeover market price. But he has also the option to sell part of his control block so long as this does not imply losing control of the company. I have contended throughout this work that allowing control enhancements is a (legal) condition for efficient separation of owner-ship and control.[9] The necessity to give the acquirer the above two options explains why the entitlement to squeeze out minority shareholders should be conditional on the making of a tender offer, and the latter should be voluntary. This arrangement forces both categories of players to reveal their preferences.

---

8 Obviously, another way to impose this restriction is to require the consideration for squeeze-out to be no lower than the bid price (i.e., a prohibition of two-tier bids). As will be illustrated in the next chapter, this is how the rule that I am advocating can be effectively operationalized in the legal discipline of takeovers. Notice that this rule differs from the solution advocated by Amihud et al (2004) in the acquisition of free-standing firms as far as the second lower bound on the squeeze-out (and the bid) price is concerned. When control has already been acquired from a controlling shareholder, this lower bound is set with reference to the market price *before the announcement* of the block transaction, and not just to the pre-bid price.

9 See *supra* Chapter 4.

The acquirer must immediately decide whether it is more profitable for him to sell or to buy non-controlling shares and trade accordingly, whereas he could always first go for the squeeze-out solution otherwise. Thanks to the same arrangement, minority shareholders are protected from pressure to tender, but they can no longer free ride. The ability of professionally informed traders to drive up the market price is constrained by the prospective acquirers' willingness to award minority shareholders a takeover premium. For the same reason, a takeover premium is allowed just to the extent that it is no impediment to a value-increasing acquisition.[10]

The reader may recognize that this solution is in fact an adaptation of the freeze-out rule advocated by Amihud et al (2004) with reference to takeovers of free-standing firms. In the context of companies with a controlling shareholder, the efficiency of squeeze-out is not constrained by the necessity to rule out negative takeover premia. Because control is transferred independently in this situation, the problem of overestimation of pre-takeover value can be corrected by stock trading after the change in control has occurred. Indeed, this same mechanism keeps *positive* takeover premia sufficiently low to make all efficient takeovers viable. All of the other constraints stay. The constraint that gains must be sufficient to compensate the incumbent's idiosyncratic PBC is intuitively more severe in the presence of controlling shareholders, given the larger size of the control premium. Furthermore, no different from free-standing firms, a consistent upper bound on diversionary PBC is required to avoid that squeeze-out of minority shareholders results in value-decreasing takeovers. Given these constraints, I claim that a rule allowing the acquirer of a control block to squeeze out minority shareholders at the higher between the pre-takeover and the post-takeover price, conditional on a tender offer being made, is the most efficient regulation of such control transactions.

Being the first to make this claim, I will explore in what follows some of its legal implications while leaving further questions open to future research.

---

10 This result obtains by backwards induction. Suppose that a prospective acquirer is just slightly more efficient than the incumbent. Since his idiosyncratic PBC are lower than the incumbent by assumption, he can only purchase the control block by making a loss. However, the squeeze-out rule I am advocating enables him to recoup his loss (and to make further gains) from subsequently trading non-controlling stock. If the stock price does not increase after the announcement of the takeover, the acquirer will just gain by buying out minority shareholders at the pre-takeover price. If the stock price goes up, or it is otherwise inflated, the acquirer will profit from selling at a premium part of his control block. In equilibrium, there is no scope for a takeover premium to prevent any better manager from initiating the acquisition – i.e., the acquirer can always extract the necessary surplus out of a value-increasing takeover. In conclusion, takeover premia are allowed by bargaining (stock trade) just to the extent that they do not hinder efficient changes in control.

7.4 Regulation of control transactions: a functional analysis

7.4.1 *The key issues*

The legal regulation of control transactions is a very complicated matter. In virtually every jurisdiction, it is determined by a complex interaction of securities regulation and corporate law. On the one hand, the goal is to make sure that, in the wake of a takeover, investors receive a sufficient amount of information to make the 'right choice': whether this choice is defined in terms of efficiency or fairness is another question (Bebchuk 1985). On the other hand, corporate law has the difficult task of making sure that control transactions can be operated in spite of objective difficulties in decision-making, but that they do not result in 'unfair' consequences for non-controlling shareholders (Coates 1999). Again, what are to be considered as fair terms of the transaction, and the relationship between fairness and efficiency in this context, are a matter of extensive debate (Easterbrook and Fischel 1991).

In practice, however, in each jurisdiction the legal discipline of control transactions arises as a particular combination of securities regulation and corporate law (Kraakman et al 2009). By taking a functional approach, we can disregard this distinction. But we have to tackle a more important problem: the apparent conflict between operability of changes in control and shareholder protection in takeover regulation. It can be argued that takeover law supports control transactions inasmuch as they are fair to minority shareholders. This is not irrelevant in a law and economics analysis of corporate governance for the same statement can be rephrased in terms of efficiency. In this perspective, the prominent goal of takeover regulation would be the optimal solution of the tradeoff between efficient allocation of corporate control and shareholder protection (Burkart and Panunzi 2008). This is how mainstream economics approaches the matter. It is now time to explore in more detail the legal implications of the alternative approach that has been developed in this study.

The analysis will be concentrated on a relatively narrow set of subjects. Only the rules having a bearing on the supposed tradeoff between the ease of the takeover process and shareholder protection will be discussed, and the discussion will be highly selective. I am going to focus on just the key elements of the theoretical framework discussed so far. These elements carry positive predictions and normative implications for the legal analysis, which are both very strong. First, they confirm some of the criticisms of mainstream economic theory toward excessive shareholder protection by takeover law. Second, they show that the market for corporate control is best supported by legal rules only concerned with efficiency of changes in control, and that this should be the main goal of takeover regulation. Third, they set shareholder protection from expropriation by the corporate controller as a precondition of an efficient takeover process; takeover regulation should pursue this goal independently of promoting a smooth market for corporate control.

The above statements translate into the following areas of functional legal analysis. They concern the regulation of each category of players in the take-over game. The first area is about the incumbent controller. Since we consider only friendly takeovers here, an entrenched controller should be given the possibility to cash in his private benefits for him to part with control. Regulation affects the ease with which both a controlling shareholder can cash in his control premium and the incumbent management can renegotiate their severance payments. Normally, this goes hand in hand with the legal discipline of entrenchment devices. The second area is perhaps the crucial one: the regulation of the acquirer's gains. This is obtained by placing legal constraints on how the company's stock can be acquired; these constraints affect both the distribution of profits and losses between shareholders and the acquirer and the probability that a change in control occurs whether it is efficient or not. The third area is shareholder protection from value-decreasing takeovers. As we know, this involves the prohibition of the sale of the manager's office and of acquisition of corporate stock below its current value. More importantly, however, an effective ban on looting is required for this purpose.

The above essential functions of takeover regulation are not necessarily in a logical order. For instance, shareholder protection from expropriation is a priority for both positive and normative analysis. The areas of takeover law are sorted in this way just for illustrative purposes. I am now going to present the typology of legal rules that belong to each area. The next chapter will discuss how these rules are actually combined in the five jurisdictions of our sample. The implications of their interaction will then be analyzed from both a positive and a normative perspective.

7.4.2 *Regulation of control rents*

7.4.2.1 *Severance payments*

So far, I have always assumed that the corporate controller could ask whatever he wanted in exchange for his parting with control. He only faced a market constraint in his ability to cash in control rents: somebody in the market for corporate control had to find it profitable to take over firm control under these conditions. I maintain that this mechanism is the optimal compromise between ex-ante and ex-post efficiency of corporate governance, subject to the only constraint that it may not result in value-decreasing takeovers – which is a matter of shareholder protection. However, in practice the ability of incumbent controllers to cash in their rents in a takeover is not unconstrained by corporate law. Indeed, corporate law may make this kind of payment extremely difficult, if not prohibit them outright (Kraakman et al 2009).

The reason why the law may be skeptical about upfront compensation of control rents is twofold. On the one hand, lawyers may regard it as nothing but a 'bribe', which – despite Coase's (1960) famous illustration of how side payments may improve the welfare of society – lawyers tend to consider as immoral *per se*. On the other hand, even apart from value judgments, compensation of control rents may be regarded as shareholders expropriation since it undoubtedly reduces their takeover gains. None of these arguments is correct: compensation of control rents does not need to be a bribe, but it is necessary to reward the investment of unverifiable entrepreneurial talent; and it may only result in shareholder expropriation when stealing is already a problem in corporate governance. However, that such compensation is treated with suspicion in many corporate jurisdictions is a matter of fact, and it cannot be neglected.

Regulation may prohibit or restrict severance payments to managers, and that happens typically when managers act in their capacity as directors. A milder version of this prohibition is preventing the controlling management from renegotiating their golden parachutes. This is no less worrisome, since we know that a significant part of the manager's incentive to put effort in the ongoing management of the company depends on his ability to claim a larger severance payment in the face of a takeover (Almazan and Suarez 2003). Regulatory restrictions on severance payments then undermine both incentive alignment and the ease of takeovers under managerial control. This is only a part of the story. Normally, these restrictions are associated with a prohibition of management from taking any action that may frustrate the success of a takeover bid, unless management is authorized by shareholders to do so. Apparently, the combination of these two restrictions should result in the incumbent management's inability to influence the outcome of takeovers through negotiations with the bidder. While this was probably the intention of rule-makers, this result is short-circuited by the power of economic incentives. We know that, despite legal restrictions, corporate controllers seeking entrenchment for reasons of firm-specific investment will anyway get entrenchment (or refrain from investing in the first place). The only consequence of these restrictions is then that they narrow the scope of feasible corporate governance arrangements, and possibly compromise their efficiency.

Having to reckon a rule of board neutrality, or even full passivity, in the wake of a takeover, managers may just have to find a different way to entrench themselves. An obvious solution is to become controlling shareholders, but this has a number of shortcomings that makes it unattractive if not as a last resort. The first drawback is the financial commitment and the resulting opportunity costs in terms of liquidity and risk diversification – not to speak about wealth constraints. This problem could be partly overcome by separating voting rights from cash flow rights, but – as we know – this solution is not always available because of either unfavorable regulation or the veto powers granted to large investors by corporate law. Finally, the same regulation that makes it difficult for managers to entrench themselves may also make it costly to be a controlling shareholder of a listed firm.

Most of these conditions characterize British regulation of corporate governance and the best practices established in the UK. The combination of these rules – in addition to other historical factors documented by Cheffins (2008) – induces the vast majority of listed companies to have relatively dispersed ownership. Controlling shareholders are rare and unlikely to emerge. Still, managers can be in control by forming coalitions powerful enough to resist an unwelcome takeover so long as they have the support of institutional investors. In addition to this, British managers are prohibited by company law from renegotiating their severance payments.[11] Hence, the corporate controllers' incentives to perform are weak and – despite the vibrant takeover activity – efficient takeovers are less frequent than they could be in the UK. These predictions will be confirmed and elaborated upon in the country-by-country analysis of the next chapter.

The British case is a peculiar one. Normally, one would expect that regulatory constraints on managerial entrenchment are sufficient for shareholder control to emerge as the only possible outcome. Then legal restrictions on severance payments would be irrelevant for the market of corporate control because the latter is operated by controlling shareholders. This is certainly correct, but the reverse is not necessarily true. In many jurisdictions, managers are allowed both to shield themselves from hostile takeovers and to renegotiate their severance payments at the time of the acquisition. However, in some countries (like the US), this allows managerial control to be workable and corporate governance to evolve from concentrated to dispersed ownership structures; and vice versa. In some others (like the Netherlands), this allows for managerial control but does not guarantee an equally smooth transition between dispersed and concentrated ownership structures. In others again (like Italy), this is not even sufficient to support managerial control. To put it succinctly, the absence of restrictions on the managers' taking an active role in takeover bargaining is neither a necessary nor a sufficient condition for managerial control and an active takeover market to be featured in corporate governance. On the one hand, managerial control needs also to be supported by a consistent legal distribution of corporate powers. On the other hand, an efficient dynamics in the allocation of corporate control also depends on how the sale of *controlling blocks* is regulated.

Normally, the sale of a control block involves both the transfer of ownership and the transfer of control powers (Easterbrook and Fischel 1982a). However, this can be problematic in those jurisdictions that deny shareholder primacy in the distribution of corporate powers. In our sample, this is applicable to the Netherlands and therefore the discussion of this problem is postponed to the specific analysis of that country. A more general problem is that corporate law very often regulates the terms in which the sale of a controlling block can be operated (McCahery et al 2004). This affects the ability for the controlling shareholder to claim a control premium in return for his rents, and thereby the ease with which takeovers may occur.

---

11 See *infra* Chapter 8.

7.4.2.2 *The control premium: 'market rule' vs. 'equal opportunity rule'*

There are mainly two kinds of regulations of the control premium (Bebchuk 1994). One is to allow the controlling shareholder to trade freely his block with no obligation to share the control premium with minority shareholders. This means that controlling and non-controlling shares are exchanged on different terms, and that the former are traded at a premium compared to the latter, for they carry the entitlement to corporate control. This is known as the 'market rule' in the sale of corporate control. It has been demonstrated that this rule maximizes the probability that efficient takeovers occur, since the incumbent faces no difficulty in having his private benefits compensated other than the acquirer's ability to reap takeover gains in the form of security benefits – a problem that must be coped with anyway. However, this rule also allows takeovers to be operated to extract further private benefits at the expense of security benefits and/or to perpetuate extraction of private benefits under shareholder control structures. This is not a problem in the framework being used here: private benefits of control may result in value-decreasing takeovers only on condition that value diversion from non-controlling shareholders is not adequately policed otherwise by corporate law. Nevertheless, this problem is considered a good rationale for the opposite regulation of the takeover premium (Burkart and Panunzi 2008). This is the so-called 'equal opportunity rule.'

The equal opportunity rule denies the controlling shareholder the entitlement to cash in a control premium with the exclusion of minority shareholders. The control block may indeed be sold at a premium over market price, but the same premium must be shared with non-controlling shareholders on equal terms. In theory, there are different ways to operationalize such a rule. In practice, it is normally implemented through the obligation for the acquirer of a control block to make a tender offer to minority shareholders for the same consideration. This is a *mandatory bid rule* with equal treatment of shareholders, whether they are controlling or not. A mandatory bid does not need to feature the obligation to share the control premium, nor does the equal opportunity rule require a mandatory bid. But the two circumstances are normally bundled together in corporate law, so the mandatory bid is – somewhat inappropriately – considered as synonymous with the equal opportunity rule (Kraakman et al 2009). I shall further speculate on the specific characteristics of the mandatory bid in the next section. What is important to notice here is that, in this configuration, the mandatory bid amounts to an effective prohibition of the controlling shareholder from getting anything more than minority shareholders get in a takeover.

What are the consequences of equal opportunities being granted to minority shareholders through a mandatory bid? The first and most unfortunate one is that it restricts the scope of feasible control transactions, in spite of their efficiency (Bebchuk 1994). Indeed, the size of the incumbent's control rents is given and unaffected by the rule. The latter just makes their compensation more difficult, since the same premium over market price must also be paid to non-controlling shareholders. As a result, many efficient takeovers will have to be foregone due to the acquirer's inability to pay such an inflated control premium, and possibly none of them will occur when the controlling shareholder's private benefits are high enough (Berglöf and Burkart 2003).

It must be acknowledged that the severity of this rule is sometimes tempered by national corporate laws, especially where the presence of controlling shareholders is largely predominant in corporate governance. This is obtained allowing for partial bids, a discount on the bid price, or simply having the mandatory bid triggered by a threshold of stock acquisition sufficiently high enough to let control transactions occur without the need to share the control premium with minority shareholders. We will discuss this sort of 'waivers' in the next chapter, since they are not allowed in many jurisdictions and some of them have recently disappeared in Europe. It is much more important to ask why this regulation is so popular even in its strictest formulation, in spite of its disruptive effects on the market for corporate control. The reason is shareholder protection.

Although the desirability of such a protection is often argued on the basis of fairness reasons, there is also an efficiency explanation. A mandatory bid with equal treatment of shareholders makes value-decreasing takeovers impossible to succeed (Bebchuk 1994). The reason is straightforward: there is no way for the acquirer to extract private benefits of any kind if he is obliged to offer non-controlling shareholders the same price that he pays for controlling shares. However, the equal opportunity rule is not the only way to achieve this goal (Burkart and Panunzi 2004). On the one hand, efficiency of all feasible takeovers obtains as well under the market rule when private benefits of the insurgent and the incumbent are of the same order of magnitude (a condition that typically holds for diversionary PBC, which depend on the legal environment rather than on the identity of controllers); but the equal opportunity rule discourages a much greater number of value-increasing transactions. On the other hand, ruling out PBC extraction is neither necessary nor desirable for the efficiency of takeovers, so long as (incremental) value diversion from minority shareholders is excluded otherwise.

7.4.3 *Regulation of the acquisition in dispersed ownership structures*

7.4.3.1 *Does the mandatory bid matter?*

When the mandatory bid carries no obligation to share the control premium, for instance because there is none in the absence of a controlling shareholder, it only affects the acquirer's gains relative to the shareholders' (Burkart and Panunzi 2004). In the takeover of a free-standing firm, the mandatory bid simply means that a would-be acquirer *must* make an *unrestricted* tender offer to non-controlling shareholders in order to gain control. It is quite intuitive that the first obligation is irrelevant to the extent that a tender offer is anyway the insurgent's best strategy to acquire a control block – which, for simplicity, we assume equal to 50% of voting shares. However, the mandatory character of the bid usually comes with regulation of the bid price, so that this cannot be lower than the price paid for previous stock purchases on the market (Kraakman et al 2009). Assuming that shareholders cannot free ride, this may undermine the acquirer's ability to profit from the acquisition of a toehold below the bid price and may, in addition, expose him to adverse fluctuations in the stock price between market purchases and the making of the bid. This solution of course benefits target shareholders conditional on a tender offer being made, but it reduces the probability that a takeover bid occurs.

The second requirement that the bid be 'any-or-all' has different implications on the takeover process depending on how the free riding problem is coped with. When the exclusionary mechanism is based on post-takeover value diversion (as in Grossman and Hart 1980), the prohibition of unrestricted offers is irrelevant provided that diversion is unconstrained. However, the prohibition prevents some value-increasing takeovers under the more reasonable assumption that the legal system constrains the acquirer's ability to divert shareholder value, thereby making restricted offers an attractive option (Burkart and Panunzi 2004). Prohibiting the latter may be nonetheless desirable in this situation, in order to prevent value-decreasing takeovers.

When free riding is instead excluded by the entitlement to squeeze out non-tendering shareholders, the mandatory bid plays a different role. At first glance, prohibition of restricted offers may seem necessary to avoid pressure to tender, and it would also be sufficient for this purpose inasmuch as the role of diversionary PBC is disallowed in takeovers – as I continue to assume it can. Yet, although coercive offers are undesirable for the efficiency of the takeover process, the mandatory bid is not necessary to avoid coercion. When the squeeze-out price is set equal to the higher between the bid and the market price, shareholders cannot be forced into value-decreasing acquisitions by a two-tier bid (Amihud et al 2004). Neither can they free ride whether they tender or not. However, it will always be in the acquirer's interest to squeeze out shareholders who do not tender, either because they do not have rational expectations or because they are rationed: a different strategy would place them back in the position to free ride.

As a result, a restricted bid makes no sense from the acquirer's standpoint, when it is associated with optimal squeeze-out. Its prohibition under a mandatory bid rule is therefore irrelevant. A partial bid may only be in the interest of the acquirer when the above squeeze-out rule is implemented imperfectly, or the acquirer is allowed to extract higher private benefits than the incumbent by looting the company. In either case, the advantage of a prohibition of restricted bids – avoidance of value-decreasing takeovers – must be balanced against its adverse consequences on the probability of efficient changes in control.

7.4.3.2 Sell-out and squeeze-out

A topic closely related to the mandatory bid is shareholders' sell-out right. This right enables minority shareholders to have their shares acquired for a fair consideration when their position has become inconvenient because of reduced liquidity of their investment or a change in control or because of both reasons. This situation typically occurs in the aftermath of a takeover bid and this is the only case being considered here. In such a case, the problem of consideration 'fairness' is solved by setting the price equal to that offered in the bid. It is often believed that the sell-out right is just the opposite of the squeeze-out right, and therefore must be granted in equal terms to minority shareholders to compensate for the entitlement given to the acquirer. This perspective, however, is misleading. Although the rules effectively mirror each other, functionally the two are very different (Kraakman et al 2009). The illiquidity argument is a partial argument in favor of the sell-out right, but under certain conditions, it turns out to be the only possible one. A much stronger argument, which enjoys the support of both academics and policymakers, is that the sell-out right may be desirable to counter pressure to tender. In this respect, the function of the sell-out right is apparently similar to that of the mandatory bid.

However, there are important differences (see Burkart and Panunzi 2004). When the squeeze-out rule departs from the optimal arrangement that we have previously described, the sell-out right is only relevant when it is triggered by a no higher percentage of stock acquisition than that sufficient to determine a change in control (which we have assumed to be 50%). This is both a necessary and a sufficient condition for the sell-out right to remove pressure to tender, whereas the mandatory bid also requires that negative takeover premia be ruled out. To this extent, the sell-out right is preferable to the mandatory bid. Nevertheless, both rules raise the cost of value-increasing acquisitions in order to prevent value-decreasing ones. This is not necessary when the squeeze-out rule is drafted in optimal terms (Amihud et al 2004). When this happens, a sell-out right is irrelevant to both the functioning and the efficiency of the takeover process, whatever the triggering threshold. The reason is threefold: (i) pressure to tender is already eliminated; (ii) neither squeeze-out nor sell-out rights are exercised in equilibrium based on rational expectations; and (iii) in the presence of noise and/or irrationality, it will always be squeeze-out to be exercised.

So far we have made a strong assumption: that the acquirer's right to squeeze-out non-tendering shareholders is triggered by the mere acquisition of control – which we still assume to be conditional on the transfer of at least 50% of the voting shares. This solution has the important advantage to let the acquirer appropriate as much as possible of the takeover gains, but not all of them, since it still allows for a positive takeover premium to be determined – in a dynamic setting – by the interaction of management's recommendations with information spillovers and bidding competition.[12] Burkart et al (1998) have argued that a squeeze-out threshold any higher than the control acquisition threshold would result in a further increase in the takeover premium, due to shareholders' ability to free ride when the latter threshold is met but the former is not. However, this argument has been shown to be incorrect (Amihud et al 2004): the only effect of a higher squeeze-out threshold is to make takeover bids conditional on that threshold being reached rather than on the mere acquisition of control.

Although this result does not affect the efficiency of takeovers under the assumption of rational expectations, the freeze-out threshold is not irrelevant in the real world. If we take the presence of noise and/or irrationality into account, too high a threshold actually lowers the chances of success of takeover bids. When, for instance, the squeeze-out threshold is set at 90% or more of the voting capital – as it is in Europe – this enables a number of players (large shareholders, arbitrageurs, and, under certain conditions, the incumbent management) to holdout for a larger premium. This is not because they can free ride, but because they may more easily make profits against noise traders or they find it otherwise profitable not to trade (Gomes 2001). Whatever the reasons for this behavior, it is allowed by a more stringent condition for the takeover's success, and it results in a number of efficient takeovers being foregone. Therefore, differently from Amihud et al (2004), a sufficiently low threshold (possibly, as low as the control acquisition threshold) is a key component of our optimal squeeze-out rule. The inefficiency of a different arrangement will be shown with reference to the UK regulation in the next chapter.

It might still be argued that a higher squeeze-out threshold protects non-controlling shareholders from value-decreasing acquisitions (Burkart and Panunzi 2004). However, since the latter are already stopped by the regulation of the freeze-out price, this is unnecessary. More in general, letting non-controlling shareholders participate in the takeover gains is neither a necessary nor a sufficient condition to have inefficient changes in control ruled out; whereas it certainly reduces the frequency of efficient takeovers.

7.4.4 *Regulation of the acquisition in concentrated ownership structures*

Is the impact of regulation of the acquisition different when control is bound to be transferred from a controlling shareholder? The answer is a qualified yes. On the one hand, it should be recalled that acquisition of non-controlling stock is not strictly necessary for a change in control to take place in this scenario. On the other hand, whether such acquisition is an option or an obligation under takeover regulation still affects the prospective acquirer's

---

12 See *supra* section 7.3.1.

incentives to initiate a takeover; this is not much different from the case of a free-standing firm. The legal solution that I advocate for this problem is also not much different, since it is based – in both situations – on the *option*, and not on the *obligation*, for the acquirer to buy out minority shareholders, conditional on shareholder protection being just sufficient to rule out value-decreasing takeovers.[13]

When takeovers are implemented through the sale of control blocks, two problems arise (Kraakman et al 2009). On the one hand, non-controlling shareholders have no say on the control transaction; on the other hand, they bear a significant part of its wealth effects, whether they are positive or negative. Lawyers and regulators, more than economists, are mostly concerned about negative effects, which they often regard as 'unfair.' To be sure, they may also be regarded as inefficient: the new controller may loot the company, either directly or by diverting profit opportunities to other group member companies; or alternatively, he may be unable or unwilling to keep shareholder value at least as high as under the previous management, for instance because he just strives for empire building. In each situation, minority shareholders would be worse off after the control shift; and the outcome would be inefficient too because – in the framework used here – it would be determined by an increase in diversionary or distortionary PBC. It is on this basis that both the fairness and the efficiency of granting minority shareholders a right of exit upon a change in control can be argued. This right of exit is implemented by a mandatory bid rule.

7.4.4.1 *Potential and limitations of the mandatory bid*

Compared to the case of acquisition of a free-standing firm, the mandatory bid has a structural difference and a theoretically optional one. The structural difference is that the obligation to make a tender offer is no longer irrelevant, even in the absence of regulation of the bid price, because in a number of situations a would-be acquirer would not make any offer and just go for the acquisition of the control block (Kraakman et al 2009). This is already a source of distortion, which I am going to elaborate upon shortly. However, the mandatory bid is intended to protect minority shareholders, and the right of exit is definitely not sufficient for this purpose: shareholders would simply have no bargaining power in a value-decreasing transaction. One option could be to set the bid price equal to the pre-takeover market price: but this would still allow for value-decreasing takeovers to the extent that the stock is undervalued. Surely the best solution would be to compel the bid to be equal to the pre-takeover *value*, instead of the *price*; but this is not possible because the pre-takeover value is not verifiable. Therefore, the bid price must be regulated with reference to the only alternative we have to the market

13 See *supra* section 7.3.2.

price: the price paid for the control block (Bebchuk 1994). It is in this way that the mandatory bid becomes more than just a right of exit for minority shareholders, for it also supplies them with the entitlement to share the control premium with the controlling shareholder (Kraakman et al 2009).

As we have seen, this configuration of the mandatory bid is unfortunate because it leads to a vast number of efficient transactions (and possibly to all of them) being foregone. The problem concerns the insurgent more than the incumbent. The latter does not really care about what is given to minority shareholders, provided that his rents are compensated. The former, however, may be unable to bring about enough security benefits to allow for private benefits' compensation to be extended to minority shareholders, in spite of (the increases in) the first kind of benefits being sufficiently large to offset (the decreases in) the second one. With respect to the goal of preventing value-decreasing takeovers, this solution is therefore an overshooting at best. Indeed, as I have shown, payment of the control premium just to the controlling shareholder is already sufficient to prevent value-decreasing takeovers on condition that at least as much as the control block is transferred and the acquirer is not allowed to divert further shareholder value.[14] While corporate law must provide for the last condition to hold, the first condition is intrinsic to the takeover process in the presence of a controlling shareholder. The mandatory bid is not necessary to rule out value-decreasing takeovers. In addition, the adverse consequences of the mandatory bid on value-increasing takeovers make it suboptimal compared to other solutions, which likewise exclude inefficient control transactions while placing fewer restraints on efficient ones (see Burkart and Panunzi 2004). In the absence of tender offers for non-controlling shares, the 'market rule' for block transactions coupled with an effective ban on incremental diversionary PBC is always one such solution.

Could alternative regulations of the mandatory bid fare better? I believe not. When it does not carry the entitlement for minority shareholders to share in the control premium, the mandatory bid cannot prevent all value-decreasing takeovers while still being counterproductive for value-increasing ones. The only condition under which this result does not obtain is an unfeasible one: the bid price set equal to the pre-takeover value. It is nonetheless interesting to study this condition, not because economists typically make unrealistic assumptions, but because this situation is illustrative of the properties that the mandatory bid may have and, even more so, of those that it may *never* have. The mandatory bid can do nothing about free riding by minority shareholders. The best that the mandatory bid could do if we knew the pre-takeover *value* would be to make sure that minority shareholders cannot suffer any loss from a change in control while they can still free ride on its benefits. As a result, non-controlling shares would never be tendered in spite of the mandatory

14 See *supra*, section 7.2.3.

character of the bid. A value-decreasing acquirer would simply refrain from purchasing the control block in the first place, since the tender offer would force him to make a loss; whereas no shares would be tendered at the pre-takeover value by shareholders who know that they can free ride on a higher post-takeover value. Ironically, the only reason why this solution would not kill off any possible takeovers at all is that changes in control can be operated by sales of controlling blocks. Still, a number of efficient takeovers would be foregone due to minority shareholders' ability to free ride and the mandatory bid, even in its ideal configuration, can simply do nothing about it.

The above result cannot be improved by any alternative configuration of the mandatory bid that we may observe in the real world, unless pressure to tender is generated. This means that the mandatory bid must be relaxed, allowing for some inefficient takeovers to take place (Kraakman et al 2009). For instance, the bidder could be enabled to offer a lower price for non-controlling stock than the price paid for the control block, to bid for less than all outstanding shares, or to combine the two strategies; no value-decreasing takeover would be allowed otherwise. This would still not be enough to create scope for value-decreasing takeovers, and then it would not generate any pressure to tender, if the acquirer is not allowed to divert more value than the incumbent from the shareholders who do not tender. Whether these conditions are also sufficient to result in a larger number of efficient takeovers than in the ideal situation (where no value-decreasing takeovers are possible and value-increasing ones are prevented by shareholders' free riding), it all depends on the legal parameters of this complicated arrangement. These are, basically, the discount on the bid price or quantity and the amount of diversionary PBC allowed by the legal system.

Without carrying these complications any further, a few points are worth making. First, the chance of this mechanism to be beneficial does not depend on the mandatory bid, but on its waivers. Second, this arrangement is the more likely to improve efficiency the stricter the mandatory bid rule is in the first place (Berglöf and Burkart 2003). Third, an alternative arrangement may replicate the outcome of the least distortive mandatory bid without necessity to generate any pressure to tender. When the threshold triggering the obligation is high enough, no tender offer needs to be made in spite of control effectively changing hands: this outcome, in which the mandatory bid is circumvented, is equivalent to setting the mandatory bid price equal to the pre-takeover value keeping the condition that diversionary PBC are disallowed.[15] Fourth, under the same condition, it is not necessary to hypothesize any tradeoff between shareholder protection from value-decreasing takeovers and promotion of value-increasing ones. As I have shown, the tradeoff hypothesis is unwarranted, and so is the attempt to cope with it through the

---

15 For the view that EU member states should use their freedom to set the mandatory bid threshold see McCahery et al (2004).

mandatory bid. On the one hand, the mandatory bid could at best protect shareholders by allowing them to free ride and can effectively do so only at the cost of further reducing the probability of efficient takeovers. On the other hand, the mandatory bid can only promote efficient takeovers to the extent that it protects shareholders imperfectly, by exposing them to the risk of value-decreasing changes in control.

On the contrary, an optimal squeeze-out rule can simultaneously promote efficient takeovers and protect shareholders from inefficient ones. If an optimal squeeze-out rule is supported by the legal system, the mandatory bid becomes a nuisance that should be simply abolished.

7.4.4.2 *Optimal squeeze-out and its regulatory impediments*

In the presence of a controlling shareholder, regulation should make squeeze-out of minority shareholders attractive enough for value-increasing acquirers without also allowing value-decreasing acquirers to profit from this option. We know that this is achieved by allowing squeeze-out to be exercised conditional upon the making of a tender offer for non-controlling shares; and by setting the squeeze-out consideration equal to the higher market price before and after the announcement of the acquisition of the control block.[16] From an economic standpoint, this is both necessary and sufficient to prevent value-decreasing takeovers from being subsidized through acquisition of non-controlling stock below its current value while allowing value-increasing acquirers to overcome free riding by minority shareholders. From a legal point of view, it is also necessary that disclosure of control block transactions is provided for and stock price manipulation is effectively prohibited. Modern systems of securities regulation normally provide sufficient guarantees that these minimal conditions for stock market efficiency are fulfilled (Kraakman et al 2009). As far as corporate law is concerned, the rule at issue is also very easy to enforce. Both constraints on the squeeze-out price are set with reference to objective market prices. Therefore, from a straight perspective of legal policy, this arrangement is very attractive, at least in the absence of interference with other rules.

Unfortunately, this interference exists in many respects. The first source of interference is the mandatory bid rule. Even if we abstract from the price constraints – which, in practice, significantly depart from the arrangement that we are considering – the mandatory character of the tender offer for non-controlling shares is problematic. According to the framework developed in this chapter, the bid should be voluntary to allow for the takeover premium to adjust to the efficient level. If the bid is mandatory and the price is just constrained by the squeeze-out rule, the bidder will still lose the option to sell part of his control block when the price increase is high enough; worse still,

---

16 See *supra* section 7.3.2.

he will have to make a tender offer at an inflated price. It can be easily demonstrated that this restores shareholders' ability to holdout for any lower price than the post-takeover value. Therefore, the mandatory bid simply short-circuits the squeeze-out's advantage in coping with the free riding problem.

A similar problem may arise from the sell-out right. In the case of a free-standing firm, sell-out is irrelevant in the presence of an optimal squeeze-out rule because it is always the latter to be exercised when shareholders do not tender. However, when control is acquired from a controlling shareholder, the acquirer may not wish to make any tender offer for non-controlling shares, which should also prevent him from squeezing them out; this is both rational and efficient when the post-announcement price is inflated. If shareholders were granted a sell-out right at the post-takeover price, triggered by the mere change in control, this would be equivalent to the mandatory bid case analyzed above. In practice, as we will see in the next chapter, such a solution is uncommon and the main corporate law jurisdictions do not allow minority shareholders to free ride on the basis of their sell-out rights (Kraakman et al 2009). In some cases, the sell-out price is set at a lower level than the post-takeover value. In the US, for instance, the appraisal right is triggered by the operation of a post-takeover merger, but it just entitles dissenting shareholders to have their shares acquired at the pre-merger price. In other cases, as in Europe, the sell-out right is triggered by a threshold of stock acquisition that is much higher than the share necessary for gaining control (between 90% and 95%). Then the acquirer may either avoid reaching that threshold or alternatively exercise the squeeze-out right when it is reached; in fact, squeeze-out and sell-out rights are normally triggered by the same threshold.

The threshold is, indeed, the third problem with our optimal squeeze-out rule. As in the case of free-standing firms, the rule always functions efficiently when the squeeze-out right is triggered by a control acquisition. The only reason why I am imposing the additional requirement that a tender offer be made is that otherwise any acquirer would always go for the squeeze-out solution to counter adverse movements in the stock price, even when it is more efficient to sell rather than to purchase stock on the market. However, the point is that when a tender offer is made (and it cannot be value-decreasing due to the regulation of the squeeze-out price) it must succeed with certainty. When this is not true, the beneficial effects of the squeeze-out rule on efficient control transactions are diminished.

Any squeeze-out threshold higher than 50% of the voting capital may lead to this problem. Whether it does or not depends on the effective ability of market players to holdout for a higher takeover premium, which would make a number of efficient transactions unprofitable for the prospective acquirer. This ability depends, in turn, on several case-specific factors (Gomes 2001). A solution cannot therefore be identified across the board. Anyway, reaching the squeeze-out threshold is a condition for a successful tender offer, so the latter is expected to be conditional upon that threshold. By and large, a threshold between 60% and 70% of the voting stock may hardly affect the probability of success. Not quite so, however, a threshold of 90% or 95%. This is likely to create enough scope for holdout by minority shareholders, thereby leading to some efficient control transactions being foregone.

A fourth source of interference with an optimal squeeze-out rule is the courts' natural skepticism towards 'an offer that shareholders can't refuse.' Two fundamental points are worth making in this respect. The first is that the courts' suspicious attitude is not without reason. We know that coercive bids can easily result in inefficient takeovers to the non-controlling shareholders' detriment. However, under the proposed squeeze-out rule, a tender offer for non-controlling shares may look like it is coercive (shareholders who do not tender will anyway be squeezed out at the same price), but in fact it is not. I have ruled out coercion by disallowing value-decreasing bids through appropriate lower bounds on the squeeze-out price (see also Amihud 2004). As Bebchuk (1987) has shown, coercion does not depend on the structure of the offer, but on pressure to tender generated by the fear that a successful bid may make non-tendering shareholders worse-off. Pressure to tender cannot be generated by a bid that is bound not to be value-decreasing, although it could be generated at an earlier stage by an inefficient sale of the control block.

This leads us to the second key point. A sufficient condition for a sale of corporate control to be inefficient is that the acquirer is able to extract a *larger* fraction of diversionary PBC from non-controlling shareholders. In our framework based on a tripartite account of PBC, this condition is also necessary for the transfer of control blocks to be value-decreasing. When this happens, it is the change in control and not the squeeze-out right that undermines the efficiency of the takeover and the wealth of non-controlling shareholders, whether a bid is made or not. This is looting and, in theory, courts should simply prevent that from occurring via takeovers. In practice, however, distinguishing between efficient and inefficient sales of control requires a high degree of sophistication. The problem is identical to the Type I/Type II errors in policing non-pro-rata distributions discussed in the previous chapters, with the peculiarity that false positives create impediments to efficient takeovers. This illustrates the tendency of unsophisticated courts and legislators to tilt the balance of takeover regulation too much in favor of shareholder protection, awarding minority shareholders the largest possible share of the takeover gains which reduces the frequency of efficient takeovers. Judges and lawyers in general often believe that shareholders are best protected in this way; but this is illusory (Macey 2008).

7.4.4.3 *The breakthrough rule*

In the next section, we will see how the problem of value-decreasing takeovers is efficiently tackled by a more focused approach to shareholder protection. But, before concluding on the distribution of the acquirer's gains, it is worth discussing a recent invention by policymakers to counter the drawbacks of the mandatory bid in controlling shareholder systems. Everybody acknowledges that the obligation to share the control premium, in all or in part, significantly reduces the probability that efficient takeovers occur. The problem is how to improve the position of prospective acquirers and make them more willing to embark on an efficient takeover, if we still want minority shareholders to get the lion's share of the takeover gains in order to avoid expropriation. One solution is to allow acquirers to extract takeover gains from the incumbent controller rather than from non-controlling shareholders. This solution is the basic idea underlying the so-called 'breakthrough' rule.[17]

So far, we have implicitly assumed that shareholder control is held with the absolute majority of the share capital, but we know that this is neither necessary nor very common. Shareholder control is normally exercised through devices – such as dual class shares, voting pacts, or pyramidal structures – which allow corporate controllers to be in charge of decision-making with an ownership stake lower than 50%. Deviations from the 'one share–one vote' arrangement affect none of the results of the previous discussion to the extent that the controlling shareholder's entrenchment was always assumed to obtain in equal terms for the incumbent and the insurgent – i.e., a sale of control can only be operated by a transfer of controlling ownership, no matter the voting leverage, provided that it stays unchanged. These deviations, however, are exactly the target of the breakthrough rule.

Ideally, the breakthrough rule provides that the 'one share–one vote' principle be restored in the wake of a takeover. This has two major consequences (Ferrarini 2006). The first is that control no longer needs to be acquired from the controlling shareholder, as a change in control may be operated through a successful bid for previously non-controlling shares. The second consequence is that the controlling shareholder is no longer able to protect his control rents to the extent that his entrenchment can be effectively broken through: since rent compensation is no longer a condition for taking over, a prospective acquirer is enabled to make larger profits in spite of a burdensome mandatory bid. Both consequences arise from the introduction of hostility in the takeover process, and therefore require that the controlling shareholder is not otherwise allowed to frustrate a takeover bid – a result easily obtained by associating the breakthrough rule with a board neutrality rule. In addition, deviations from 'one share–one vote' should be in place for the breakthrough rule to have any impact.

---

17 See McCahery et al (2004); Mülbert (2004); and Kraakman et al (2009). The breakthrough rule was proposed by the High Level Group of Company Law Experts led by Professor Jaap Winter in 2002. The basic idea of the breakthrough rule was to 'level the playing field' in European takeover regulation, complementing the board neutrality rule (suitable for contestability of managerial control structures) with equivalent regulations also exposing controlling shareholders to hostile takeovers. This rule was adopted in less stringent terms by the Takeover Bid Directive (2004/25/EC), which will be discussed in the next chapter.

The breakthrough rule is impractical and makes little economic sense (Coates 2004). From an economic standpoint, it could only be interpreted as a way to trade ex-post for ex-ante efficiency. As we know, idiosyncratic control rents draw a wedge between the two. They are needed to feature corporate control with adequate incentives at the outset, but they turn out to be an impediment to efficient changes in control to be operated at a later stage. In Chapter 4, I have extensively argued in favor of contractual freedom for the solution of this tradeoff in order to allow for efficient modes and degrees of separation between ownership and control to be determined by stock placement with the investing public.[18] This basically means that both separation of control rights from ownership (managerial entrenchment devices) and separation of voting rights from cash flow rights (deviations from 'one share–one vote') should be freely established in connection with the sale of stock on the market. However, these arrangements should not allow for subsequent modifications being unilaterally implemented in *either* direction.

When no role is acknowledged to idiosyncratic control rents (and entrepreneurship) in corporate governance, the proposition that corporate law should not be mandatory with respect to the security-voting structure established at the outset becomes questionable (see Grossman and Hart 1988). However, the prohibition of unilateral renegotiations in the same respect is out of the question because it is bound to be opportunistic (Ferrarini 2006). Allowing shareholders to turn down existing deviations from 'one share–one vote' would exactly amount to such an opportunistic renegotiation, aimed at expropriating the controlling shareholder of the rents that – for whatever reason – were promised to him in the first place. It is for this reason that the breakthrough rule makes no economic sense.

This also explains why the breakthrough rule is not practical: it cannot achieve its purpose, if not in the very short run, and only creates distortions in the long run.[19] When a breakthrough rule is first introduced, it may disrupt some existing control structures. This result, however, depends on the rule being effectively able to impose a 'one share–one vote' security-voting structure when a takeover bid is made. The rule obviously loses its bite when at least one device for leveraging voting power is left out, since controlling shareholders will be expected to turn exactly to that device. Pyramidal structures are the case in point. On the one hand, they are hardly affected by any breakthrough rule, unless the rule is allowed to be as powerful as to compel dissolution of corporate groups – which is unlikely. On the other hand, pyramidal structures may easily be created (or expanded) at the corporate controller's initiative. This is the reason why pyramids were characterized as perhaps the most dangerous among the instruments for leveraging voting power in Chapter 4. Ironically, the introduction of a breakthrough rule may

---

18 See *supra* Chapter 4, section 4.6.2.
19 See L.A. Bebchuk and O. Hart, "A Threat to Dual-Class Shares," *Financial Times*, May 31, 2002.

just led to the proliferation of pyramidal structures, instead of easing the takeover process.

Even leaving out the pyramid problem and assuming that regulation outperforms controlling shareholders' ability to suddenly switch to alternative techniques for leveraging voting or control power, entrenchment is unlikely to be eliminated on a structural basis by the breakthrough rule. On the one hand, controlling shareholders can always entrench themselves by holding 50% of the company's stock. This solution is costly, but it may be considered preferable to the exposure to hostile takeover in the presence of high control rents. On the other hand, whatever the degree of contestability of corporate control determined by the breakthrough rule in spite of its deficiencies, this will just be temporary. After the first impact of the rule, the expectations of the players will adjust to its existence. All deviations from 'one share–one vote' that can be effectively reneged ex-post will be regarded as insufficient basis for a credible commitment ex-ante: this is equivalent to their prohibition at the outset. When deciding whether and on what terms to take their company public, controlling shareholders will therefore resort just to arrangements that make the desired distribution of corporate powers resistant to any breakthrough rule. If there is no such distribution, controllers will either refrain from non-contractable investments in entrepreneurship, hold on to 50% of ownership, or refrain from going public altogether.

In conclusion, the breakthrough rule confirms that contestability of corporate control cannot be imposed by regulation: the only effect that can be expected from regulatory restrictions on the corporate controller's entrenchment, either ex-ante or ex-post, is a lower degree of separation of ownership and control.

7.4.5 *Shareholder protection*

7.4.5.1 *Looting as a determinant of inefficient takeovers*

Shareholder protection does not need to be distortive of either separation of ownership control or the efficiency of the takeover process. It can be reconciled with both entrenchment of corporate control and the absence of restraints on value-increasing takeovers. This compatibility is a fundamental underpinning of an efficient takeover regulation. Throughout the foregoing discussion, I have already mentioned what the functional elements of shareholder protection should be in this framework. Let us now put them in a bit of a structure, highlighting the most prominent legal instruments by which they are implemented in the discipline of control transactions. These instruments will be discussed in more detail in the following country-by-country analysis.

The first problem is diversionary PBC. In an ideal system of corporate governance there would be none. However, there is no set of institutional and legal constraints in which non-pro-rata distributions can be ruled out. The tradeoff between Type I and Type II errors in policing stealing by the corporate controller can be optimized, but never eliminated. In addition, as we have seen, some legal systems perform better than others do on this account. Let us take both these results as a constraint in the analysis of the takeover process. On the one hand, allowing takeovers to function on the basis of value diversion is neither entirely feasible ex-post nor desirable ex-ante. On the other hand, takeovers are not the right tool to address the imperfections in the legal policing of non-pro-rata distributions; I will elaborate on this statement shortly.

If the amount of diversionary PBC in the ongoing management of listed companies is given, one should just be concerned that takeovers do not result in their increase (Bebchuk 1994). Constant diversion of shareholder value affects neither the probability of takeovers nor their efficiency, whereas its increase may determine their inefficiency. Of course, this scenario is the more unlikely the better diversionary PBC are policed by corporate law and related institutions (the lower the bound set on their extraction). However, upon a more careful investigation, the problem of shareholder value extraction through inefficient takeovers has a more general implication.

Assume for one moment that the incumbent controller is utmost honest (i.e., diversionary PBC are nil). This cannot depend on the legal system, which can at most set an upper bound on non-pro-rata distributions. Faced with a takeover proposal, our controller may find the temptation to cheat on shareholders irresistible. On the one hand, he may face no reputation constraint, for instance because this is the last corporate transaction before his retirement (a so-called 'endgame problem').[20] On the other hand, the legal system will anyway give the insurgent some leeway to expropriate shareholders for the simple reason that the incumbent is diverting nothing by assumption. Therefore, incumbent and insurgent can always reach an agreement on how to split the gains arising from expropriation of non-controlling shareholders in a control transaction, no matter how tightly ongoing diversion of shareholder value is constrained by corporate law. Such a takeover may be inefficient both ex-post and ex-ante: ex-post, because the insurgent may end up decreasing the overall firm value, and nonetheless find the takeover profitable to the extent that opportunity costs on *his* security benefits are more than compensated by higher diversion; ex-ante, because even if the transaction is merely redistributive of firm value, shareholders will be less willing to buy corporate stock under these conditions.

This extreme example illustrates the more general problem with diversionary PBC in the takeover process. First, the problem does not depend on the amount of diversion, but on its increase. Second, in the context of friendly takeovers, collusion between the incumbent and the insurgent is required. Third, incremental diversion is constrained by the scope for non-pro-rata distributions allowed by the legal system, but it is ultimately determined by

20 See e.g. Rock and Wachter (2001).

the terms of the control transaction. Let us define 'looting' as broadly as to include any instance of incremental diversion of shareholder value that may be involved by a control transaction. Let us also assume, for the moment, that the looter is as good a manager as the previous controller. The former may nonetheless purchase control from the latter if he bribes him high enough. For this strategy to be profitable, the cost of the bribe must be offset by incremental diversion involved with the control transaction.

7.4.5.2 The role of fiduciary duties in control transactions

Consider first the takeover of a free-standing firm and recall that the regulation of post-takeover squeeze-out should not allow the purchase of non-controlling shares on any more favorable terms than those concerning the acquisition of controlling ownership. Our looter would still have two options for making profits at the expenses of non-controlling shareholders. The first is to bid for the company's stock less than it is worth, squeeze-out non-tendering shareholders at the same price, and loot the rest of the firm's value (Bebchuk 1987). The success of this strategy requires collusion with the incumbent management, which is supposed to have inside information about the company's stock being undervalued. The only reason why insiders should do this is that they trade a lower bid price for a higher severance payment; the only way in which they can do this is by restricting actual or potential competition among bidders. The second option does not require collusion with the incumbent management, although collusion might be useful for the looter. The looter may simply acquire just enough shares to become the controlling shareholder and refrain from purchasing non-controlling stock (Kraakman et al 2009). The company need not be undervalued. The controller may subsequently force minority shareholders into a merger with a fully-owned subsidiary, in which either the value of their stock is diluted or they are otherwise frozen out for a lower consideration than the pre-takeover stock price (Bebchuk 1987). When the incumbent management colludes, the terms of this strategy may even be pre-arranged at the takeover stage.

Both looting strategies can be prevented by an appropriate configuration of fiduciary duties (see Easterbrook and Fischel 1991). As far as the first strategy is concerned, courts should just check whether the incumbent management is restricting competition for corporate control in order to increase the size of the severance payment. This behavior (playing favorites with the bidder that offers the most for the controlling position, but the least for the stock) would amount to outright breach of the duty of loyalty and it can be challenged on grounds of procedural fairness. Notice, however, that the definition of procedural unfairness should be broad enough as to include collusion also in the absence of competing bids – to the extent that stopping potential competition is sufficient to let the company be acquired below its value. The second strategy can be policed instead by the fiduciary duties of the controlling shareholder (Kraakman et al 2009). The latter will have quite a hard time in forcing minority shareholders into an unfavorable merger when his position on both sides of the transaction requires that 'entire fairness' of its substantive terms be proven in court. This might be somewhat easier when the terms are pre-arranged at the takeover stage so that these terms look more like the outcome of an arm's length transaction. However, courts may be inclined to review the substantive terms of the transaction when they suspect collusion (as in the US);[21] or they may require that the transaction be approved by would-be minority shareholders (as in the UK).[22]

Looting may seem easier when control is transferred by a controlling shareholder; but it is not easy at all if only fiduciary duties are strictly enforced. To start with, acquisition of undervalued stock is no option, at least to the extent that this is also prevented with reference to non-controlling shares. As we know, the last condition is satisfied by an appropriate configuration of the squeeze-out right. Then, both the seller and the acquirer should be subject to the fiduciary duties of the controlling shareholder. If this is true, the conscious sale of corporate control to a looter would not escape a judgment of procedural unfairness, whereas any looting attempt by the purchasing controlling shareholder would be carefully scrutinized under a strict standard of substantive fairness.[23] Assume that the sale of the control block is regulated by the market rule, so that any premium above the stock market price would be legitimate. What would not be legitimate is that this premium incorporates compensation for allowing the acquirer to loot the company. This would hardly be explicit in the terms of the transaction. The latter, however, should be regarded as procedurally unfair so long as it has no business purpose other than collusion for minority shareholders expropriation (see Bainbridge 2002). The standards regulating the acquirer's behavior should be stricter, no different from the case for acquisition of a free-standing firm. Any subsequent organic change in the corporate structure, or even worse a takeout of minority shareholders, should be possible only on condition that non-controlling shareholders are no worse off: either they knowledgeably approve the transaction, or the controlling shareholder has to prove its substantive fairness.

7.4.5.3 *Can takeovers simply lead to worse management?*

The conditions for looting to be profitable become stricter when – as is normally the case – the looter has no good managerial skills and he can only make the firm's management worse. Fiduciary duties cannot perform any worse in preventing inefficient takeovers under this more realistic assumption. However, the scenario changes when no looting is involved and the prospective acquirer is simply a worse manager. Fiduciary duties are ill equipped to tackle

21 See *infra* Chapter 8, section 8.2.1.
22 See *infra* Chapter 8, section 8.3.3.
23 See *supra* Chapters 5 and 6.

lack of skill or diligence – what I have labeled distortionary PBC. But can any such acquisition succeed? I do not believe it can if only corporate law prohibits the sale of office – which it normally does. I have already shown that, unless looting is at play, no acquirer may profit from a value-decreasing takeover if, in order to gain control, he has to acquire an ownership stake that is no lower than the incumbent's and to compensate his control rents upfront. These conditions are always met when takeovers are friendly and the acquirer cannot just purchase the controller's office.

A necessary corollary of the sale of office prohibition, in the acquisition of a free-standing firm, is that the incumbent management cannot play favorites with bidders concerning the size of severance payments because this may allow the firm's stock to be acquired below its value; we know that policing this kind of collusion is also necessary to prevent looting. Finally, the acquirer must not be allowed to subsidize a value-decreasing takeover through compulsory acquisition of non-controlling shares or outright diversion of their value.

In conclusion, when the sale of office is prohibited, a ban on looting is both a necessary and a sufficient condition for value-decreasing takeovers to be ruled out. Post-takeover squeeze-out does not affect this result, but only maximizes the probability of value-increasing takeovers, when it is regulated efficiently.

7.4.5.4 *Can takeover regulation substitute for weak fiduciary duties?*

Two potential objections to this reasoning can be anticipated. The first is that legal systems that perform poorly in policing ongoing extraction of diversionary PBC cannot be reasonably expected to provide an effective ban on looting in takeovers. This makes sense, and indeed represents the strongest argument in favor of the mandatory bid rule in spite of its many drawbacks (Enriques and Gatti 2007). If we assume that corporate law is unable to set a sufficiently low upper bound on the controller's ability to implement non-pro-rata distributions, only controlling shareholder systems are feasible in corporate governance (Bebchuk 1999). Then the risk is high that takeovers result in further inefficiency, both ex-ante and ex-post, due to looting. In order to ensure some investors' confidence, it might be preferable to prevent this result from occurring by compelling the control premium to be shared with minority shareholders in the event of a takeover. This rule is easy to enforce in spite of corporate law's deficiencies in coping with stealing by controlling shareholders (Gilson 2006).

However, there are both practical and logical counter arguments. The practical ones are that the rule has a very high cost in terms of efficiency of the takeover process, and that a more efficient dynamics of control allocation can only be allowed to the extent that the mandatory bid is circumvented or made less burdensome: either solution cannot avoid the risk of value-decreasing takeovers. The logical counter argument is that policing diversionary PBC through takeover regulation is inappropriate: the problem of non-pro-rata distributions is both broader and different from the efficiency of changes in control. Non-pro-rata distributions have only side-effects on the market for corporate control. Stealing in corporate governance should be addressed by different legal tools. In conclusion, what can only be conceded to this position is that improvement of these tools is a precondition for a more liberal approach to takeover regulation (see also Kraakman et al 2009).

This leads me to the second potential objection: the approach to shareholder protection that I am advocating is based on incremental diversion being ruled out from takeovers, but can do nothing to decrease the amount of diversionary PBC in the system. Apparently, an alternative regulation may also achieve this result. According to Professor Gilson (2006), the combination of the mandatory bid with the breakthrough rule may allow cross-border acquisitions to eliminate progressively diversionary PBC. This result is derived combining two constraints: one on the incumbent's ability to protect his private benefits (breakthrough) and another on the insurgent's ability to extract his own (mandatory bid). Under these conditions, takeovers are efficient when the acquirer is committed to transforming previous diversion in future firm residual; and they are profitable to the extent that the acquirer can share with tendering shareholders the expected benefits from doing so.

However, there are a number of problems with this mechanism, which make it unlikely to produce the desired outcome. First, there is no legal system that can possibly guarantee a full commitment to no diversion of shareholder value; this turns the goal of elimination of diversionary PBC into, at best, their reduction. Second, as we have seen, the breakthrough rule can never be entirely effective in disrupting rent protection, whether this would be efficient (as in the case of diversionary PBC) or not (as in the case of idiosyncratic PBC). Third, Professor Gilson does not consider the possibility that idiosyncratic control rents are *also* involved on both the incumbent and the insurgent's side.[24] As he recognizes, hostile acquisitions are both undesirable and likely to be short-circuited when the 'good kind' of PBC determines the presence of controlling shareholders.[25] The problem is that the same conclusion holds when the two kinds of private benefits are simultaneously at play and the relative proportions are not known. It would be unrealistic to assume that control only features diversionary PBC in this case. Therefore, seeking reduction of diversionary PBC through an artificial injection of hostility in the takeover process may ultimately undermine the efficient protection of control rents in corporate governance.

---

24 See instead Coates (2004) for the explicit discussion of this hypothesis.
25 "In contrast, the breakthrough rule's threat to control in efficient controlling shareholder systems would be substantially more muted. Because of the low level of pecuniary private benefits of control in an efficient controlling shareholder system, there would be no easy source of premiums for would-be bidders" Gilson (2006: 1677).

8 Comparative takeover law

8.1 Two opposite models of takeover regulation

After the extensive discussion of the functional elements in the previous chapter, the analysis of takeover regulation is going to be relatively straightforward from both a positive and a normative standpoint. Yet takeover regulation is a relatively recent phenomenon. It has emerged to cope with the new problems arising from the increase in the frequency of changes in control brought about by likewise increasing separation of ownership and control. The two phenomena are in fact related, and their relationship is supported by the stock market development that nurtures both firms' access to equity finance and vibrant markets for corporate control (Mayer and Sussman 2001). The characteristics of this relationship, and its bearing on the patterns of economic growth, are far beyond the scope of this inquiry. However, it is no coincidence that takeover regulation was established in those countries that experienced, before others, extensive separation of ownership and control, and still lead the rest of the world in this particular respect. These countries are the United Kingdom and the United States.

In the second half of the twentieth century, it became evident in both countries that separation of ownership and control was creating a market for corporate control on the side of the stock market (Coffee 2001b). Paralleling the shrinkage of controlling ownership, hostile takeovers became not only a matter of academic debate, but also an opportunity for profits that were unimaginable in connection with more traditional patterns of stock trading. This created two separate, and in a sense opposite, concerns: on the one hand, the concern that corporate control becomes unstable, forcing managers to forego long-term investments for short-term stock returns (Shleifer and Vishny 1990); on the other hand, the concern of corporate ownership being under-protected, which exposes shareholders to the risk of not being dealt with fairly (Franks et al 2009). Takeover regulation was initially established to address these concerns, narrowing the scope for hostile acquisitions (Armour and Skeel 2007). In the US, securities regulation placed a number of constraints on the rider's ability to profit from pre-bid purchases and from any discriminatory structure of the tender offer.[1] In

---

1 The Williams Act was passed in 1968, introducing a federal discipline of tender offers. The Securities Act of 1934 was amended accordingly. See Easterbrook and Fischel (1991).

the UK, the rider was even obliged to make an 'any or all' bid for outstanding shares in order to take over – a solution which was never introduced in American law.[2] Then, American state laws enabled the board of directors to provide further safeguards against hostile acquisitions, and so did Delaware courts; whereas the British regulation preferred having the hurdles of the mandatory bid tempered by the prohibition of directors from frustrating a takeover attempt.

Nowadays, American and British law provide two opposite models of takeover regulation (Kraakman et al 2009). The historical roots of this divergence have been very nicely illustrated in both the economic and the legal literature of the past few years.[3] Here I just want to avoid one typical misunderstanding arising from the comparisons of Anglo-American takeover regulation: that regulation in the US is just management-oriented (or captured), since it allows contestability of corporate control to be restricted; whereas the British regulation is just more shareholder-oriented, for it has been influenced by the long-standing power of institutional investors, and then it promotes contestability. This would be a superficial account of two models of takeover regulation that have proven, at least so far, to be the best in the world. Corporate governance in both the US and the UK is characterized by vibrant markets for corporate control. However, none of them is actually driven by hostile takeovers, which – despite the appearance – are very exceptional events in both countries (Schwert 2000; Weir and Laing 2003).

Therefore, the performance of takeover regulation does not depend mainly on whether and to what extent it promotes contestability. It depends much more on how smoothly regulation allows takeovers to be operated on a negotiated basis, because this is the way in which the overwhelming majority of changes in control are operated. Corporate controllers cannot be prevented from entrenching themselves if they so wish; however, they can be induced to part with control when this is efficient.

Having already suggested that the American regulation may perform somewhat better in this respect, I shall elaborate upon this shortly. But it is worth noting that, in both the US and the UK, takeover regulation forms a system with the rest of the institutional and legal discipline of corporate governance. In Britain, the mandatory bid and the requirement that takeovers cannot be frustrated by the incumbent management may be regarded as distortions of a more efficient market mechanism. However, neither do they inhibit the incumbent management's actual involvement in the takeover process nor do they prevent, for the most part, efficient control transactions

2 See the City Code on Takeovers and Mergers (September 2011) – hereinafter the City Code – providing that takeover bids must be unrestricted, save for exceptional circumstances, and that they are mandatory when the 30% threshold of share ownership is surpassed by a person or a group of shareholders acting in concert.
3 See for instance Franks et al (2005), Armour and Skeel (2007), and Cheffins (2008).

from taking place. None of these results may hold if the British environment was not also very unfavorable to controlling shareholdings. In a sense, the bias against controlling shareholders may be regarded as perhaps the only distortion in the British discipline of corporate governance. The UK takeover regulation pretty well fits this system (although it can be improved); but the same takeover regulation may have disruptive effects on the dynamics of control allocation when it is applied to a corporate governance characterized by the dominant presence of controlling shareholders. This is, in essence, the mistake of having followed the British model in the European regulation of takeovers. We will come to this issue after a more detailed comparison of takeover regulation in the US and the UK.

8.2 The discipline of control transactions in the US

We have seen in the foregoing chapters that one point of strength of the American discipline of corporate governance lies in its being equally suitable to managerial and shareholder control, when both the distribution of control powers and the prevention of their abuse are considered. The same basically holds for the discipline of control transactions. This time, let us consider managerial control and shareholder control separately. It will be shown that US takeover regulation performs equally well in preventing value-decreasing changes in control and in promoting value-increasing ones when a controlling shareholder or professional managers are in charge.

8.2.1 *Takeover of free-standing firms*

8.2.1.1 *The management's bargaining power*

American managers traditionally face few constraints on their ability to cash in control rents via a takeover (Kraakman et al 2009).[4] Golden parachutes are customarily a part of the manager's compensation package (Kahan and Rock 2002); and they can be renegotiated in the event of an acquisition (Almazan and Suarez 2003). The empirical evidence shows that these renegotiations are a part of the takeover bargaining strategy, and that they systematically determine a lower takeover premium for outside shareholders (Hartzell et al 2004). However, it is unclear from regression analysis whether severance payments and other benefits from the incumbent management's exit come at the expense of target shareholders. It actually seems that renegotiation of severance payments is more than offset by reduction of the takeover premium. On the one hand, this means that "acquirer-paid sweeteners" reduce the overall cost of acquisitions; on the other hand, this may involve that target shareholders are being exploited

---

4 But see *infra* on the changes recently introduced by the Dodd-Frank Act.

by trading higher severance payments for lower takeover premia (Bebchuk and Fried 2004).

However, corporate law in the US prevents managers, at least in their capacity as directors, from playing this kind of trick with shareholders. There are several elements of Delaware case-law which make sure that directors cannot trade higher severance payments for a lower takeover bid, even though they otherwise enjoy a considerable degree of freedom in bargaining over both their golden parachutes and shareholders' takeover premium *separately*. Simply put, they can do anything except colluding with the bidder on severance payments, because they are strictly prohibited from restricting bidding competition in such a fashion. In negotiating an acquisition, there are a number of legal constraints on the management's ability to collude with the acquirer.

A first constraint is that a reasonable investigation has to be made on possible alternatives for a plainly negotiated deal to go through safely (Bainbridge 2002). This is especially required by Delaware courts when the reputational incentives of the CEO – who gives the green light to the acquisition and is also supposed to exert a considerable influence over the other board members – are weakened by his being at the end of his career (a typical endgame problem which makes hidden conflict of interest the most worrisome) (Rock and Wachter 2001). Although the failure to conduct this investigation on potential bidders is regarded as a breach of the duty of care, and not of the duty of loyalty, the result is unchanged. The only positive significance attached by law and economics commentators to the famous *Smith v. Van Gorkom* decision,[5] in spite of the contradictions with the business judgment rule, is that it may counter the tendency of incumbent managers to conceal a sale of office under the appearance of an arm's length control transaction, which may be especially problematic when they are in their last period of play.

Even in the absence of the *Van Gorkom* ruling, the management should be very careful in negotiating side payments in exchange for low bids. "Where side payments persuade the target's board to accept a low initial offer, a second bidder may – and often does – succeed by offering shareholders a higher-priced alternative" (Bainbridge 2002: 650). Then the game would be over because in this case Delaware law compels directors to simply accept the highest bid. Bidding competition triggers the *Revlon* standard, according to which the board should behave like a neutral auctioneer.[6] Does this mean that directors have *always* to seek for the highest takeover premium for shareholders? The answer, in general, is no. This is indeed the peculiarity of Delaware law when it comes to takeover regulation. Facing

---

5 Smith v. Van Gorkom, 488 A.2d 858 (Del.Sup.1985), discussed *supra* Chapter 6, section 6.2.2.
6 Revlon, Inc. v. MacAndrews and Forbes Holdings, Inc., 506 A.2d 173 (Del.Sup.1986), discussed *supra* Chapter 4, section 4.3.1.

an unwanted takeover bid, directors may 'just say no.' On condition that this does not absolutely prevent the firm from being acquired in the future, this decision will be upheld by Delaware courts under the business judgment rule.[7]

This is how American directors came to enjoy so much bargaining power in corporate acquisitions. When the time to sell has come, 'saying no' could always be the best strategy to start negotiations (Schwert 2000). Then the bargaining would start and it may initially also concern the severance payment. When a competing bid materializes, the bargaining power of incumbent management would stop. However, as we have seen in the previous chapter, competition would also be against the interest of the first bidder. Therefore, the insurgent and the incumbent are most likely to settle for a severance payment high enough to induce management to part with control and a takeover premium attractive enough to allow the bid to be uncontested and successful.[8]

This strategy is compatible with a number of phenomena that we observe in the takeover practice, like for instance the attraction by the management of a favored bid (so-called 'white knight'). Short of promoting real competition, white knights, greenmail, and similar tactics could simply serve the purpose to raise the incumbent management's outside option. If that is the case, these techniques are to be regarded as a part of the bargaining strategy of the management (Shleifer and Vishny 1986b).

In the aftermath of the global financial crisis, US securities regulation has placed some additional constraints on the ability of managers to bargain for a severance payment. The Dodd-Frank Act of 2010 has introduced "say on pay" on all forms of managerial remuneration, including golden parachutes.[9] Particularly, as far as the latter are concerned, all arrangements in connection with a change in control need to be subject to an advisory shareholder vote if they have not already been through such a vote before. Say-on-pay votes are compulsory, but they are not binding on the board. Still, unfavorable say-on-pay votes are not irrelevant because they may be a first step towards a campaign of vote withholding at the annual elections.[10] In the context of takeovers, it is hard to predict what the impact of "say on golden parachutes" would be, also because the new rules are being first applied at the time of writing. However, because of the endgame situation, a non-binding vote on severance payments may have a limited impact on the managers' ability to claim compensation of their control rents. Whether this will be actually the case is an empirical question that can be answered only in the next few years.

---

7 See *supra* Chapter 4, section 4.3.1.
8 See *supra*, Chapter 7, section 7.3.1.
9 See Section 951 of Dodd-Frank Act 2010 (as implemented by the SEC Releases Nos. 33-9178 and 34-63768 on Jan 25, 2011).
10 See *supra* Chapter 4, section 4.3.1.

8.2.1.2 *Freeze-outs and shareholder protection*

The American discipline of the incumbent's behavior conforms to the key functional elements of an efficient takeover regulation. The option of management entrenchment is coupled with the possibility to renegotiate severance payments, whereas opportunistic renegotiation at the shareholders' expense is constrained by a meaningful prohibition of the sale of office.

What about the acquirer's gains? In the US, this problem is tackled by a complicated body of rules, which results in a rather unique discipline of freeze-outs. This discipline makes sure that non-controlling shareholders cannot be made worse-off by a takeover, whereas the acquirer is entitled to reap all the gains necessary to motivate an efficient change in control. Takeover premia are determined independently by the pattern of negotiations between the bidder and the incumbent board described above. As a result, this legal arrangement maximizes the chances that value-increasing acquisitions go through, while ensuring that value-decreasing takeovers cannot be subsidized by inefficient freeze-out of non-tendering shareholders. The residual possibility that takeovers feature higher diversionary private benefits of control (PBC) is also excluded by a strict enforcement of the controlling shareholder's fiduciary duties, which result in an effective ban on post-takeover looting. The latter will be discussed later.

A major source of uniqueness of the American discipline of freeze-out is the traditional absence of a discipline of legal capital (Enriques and Macey 2001). This implies that shareholders can easily exit the company receiving cash out of the corporate treasury. One typical way to do this is the so-called cash-out merger, by which minority shareholders receive cash as consideration while the controlling shareholder gets all the shares of the surviving company (which is normally a wholly owned subsidiary) (Hamilton 2000). The transactional technique may vary, but the key problem is always the adequacy of the consideration received by minority shareholders. For this reason, originally, corporate law used to require unanimous shareholder approval of mergers. Given the evident hold-up potential of this rule, it was rapidly replaced with majority approval. Most American states – including Delaware – today require only 50% of outstanding shares to approve a merger, although a few states still require a 2/3 majority (see Bainbridge 2002). In exchange for that, the possibility for dissenting shareholders to have their share judicially appraised was introduced in statutory law (Easterbrook and Fischel 1991). The bottom line is that the ability to operate a cash-out merger is now generally conditional on the acquisition of the absolute majority of outstanding shares. As it has been efficaciously pointed out, this is a form of "private eminent domain," which is only apparently tempered by the statutory appraisal right (Bainbridge 2002: 352). Indeed, this right provides minority shareholders with a very weak protection from receiving an inadequate consideration for their shares.

A thorough illustration of the appraisal right would lead us far away from the focus of this discussion. In general, the exercise of the appraisal right confronts individual shareholders with both high costs – they are not entitled to a class proceeding – and a number of 'traps for the unwary' – they may only seek appraisal between *refusing* to tender and voting *against* the merger (Hamilton 2000). More importantly, in takeovers, the appraisal remedy does not entitle shareholders to participate in *any* of the gains at stake. "In practice, shareholders have no reason to expect that the court's appraisal will be larger than an offer price which exceeds the pre-offer share price" (Amihud et al 2004). Therefore, in spite of the appraisal right, freeze-out is a credible threat that shareholders may be exploited by a takeover. That is, freeze-outs backed by an appraisal remedy still generate pressure to tender (Bebchuk 1987). The only possible constraint arising from the appraisal right is that negative takeover premia are disallowed. In terms of our functional framework, this is equivalent to a sell-out right setting the pre-takeover price as a lower bound on the bid price. The hurdles of individual enforcement of this right make it quite a shaky condition for takeovers to be only value-increasing; in any case, the condition is not sufficient. Fortunately, the statutory appraisal is neither the end of the freeze-out story in the US, nor the most important part of it.

The core of freeze-out law in the US lies in the fiduciary duties judicially imposed on both the target board and the acquirer, as soon as he becomes a controlling shareholder (Kraakman et al 2009). In the leading case *Weinberger v. UOP*, the Supreme Court of Delaware ruled that a freeze-out merger must satisfy an 'entire fairness' standard, including simultaneously 'fair price' and 'fair dealing.'[11] On the one hand, this strengthens the lower bound on the squeeze-out consideration set by the appraisal right equal to the pre-takeover price: despite *Weinberger*'s opining to the contrary – which was subsequently overruled – a freeze-out merger does not preclude the enforcement of fiduciary duties through derivative litigation.[12] On the other hand, "the test is not a bifurcated one."[13] Thus, once fair dealing is in question, the requirement of fair price must also be satisfied in order for freeze-out to be legal. An acquirer will have little chance to meet these requirements after he becomes a

---

11 Weinberger v. OUP, Inc., 457 A.2d 701 (Del.Sup.1983).

12 Technically, *Weinberger* is a complicated opinion. It overruled a number of precedents, but only did so prospectively. Under *Singer*, the statutory appraisal was not the sole remedy available to disgruntled shareholders in a cash-out merger. Singer v. Magnavox Co., 380 A.2d 969 (Del.Sup.1977). *Weinberger* still granted shareholders a cause of action on equitable grounds, but ruled that, for the future, shareholder remedies should have been confined to those available under the statutory appraisal procedure (which, as we know, does not allows for a class action). The Supreme Court of Delaware did not hold on this position for long. In *Rabkin*, it ruled that *Weinberger* only precluded class (derivative) actions challenging fairness of the price. Rabkin v. Philip A. Hunt Chemical Corp., 498 A.2d 1099 (Del.Sup.1985). At least in Delaware, fair dealing can still be questioned at common law. In contrast, § 13.02 of the Revised Model Business Corporation Act (MBCA) makes the appraisal remedy exclusive "unless the action is unlawful or fraudulent with respect to the shareholders or the corporation." See Bainbridge (2002: 358–360).

13 Weinberger v. OUP, Inc., 457 A.2d 701, 713 (Del.Sup.1983).

controlling shareholder. He would be on both sides of the freeze-out transaction then, and this would automatically exclude fair dealing in the absence of independent approval.[14] If we reason by backwards induction, this is extremely risky for a would-be acquirer, since the failure to obtain approval by the majority of (remaining) minority shareholders will compromise the legality of the cash-out merger and, in turn, the profitability of the takeover. However, the acquirer also has the option of negotiating the freeze-out merger as a follow-up of the takeover bid, when he is not yet a controlling shareholder and the fiduciary duties apply to the target board only (Amihud et al 2004). This solution requires the cooperation of the target board and that the squeeze-out price is set somewhat higher than the pre-takeover price, but in any case equal to the bid price.

Board cooperation is no problem in our framework, since it is bound to obtain for the takeover to be operated, at the end of the day, as a friendly deal. To understand why the squeeze-out price must rise up to the level of the bid price, consider instead the following circumstances. First, Delaware judges consider freeze-out too dangerous to be protected by the business judgment rule at any rate: this means that fair dealing may only result in a shift of the burden of proof – i.e., disgruntled shareholders may still prove that the freeze-out consideration was unfair (Kraakman et al 2009). Second, the target board can satisfy the fair dealing requirement by negotiating with the bidder the terms of the post-takeover merger, submitting the agreement to an independent special-purpose committee, and, on condition that the special committee endorses it (which it will normally do), have the merger approved by shareholders.[15] This last requirement is considered implicitly satisfied when the majority of shareholders of a free-standing firm tender their shares, provided that there is no coercion. Third, shareholders may still challenge the transaction on grounds that freeze-out consideration is unfair, when the latter is any lower than the bid price. However, when the two are equal, neither the coercion of the bid nor the unfairness of the freeze-out price can be invoked to question the validity of the deal – provided that none of them is lower than the current stock price.[16] This is how freeze-out law in the US is interpreted as requiring that the squeeze-out price be equal to the highest between the bid and the market price (Amihud et al 2004).

---

14 When there is a controlling shareholder the requirement of independent approval of conflicting transactions is met when a majority of minority shareholders (hereinafter MOM) approve the deal on the basis of adequate information about its terms. To this purpose, an opinion should be issued by a special-purpose committee (SC) of independent directors. See Bainbridge (2002).

15 Kahn v. Lynch Communication Systems, 638 A.2d 1110, 1117 (Del.Sup.1994).

16 This issue is quite technical as a matter of civil procedure and it is not really necessary to discuss it in detail. It is only worth noting that coercion impinges on fair dealing, which is easier to challenge in the courts. On the contrary, fairness of price can only be challenged in a statutory appraisal proceeding when fair dealing is not in question. When the squeeze-out price is equal to the bid, the transaction can hardly be attacked on either ground.

It is important to emphasize that such an arrangement would not be available to the acquirer at a later stage, namely when he has become a controlling shareholder: normally, he will have either to prove 'entire fairness' of freeze-out or to seek approval by a majority of *remaining* minority shareholders in order to shift the burden of proof. The importance of this remark will get clearer in the analysis of sales of control blocks. Conversely, the developments of Delaware case-law have made somewhat easier to implement the above mechanism of pre-arranged freeze-out. The issue is known under the heading of *Siliconix* and its progeny, and it has been quite debated in the American legal literature (Subramanian 2007). After the Chancery Court's ruling in *Siliconix* (confirmed, one month later, by the Supreme Court in *Glassman*), Delaware courts do no longer apply the entire fairness test for reviewing freeze-outs, so long as they are implemented through a short-form merger follow-up to a tender offer and the consideration is equal to the bid price.[17] The advantage of a short-form merger is that it does not require approval by either the target's board or its shareholder.[18] The disadvantage is that at least 90% of outstanding shares are needed to operate it.[19] All in all, the new judicial safe harbor adds little to the ability of the acquirer of a free-standing firm to efficiently squeeze-out minority shareholders, save that making the bid conditional on 90% of the shares being tendered might be desirable for the deal to be insulated from shareholder litigation. However, this ruling may have important implications in acquisitions from controlling shareholders, which – at least to my knowledge – have not yet been completely explored.

8.2.1.3 *Are shareholders protected any further?*

To conclude about the acquirer's gains, it should be noticed that American law does not otherwise feature distortions of the takeover process. To start with, there is no general requirement of a mandatory bid. Federal regulation does not even prevent restricted bids, so long as shareholder rationing is executed pro-rata and not on a 'first-come, first-served' basis (Armour and Skeel 2007). The federal requirement that all tendering shareholders shall be granted equal treatment does not alter the overall picture. The substantial disclosure obligations imposed on both the bidder and the target's board by securities regulation indeed affect the overall cost of takeovers, but I am not considering this problem here. Still, some constraints on the structure of the bid do arise under state law, and at first glance, they may seem to be equivalent to a mandatory bid (Berglöf and Burkart 2003). Upon a more careful

---

17 In re Siliconix, Inc. Shareholders Litigation, 2001 WL 716787 (Del.Ch.2001); Glassman v. Unocal Exploration Corp., 777 A.2d 242 (Del.Sup.2001).

18 In a short-form merger, minority shareholders are only entitled to the appraisal of their shares (Kraakman et al 2009).

19 DGCL § 253(a) and MBCA § 11.05.

investigation, however, they turn out to be irrelevant so long as the bid is operated as a part of a negotiated deal with the target's board.

Many states feature anti-takeover statutes in their corporate law.[20] So-called 'fair price' provisions are an illustrative example. By and large, these provisions – which may alternatively be included in the company's articles of incorporation – confer upon shareholders the right to be bought out at the highest price paid by a rider in the acquisition of corporate control. Apparently, this amounts to a sell-out right in the worst possible configuration for the acquirer, since it may force him to give up most of the takeover gains and possibly all of them. In addition, fair price provisions exclude the possibility of two-tier offers since the squeeze-out option is superseded by a more favorable sell-out right. However, this right is only triggered by unwanted acquisitions and has therefore the same practical effect of a poison pill. That is, it forces would-be acquirers to come to terms with the target's board. As a result, two-tier bids are of no use in any case: they cannot be used to overcome the board's resistance (which is always allowed, if not required, by Delaware courts in the presence of a coercive bid);[21] they cannot be featured by a negotiated deal, because coercion would make such a deal illegal. It is thus unsurprising that two-tier bids have disappeared from the takeover practice in the US (Amihud et al 2004). In addition, fair price statutes or charter provisions have no effect on the structure of a takeover bid, provided that it is negotiated with the incumbent board. Indeed, in other states (like in Delaware), these provisions are replicated by statutes that more explicitly prevent raiders from operating 'business combinations' (including a freeze-out merger) for some time, in the absence of previous agreement with the target board or subsequent approval by a super-majority of minority shareholders.[22]

Finally, the sophistication of Delaware courts in enforcing fiduciary duties prevents takeovers from being driven by diversion of shareholder value. To start with, the acquirer cannot collude with the target's board for looting the company, because – as we have seen – the fiduciary obligations of the board

---

20 State anti-takeover legislation is a big issue in the history of US corporate law. It involves a number of legal technicalities which are not even touched upon here. There are at least three generations of anti-takeover statutes. The first one – giving state officers veto power over the acquisition of any company doing business in the state – was declared unconstitutional by the US Supreme Court. Edgar v. MITE Corp., 457 U.S. 624, 102 S.Ct. 2629, 73 L.Ed.2d 269 (1982). The second generation – including 'fair price' statutes – was upheld by the Supreme Court in CTS Corp. v. Dynamics Corp., 481 U.S. 69, 107 S.Ct. 1637, 95 L.Ed.2d 67 (1987). The third-generation statutes – so-called 'business combination statutes' – have considerably more bite on unwanted takeovers, since they prevent the acquirer from operating a merger in the absence of approval by either the board (before the acquisition) or a super-majority of minority shareholder (after the acquisition). Delaware has enacted a statute of this type. See *infra* in the text and Bainbridge (2002) for more details.

21 Unocal Corp. v. Mesa Petroleum Co., 493 A.2d 946 (Del.Sup.1985).

22 DGCL § 203. Note that § 203 may be opted out by the articles of incorporation. In addition, the restrictions on business combinations are waived conditional upon acquisition of 85% of the stock which is not under the insiders' control.

exclude any form of collusion with bidders. More importantly, however, the acquirer is effectively prevented from looting the company on his own. On the one hand, when he acts in his capacity as controlling shareholder, the acquirer is prevented from entering into any transaction that may deprive minority shareholders of anything belonging to them. Whenever a potential conflict of interest is involved, the transaction must be approved by a majority of the minority or, alternatively, it requires that entire fairness be proved by the controlling shareholder.[23] On the other hand, exploiting minority shareholders through unfavorable freeze-out terms is also not an option, because this kind of transaction is likewise subject to the entire fairness standard of review.[24] This point is better illustrated with reference to the sale of control blocks.

8.2.2 Taking over from a controlling shareholder

8.2.2.1 Regulation of control sales

In the US, the sale of control blocks is regulated by the market rule (Bebchuk 1994). Acquirers have neither to make a tender offer for non-controlling stock nor to provide minority shareholders with equal opportunities as to the control transaction (Kraakman et al 2009). On the one hand, this implies that the incumbent may cash in his control rents through bargaining with the insurgent, which will actually result in a change in control inasmuch as it leaves the latter with a sufficient share of the takeover gains. On the other hand, minority shareholders have no right of exit, nor are they entitled to share in the control premium at any rate. The question that naturally arises is how shareholders are otherwise protected from value-decreasing changes in control that, apparently, could just be imposed upon them. This question has not been neglected by American courts, which occasionally 'flirted' with the equal opportunity rule (Easterbrook and Fischel 1991). However, the latter rule has never become a part of the US states common law.

Both courts and commentators tend to regard sales of control blocks on the free market as transactions that are normally beneficial to minority share-holders, in that they essentially feature an efficient dynamics of control allocation. This view is supported by the empirical evidence, at least that regarding block trades in the US (Holderness 2003). As a result, one funda-mental principle of American corporate law is that controlling shareholders are free to dispose of their stock as they wish, and they may decide to sell or not to sell corporate control without consulting the minority. This principle is rather unique in the discipline of listed firms by most developed countries, but – even in the US – it is not without exceptions.

23 See *supra* Chapter 6, section 6.2.2.
24 Weinberger v. OUP, Inc., 457 A.2d 701 (Del.Sup.1983).

To start with, a controlling shareholder is not entitled to sell to a looter. This may seem rather obvious in case of outright fraud, but the transaction may also be challenged on grounds of gross negligence or misrepresentation of material facts. By and large, a *Van Gorkom*-type suit might be brought on the first grounds, not because the controlling shareholder has a positive duty to investigate, but because courts would hold him liable when it was apparent from the transaction terms that it had hardly any business purpose other than looting (Rock and Wachter 2001). A class action might be brought on the second grounds, when the sale is operated in connection with trading on the market and it is not timely and properly disclosed (Hamilton 2000).

Second, a controlling shareholder is prohibited (as is the management) from selling the office. The prohibition has little bite given the acquirer's ability to take control of the board without cooperation by the seller, as soon as he purchases the majority of voting stock. The prohibition is only useful to guarantee that no change in control can take place without transfer of controlling ownership (Easterbrook and Fischel 1991).

Third, recent developments in Delaware case-law suggest that a somewhat stricter approach to the payment of the control premium is in the making. In 2005, the Chancery Court held that entire fairness of a merger granting a 10% premium on high-voting shares was a triable issue, at least in the absence of properly independent approval by a special-purpose committee; but the case never went to trial.[25] In 2009 the Chancery Court again ruled that a controlling shareholder is entitled to a control premium; such transactions are entitled to the protection of the business judgment rule so long as there are robust procedural protections for the minority shareholders.[26] However, in 2012, Vice-Chancellor Glasscock ruled that even in the presence of these procedural safeguards, the conflicts of interest of the controlling shareholder in selling the company for a control premium may come under judicial scrutiny.[27] Although Delaware law still allows controllers to negotiate a control premium, the judiciary has become increasingly suspicious of differential treatments of non-controlling shareholders.

8.2.2.2 *Protection of minority shareholders*

Much more important is that, however control is transferred, the acquirer is prevented from abusing minority shareholders. As I showed in Chapter 6, the

---

25 The Chancery Court considered, in a summary judgment action, a stockholder challenge to the acquisition of Tele-Communication, Inc. (TCI) by AT&T Corp., in which TCI's controller demanded for his Class B (super-voting) shares a 10% premium to Class A shares. See In re Tele-Communications, Inc. Shareholders Litigation, 2005 WL 3642727 (Del.Ch. Dec. 21, 2005, revised Jan. 10, 2006).

26 In re John Q. Hammons, Inc. Shareholder Litigation, C.A. No. 758-CC (Del.Ch. Oct. 2, 2009).

27 In re Delphi Financial Group Shareholder Litigation, C.A. No. 7144-VCG (Del.Ch. Mar. 6, 2012).

strictness of fiduciary duties in the US provides an effective upper bound on the controlling shareholder's ability to siphon off assets from the company. If we take into account that courts also police collusion, especially when it comes to looting, it is unlikely that sales of control blocks can be motivated by the acquirer's ability to extract higher diversionary PBC than the seller. Still, as we know, a majority shareholder is entitled by American law to freeze-out minority shareholders. The fiduciary duties prevent him from choosing this strategy on unfavorable terms to minority shareholders.

When a controlling shareholder is in charge, the demanding requirements of *Weinberger* apply. To start with, shareholders cannot be frozen out at any lower consideration than the market price. More importantly, there is no price that guarantees that the transaction is entirely fair, which is something that the controlling shareholder has almost no chance of proving so long as he profits from the transaction – a necessary condition from entering into it in the first place. The only possible way out of this bind is seeking a shift of the burden of proof through approval by a majority of the minority, which can be characterized as fair dealing so long as it is supported by the opinion of a special-purpose committee guaranteeing independent information.[28] Then, a freeze-out merger can go through only for a higher consideration than the market price. Proving unfairness of such consideration in the presence of independent approval is nearly as hard as proving the contrary in its absence: there is no such thing as an objective 'fair price' for the company's stock.

8.2.2.3 Post-takeover freeze-out: the short-form merger solution

While the above arrangement protects minority shareholders from expropriation, it does not protect the acquirer of a control block from shareholders free riding: the majority of the minority requirement still gives shareholders the opportunity to holdout. We know that coping with the free rider problem is no less important for the efficiency of the takeover process.[29] The American system of fiduciary duties may also provide a way out of this problem. The post-*Siliconix* developments of Delaware case-law allow controlling shareholders to avoid the review of freeze-out transactions under the entire fairness standard, if only these transactions are implemented by a particular tender offer for non-controlling shares and the requirement of fair dealing is fulfilled.[30]

The deal can be structured as follows. After gaining control of the company, and *whenever he finds it profitable*, the acquirer makes a tender offer for non-controlling stock combined with pre-arrangement of freeze-out of non-tendering shareholders at the *same* price. Normally, this transaction would be

---

28 Kahn v. Lynch Communication Systems, 638 A.2d 1110 (Del.Sup.1994).
29 See *supra* Chapter 7, section 7.3.2.
30 In re Siliconix, Inc. Shareholders Litigation, 2001 WL 716787 (Del.Ch.2001).

subject to the entire fairness standard.[31] But there is a way to escape this. Freeze-outs are no longer regarded as conflicted interest transactions when they are executed as a short-form merger, since the controlling shareholder (the parent company) has the statutory entitlement to perform it without both a conflicted shareholder vote and an equally conflicted board approval by the subsidiary.[32] A vote of neither body is required when the parent company owns at least 90% of the outstanding stock.[33] Therefore, the next step is making the bid conditional on acquisition of at least 90% of the company's shares.

At common law, judges are constrained by statutes, but they need not otherwise refrain from applying fiduciary duties. Although a freeze-out merger cannot involve a breach of fiduciary duties when it is executed in the short-form, a tender offer conditional on enabling a short-form merger potentially could.[34] The requirements of fair dealing and fair price are then restored at the bid stage, albeit in a very special configuration.[35] The fair dealing requirement is met by tendering by the majority of minority shareholders, provided that they are adequately informed by a special-purpose committee and that the opinion of the latter is not tainted by "retributive threats" by the controlling shareholder.[36] An additional requirement of fair dealing is that the bid be non-coercive: for this reason, the bid and the freeze-out price must coincide. But what about fair price?

A non-coercive bid can only be successful when it offers shareholders a consideration somewhat higher than the current market price. Disgruntled shareholders would have a hard time proving the unfairness of such a consideration, and would only get a lower one if they seek appraisal of their shares. As a result, shareholders will accept the deal when the premium is attractive enough, and the controller would refrain from offering any premium when the stock price is already too high. It is also worth noting that the

---

31 The peculiarity of this freeze-out transaction is that the requirement of independent shareholder approval may be considered implicitly met if a majority of the minority has tendered their shares based on independent advice by a SC of outside directors. However, under *Kahn*, this would only be sufficient to shift the burden of proof while having no impact on the standard of review. It is exactly this point that has changed after *Siliconix*. See Subramanian (2007).

32 Glassman v. Unocal Exploration Corp., 777 A.2d 242 (Del.Sup.2001).

33 DGCL § 253(a).

34 The empirical evidence about the wealth effects of post-*Siliconix* freeze-outs on target shareholders is mixed. Two independent studies report opposite results. For the view that these transactions are detrimental to minority shareholders, see Subramanian (2007); for the contrary view see Bates et al (2006).

35 This result obtains as a doctrinal combination of *Siliconix* (in the presence of fair dealing, the entire fairness standard of review does not apply to tender offer freeze-outs) and *Glassman* (short-form mergers are not subject to entire-fairness review). See Subramanian (2005) for a comprehensive explanation.

36 See In re Pure Resources Shareholders Litigation, 808 A.2d 421 (Del.Ch.2002). The court has also clarified that the MOM tender condition must be non-waivable.

controller cannot profit from a post-takeover price lower than the pre-takeover one, when he has just acquired a control block: in this case, it would be relatively easy for shareholders to demonstrate that the bid price was unfair, given the circumstances of the acquisition, in spite of any appearance of fair dealing.[37]

In conclusion, the current state of American law matches the optimal regulation of squeeze-out that I have advocated, also as far as the sale of control blocks is concerned. The optimal squeeze-out rule is conditional on the making of a tender offer for non-controlling shares and sets the minimum consideration at the highest between the pre-takeover and the post-takeover market price.[38] To be sure, a threshold of 90% is imposed for the freeze-out to go through safely in the US. According to the framework developed in the previous chapter, this may be too stringent a requirement because it allows for some value-increasing takeovers to be prevented by minority shareholders' holdout. This might not be much of a problem given the high rate of dispersion of non-controlling ownership in the US. Nevertheless, it still seems advisable for statutory law to set the threshold of short-form mergers to a somewhat lower level.

8.3 The discipline of control transactions in the UK

8.3.1 A summary of the UK style

Takeover regulation in the UK is somewhat less intricate. Rules are clearly set at the statutory level, by securities regulation, or by self-regulation having traditionally a binding character: there is almost no chance of doing business at the London Stock Exchange without complying with the Takeover Code.[39]

37 Such a deal would not easily go through in the first place. No SC would be able to support it without facing a considerable risk of liability. Even if the deal was consummated on these terms, most probably a disgruntled minority shareholder would be able to bring a class action suit against the original sale of control block on grounds of looting.
38 See *supra* Chapter 7, section 7.3.2.
39 The preamble of the first edition of the City Code on Takeovers and Mergers (1968) is illustrative of this point:

> The Code has not, and does not seek to have, the force of law, but those who wish to take advantage of the facilities of the securities markets in the United Kingdom should conduct themselves in matters relating to takeovers according to the Code. Those who do not so conduct themselves cannot expect to enjoy those facilities and may find that they are withheld.

The Code was the result of the pressure exerted by institutional investors faced with the emergence of the new techniques of hostile acquisitions (Cheffins 2008). These were perceived as disruptive of the relationship between investors and firm control, which had just turned from controlling shareholders to professional management (Franks et al 2005). The City Code issued in 1968 was Britain's second try to deal with this problem as a matter of self-regulation, under the (credible) threat that legislation would have stepped in

Actually, this very special kind of self-regulation is the most important source of discipline of control transactions in the UK. Nowadays, it has been given statutory authority in order to comply with the takeover law at the EU level, but nothing else has changed in the form or substance of regulation.[40] The rules are contained in the *City Code on Takeovers and Mergers*,[41] and they are enforced by the homonymous *City Panel* under the ultimate threat of excluding infringers from the core of British finance: that is 'The City,' the one square mile district where London's business community is located (Armour and Skeel 2007).

Professors Armour and Skeel have so nicely elaborated on the virtues of such an enforcement mechanism that we can just focus on the rules as if they were dictated by the law, but enforced in a virtually perfect manner. The only thing is that other sources of British law also have an impact on takeovers, whereas the judiciary has almost none (Armour 2010). While the former circumstance is often overlooked, the latter is now recognized as another prominent difference from the American regulation of corporate governance (Kraakman et al 2009).[42] In the takeover context, this suffers perhaps just a

---

otherwise. The Bank of England's first attempt to issue a softer body of recommendations ('Notes on Amalgamation of British Business') had just failed a few years earlier: these recommendations remained a dead letter. The Code took the matter more seriously, by issuing a number of bright-line rules backed by general principles, and entrusting adjudication of disputes about the application of the rules (and, subsequently, their update) to a body of individuals: the City Panel on Takeovers and Mergers. Thanks to this enforcement mechanism, as a matter of fact, the Code is complied with in every control transaction involving a British listed firm as a target. See Armour and Skeel (2007).

40 For the first time since the establishment of the City Panel, the Code on Takeovers and Mergers has now statutory authority. See Companies Act of 2006, §§ 942–965. This was required by the European Takeover Directive. The most important effect of this innovation is that the rules and the decisions issued by the City Panel are now also *legally* binding, so that the Panel has new powers to request court enforcement of its rulings. Still, a peculiarity of British takeover regulation is that breaches of the City Code provide no grounds for civil litigation, and complaints need to always be addressed to the City Panel in the first place.

41 The 10th edition of the City Code came into force on 19 September 2011, including a significant but not radical revision of the takeover rules aimed at strengthening the protection of target shareholders. None of the new rules concerns the general issues discussed in the text.

42 According to Armour and Skeel (2007), in the 1960s and the early 1970s, the UK common law on takeover defenses was remarkably similar to the opinions written by Delaware judges in the following decades. See Hogg v. Cramphorn [1967] Ch 254 (directors cannot take actions having the *primary* purpose of entrenching their control position); and Howard Smith Ltd v. Ampol Petroleum Ltd [1974] AC 821 (frustrating actions are not considered as breach of director's duty when they are *primarily* motivated by a legitimate business purpose). Since British courts were traditionally not inclined to second-guess the merits of business purpose, the above combination resembles the proportionality test of Unocal Corp. v. Mesa Petroleum Co., 493 A.2d 946 (Del.Sup.1985). Afterwards, the role of British judiciary was superseded by the institution of the City Panel, aggressively enforcing the principle and the rules of board neutrality. The real question is, therefore, why nothing like

minor exception: the existing, but very limited role played by the courts in upholding takeovers operated as schemes of arrangement.[43] We will come to that after discussing the most common way to operate a change in control in the UK: a takeover bid for all of outstanding shares.

8.3.2 Takeover bids in the acquisition of free-standing firms

8.3.2.1 The uneasy life of controlling shareholders in the UK

The City Code requires that an 'any or all' bid for outstanding shares be made for the acquisition of a listed firm. This requirement applies in two circumstances: when somebody *wishes* to gain control of a company through a tender offer; and when somebody *does* acquire more than 30% of a company's stock.[44] Tricky as it may appear, the bid is mandatory only in the last circumstance. In the first one, the bid is actually voluntary: regulation only constrains its structure and, possibly, its price. The underlying principle is that shareholders shall be granted equal treatment in takeovers (Davies 2008). However, the same principle is implemented differently whether a free-standing or a shareholder-controlled firm is acquired. In the first case, regulation only prevents the tender offer from being restricted and any lower than the price paid in pre-bid purchases on the market;[45] partial offers are only allowed upon the Panel's authorization, and only when the bid is for less than 30%.[46] In the second case, regulation is much more demanding: not only must minority

that happened in the US. According to Armour and Skeel, US federal legislation was the reason. As the authors conclude on this point:

> This, as we have explained, is a result of federal legislation which prevented institutional investors from developing sufficiently close links with one another to make collective action on this scale feasible in the US, together with federal regulation that displaced an earlier tradition of self-regulation in the securities markets. There is an irony, therefore, in calls for federal legislation to remedy the perceived 'problem' of Delaware takeover law: in our view, it is federal legislation that is fundamentally responsible for the perceived problem.

43 See *infra*, section 8.3.3.
44 See, respectively, Rules 10 and 36 and Rule 9.1(a) of the City Code. Likewise, a shareholder who already owns between 30% and 50% of the stock has to make an 'any or all' bid if he "acquires an interest in any other shares which increases the percentage of shares carrying voting rights in which he is interested."
45 In the presence of pre-bid purchases, the City Code regulates both the *level* and the *nature* of the consideration to be offered in voluntary bids. As far as the price is concerned, the offer cannot be on less favorable terms than those of purchases within the three-month period before the bid is announced. Rule 6.1 of the City Code. As far as the nature of the consideration is concerned, the Code requires that cash be offered at least as an option when pre-bid purchases for cash exceed 10% of any class of shares within the previous 12 months. Rule 11.1 of the City Code.
46 Rule 36 of the City Code.

shareholders be granted a right of exit upon a change in control, but this right cannot be offered on any less favorable terms than those of the acquisition of the control block, which includes a premium over the market price.[47]

Combined with the otherwise unfavorable regulation of the ongoing exercise of shareholder control, the mandatory bid is a prominent determinant of the rarity of controlling shareholders among firms listed in the UK. But notice that the opposite would probably have happened in the absence of this combination – as it happens in most parts of continental Europe (Becht and Mayer 2001). Short of the historical factors that have contributed to separation of ownership and control in the UK (Cheffins 2008), today a British controlling shareholder would find it more difficult than a continental colleague not only to part with control at a premium, but also to exercise control on an ongoing basis. The Listing Rules and the UK Corporate Governance Code jointly constrain a significant shareholder's ability to control the board of directors.[48] It is for this reason that British entrepreneurs face the choice of either parting with control when they go public (see e.g. Brennan and Franks 1997) or refraining from going public when the stock returns are insufficient to compensate for their control rents. These rents can hardly be exploited, protected, or cashed in by a controlling shareholder of a British listed company (Mayer 1999). On the contrary, the injection of the mandatory bid in otherwise unaltered corporate governance systems in continental Europe only affects the cashing-in phase.

I will discuss continental Europe in the last sections of this chapter. Here it is important to emphasize that the disfavor towards controlling shareholders in Britain also affects the way in which the takeover of free-standing firms is operated. The success of a takeover bid depends on the ability of the acquirer to avoid being stuck in the inconvenient position of controlling shareholders – i.e., on his ability to either take the company private or to otherwise cash-out minority shareholders. This circumstance affects, in turn, the ability of the incumbent management to resist an unwanted takeover.

The disfavor of UK corporate governance towards controlling shareholders is a main source of empowerment for a management opposing takeover. Controlling the board of directors and a non-negligible amount of voting rights, managers can make it difficult for a bidder to reach the threshold of acceptances that allows a squeeze-out. In the UK, a successful bidder is only able to buy out non-tendering shareholders if 90% of the outstanding shares (excluding the bidder's) are tendered. Alternatively, the would-be acquirer must agree with the incumbent board on a scheme of arrangement, which *inter alia* needs to be approved by 75% of the outstanding shares (once again, excluding the bidder's). Otherwise, the presence of minority shareholders would make the acquirer subject to all the restrictions of decision rights faced

---

47 Rule 9 of the City Code.
48 See *supra* Chapter 4, section 4.3.2.

by a controlling shareholder of a listed company.[49] Unsurprisingly, the vast majority of takeover bids voluntary made for the acquisition of a free-standing firm in the UK are conditional on the 90% of outstanding shares being tendered (Franks et al 2001). Friendly deals are instead increasingly implemented as schemes of arrangement (Payne 2011). Given the difficulties faced by controlling shareholders in exerting effective control on UK boards, the squeeze-out of minority shareholders plays a key role in the British takeover regulation.

8.3.2.2 *The structure of voluntary bids and takeover resistance*

This functional feature of UK takeover law has a number of important implications. To start, the City Code's insistence on tender offers being 'any or all' is superfluous whenever control is at stake.[50] The bidder cannot make any lower offer than the price paid in the acquisition of a toehold;[51] he needs anyway to purchase 90% of the stock *via the takeover bid* to perform a squeeze-out;[52] and the consideration of the latter must be equal to the bid price.[53] This implies that partial offers would make no sense anyway, provided that two-tier bids are prohibited by statutory law.[54] Secondly, the hurdles faced by the bidder in reaching the critical 90% threshold enables the management to resist a hostile takeover, in spite of the board being prohibited by the City Code from taking frustrating actions, with respect to actual or imminent bids, in the absence of a specific authorization by the general meeting of shareholders.[55] This is often sufficient to provide the board with some bargaining power in the face of an unwanted takeover bid.

The board is not otherwise entitled to implement defensive tactics. Post-bid resistance would have little chance to be upheld by shareholders, whereas pre-bid defenses – which are theoretically legal – are almost never established since they have been opposed for decades by institutional investors (Cheffins 2008). The high threshold for squeeze-out is often sufficient for board resistance because of two reasons. First, board members in the UK account on average for more than 10% of share ownership (Goergen and Renneboog 2001). This enables managers to form coalitions powerful enough to block a takeover without taking any frustrating action: they simply would not

---

49 Delisting also require a super-majority vote of 75% of the shares. See Kraakman et al (2009).
50 The Panel may allow partial bids only on condition that they cannot result in accumulation of a share block accounting for more than 30% of voting rights. See Rule 36 of the City Code.
51 Rule 6 of the City Code.
52 Companies Act (CA) 2006 § 979.
53 CA 2006 § 986.
54 CA 2006 § 974.
55 Rule 21 of the City Code.

tender.[56] Second, in every case in which board ownership is below average, management may still counter an unwanted bid by issuing an unfavorable recommendation to shareholder and/or taking other actions which do not amount to frustration (e.g. seeking a 'white knight'). The City Code does not mandate absolute 'board passivity,' only 'board neutrality' (Kraakman et al 2009). In fact, very few takeovers manage to go through in the UK when the board of directors keeps on objecting as strongly as they are allowed to do.

This only tells us *how* British managers can force bidders to come to terms with them. Note that so far takeovers of free-standing firms seem to work in the UK not so differently from the US. The major difference depends neither on the regulation of the bid (which is only slightly more burdensome) nor on that of board resistance (which is formally disallowed in the UK), but rather on the threshold for minority shareholders' squeeze-out. Still, squeeze-out is preferably operated at 90% also in the US. What we still do not know is *why* British managers wish to resist a takeover bid – i.e., what they are allowed to bargain for.

Here lies a fundamental difference between takeovers in the UK and in the US. Under UK company law, board members are prevented from renegotiating severance payments ("payments for loss of office") in the wake of takeovers, unless renegotiation is approved by the general meeting of shareholders (Kraakman et al 2009).[57] Let us assume that this is sufficient to rule out renegotiation. The acquirer-paid sweeteners that are so common in the US (Bebchuk and Fried 2004) would not be possible (and they are in fact unheard of in the British takeover practice). Does this mean that, in Britain, managers have no better option to extract PBC than to entrench themselves? This would be a too hasty conclusion and it is in fact contradicted by the empirical evidence. Both the US and the UK feature perhaps the highest levels of takeover activity in the world. However, the US outperforms the UK in terms of takeover activity when the frequencies are corrected for the relative size of the stock markets. In neither of the two countries do deals *concluded* as hostile account for more than half a percentage point – although the score in the UK is somewhat higher than in the US (Armour and Skeel 2007). These figures are quite suggestive of what may be actually going on.

Hostile takeovers are very exceptional events everywhere (Becht et al 2007). They might be slightly more frequent in the UK, which reflects the stricter regulatory constraints on board resistance. But, on the one hand, the difference is negligible and, on the other hand, the real meaning of hostility is open to question (Schwert 2000). What matters is that the market of corporate control is very active in both countries, where it is normally operated through friendly deals. Then the impact of regulation on this kind of deal, more than on hostile

---

56 See *supra* Chapter 4, section 4.3.2.
57 §§ 215–222 of CA 2006.

takeovers, is what ultimately determines the functioning of the market of corporate control and its size and performance in either place. In spite of their inability to renegotiate severance payments, some British managers may have to cash in their control rents as a precondition of their parting with control. When the quality of management is not up to expectations (that is, managers are seriously underperforming), given that the size of the pie is shrinking there would be nothing to renegotiate. One should recall from Chapter 3 that the best strategy for a lazy or otherwise unskilled manager is just to take the present value of his pre-arranged compensation package and leave the steering wheel to a better manager.[58] The empirical evidence about changes in control in the UK seems to confirm this result (Franks et al 2001). The worst performing firms exhibit higher board turnover. However, takeovers appear to be otherwise 'unfocused' in the UK: not only are they not targeted to poorly performing firms, but they also score comparatively worse than in the US in this particular respect. It seems, then, that the British market for corporate control is both smaller in size and less performing compared to the US. This suggests that comparatively more value-increasing takeovers are foregone. The big question is why?

8.3.2.3 *Takeover premia as renegotiated severance payments*

Value-decreasing acquisitions are no possible explanation of underperformance of the market for corporate control in the UK, since takeover regulation effectively prevents these from occurring in Britain. The principle of equal treatment of shareholders is so carefully implemented that no rider can profitably take over unless he is bound to increase shareholder value. The problem is that takeovers need to increase *significantly* the firm value to be profitable for the acquirer.[59] This is only apparently due to the necessity to acquire 100% of the company's stock. We know that this would always be the best strategy for a truly value-increasing bidder, provided that he can so exclude shareholders from any part of the takeover gains.[60] The real reason is that exclusion of non-controlling shareholders from the takeover gains can only be imperfectly performed because of company law's discipline of control premia and severance payments.

When managers are performing sufficiently well to be credibly committed to renegotiate compensation of their control rents, but still sufficiently bad for a takeover to be efficient,[61] they are not allowed to negotiate their severance payments separately from the takeover premium in the UK. Of course, this would not be a problem if takeovers were only hostile. But hostile takeovers

---

58 See *supra* Chapter 3, section 3.3.3.

59 This is the major drawback of a strict implementation of the principle of shareholders' equal treatment. See Kraakman et al (2009).

60 See *supra* Chapter 7, section 7.2.2.

61 See *supra* Chapter 3, section 3.3.3.

are not so common and – whenever entrepreneurship matters in listed companies – they may be not desirable. As a result, incumbent managers are able to hold out for their control rents in their capacity as (coalition of) shareholders, and possibly to induce other shareholders to do the same, until the takeover premium gets high enough. Since the takeover premium accrues in equal terms to all of the target's stockholders, and not just to those in control, this may explain how legal protection of minority shareholders in the UK leads to moderately value-increasing takeovers being foregone. Notice that this result does not hold for the US too, because both the power of incumbent managers to claim compensation of control rents and their profits from doing so do not depend on shareholding.[62] An appropriate regulation of side-payments in takeovers, more than their outright ban, would therefore be more efficient as it would allow more gains from trade to be captured, no matter of how they are divided.

In a sense, this approach can be interpreted as one more salute to the work of Ronald Coase.

8.3.3 *Takeover as scheme of arrangement*

Since a takeover bid is not mandatory for the acquisition of a free-standing firm, a would-be acquirer may prefer to use a different technique. In the UK, the alternative to a tender offer is a takeover implemented by a scheme of arrangement. This option is often neglected by the international literature, but is important and also relatively popular.[63] It is in fact a way to overcome some of the rigidities of takeover bids.

The procedure is regulated by the Companies Act, although a scheme of arrangement allows no exception to the mandatory provisions of the City Code (most notably, a scheme cannot be used to avoid the mandatory bid) and the disclosure requirements are anyway triggered by the takeover purpose, no different from a tender offer. That being said, takeovers implemented as schemes of arrangement do not significantly alter the picture of takeover regulation in the UK, especially as regards the cashing in of control rents. Schemes of arrangement make this no easier, since they do not allow controllers to get anything that is not given to each class of shareholders on equal terms. To be sure, compared to a tender offer, schemes of arrangement may considerably empower non-controlling shareholders relative to both the management and the prospective acquirer. It is probably for this reason that they are somewhat less popular than takeover bids, and they are mostly employed when shareholders are very dispersed or otherwise out of reach, or for tax reasons.

---

62 See *supra* section 8.2.1.

63 I wish to thank Professor Julian Franks for having suggested me this line of inquiry in a personal talk about the dissertation on which this book is based. See Payne (2011) for a comprehensive legal discussion of takeovers as schemes of arrangement.

The scheme of arrangement is a far-reaching procedure, which can be used to bind dissenting or apathetic shareholders to a number of decisions (Davies 2008). Here I just consider its use to operate a takeover. A typical scheme of arrangement implementing a change in control would involve the existing shareholders in the target company transferring their shares to the acquirer in consideration of a cash payment or of an issue of shares in the acquiring company. Summarizing from legal formalism, this scheme basically results in a takeover being directly implemented through a merger.[64] The board must agree to this purpose, since its cooperation is required to call one or more shareholder meetings for the approval of the scheme. Overcoming the board's reluctance by a shareholder resolution is not an option, since – as we are about to see – the higher the insurgent's voting power, the lower the chances that a takeover can succeed as a scheme of arrangement. Therefore, the friendly character of the takeover holds even more strictly in this scenario.

A consenting board is far from sufficient for the deal to go through. The target management is not completely in control of the implementation of the scheme, because it requires that the competent court convenes one or more shareholder meetings and that the court sanctions the deal upon its approval by shareholders (Davies 2008). Courts, however, mainly check the regularity of the procedure and that shareholders are adequately informed about the deal. In this respect, additional checks are independently performed by the Takeover Panel based on the provisions of the City Code (Payne 2011). Therefore, the last word about schemes of arrangement rests with shareholders: they are the pivots of the transaction.

The Companies Act 2006 provides that an "arrangement" between the company and its "members" must be approved by a majority in number representing 75% in value of the shareholders present and voting either in person or by proxy.[65] To this purpose, a vote must be held separately for each class of shareholders. Let us draw, for simplicity, from the presence of multiple classes of shares – a situation not so common among British listed firms. The crucial point is that the shares held by the would-be acquirer are considered as belonging to a *separate class*, so that they do not count for the approval of the scheme. As a result, the acquirer may only count on the board's ability to gather enough independent support for the proposal at the shareholder meeting.

Somewhat ironically, the higher the acquirer's ownership stake in the company, the higher the chance that he will fail: this would make it easier for one or more dissenting shareholders to account for 25% of the shares that can be voted. But the final outcome also depends on the number of shares that are actually voted. In summary, a scheme of arrangement has the advantage that dissenting shareholders may be more easily squeezed-out than by a takeover

---

64 There is no statutory merger in UK company law. See Kraakman et al (2009).
65 §§ 895–899 of CA 2006. The key provisions are contained in CA 2006 § 899.

bid, due to the difference in thresholds of acceptance of the deal and in how they are calculated. The disadvantage is that the scheme is much riskier. Notably, this strategy failed as an attempt to squeeze out minority shareholders of a company already controlled by a *majority* shareholder (a scheme of arrangement is no option when controlling ownership is between 30% and 50%, because then any increase in the controller's stake triggers the mandatory bid).[66] In that case, the majority shareholder had finally to launch a takeover bid to take the company private.[67] It is for this reason that, before being 'trapped' into the position of majority shareholder, a prospective acquirer may prefer to go for a takeover bid from the very beginning.

Finally, there is no reason to expect that, compared to a tender offer, a scheme of arrangement would result in a lower takeover premium. Company law requires that any interest of directors in the transaction be disclosed and approved by shareholders together with the deal.[68] This has an effect equivalent to the discipline of payments for loss of office in the wake of a takeover bid. Also in this scenario, then, managers are prevented from renegotiating separately any severance payment. What they can do – as in the face of a tender offer – is to use their bargaining power to claim compensation in the form of a takeover premium shared with the rest of shareholders. Shareholders would not object to this kind of directors' interest in the transaction because it is perfectly aligned with theirs. I have already highlighted the adverse consequences of this result of British regulation on the probability of value-increasing takeovers.

8.3.4 Why the mandatory bid does little harm in the UK (and what else may be more harmful)

If the picture of British takeover regulation is shadowed by the above remarks as far as the acquisition of free-standing firms is concerned, it becomes very dark in the case of takeovers of shareholder-controlled listed companies. Here a different regulation applies. Changes in control involving the transfer of a 30% stake or higher trigger a mandatory 'any or all' bid feature, with equal opportunity to be granted to minority shareholders; and there is basically no way to get round this rule.[69] This means that, unless control is allowed to

---

66 Rule 9.1(b) of the City Code. Notice that, differently from voluntary bids, mandatory bids must be *unconditional* (more precisely, they cannot include any condition other than as to the need for 50% acceptance and the authorization by competition authorities – Rules 9.3 and 9.4 of the City Code). As a result, the mandatory bid by a controlling shareholder cannot be conditioned on 90% of voting shares being acquired – the threshold for operating a minority squeeze-out.

67 See, for illustration of events, *Dick's Tricks at Harvey Nicks*, 12 November 2002, available at www.webb-site.com (last accessed 26 June 2012).

68 CA 2006 § 897.

69 See the detailed discipline provided for by Rule 9 of the City Code. Exemptions from the mandatory bid may be granted only by the City Panel under a very limited set of circumstances. See City Code, Section F, Notes on dispensation from Rule 9.

change hands below that threshold, no scope is left by regulation for private negotiations over the control premium. The latter may only be paid as inducement to part with control to the extent that the same offer is extended to non-controlling shareholders.

This is consistent with the regulation of controlling management's severance payments illustrated above. However, the size of the control rents at stake is incomparable in the two scenarios. The bottom line is that, in the presence of a controlling shareholder, the obligation to share the control premium with non-controlling shareholders may simply make no takeover profitable enough to pay that price while leaving the acquirer better off, unless takeover gains are of extraordinarily large magnitude.[70]

However, as we have seen in Chapter 4, the position of controlling shareholders is quite inconvenient in the UK system of corporate governance. In fact, controlling shareholders are very rare among British listed companies. It is therefore not worthwhile discussing the mandatory bid any further, as the vast majority of takeover bids in the UK are in effect voluntary. But one point is worth making as a conclusive remark. British regulation does not allow significant control rents to be cashed in through a change in control, and this is one of the reasons why high control rents are simply not featured by corporate governance in the UK.[71] Apart from the inefficiencies that it generates in the takeover process, this regulatory disfavor towards private benefits of control also restricts the set of choices available for separating ownership and control.

As one British economist has authoritatively argued, the drawback of this solution may be the inability of the institutional system in the UK to support economic activities that financial markets cannot fully reward (Mayer 1999). Professor Mayer nicely attributes this to a British predilection for eunuchs ("responsibility without power") over harlots ("power without responsibility"). The present study being concerned with positive and normative analysis of law, more than with its cultural determinants, I can only conclude by speculating that the current state of British corporate governance may result in too high a degree of ownership dispersion compared to what would be efficient. This is due to a strong bias against controlling shareholders.

8.4 The European Directive on takeover bids

8.4.1 *The failure of harmonization*

It took almost 15 years of negotiations between Member states, but finally a European takeover regulation was established in April 2004 with the Takeover Directive.[72] The history of the Thirteenth Directive on European company

---

70 See *supra* Chapter 7, section 7.4.4.
71 This point was already made long ago by Professors Franks and Mayer (1990).
72 Directive 2004/25/EC of the European Parliament and of the Council of 21 April 2004 on takeover bids (hereinafter Takeover Directive).

law is well known (see McCahery et al 2004). Its enactment was preceded by the dismissal by the Parliament of a former proposal aimed at creating a 'level playing field' as far as the regulation of takeovers was concerned. This was the first failure of the harmonization attempt. Then the Directive could only be passed as a compromise between opposite positions of the Member states, by providing them with a number of options for its implementation.[73] As a result, a second failure of harmonization is in the making. Member states have exercised the options available to implement the Directive without significant departures from their regulatory traditions (see Davies et al 2010).

From a theoretical perspective, the adoption and implementation of the Takeover Directive raises a number of interesting questions, regardless of its contents (see Enriques and Gatti 2006): the allocation of institutional competence for takeover legislation (centralization v. decentralization); whether harmonization is preferable to regulatory competition; and whether these are truly crucial issues in corporate governance, or convergence and divergence of regulation occurring on a rather different basis. In Chapter 6, I have suggested that the latter might be the case. I have shown that, at least as far as the legal discipline of self-dealing is concerned, national regulations seem to address similar functional problems. Although different countries are influenced by legal comparison, ultimately they evolve along their own path. European harmonization is most unpromising and unlikely to succeed in that field. But whether the European legislator could fare any better in takeover regulation is just a too complicated question to be answered here. While self-dealing is mostly confined to a national dimension, thereby suggesting that freedom of incorporation may be the right way to address institutional diversity, corporate acquisitions obviously are not quite so, and therefore the case for harmonization is, *prima facie*, stronger.

Issues of federalism and regulatory competition in corporate governance would deserve a separate inquiry anyway. Here we need to cope with a more severe problem concerning the European regulation of takeovers. Even assuming that an optimal model of regulation exists, the European Union has simply chosen the wrong one. The basic idea underlying the Takeover Directive, in both the original and the compromised version, is that of transplanting the British discipline of corporate control transactions in the

---

73 The European Commission's proposal of a revised Takeover Directive was largely based on the first report of the High Level Group of Company Law Experts chaired by Professor Jaap Winter. The Commission set up this group after the European Parliament failed to pass the first proposal of a Takeover Directive in a second reading. However, the proposal faced the strong opposition of a number of Member states, most notably from Nordic Countries. As a result, the proposal was substantially amended by the European Parliament, and subsequently adopted in the amended configuration despite of the Commission's opposition. Most important modifications of the original proposal include optionality of the board neutrality and the breakthrough rules, a complicated two-tier mechanism of opt-in/opt-out, and the introduction of the principle of reciprocity. All of this will be briefly discussed in the next section.

other Member states (see Hopt 2006). This model, however, has not been completely understood: on the one hand, its suitability to dispersed ownership structures depends on the interaction with other legal rules that have nothing to do with the discipline of takeovers; on the other hand, the same model is unsuitable for creating an active market of corporate control in concentrated ownership structures.

To be sure, European regulators were aware of the second problem, and of its particular severity for most countries of continental Europe. So they tried to get round it, by introducing an element unknown to British regulation as to any other legislation in the world: the breakthrough rule, which – at least in the intentions of the experts who invented it – was supposed to create dispersed ownership and control structures where there was none (Mülbert 2004).

Not only is the attempt to force dispersion of ownership theoretically unfounded, as was just pointed out with reference to the UK, more importantly, the breakthrough rule was the wrong way to try.[74] Unsurprisingly that attempt failed and it contributed significantly to the dismissal of the Commission's original proposal. We know from the previous chapter that no breakthrough rule could have possibly succeeded in imposing full contestability of corporate control in the long run. Also, according to some commentators (Coates 2004), the breakthrough rule would have affected relatively few companies. Nevertheless, the idea that existing patterns of corporate control could be disrupted was simply unacceptable to some Member states. What today remains of the Takeover Directive is a patchwork of mandatory rules, waivers, and optional provisions, which overall still attempt to emulate as closely as possible the British model of takeover regulation (Enriques and Gatti 2007).

The overall result is unfortunate. Options and permissible waivers only partly allow Member states to adapt that model to the prevailing features of corporate governance in their country. Effectively, they may choose to restrict contestability nearly as much as they wish (Enriques 2006). But we know that contestability is not the right question for the efficiency of takeover regulation. On the contrary, the regulatory attitude towards contestability (whether pro-takeover or anti-takeover) is ultimately a source of distortion. When it comes to the crucial point – the ease of (friendly) takeovers – Member states enjoy much less freedom. The most prominent achievements of the Takeover Directive in terms of harmonization concern shareholder protection (Ventoruzzo 2006). The establishment of an active market for corporate control is sacrificed to that goal via the adoption across the board of a British-style mandatory bid rule. The adverse consequences of this choice are more evident the more the prevailing ownership structures at the national level depart from those characterizing the UK.

---

74 See *supra* Chapter 7, section 7.4.4.

8.4.2 *The contents of the Takeover Directive*

A brief illustration of the main provisions of the Takeover Directive is in order, before discussing their impact on the three remaining countries of our sample. As I mentioned, the mandatory core of the Directive is shareholder protection, interpreted as a principle of equal treatment of shareholders in the wake of a takeover, which may not suffer exceptions in the implementation at the national level.[75] The mandatory bid is the prominent application of this principle.

8.4.2.1 *Mandatory bid*

Upon a change in control, minority shareholders must be offered an equal opportunity to exit compared to the controlling shareholder. To this purpose, an obligation to make an 'any or all' tender offer is triggered by the acquisition of a percentage of voting rights sufficient to determine a change in control; and the bid price is set equal to the highest consideration paid for the acquisition of the control block over a period between 6 and 12 months before the triggering event.[76] Specification of the percentage of voting rights that qualifies as a triggering event (i.e., the threshold of the mandatory bid) is left to the Member states.[77] However, this is not the only degree of freedom that Member states enjoy in the implementation and the application of the mandatory bid: some aspects of the mechanism established in the Directive may be waived on condition that the principle of equal treatment of shareholders is otherwise preserved.[78]

The mandatory bid must be put in context. To start with, the obligation is superseded in the acquisition of a free-standing firm. Here the tender offer will be voluntary, although the discipline of the mandatory bid still prescribes that the offer be unrestricted.[79] This is the first requirement that can be waived at the national level. Partial bids are allowed by the general derogation clause of the Directive, on condition that they are neither discriminatory (acceptances must be satisfied pro-rata) nor otherwise coercive (two-tier bids are prohibited at any rate).[80]

Partial bids may be likewise permitted on the same conditions in the presence of a controlling shareholder, but they cannot allow for outright circumvention of the obligation to share the control premium with minority shareholders. An explicit corollary of the binding principle of equal treatment in the Directive is that "if a person acquires control of the

---

75 See Takeover Directive, Recital 9 and art. 3.1(a) (General Principle 1).
76 Art. 5.1 and art. 5.4 of the Takeover Directive.
77 Art. 5.3 of the Takeover Directive.
78 Art. 4.5 of the Takeover Directive.
79 Art. 5.2 of the Takeover Directive.
80 See Recital 9, art. 3.1(a), and art. 4.5 of the Takeover Directive.

company, the other holders of securities must be protected."[81] Thus, partial bids may not allow for the control block to be traded on different terms from non-controlling shares, but only for the latter to be entitled to limited participation in the control premium provided that this participation is pro-rata.

Derogations are also allowed, but on a different basis, as far as the price of the mandatory bid (which must be unrestricted in any case) is concerned. The national Security Authority may set the bid price either higher or lower than the level set by the Directive "in circumstances and in accordance with criteria that are clearly determined."[82] If we take both the case-by-case approach and the objectivity of criteria seriously, this leaves Member states with limited margins of action. This provision importantly constrains the ability of Member states to relax the mandatory bid rule in order to ease the transfer of controlling blocks (Kraakman et al 2009).

8.4.2.2 Pre-bid and post-bid defenses

Two other key provisions of the directive are instead optional. These are the regulation of post-bid and pre-bid defenses that may be set up by the target company.[83] The first is the prohibition of the board from frustrating a takeover bid in the absence of authorization by the shareholder meeting.[84] The second is the (in)famous breakthrough rule.[85] The two provisions are intended to complement each other: the first is clearly modeled after the principle of board neutrality established by the British City Code; the second is aimed at replicating the conditions of corporate governance in the UK. The goal is to prevent both the board and controlling shareholders from hindering contestability.

In the face of a takeover bid, the incumbent needs to count on existing restrictions on either the transfer of shares or the exercise of voting rights; alternatively, the board must be authorized by the general meeting to take defensive measures. The breakthrough rule provides that restrictions on the transfer of securities be set aside upon the making of a tender offer, while restrictions on the exercise of voting rights have no effect in the shareholder meeting which decides upon defensive measures.[86] The latter provision applies to all the restrictions established either contractually or in the corporate charter, and it downgrades to one the power of multiple-voting shares.[87]

---

81 Art. 3.1(a) of the Takeover Directive.
82 Art. 5.4, 2nd paragraph, of the Takeover Directive.
83 Art. 12.1 of the Takeover Directive.
84 Art. 9 of the Takeover Directive.
85 Art. 11 of the Takeover Directive.
86 Art. 11.2 and art. 11.3 of the Takeover Directive.
87 It should be noted that the wipeout of restrictions on voting power suffers an important exception. 'One share–one vote' shall not be restored with respect to "securities where the restrictions on voting rights are compensated for by specific pecuniary advantages." Art.

Assuming that this is sufficient to short-circuit the frustration of the bid, the restrictions in place could still prevent a successful bidder from taking over the company's control. Therefore, the breakthrough rule also provides that restrictions on both the transfer and the exercise of voting rights – including multiple votes – are either repealed *ope legis* or may be removed by the acquirer, on condition that he holds at least 75% of the voting shares following the bid and equitable compensation is offered to the beneficiaries of those restrictions.[88] Terms and procedure of this compensation are to be established by the Member states.[89]

Both the breakthrough and the board neutrality rules are subject to a complicated mechanism of opting-out, at the level of Member states, and opting-in, at the company level.[90] That is, Member states may choose not to implement either provision as mandatory; but they must allow the companies under their jurisdiction to uphold each of them in the corporate charter.[91] It is established that opting-in at the company's level should be reversible, which is unsurprising given that either rule would have to be implemented as a charter amendment. Consequently, both the breakthrough and the board neutrality rule may not feature a credible commitment unless they are implemented as mandatory in national corporate laws. While the majority of EU Member states have implemented the rule of board neutrality in this fashion, hardly any of them has endorsed the breakthrough rule as a mandatory provision (Kraakman et al 2009).[92] The breakthrough rule apparently fares no better at the company level: companies seem to find it uninteresting (Davies et al 2010). Finally, the application of both rules, on either a mandatory or a voluntary basis, may be suspended in the absence of reciprocity by the bidder.[93] This is an additional option given to the Member states and indirectly, to the companies. Reciprocity on these matters hardly makes economic sense (Becht 2004). Still, the reciprocity clause has an impact on the strength with which the board neutrality and possibly the breakthrough rules are effectively implemented (Davies et al 2010). Reciprocity may also affect the individual company's strategy on whether to opt in to either rule (Kraakman et al 2009).

11.6 of the Takeover Directive. This basically implies that most kinds of limited-voting and non-voting stock can be set out of the scope of the rule, even when the latter is not opted out of.

88 Art. 11.4 of the Takeover Directive. Also in this case the provision does not apply to restrictions compensated by specific pecuniary advantages.

89 Art. 11.5 of the Takeover Directive.

90 Art. 12.1 and art. 12.2 of the Takeover Directive.

91 See Recital 21 of the Takeover Directive.

92 The opt-out countries notably include the UK. There are exceptions, though, namely the Baltic states and – until 2008 – Italy: these countries adopted a mandatory breakthrough rule.

93 Art. 12.3 of the Takeover Directive.

8.4.2.3 *Squeeze-out and sell-out*

There are a few other provisions in the Takeover Directive having an impact on the framework of analysis developed in this book. One is the disclosure of all existing arrangements concerning corporate control and its transfer.[94] This disclosure is a precondition for the efficient functioning of the market for corporate control (Kraakman et al 2009). The regulation of the squeeze-out and sell-out rights is even more important. The Directive provides that the two rights should be equally triggered by a 90% threshold of both ownership and voting rights reached after a takeover bid, no matter whether the bid is voluntary or mandatory.[95] Member states may, however, raise that threshold in their company laws, provided that it does not exceed 95%.[96] The squeeze-out consideration is considered fair inasmuch as it is equal to the bid price, even though the additional requirement that at least 90% of voting shares be effectively tendered at that price is established in case of a voluntary bid.[97] In implementing both rights, Member states have only limited discretion as to the threshold. As we are about to see, this part of the EU regulation only results in minor changes for the jurisdictions of our sample; but it may prevent these countries from choosing a more efficient approach to the dynamics of control allocation in the future.

8.5 Takeover regulation in continental Europe

8.5.1 *Takeovers and their discipline in Sweden*

8.5.1.1 *Pre-empting the European legislator*

The Swedish approach to the implementation of the Takeover Directive is open to interpretation. According to some commentators, the Swedish case supports the thesis of convergence of takeover regulation towards the British standard, regarded – at least in Europe – as the prevailing one (Ventoruzzo 2006). Sweden introduced both the mandatory bid and the rule of board neutrality, originally on a voluntary basis, and, about one year before the Directive came into force, on the basis of mandatory self-regulation. As I mentioned in Chapter 6, self-regulation is no less binding than corporate and securities law for Swedish listed companies. Like the UK, Sweden had subsequently to give statutory authority to these regulations in order to comply with the Directive, but nothing else was changed in the contents or the basic enforcement mechanism. However, Sweden had little reason to switch spontaneously to such a restrictive regulation of takeovers and a very

---

94 Art. 10 of the Takeover Directive.
95 Art. 15 and art. 16 of the Takeover Directive.
96 Art. 15.2 and art. 16.2 of the Takeover Directive.
97 Art. 15.5 of the Takeover Directive.

good one not to do it (Kraakman et al 2009). While the effective protection of minority shareholders has never been a problem in Swedish corporate governance, the mandatory bid was a serious challenge to the market for corporate control, given the absolute prevalence of controlling shareholders in the structure of corporate ownership (Skog 2004). Yet, despite the peculiarities of national corporate governance, Sweden had no choice but to follow the European trend, especially when it became clear that the Takeover Directive would have been approved in one way or another.

This perspective explains too why many other European countries started to reckon with the British model of takeover regulation before the European Directive compelled them to do so (Grundmann 2005). But this is only one part of the story. Introducing a British-style takeover regulation, national legislators anticipated the European one: on the one hand, this gave them the opportunity to adapt the model to the features of their country's corporate governance; on the other hand, this strategy conferred upon them bargaining power in the negotiations about the EU legislation. If anything, Sweden was even smarter in this respect. On the one hand, together with other Scandinavian countries, it contributed to the failure of the original attempt to impose the breakthrough rule as mandatory, which would have had disruptive effects on the Swedish system. On the other hand, Sweden made sure that the introduction of the mandatory bid was the least troublesome for its market for corporate control.

8.5.1.2 *How to neutralize the mandatory bid: two-stage acquisitions*

When the mandatory bid was first introduced as a recommendation in 1999, Sweden had a higher threshold than the majority of European countries, namely 40% of the voting power. In September 2003, the threshold was lowered to 30% by the Swedish *Näringslivets Börskommitté*, which was in charge of takeover regulation before the Takeover Act came into force in July 2006.[98] The substantive contents of takeover regulation in Sweden are essentially unchanged since then. Detailed rules are issued by the stock exchanges, mainly the NASDAQ-OMX Nordic Stock Exchange; the current rules are in force since 2009.[99] Importantly, the enforcement of takeover regulation is entirely delegated to the Swedish Securities Council, which works quite similarly to the UK Takeover Panel. The main sanction at the Council's disposal is the ability to issue public statements regarding a company's compliance (Petersson and Thomsen 2011). In the Swedish culture, this threat is very effective. The Securities Council issues statements on

---

98 The Takeover Act – *Lag (2006:451) om offentliga uppköpserbjudanden på aktiemarknaden*, Act (2006:451) on Public Purchase Offers in the Stock market – is not available in English.

99 A revision of the Takeover Rules is being considered at the time of writing, but it is not likely to be implemented before the end of 2012. Also, the revision will not concern the general issues being discussed in this section.

matters of interpretations and contentious issues. The Council also has authority to grant exemptions from the mandatory bid rules, which it has done quite often.[100]

In the absence of an exemption, an acquirer willing to take over from a controlling shareholder having more than 30% of voting power has in principle to make a tender offer for all outstanding stock at the highest price paid for each class of shares in the previous six months.[101] The question is how this person can possibly avoid extending the payment of the control premium to all minority shareholders, especially when the burden of this obligation would induce him to refrain from taking over in the first place. The only possible answer is that the control transaction must be structured in such a way as to avoid triggering the mandatory bid. This can be done following the tradition of corporate acquisitions in Sweden. In order to understand this, we need to step back to the takeover practice before the introduction of the mandatory bid.

Before the introduction of the mandatory bid, acquisitions in Sweden used to be operated in two stages (Agnblad et al 2001). The first stage was the transfer of the control block at a freely negotiated price. The second step was an unrestricted tender offer for non-controlling shares, conditional on the acquisition of 90% of the outstanding stock: this is in fact the threshold traditionally established by Swedish corporate law for the minority's squeeze-out (Skog and Fäger 2007). It should be noticed that this result was possible in the absence of restrictive regulation of takeovers: at that time, the mandatory bid was only a non-binding recommendation. This free-market result indirectly confirms the optimality of the takeover mechanism that was illustrated in the previous chapter with reference to controlling shareholder systems. Swedish corporate governance features very little, if any, scope for diversionary PBC, so that there is essentially no risk that takeovers are value-decreasing – at least, not as far as the target shareholders are concerned. Introducing a takeover regulation, the Swedish authorities had the difficult task to preserve this mechanism in spite of the constraints that were coming from the EU. So they did through the regulation of voluntary bids, which are regarded by the Directive as a valid exception to the mandatory bid.

Acquisitions can still be operated in two stages in Sweden. Nowadays they may even need to be operated in such a fashion in order to avoid the mandatory bid. As before, the acquirer will have to purchase a toehold from the controlling shareholder, but now this must necessarily account for less than 30% of the voting rights. The rest will have to be purchased together with non-controlling shares via a voluntary tender offer. When the threshold is surpassed by way of an unrestricted voluntary bid, the mandatory bid does not apply. However, the price of voluntary bids is also regulated. In the presence of pre-bid

---

100 See the official website of the Swedish Securities Council (www.aktiemarknadsnamnden. se/in-english__50, last accessed on 26 June 2012).
101 Takeover Rule II.21.

purchases, both the voluntary and the mandatory bid must offer a consideration no lower than the highest price paid in the previous six months.[102] Thus the bidder has to wait half a year if he wants to avoid the tender offer being overpriced. Apparently, this is not much of a change for the Swedish takeover tradition, whose "remarkable feature . . . is that the bidder often has a substantial long-term toehold in the target firm" (Agnblad et al 2001: 247). This makes sense in a context where takeovers are mainly friendly. Both stages of the control transaction need to be negotiated at the outset between the incumbent and the insurgent controllers. The friendly character of the vast majority of takeovers appears to be a feature of the Swedish market for corporate control, which is otherwise quite active (Skog 2004).

Other elements of regulation support, or are no impediment to, the functioning of takeovers according to this mechanism. Swedish best practices pre-empted the Takeover Directive also in introducing a rule of board neutrality, which is now in the law and is further elaborated in the takeover rules.[103] This does not undermine the controlling shareholder's ability to fend off a hostile takeover because he could always count on sufficient voting rights to uphold defensive measures, should they ever be necessary. On the other hand, because the general corporate law does not support managerial control, virtually every Swedish company has one or more large shareholders in control. The Swedish legislator protected instead both the typical ownership structure and the takeover market from potential (albeit temporary) disruption by opting out of the breakthrough rule. Swedish firms are quite unlikely to opt in although, in theory, they are permitted to do so. Companies would rather restructure dual-class security-voting arrangements, as they have partly started to do (Henrekson and Jakobsson 2012), instead of suddenly exposing themselves to hostile takeovers.

In conclusion, as it was long advocated by Rolf Skog (2004), the Swedish takeover market remains perfectly compatible with controlling shareholdings, even when these are supported by dual-class shares structures. As in the past, dual-class shares are allowed differential treatment in takeover bids (under certain conditions).[104] However, this would be generally insufficient to avoid the sharing of the control premium involved by the mandatory bid mainly because takeover bids cannot be restricted to just one class of shares. Dual-class shares may contribute to the cashing in of the control premium when the transaction is structured in two stages; the differential treatment in the tender offer stage is not strictly necessary for this purpose. Even before the introduction of takeover regulation, the vast majority of voluntary bids addressed to dual-class targets did not differentiate between classes of shares (Agnblad et al 2001).

---

102 Takeover Rule II.13.
103 Takeover Rule II.19.
104 Takeover Rule II.11.

8.5.1.3 *What is wrong with Swedish corporate governance?*

Little more can be said about takeover regulation in Sweden, save that perhaps the weakness of Swedish corporate governance does not depend on it. The Swedish system seems to have coped pretty well with the constraints set by the Takeover Directive. It can be predicted that the smoothness of the takeover process will not be much affected by compliance with the EU regulations, even though they constrain the national legislator's ability to improve that smoothness in the future. The lower bound on the squeeze-out threshold is a prominent example in this regard, regardless of the 90% figure actually corresponding to the Swedish tradition. But this is a negligible problem compared to the side effects that distribution of legal powers, under Swedish corporate law, has on the efficient dynamics of control allocation.

The reader may recall that the distribution of powers does not allow for managerial control of listed companies in Sweden.[105] This means, in turn, that dispersion of ownership nurtured by a sequence of changes in control unavoidably faces a lower bound. It can be expected that, when this limit is reached, idiosyncratic control rents no longer play a substantial role in corporate governance. However, the impossibility of transition to managerial control limits the incumbent controller's ability to cash them in.[106] As a result, control is stuck in families for generations, ownership and control are probably more concentrated than it would be desirable, and fewer and more 'unfocused' takeovers occur than would be efficient (Cronqvist and Nilsson 2003). Mismanagement of free cash and empire building – all instances of distortionary PBC – do not exactly arise from the takeover process, but from its failure to determine an efficient evolution of the ownership structure. Extraction of higher perquisites is the only way to profit from control when its rents cannot otherwise be cashed in.

This interpretation is borne out by the data showing that Swedish companies are mainly involved in highly mature businesses; and that their finance and acquisitions are affected more by traditional 'agency costs' than by expropriation of minority shareholders (Holmén and Högfeldt 2004). I subscribe to the view of some Swedish commentators that distortionary PBC, not diversion of shareholder value, could be the real problem of corporate governance in Sweden (Holmén and Högfeldt 2009). I can only speculate that this is determined by the failure of corporate law to provide sufficient entitlements for managerial control, rather than by a too liberal attitude towards pyramids or dual class shares for which Sweden is traditionally blamed. The recent empirical evidence on how Swedish capitalism has failed to evolve despite the decreasing importance of control-enhancing mechanisms seems to support this conclusion (Henrekson and Jakobsson 2012).

---

105 See *supra* Chapter 4, section 4.4.1.
106 See *supra* Chapter 3, section 3.7.3.

8.5.2　*A new takeover regulation in the Netherlands*

As far as takeover regulation is concerned, the Netherlands is again a peculiar case. One reason is that the Netherlands used to have a minimal takeover regulation and no mandatory bid before the Takeover Directive was implemented. The second difficulty is that, differently from other countries in continental Europe, corporate governance in the Netherlands features both managerial and shareholder control, which are obviously affected by takeover regulation in different fashions. Third, assessing the impact of takeover regulation in the Netherlands is more difficult due to the complications in the legal distribution of corporate powers, particularly those due to the stakeholder orientation of Dutch company law. As we saw in Chapter 4, these are the key legal underpinnings of the Dutch model of corporate governance. Therefore, let us consider separately the issues of takeover resistance and of the mandatory bid with reference to companies that have, or have not, a controlling shareholder.

8.5.2.1　*When the management is in charge*

Takeover resistance is the key issue under managerial control. The latter would even be difficult to sustain if managers had no way to shield themselves from a hostile takeover. The Dutch legislator has then chosen to opt out of both the board neutrality and the breakthrough rules (Davies et al 2010). To be sure, the Dutch Government originally flirted with both rules. In the first bill of implementation of the Takeover Directive, not only was a hostile takeover bid no longer allowed as an exception to the duty of the *Administratiekantoor* to issue a proxy to holders of depository receipts, but also priority shares (carrying preferential nomination rights) and protective preference shares (allowing dilution of unwelcome bidders) were bound to be neutralized upon at least 75% of the share capital being tendered to the bidder.

The Dutch Parliament rejected that proposal. In addition, neither the Government nor the Parliament have ever questioned the principle, established by the judiciary since the time of the battle over control of Gucci, that the board may take frustrating actions in the interest of the company and of its *stakeholders*.[107] Individual companies may still opt in to the board neutrality and/or the breakthrough rules in their articles of association. However, this would be no exception to the principles firmly established in the case law that the board may resist takeover when this is in the interest of the company's stakeholders as a whole. Opting in the two rules in question is therefore even more unlikely for Dutch companies than anywhere else in Europe. This is confirmed by the company practice (Bekkum et al 2010). The Dutch Takeover Act specifically takes into account the traditional takeover defenses supported by corporate law. For instance, the obligation of the *Administratiekantoor* to

---

107 See *supra* Chapter 4, section 4.3.3.

issue a proxy to the holders of depository receipts is suspended pending a hostile bid; and the holder of depository receipts as a result of defensive measures implemented by a target company is exempted from the mandatory bid. However, it seems that companies have spontaneously decided to decrease the number if not the intensity of takeover defenses due to the market pressure by institutional investors (de Jong et al 2010). This applies particularly to the depository receipts.

The introduction of the mandatory bid into Dutch law is not really problematic so long as the target's ownership is dispersed; the acquirer will always be smart enough to avoid triggering it. As could be expected, takeover bids after the implementation of the Directive have continued to be mainly voluntary, where the price can be freely agreed upon between the acquirer and the incumbent management. The expertise of the Enterprise Chamber of the Amsterdam Court of Appeals – as well as the ease of activating a proceeding before it – can be expected to provide sufficient constraints against value-decreasing takeovers.[108] To be sure, the option to request a proceeding in front of the Enterprise Chamber can be used strategically to block an unwelcome takeover, particularly by the Work Council whose powers have been strengthened recently.[109] In addition, coercive bids are traditionally impossible under Dutch corporate law because of the restrictive regulation of the minority's squeeze-out.[110] This feature is unchanged after the implementation of the Takeover Directive, which compels Member states to provide for post-bid squeeze-out while regulating the consideration in such a way as to exclude coercive bids.

The approach of the Dutch legislator was quite conservative in this respect. Both squeeze-out and sell-out rights, for a consideration equal to the bid price, are triggered by the acquisition of 95% or more of the outstanding shares. This has resulted in the introduction of a sell-out right where there was none (Timmerman and Doorman 2002), and in the squeeze-out right being modified in the price regulation: the Enterprise Chamber will continue to be in charge of the proceeding, but a consideration equal to the bid price will have to be considered as fair under the conditions established by the Directive.[111] Needless to say, a lower threshold for the exercise of squeeze-out could ease the takeover process without undermining investor protection. Still, 90% is the lowest figure allowed by the Takeover Directive.

---

108 See *supra* Chapter 6, section 6.3.3. It should be remembered that the Enterprise Chamber has exclusive jurisdiction on the Inquiry Procedure. Over the last few years, this procedure has become very popular in the takeover context as it can be activated on grounds of mismanagement pending a takeover bid. See Meinema (2003) and Bekkum et al (2010).

109 See DeBrauw Blackstone Westbroek Newsletter, *Bills on shareholders' and works council's rights become law*, 1 July 2010.

110 Squeeze-out traditionally requires the intervention of the Enterprise Chamber and is quite burdensome. See Timmerman and Doorman (2002).

111 Importantly, that requires that at least 90% of the shares (excluding those already in possession of the bidder) be acquired through the bid (Bekkum et al 2010).

One important legal friction affecting the takeover of free-standing firms in the Netherlands has nothing to do with the Directive. It is about regulation of severance payments. Traditionally management compensation could be handled entirely at the level of the supervisory board. Since 2004, all aspects of management remuneration – including severance payments – must be disciplined according to a policy endorsed by the shareholder meeting. With the aim to limit the high costs of board members' dismissal, the Dutch Government even considered setting an upper bound to the management's golden parachutes, based on a compensation formula adopted by Sub-district Courts in labor cases (the "Dutch cantonal formula," so-called *Kantonrechtersformule*). This proposal has never become law, although some companies have spontaneously chosen to establish their remuneration policy on that basis. The upper bound on management's severance payments is set instead by the Corporate Governance Code, which as we know is both binding on an "apply-or-explain" basis and complied with by the vast majority of Dutch listed firms.[112] According to the Code, golden parachutes cannot exceed the amount of one-year salary, which can be raised up to a two-year amount in particular circumstances. The Dutch Monitoring Commission on Corporate Governance reported that some companies that failed to comply with these rules in 2009 explained that on the necessity to honor existing contracts. The Dutch legislator is thus considering regulating the whole matter of managerial remuneration by law, including a duty for the supervisory board to revise the bonuses contracted for in case of changes in control.[113] This situation gives the incumbent management limited, if any, ability to renegotiate severance payments in the event of a takeover. This circumstance forces would-be bidders willing to lure managers into parting with control to offer a higher takeover premium and to forego takeover when this premium would be too high compared to the gains at stake.

8.5.2.2 How can controlling shareholders tackle the mandatory bid?

In the presence of a controlling shareholder, neither takeover resistance nor golden parachutes really affect the functioning of the market for corporate control. The latter is naturally operated on the basis of negotiated deals. However, the mandatory bid potentially affects this operation. An acquirer who crosses the threshold of 30% of voting rights has to bid for all of the outstanding shares at a price deemed to be equitable. The price is determined to be fair when it corresponds with the highest consideration paid by the bidder for stock acquisitions over the preceding 12 months. In principle, these rules disallow the payment of a control premium, which discourages changes in control altogether. Such a discipline of control transactions is

---

112 See *supra* Chapter 6, section 6.3.3.
113 See DeBrauw Blackstone Westbroek Newsletter, *Remuneration and legal position of directors of Dutch listed companies and financial institutions*, January 2011.

particularly burdensome for the efficiency of concentrated ownership structures. Unless there are ways to get around it. The Dutch Securities Authority (*Autoriteit Financiële Markten*) can indeed grant an exemption from the mandatory bid in some specific circumstances.

In the Netherlands, there are few opportunities to circumvent the mandatory bid when a control block is transferred. The easiest situation is when the controlling ownership is lower than 30%. In this case, the acquirer would be allowed to purchase this block at a premium without having to pay the same control premium to minority shareholders. He may then decide whether to make a voluntary bid for the rest of the company's shares. The law establishes that passing the 30% threshold through a voluntary, 'any or all' tender offer does not trigger the mandatory bid; under these circumstances, the price is not regulated. Still, a mandatory bid obligation might be imposed on the acquirer by the Enterprise Chamber. To avoid this risk, a prospective acquirer should be careful with building up a toehold in the target company. Or alternatively, the acquirer should wait one year after purchasing the initial stake before launching a voluntary bid for the rest of the shares and trying to take the company private.

Often a controlling shareholder would account for more than 30% of share capital. The Dutch discipline is constructed is such a way that little, if anything, can be done to get around the mandatory bid when there is a change in control of that size. The transfer, in any form, of 30% or more of the voting power triggers the mandatory bid, which in turn raises the cost of changes in control undermining the viability of possibly many of them. In this situation, the only possibility is taking the company private *before* control is transferred. This is possible for existing controlling shareholders and their family, because those already controlling more than 30% of voting power before 28 October 2007 are practically exempted from the mandatory bid when they increase their stake. After a recent reform, this increase can also be implemented by means of accessions to a consortium of control persons. In addition, the mandatory bid can be waived if a transfer of control is approved by shareholders with a 90% majority (so-called whitewash).[114]

All in all, transferring a controlling stake of 30% or more is bound to be expensive in one way or another. It is a much better strategy to stay below the mandatory bid threshold, when possible. This should not be a problem for corporate controllers given the wide array of legal instruments to fend off unwelcome bids. Indeed, in 2005, only about 11% of listed firms in the Netherlands had a shareholder holding between 30% and 50% of voting power. The percentage is nearly halved compared to 1992 (de Jong et al 2010). This suggests a strong trend to reduce the size of large shareholdings below 30%, which is more consistent with the current state of Dutch corporate law.

---

114 See DeBrauw Blackstone Westbroek Newsletter, *Amended Dutch Public Offer Rules in force as of 1 July 2012*, 13 June 2012.

8.5.2.3 *The Dutch 'structure regime' and the takeover process*

Another impediment to the efficient functioning of the market for corporate control does not depend on the implementation of the Takeover Directive, but rather on the tradition of the Dutch model. Under both managerial and shareholder control, the structure regime undermines the acquirer's ability to replace the members of the management and the supervisory board, in spite of his being in control of the majority – or even all – of voting rights. Even under the new regime, the shareholder meeting is not entitled to place binding nominations, but only to veto the supervisory board's choice; and the power of appointing new board members, upon dismissal of the old ones, resides only with the Enterprise Chamber.[115] As was illustrated in Chapter 4, this is not an impediment for the controlling shareholder to exercise ongoing control in the long run; but it can indeed be an impediment to changes in control that require a quick replacement of the management. For this purpose, full control of the supervisory board would be necessary.

The structure regime is traditionally associated with the entrenchment of Dutch managers (Becht et al 2007), but it is unnecessary for this purpose. Managerial control may otherwise avail itself of both a favorable distribution of powers and takeover resistance. In the Netherlands not many listed companies are effectively subject to the structure regime; still, many of these companies are under managerial control. The structure regime is not really needed to support separation of ownership and control. However, it creates frictions that may undermine the efficiency of the takeover process. Therefore it would be worthwhile considering repealing the structure regime or at least, allowing its suspension in the wake of a takeover, so that the acquirer faces no rigidities in replacing the incumbent management. Unfortunately, although the Dutch legislator is going to introduce for all companies the possibility to opt in to a one-tier board structure, the structure regime will continue to apply to those companies that do not manage to opt out of it. In this case, the nomination rights that normally pertain to the supervisory board would be transferred to the non-executive directors in a one-tier structure. This would continue to undermine the smoothness of takeovers, both friendly and hostile.

8.5.3 *The implementation of the Takeover Directive in Italy*

The Italian case may be regarded as both an easy and a difficult one. It may look easy because corporate governance only features controlling shareholders (or coalitions thereof) and takeover regulation included the key elements of the European Directive already for more than a decade before its coming into force.[116] However, the Italian case is difficult because the patterns of separation

---

115 See *supra* Chapter 4, section 4.3.3.
116 The first comprehensive body of takeover regulation was introduced in Italy in 1992 (Act No. 149/1992 – "Disciplina delle offerte pubbliche di vendita, sottoscrizione, acquisto e

of ownership and control are strongly influenced by the long-standing weakness of the discipline of conflicted interest transactions and by the absence of a distribution of corporate powers supporting managerial control.[117] Both factors contribute to ownership concentration and stock market under-development, but – even more importantly – they constrain the efficiency of the takeover process. As I mentioned, the solution of these two problems has to be regarded as a precondition for an efficient regulation of the market of corporate control.[118] I shall start by assuming that they can be tackled in the ways I have illustrated in the previous chapter. This may be regarded as overly optimistic, of course. Therefore, in the end, I shall consider the implications of unresolved expropriation of minority shareholders for takeover regulation.

8.5.3.1 The 'Italian model' of takeover regulation

Italy implemented the Takeover Directive in various phases making extensive use of the optional arrangements provided for regarding the board neutrality and the breakthrough rule. Originally, Italy implemented both these rules as mandatory, which was quite exceptional particularly as regards the breakthrough.[119] In the wake of the financial turmoil of 2008 the discipline was radically changed because Italian law opted out of both rules; individual companies could opt in either rule in their articles of association, but the default was that none applied.[120] Finally, in 2009, the implementation of the board neutrality rule was changed again, but in a rather unique fashion compared to the rest of the EU countries:[121] board neutrality (but not also the breakthrough rule) became default; it is up to individual companies to opt out of it. Reciprocity has been maintained as an option for individual companies that apply the board neutrality and/or the breakthrough rule (Davies et al 2010).

Remarkably, in several aspects takeover regulation in Italy was already anticipating the Directive before its implementation. Since 1998, a manda-tory bid is in place. This is triggered when a threshold of 30% of voting rights

---

scambio di titoli"). The 1992 legislation provided – *inter alia* – for both a mandatory bid (to be imposed by the National Securities Authority – *Consob* – without a fixed threshold) and absolute board passivity pending a hostile bid. The current regulation is established by the Legislative Decree No. 58/1998 ("Testo unico delle disposizioni in materia di intermediazione finanziaria"), which has introduced a threshold of 30% of voting capital triggering the mandatory bid, substituted board neutrality for board passivity, and provided for a mini-breakthrough rule concerning voting pacts.

117 See *supra* Chapter 4, section 4.4.1; and Chapter 6, section 6.3.5.
118 See *supra* Chapter 7, section 7.1.
119 Legislative Decree No. 229/2007 amending the Legislative Decree No. 59/1998 effective 28 December 2007.
120 Decree-Law No. 185/2008 effective 29 November 2008 (converted by Law No. 2/2009).
121 Legislative Decree No. 146/2009 effective 6 November 2009.

is surpassed; exceptions are very limited.[122] Also before the first phase of implementation of the Directive, defensive measures could only be taken by the board in the presence of shareholder authorization with at least a 30% majority.[123] However, the bid price was not regulated as strictly as in the UK and later, by the Takeover Directive for the entire EU. Before 2008, the price was set equal to the average between the highest consideration paid for pre-bid acquisitions and the market price weighted-average in the 12 months preceding the bid.[124] Alternatively, the acquirer could have sought a quantity discount by making a partial, non-discriminatory bid for at least 60% of outstanding stock. This option has also been maintained after the implementation of the Directive. However, it is only available in the absence of significant pre-bid purchases and conditional on the approval by the shareholder meeting (without the votes held by controlling shareholders) and the authorization by the Securities Authority (*Consob*).[125]

Even before the board neutrality rule ceased to be mandatory in 2009, the regulation of takeover defenses in Italy has never been as strict as it looked. Most controlling shareholders in Italy hold (directly or through coalitions) more than 30% of the voting rights, and are otherwise entrenched when they do not. In addition, some financial instruments introduced by the corporate law reform in 2004 could have been used with anti-takeover purposes: they may escape the hurdles of the board neutrality rule if they are issued before a bid is launched.[126] However, probably because these instruments cannot support ongoing managerial control, but only its defense, they have had little impact on the governance of listed firms (Enriques 2006).

Before the Directive, takeover regulation in Italy featured an interesting compromise between shareholder protection and the promotion of an active market for corporate control (Kraakman et al 2009). On the one hand, the mandatory bid was made relatively uneasy to circumvent whenever control was exercised with more than 30% of the voting rights. Splitting the control block would not help, since pre-bid purchases also affect the price of voluntary bids under Italian law. Although, under certain conditions, mergers and other organic changes could (and still can) allow a change in control to escape the mandatory bid.[127] On the other hand, regulation did not compel full sharing of the control premium with minority shareholders. A discount was allowed on the price or the quantity of the bid, thereby easing the takeover process at least in those cases where the control premium was not too high relative to the inefficiencies of management.[128] This strategy had to stop

---

122 Art. 106(1) Legislative Decree No. 58/1998.
123 Art. 104 Legislative Decree No. 58/1998.
124 Art. 106(2) Legislative Decree No. 58/1998.
125 Art. 107 Legislative Decree No. 58/1998.
126 See *supra*, Chapter 4, section 4.4.2.
127 See art. 106(5) Legislative Decree No. 58/1998 and art. 49 Consob Reg. No. 11971/1999.
128 See art. 106(2) and art. 107 Legislative Decree No. 58/1998.

with the implementation of the Takeover Directive (which compels the mandatory bid price to be equal to the highest price paid in the 12 months preceding the bid); but anyway, it was not particularly successful. Although some more dynamism was initially observed in the ownership structure of listed companies after the enactment of the Decree 58/1998 (the "Draghi Law"), it seems that changes in control overall continue to take place below the mandatory bid threshold or they do not occur at all (Bianchi and Bianco 2006).

Perhaps two mistakes were made in drafting the Italian takeover regulation. The first one was to expect that contestability of corporate control would have eventually emerged thanks to these rules. To this purpose, not only was the rule of board neutrality laid down (in spite of its little usefulness in concentrated ownership structures), but Italy was one of the first countries to introduce a mini-breakthrough rule. Shareholder agreements as to both the voting and the transfer of shares have no effect in the wake of a tender offer, and may be definitively set aside when the bid is successful.[129] As it turns out, none of these measures have managed to stimulate contestability. It seems that hardly any listed company is managed without the support of a controlling shareholder or a coalition of them. Contestability cannot be imposed. The second mistake was to consider a strict takeover regulation a substitute for an effective discipline of related-party transactions and similar conflicts of interest. Rightly, in 1998, the problem of minority shareholders expropriation was considered more important than the adverse effects of the mandatory bid on the dynamics of control allocation. In this perspective, the rules that were established back then could be regarded as a good compromise, until a more efficient discipline of diversionary PBC became available. However, after fifteen years, a change in approach is in order: takeover regulation is not the right tool for policing shareholder expropriation, and should be freed from this concern in order to support an efficient market for corporate control.

8.5.3.2 *Activating the market for corporate control*

Separating the protection of minority shareholders from the regulation of takeovers is certainly not in the spirit of the Takeover Directive, although – from a normative perspective – it should be. Given this circumstance, the Italian policymakers should attempt to make the EU regulation as little burdensome as possible for the market for corporate control. Unfortunately, the Takeover Directive does not provide much opportunity to do so. Italy had to repeal its peculiar regulation of the bid price and the *Consob* has only limited discretion to allow discounts on the bid price. The option of partial bids could instead be maintained as it is considered compatible with the Takeover Directive. This is hardly enough to stimulate an active market

---

129 Art. 123(3) Legislative Decree No. 58/1998.

for corporate control. The Italian regulation should use any possible margin of discretion in order to allow efficient changes in control to get around the mandatory bid. One immediate solution would be to set the mandatory bid threshold at a higher level. However, this seems to be quite unfeasible, given the convergence of the near totality of EU jurisdictions towards the 30% threshold.[130]

As an alternative, voluntary bids could be liberalized. Currently, unless the acquirer goes straight for the partial bid option, voluntary bids do not allow price regulation to be easily escaped. However, the Takeover Directive definitively allows for this possibility, at least when the voluntary bid is unrestricted. The Italian regulation might ease the transfer of controlling blocks by legalizing the following strategy. Payment of the control premium is allowed inasmuch as it concerns less than 30% of the outstanding capital. The control premium needs *not* be paid to minority shareholders when their shares are acquired by means of a subsequent tender offer. To this purpose, the price of both voluntary bids and of subsequent purchases should be unregulated – or at least, it should be regulated in such a way as to allow for two-stage acquisitions with a window no larger than six months. The reader can recognize the Swedish solution here.[131]

There are two important requirements for the above mechanism to be an effective acquisition strategy. The first is that the acquirer of the control block should be entitled both to exercise and to defend corporate control with less than 30% of the voting rights so long as this is needed. Partly this depends on the distribution of corporate powers; but let us leave this problem here. More importantly, the acquirer needs to be able to shield the company from another takeover (which may well be hostile) until he can make a tender offer for the rest of the shares. The current regime of board neutrality and breakthrough rule in Italy clearly allows for such a strategy. Italian companies can and sometimes do opt out of the board neutrality rule, whereas the breakthrough needs to be opted in, which no company does. Apart from the mini-breakthrough of voting pacts, which remains mandatory, companies that are not subject to either of these rules can be good targets for a friendly acquisition below the mandatory bid threshold, ironically just because they would not be good targets for a hostile takeover after the first stage of the acquisition (when only less than 30% of voting power can be acquired). In a sense, this mechanism can be interpreted as a first step towards the emergence of managerial control, although this could only be established in the long run upon an appropriate regulation of both distribution of corporate powers and conflicted interest transactions.[132]

130 See European Commission, *Report on the Implementation of the Directive on Takeover Bids*, 2007, Annex 2.

131 See *supra* section 8.5.1.

132 See *supra* Chapters 4 and 6. In the example, the acquirer still would have to consolidate his position as soon as he can launch a voluntary bid without price regulation.

The second requirement is that the acquirer must find it profitable to make a tender offer for non-controlling shares. A necessary condition for this is that the takeover is value-increasing, because otherwise the acquirer would have no interest in buying-out minority shareholders. Let us assume this is the case for a moment. The best of all worlds would be if the acquirer was entitled to decide freely whether to make the bid or not, and on what terms, immediately after the acquisition of the control block or of a part of it.[133] But this would not likely be compatible with the Takeover Directive in the present configuration. One possibility is that the acquirer should wait, as in Sweden, for at least six months for overcoming the regulatory restrictions on the bid price.[134] This would already place an important constraint on the acquirer's ability to profit from the tender offer: the market price may just rise too much meanwhile, if he is really going to improve the management.

The odds of making a successful bid for non-controlling stock are even more importantly affected by the rules governing the purchase of the shares that are not tendered. Here comes the importance of the regulation of squeeze-out. If the bidder has no good chances to buy out minority shareholders and to prevent them from free riding, he may forego the bid (and the acquisition) in the first place. After implementing the Takeover Directive, the Italian regulation of post-bid squeeze-out has become somewhat less strict than before. The triggering threshold used to be as high as 98% and the consideration had to be determined upon appraisal by an expert appointed by the court. Now, when at least 90% of the shares are acquired via a tender offer and 95% of share capital is reached, the bidder is entitled to squeeze out the remaining shareholders at the bid price. This solution is probably as conservative as it could be given the Takeover Directive. While the strictness of the squeeze-out rules can be explained by the traditional concern for expropriation of minority shareholders, this considerably limits the takeover activity. The Italian legislator should consider relaxing this discipline as soon as the concern that acquisitions are value-decreasing becomes less severe.

8.5.3.3 *Looting and the broader set of problems of Italian corporate governance*

Although it is embarrassing to say for an Italian, we cannot yet safely assume that takeovers are not value-decreasing in Italy. This does not just depend on the regulation of squeeze-outs (a value-decreasing acquirer would simply not go for the purchase of non-controlling shares), but on a number of legal and institutional shortcomings that determine the corporate controller's ability to

---

133 See *supra* Chapter 7, section 7.3.2. The American regulation (*supra* section 8.2.2) is the one coming closest to that framework.

134 No such requirement is explicitly established by the Takeover Directive. However, compare art. 5.2 with the general principle of equal treatment of shareholders, as enunciated in art. 3.1(a) of the Takeover Directive.

effect non-pro-rata distributions. I have extensively reviewed these short-comings in Chapter 6. However, the core of the problem is more about how corporate control is exercised on an ongoing basis than in how it is transferred. This is one of the key arguments of the present study. In the presence of diversionary PBC, the market for corporate control cannot be assumed to work efficiently. However, this is not a good reason to dismiss the efficiency of takeovers as unimportant.

The highest priority for Italian corporate law is to police diversionary PBC, but this should not come at the expenses of equally important issues. As regards takeovers, it is essential to make sure that acquisitions do not result in an increase of non-pro-rata distributions.[135] The significant progress in the Italian discipline of conflicted interest transactions provides indirect support for this condition, at least as far as the ongoing management is concerned; this support was probably not available fifteen years ago (Enriques 2009). This may still be insufficient to rule out value-decreasing takeovers. However, policymakers should address looting directly instead of trying to prevent it making takeovers indistinctively expensive for looters as well as for efficient would-be acquirers. This may be too high a price to pay to protect minority shareholders (Kraakman et al 2009). Having this rigidity tempered by a less burdensome configuration of the mandatory bid is only an imperfect solution, which is also difficult to reconcile with the Takeover Directive as it stands.

The comparative picture suggests a better alternative: having control trans-actions scrutinized by the judiciary under the same 'no shareholder diversion' standard as in the ongoing exercise of corporate control.[136] This requires both easy access to court redress by shareholders (or their representatives). But courts also need to have sufficient expertise to dismiss nuisance litigation in a summary judgment, on the one hand, and to 'smell out' the most sophisti-cated instances of looting, on the other. We have seen that the two countries of our sample that go for this solution – the US and the Netherlands – allow for both appropriate procedural rules and a specialized judiciary to police conflicts of interest also regarding control transactions.

None of these tools is currently available under Italian corporate law or at least, not entirely. There is only a slight chance that this situation will change in the future with the new forms of private enforcement that have been recently introduced.[137] The Italian legislation should take stock of the recent improvements in the policing of diversionary PBC, by allowing first for their consolidation, and subsequently for their extension to corporate control transactions. Also in this context, the judicial oversight could be limited to the risk of value diversion, and allow for as little interference as possible with business judgment (i.e., the merits of a change in control). Then the approach to takeover regulation could be safely liberalized inasmuch as this is allowed

---

135 See *supra* Chapter 7, section 7.2.3.
136 See *supra* Chapter 7, section 7.4.5.
137 See *supra* Chapter 6, section 6.3.5.

by the EU law.[138] The next and final step towards a more efficient regulation of corporate governance would be a more even distribution of corporate powers, allowing control to be exercised by the board of directors also in the absence of a controlling shareholder. As was illustrated in Chapter 4, this may require little more than a reform of the proxy voting system.[139]

---

138   For the view that EU law should also become more enabling with respect to takeovers, see recently Enriques et al (2012).
139   See *supra* Chapter 4, sections 4.4.1 and 4.6.1.

Concluding remarks

As in Pacces (2007), I have divided the conclusions of this study into ten propositions. The last section of these conclusions aims instead to suggest a few avenues for future research in the law and economics of control powers.

1 Corporate governance is not just a relationship between principals and agents

Historically, the agency theory was a major turning point in the economic and legal analysis of corporate governance. Before, economic theory was hardly able to explain why corporate finance mattered besides different taxation of debt and equity. Legal theory was ultimately unable to explain what was wrong with separation of ownership and control. With the emphasis on asymmetric information between managers and financiers, principal–agent models identified in agency costs the explanation of both issues, and in their minimization the virtue of the corporate contract. The law and economics of corporate governance was born under this premise. Managers were regarded as agents of shareholders, creditors, and other firm constituencies, but the open-ended structure of the equity contract made incentive alignment with shareholder interest the fundamental issue: shareholders needed to have sufficient powers to hold managers accountable. In spite of subsequent developments in economic theory, the law and economics of corporate governance is still a prisoner of this view.

What I have attempted to demonstrate in this book is that the above view is incomplete, and in some respects it turns out even to be wrong. This view does not fully match the empirical evidence. Principal–agent models can explain different choices of ownership and capital structure at the firm level, but cannot tell why these choices exhibit structurally different patterns across countries. The absolute prevalence of controlling shareholders outside the US and the UK is a remarkable challenge to the agency framework. One explanation of this circumstance, which is still consistent with the principal–agent framework, is that in some countries corporate law fails to support minimization of agency costs. This is the gist of the 'law matters' argument.

From a purely theoretical perspective, traditional principal–agent models are incomplete because they do not allow institutions and the law to play a significant role. Incomplete does not necessarily mean wrong. The more recent elaboration on contractual incompleteness has tried to fix the inconsistencies of the agency framework while preserving the original insight. Apparently, managers may still be regarded as agents of shareholders in this perspective. However, given the imperfections of the corporate contract, corporate law is necessary to protect dispersed shareholders from expropriation and to empower them vis à vis the management. When it fails to achieve this goal, controlling shareholders are the only option for incentive alignment.

As I have shown, this view – the 'law matters' version of the agency framework – fares no better in spite of its popularity. On the legal side, ownership concentration also prevails in those jurisdictions that, besides protecting shareholders from expropriation, empower them the most. Sweden is a case in point. On the economic side, the underpinnings of this modified agency framework are also contradicted by the empirical evidence. Under contractual incompleteness, shareholders are supposed to delegate control rights to corporate controllers, and the law should guarantee that they could withdraw from that delegation at any time. Whatever the contents of the law are in this regard, there is virtually no place in the world where shareholders can count on that. Both lawyers and economists tend to blame this as a major distortion in corporate governance, but the fact is that hostility in real-world takeovers is highly exceptional.

The ultimate reason why the agency paradigm does not fully explain corporate governance is that *control matters*. Control rights may not always be delegated by the owners, but sometimes retained as entitlements by an entrepreneur-manager. This is the *first conclusion* of the present inquiry; it also explains why and to what extent the agency approach is flawed.

That being said, the principal–agent framework still captures at least two prominent features of corporate governance. One is that the corporate controller's incentives need to be aligned with the interest of shareholders, for they would not invest otherwise. The other is that incentive alignment can only be achieved as a second best. The crucial difference highlighted by the present study is that incentive-compatibility is not necessarily obtained by allocating powers to shareholders; it can occur equally well when the abuse of the same powers by corporate controllers is constrained. In this perspective, managers and controlling shareholders can no longer be considered as agents, as if they were sort of employees of investors. Surely, they do not consider themselves as being in such a position when they play an entrepreneurial role.

2 Entrepreneurship is a major omission in incomplete contracts theories of separation of ownership and control

At least since Ronald Coase's famous article of 1937, the theory of the firm was separated from the theory of entrepreneurship. However, it is remarkable how Coase – building more on legal theory than on an economic theory that did not yet exist – intended the firm relationships as closer to those established between a master and his servants than to those between agents and principals (Coase 1937: 392). About thirty years later, the founding father of corporate law and economics – Henry Manne – inaugurated the study of the market for corporate control by claiming that control of corporations should be treated like any other commodity. In spite of his contention that authority, not consensus, explained the nature of the firm, Coase is considered as the intellectual father of the nexus of contracts theory of the firm, which later provided the basis for the agency approach to corporate governance. Manne is considered as the first author to have advocated the virtue of hostile takeovers; but his oft-cited paper (Manne 1965) contains no such advocacy and rather points to negotiations for mergers as a way to allocate control to the best available manager. Neither of these authors explicitly discussed entrepreneurship. Yet both of them clearly had entrepreneurs in mind when they analyzed, respectively, the exercise of authority in firm management and the discovery of profit opportunities in corporate takeovers.

Uncertainty is the ultimate reason why entrepreneurs exist: they may be especially skilled individuals or visionaries, but the fact is that they look beyond what markets already give a price to. Every day, most entrepreneurs fail and only a few of them are successful: we owe economic progress to the latter, but they may never get their chance in the absence of the former. Uncertainty is also the reason why contracts are incomplete and firms need to exist as hierarchical organizations alternative to markets. Perhaps the most curious thing about the study of uncertainty is that it resulted in two theories of the same phenomenon that hardly speak to each other. The *second conclusion* of the present work is that a thorough understanding of corporate governance requires integration of the theory of the firm with the theory of *entrepreneurship*.

Mainstream economics is with the theory of the firm, which took up the heritage of the neoclassical paradigm. That paradigm already featured the problem of rewards to inventiveness in price theory, but only managed to describe the firm as a "black box." More recent economics of contractual incompleteness has integrated Marshall's (1893) notion of quasi-rents in the theory of the firm: non-contractable rewards to inventiveness, more customarily described as firm-specific investments, are appropriated in the form of quasi-rents by the owner(s) of the enterprise. This approach had the remarkable merit to explain why firms exist and grow, but not how they may be owned by non-controlling shareholders. Explaining separation of ownership and control in this framework required that asset-specificity be centered in shareholders' investments, not in the manager's. As a result, shareholders had ultimate authority over the firm's assets, and just delegated their daily management. Protection of managerial firm-specific investment was deemed unimportant in public companies because entrepreneurial inventiveness was not considered an issue compared with the problem of managers' incentives alignment with the owner's interest.

The conflict with the parallel theory of entrepreneurship is striking. One prominent result of this theory is separation of entrepreneurs from the capitalists. According to Kirzner (1979), ownership is never a condition for entrepreneurship. The corporation is considered a way to ease the access of entrepreneurial talent to large-scale financing. This implies that returns on entrepreneurship need also to be separated from returns on shareholders' capital. Following the traditional controversy between Neo-Austrian and neoclassical economics, the theory of entrepreneurship does not specify how rewards to entrepreneurial talent are appropriated; it only contends that – in some way or another – they are. The very process of appropriation is what ultimately motivates entrepreneurship and economic progress, at least until the same process makes entrepreneurs obsolete. Despite Schumpeter's (1947) famous prophecy about the destiny of capitalism, we have not yet experienced such obsolescence. 'Creative destruction' of entrepreneurs seems to go on endlessly, and the only thing we know about this process is that it is inherently unpredictable.

I am not the first who has tried to integrate entrepreneurship in mainstream economics of corporate governance. Clearly, the only possible way to operationalize this intuition is through the notion of quasi-rents as a reward of managerial choices under uncertainty. Some have tried to overcome the hurdles of the property rights approach by hypothesizing a state-contingent allocation of control rights (carrying conditional entitlements to quasi-rents) between managers and shareholders (e.g. Burkart et al 1997). Others have followed Oliver Williamson's intuition of 'forbearance' in enforcement of legal entitlements, and hypothesized sources of power alternative to ownership in a comprehensive stakeholder theory of the firm (e.g. Rajan and Zingales 1998b). I have not found these explanations entirely convincing, and I have therefore advocated a different one. Rewards to entrepreneurial talent can be appropriated in the non-contractable form of private benefits of control. Corporate law may support this result providing entitlements to firm control separated from ownership of the corporation.

3 Private benefits of control and control entrenchment are not always 'bad' for corporate governance

I had a difficult case in challenging the conventional wisdom that private benefits of control are a curse for corporate governance. The idea that private benefits may play a beneficial role conflicts with both the lawyers' view of shareholder democracy and the economists' reliance on principal–agent models. Albeit for different reasons, both views contend that shareholders as a whole should be ultimately in charge of corporate governance and that fighting extraction of private benefits of control should be a major goal of corporate law. Yet, both fairness and efficiency of this ideal picture are contradicted by the empirical evidence. Non-controlling shareholders may live with their being powerless so long as they earn conspicuous returns on their investment. Many companies featuring generations of controlling shareholders or a self-perpetuating management are both profitable for investors and reward controllers with private benefits on top of that. It may seem cynical, but there seems to be no such thing as a shareholder democracy in the real world. It may seem heretical, but shareholders do not always stand to gain all of the firm's residual (alias, profits). Regardless of whether these outcomes can be considered 'fair,' the only way to reconcile this evidence with efficiency is to allow private benefits of control to also perform some beneficial role in corporate governance. *The third conclusion* of this investigation is that *private benefits of control* not only can, but sometimes must perform such a beneficial role.

In principal–agent models, private benefits of control always come at the expense of non-controlling shareholders. They depend either on 'stealing' or on 'shirking' by the corporate controller. Following Mayer (1999), I have characterized these two categories of private benefits as diversionary and distortionary with respect to shareholder value. If we take the latter as a criterion for welfare analysis, these benefits cannot but have adverse effects on the efficiency of corporate governance. However, distortionary private benefits are an unavoidable consequence of separation of ownership and control. They might be 'ugly' for this reason, but we have to live with them. Diversion and distortion of shareholder value are not the only way in which private benefits of control may be generated, although these are the only two sources allowed by the agency framework. If we depart from that framework and take a straightforward incomplete contracts perspective, we can assume that part of the firm value is neither observable nor verifiable. This part is therefore excluded from shareholder value and accounts for the value of entrepreneurship in the corporate enterprise. These are profits 'in the entrepreneur's head' and have no value whatsoever for outside shareholders, at least until they become observable by somebody else. I have defined this value as idiosyncratic private benefits of control. Consideration for entrepreneurship in the exercise of corporate control is the reason why corporate governance needs to support them, at least potentially. Their idiosyncrasy to the corporate controller is the reason why initially their extraction does not reduce shareholder wealth.

This still does not tell us why these private benefits are good for corporate governance. In order to provide incentives to entrepreneurship in corporate governance, they need to be appropriable by the corporate controller. I am not making the heroic assumption that managers or controlling shareholders are less greedy than investors. However, they may be more patient. It could be that idiosyncratic private benefits of control account for some incommensurable physic satisfaction; to be sure, they are sometimes characterized in this fashion. However, in the wake of a change in control, profits that are still to be realized come out of the entrepreneur's head: they become a tangible issue inasmuch somebody else is willing to pay for taking a chance on them. The quasi-rent nature of idiosyncratic private benefits becomes apparent in this circumstance. The market for corporate control makes them both valuable and appropriable. If we considered only the takeover stage, their appropriation would be simply a matter of distribution. If we consider them as a prospective reward to the investment of entrepreneurial talent, efficiency requires that they be appropriated by the incumbent controller. The latter would not make any firm-specific investment under a different arrangement. Incumbents can only appropriate control rents when they cannot be ousted against their will; that is, when control is entrenched. Idiosyncratic private benefits may thus explain how entrenchment of corporate control can be efficient in corporate governance. Entrenchment is what allows idiosyncratic private benefits to play a motivational role for entrepreneurship.

Entrenchment of corporate control has two major implications for corporate governance. One is that separation of ownership and control can only take place to the extent that corporate law supplies entitlements to corporate control independently of ownership. The second implication of entrenchment is that hostile takeovers are disallowed; in this situation the market for corporate control can only be operated by friendly takeovers. These two implications are broadly consistent with the empirical evidence about the functioning and the regulation of corporate ownership and control. However, both implications are often challenged by economic theorists and legal policymakers.

4 The market for corporate control can be efficiently operated by friendly takeovers

According to a quite standard view of corporate governance, when the corporate controller is entitled to shield himself from hostile takeover, shareholders lose twice: their shares are worth less because of excessive consumption of control perquisites; and they forego the opportunity of profitable tender offers by more efficient managers willing to take over. Apparently, both circumstances raise the agency costs of separation of ownership and control. As I hope to have demonstrated, this is not the only possible way to look at the market for corporate control. This view does not explain why the vast majority of non-controlling shareholders still invest in spite of control entrenchment. Therefore, this view must be incomplete, if not misguided.

In an incomplete contracting perspective, corporate governance features a little more than agency costs. The latter are included in the notion of private benefits of control; but this is broader and also allows for protection of control rents to be efficient. To rephrase the fundamental insight of the agency theory, the opportunity cost of the incumbent's consumption of distortionary private benefits will rise, all else being equal, as soon as a more efficient controller appears on the market. This problem is ideally dealt with by the market for corporate control, which should provide for dynamic minimization of distortionary private benefits over time. When nothing else than these benefits is at play, hostile takeovers would be the solution. But this is not always what the empirical evidence tells us. Something else must be at play when control contestability is ruled out at the outset. In order to interpret this kind of situation, I have introduced a tripartite account of private benefits of control. This complicates the picture considerably.

Hostile takeovers are sometimes not good. Particularly when entrepreneurship is at play, they would be disruptive of idiosyncratic private benefits whose protection is efficient. In these situations, hostile takeovers must be disallowed. Friendly takeovers become the only option under entrenchment of corporate control, and they may do quite as well. The problem is that idiosyncratic private benefits create a wedge between the interest of non-controlling shareholders in maximizing their returns and the controllers' concern for reward of their firm-specific investments. The market for corporate control can still minimize distortionary private benefits under this constraint, when it allows for changes in control to be operated on condition that the incumbent's control rents are compensated. This would imply that control changes hands if and only if insurgents can both make the company more profitable and compensate incumbents of their previous efforts in bringing the firm to the current state of development. Unfortunately, diversionary private benefits also interfere with this mechanism, and may compromise its constrained efficiency. In the presence of such benefits, control may end up being allocated to the best 'thief' of minority shareholders, instead of to the best available manager of the firm (Bebchuk et al 2000).

An appropriate set of constraints on the extraction of diversionary private benefits of control is therefore a precondition for the efficient functioning of the market for corporate control, as it is for efficient separation of ownership and control. If corporate law permits an allocation of powers that preserves the incumbent's idiosyncratic rents, it should also prevent control rents from being extracted in the form of diversion of shareholder value by regulating the abuse of the same powers. These are two necessary conditions for efficient corporate governance, but they are not sufficient. Corporate controllers should be proactively induced to part with control when a more efficient manager is available. The only way in which this can be reconciled with protection of idiosyncratic control rents ex-ante is allowing the market for corporate control to be operated through side payments ex-post. These payments are, alternatively, golden parachutes in managerial control structures and control premia in controlling shareholder structures. This may sound weird to lawyers, but – at least on condition that stealing is effectively curbed by the legal system – side payments should not be merely regarded as 'bribes': they are actually necessary to capture gains from trade, which in turn promote the efficient allocation of corporate control. One prominent implication of uncertainty about the prospective value of corporate control – depending on my previous assumptions about entrepreneurship – is that the amount of these payments cannot be determined at the outset, but must be freely bargained for at the takeover stage.

The market for corporate control is thus understood as an application of the Coase Theorem. If takeover bargaining was frictionless, corporate law should do nothing else than define the entitlements to corporate control. The presence of transaction costs explains not only why the allocation and the regulation of these entitlements matter, but also why further discipline of control transactions is required to cope with the frictions in the takeover process. Besides the specific implications for takeover regulation, *the fourth conclusion* of this book is that a market for corporate control based on a smooth sequence of *friendly acquisitions* can guarantee the dynamic efficiency of control allocation. This mechanism requires that, in the presence of entrepreneurship, the incumbent's control rents are compensated at every stage and that value diversion from minority shareholders is always disallowed.

This result builds on the few models that have treated entrenchment of corporate control under a narrower set of assumptions. Some of them consider control rents as a non-contractable reward for managerial effort. Bundling issues of deferred compensation with the dynamics of the market of corporate control, I have speculated that the results may differ from those achieved by the narrower existing literature. The bottom line is that shareholder value maximization under entrenchment of corporate control could be simply constrained-efficient. The constraint is given by the size of idiosyncratic control rents necessary to motivate the investment of entrepreneurial talent under uncertainty. An assumption consistent with the theory of entrepreneurship is that this size is decreasing over the firm's lifecycle. This may involve that the constraint always remains sufficiently binding to rule out contestability. However, different sizes of idiosyncratic private benefits explain the choice of different ownership structure. In this perspective, both this choice and its evolution in a sequence of changes in control are endogenous to any particular business.

Corporate law may make these choices suboptimal depending on how it regulates, or fails to regulate, the three kinds of private benefits affecting exercise, abuse, and transfer of corporate control. This is how I have derived three fundamental functions of corporate law in an economic perspective: (i) supporting control (protection of idiosyncratic private benefits); (ii) protecting investors (constraining extraction of diversionary private benefits); and (iii) promoting the market for corporate control (minimization of distortionary private benefits).

5 Directors' autonomy from the shareholder meeting is a legal precondition for managerial control

The theoretical framework that I have introduced in this book challenges some of the main tenets of the law and economics of corporate governance. One of these mantras is that corporate law should empower non-controlling shareholders. Having rejected the agency-based framework of delegation of control rights from shareholders to the management, I have claimed that in certain situations corporate law may have to do exactly the opposite: empower corporate controllers. The rationale of this assertion has already been summarized in the previous propositions. Entrepreneurs concerned with idiosyncratic private benefits of control may only go public with an ownership structure that supports both the ongoing exercise of corporate control and its protection from hostile takeover. Corporate law determines how much ownership entrepreneurs can sell to the investing public without risk of losing control, by providing control rights only partly related to ownership, or even not at all. In a sense, corporate law complements the system of ownership entitlements established under property law. How these entitlements are allocated between participants in the corporate enterprise depends on the legal distribution of corporate powers. The *fifth conclusion* of this book is that some *distributions of powers* are suitable to dispersed ownership structures, whereas others only allow for controlling shareholdings. Ideally, both kinds of distributions should be provided for by corporate law.

This conclusion is two-sided. On the positive account, distribution of powers may affect the workability of managerial control and shareholder control systems; on the normative side, too, an inflexible distribution of powers may bias the selection of corporate governance patterns and induce suboptimal choices. Specifically, an entrepreneur may wish to go public with a certain ownership structure. When the uncertainty of the business is high, and idiosyncratic control rents are likewise high, retaining a controlling shareholding can be a most efficient way to place equity with the investing public. Conversely, when idiosyncratic private benefits are of a limited size, selling virtually all of the company's stock to the investing public could be more efficient. The lack of legal entitlements to either managerial or shareholder control may induce respectively less and more separation of ownership and control than would be efficient. In the first scenario, entrepreneurs are prevented from deconcentrating ownership by the legal inability to keep control uncontested under managerial control; in the second, they may choose not to take a highly innovative business public, or to forego it altogether, because the legal system does not support controlling shareholders in listed companies. The study of corporate law in a sample of five jurisdictions not only supports the positive account, but also provides the basis for normative assessment.

The analysis of distribution of decision rights between the two major bodies of the corporate structure shows that managerial control of publicly held companies is only featured in those jurisdictions that empower the board of directors relative to the general meeting of shareholders. What matters is whether directors may avail themselves of sufficient powers to make sure that they are reappointed to office, that they can have favored resolutions passed by the general meeting, and – most importantly – that they cannot be ousted midterm against their will. The three jurisdictions of the sample that feature managerial control (namely, the US, the UK, and the Netherlands) provide directors with a favorable distribution of power in all of the above-mentioned respects. The other two jurisdictions of the sample – Sweden and Italy – fail to support managerial control with one or more of the necessary entitlements. The weakness of the board of directors relative to the general meeting is one fundamental reason why corporate governance can only feature controlling shareholders in those countries. Contrary to what is often contended by at least one part of the legal and economic literature, issues of board structure and stakeholder involvement in the appointment of board members (which both vary considerably between the five jurisdictions) turn out to be of secondary importance.

The legal configuration of entitlements supporting managerial control varies across jurisdictions. In the UK, the regulation and best practices governing listed firms are very unfavorable to controlling shareholders; this circumstance seems to explain a lot about how directors ultimately manage to be in control. Dutch corporate law allegedly empowers stakeholders, but this – at least in the absence of a controlling shareholder – only results in directors' autonomy from the general meeting because of a number of legal devices. American law makes directors extremely powerful when ownership is dispersed, but does not deny controlling shareholders the opportunity to hold directors accountable whenever ownership is coalesced. A number of items of Delaware law and in the federal regulation of proxy voting put the board in the driving seat (although a bit less now than before); but board powers are easily superseded whenever a change in control is agreed upon. Dutch law does not have this feature because of the remaining rigidities of its traditional governance model for large companies. Apart from that, both American and Dutch corporate law as regards distribution of powers display more virtue than they are usually credited for, since they equally support managerial and shareholder control. The opposite result holds for UK law, which supports managerial control as much as it opposes shareholder control.

Two basic policy guidelines for corporate jurisdictions that do not support managerial control can be derived from the analysis of those that do. The first is that corporate law should allow the board of directors to take all relevant decisions about firm management (including those as to whether or not to sell control of the company, but excluding those involving other conflicts of interest) without shareholders having more than to rubberstamp them, at least so long as they are dispersed and therefore unwilling to actively participate in firm control. Italian corporate law is not so far from achieving this result, and may just need a reform of the proxy voting system to that purpose. On the contrary, Swedish law seems to have a much longer way to go before it can allow for management to be in charge in the absence of a controlling shareholder.

The second policy implication is that legal reforms aimed at fostering managerial control should not create the opposite bias against shareholder control. Since ownership can be in principle either too dispersed or too concentrated because of corporate law's rigidities, neither bias is good. The weakness of the otherwise celebrated British model of listed companies is that it does not really supports controlling shareholders. On the contrary, the fundamental strength of the usually criticized American and Dutch models of corporate governance is that they are neutral. They allow companies that go public to choose freely between managerial and shareholder control.

6 A 'one share–one vote' rule is not desirable for efficient separation of ownership and control

In a sense, the dichotomy between managerial and shareholder control is an oversimplification of the choice between ownership structures. Dispersed ownership is also compatible with controlling shareholders. But then voting rights have to be separated from ownership stakes or, at least, the two must not stand in a relation of strict proportionality. From a purely positive standpoint, the principle of proportionality in security-voting structures – also known as 'one share–one vote' – sets a constraint on the ability of controlling shareholders to deconcentrate ownership. If they wish to stay safe as controlling shareholders, they may not sell more than a half of the share capital to the investing public. Any further dilution of controlling ownership would involve the risk of a hostile takeover.

Very few commentators analyze 'one share–one vote' in this perspective, and this is probably because most people think that the positive account is just a trivial issue compared with the normative one. Allowing more than one vote to be cast per share is often considered unfortunate from both a legal and an economic standpoint. However, the matter has always been very controversial. Interpreting 'one share–one vote' under the broader heading of legal distributions of corporate powers allows putting the matter in the right perspective.

Under the assumption I have made, that entrepreneurship matters, the choice of ownership structure based on the size of idiosyncratic private benefits faces a discontinuity. Investors' willingness to pay for non-controlling stock is decreasing in the amount of anticipated control rents, and this is why controlling shareholders are the only outcome financially consistent with positive control premia. However, when idiosyncratic private benefits are low enough, investors may purchase all of the outstanding stock under the promise of a lower bound on their compensation. This is how golden parachutes may substitute for control premia and transition from shareholder control to managerial control can be operated. Distribution of powers in corporate law does not only affect the legal feasibility of this transition, but also determines how far separation of ownership and control can go under shareholder control until time for transition is ripe. It does so by allowing departure from the 'one share–one vote' arrangement. The *sixth conclusion* of the present reserach is that *'one share–one vote' regulation* in corporate law restricts the range of choices as to separation of ownership and control, and may force the adoption of suboptimal ownership structures.

This conclusion is less striking than the previous one. It has also been authoritatively advocated – among others – by Professors Grossman and Hart (1988) who otherwise demonstrated, under certain assumptions, the optimality of 'one share–one vote' for a contestable market for corporate control. Faced with the popularity of disproportional security-voting structures in the real world, reputable academics do not dare to argue in favor of contestability across the board. As a matter of fact, more than of theory, the majority of them are uncomfortable with mandatory 'one share–one vote' regulations. The framework of the present analysis, which disallows contestability on efficiency grounds, brings about clearer conclusions about one share–one vote rules. These conclusions parallel the discussion of the legal underpinnings of managerial control.

First, shortage of legal entitlements to corporate control undermines its separation from ownership: as a weak board of directors makes managerial control legally unviable, restrictions on the disproportionality of security-voting structures may prevent wealth-constrained controlling shareholders from going public. This is particularly problematic in Italy where, in spite of the reforms aimed at increasing the flexibility of the corporate structure, dual-class shares are still unattractive because of an old-fashioned regulation. On the one hand, multiple voting shares are prohibited and, despite the appearance, limited-voting shares do not perform equally well in enhancing the controlling shareholder's voting power. On the other hand, limited-voting shares cannot account for more than 50% of share capital.

Second, the corporate structure allows for different techniques for separating voting rights from ownership; but normally regulation can only tackle some of them. Once again, non-neutrality in distribution of powers may have adverse consequences on efficiency. For instance, mandatory proportionally of the security-voting structure can be circumvented by pyramidal group structures, which are more difficult to regulate. While pyramids are inherently suitable to midstream leveraging of voting power, dual-class shares are more easily prevented from harming existing shareholders by the discipline of share capital (as in Europe) or by an explicit ban on unilateral recapitalizations (as in the US). Once again, this is still a problem in Italy, where listed companies with significantly dispersed ownership are often controlled through pyramidal group structures. This situation may even be made worse by the negative attitude of national policymakers towards somewhat less dangerous techniques of enhancement of shareholder control, like voting pacts. Conversely, the frequency of pyramidal structures in Sweden may owe as little to regulatory restrictions on dual-class shares as much to the unavailability of legal support for managerial control. The bottom line is that, before considering regulation of pyramidal structures in corporate governance, the biases in the legal distribution of corporate powers should be removed.

A third and related point is that contestability of corporate control cannot be imposed by regulation because it can always be short-circuited at the firm level. As it turns out, control of the majority of companies is seldom made contestable when they first go public, no matter how strict the regulation of 'one share–one vote' is. The argument that, as a matter of principle, control of listed firms *should be* contestable is a recurring source of mistakes by policymakers. In the 1980s, the SEC was about to "kill shareholders with kindness" attempting to prohibit dual-class shares among companies listed in

American stock exchanges.[1] In the 2000s, the European legislator likewise attempted to 'breakthrough' disproportional security-voting structures. As academics argued in both circumstances, these regulatory initiatives, if successful, would have been most likely either to be circumvented by alternative (but not necessarily more desirable) arrangements or to induce less and less firms to go public.[2] Luckily, or perhaps unavoidably, both attempts ultimately failed. The lesson from the American experience is that regulation ended up addressing only the right problem: midstream changes in security-voting structures. After having tried to promote, instead of prevent, these midstream changes with an economically unfounded breakthrough rule, hopefully the EU legislation will also find its way to put the problem of 'one share–one vote' in the right perspective.

7　An efficient discipline of related-party transactions is necessary, but not sufficient, for separation of ownership and control

Separation of ownership and control requires both willing sellers and willing buyers of the company's stock. The argument that in some companies corporate controllers, and not minority shareholders, should be empowered by corporate law is grounded on the protection of idiosyncratic control rents. This explains the first part of the statement. The second part is equally important. Once controllers have all the decision-making powers, non-controlling shareholders must be provided with a meaningful guarantee that those powers are not abused for expropriation purposes. According to the mainstream view, this is the only relevant issue for the economics of corporate law. On the assumption that protection of control rents is unimportant for the efficiency of corporate governance, controllers have no reason to be empowered. On the contrary, controllers are naturally empowered by a number of circumstances depending on delegation of decision rights by dispersed and rationally apathetic shareholders. Therefore, corporate law should constrain the exercise of control powers or, even worse, reallocate them from controllers to non-controlling shareholders. This is how law is supposed to 'matter' in corporate governance. I have shown that this view is incomplete. The *seventh conclusion* of this work is that *legal protection of non-controlling shareholders* is a necessary, but not sufficient condition for separation of ownership and control (and for its efficiency).

The importance of managerial firm-specific investments under contractual incompleteness is the reason why it is not sufficient: corporate law must also *enable* the corporate contract to protect those investments independently of

---

1　Oliver Hart, "SEC May Kill Shareholders with Kindness" in *The Wall Street Journal*, July 14, 1988.
2　Lucian Bebchuk and Oliver Hart, "A Threat to Dual-Class Shares" in *Financial Times*, May 31, 2002.

corporate ownership, and it can only do so by providing a sufficiently broad range of entitlements to control power. This is the reason why legal protection of non-controlling shareholders is necessary, too. Differently from other commercial contracts, decision rights in the controller–shareholder relationship are barely constrained by the corporate contract. Long-term supply or credit contracts may include few or many provisions; they are possibly renegotiated in the face of unforeseen contingencies, but cannot be unilaterally amended. Corporate charters are almost empty at their core; virtually none of their provisions is governed by unanimity, and control powers include the ability to have them amended when new circumstances materialize. The spectacular flexibility of the corporate contract parallels the substitution of authority for consensus, which is the ultimate reason why firms are established to cope with relationships that markets cannot support. The flip side of the coin is that the corporate contract cannot be a source of credible commitment for controllers. In order to induce non-controlling shareholders to invest in spite of that, credible commitments need to be established on the basis of institutions that are out of the controller's reach. Corporate law's rules qualify to the extent that they are mandatory or, if they are default rules, they are crafted in such a way that they cannot be opted out unilaterally by the corporate controller. However, these constraints on the controller's decision-making power should not exceed the domain of conflicts of interest that may result in shareholder expropriation. Regulation of related-party transactions is the case in point.

The framework of the present analysis provides an explanation of why corporate law should be as enabling as possible as far as distribution of powers is concerned, whereas it should be much stricter when it comes to constraining the direct or indirect tunneling of shareholder value to the controller's pockets. The mandatory/enabling balance of corporate laws is perhaps the favorite matter of debate for lawyers, while it is often dismissed as an unimportant issue by economists. The former tend to view incompleteness of the corporate contract as a case for gap-filling or a reason to overreach, by regulation, the unintended creation of control powers. Economists are definitely more comfortable with power in the governance of the firm and consider law simply as a device to correct for allocations of control rights which are un-favorable to the shareholders. Either view only captures one aspect of a twofold problem. Both power and law matter in corporate governance. Law needs to support control power and to constrain its abuse. Power needs to be *allocated* to corporate controllers in order for them to have authority over assets that they do not own; but it needs also to be *regulated* in order for shareholders not to be expropriated of assets that they do not control. Answering the question of what the mandatory/enabling balance should be in corporate law also explains why legal protection of outside shareholders is necessary, but not sufficient, for separation of ownership and control.

This contention is supported by the empirical evidence at least as far as the five-country case study of this book is concerned. In all the jurisdictions considered, the discipline of related-party transactions is essentially mandatory. A reliable enforcement of this discipline is a precondition for non-controlling ownership, but separation of ownership and control also requires that suitable distributions of powers be enabled. The sophisticated system of fiduciary duties administered by Delaware courts cannot be opted out unless by a reincorporation decision that hardly any shareholder would accept. Combined with securities regulation at the federal level, this system is as strictly enforced as to disallow most instances of diversion of shareholder value; but it is also flexible enough to allow control power to be exerted in either dispersed or concentrated ownership structures. Perhaps unconventionally, I have shown that non-controlling shareholders are fairly well protected from expropriation under Dutch corporate law, too. While statutory law provides for distributions of powers also suitable to managerial control, good protection of non-controlling shareholders is obtained in the Netherlands through the elaboration of case law by a specialized judiciary. The Dutch discipline of non-pro-rata distributions is remarkably similar to Delaware law and so are the venues for private enforcement, in spite of the significant differences in civil procedure.

I have also reconsidered the legal underpinnings of the excellent protection of minority shareholders in Sweden. The stability of a powerful system of social norms ultimately relies upon a set of enforceable anti-expropriation rules as a credible threat. Still, controlling shareholders are the only governance solution supported by the legal distribution of corporate powers. Italian corporate law shares the same problem. On top of this, despite the significant improvements in the discipline of related-party transactions, Italy may still fail to protect minority shareholders effectively because of a formalistic adjudication by the (unspecialized) judiciary, too little scope for private enforcement, and weak social norms. Italy may be the only country of our sample that still supports the standard 'law matters' argument; but, even there, the unchanged patterns of corporate governance in spite of the recent improvements in shareholder protection suggest that something else is at play.

Britain is a strange case. On the one hand, shareholder protection from outright theft relies on a few mandatory provisions in company law and in the regulation of listed companies. On the other hand, this protection is not enforced in courts, through the existing discipline of related-party transactions, but it depends rather on the power of non-controlling shareholders to veto these transactions and to oust directors who fail to bring them to their attention. These powers are hardly ever exercised. Still, they provide the institutional investor with a sufficiently credible threat to police managerial disloyalty. The only drawback of this arrangement is that, as in the rest of the discipline of listed companies in the UK, it may overly constrain discretion in corporate management. But this is another, and more complicated, story.

8 Shareholder protection by corporate law does not necessarily mean shareholder empowerment in corporate governance

Ideally, one would wish that control powers are exercised with the broadest possible discretion and that controllers are only accountable to outside shareholder for mischief – that is, they are prevented from stealing. The case for making controllers also accountable for negligence – that is, shirking – is particularly weak in corporate governance. The standard argument in corporate law and economics is that judges are ill equipped to review business judgment. Finding that this argument would equally apply to many pro-fessional judgments, which are yet subject to enforceable standards of diligence, I have shown that the rationale of the so-called business judgment rule (a functional principle of judicial abstention from second-guessing the quality of corporate management) is rather to prevent adjudication with a hindsight bias.

Any business decision could be regarded as very clever when it turns out to be profitable, and blamed for utmost negligence when it turns out badly. The fact is that diligence is inherently indeterminate ex-ante when decisions – like typically those by entrepreneurs – are taken under uncertainty. Differently from the risks of a surgery, uncertainty of a business venture cannot be assigned a probability by definition. This is the reason why legal liability of corporate controllers should only be established for disloyalty. Unfortunately, this is also the reason why policing disloyalty is only possible at the cost of some second-guessing. Related-party transactions may have plenty of business purpose, but they may also result in expropriation of outside shareholders. At the end of the day, nobody can scrutinize the diversionary potential of business decisions without interfering with its merits. Any regulation of related-party transactions involves a tension between discretion and accountability of corporate control.

Another, perhaps more conventional, way to interpret this tension is the tradeoff between false positives (innocent being convicted) and false negatives (guilty being acquitted) in the enforcement of shareholder protection against stealing. In whatever configuration, this tradeoff cannot be eliminated, but an efficient regulation of related-party transactions should provide for its optimization. I have shown that, as far as accountability is concerned, systems based on independent scrutiny of conflicting interest transactions may fare as well as those based on empowerment of non-controlling shareholders in decision-making. However, the former normally outperform the latter as far as discretion in the exercise of business judgment is concerned. The *eighth conclusion* of this book is that *shareholder protection* from expropriation should not be confused with *shareholder empowerment* in corporate governance. As it turns out, empowering non-controlling shareholders may add little to their protection from expropriation and only result in too conservative management strategies that ultimately undermine profitability of shareholder investments.

The majority of jurisdictions in our sample go for a strategy of independent scrutiny of related-party transactions. This may be based on approval by disinterested directors ex-ante, judicial review ex-post, or a combination of both. The US features the most sophisticated combination. Delaware courts do not trust disinterested director approval entirely, so long as it is not proven to be really independent of the corporate controller; and securities class actions before federal courts are also often an option for disgruntled shareholders (or, more precisely, for their lawyers). The bite of both securities and corporate litigation under US law raises as little concerns of false negatives (apart from large-scale, one-shot appropriations in the Enron-style, which no legal system could possibly prevent) as moderately serious ones concerning false positives. At least as far state law is concerned, the business judgment rule shields pretty well corporate controllers from unfounded litigation.

The problem of false positives is potentially more severe in the UK where, instead of having directors and/or a skilled judiciary to do the job, all substantial related-party transactions need to be ultimately approved by non-controlling shareholders. Effectively, these transactions only manage to go through with the support of institutional investors. Those investors naturally abstain from business judgment, but may nonetheless induce the management to forego profitable strategies when they have any interest (perhaps different from that of the other shareholders) in having a say on management issues.

Both the American and the British systems could be improved by separating the professional monitoring of conflicted interest transactions from the empowerment of either non-controlling shareholders or of their lawyers working on a contingent-fee basis. I have argued that independent directors could be a good solution, so long as they are neither nominated nor appointed by the corporate controller. Differently from other proposals in the same vein, I have contended that they should exclusively be in charge of approving transactions that involve significant risk of shareholder expropriation.

The US and the UK feature two different approaches to shareholder protection, which are often regarded as models for the rest of the world. Yet, at least one country of our sample seems to perform even better than Anglo-American law as far as shareholder protection is concerned. This is Sweden. To be sure, the optimal balance between discretion and accountability in Sweden is due to a rather unique combination of social norms and legal rules. However, it is also supported by a consistent regulation. The introduction of independent directors by a *de facto* binding Corporate Governance Code follows exactly the guidelines of no-interference with the exercise of corporate control and exclusion of corporate controllers from the appointment process. The other countries of the sample perform worse on this account. The Dutch Corporate Governance Code, whose compliance is regulated by a legally enforceable 'comply-or-explain' principle, relies on the formal independence of all the members of the supervisory board; however, the majority of them must be necessarily part of the control chain. Nevertheless, in the Netherlands, a sophisticated judiciary and aggressive tools for private enforcement compensate for the weakness of internal controls. None of the above features is so far available under Italian corporate law, for which strengthening the independence of internal controls, improving the quality of adjudication, and enhancing private enforcement are top priorities.

9 Efficiency of takeover regulation requires an optimal discipline of minority shareholders' squeeze-out

Similar conclusions regarding the allocation and the regulation of control powers apply to the market for corporate control, but with a complication. The operation of takeovers brings in a third player: the acquirer. When a takeover bid is made, the would-be acquirer is neither in control nor, in principle, a significant shareholder. However, in order to succeed, he has both to induce the incumbent to part with control and to purchase stock from non-controlling shareholders in such a way as to make takeover profitable for him. The first condition follows from the assumption that protection of control rents matters in corporate governance, and therefore the market for corporate control is normally operated by friendly acquisitions. Still, when only friendly takeovers are considered, the second problem remains. Prospective acquirers need to have sufficient incentives to seek for potential targets, thereby initiating the takeover process. These incentives are only available to the extent that acquirers can make profits on the stock market through the acquisition of undervalued shares.

The ultimate problem of the market for corporate control is the distribution of takeover gains between the acquirer and the existing shareholders. This problem is normally understood as a tradeoff between efficient allocation of corporate control and protection of non-controlling shareholders. By making the incumbent also participate in the distribution of takeover gains, I show that the tradeoff becomes different: it is between ex-ante efficiency of rent protection and ex-post maximization of shareholder value. This tradeoff may be solved dynamically, through a process of value-increasing acquisitions conditional on compensation of existing control rents. In order for this process to be as smooth as possible, most of the remaining gains should be allocated to prospective acquirers. Protection of non-controlling shareholders is unnecessary so long as looting is disallowed and there is potential competition among bidders. Under these conditions, minority shareholders are efficiently excluded from the takeover gains. The *ninth conclusion* of this book is that the market for corporate control can be optimally operated by *squeeze-out* of minority shareholders, so long as regulation prevents them from being exploited by this mechanism.

Once the market for corporate control is interpreted as an application of Coasian bargaining, it might not be entirely clear why it should be regulated at all. The reason is that the Coase Theorem does not apply in its strongest formulation due to the presence of transaction costs. This has two prominent implications: controllers, acquirers, or both (if they collude) may go for value-decreasing takeovers when shareholders do not knowledgeably participate in the bargaining; shareholders participation in the bargaining may instead prevent value-increasing takeovers when they do not manage to coordinate on how to split the gains efficiently. Because of these two circumstances takeovers may generate two opposite problems, respectively known as pressure to tender and free riding, which are the ultimate reason for regulatory intervention. Financial economics tends to identify the solution in some optimal amount of pressure to tender that keeps free riding sufficiently low. As a result, some value-decreasing takeovers are allowed and some value-increasing takeovers are foregone.

However, the economic analysis of takeover regulation has shown that, at least in dispersed ownership structures, the free riding problem can be solved without generating pressure to tender if successful bidders are allowed to squeeze out non-tendering shareholders at the higher between the bid and the market price. I have elaborated this result under the assumption of (potential) bidding competition. Thanks to the incumbent's involvement in bargaining, the efficient outcome obtains in spite of appropriation of a moderately positive takeover premium by shareholders. I have also extended the analysis of squeeze-outs to the sale of controlling blocks in concentrated ownership structures, where changes in control are normally analyzed by abstracting from problems of free riding and pressure to tender. I have demonstrated that allowing, but not forcing, the purchaser to make a tender offer for non-controlling shares maximizes the probability of value-increasing takeovers without generating pressure to tender. This conclusion holds true if squeeze-out can be operated at the higher between the bid and the market price before the announcement of takeover. When takeovers are friendly, the efficiency of the above squeeze-out rules requires that looting be otherwise disallowed. In dispersed ownership structures, incumbents and insurgents must also be prevented from restricting bidding competition by colluding on severance payments. Besides efficiently regulating squeeze-outs, corporate law should also meet these requirements.

Takeover regulation is the only item of the present book where the five-country tournament has just one winner: this is the US. There is a special reason for that. Takeovers are a relatively recent phenomenon, and the two jurisdictions that first addressed it still provide the two fundamental models of legal discipline. The UK model has lately become (with modifications) the European model, but unfortunately – at least according to the framework developed here – it performs comparatively worse than the American one. British regulation does allow for minority squeeze-out. However, on the one hand, it sets ownership of 90% of outstanding shares as the minimum threshold for its operation; this still gives minority shareholders the opportunity to holdout when they are large enough. On the other hand, the squeeze-out option is superseded by the mandatory bid when controlling blocks are transferred; this could be a serious impediment to the market for corporate control if controlling shareholdings were not otherwise disfavored by British regulation of listed firms. American law does not feature any of these constraints. Both federal and state laws do not interfere with mandatory bid requirements, whereas Delaware courts have found their way to regulate squeeze-outs exactly as they should be. To be sure, a 90% threshold is also set by Delaware law for squeeze-outs by a person who has already become controlling shareholder. This requirement is unnecessary; but it is also not particularly harmful, given the low concentration of non-controlling ownership in the US.

That being said, both models of takeover regulation are consistent with the law governing listed companies. Corporate law in both the US and the UK includes sufficient constraints on looting; this makes value-decreasing takeovers very unlikely. If anything, UK law achieves this result at the price of making value-increasing deals more difficult to go through. In addition, the high squeeze-out threshold under British law is practically the only defense for incumbent management against hostile takeovers. This could not be changed unless US-style takeover defenses were introduced. The other European jurisdictions of the sample do not necessarily face these constraints. Some of them did not even have a takeover regulation a few years ago, let alone a discipline of takeover defenses. Also, they may not worry about the efficiency of friendly takeovers, when the high standards of protection of minority shareholders are already sufficient to rule out looting. Nowadays, however, they face constraints from a different source, which is EU law. The Takeover Directive has not only imposed a mandatory bid rule, which interferes with the squeeze-out mechanism and normally short-circuits its virtues; but has also set at 90% the minimum threshold for post-takeover squeeze-outs. This solution may possibly make sense for those countries – like Italy – where the standards of protection of minority shareholders are traditionally low, although its rigidity limits the future ability of national regulators to compromise investor protection with the goal of promoting efficient changes in control. The adverse consequences of the mandatory bid on the efficiency of the market for corporate control are most severe where ownership is more concentrated. Therefore, it is at least risky to impose such a regime in continental Europe, where – with the exception of the Netherlands and perhaps a few other countries – corporate ownership is most typically concentrated.

10 When control is entrenched and non-controlling shareholders are protected from expropriation, unequal treatment of shareholders is preferable to the mandatory bid

The general principle of equal treatment of shareholders is featured by virtually any corporate jurisdiction. It is hardly questionable in economic analysis of law, and with good reason. A fundamental tenet of the incentive-compatibility of corporate governance is that shareholders, whether they are controlling or not, must participate in the firm's residual pro-rata. This explains why an outright prohibition of non-pro-rata distributions (what I have referred to as diversionary private benefits of control) makes sense in corporate law. Yet this reasoning only applies to verifiable profits, not also to that part of the firm value that owes its existence to unverifiable entrepreneurial talent. Appropriation of this value does not contradict the rationale of equal treatment of shareholders, although it may conflict with the application of the same principle to takeovers. The implications of entrepreneurship for the market for corporate control are that incumbents must cash in their idiosyncratic private benefits and insurgents must be able to appropriate the remainder of the differences between current and prospective shareholder value. Otherwise, neither would incumbents part with control nor would insurgents bother to uncover new profit opportunities in potential takeover targets. These players need to get more than non-controlling shareholders do in takeovers. However, the rationale of this preferential treatment is their capacity as active entrepreneurs, not as passive shareholders. In principle, corporate controllers may play an entrepreneurial role regardless of how much stock they hold. In this case controlling and non-controlling shareholders play two structurally different roles in takeovers. Likewise, they should be treated differently.

For reasons of fairness, the majority of legal scholars would probably refuse to reconsider equal treatment of shareholders in the above perspective. The legal economists' concern for efficiency leads to a more balanced position. They recognize that private benefits of control are necessary to operate the market for corporate control, but they are also worried that the quest for private benefits may result in value-decreasing takeovers. The two positions tend to converge in advocating the case for mandatory bid regulation, at least in a configuration sufficiently flexible to allow acquirers (and possibly incumbents too) to appropriate some part of the takeover gains. Takeover regulation is then understood as a tradeoff between shareholder protection and the efficient allocation of corporate control. This contention is affected by confusion between different categories of private benefits of control. By disentangling three categories of these benefits, I have shown that the above tradeoff is unwarranted.

Specifically, when corporate control is entrenched for reason of efficient rent protection, value-decreasing takeovers mainly depend on incremental extraction of diversionary private benefits (looting), which must be disallowed by regulation in order for the market for corporate control to work efficiently. Then takeover regulation should only worry about efficient allocation of corporate control. Takeovers should let incumbents cash in their idiosyncratic private benefits whereas insurgents should appropriate sufficient gains in shareholder value to minimize distortionary private benefits. The *last* – and perhaps the most important – *conclusion* of this study is that *equal treatment of shareholders* unnecessarily interferes with the takeover mechanism. Shareholder protection in takeovers may undermine the operation of the market for corporate control not because there is too much or too little of it, but rather, because it is implemented in the wrong fashion. This makes the case for mandatory bid regulation extremely weak, if not completely unfounded.

The comparison of the US and the UK – the two countries of the sample featuring the most active market for corporate control – is illustrative of this point. Takeover regulation in the US does not feature a mandatory bid, since it does not require equal treatment of controllers and non-controlling shareholders. Protection of the latter is implemented by a strict enforcement of fiduciary duties instead of a regulation of control premia, severance payments, or the structure of tender offers. Corporate law eases an efficient dynamics of control allocation by allowing relatively unrestricted negotiations upon these variables, whatever the ownership structure. Conversely, the discipline of takeovers in Britain is based on a mandatory bid as a consequence of a strict principle of equal treatment of shareholders. Negotiations upon control premia and managerial severance payments are hence not allowed to ease the takeover process. On top of this, becoming controlling shareholders is not only more expensive because of the mandatory bid, but also unattractive due to the consequences of holding a controlling position under the UK rules and best practices governing listed companies. In a sense, the circumstance that a bidder would not like to be stuck in a controlling shareholder position, together with the hurdles to implement a going private transaction, provides the management with some power to resist unwanted acquisitions despite the formal prohibition of takeover defenses. As a result, takeovers in the UK allow little more hostility than in the US, but the empirical evidence shows that they are much less targeted to managerial underperformance.

However, perhaps surprisingly, the activity of the market for corporate control is only slightly lower in Britain than in the US when the different size of the economy is accounted for. There is an explanation for that: controlling shareholdings are the most sensitive to the adverse effects of the mandatory bid, but they are very infrequent among UK listed companies. The problem of regulation of corporate governance in the UK is that it opposes the extraction of private benefits across the board, no matter what efficient properties they may have, and therefore it may be unsuitable to highly innovative business that requires higher ownership concentration and idiosyncratic private benefits in order to be carried out efficiently. The British case illustrates the potentially adverse consequences of relying exclusively on the principal–agent framework to interpret corporate governance. The only reason why the UK bias against controlling shareholders has not resulted in a visible underperformance of corporate governance is the peculiar consistency of the British model. However, this is based on a combination of culture, legal rules and historical evolution of corporate ownership that could hardly be replicated elsewhere.

The drawbacks of the mandatory bid are much more severe in continental Europe, where ownership structures are typically more concentrated than in Britain. In this situation the inability to negotiate a control premium separately from minority shareholders may just force corporate control to remain stuck in suboptimal allocations. I have shown that the attempt by the EU Takeover Directive to level the playing field based on the UK model of regulation of control transactions has been unfortunate. On the one hand, that attempt has remarkably failed in the purpose to replicate the conditions of corporate governance in the UK through the adoption of breakthrough and board neutrality rules, which became eventually optional. On the other hand, the ability of European jurisdictions to support an efficient market for corporate control may actually depend on how the very core of harmonization – the mandatory bid – can be circumvented.

Within our sample, Sweden and the Netherlands seem to have succeeded in keeping the traditional features of their rather liberal market for corporate control, in spite of the regulatory constraints established at the EU level. Although the discipline of control transactions could be improved in both countries taking stock of the more sophisticated American example, takeover regulation is not a major problem for corporate governance in either of them. Swedish law simply does not feature possibilities for evolution towards managerial control, whereas the Dutch structure regime remains a source of unnecessary rigidities for the takeover process. Italian law has problems similar to Sweden concerning the distribution of corporate powers; but the Italian case is still complicated by the traditional weakness of shareholder protection from expropriation. In spite of that, it may be advisable to find a way out of the hurdles of the mandatory bid in Italy, assuming that the minimal conditions to prevent incremental value diversion are met by the recent, significant improvements in the discipline of related-party transactions. This assumption could be warranted particularly if the improvements in substantive law will soon be matched by a tighter and more reliable enforcement.

12 Ideas for future research

To conclude, based on the results of the present inquiry, I shall mention a few promising avenues for future research in the law and economics of control powers.

The thesis that the corporate structure supports not only investor protection, but also the exercise of control powers, has an important implication that would be interesting to explore: the *nature of the public company*. The principal–agent approach to separation of ownership and control has made the long-standing legal debate on the nature of the corporation progressively outdated. For a long time now, supporters of the institutional nature of the corporate structure have had a difficult case against the prevailing nexus of contracts paradigm. The intrinsic limitations of the agency approach in the interpretation of corporate governance may reopen the door to institutionalism in corporate law.

In this book, I have shown that the legal personality of the corporation may be more than a fiction. After all, this fiction enables managers or controlling shareholders to be in control of assets that they do not own. However, I have not pushed the reasoning so far as to deny the contractual nature of the corporate enterprise. I doubt whether there are sufficient grounds for it to be denied. The publicly held corporation seems indeed to rely on a peculiar set of entitlements complementing the property rights system. But these entitlements are not created once and for all with the corporation. The separation of ownership and control ultimately derives from choices made by the corporate contract; I have only argued that corporate law should support these choices. This parallels the fundamental question of how institutions are created and evolve over time in the economy and the society (North 1990). Solving this puzzle is a major challenge for both legal and economic institutionalism. Corporate governance may be the right domain for a fruitful dialogue.

A related question is the *evolution* of the *ownership structure* of corporate enterprises. In this study, I have made a fundamental assumption and a conjecture, which are both based on the theory of entrepreneurship. The assumption is that rewards to entrepreneurship may also be important in the corporate governance of listed companies; that these rewards come in the form of private benefits of control; and that these benefits endogenously determine the ownership structure in the absence of legal shortcomings or needless constraints. The conjecture is that the private benefits of control rewarding entrepreneurship are asymptotically decreasing with the uncertainty during a firm's lifecycle. This may result in a progressive dispersion of the ownership structure based on a sequence of efficient changes in control, so long as the latter are not hampered by legal impediments. While some theoretical and empirical studies support my endogeneity assumption, no dynamic analysis of corporate governance I am aware of has so far investigated my conjecture.

This book's results about the efficiency of the takeover process, and its normative implications on takeover regulation, are ultimately based on that intuition. Theoretical models that have analyzed the takeover dynamics under entrenchment of corporate control allow private benefits of control to be, at best, neutral to social welfare. Although I have questioned the results drawn on this basis throughout this book, a *formal integration of private benefits* motivating the investment of entrepreneurial talent awaits future research in the economic theory of corporate governance. This may also allow reconsidering the empirical question of whether one or more optimal ownership structures exist at any geographical or industrial level. I suspect that the answer may vary depending on the stage of economic development. But then, the role of corporate laws in fostering economic growth through separation of ownership and control should also be reconsidered, possibly by extending the framework of the present investigation to developing and transition economies. Needless to say, the theoretical, the empirical, and the legal accounts should not be treated as separate lines of inquiry.

The ownership structure is also worth exploring from a different, purely *empirical* angle. In this respect, we do not yet have sufficient knowledge to determine with precision how listed firms are owned and controlled in different countries. Based on Pacces (2007), the summary picture of owner-ship and control presented in this book relies heavily on information pro-vided at the national level and aggregated, with difficulty, in the few empirical studies available in the literature. On this basis I have only managed to draw a parsimonious distinction between controllers and non-controlling shareholders. In addition, this had to be limited to a relatively narrow sample of countries making reference to data that are now more than fifteen years old.

I believe that updating, improving, and making comparable our knowledge about ownership and control of listed companies around the world is one of the more urgent topics for research in corporate governance. This would, for instance, allow us to distinguish between corporate controllers and between non-controlling shareholders based on their identity. I did not find the available evidence sufficiently reliable to endeavor such a distinction. However, this may have promising implications for the study of certain categories of non-controlling owners and of controlling shareholders from both a legal and an economic viewpoint. Without speaking about the tons of research questions that one such knowledge would enable to investigate, I could only mention that information about how companies are effectively controlled in different countries would allow designing of a number of quasi experiments in corporate and financial law. Given the amount of legal change triggered by the first phase of the law and finance scholarship, this way to study the effects of laws could become the next round of law and finance approach.

One final question for future research is the *mechanisms of production of corporate laws* in both a national and an international perspective. Having to confront with the very core of the mainstream approach to corporate governance – the principal–agent framework – this book has only taken a public interest approach. A growing body of law and economics scholarship deals instead with the role of vested interests in the evolution of corporate laws. This scholarship analyzes how the production of legal rules is influenced and constrained by private constituencies, public bodies, and regulatory competition. The importance of this approach cannot be overstated. It would be simply naïve to assume that improvements in the quality of legal rules are driven by the intelligence and the benevolence of policymakers. The regulatory swings before and after the global financial crisis of 2007–2009 clearly show that the key determinants of both regulation and deregulation are others, and they depend mainly on the relative strength of interest groups in a given point in time. If the economic analysis of law is to identify recipes to improve the welfare of society, it would be foolish to neglect the role of political economy in the implementation of these recipes.

At the same time, our knowledge is very often affected by a conventional wisdom that is more resistant to change than vested interests. This applies even more forcefully to the scientific knowledge. If we consider ourselves – academics – *homines oeconomici* not differently from managers, shareholders, lawmakers and bureaucrats, questioning the established knowledge may not always be in our best interest. At the very least, this strategy would make it harder for us to earn tenure. The countervailing, prospective benefits could be ideally rewarding for an 'entrepreneurial' researcher as well as for society. For instance, showing that the world is not working as most people think it does could be a first step towards improving the world. The crucial point, however, is that it is not easy to make an impact in the market for ideas; and this is not only because certain ideas may be resisted by vested interests. As Keynes (1936) put it:

> [T]he ideas of economists and political philosophers, both when they are right and when they are wrong, are more powerful than is commonly understood. Indeed the world is ruled by little else. Practical men, who believe themselves to be quite exempt from any intellectual influences, are usually the slaves of some defunct economist. Madmen in authority, who hear voices in the air, are distilling their frenzy from some academic scribbler of a few years back. I am sure that the power of vested interests is vastly exaggerated compared with the gradual encroachment of ideas. Not, indeed, immediately, but after a certain interval; for in the field of economic and political philosophy there are not many who are influenced by new theories after they are twenty-five or thirty years of age, so that the ideas which civil servants and politicians and even agitators apply to current events are not likely to be the newest. But, soon or late, it is ideas, not vested interests, which are dangerous for good or evil.

References

Adams, R. and Ferreira, D. 2008, "One Share–One Vote: The Empirical Evidence", *Review of Finance*, vol. 12, no. 1, pp. 51–91.

Adams, R. and Ferreira, D. 2007, "A Theory of Friendly Boards", *Journal of Finance*, vol. 62, no. 1, pp. 217–250.

Adams, R.B., Hermalin, B.E. and Weisbach, M.S. 2010, "The Role of Boards of Directors in Corporate Governance: A Conceptual Framework and Survey", *Journal of Economic Literature*, vol. 48, no. 1, pp. 58–107.

Aghion, P. and Bolton, P. 1992, "An Incomplete Contracts Approach to Financial Contracting", *Review of Economic Studies*, vol. 59, no. 3, pp. 473–494.

Aghion, P. and Tirole, J. 1997, "Formal and Real Authority in Organizations", *Journal of Political Economy*, vol. 105, no. 1, pp. 1–29.

Agnblad, J., Berglöf, E., Högfeldt, P. and Svancar, H. 2001, "Ownership and Control in Sweden: Strong Owners, Weak Minorities, and Social Control" in *The Control of Corporate Europe*, eds. F. Barca and M. Becht, Oxford University Press, Oxford, pp. 228–258.

Akerlof, G.A. 1970, "The Market for "Lemons": Quality Uncertainty and the Market Mechanism", *Quarterly Journal of Economics*, vol. 84, no. 3, pp. 488–500.

Almazan, A. and Suarez, J. 2003, "Entrenchment and Severance Pay in Optimal Governance Structures", *Journal of Finance*, vol. 58, no. 2, pp. 519–547.

Almeida, H. and Wolfenzon, D. 2006, "A Theory of Pyramidal Ownership and Family Business Groups", *Journal of Finance*, vol. 61, no. 6, pp. 2637–2681.

Amihud, Y., Kahan, M. and Sundaram, R.K. 2004, "The Foundations of Freezeout Laws in Takeovers", *Journal of Finance*, vol. 59, no. 3, pp. 1325–1344.

Arcot, S., Bruno, V. and Faure-Grimaud, A. 2010, "Corporate Governance in the UK: Is the Comply or Explain Approach Working?", *International Review of Law and Economics*, vol. 30, no. 2, pp. 193–201.

Arkes, H.R. and Schipani, C.A. 1994, "Medical Malpractice v. the Business Judgement Rule: Differences in Hindsight Bias", *Oregon Law Review*, vol. 73, no. 3, pp. 587–638.

Arlen, J. and Talley, E.L. 2003, "Unregulable Defenses and the Perils of Shareholder Choice", *University of Pennsylvania Law Review*, vol. 152, no. 2, pp. 577–666.

Armour, J. 2010, "Enforcement Strategies in UK Corporate Governance: A Roadmap and Empirical Assessment" in *The Law and Economics of Corporate Governance: Changing Perspectives*, ed. A.M. Pacces, Edward Elgar Publishing, Cheltenham, pp. 213–263.

Armour, J., Black, B.S., Cheffins, B.R. and Nolan, R. 2009a, "Private Enforcement of Corporate Law: An Empirical Comparison of the United Kingdom and the United States", *Journal of Empirical Legal Studies*, vol. 6, no. 4, pp. 687–722.

Armour, J., Deakin, S., Sarkar, P., Siems, M. and Singh, A. 2009b, "Shareholder protection and stock market development: an empirical test of the legal origins hypothesis", *Journal of Empirical Legal Studies*, vol. 6, no. 2, pp. 343–380.

Armour, J., Deakin, S. and Konzelmann, S.J. 2003, "Shareholder Primacy and the Trajectory of UK Corporate Governance", *British Journal of Industrial Relations*, vol. 41, no. 3, pp. 531–555.

Armour, J. and Skeel, D.A. 2007, "Who Writes the Rules for Hostile Takeovers, and Why? The Peculiar Divergence of US and UK Takeover Regulation", *Georgetown Law Journal*, vol. 95, no. 6, pp. 1727–1794.

Atanasov, V., Black, B. and Ciccotello, C.S. 2011, "Law and Tunneling", *Journal of Corporation Law*, vol. 37, pp. 1–49.

Ayres, I. 2006, "Menus Matter", *The University of Chicago Law Review*, pp. 3–15.

Bainbridge, S.M. 2011, "Dodd-Frank: Quack Federal Corporate Governance Round II", *Minnesota Law Review*, vol. 95, pp. 1779–1821.

Bainbridge, S.M. 2008, *The New Corporate Governance in Theory and Practice*, Oxford University Press, New York, NY.

Bainbridge, S.M. 2006, "Director Primacy and Shareholder Disempowerment", *Harvard Law Review*, vol. 119, no. 6, pp. 1735–1758.

Bainbridge, S.M. 2002, *Corporation Law and Economics*, Foundation Press, New York, N.Y.

Bainbridge, S.M. 2000, "Insider Trading" in *Encyclopedia of Law and Economics*, eds. B. Bouckaert and G. De Geest, Elgar, Cheltenham, pp. 772–812.

Bank, S. and Cheffins, B.R. 2008, "Tax and the Separation of Ownership and Control", *Tax and Corporate Governance*, pp. 111–161.

Barca, F. and Becht, M. 2001, *The Control of Corporate Europe*, Oxford University Press, Oxford.

Bates, T.W., Lemmon, M.L. and Linck, J.S. 2006, "Shareholder Wealth Effects and Bid Negotiation in Freeze-out Deals: Are Minority Shareholders Left out in the Cold?", *Journal of Financial Economics*, vol. 81, no. 3, pp. 681–708.

Baumol, W.J., Panzar, J.C., Willig, R.D. and Bailey, E.E. 1982, *Contestable Markets and the Theory of Industry Structure*, Harcourt Brace Jovanovich, New York, N.Y.

Baums, T. 2007, "European Company Law Beyond the 2003 Action Plan", *European Business Organization Law Review*, vol. 8, no. 1, pp. 143–160.

Baums, T. 2000, *General Meetings in Listed Companies: New Challenges and Opportunities*, Working Paper No. 103, Frankfurt University, Institut für Bankrecht.

Baums, T. and Scott, K.E. 2005, "Taking Shareholder Protection Seriously – Corporate Governance in the United States and Germany", *American Journal of Comparative Law*, vol. 53, no. 1, pp. 31–76.

Bebchuk, L.A. 2007, "The Myth of the Shareholder Franchise", *Virginia Law Review*, vol. 93, no. 3, pp. 675–732.

Bebchuk, L.A. 2005, "The Case for Increasing Shareholder Power", *Harvard Law Review*, vol. 118, no. 3, pp. 833–914.

Bebchuk, L.A. 2003a, "Why Firms Adopt Antitakeover Arrangements", *University of Pennsylvania Law Review*, vol. 152, no. 2, pp. 713–753.

Bebchuk, L.A. 2003b, "The Case for Shareholder Access to the Ballot", *The Business Lawyer*, vol. 59, no. 1, pp. 43–66.

Bebchuk, L.A. 2003c, "Symposium on Corporate Elections", *Harvard Law School John M. Olin Center for Law, Economics and Business Discussion Paper Series*, The Berkeley Electronic Press Host, Berkeley, October 23, 2003 (transcripts).

Bebchuk, L.A. 2002, "The Case against Board Veto in Corporate Takeovers", *University of Chicago Law Review*, vol. 69, no. 3, pp. 973–1035.

Bebchuk, L.A. 1999, *A Rent-Protection Theory of Corporate Ownership and Control*, NBER Working Paper No. 7203, National Bureau of Economic Research.

Bebchuk, L.A. 1994, "Efficient and Inefficient Sales of Corporate Control", *Quarterly Journal of Economics*, vol. 109, no. 4, pp. 957–993.

Bebchuk, L.A. 1989a, "Foreword: The Debate on Contractual Freedom in Corporate Law", *Columbia Law Review*, vol. 89, no. 7, pp. 1395–1415.

Bebchuk, L.A. 1989b, "Limiting Contractual Freedom in Corporate Law: The Desirable Constraints on Charter Amendment", *Harvard Law Review*, vol. 102, no. 8, pp. 1820–1860.

Bebchuk, L.A. 1989c, "Takeover Bids Below the Expected Value of Minority Shares", *Journal of Financial and Quantitative Analysis*, vol. 24, no. 2, pp. 171–184.

Bebchuk, L.A. 1987, "Pressure to Tender: An Analysis and a Proposed Remedy", *Delaware Journal of Corporate Law*, vol. 12, no. 3, pp. 911–949.

Bebchuk, L.A. 1985, "Toward Undistorted Choice and Equal Treatment in Corporate Takeovers", *Harvard Law Review*, vol. 98, no. 8, pp. 1695–1808.

Bebchuk, L.A. 1982, "The Case for Facilitating Competing Tender Offers: A Reply and Extension", *Stanford Law Review*, vol. 35, no. 1, pp. 23–50.

Bebchuk, L.A., Coates, J.C. and Subramanian, G. 2002, "The Powerful Antitakeover Force of Staggered Boards: Further Findings and a Reply to Symposium Participants", *Stanford Law Review*, vol. 55, no. 3, pp. 885–917.

Bebchuk, L.A. and Cohen, A. 2005, "The Costs of Entrenched Boards", *Journal of Financial Economics*, vol. 78, no. 2, pp. 409–433.

Bebchuk, L.A. and Cohen, A. 2003, "Firms' Decisions Where to Incorporate", *Journal of Law and Economics*, vol. 46, no. 2, pp. 383–425.

Bebchuk, L.A. and Fried, J.M. 2004, *Pay without Performance: The Unfulfilled Promise of Executive Compensation*, Harvard University Press, Cambridge, MA.

Bebchuk, L.A. and Hamdani, A. 2009, "The Elusive Quest for Global Governance Standards", *University of Pennsylvania Law Review*, vol. 157, no. 5, pp. 1263–1317.

Bebchuk, L.A. and Hamdani, A. 2002, "Optimal Defaults for Corporate Law Evolution", *Northwestern University Law Review*, vol. 96, no. 2, pp. 489–520.

Bebchuk, L.A. and Hart, O.D. 2001, *Takeover Bids vs. Proxy Fights in Contests for Corporate Control*, NBER Working Paper No. 8633, National Bureau of Economic Research.

Bebchuk, L.A. and Hirst, S. 2010, "Private Ordering and the Proxy Access Debate", *The Business Lawyer*, vol. 65, no. 2, pp. 329–360.

Bebchuk, L.A. and Kahan, M. 1990, "A Framework for Analyzing Legal Policy Towards Proxy Contests", *California Law Review*, vol. 78, no. 5, pp. 1073–1135.

Bebchuk, L.A., Kraakman, R.H. and Triantis, G. 2000, "Stock Pyramids, Cross-Ownership, and Dual Class Equity: The Mechanisms and Agency Cost of Separating Control from Cash-flow Rights" in *Concentrated Corporate Ownership, A NBER Conference Report*, ed. R.K. Morck, University of Chicago Press, Chicago, IL, pp. 295–315.

Bebchuk, L.A. and Roe, M.J. 1999, "Theory of Path Dependence in Corporate Ownership and Governance", *Stanford Law Review*, vol. 52, no. 1, pp. 127–170.

Bebchuk, L.A. and Zingales, L. 2000, "Ownership Structures and the Decision to Go Public: Private versus Social Optimality" in *Concentrated Corporate Ownership, A NBER Conference Report*, ed. R.K. Morck, University of Chicago Press, Chicago, IL, pp. 55–75.

Becht, M. 2004, "Reciprocity in Takeovers" in *Reforming Company and Takeover Law in Europe*, eds. G. Ferrarini, K.J. Hopt, J. Winter and E. Wymeersch, Oxford University Press, New York, NY, pp. 647–675.

Becht, M., Bolton, P. and Röell, A. 2007, "Corporate Law and Governance" in *Handbook of Law and Economics*, eds. A.M. Polinsky and S. Shavell, Elsevier North-Holland, Amsterdam, pp. 829–943.

Becht, M., Franks, J., Mayer, C. and Rossi, S. 2009, "Returns to Shareholder Activism: Evidence from a Clinical Study of the Hermes UK Focus Fund", *Review of Financial Studies*, vol. 22, no. 8, pp. 3093–3129.

Becht, M. and Mayer, C. 2001, "Introduction" in *The Control of Corporate Europe*, eds. F. Barca and M. Becht, Oxford University Press, Oxford, pp. 1–45.

Becker, G.S. 1968, "Crime and Punishment: An Economic Approach", *Journal of Political Economy*, vol. 76, no. 2, pp. 169–217.

Bekkum, J. van, Hijink, J.B.S., Schouten, M.C. and Winter, J.W. 2010, "Corporate Governance in the Netherlands", *Electronic Journal of Comparative Law*, vol. 14, no. 3 (December 2010), pp. 1–35.

Berglöf, E. and Burkart, M. 2003, "European Takeover Regulation", *Economic Policy*, vol. 18, no. 36, pp. 171–213.

Berle, A.A. and Means, G.C. 1932, *The Modern Corporation and Private Property*, MacMillan, New York, NY.

Bertrand, M., Mehta, P. and Mullainathan, S. 2002, "Ferreting Out Tunneling: An Application to Indian Business Groups", *Quarterly Journal of Economics*, vol. 117, no. 1, pp. 121–148.

Bhagat, S. and Black, B.S. 2002, "The Non-Correlation between Board Independence and Long-Term Firm Performance", *Journal of Corporation Law*, vol. 27, no. 2, pp. 231–274.

Bhagat, S. and Black, B.S. 1999, "The Uncertain Relationship Between Board Composition and Firm Performance", *Business Lawyer*, vol. 54, pp. 921–953.

Bianchi, M. and Bianco, M. 2006, *Italian Corporate Governance in the Last 15 Years: From Pyramids to Coalitions?*, ECGI-Finance Working Paper No. 144/2006.

Bianchi, M., Bianco, M., Giacomelli, S., Pacces, A.M. and Trento, S. 2005, *Proprietà e controllo delle imprese in Italia*, Il Mulino, Bologna.

Black, B.S. 2001, "The Legal and Institutional Preconditions for Strong Securities Markets", *UCLA Law Review*, vol. 48, no. 4, pp. 781–855.

Black, B.S. 1990, "Shareholder Passivity Reexamined", *Michigan Law Review*, vol. 89, no. 3, pp. 520–608.

Black, B.S., Cheffins, B.R. and Klausner, M. 2006, "Outside Director Liability: A Policy Analysis", *Journal of Institutional and Theoretical Economics*, vol. 162, no. 1, pp. 5–20.

Black, B.S. and Coffee, J.C. 1994, "Hail Britannia?: Institutional Investor Behavior Under Limited Regulation", *Michigan Law Review*, vol. 92, no. 7, pp. 1997–2087.

Blair, M.M. and Stout, L.A. 2001, "Trust, Trustworthiness, and the Behavioral Foundations of Corporate Law", *University of Pennsylvania Law Review*, vol. 149, no. 6, pp. 1735–1810.

Blair, M.M. and Stout, L.A. 1999, "A Team Production Theory of Corporate Law", *Virginia Law Review*, vol. 85, no. 2, pp. 247–328.

Bolton, P. and von Thadden, E.L. 1998, "Blocks, Liquidity, and Corporate Control", *Journal of Finance*, vol. 53, no. 1, pp. 1–25.

Boot, A.W.A., Gopalan, R. and Thakor, A.V. 2006, "The Entrepreneur's Choice between Private and Public Ownership", *Journal of Finance*, vol. 61, no. 2, pp. 803–836.

Boot, A.W.A. and Macey, J.R. 2004, "Monitoring Corporate Performance: The Role of Objectivity, Proximity, and Adaptability in Corporate Governance", *Cornell Law Review*, vol. 89, no. 2, pp. 356–393.

Braendle, U.C. 2006, "Shareholder Protection in the USA and Germany – "Law and Finance" Revisited", *German Law Journal*, vol. 7, no. 3, pp. 257–278.

Brandeis, L.D. 1914, *Other People's Money and How the Bankers Use It*, Reprint 2009, Cosimo Classics, New York, NY.

Bratton, W.W. and McCahery, J.A. 2001, "Incomplete Contracts Theories of the Firm and Comparative Corporate Governance", *Theoretical Inquiries in Law*, vol. 2, no. 2, pp. 745–782.

Brennan, M.J. and Franks, J. 1997, "Underpricing, Ownership and Control in Initial Public Offerings of Equity Securities in the UK", *Journal of Financial Economics*, vol. 45, no. 3, pp. 391–413.

Broman, C. and Granström, M. 2003, "Sweden" in *International Civil Procedure*, ed. S. Grubbs, Kluwer Law International, The Hague, pp. 705–729.

Burkart, M. and Lee, S. 2008, "One Share–One Vote: The Theory", *Review of Finance*, vol. 12, no. 1, pp. 1–49.

Burkart, M., Gromb, D. and Panunzi, F. 2000, "Agency Conflicts in Public and Negotiated Transfers of Corporate Control", *Journal of Finance*, vol. 55, no. 2, pp. 647–677.

Burkart, M., Gromb, D. and Panunzi, F. 1998, "Why Higher Takeover Premia Protect Minority Shareholders", *Journal of Political Economy*, vol. 106, no. 1, pp. 172–204.

Burkart, M., Gromb, D. and Panunzi, F. 1997, "Large Shareholders, Monitoring, and the Value of the Firm", *Quarterly Journal of Economics*, vol. 112, no. 3, pp. 693–728.

Burkart, M. and Panunzi, F. 2008, "Takeovers" in *Handbook of European Financial Institutions and Markets*, eds. X. Freixas, P. Hartmann and C. Mayer, Oxford University Press, New York, NY, pp. 265–296.

Burkart, M. and Panunzi, F. 2004, "Mandatory Bids, Squeeze-out, Sell-out and the Dynamics of the Tender Offer Process" in *Reforming Company and Takeover Law in Europe*, eds. G. Ferrarini, K.J. Hopt, J. Winter and E. Wymeersch, Oxford University Press, New York, NY, pp. 737–765.

Burkart, M. and Panunzi, F. 2001, *Agency Conflicts, Ownership Concentration, and Legal Shareholder Protection*, CEPR Discussion Paper No 2708 (on file with author).

Canoya, M., Riyanto, Y.E. and Van Cayseele, P. 2000, "Corporate Takeovers, Bargaining and Managers' Incentives to Invest", *Managerial and Decision Economics*, vol. 21, no. 1, pp. 1–18.

Carney, W.J., Shepherd, G.B. and Shepherd, J.M. 2010, "Delaware Corporate Law: Failing Law, Failing Markets" in *The Law and Economics of Corporate Governance: Changing Perspectives*, ed. A.M. Pacces, Edward Elgar Publishing, Cheltenham, pp. 23–67.

Cheffins, B.R. 2008, *Corporate Ownership and Control: British Business Transformed*, Oxford University Press, New York, NY.

Chemmanur, T.J. and Jiao, Y. 2012, "Dual class IPOs: A theoretical analysis", *Journal of Banking and Finance*, vol. 36, pp. 305–319.

Chirinko, R., Van Ees, H., Garretsen, H. and Sterken, E. 2004, "Investor Protections and Concentrated Ownership: Assessing Corporate Control Mechanisms in the Netherlands", *German Economic Review*, vol. 5, no. 2, pp. 119–138.

Choi, S.J. 2004, "The Evidence on Securities Class Actions", *Vanderbilt Law Review*, vol. 57, no. 5, pp. 1465–1528.

Claessens, S., Djankov, S., Fan, J.P.H. and Lang, L.H.P. 2002, "Disentangling the Incentive and Entrenchment Effects of Large Shareholdings", *Journal of Finance*, vol. 57, no. 6, pp. 2741–2771.

Clark, R.C. 1986, *Corporate Law*, Little, Brown and Comapny, Boston, MA.

Coase, R.H. 1992, "The Institutional Structure of Production", *American Economic Review*, vol. 82, no. 4, pp. 713–719.

Coase, R.H. 1960, "The Problem of Social Cost", *Journal of Law and Economics*, vol. 3, pp. 1–44.

Coase, R.H. 1937, "The Nature of the Firm", *Economica*, vol. 4, no. 16, pp. 386–405.

Coates, J.C. 2004, "Ownership, Takeovers and EU Law: How Contestable Should EU Corporations Be?" in *Reforming Company and Takeover Law in Europe*, eds. G. Ferrarini, K.J. Hopt, J. Winter and E. Wymeersch, Oxford University Press, New York, NY, pp. 677–709.

Coates, J.C. 1999, "'Fair Value' as an Avoidable Rule of Corporate Law: Minority Discounts in Conflict Transactions", *University of Pennsylvania Law Review*, vol. 147, no. 6, pp. 1251–1359.

Coffee, J.C. 2006a, *Gatekeepers: The Role of the Professions in Corporate Governance*, Oxford University Press, New York, NY.

Coffee, J.C. 2006b, "Reforming the Securities Class Action: An Essay on Deterrence and Its Implementation", *Columbia Law Review*, vol. 106, no. 7, pp. 1534–1586.

Coffee, J.C. 2005, "A Theory of Corporate Scandals: Why the USA and Europe Differ", *Oxford Review of Economic Policy*, Vol. 21, no. 2, pp. 198–211.

Coffee, J.C. 2004a, "Gatekeeper Failure and Reform: The Challenge of Fashioning Relevant Reforms", *Boston University Law Review*, vol. 84, no. 2, pp. 301–364.

Coffee, J.C. 2004b, "Partnoy's Complaint: A Response", *Boston University Law Review*, vol. 84, no. 2, pp. 377–382.

Coffee, J.C. 2001a, "Do Norms Matter? A Cross-Country Evaluation", *University of Pennsylvania Law Review*, vol. 149, no. 6, pp. 2151–2178.

Coffee, J.C. 2001b, "The Rise of Dispersed Ownership: The Roles of Law and the State in the Separation of Ownership and Control", *Yale Law Journal*, vol. 111, no. 1, pp. 1–82.

Coffee, J.C. 1991, "Liquidity Versus Control: The Institutional Investor As Corporate Monitor", *Columbia Law Review*, vol. 91, no. 6, pp. 1277–1368.

Coffee, J.C. 1989, "The Mandatory/Enabling Balance in Corporate Law: An Essay on the Judicial Role", *Columbia Law Review*, vol. 89, no. 7, pp. 1618–1691.

Coffee, J.C. 1987, "The Regulation of Entrepreneurial Litigation: Balancing Fairness and Efficiency in the Large Class Action", *University of Chicago Law Review*, vol. 54, no. 3, pp. 877–937.

Coffee, J.C. 1985, "The Unfaithful Champion: The Plaintiff as Monitor in Shareholder Litigation", *Law and Contemporary Problems*, vol. 48, no. 3, pp. 5–81.

Cohen, L. 1998, "Holdouts" in *The New Palgrave Dictionary of Economics and The Law*, ed. P. Newman, Macmillan, London, pp. 236–240.

Consolo, C. 2009, "Come cambia, rivelando ormai a tutti e in pieno il suo volto, l'art. 140-bis e la *class action* consumeristica", *Corriere Giuridico*, vol. 10, pp. 1297–1308.

Cools, S. 2005, "The Real Difference in Corporate Law between the United States and Continental Europe: Distribution of Powers", *Delaware Journal of Corporate Law*, vol. 30, no. 3, pp. 697–766.

Cooter, R.D. and Ulen, T. 2011, *Law and Economics*, 6th edn, Pearson/Addison Wesley, Boston, MA.

Crespi, R. and Renneboog, L. 2010, "Is (Institutional) Shareholder Activism New? Evidence from UK Shareholder Coalitions in the Pre-Cadbury Era", *Corporate Governance: An International Review*, vol. 18, no. 4, pp. 274–295.

Crespi-Cladera, R. and Garcia-Cestona, M.A. 2001, "Ownership and Control of Spanish Listed Firms" in *The Control of Corporate Europe*, eds. F. Barca and M. Becht, Oxford University Press, Oxford, pp. 207–227.

Cronqvist, H. and Nilsson, M. 2003, "Agency Costs of Controlling Minority Shareholders", *Journal of Financial and Quantitative Analysis*, vol. 38, no. 4, pp. 695–719.

Culpepper, P.D. 2007, "Eppure, non si muove: Legal change, institutional stability and Italian corporate governance", *West European Politics*, vol. 30, no. 4, pp. 784–802.

Daines, R. and Klausner, M. 2001, "Do IPO Charters Maximize Firm Value? Antitakeover Protection in IPOs", *Journal of Law, Economics, and Organization*, vol. 17, no. 1, pp. 83–120.

Davies, P.L. 2008, *Gower and Davies: The Principles of Modern Company Law*, 8th edn, Sweet and Maxwell, London.

Davies, P.L. 2002, *Introduction to Company Law*, Oxford University Press, Oxford.

Davies, P.L., Schuster, E. and Van de Walle de Ghelcke, E. 2010, "The takeover directive as a protectionist tool?" in *Company Law and Economic Protectionism: New Challenges to European Integration*, eds. U. Bernitz and W. Ringe, Oxford University Press, Oxford, pp. 105–160.

de Jong, A., Kabir, R., Marra, T. and Röell, A. 2001, "Ownership and Control in the Netherlands" in *The Control of Corporate Europe*, eds. F. Barca and M. Becht, Oxford University Press, Oxford, pp. 188–206.

de Jong, A., Mertens, G. and Roosenboom, P. 2006, "Shareholders' Voting at General Meetings: Evidence from the Netherlands", *Journal of Management and Governance*, vol. 10, no. 4, pp. 353–380.

de Jong, A. and Röell, A. 2005, "Financing and Control in The Netherlands: A Historical Perspective" in *A History of Corporate Governance Around the World: Family Business Groups to Professional Managers*, ed. R.K. Morck, University of Chicago Press, Chicago, IL, pp. 467–506.

de Jong, A., Röell, A. and Westerhuis, G. 2010, "Changing National Business Systems: Corporate Governance and Financing in the Netherlands, 1945–2005", *Business History Review*, vol. 84, no. 4, pp. 773.

Demsetz, H. 1983, "The Structure of Ownership and the Theory of the Firm", *Journal of Law and Economics*, vol. 26, no. 2, pp. 375–390.

Demsetz, H. and Lehn, K. 1985, "The Structure of Corporate Ownership: Causes and Consequences", *Journal of Political Economy*, vol. 93, no. 6, pp. 1155–1177.

den Hertog, J. 2012, "Economic theories of regulation" in *Regulation and Economics*, eds. A.M. Pacces and R.J. Van den Bergh, Encyclopedia Law and Economics, 2 edn, Edward Elgar, Cheltenham, pp. 25–95.

Djankov, S., La Porta, R., Lopez-de-Silanes, F. and Shleifer, A. 2008, "The Law and Economics of Self-Dealing", *Journal of Financial Economics*, vol. 88, no. 3, pp. 430–465.

Donald, D.C. 2004, *The Nomination of Directors under U.S. and German Law*, Working Paper No. 21, Frankfurt University, Institute for Law and Finance.

Dooley, M.P. 1992, "Two Models of Corporate Governance", *The Business Lawyer*, vol. 47, no. 2, pp. 461–527.

Dotevall, R. 2003, "Liability of Members of the Board of Directors and the Managing Director – A Scandinavian Perspective", *International Lawyer*, vol. 37, no. 1, pp. 7–22.

Dyck, A. and Zingales, L. 2004, "Private Benefits of Control: An International Comparison", *Journal of Finance*, vol. 59, no. 2, pp. 537–600.

Easterbrook, F.H. and Fischel, D.R. 1991, *The Economic Structure of Corporate Law*, Harvard University Press, Cambridge, MA.

Easterbrook, F.H. and Fischel, D.R. 1983, "Voting in Corporate Law", *Journal of Law and Economics*, vol. 26, no. 2, pp. 395–427.

Easterbrook, F.H. and Fischel, D.R. 1982a, "Corporate Control Transactions", *Yale Law Journal*, vol. 91, no. 4, pp. 698–737.

Easterbrook, F.H. and Fischel, D.R. 1982b, "Auctions and Sunk Costs in Tender Offers", *Stanford Law Review*, vol. 35, no. 1, pp. 1–21.

Easterbrook, F.H. and Fischel, D.R. 1981, "The Proper Role of a Target's Management in Responding to a Tender Offer", *Harvard Law Review*, vol. 94, no. 6, pp. 1161–1204.

Edmans, A. and Manso, G. 2011, "Governance Through Trading and Intervention: A Theory of Multiple Blockholders", *Review of Financial Studies*, vol. 24, no. 7, pp. 2395–2428.

Eisenberg, M.A. 1997, "The Director's Duty of Care in Negotiated Dispositions", *University of Miami Law Review*, vol. 51, no. 3, pp. 579–604.

Eisenberg, M.A. 1993, "The Divergence of Standards of Conduct and Standards of Review in Corporate Law", *Fordham Law Review*, vol. 62, no. 3, pp. 437–468.

Eisenberg, M.A. 1989, "The Structure of Corporation Law", *Columbia Law Review*, vol. 89, no. 7, pp. 1461–1525.

Enriques, L. 2009, "Corporate Governance Reforms in Italy: What Has Been Done and What Is Left to Do", *European Business Organization Law Review*, vol. 10, no. 4, pp. 477–513.

Enriques, L. 2006, "EC Company Law Directives and Regulations: How Trivial Are They?", *University of Pennsylvania Journal of International Economic Law*, vol. 27, no. 1, pp. 1–78.

Enriques, L. 2005, "Quartum non datur: appunti in tema di 'strumenti finanziari partecipativi' in Inghilterra, negli Stati Uniti e in Italia", *Banca Borsa Titoli di Credito*, vol. 68, pp. 166–183.

Enriques, L. 2003, "Bad Apples, Bad Oranges: A Comment from Old Europe on Post-Enron Corporate Governance Reforms", *Wake Forest Law Review*, vol. 38, no. 3, pp. 911–934.

Enriques, L. 2002, "Do Corporate Law Judges Matter? Some Evidence from Milan", *European Business Organization Law Review*, vol. 3, no. 4, pp. 756–821.

Enriques, L. 2000, "The Law on Company Directors' Self-Dealing: A Comparative Analysis", *International and Comparative Corporate Law Journal*, vol. 2, pp. 297–333.

Enriques, L. and Gatti, M. 2007, "EC Reforms of Corporate Governance and Capital Markets Law: Do They Tackle Insiders' Opportunism?", *Northwestern Journal of International Law and Business*, vol. 28, pp. 1–33.

Enriques, L. and Gatti, M. 2006, "The Uneasy Case for Top-Down Corporate Law Harmonization in the European Union", *University of Pennsylvania Journal of International Economic Law*, vol. 27, no. 4, pp. 939–998.

Enriques, L., Gilson, R.J. and Pacces, A.M. 2012, "The Case for an Unbiased Takeover Law", unpublished manuscript. (on file with author.)

Enriques, L. and Macey, J.R. 2001, "Creditors Versus Capital Formation: The Case against the European Legal Capital Rules", *Cornell Law Review*, vol. 86, no. 6, pp. 1165–1204.

Enriques, L. and Volpin, P.F. 2007, "Corporate Governance Reforms in Continental Europe", *Journal of Economic Perspectives*, vol. 21, no. 1, pp. 117–140.

Faccio, M. and Lang, L.H.P. 2002, "The Ultimate Ownership of Western European Corporations", *Journal of Financial Economics*, vol. 65, no. 3, pp. 365–395.

Fama, E.F. and Jensen, M.C. 1983a, "Separation of Ownership and Control", *Journal of Law and Economics*, vol. 26, no. 2, pp. 301–325.

Fama, E.F. and Jensen, M.C. 1983b, "Agency Problems and Residual Claims", *Journal of Law and Economics*, vol. 26, no. 2, pp. 327–349.

Ferrarini, G. 2006, *One Share–One Vote: A European Rule?*, ECGI Law Working Paper No. 58, SSRN.

Ferrarini, G. and Giudici, P. 2005, *Financial Scandals and the Role of Private Enforcement: The Parmalat Case*, ECGI Law Working Paper No. 40.

Field, L.C. and Karpoff, J.M. 2002, "Takeover Defenses of IPO Firms", *Journal of Finance*, vol. 57, no. 5, pp. 1857–1889.

Fisch, J.E. 2000, "The Peculiar Role of the Delaware Courts in the Competition for Corporate Charters", *University of Cincinnati Law Review*, vol. 68, no. 4, pp. 1061–1100.

Fox, M.B. and Heller, M.A. 2006, "What Is Good Corporate Governance?" in *Corporate Governance Lessons from Transition Economy Reforms*, eds. M.B. Fox and M.A. Heller, Princeton University Press, Princeton, NJ, pp. 3–31.

Franks, J. and Mayer, C. 2002, "Corporate Governance in the UK – Contrasted with the US System", *Cesifo Forum*, vol. 3, no. 3, pp. 13–22.

Franks, J. and Mayer, C. 1990, "Capital Markets and Corporate Control: A Study of France, Germany and the UK", *Economic Policy*, vol. 5, no. 1, pp. 189–231.

Franks, J., Mayer, C. and Renneboog, L. 2001, "Who Disciplines Management in Poorly Performing Companies?", *Journal of Financial Intermediation*, vol. 10, no. 3–4, pp. 209–248.

Franks, J., Mayer, C. and Rossi, S. 2009, "Ownership: Evolution and Regulation", *Review of Financial Studies*, vol. 22, no. 10, pp. 4009–4056.

Franks, J., Mayer, C. and Rossi, S. 2005, "Spending Less Time with the Family: The Decline of Family Ownership in the UK" in *A History of Corporate Governance Around the World: Family Business Groups to Professional Managers*, ed. R.K. Morck, University of Chicago Press, Chicago, IL, pp. 581–607.

Gadhoum, Y., Lang, L.H.P. and Young, L. 2005, "Who Controls US?", *European Financial Management*, vol. 11, no. 3, pp. 339–363.

Garoupa, N. 1997, "The Theory of Optimal Law Enforcement", *Journal of Economic Surveys*, vol. 11, no. 3, pp. 267–295.

Garry, P.M., Spurlin, C.J., Owen, D.A., Williams, W.A. and Efting, L.J. 2004, "The Irrationality of Shareholder Class Action Lawsuits: A Proposal for Reform", *South Dakota Law Review*, vol. 49, no. 2, pp. 275–312.

Gevurtz, F.A. 1994, "The Business Judgment Rule: Meaningless Verbiage or Misguided Notion?", *Southern California Law Review*, vol. 67, no. 2, pp. 287–337.

Gilson, R.J. 2006, "Controlling Shareholders and Corporate Governance: Complicating the Comparative Taxonomy", *Harvard Law Review*, vol. 119, no. 6, pp. 1642–1679.

Gilson, R.J. 1987, "Evaluating Dual Class Common Stock: The Relevance of Substitutes", *Virginia Law Review*, vol. 73, no. 5, pp. 807–844.

Gilson, R.J. 1982, "Seeking Competitive Bids Versus Pure Passivity in Tender Offer Defense", *Stanford Law Review*, vol. 35, no. 1, pp. 51–67.

Gilson, R.J. and Kraakman, R.H. 1991, "Reinventing the Outside Director: An Agenda for Institutional Investors", *Stanford Law Review*, vol. 43, no. 4, pp. 863–906.

Gilson, R.J. and Kraakman, R.H. 1984, "The Mechanisms of Market Efficiency", *Virginia Law Review*, vol. 70, no. 4, pp. 549–644.

Goergen, M. and Renneboog, L. 2001, "Strong Managers and Passive Institutional Investors in the UK" in *The Control of Corporate Europe*, eds. F. Barca and M. Becht, Oxford University Press, Oxford, pp. 259–284.

Gomes, A. 2001, *Takeovers, Freezeouts, and Risk Arbitrage*, Working Paper, University of Pennsylvania.

Gompers, P.A., Ishii, J.L. and Metrick, A. 2010, "Extreme Governance: An Analysis of Dual-Class Firms in the United States", *Review of Financial Studies*, vol. 23, no. 3, pp. 1051–1088.

Gordon, J.N. 1989, "The Mandatory Structure of Corporate Law", *Columbia Law Review*, vol. 89, no. 7, pp. 1549–1598.

Gordon, J.N. 1988, "Ties that Bond: Dual Class Common Stock and the Problem of Shareholder Choice", *California Law Review*, vol. 76, no. 1, pp. 1–85.

Gordon, M. 2002, "Takeover Defenses Work – Is That Such a Bad Thing", *Stanford Law Review*, vol. 55, no. 3, pp. 819–837.

Grossman, S.J. and Hart, O.D. 1988, "One Share–One Vote and the Market for Corporate Control", *Journal of Financial Economics*, vol. 20, pp. 175–202.

Grossman, S.J. and Hart, O.D. 1986, "The Costs and Benefits of Ownership: A Theory of Vertical and Lateral Integration", *Journal of Political Economy*, vol. 94, no. 4, pp. 691–719.

Grossman, S.J. and Hart, O.D. 1980, "Takeover Bids, the Free Rider Problem, and the Theory of the Corporation", *Bell Journal of Economics*, vol. 11, no. 1, pp. 42–64.

Grossman, S.J. and Stiglitz, J.E. 1980, "On the Impossibility of Informationally Efficient Markets", *American Economic Review*, vol. 70, no. 3, pp. 393–408.

Grundmann, S. 2005, "The Market for Corporate Control: The Legal Framework, Alternatives, and Policy Considerations" in *Corporate Governance in Context: Corporations, States, and Markets in Europe, Japan, and the US*, eds. K.J. Hopt, E. Wymeersch, H. Kanda and H. Baum, Oxford University Press, New York, NY, pp. 421–446.

Gulati, M. 1999, "When Corporate Managers Fear a Good Thing Is Coming to an End: The Case of Interim Nondisclosure", *UCLA Law Review*, vol. 46, no. 3, pp. 675–756.

Hamdani, A. 2004, "Gatekeeper Liability", *Southern California Law Review*, vol. 77, no. 1, pp. 53–122.

Hamilton, R.W. 2000, *The Law of Corporations*, West Group, St. Paul, MN.

Hansmann, H. 2006, "Corporation and Contract", *American Law and Economics Review*, vol. 8, no. 1, pp. 1–19.

Hansmann, H. 1996, *The Ownership of Enterprise*, Harvard University Press, Cambridge, MA.

Hansmann, H. and Kraakman, R.H. 2001, "The End of History for Corporate Law", *Georgetown Law Journal*, vol. 89, no. 2, pp. 439–468.

Hart, O.D. 2001, "Financial Contracting", *Journal of Economic Literature*, vol. 39, no. 4, pp. 1079–1100.

Hart, O.D. 1995, *Firm, Contracts, and Financial Structure*, Oxford University Press, New York, NY.

Hart, O.D. 1989, "An Economist's Perspective on the Theory of the Firm", *Columbia Law Review*, vol. 89, no. 7, pp. 1757–1774.

Hart, O.D. and Moore, J. 1990, "Property Rights and the Nature of the Firm", *Journal of Political Economy*, vol. 98, no. 6, pp. 1119–1158.

Hart, O.D. and Moore, J. 1988, "Incomplete Contracts and Renegotiation", *Econometrica*, vol. 56, no. 4, pp. 755–785.

Hartzell, J.C., Ofek, E. and Yermack, D. 2004, "What's in It for Me? CEOs Whose Firms Are Acquired", *Review of Financial Studies*, vol. 17, no. 1, pp. 37–61.

Hellwig, M. 2000, "On the Economics and Politics of Corporate Finance and Corporate Control" in *Corporate Governance: Theoretical and Empirical Perspectives*, ed. X. Vives, Cambridge University Press, Cambridge, pp. 95–134.

Henrekson, M. and Jakobsson, U. 2012, "The Swedish Corporate Control Model: Convergence, Persistence or Decline?", *Corporate Governance: An International Review*, vol. 20, no. 2, pp. 212–227.

Hermalin, B.E. and Weisbach, M.S. 2003, "Boards of Directors as an Endogenously Determined Institution: A Survey of the Economic Literature", *Economic Policy Review*, vol. 9, no. 1, pp. 7–26.

Hertig, G. 2010, "Comparative Law and Finance: Past, Present, and Future Research: Comment", *Journal of Institutional and Theoretical Economics*, vol. 166, no. 1, pp. 145–148.

Hertig, G. 2005, "On-Going Board Reforms: One Size Fits All and Regulatory Capture", *Oxford Review of Economic Policy*, vol. 21, no. 2, pp. 269–282.

Hirschman, A.O. 1970, *Exit, Voice, and Loyalty: Responses to Decline in Firms, Organizations, and States*, Harvard University Press, Cambridge, MA.

Holderness, C.G. 2009, "The Myth of Diffuse Ownership in the United States", *Review of Financial Studies*, vol. 22, no. 4, pp. 1377–1408.

Holderness, C.G. 2003, "A Survey of Blockholders and Corporate Control", *Economic Policy Review*, vol. 9, no. 1, pp. 51–64.

Holderness, C.G. and Sheehan, D.P. 1988, "The Role of Majority Shareholders in Publicly Held Corporations: An Exploratory Analysis", *Journal of Financial Economics*, vol. 20, pp. 317–346.

Holmén, M. and Högfeldt, P. 2009, "Pyramidal Discounts: Tunneling or Overinvestment?", *International Review of Finance*, vol. 9, no. 1–2, pp. 133–175.

Holmén, M. and Högfeldt, P. 2004, "A Law and Finance Analysis of Initial Public Offerings", *Journal of Financial Intermediation*, vol. 13, no. 3, pp. 324–358.

Holmström, B. and Kaplan, S.N. 2001, "Corporate Governance and Merger Activity in the United States: Making Sense of the 1980s and 1990s", *Journal of Economic Perspectives*, vol. 15, no. 2, pp. 121–144.

Holmström, B. and Nalebuff, B. 1992, "To The Raider Goes The Surplus? A Reexamination of the Free-Rider Problem", *Journal of Economics and Management Strategy*, vol. 1, no. 1, pp. 37–62.

Hooghiemstra, R. and van Manen, J. 2004, "The Independence Paradox: (Im)possibilities Facing Non-Executive Directors in The Netherlands", *Corporate Governance: An International Review*, vol. 12, no. 3, pp. 314–324.

Hopt, K.J. 2011, "Comparative corporate governance: The state of the art and International Regulation", *American Journal of Comparative Law*, vol. 59, no. 1, pp. 1–73.

Hopt, K.J. 2006, "Modern Company and Capital Market Problems: Improving European Corporate Governance after Enron" in *After Enron, Improving Corporate Law and Modernising Securities Regulation in Europe and the US*, eds. J. Armour and J.A. McCahery, Hart Publishing, Portland, OR, pp. 445–496.

Hopt, K.J. 2005, "European Company Law and Corporate Governance: Where Does the Action Plan of the European Commission Lead?" in *Corporate Governance in Context: Corporations, States, and Markets in Europe, Japan, and the US*, eds. K.J. Hopt, E. Wymeersch, H. Kanda and H. Baum, Oxford University Press, New York, NY, pp. 119–214.

Jackson, H.E. and Roe, M.J. 2009, "Public and Private Enforcement of Securities Laws: Resource-Based Evidence", *Journal of Financial Economics*, vol. 93, no. 2, pp. 207–238.

Jensen, M.C. 2001, "Value Maximization, Stakeholder Theory, and the Corporate Objective Function", *European Financial Management*, vol. 7, no. 3, pp. 297–317.

Jensen, M.C. 1993, "The Modern Industrial Revolution, Exit, and the Failure of Internal Control Systems", *Journal of Finance*, vol. 48, no. 3, pp. 831–880.

Jensen, M.C. 1986, "Agency Costs of Free Cash Flow, Corporate Finance, and Takeovers", *American Economic Review*, vol. 76, no. 2, pp. 323–329.

Jensen, M.C. and Meckling, W.H. 1976, "Theory of the Firm: Managerial Behavior, Agency Costs and Ownership Structure", *Journal of Financial Economics*, vol. 3, no. 4, pp. 305–360.

Jensen, M.C. and Ruback, R.S. 1983, "The Market for Corporate Control: The Scientific Evidence", *Journal of Financial Economics*, vol. 11, no. 1–4, pp. 5–50.

Jitta, M.J. 2004, "Procedural Aspects of the Right of Inquiry" in *The Companies and Business Court from a Comparative Law Perspective*, eds. M.J. Jitta, L. Timmerman, G. Kemperink, et al, Kluwer, Deventer, pp. 1–42.

Johnson, S., La Porta, R., Lopez-de-Silanes, F. and Shleifer, A. 2000, "Tunneling", *American Economic Review*, vol. 90, no. 2, pp. 22–27.

Kabir, R., Cantrijn, D. and Jeunink, A. 1997, "Takeover Defenses, Ownership Structure and Stock Returns in the Netherlands: An Empirical Analysis", *Strategic Management Journal*, vol. 18, no. 2, pp. 97–109.

Kahan, M. and Rock, E.B. 2011, "The Insignificance of Proxy Acces", *Virginia Law Review*, vol. 97, pp. 1347–1475.

Kahan, M. and Rock, E.B. 2002, "How I Learned to Stop Worrying and Love the Pill: Adaptive Responses to Takeover Law", *University of Chicago Law Review*, vol. 69, no. 3, pp. 871–915.

Karnell, G. 1981, "The Law of Associations, with Special Regard to Company Law" in *An Introduction to Swedish Law*, ed. S. Strömhold, Kluwer, Hingham, MA, pp. 303–356.

Karpoff, J.M., Scott Lee, D. and Martin, G.S. 2008, "The consequences to managers for financial misrepresentation", *Journal of Financial Economics*, vol. 88, no. 2, pp. 193–215.

Kemperink, G. 2004, "The Companies and Business Court and Codetermination Law" in *The Companies and Business Court from a Comparative Law Perspective*, ed. M.J. Jitta, Kluwer, Deventer, pp. 59–91.

Keynes, J.M. 1937, "The General Theory of Employment", *Quarterly Journal of Economics*, vol. 51, no. 2, pp. 209–223.

Keynes, J.M. 1936, *The General Theory of Employment, Interest and Money*, Reprint 2008, BN Publishing, Milton Keynes, UK.

Kirzner, I.M. 1979, *Perception, Opportunity and Profit: Studies in the Theory of Entrepreneurship*, University of Chicago Press, Chicago, IL.

Klausner, M. 2004, "The Limits of Corporate Law in Promoting Good Corporate Governance" in *Restoring Trust In American Business*, eds. J.W. Lorsch, L. Berlowitz and A. Zelleke, MIT Press, Cambridge, MA, pp. 91–98.

Klein, B., Crawford, R.G. and Alchian, A.A. 1978, "Vertical Integration, Appropriable Rents and the Competitive Contracting Process", *Journal of Law and Economics*, vol. 21, no. 2, pp. 297–326.

Klick, J. 2010, "The Perils of Empirical Work on Institutions", *Journal of Institutional and Theoretical Economics (JITE)*, vol. 166, no. 1, pp. 166–170.

Knight, F.H. 1921, *Risk, Uncertainty and Profit*, Houghton Mifflin, Boston, MA.

Knoeber, C.R. 1986, "Golden Parachutes, Shark Repellents, and Hostile Tender Offers", *American Economic Review*, vol. 76, no. 1, pp. 155–167.

Kortmann, J.S. and Bredenoord-Spoek, M.G. 2011, "The Netherlands: Hotspot for Class Actions?", *Global Competition Litigation Review*, vol. 4, no. 1, pp. 13–17.

Kraakman, R.H. 1986, "Gatekeepers: The Anatomy of a Third-Party Enforcement Strategy", *Journal of Law, Economics, and Organization*, vol. 2, no. 1, pp. 53–104.

Kraakman, R.H., Armour, J., Davies, P.L., Enriques, L., Hansmann, H., Hertig, G., Hopt, K.J., Kanda, H. and Rock, E.B. 2009, *The Anatomy of Corporate Law: A Comparative and Functional Approach*, 2nd edn, Oxford University Press, Oxford and New York.

La Porta, R., Lopez-de-Silanes, F. and Shleifer, A. 2008, "The economic consequences of legal origins", *Journal of Economic Literature*, vol. 46, no. 2, pp. 285–332.

La Porta, R., Lopez-de-Silanes, F. and Shleifer, A. 2006, "What Works in Securities Laws?", *Journal of Finance*, vol. 61, no. 1, pp. 1–32.

La Porta, R., Lopez-de-Silanes, F. and Shleifer, A. 1999, "Corporate Ownership around the World", *Journal of Finance*, vol. 54, no. 2, pp. 471–517.

La Porta, R., Lopez-de-Silanes, F., Shleifer, A. and Vishny, R.W. 2002, "Investor Protection and Corporate Valuation", *Journal of Finance*, vol. 57, no. 3, pp. 1147–1170.

La Porta, R., Lopez-de-Silanes, F., Shleifer, A. and Vishny, R.W. 2000, "Investor Protection and Corporate Governance", *Journal of Financial Economics*, vol. 58, no. 1–2, pp. 3–27.

La Porta, R., Lopez-de-Silanes, F., Shleifer, A. and Vishny, R.W. 1998, "Law and Finance", *Journal of Political Economy*, vol. 106, no. 6, pp. 1113–1155.

La Porta, R., Lopez-de-Silanes, F., Shleifer, A. and Vishny, R.W. 1997, "Legal Determinants of External Finance", *Journal of Finance*, vol. 52, no. 3, pp. 1131–1150.

Laeven, L. and Levine, R. 2008, "Complex Ownership Structures and Corporate Valuations", *Review of Financial Studies*, vol. 21, no. 2, pp. 579–604.

Laffont, J. and Tirole, J. 1988, "Repeated Auctions of Incentive Contracts, Investment, and Bidding Parity with an Application to Takeovers", *RAND Journal of Economics*, vol. 19, no. 4, pp. 516–537.

Langevoort, D.C. 2001, "The Human Nature of Corporate Boards: Law, Norms, and the Unintended Consequences of Independence and Accountability", *Georgetown Law Journal*, vol. 89, no. 4, pp. 797–832.

Levine, R. 1999, "Law, Finance, and Economic Growth", *Journal of Financial Intermediation*, vol. 8, no. 1–2, pp. 8–35.

Levine, R., Loayza, N. and Beck, T. 2000, "Financial Intermediation and Growth: Causality and Causes", *Journal of Monetary Economics*, vol. 46, no. 31, pp. 77.

Listokin, Y. 2010, "If you give shareholders power, do they use it? An empirical analysis", *Journal of Institutional and Theoretical Economics*, vol. 166, no. 1, pp. 38–53.

Listokin, Y. 2009, "What Do Corporate Default Rules and Menus Do? An Empirical Examination", *Journal of Empirical Legal Studies*, vol. 6, no. 2, pp. 279–308.

Loss, L. 1983, *Fundamentals of Securities Regulation*, Little, Brown and Company, Boston, MA.

Lowenfels, L.D. and Bromberg, A.R. 1997, "Controlling Person Liability Under Section 20(a) of the Securities Exchange Act and Section 15 of the Securities Act", *The Business Lawyer*, vol. 53, no. 1, pp. 1–33.

Macey, J.R. 2008, *Corporate Governance: Promises Kept, Promises Broken*, Princeton University Press, New Jersey, NJ.

Mahoney, P. 1995, "Mandatory Disclosure As a Solution to Agency Problems", *University of Chicago Law Review*, vol. 62, no. 3, pp. 1047–1112.

Manne, H.G. 2005, "Insider Trading: Hayek, Virtual Markets, and the Dog that did not Bark", *Journal of Corporation Law*, vol. 31, no. 1, pp. 167–185.

Manne, H.G. 1966, *Insider Trading and the Stock Market*, Free Press, New York, NY.

Manne, H.G. 1965, "Mergers and the Market for Corporate Control", *Journal of Political Economy*, vol. 73, no. 2, pp. 110–120.

Manning, B. 1984, "The Business Judgement Rule and the Director's Duty of Attention: Time for Reality", *The Business Lawyer*, vol. 39, no. 4, pp. 1477–1501.

Manso, G. 2011, "Motivating Innovation", *The Journal of Finance*, vol. 66, no. 5, pp. 1823–1860.

Marshall, A. 1893, "On Rents", *Economic Journal*, vol. 3, no. 9, pp. 74–90.

Martynova, M. and Renneboog, L. 2008, "A Century of Corporate Takeovers: What Have We Learned and Where Do We Stand?", *Journal of Banking and Finance*, vol. 32, no. 10, pp. 2148–2177.

Mattil, P. and Desoutter, V. 2008, *Butterworths Journal of Banking and Financial Law*, vol. (October 2008), pp. 484–488.

Maug, E. 2001, "Ownership Structure and the Life-Cycle of the Firm: A Theory of the Decision to Go Public", *European Finance Review*, vol. 5, no. 3, pp. 167–200.

Mayer, C. 1999, *Firm Control*, Inaugural Lecture at the University of Oxford (February 18, 1999), Oxford.

Mayer, C. and Sussman, O. 2001, "The Assessment: Finance, Law, and Growth", *Oxford Review of Economic Policy*, vol. 17, no. 4, pp. 457–466.

McCahery, J.A., Renneboog, L., Ritter, P. and Haller, S. 2004, "The Economics of the Proposed European Takeover Directive" in *Reforming Company and Takeover Law in Europe*, eds. G. Ferrarini, K.J. Hopt, J. Winter and E. Wymeersch, Oxford University Press, New York, NY, pp. 575–646.

McCahery, J.A. and Vermeulen, E.P.M. 2005, "Corporate Governance Crises and Related Party Transactions: A Post-Parmalat Agenda" in *Corporate Governance in Context: Corporations, States, and Markets in Europe, Japan, and the US*, eds. K.J. Hopt, E. Wymeersch, H. Kanda and H. Baum, Oxford University Press, New York, NY, pp. 228–230.

Meinema, M. 2003, "Mandatory and Non-Mandatory Rules in Dutch Corporate Law", *Electronic Journal of Comparative Law*, vol. 6.4, pp. 199–224.

Merryman, J.H. 1969, *The Civil Law Tradition: An Introduction to the Legal Systems of Western Europe and Latin America*, Stanford University Press, Stanford, CA.

Milhaupt, C.J. and Pistor, K. 2008, *Law and Capitalism: What Corporate Crises Reveal about Legal Systems and Economic Development Around the World*, University of Chicago Press, Chicago and London.

Morck, R.K., Shleifer, A. and Vishny, R.W. 1988, "Management Ownership and Market Valuation: An Empirical Analysis", *Journal of Financial Economics*, vol. 20, pp. 293–315.

Morck, R.K., Wolfenzon, D. and Yeung, B. 2005, "Corporate Governance, Economic Entrenchment, and Growth", *Journal of Economic Literature*, vol. 43, no. 3, pp. 655–720.

Morck, R.K. and Yeung, B. 2005, "Dividend Taxation and Corporate Governance", *Journal of Economic Perspectives*, vol. 19, no. 3, pp. 163–180.

Mülbert, P.O. 2004, "Make It or Break It: The Break-Through Rule as a Break-Through for the European Takeover Directive?" in *Reforming Company and Takeover Law in Europe*, eds. G. Ferrarini, K.J. Hopt, J. Winter and E. Wymeersch, Oxford University Press, New York, NY, pp. 711–736.

Myers, S.C. 1977, "Determinants of Corporate Borrowing", *Journal of Financial Economics*, vol. 5, no. 2, pp. 147–175.

Myerson, R.B. 1983, "Mechanism Design by an Informed Principal", *Econometrica*, vol. 51, no. 6, pp. 1767–1797.

Nenova, T. 2003, "The Value of Corporate Voting Rights and Control: A Cross-Country Analysis", *Journal of Financial Economics*, vol. 68, no. 3, pp. 325–351.

Nicodano, G. 1998, "Corporate Groups, Dual-Class Shares and the Value of Voting Rights", *Journal of Banking and Finance*, vol. 22, no. 9, pp. 1117–1137.

Nicodano, G. and Sembenelli, A. 2004, "Private Benefits, Block Transaction Premiums and Ownership Structure", *International Review of Financial Analysis*, vol. 13, no. 2, pp. 227–244.

North, D.C. 1990, *Institutions, Institutional Change and Economic Performance*, Cambridge University Press, Cambridge.

Pacces, A.M. 2011, "Controlling the Corporate Controller's Misbehaviour", *Journal of Corporate Law Studies*, vol. 11, no. 1, pp. 177–214.

Pacces, A.M. 2009, *Control Matters: Law and Economics of Private Benefits of Control*, ECGI-Law Working Paper 131/2009.

Pacces, A.M. 2007, *Featuring Control Power: Corporate Law and Economics Revisited*, PhD Dissertation, Erasmus University Rotterdam.

Pacces, A.M. 2000, "Financial Intermediation in the Securities Markets: Law and Economics of Conduct of Business Regulation", *International Review of Law and Economics*, vol. 20, no. 4, pp. 479–510.

Pagano, M. and Röell, A. 1998, "The Choice of Stock Ownership Structure: Agency Costs, Monitoring, and the Decision to Go Public", *Quarterly Journal of Economics*, vol. 113, no. 1, pp. 187–225.

Pagano, M. and Volpin, P.F. 2005, "The Political Economy of Corporate Governance", *American Economic Review*, vol. 95, no. 4, pp. 1005–1030.

Pardolesi, R., A.M.P. (alias Alessio M. Pacces) and Portolano, A. 2004, "Latte, lacrime (da coccodrillo) e sangue (dei risparmiatori). Note minime sul caso Parmalat", *Mercato, Concorrenza, Regole*, vol. 1/04, pp. 193–216.

Paredes, T.A. 2004, "A Systems Approach to Corporate Governance Reform: Why Importing U.S. Corporate Law Isn't the Answer", *William and Mary Law Review*, vol. 45, no. 3, pp. 1055–1157.

Paredes, T.A. 2003, "Blinded by the Light: Information Overload and Its Consequences for Securities Regulation", *Washington University Law Quarterly*, vol. 81, no. 2, pp. 417–485.

Partnoy, F. 2004, "Strict Liability for Gatekeepers: A Reply to Professor Coffee", *Boston University Law Review*, vol. 84, no. 2, pp. 365–375.

Partnoy, F. 2001, "Barbarians at the Gatekeepers?: A Proposal for a Modified Strict Liability Regime", *Washington University Law Quarterly*, vol. 79, no. 2, pp. 491–547.

Payne, J. 2011, "Schemes of Arrangement, Takeovers and Minority Shareholder Protection", *Journal of Corporate Law Studies*, vol. 11, no. 1, pp. 67–97.

Petersson, H. and Sandberg Thomsen, E. 2011, "Sweden" in *The Corporate Governance Review*, ed. W.J.L. Calkoen, Law and Business Research, London, pp. 296–307.

Polinsky, A.M. and Shavell, S. 2000, "The Economic Theory of Public Enforcement of Law", *Journal of Economic Literature*, vol. 38, no. 1, pp. 45–76.

Posner, R.A. 2011, *Economic Analysis of Law*, 8th edn, Aspen Publishers, New York, NY.

Posner, R.A. 1972, *Economic Analysis of Law*, 1st edn, Little, Brown and Company, Boston, MA.

Rajan, R.G. and Zingales, L. 2003, "The Great Reversals: The Politics of Financial Development in the Twentieth Century", *Journal of Financial Economics*, vol. 69, no. 1, pp. 5–50.

Rajan, R.G. and Zingales, L. 2001, "The Firm as a Dedicated Hierarchy: A Theory of the Origins and Growth of Firms", *Quarterly Journal of Economics*, vol. 116, no. 3, pp. 805–851.

Rajan, R.G. and Zingales, L. 2000, "The Governance of the New Enterprise" in *Corporate Governance: Theoretical and Empirical Perspectives*, ed. X. Vives, Cambridge University Press, Cambridge, pp. 201–232.

Rajan, R.G. and Zingales, L. 1998a, "Financial Dependence and Growth", *American Economic Review*, vol. 88, no. 3, pp. 559–586.

Rajan, R.G. and Zingales, L. 1998b, "Power in a Theory of the Firm", *Quarterly Journal of Economics*, vol. 113, no. 2, pp. 387–432.

Ravina, E. and Sapienza, P. 2010, "What Do Independent Directors Know Evidence from Their Trading", *Review of Financial Studies*, vol. 23, no. 3, pp. 962–1003.

Ribstein, L.E. 2006, "Fraud on a Noisy Market", *Lewis and Clark Law Review*, vol. 10, no. 1, pp. 137–168.

Ribstein, L.E. 2002, "Market vs. Regulatory Responses to Corporate Fraud: A Critique of the Sarbanes-Oxley Act of 2002", *Journal of Corporation Law*, vol. 28, no. 1, pp. 1–67.

Ricketts, M. 2003, *The Economics of Business Enterprise: An Introduction to Economic Organisation and the Theory of the Firm*, 3rd edn, Elgar, Cheltenham.

Rock, E.B. 2002, "Securities Regulation as Lobster Trap: A Credible Commitment Theory of Mandatory Disclosure", *Cardozo Law Review*, vol. 23, no. 2, pp. 675–704.

Rock, E.B. 1997, "Saints and Sinners: How Does Delaware Corporate Law Work", *UCLA Law Review*, vol. 44, no. 4, pp. 1009–1107.

Rock, E.B. 1991, "The Logic and (Uncertain) Significance of Institutional Shareholder Activism", *Georgetown Law Journal*, vol. 79, no. 3, pp. 445–506.

Rock, E.B. and Wachter, M.L. 2001, "Islands of Conscious Power: Law, Norms, and the Self-Governing Corporation", *University of Pennsylvania Law Review*, vol. 149, no. 6, pp. 1619–1700.

Roe, M.J. 2003, *Political Determinants of Corporate Governance: Political Context, Corporate Impact*, Oxford University Press, Oxford.

Roe, M.J. 2002, "Corporate Law's Limits", *Journal of Legal Studies*, vol. 31, no. 2, pp. 233–271.

Roe, M.J. 2001, "Rents and Their Corporate Consequences", *Stanford Law Review*, vol. 53, no. 6, pp. 1463–1494.

Roe, M.J. 1998, "Backlash", *Columbia Law Review*, vol. 98, no. 1, pp. 217–241.

Roe, M.J. 1994, *Strong Managers, Weak Owners: The Political Roots of American Corporate Finance*, Princeton University Press, Princeton, NJ.

Romano, R. 2005, "The Sarbanes-Oxley Act and the Making of Quack Corporate Governance", *Yale Law Journal*, vol. 114, no. 7, pp. 1521–1611.

Romano, R. 2001, "Less is More: Making Institutional Investor Activism a Valuable Mechanism of Corporate Governance", *Yale Journal of Regulation*, vol. 18, no. 2, pp. 174–251.

Romano, R. 1991, "The Shareholder Suit: Litigation without Foundation?", *Journal of Law, Economics, and Organization*, vol. 7, no. 1, pp. 55–87.

Romano, R. 1989, "Answering the Wrong Question: The Tenuous Case for Mandatory Corporate Laws", *Columbia Law Review*, vol. 89, no. 7, pp. 1599–1617.

Roosenboom, P. and Van der Goot, T. 2003, "Takeover Defences and IPO Firm Value in the Netherlands", *Europen Financial Management*, vol. 9, no. 4, pp. 485–511.

Rubinfeld, D.L. and Scotchmer, S. 1998, "Contingent Fees" in *The New Palgrave Dictionary of Economics and the Law*, ed. P. Newman, Macmillan, London, pp. 415–420.

Schaefer, H.B. 2000, "The Bundling of Similar Interests in Litigation. The Incentives for Class Action and Legal Actions Taken by Associations", *European Journal of Law and Economics*, vol. 9, no. 3, pp. 183–213.

Scharfstein, D. 1988, "The Disciplinary Role of Takeovers", *Review of Economic Studies*, vol. 55, no. 2, pp. 185–199.

Schnitzer, M. 1995, "Breach of Trust" in Takeovers and the Optimal Corporate Charter", *Journal of Industrial Economics*, vol. 43, no. 3, pp. 229–259.

Schuit, S.R., Bier, B., Verburg, L.G. and Ter Wisch, J.A. 2002, *Corporate Law and Practice of the Netherlands: Legal and Taxation*, 2nd edn, Kluwer Law International, The Hague.

Schumpeter, J.A. 1947, *Capitalism, Socialism, and Democracy*, 2nd edn, Allen and Unwin, London.

Schwert, W.G. 2000, "Hostility in Takeovers: In the Eyes of the Beholder?", *Journal of Finance*, vol. 55, no. 6, pp. 2599–2640.

Shavell, S. 2004, *Foundations of Economic Analysis of Law*, Harvard University Press (Belknap), Cambridge, MA.

Shavell, S. 1993, "The Optimal Structure of Law Enforcement", *Journal of Law and Economics*, vol. 36, no. S1, pp. 255–287.

Shleifer, A. and Summers, L.H. 1988, "Breach of Trust in Hostile Takeovers" in *Corporate Takeovers: Causes and Consequences*, ed. A.J. Auerbach, University of Chicago Press, Chicago, IL, pp. 65–88.

Shleifer, A. and Vishny, R.W. 1997, "A Survey of Corporate Governance", *Journal of Finance*, vol. 52, no. 2, pp. 737–783.

Shleifer, A. and Vishny, R.W. 1990, "Equilibrium Short Horizons of Investors and Firms", *American Economic Review*, vol. 80, no. 2, pp. 148–153.

Shleifer, A. and Vishny, R.W. 1989, "Management Entrenchment: The Case of Manager-Specific Investments", *Journal of Financial Economics*, vol. 25, no. 1, pp. 123–139.

Shleifer, A. and Vishny, R.W. 1988, "Value Maximization and the Acquisition Process", *Journal of Economic Perspectives*, vol. 2, no. 1, pp. 7–20.

Shleifer, A. and Vishny, R.W. 1986a, "Large Shareholders and Corporate Control", *Journal of Political Economy*, vol. 94, no. 3, Part 1, pp. 461–488.

Shleifer, A. and Vishny, R.W. 1986b, "Greenmail, White Knights, and Shareholders' Interest", *RAND Journal of Economics*, vol. 17, no. 3, pp. 293–309.

Siems, M. 2005, "Numerical Comparative Law – Do We Need Statistical Evidence in Order to Reduce Complexity?", *Cardozo Journal of International and Comparative Law*, vol. 13, no. 2, pp. 521–540.

Siems, M. and Deakin, S. 2010, "Comparative Law and Finance: Past, Present, and Future Research", *Journal of Institutional and Theoretical Economics JITE*, vol. 166, no. 1, pp. 120–140.

Skeel, D.A. 2001, "Shaming in Corporate Law", *University of Pennsylvania Law Review*, vol. 149, no. 6, pp. 1811–1868.

Skog, R. 2004, "The European Union's Proposed Takeover Directive, the 'Breakthrough' Rule and the Swedish System of Dual Class Common Stock", *Scandinavian Studies in Law*, vol. 45, pp. 293–306.

Skog, R. 1994, *Setting Up a Business in Sweden*, Juristförlaget, Stockholm.

Skog, R. and Fäger, C. 2007, *The Swedish Companies Act: An Introduction*, Norstedts Juridik, Stockholm.

Smith, A. 1776, *The Wealth of Nations*, Cannan edn, The Modern Library, New York.

Spamann, H. 2010, "The" Antidirector Rights Index" Revisited", *Review of Financial Studies*, vol. 23, no. 2, pp. 467–486.

Spamann, H. 2006, *On the Insignificance and/or Endogeneity of La Porta et al.'s 'Anti-Director Rights Index' under Consistent Coding*, Working Paper No. 7, Harvard Law School (Fellows Series).

Stapledon, G.P. 1996, *Institutional Shareholders and Corporate Governance*, Clarendon Press, Oxford.

Stigler, G.J. 1989, "Two Notes on the Coase Theorem", *Yale Law Journal*, vol. 99, no. 3, pp. 631–633.

Stigler, G.J. 1966, *The Theory of Price*, 3rd edn, Macmillan, New York, NY.

Subramanian, G. 2007, "Post-Siliconix Freeze-Outs: Theory and Evidence", *Journal of Legal Studies*, vol. 36, no. 1, pp. 1–26.

Subramanian, G. 2005, "Fixing Freezeouts", *Yale Law Journal*, vol. 115, no. 1, pp. 2–70.

Timmerman, L. 2004, "Review of Management Decisions by the Courts, Seen Partly from a Comparative Legal Perspective" in *The Companies and Business Court from a Comparative Law Perspective*, ed. J.M. Jitta, Kluwer, Deventer, pp. 59–91.

Timmerman, L. and Doorman, A. 2002, "Rights of Minority Shareholders in the Netherlands", *Electronic Journal of Comparative Law*, vol. 6.4, pp. 181–211.

Tirole, J. 2006, *The Theory of Corporate Finance*, Princeton University Press, Princeton, NJ.

Tirole, J. 2001, "Corporate Governance", *Econometrica*, vol. 69, no. 1, pp. 1–35.

Tirole, J. 1999, "Incomplete Contracts: Where Do We Stand?", *Econometrica*, vol. 67, no. 4, pp. 741–781.

Van der Elst, C. 2008, *Shareholder Mobility in Five European Countries*, ECGI-Law Working Paper 104/2008.

Ventoruzzo, M. 2011, "Empowering Shareholders in Dirctors' Elections: A Revolution in the Making", *European Company and Financial Law Review*, vol. 8, no. 2, pp. 105–144.

Ventoruzzo, M. 2006, "Europe's Thirteenth Directive and U.S. Takeover Regulation: Regulatory Means and Political and Economic Ends", *Texas International Law Journal*, vol. 41, no. 2, pp. 171–221.

Ventoruzzo, M. 2004, "Experiments in Comparative Corporate Law: The Recent Italian Reform and the Dubious Virtues of a Market for Rules in the Absence of Effective Regulatory Competition", *Texas International Law Journal*, vol. 40, no. 1, pp. 113–156.

Weir, C. and Laing, D. 2003, "Ownership Structure, Board Composition and the Market for Corporate Control in the UK: An Empirical Analysis", *Applied Economics*, vol. 35, no. 16, pp. 1747–1759.

Williamson, O.E. 1991, "Comparative Economic Organization: The Analysis of Discrete Structural Alternatives", *Administrative Science Quarterly*, vol. 36, no. 2, pp. 269–296.

Williamson, O.E. 1985, *The Economic Institutions of Capitalism: Firms, Markets, Relational Contracting*, Collier Macmillan, London.

Williamson, O.E. 1979, "Transaction-Cost Economics: The Governance of Contractual Relations", *Journal of Law and Economics*, vol. 22, no. 2, pp. 233–261.

Wymeersch, E. 2005, "Implementation of the Corporate Governance Codes" in *Corporate Governance in Context: Corporations, States and Markets in Europe, Japan, and the US*, eds. K.J. Hopt, E. Wymeersch, H. Kanda and H. Baum, Oxford University Press, New York, NY, pp. 403–419.

Wymeersch, E. 2003, "Do We Need a Law on Groups of Companies?" in *Capital Markets and Company Law*, eds. K.J. Hopt and E. Wymeersch, Oxford University Press, New York, NY, pp. 573–600.

Yarrow, G.K. 1985, "Shareholder Protection, Compulsory Acquisition and the Efficiency of the Takeover Process", *Journal of Industrial Economics*, vol. 34, no. 1, pp. 3–16.

Yermack, D. 2010, "Shareholder Voting and Corporate Governance", *Annual Review of Financial Economics*, vol. 2, no. 1, pp. 103–125.

Zingales, L. 2005, "The Importance of Bad News" in *Corporate Governance in the US and Europe*, eds. G. Owen, T. Kirchmaier and J. Grant, Palgrave Macmillan, Basingstoke, pp. 96–100.

Zingales, L. 2000, "In Search of New Foundations", *Journal of Finance*, vol. 55, no. 4, pp. 1623–1653.

Zingales, L. 1998, "Corporate Governance" in *The New Palgrave Dictionary of Economics and the Law*, ed. P. Newman, Macmillan, London, pp. 497–503.

Zingales, L. 1995, "Insider Ownership and the Decision to Go Public", *Review of Economic Studies*, vol. 62, no. 3, pp. 425–448.

Zweigert, K. and Kötz, H. 1998, *Introduction to Comparative Law*, 3rd edn (translated from German by T. Weir), Oxford University Press, Oxford.

Index